HEROIC IMAGINATION
THE CREATIVE GENIUS OF EUROPE
FROM WATERLOO (1815)
TO THE REVOLUTION OF 1848

By Frederic Ewen

BERTOLT BRECHT, HIS LIFE, HIS ART, AND HIS TIMES
THE POETRY AND PROSE OF HEINRICH HEINE
THE PRESTIGE OF SCHILLER IN ENGLAND
BIBLIOGRAPHY OF EIGHTEENTH-CENTURY ENGLISH LITERATURE

*

with David Ewen
MUSICAL VIENNA

*

with Phoebe Brand and John Randolph
dramatic adaptations of
JAMES JOYCE'S A PORTRAIT OF THE ARTIST AS A YOUNG MAN
THOMAS MANN'S THE MAGIC MOUNTAIN

Heroic Imagination

THE CREATIVE GENIUS OF EUROPE
FROM WATERLOO (1815) TO THE
REVOLUTION OF 1848

by Frederic Ewen

CITADEL PRESS   SECAUCUS, N.J.

First edition
Copyright © 1984 by Frederic Ewen
All rights reserved
Published by Citadel Press
A division of Lyle Stuart Inc.
120 Enterprise Ave., Secaucus, N.J. 07094
In Canada: Musson Book Company
A division of General Publishing Co. Limited
Don Mills, Ontario
Manufactured in the United States of America by
The Book Press, Brattleboro, VT

Library of Congress Cataloging in Publication Data

Ewen, Frederic, [date]
    Heroic imagination.

    Includes index.
    1. Europe—Intellectual life—19th century.
2. Romanticism—Europe. I. Title.
CB204.E94   1984   940.2'82   84-1809
ISBN 0-8065-0895-7

For My Students

Whose interest, loyalty, and encouragement throughout many years made teaching a privilege and learning a joy.

Contents

Acknowledgments

The author wishes to thank the publishers and authors listed below for permission to quote from coyright materials:

BASIL BLACKWELL (Oxford): J.H. Whitfield: *Giacomo Leopardi*. Basil Blackwell, Oxford, 1954.

J.M. DENT & SONS LTD (London): Archibald Colquhoun: *Manzoni and His Times*. London, J.M. Dent & Sons Ltd., 1954.

DOUBLEDAY & COMPANY: Henri Troyat: *Pushkin*. Translated by Nancy Amphoux. English translation copyright © 1970 by Doubleday & Company, Garden City, N.Y. 1970. Reprinted by permission of the publisher.

HARVARD UNIVERSITY PRESS: *The Letters of John Keats*. Edited by Hyder E. Rollins. Copyright Harvard University Press, Cambridge, Mass., 1958.

ERNEST J. SIMMONS: *Pushkin*. Copyright Harvard University Press, Cambridge, Mass., 1937.

ALFRED A. KNOPF, INC.: *The Memoirs of Chateaubriand*. Selected, translated, and Introduction by Robert Baldick. Copyright Alfred A. Knopf, Inc., New York, 1961.

MACMILLAN PUBLISHING CO., INC.: *The Works of Joseph DeMaistre*. Edited and translated by Jack Lively. Copyright © 1965 by Jack Lively. Macmillan Publishing Company, Inc., New York, 1965.

MRS. ELSIE D. MAGARSHACK (London): Permission to reprint from David Magarshack, *Pushkin. A Biography*. Copyright Grove Press, New York, 1967.

METHUEN & CO., LTD (London): *Pushkin on Literature*. Selected, translated and edited by Tatiana Wolff. Methuen & Co., Ltd., London, 1971.

THE NEW AMERICAN LIBRARY: *Giacomo Leopardi: Selected Prose and Poetry*. Edited, translated, and introduced by Iris Origo and John Heath-Stubbs. Copyright The New American Library, New York, 1967.

OXFORD UNIVERSITY PRESS: *The Letters of John Keats*. Edited by Maurice Buxton Forman. Oxford University Press, 1952.

RANDOM HOUSE, INC.: Antonina Vallentin: *This I Saw: The Life and Times of Goya*. Translated by Katherine Woods. Copyright Random House, Inc., New York, 1949.

CHARLES SCRIBNER'S SONS: Jules Eckert Goodman: *The Road to Monte Cristo*. Copyright © 1956 by Jules Eckert Goodman. Reprinted with the permission of Charles Scribner's Sons.

STANFORD UNIVERSITY PRESS: Anatole G. Mazour: *The First Russian Revolution, 1825*. Copyright Stanford University Press, 1963.

Prologue

In the theatre of man's life it is reserved
only for God and his angels to be lookers-on.
— Francis Bacon —

Every age is both offspring and parent, legatee and testator, product
and producer. But there are ages that more than others carry
distinctive imprints of the future, and may assert an indisputable
right to a primacy of influences. Such is the nineteenth century,
considered as a forebear of some of the most illustrious achievements
of our day.

In this respect, the first half of the nineteenth century is
remarkable. Its pioneering accomplishments, especially in the
sciences, are astounding, and the catalogue of its innovations
extraordinary. Consider, for example, that it was in the first decade
of that century that John Dalton established his atomic theory in
chemistry; that in the second decade the French physicist Ampère
developed the science of electro-magnetism, and Cuvier published
his epochal treatise on fossils; that in December 1831 Charles
Darwin set forth on his memorable voyage on the "Beagle."

When we turn to the world of art, poetry, painting, music —
culture in general — the phenomenon is no less astounding. Here,
too, we encounter an assemblage of almost incomparable greatness:

We are in the presence of Beethoven and Goethe; Byron and Blake; Balzac, Goya, Pushkin, Heine, Liszt, Chopin and Berlioz, Stendhal and George Sand, among others. This is a time when national genius transcends national boundaries, and spirits communicate across vast distances, affecting or being affected by those of other lands: Thus, figuratively, Byron speaks to Pushkin in Russia; Goethe to Sir Walter Scott and Carlyle; Heine to France; George Sand to the England of George Eliot.

Yet it was not in a peaceful world that this wide manifestation of creativity took place. The century opened amidst wars and upheavals, that lasted almost unintermittently from 1789, the outbreak of the French Revolution, to 1815, Waterloo and the downfall of Napoleon. Thereafter the "Restoration" that sought to bring back the old order preceding the French Revolution, and hoped by restoring the displaced ruling houses, once more to assure stability and peace, found for all its absolute power that irreversible changes had taken place. Two more revolutions followed in the half-century.

The "old" world was gone, and a "new" one was in the making. New forces, new elements, new alignments arose that were destined ultimately to spell the doom of absolutism.

We might say that the principal sources of that irreversible change could be called, symbolically, Paris and Manchester: Paris, mother of revolutions in the political sphere; and Manchester standing for the ultimate triumph of the Industrial Revolution. But not least of the revolutionary forces now come to the fore is the revolution of and in the mind, revolution in what we may call the "collective consciousness" of peoples.

Not since the Reformation had there been such an unmooring of ideas, beliefs, customs and behavior. A "collective consciousness" is the sum-total of beliefs and goals peculiar to particular groups within a society. Subjected to new conditions, pressures, and problems the mind of a human being is forced into new moulds.

And now, History was shaping ever larger segments of the population into an ever greater awareness of conflicting issues, interests, and needs; shaping them as well into a greater awareness of their own individual and social selves. When, as in the first half of the century, human beings are uprooted, say, from the land, and brought into factories, to constitute new aggregations, with new interests and new problems, they reshape their consciousness as collective human beings. And this, too, constitutes one of the most significant elements toward change. With the extension of sources and means of communication, the press, public debate, the sermon; with ever-enlarged access to new ideas, a crystallized "collective consciousness" may in turn become a viable instrument in the battles that lie ahead. Consciousness translated into action can itself make history.

In the formation, or better, the reformation of that "collective consciousness" the role of the artist, philosopher, poet, political and social thinker becomes ever more crucial as the arena of problems widens. After all, they too, are products and heirs of a precedent consciousness, and soon to be fashioners thereof through their varied utterances, their art, their science, their philosophies.

The present study is concerned with the fruits of the interaction of the public "collective consciousness" with the creative consciousness of the individual, the private creator.

If I may borrow a figure taken from Stendhal, and transplant it into this new context, I would say that art is like a branch of a tree (that is, the artist's individual endowment) which is plunged into the depths of a mine (the world outside), and which emerges, as Stendhal puts it "covered with an infinity of sparkling diamonds," branch and diamonds being the finished product, the work of art. This process Stendhal called "crystallization."

And it is this "crystallization" that the present book will attempt to describe.

*

In preparing this work I have contracted many debts, some of which it will be impossible to list fully, such as, for example, that to the numerous writers whose contributions I have used, and which I can only acknowledge by a bibliographical entry. Such too is my debt to my colleagues at various institutions, in whose company many of the ideas contained in the following pages were once passionately argued. Unfortunately, too many of them are no longer here to accept a posthumous, but deeply felt tribute.

I am happy to express my thanks to Dr. Eve Vassiliades, whose linguistic gift helped me greatly; to Lillian and Edmund Hennefeld for reading the entire manuscript and offering many useful suggestions; to Petra and Joel Ewen for placing their technical resources and knowledge at my disposal; to Teresa Bennett of the Mexitype Corporation for excellent typesetting. I wish to thank the directors of the libraries of Columbia University, Harvard University, the New York Public Library, the Bibliothèque Nationale of Paris, and the British Museum for the use of their rich resources. I am also grateful to the officers and staff of the Citadel Press for preparing the book for publication with exemplary care.

To my wife, Miriam Gideon, my debt exceeds telling, and I shall merely content myself with saying that she made the writing of this book an exhilarating adventure.

FREDERIC EWEN

New York City
August 1983

NOTE

Unless otherwise indicated, translations
in the following pages are by Frederic Ewen.

Part One

WATERLOO AND AFTER

I.

THE ANGUISH OF TRANSITION
AND WATERLOO

I.

THE ANGUISH OF TRANSITION

I.

THE ANGUISH OF TRANSITION

As in human life, so too in the life of a society, a nation, a community, periods of transition are frequently marked by anguish, pain, disturbance, and doubt. The old and the new contend for mastery; the struggle is still undecided; and the "child" — to use a somewhat different figure — is changing into man or woman —and in the process of "becoming" something else, experiences deep pangs, conflicts, and anxieties. Internal chaos contends with what appears a chaos without — and the quest for order, the quest for internal and external security are not easily attained. The dynamism of life proceeds — things, conditions, human beings constantly change — though such change is not always or immediately apparent. However, often changes are rapid, and the clash between that which was and that which is or is about to be becomes sharpened, often even desperate. At such times defeats seem almost more numerous than victories. At such moments the passions of an earlier day subside or are extinguished, and disenchantment seeks a quietus — a resting place, a retreat...

But the creative impulses within mankind are never really totally submerged or quenched. The need to "create" transcends the obstacles that would bar its way. In such a process, creation may take on the color of the world surrounding it, and its crystallization in art expresses poignantly the anguish and torment of the creator and his times.

It is therefore not surprising — but always exhilarating — to find in such periods of stress great genius and great inventions, art works, discoveries and vital experiments. Even when they reveal profoundest despair or despondency, such creations are affirmative acts, for they testify to the indestructibility of human capacities.

There is, however, pathos in such ages — pathos of premature deaths or isolation of the creative genius — especially when a hostile or indifferent society denies it acceptance, or shrinks from it. For great genius is like a volcano or an earthquake. It terrifies. But unlike those phenomena, genius is productive, though at the moment one might only be aware of the ravages it spreads.

Such a transitional world appears as if it were dismembered. The potential and actual are at war. Unresolvable contradictions haunt its denizens. What can one make of a world in which extraordinary discoveries and inventions that apparently draw the world together into some unity, that create sources of well-being and power, and overnight enrich entire populations — at the same time give birth to over-crowded cities, wretched habitations which displace communities, and instead of shouts of jubilation, draw forth pitiful cries and plaints. How is one to reconcile the promises held forth by two revolutions — that in America and that in France — at the end of the eighteenth century, with the monstrous evidences of cupidity, new tyrannies, new absolutisms?

Where, one asks, is that brotherhood of human kind so recently proclaimed? Greed appears to be stalking the lands as never before — though the old lords of the blood have given way. Yet, here are new lords in power — the lords of the money-marts...

Where is one to turn? Past, Present, and Future — each of these wars with its claims, problems, and solutions. Go back to the Past? Come to terms with the Present? Or, instead, indulge in dreams — dreams of the seemingly impossible — yet look ahead and strive, strive?...

II.

WATERLOO AND AFTER

II.

WATERLOO AND AFTER

Where the Revolution surrendered her sword.
— Edgar Quinet —

"On June 18, 1815, I left Ghent about noon by the Brussels gate; I was going to finish my walk alone on the highroad. I had taken Caesar's *Commentaries* with me and I strolled along, immersed in my reading. I was over two miles from the town when I thought I heard a dull rumbling; I stopped and looked up at the sky, which was fairly cloudy, wondering whether I should walk or turn back toward Ghent for fear of a storm. I listened, I heard nothing more but the cry of a moor-hen in the rushes and the sound of the village clock. I continued on my way: I had not taken thirty steps before the rumbling began again, now short, now drawn out and at irregular intervals; sometimes it was perceptible only through a trembling of the air, which was so far away that it communicated itself to the ground as it passed over those vast plains. The detonations, less prolonged, less undulating, less interrelated than those of thunder, gave rise in my mind to the ideas of a battle. I found myself opposite a poplar at the corner of a hop-field. I crossed the road and leant against the trunk of the tree, with my face turned in the direction of Brussels. A southerly wind sprang up and brought me more distinctly the sound of artillery. That great battle, nameless as yet, to whose echoes I was listening at the foot of a poplar, and for whose unknown obsequies a village clock had just struck, was the Battle of Waterloo."[1]

It is in these words that the great romantic, Vicomte François-René Chateaubriand, describes the sound of the guns that were to

11

mark one of the major turning points in the history of the modern
world. For with the fall of Napoleon Bonaparte, and his exile to St.
Helena, ends one stupendous period of world-history. Another,
equally stupendous, is about to begin.

What followed immediately upon Waterloo has been somewhat
euphemistically called the "Restoration". In reality, it was the
second of that name, for the first "Restoration" had been
unpredictably interrupted by the return of Napoleon from Elba
some time before, and was followed by the "Hundred Days" that threw
the seemingly victorious powers into a panic. But now, there could
be no further doubt. Napoleon — that Monster or Titan, as he was
variously designated by foe or friend — had been finally crushed.
Now it might seem as if past history — that of the last thirty or so
years, from the French Revolution on, with all its terrifying and
confusing aftermaths, Napoleon and the Napoleonic Empire — was
but a bad dream, from which the world might awaken to a sunny
and untroubled new dawn. For over twenty-five years Europe had
been witnessing war and desolation. The "Corsican upstart" had
succeeded in toppling monarch after monarch.

Eighty-five million, five-hundred thousand souls recognized his sovereignty
or that of his family. Half the population of Christendom obeyed him; his
orders were carried out over an area of nineteen degrees latitude and thirty
degrees longitude.[2]

Only England had remained immune to his despoilment and
invasion...Like the rest of the world, she looked forward to the
"new day".

The "new day" was to bring back the Old Order..."the good,
old times".

The British Tory magazine, the *Quarterly Review*, exulted.
"The Volcano is now extinguished...And now we may approach
the crater with perfect security."[3]

Now that fictive entity of victorious nations, Russia, Prussia,
and Austria, the so-called "Holy Alliance", proclaimed "Christian

love", and in the role of "the plenipotentiaries of Providence", vowed an indissoluble "brotherhood" — "to help one another like fellow-countrymen", that is, to make sure that nothing was to be allowed to subvert the return to the status-quo. England held aloof from the "Holy Alliance", but joined a "Quadruple Alliance", with the three others, "for the maintenance of the existing state of things." And so, at the Congress of Vienna of 1814 and the Peace Conference of Paris of 1815, they proceeded to redraw the map of Europe. Once more Poland was cut up — Russia, Prussia, and Austria getting a slice each. In addition, Austria was awarded the provinces of Venetia, Dalmatia, and Lombardy. The kingdoms of Sardinia and Sicily were resurrected. As for that inchoate mélange of states called "Germany" — it was now a patchwork of thirty-nine separate and sovereign units, leagued together in a German Confederation. Its heart was Vienna. Here sat Prince Metternich — the policeman of Europe. His function — to see that nothing changed. The specter of Revolution was never to rise again. At least so he thought, and so he hoped.

French émigrés began hurrying back to their country, eager to retrieve that "sweetness of life" that Talleyrand had said characterized the period before 1789. They came to reclaim estates, chateaux, and huge fortunes that they felt constituted their rightful reparations for sorrows sustained under the Revolution and Napoleon. They also came to exact vengeance and inaugurate their own "White Terror."

But only on the surface was this return to a "status-quo" truly a Restoration. For the world had changed radically since 1789, and the Idea of Revolution was not so easily extirpated. Revolution — in one form or another was to be the special earmark of the nineteenth century — as the events of 1830, 1848, and 1871 were to prove — and it was to become a reality in the twentieth. Of course, there were portents present even in 1815, but there were few prescient enough to sense them. Who could then have predicted what mighty roles on the world stage were to be played by such nations as England, Russia, and Prussia?

Of England's coming importance there had been premonitory signs enough. She had been the first country in the world to industrialize on a large scale; and now, after the Napoleonic Wars, she stood forth as the strongest of all the nations. Her own territories had remained untouched by the ravages of war; and by 1815, in the words of one historian, "she had gained the most complete victory of any power in the entire history of the world, having emerged from the twenty years of war against France as the *only* industrialized economy, the *only* naval power ... and virtually the *only* colonial power in the world."[4]

The French Revolution and the Industrial Revolution were the irrefragable realities of the years to come. Of no lesser influence on the minds of the nineteenth century was the Napoleonic Idea and its persistence. The idea of the French Revolution had, in its own day, swept artists, scientists, philosophers, and statesmen. It had inflamed the imagination of poets like Schiller, Burns, Wordsworth, Coleridge, William Blake; of philosophers like Kant, Fichte, and Hegel. As for France, the Revolution was to remain an irrepressible battle cry for the rest of the century.

Of those revolutionary days, William Wordsworth had sung,

> Bliss was it in that dawn to be alive,
> But to be young was very Heaven!

And the German philosopher Fichte had declared his readiness to take up arms in defense of the French Republic:

I give myself hereby with all that I have and can into the hands of the Republic; not in order to gain from her something but in order to be of use to her if I can ... It is clear from now on, only the French Republic can be the fatherland of the righteous man, to which he may dedicate his powers ... Not only the dearest hopes of mankind, but its very existence is tied up with its victory.[5]

And Hegel celebrated the great event by seeing in it the triumph of Reason — "a glorious dawn."

The world had changed and was changing radically. What was the nature of those changes?

For one, the growth of Europe's population. Within a hundred years following 1750, the population had doubled, rising from approximately 140 million to 257 million. In 1800 there were only around twenty-two towns in Europe with a population exceeding 100,000. In 1850 there were forty-seven such, and of these twenty-eight were in England. London showed an increase of over one million inhabitants in that period, Paris doubled its population to reach one million, at the same time.

To describe the changes — the new productions, inventions, ideas, changes in human relations — a new vocabulary comes into being — and the extent of such changes can be measured superficially by the incursion of such terms as industry and industrialist; industrial revolution; factory and working-classes; middle classes and capitalist; capitalism, aristocracy, liberal, conservative; nationality; pauperism, proletariat, strikes; engineer; socialism and communism . . . [6]

And perhaps most important of all — revolution in technology brought about by changes in the sources of energy and their practical application to nature and mankind. To effect significant changes in the structure of the economy these new sources require application by means of machinery and capital. The combination of these elements produced a revolution in the life of humanity to an extent unprecedented in the history of the Western world. The rapid transformation in our own way of life today through the application of atomic energy must not blind us to the equally exciting and terrifying impact of steam, the steam engine, and later, of electricity. If our senses and imagination are dulled today by meteoric new discoveries, inventions and exploits — let us not look with condescension on the awe and terror that accompanied the thirty-mile an hour speed of the first railway, as it made its thunderous whirlwind journey between Stockton and Darlington in 1825. How could even James Watt himself, in 1765, have foreseen the

consequences of his invention of the steam engine? For by means of
the railroad, coal could now be transported from coal-mine to other
mines — the iron output could be raised, and with it the mass
production of steel undertaken. Sadder to remember, the railroad
would change the character of war and warfare.

Steam drove the machine, and the machine became King. Such
technological triumphs as England now exhibited had never been
witnessed before. England was at the head of nations with respect to
industry and commerce. The Napoleonic Wars had made it possible
for her to eliminate all her major rivals, with the likely exception of
the still very young North American republic. England's cotton
industry penetrated many corners of the earth — an industry that
attracted capital — an industry that made for colonial expansion. It
has been justly remarked that cotton and colonial expansion were
the two motive forces of the Industrial Revolution.

But the terrifying and wonderful machine that had been
brought into being was a human product, invented by human
beings, owned and served by human beings, capable of being
changed and developed by them, but also capable of changing them,
their environment, and their history. Like all great inventions and
innovations it will have its constructive as well as destructive
aspects. Old, less profitable or efficient methods, systems, arrange-
ments will be doomed. The new cotton industry will kill off the
hand-weaving industry; it will turn the hand-loom worker into a
factory hand; and often, in times of crisis, it will throw him out into
the streets. The process is inexorable, irresistible. Industry is King!
Industry will take over farming — though much more gradually —
and turn the formerly independent middle-class farmer either into a
tenant-farmer or into an agricultural laborer.

England became the marvel of the century — the foremost
producer of cotton, of coal; the world's foremost commercial and
industrial nation — the dominant colonial power. She seemed
destined to rule the world...

The earmark of the nineteenth century: — Struggle...

The ostensible "calm" following 1815 — the "peace" that was being guaranteed by the Concert of European States — the "balance of powers" by which they expected to fortify the Restoration — these only hid the underlying stirrings and unrest that were to intensify into an unpredictable explosive power.

There will be struggle among nations — struggle for colonial domination — struggle for world-power.

Struggles within nations — struggles for national independence.

And of no lesser intensity — struggles between "classes" of society. A new class, offspring of the English and French Revolutions — the "middle" class, or "bourgeoisie" — had achieved a measure of power. Industrialists, traders, bankers — soon to be known as "capitalists" — are now sufficiently strong to throw down challenges to the prepotent upper or landed classes, and demand their share of political control. Soon, these, in turn, will be confronted by a dreaded, and eventually formidable adversary, brought into being by the Industrial Revolution — the so-called "proletariat" — the working classes. Great clashes are in the offing...

The aristocracy of the "blood" will be faced by a new aristocracy — the new princes of high finance and industry. The latter have powerful weapons in their armories — Money. They too will have other armaments — ideological weapons which they will press into service — ideas: theological, metaphysical, political, scientific, social, which they will soon turn against new adversaries, as interests oppose interests... Arts and letters, too, will be drawn into these conflicts. Problems and struggles provoke and awaken a new consciousness...

Rarely before in the history of the world had the European consciousness been so sharply tested and strained, and forced to respond to the stresses, turbulences and excitements that now prevailed — mounting indeed, one might say, with ever-accumulating intensity. In one of those paradoxes, so replete in history, the Napoleonic Empire, that had striven to unify Europe under one aegis, and then had crumbled, had despite all, brought about a new kind of interrelation of European beings — politically, intellectually, and artistically — a novel kind of interdependence and interchange. Physically it might be symbolized by the presence of the Tsar of Russia in Paris: as before, it might have been symbolized by the presence of Napoleon in Russia. Intellectually and practically, it was to be marked by the flow of ideas across the many barriers of a reestablished Europe. Such an internationalization was in time to embrace many interests: cultural, technological, scientific, mechanical — and, not least, social and political.

The rapid historical changes wrought upon the human consciousness as rapidly changing history. Living within history, it was forced to grapple with the meaning and nature of history, particularly with new manifestations, as they became more and more evident. A society such as had come into being now, that was redistributing its population, increasing its concentration in cities, which were becoming major manufacturing or commercial centers, cities across whose horizons smoke-stacks belched forth thick smoke, whose inhabitants were seen daily trooping to and from work, living together in close quarters, such a society makes visible problems formerly hidden or undiscovered: in fact concentrates them in a way not so easily perceptible in a feudal, agrarian society of widely dispersed villages and hamlets.

Of course, such phenomena did not occur overnight.

A new phenomenon, no less serious, becomes apparent — that of economic booms and recessions. After 1815, economic crises follow one another at practically ten-year intervals. By 1870, they will have become world-wide in their effects. The ever-widening gulf between those who have and those who have not will stand out glaringly. The hovels of the newly risen slums will cry out against the lavish palaces of the great financiers, the Barings of England, the Hochs of Amsterdam, the Rothschilds, the Foulds and the Laffittes of France — against the vast holdings of the still semi-feudal landowners. History posed the question: Shall the poor always be with us? And demanded an answer.

Whatever unrest might bridle against oppressions, it was barely articulate as yet. In the Ballhausplatz in Vienna sat Prince Clemens Wenzel Lothar von Metternich-Winneburg — guardian of the peace and security of the German Federation of states and of Austria; a brilliant diplomat, now, in 1815, forty-two years old. As one of the principal architects of the policies of the Restoration, he also regarded himself, in his own words as a "species of moral power in Germany, and perhaps in Europe." He surrounded himself with brilliant coadjutors, most of them one-time liberals and fervent Romantics — figures like Adam Müller, Friedrich Gentz, and Friedrich Schlegel. Needless to say, he also had police and armies at his beck and call. His surveillance extended from Sicily to the English Channel. Of course, he had journalists and journals in his pay, or under his control, and a rigid press censorship at his service, as well as a strict supervision of universities and their faculties, and occasionally, even inquisitorial commissions.

Where revolutionary stirrings turned into menaces, he would invoke protocols endorsed by Austria, Russia and Prussia, which empowered joint interventions in such areas. Thus, in 1820, insurrections in Naples and Spain were quickly suppressed. The French sent troops and restored the ousted Bourbon monarch to the Spanish throne in 1823.

Metternich believed that "man's nature is immutable." Though scarcely a devout Catholic, he saw himself aided by the Lord's intervention to advance his designs. "Drag through the mud the name of God and the power instituted by His divine decrees, and the Revolution will prepare!" He abhorred the idea of a social contract and the rights of man. "Speak of a social contract, and the Revolution is accomplished." "Two words will suffice to create evil: Liberty and Equality." He hated Napoleon Bonaparte and the middle classes with equal fervor. In the latter he foresaw the seeds of disintegration of religion, morality, and political society.

With justice, and not without some concern, he kept a sharp look-out on the motherland of revolutions — France. France was the land of ideologues — and what new ideas might she not be breeding and worse, put into practice there? ... England deserved careful watching, too. Had not that country fathered the first bourgeois revolution in the seventeenth century? What might not that land of "shop-keepers" and traders be capable of, with her sharp look-out for her own materialistic interests? And her diplomats and statesmen! — as sharp and Machiavellian as the great Metternich himself? ...

II.

ENGLAND
"THE SCEPTERED ISLE" AND
"THE DARK SATANIC MILLS"

I.

"THE SCEPTERED ISLE"

I.

"THE SCEPTERED ISLE"

An old mad, blind, despised and dying king —
Princes, the dregs of their dull race, who flow
Through public scorn — mud from a muddy spring;
Rulers who neither see, nor feel, nor know,
But leechlike to their fainting country cling,
Till they drop, blind in blood, without a blow;
A people starved and stabbed in the untilled field —
An army, which liberticide and prey
Makes as a two-edged sword to all who wield;
Golden and sanguine laws which tempt and slay;
Religion Christless, Godless — a book sealed;
A Senate — Time's worst statute unrepealed;
Are graves, from which a glorious Phantom may
Burst, to illumine our tempestuous day.
— Shelley, "England in 1819" —

Because England was at this time the most advanced nation industrially and commercially; and because she had the most advanced industrial and manufacturing class, and the most numerous workers engaged in industry, she was bound to show in the sharpest light the clashes and contradictions that were to be the earmarks of all future industrial societies.

Surely, so many an Englishman thought, there must be a Divine Dispensation that was working in favor of that land, and it would be sinful to interfere with it. A natural or divine order — so the great political thinker Edmund Burke believed — had decreed that there were necessaries of life "which it has pleased the Divine Providence for a while to withhold" from the poor. Or they might approve, with Adam Smith, of that "invisible hand" that guided the equitable "distribution of the necessaries of life."[8]

25

Was not what England had achieved within a very short space of time cause for pride and exultation — a miracle? There were the new mills and the new cities that had grown up in Lancashire and in Scotland. The roar of the Manchester factories could be heard around the world. There was the breath-taking wool industry of West Riding; and the linen and silk manufactures elsewhere. There were the astonishing advances in iron and coal mining, and in the smelting industries. The history of the English industrial development of that and the following periods had, in Friedrich Engels's words, "no counterpart in the annals of humanity."9

So much for the pride of the things achieved. But there was less pride when the English looked up at their ruling class. Never before, not even during the reign of the Stuarts, had England been governed by a royal house so utterly corrupt, profligate, and, in part, lunatic. In 1810 George III had been publicly recognized as insane. A regency bill of 1811 had entrusted the supreme government to the hand of the Prince of Wales, another George, who had in 1785 married a Catholic, Mrs. Fitzherbert, without the King's consent; and who in 1795 had been constrained to marry a German princess, Caroline. The Prince continued living with Mrs. Fitzherbert until 1803, and supplied England and British history with one of their most shameful scandals.

It was indeed difficult to decide which one of the many sons of George III was the most dissolute, the greatest spendthrift, or produced the most numerous brood of bastards on his mistresses. The Prince Regent was high on the list. Nor did he lack lickspittles who were ready to celebrate him with these words: "You are the glory of the People — You are the Maecenas of the Age . . . You are an Adonis in loveliness." The poet-laureate, Robert Southey, once an ardent revolutionary, was one of his most dedicated celebrants, for which he was to receive an exemplary drubbing from the pen of Byron. It would be interesting to know what the operatives in the Lancashire mills, who labored so that the Regent might whore in luxury, thought of their rulers.

To cast aspersions on royal conduct was, of course, *lèse-majesté*. Leigh Hunt, friend of Shelley and Keats, who with his brother was editor of the intrepid periodical, the *Examiner*, dared to write in 1812 that

this redoubtable Adonis in Loveliness was a corpulent gentleman of fifty! . . . This delightful, blissful, wise, and pleasurable, honorable, virtuous, true and immortal PRINCE was a violator of his word, a libertine over head and ear in debt and disgrace, a despiser of domestic ties, the companion of gamblers and demireps, a man who has just closed a half century without one single claim on the gratitude of his country and the respect of posterity.[10]

For which piece of plain-speaking, both Leigh Hunt and his brother were sentenced to two years' imprisonment in 1813.

It would be useless to follow the Prince Regent in his sexual peregrinations, which included ladies of both high and low estate. What a royal household his must have been! In his apartments, the mad George III, his father, raved, and had to be forcefully restrained. At last the longed-for death of the King, in 1820, freed the son so that he might rid himself of his wife, Caroline, herself no mean free-wheeling sexual adventuress. Could royal comedy have proceeded farther? A Royal whoremonger charging a Royal whore with whoredom! The people sided with poor Caroline, and the brilliant defense by Brougham brought a vindication for her; but hapless woman — she died in July 1821, with the title of Queen-Consort still intact. George IV grew fat, gouty, and moved in a wheelchair, not less promiscuous than before; to get on his horse, he was heaved up with a mechanical contrivance; and he managed to survive till 1830. Ominous year! . . .

His brothers, the Duke of York, and the Duke of Cumberland, were no better. The reigning king of sartorial style was none other than Beau Brummel, the Prince-Regent's one-time favorite, who was on such familiar footing with his master that he could tell him "Wales, ring the bell."[11]

When he was Prince-Regent, his father, George III, once reproved him for his late rising. "I find, Sir," the son responded, "however late I rise, that the day is long enough for doing nothing."[12]

Almost at the same time, Robert Owen, the Utopian, was writing:

Children at this time were admitted into the cotton, wool, flax and silk mills, at six, and sometimes even at five years of age. The time of working, winter and summer, was unlimited by law, but usually it was fourteen hours per day — in some fifteen, even, by the most inhuman and avaricious, sixteen hours.

II.

"THE DARK SATANIC MILLS"

II.

"THE DARK SATANIC MILLS"

And did those feet in ancient time
Walk upon England's mountain green:
And was the holy Lamb of God
On England's pleasant pastures seen!

And did the Countenance Divine
Shine forth upon our clouded hills!
And was Jerusalem builded here
Among these dark Satanic Mills?

Bring me my Bow of burning gold:
Bring me my Arrows of desire:
Bring me my Spear: O clouds unfold!
Bring me my Chariot of Fire!

I will not cease from Mental Fight,
Nor shall my Sword sleep in my hand
Till we have built Jerusalem
In England's green and pleasant land.

— William Blake, "Milton," 1804 —

When news of the abdication of Napoleon Bonaparte reached England, the Prince-Regent made ready to celebrate the event. Louis XVIII of France was then living in luxurious emigration in Hartwell, Buckinghamshire, and the British monarch escorted reestablished French majesty to London. What more proper than they should joyfully embrace on such a Restoration — and properly decorate each other? The King of France invested the Prince-Regent with the order of Saint-Esprit, and the Prince-Regent bestowed upon the Bourbon the Order of the Garter.

31

The satirist who called himself Peter Pindar wrote:

> And France's hope and Britain's heir,
> Were, in truth, a most congenial pair;
> Two round, tunbellied, thriving rakes,
> Like oxen fed on linseed cakes.[14]

Yet, at that moment England had cause for worry. Her largest customer and consumer of her goods — War — was no more. That great production that had gone into the making and continuing of war, and aiding others to do likewise, and had kept enriching her native manufacturers and landlords, was now at a temporary standstill. There had been intermittent crises even during the "boom" years of war. But concomitantly with the high development of technology, machinery, and production, there also had been a steadily rising cost of living, approximately 90% between 1790 and 1813, and falling thereafter; but then rising again until 1825. Wages, already low in 1793 (amounting to between 8s. and 9s. weekly), had risen and fallen. But no matter what the rise, both the agricultural worker and the factory operative, were miserably underpaid. The national debt rose from nine million pounds to over thirty-one; and since the money therefor came from the excise and custom taxes, the debt weighed most heavily on buyers of essential commodities. With the abolition of the income tax, such a burden was aggravated so far as the unpropertied were concerned.

The result — frequent periods of starvation.

There had been serious disturbances among the working population before 1815, and among agrarian workers as well. The rapid industrialization of the country had grievously injured domestic manufacture, especially in the hand-looming industry. It was these domestic weavers who sparked and participated in the so-called "Luddite" insurrections, with the avowed purpose of destroying the new machinery that was causing them such desolation and misery. Severely repressed as they were — for hanging was not deemed too severe a punishment for such infractions — they continued for years, till overshadowed by the larger demonstrations after 1815, when even the new machinery was not able to keep workers from unemployment and starvation.

And with the peace — came the "bad years." The price of wheat declined by almost 50% in 1815. Such panic as now took place among the proprietary agrarian interests had not been seen in a long time. The response to this crisis was immediate. It was the passage by Parliament of the notorious Corn Law, which regulated the profitable sale of the product at home — in other words, decreeing that until the wheat price in England rose to say 80s. a quarter, no foreign wheat could be imported to compete with it.

So that the already impoverished part of the British population was forced to pay more for their bread. The anti-Corn Law agitation of subsequent years became one of the most potent incentives to popular solidarity.

No lesser was the panic of the industrialists in the face of a catastrophic rate of unemployment. The armies of the "idle" (there is always a suitable euphemism in those circumstances!) were now swelled by large numbers of returning soldiers. Who was to pay for their relief? In Birmingham alone, during 1816-1817, practically one-fifth of the population received weekly relief. Situations in other industrial towns and cities were scarcely better. The "silence of unmingled desolation" — as one contemporary described the tomb-like quiet and misery of those days — was to recur at frequent intervals.

Fear of revolution had been successfully invoked in the 1790's. Now it was mobilized with all energies, so that any visible signs of discontent might be annulled at once. Parliament, at the behest of manufacturers and landlords, suspended the Habeas Corpus Act in 1817 and 1818, and hastened to enforce the Combination Acts of 1799 and 1800, which prohibited the organization of workers, or any suspect association; restricted the freedom of oral and written utterances, and subjected violators to fines, imprisonment, and even deportation.

Yet protest was by no means stifled ...

There was the Spa Field monster demonstration of London, in 1816, addressed by the fiery and irrepressible orator Henry Hunt. There was the Lancashire procession of handloom weavers, who set out for London carrying their own blankets (hence called "Blanketeers"), petitioning for relief and reform, and work, who were dispersed before they were able to set out. The most flagrant and notorious incident of those days occurred on August 16, 1819, at St. Peter's Field, Manchester, at which thousands of demonstrators were attacked by the yeomanry and soldiery, spurred on by the clergy, and in which eleven persons were killed and hundreds injured. This was the "Peterloo" massacre — named after Waterloo. The martyrology of the unknown and unchronicled "heroes" of such actions escapes the notice of historians.

Luckily, other names have survived. That, for example of Henry Hunt, sentenced to two and a half years' imprisonment for his participation in the St. Peter's Field demonstration. There is the indomitable publicist and editor of *The Republican,* Richard Carlile, who spent over nine years in jail, during his lifetime. Nor can one forget William Cobbett, and his *Political Register,* as well as Leigh Hunt and his brother. There is John Gast, editor of the *Gorgon,* the first trade-union newspaper. And there were the many editors and distributors of cheap pamphlets and papers, which their enemies referred to as "two-penny trash," who defied the law with their "unstamped" — untaxed publications. These were eagerly read, and listened to when read by others, by shoemakers, tradesmen, artisans, millworkers and miners.[15]

Considering the formidable oposition they faced, and the severe penalties that were being imposed, the sporadic, unorganized insurgents could not but fail — though they might cause occasional panic. Politically immature, without a voice in Parliament (it would be almost three-quarters of a century before they would be enfranchised), they encountered monolithic powers, with unlimited forces of law and men at their command. Until 1851 the landed interests represented the most powerful political force in England, a vast hierarchy that in descending order included the landed aristocracy, the great land-owners without title, the country gentlemen, the tenant farmers, the small land-owners, down to the agrarian laborers. They also enjoyed the support of the attending professions and tradesmen who ministered to their wants and their health, as well as a great preponderance of the clerical religious establishment. The extent and duration of their power may be gauged by the fact that even as late as 1873, fewer than seven thousand individuals owned four-fifths of the land in the United Kingdom.[16]

Their political and social control, it may be guessed, was vast. Two-thirds of the political representation of England and Wales was in the hands of 177 individuals; seven thousand clerical livings out of a total of eleven thousand were in the hands of the aristocracy and the gentry.

It was a solid body this, a Tory group well entrenched in Parliament, and well protected by such figures in the Cabinet as Lord Liverpool, Castlereagh, Sidmouth and Lord Ellenborough, and in the courts by the Treasonable Practice Bill, the Combinations Acts, the rigid press censorship, suspensions of the Habeas Corpus — all backed by the yeomanry, soldiery, and the clergy. The Bishops in the House of Lords could be relied on to oppose any movement for the reform of the parliamentary structure.

Tory power resided in the House of Lords, where two or three hundred peers could reject any measures passed by the House of Commons. In 1815 nearly all members of the British Parliament were landed proprietors, who profited from the highly restrictive franchise (note: London was represented by four members, while Cornwall had forty-four!), the corrupt rotten boroughs, bribery and patronage.

Tories regarded themselves as the defenders of royal prerogatives against Parliament. Until their preeminence was challenged by the rising power of the manufacturers, traders and bankers, they were the true rulers of England. But they were unlike the French Bourbons. They remembered and they learned. When pressed, they would be persuaded to share power, but they knew how to retain it for a long time. Thus they stamped the age with the seal of "compromise."

III.

ROMANTICISM, REVOLUTION, AND THE POETS
Wordsworth — Blake — Byron — Keats — Shelley

ROMANTICISM, REVOLUTION,
AND THE POETS

1.

The complex literary, artistic, and philosophic movement called "Romanticism" had its beginnings before the outbreak of the French Revolution, but it reaches its full fruition through the impact of that world-historic event. It is a part of that great historic breakthrough which is marked by a widening of human consciousness — a flowering of self-awareness, as well as a deepening sense of human interrelations in a changed and changing world. It reflects a fresh sense of the meaning of the "ego" — expressive not only of its own desires, visions, and feelings; but also of its relation to the world around it — nature, both animate and inanimate; and humanity. It reflects its heightened sense of the infinite possibilities that lie within human beings individually and socially. Its consciousness is directed toward the present and the future. The "I" acquires a new importance and dignity. Its vision is international, as never before; it is also "national," in its discovery of a national past, a national history, a national culture in which it can take pride. In its manifestations, "Romanticism" is marked by this consciousness of "change" — of freedom, of experiment, of discovery of new ways of expression, new territories of experience, as well as — paradoxically — a searching of history for older forms to be reshaped. The "I" of the present seeks to understand the "I" of the past. The sense of the importance of the individual, self-examination, "history of the soul", as it were, dominates the creative spirit. Autobiography acquires a new dignity and meaning — sparked by such creations as Rousseau's *Confessions* and Goethe's *Dichtung und Wahrheit*. At first self-development and

Revolution become almost synonymous . . . Political "declarations of independence" or of "the rights of man" have their counterparts in literary, artistic, and philosophical manifestoes.

These are the "universals" of Romanticism, wherever it may make its appearance. The specifics may vary from land to land, from age to age, but even these will be understood within the context of the political, social and moral environment of the particular country.

It was natural that England should have been the advance guard of Romanticism, for here a revolutionary climate had already been established in the Great Revolution of the seventeenth century — the first "bourgeois" revolution of the western world. The modern novel was the offspring of that "bourgeois" transformation, and England's other pre-romanticists set the stage for an international romantic insurgence. No less a figure than Rousseau had come under British influence, though his own individual genius had made him France's leading pre-Romantic. But all these individual streams were finally strengthened by the events in France to make for a full flood.

If the essence of Romanticism is "freedom" — its central themes are entwined around the new conception of "people" and "brotherhood" — now envisioned not as phantasms, but as realities. For hadn't the "people" in common action toppled the rotting feudalism of France? Hadn't the "people" in far off America proclaimed with pride their making of a "more perfect union"? It was under this double inspiration that the Scottish poet Robert Burns celebrated in a new "Marseillaise" and in his Scottish tongue the equality of humankind — "A Man's a Man for a' That" — and scorning rank as the mere "guinea stamp," proclaimed a universal humanitarianism; and with his incomparable satiric pen scourged oppression, hypocrisy, and fanaticism. Yes, in poetry the "people" were finding their most dedicated allies . . .

Was France destined to be the New Jerusalem — the realized dream of a new, ideal commonwealth? The young poets and writers of the early 1790's believed so; radical preachers spoke of the new day. Young Coleridge and young Robert Southey in their daydreams thought to emigrate to America and there establish an ideal new community on the banks of the Susquehanna River (the name sounded so beautiful!) — a state to be called "Pantisocracy" — "rule by all" — and they marshalled plans, which of course all came to naught, as the practical demands of life wrought havoc with the dream. They sublimated it in ebullient poetry.

Young William Wordsworth went to France in 1791, to see for himself — and he remained there to the end of the following year, at the time of the great upheaval, mostly in Blois and Orléans. In France he fell in love with a young French woman, Annette Vallon, and had a child by her. This was to remain the most recondite secret of his life, unsuspected by a worshiping posterity, who came to regard him as the moral prophet of the age. But out of his experiences in revolutionary France came what was to be his greatest single poem, which he set down in 1804, at the height of his poetic career, and which he completed in 1805. The histroy of that long poem is no less interesting than the experiences he was to record, for it was not published till 1850, the year of the poet's death, in a radically revised version. The unpublished version in 1805 did not come to light until much later. Neither version mentions his love experience, but both represent an extraordinary poetic self-revelation — as the title shows: *The Prelude, or The Growth of a Poet's Mind,* — a study of the evolution of a poet under the impact of the new forces at work at the time, particularly the Revolution in France. *The Prelude* was Wordsworth's private testament, as the celebrated *Lyrical Ballads* of 1798 — the joint little volume of poems by Coleridge and Wordsworth — was to be their public testament —a precious and radical manifesto of the new poetry. The *Preface* composed by Wordsworth set forth its theory of the form, language and content that their poetic creations involved — the break with eighteenth century formal poetic diction, the need for replacing it with the language of common speech heightened to poetry, and the new perceptions of the relation of poetry to Man, Nature, and ordinary human experiences.

We look to the *Prelude* for the sources of the radical new poetry. We read in the two versions the great changes that had come over Wordsworth in the course of the nigh half-century, after his "disenchantment", when more and more gradually he turned into a hide-bound Tory, and became poet-laureate and thoroughly "Victorian."

But the flames of youth, like the flames of a first love, are never totally quenched, and even in the version of 1850 they still burn — though less fiercely — in many lines that he could not erase. Much of the incandescent eloquence of an earlier day remains.

It is with the early version that we are primarily concerned here — for it represents a contemporary confession, drawn out of the immediate contacts and conflicts of 1791 and 1792, wrought out with glow of youth's inspirations.[17]

Who can ever forget the great lines,

> O pleasant exercise of hope and joy!
> For great were the auxiliars which then stood
> Upon our side, we who were strong in love;
> Bliss was it in that dawn to be alive,
> But to be young was very Heaven...
> Not favour'd spots alone, but the whole earth
> The beauty wore of promise...

when men and women

> Were call'd upon to exercise their skill
> Not in Utopia, subterraneous Fields,
> Or some secreted Island, Heaven knows where,
> But in the very world which is the world
> Of all of us, the place in which, in the end,
> We find happiness, or not at all...

when he, too, seemed assured

> ... that time would soon set all things right,
> Prove that the multitude had been oppressed,
> And would be so no more...

He hated the bulwarks of the aristocracy,

> ... where will of One
> Is law for all,

and his heart went out with love of the "abject multitude", whose misery and wretchedness horrified him, and he came to believe

> ... that poverty
> would in a little time
> Be found no more,

that honest toil would receive its rightful reward, and the people would share in governing themselves, and that, finally, "better days to all mankind" would come.

The young poet dreams of "the unity of man."

Then came the great shock: Britain declared war against revolutionary France! — a war against regenerated France! "Unworthy service!" he cried, and rejoiced when his country's armies suffered their first defeats!

He was no less intensely outraged by the British government's domestic policies — the political repressions at home of dissidents, supporters and defenders of the French Revolution, when in 1793 the Habeas Corpus Act was suspended, and when members of the democratic Corresponding Society, proponents of political reform, men like Hardy, Horne Tooke and Thelwall were prosecuted. This was the time when an enraged mob, inflamed by anti-French feeling, set fire to the house of Joseph Priestley, philosopher, scientist, and radical thinker.

Wordsworth was unsparing in his condemnation:

Our Shepherds ... at the time
Thirsted to make the guardian Crook of Law
A tool of Murder; they who ruled the State,
Though with such awful proof before
    their eyes
That he who would sow death, reaps death,
    or worse,
And can reap nothing better, child-like long'd
To imitate, not wise enough to avoid,
Giants in their impiety alone,
But in their weapons and their warfare base
As vermin working out of reach, they leagu'd
Their strength perfidiously, to undermine
Justice, and make an end of Liberty.

All his passion was still alive in 1804, when disenchantment
had already set in as a result of the French "Reign of Terror" of the
years 1793 and 1794; and the succeeding reaction, when he could
still describe his feelings, as "Creed which the shameful years have
not annulled." But with time he grew more and more conservative,
and when he came to revise the great poem of 1805 he attenuated
many of the most eloquent passages, like the one quoted above.
Censure of England gave way to a retraction, and he no longer
condemned the persecution of British radicals, and capped his
political and social tergiversation by adding a eulogy of Edmund
Burke, whose *Reflections on the Revolution in France* had been the
virulent, though eloquent, call to battle against the French
Revolution. Wordsworth's revisions were part of that pattern of
retreat that was exemplified in his attacks in later life on the Reform
Bill, on Catholic emancipation, his defense of capital punishment,
and culminated in the composition of his dreary *Ecclesiastical
Sonnets*. He preached submission to Custom, Institutes and Laws
"hallowed by time," and scourged "exploding upstart Theory", and
insisted upon "the allegiance to which men are born."[18] Forgotten

were the "auxiliars" of former days who had battled in the same
cause as he: Mary Wollstonecraft, with her fervent *Vindication of
the Rights of Woman* of 1792; and her future husband, William
Godwin's *Political Justice*, that remarkable defense of "philosophical" anarchism, inspired by the French Revolution; or Thomas
Paine, whose *Rights of Man* had replied to Burke's pamphlet ... A
younger generation of poets, writers like Shelley and Browning,
were to bewail the great poet's "apostasy."

But the fresh wells of poesy Wordsworth and Coleridge had
opened to posterity were never to be shut up. New feelings, new
imagery, new music — were to fructify English poetry for decades to
come, as divergent streams fed upon these sources. It is to these
masters — as well as to Robert Burns — that their great successors
looked for their inspiration — both moral, and aesthetic.

2.

> There is no other God than the God who is the
> intellectual foundation of Humanity.
> — William Blake, *Jerusalem* —

On the 16th of August 1803 William Blake wrote to his friend and patron, Thomas Butts, from the Sussex town of Felpham, where he was then residing:

I am at present in a bustle to defend myself against a very unwarrantable warrant from a Justice of Peace in Chichester, which was taken out against me by a private in Capt. Leathes's troop of 1st or Royal Dragoons, for an assault & seditious words.[19]

A boisterous and rude soldier, named Scholfield, claimed that Blake had abused King, and the Army, and lauded Bonaparte. At a subsequent trial Blake was cleared of the accusations, but he was not soon to forget the injury. The perjuring soldier was never to know that the poet was to immortalize him in his prophetic verses. Whether he had ever uttered those "seditious" sentiments in the streets of Felpham remains doubtful. But there can be no doubts about those sentiments: they were Blake's, and had the government of George III been more aware of him as a poet, and been able to penetrate more deeply into his symbolic words and drawings, matters might have grown more serious.

He was, after all, the most intransigeant revolutionary poet (Shelley, perhaps, excepted) of the entire Romantic Movement — by age belonging to the "older" group (he was born in 1757), and in spirit (he died in 1827) with the younger Romantics, whom he outlived. His own partial obscurity as a person, and the apparent obscurity of his creations saved him from the persecutions that fell to the lot of Joseph Priestley, and Thomas Paine, whom he knew well; but also reserved for him the tragic fate of "enjoying" posthumous glory. He was rarely to reap the fruits of his labors, whether as artist or poet; and he was often on the brink of poverty... He was not to be "rediscovered" until a generation or two after his death: by the Pre-Raphaelites; thereafter to be apotheosized by the poet Swinburne in a celebrated study.

His life ran concurrently with a vast expansion of the British Empire, and the efflorescence of the Industrial Revolution. One habitually thinks of William Blake as the humble recluse, working at his engraving, designing, painting, and writing and altogether removed from the workaday world and history. Nothing could be more misleading. He was a part of the vast historic movement of his day, and cannot be understood without reference to the history of his times. He was not only aware of what was happening, but he was deeply involved in understanding and reinterpreting it. As he was growing up, a triumphant Britain could boast of having broken the power of France in India, Canada, in the West Indies. When he was three years old, George III ascended the throne. When he was four, "the child Blake saw his first vision of God, and screamed..."[20]

Thereafter he saw many, many "visions," to the dismay of his family; meeting throughout his life with the indulgent astonishment and forbearance of his friends and acquaintances, sometimes awing them at the self-possession and simplicity and conviction with which he spoke of them. Perplexed as his father, a simple hosier, might have been, he was perceptive enough to recognize the boy's artistic talent, and apprenticed him to an engraver. Little did he realize in what manifold ways a genius would come into being — as a skilled artisan, craftsman, designer, painter, printer, and — of all things — as poet, a genius that would encompass three worlds and somehow amalgamate them — the workaday world of the drudge engraver, — the world of "visions," and the world of artistic and poetic creation...

Blake had no formal education except in art: in all else he was self-taught, and in his own wide-ranging, frequently strange way he assimilated a large body of knowledge — wide enough to dismay his

later critics and commentators intent on tracing Blake's "sources."
In his fusion of his own form of "religiousness" and radicalism, he
was the heir of the Puritan Revolution, particularly its left-wing and
communistic elements, like the Levellers and the Diggers with their
millenarian dreams; and he appears also to have drawn on the
antinomian mystics and pietists of the Continent: men like Jacob
Boehme; the alchemical ideas of Paracelsus; the wide-ranging and
extravagant ideas of Swedenborg. He may even have been acquainted
with the heretical conceptions of the Gnostics, and of the Hebrew
Cabbala. But in his own typical fashion, his wandering in these
ethereal and far-flung regions did not keep him from living in the
lower terrestrial realms and from the ideas of his contemporaries,
political and religious non-conformists like his printer Joseph
Johnson, in whose rooms he came to know such dissidents as Tom
Paine, Joseph Priestley, Mary Wollstonecraft — figures deemed
dangerous in the eyes of the established authorities. These too were
significant contributors to his "education." They were supporters of
the American, and later of the French Revolution, and many of
them paid dearly for their dissidence. The two worlds of vision and
reality were never apart for Blake; nor was there an ambivalence in
his personality; the visionary and the practical were never separate,
and never at odds within him. No man was more "devout" —
religious, one might say — in his own heterodox way — than Blake;
no man more heterodox in his pieties. He saw miracles where other
men only saw the commonplace, as in the case of Tom Paine, of
whose *Common Sense* he said:

Is it a greater miracle to feed five thousand men with five loaves, than to
overthrow all the armies of Europe with a small pamphlet?[21]

He spoke of himself as a "soldier of Christ." And in his
uninhibited way wrote to his friend and patron, Thomas Butts:

I am not ashamed, afraid, or averse to tell you what ought to be told: That I
am under the direction of Messengers from Heaven, daily and nightly . . . If
we fear to do the dictates of our Angels, and tremble at the tasks set before

us; if we refuse to do spiritual acts because of natural fears or natural desires! who can describe the dismal torments of such a state! — I too well remember the threats I heard: "If you, who are organised by Divine Providence for spiritual communion, refuse and bury your talent in the earth, even though you should want natural bread, sorrow and desperation pursues you through life, after death shame and confusion of face to eternity. Every one in Eternity will leave you, aghast at the man who was crowned with the glory and honor by his brethren, and betrayed their cause to their enemies. You will be called the base Judas who betray'd his friend! ... [22]

He was the heir of the Hebrew Prophets, and he spoke with their accents, and often with their eloquence. His Bible was the New Testament Book of Revelation. His vision of the apocalypse embraced the emergence of a new Jerusalem, not one where the graves opened to restore dead bodies, but one that would transform the death in life of man on earth to a newly recovered emancipation and internal and external harmony. In his quest he became the fiery transvaluator of values, uprooted the traditional clichés and credos of established society — its morality, its social thought, its religious and ethical values ...

Physically, the world was bounded for him by a circuit that included no more than the city of London, and the Sussex town of Felpham where he spent three years. London was *his* city; and in and through London he viewed the world. London was his world. His most touching and comprehensible poems were of London, its inhabitants, its men, women and children. Here he saw in microcosm, the macrocosmic forces of his cosmic voyagings — good and evil — terrors and joys. From London he looked out and saw and encompassed the rest of the world — America, France, Asia, Africa ...

To express his "vision" of the world, Blake formulated a dialectical mythology, peopling it with symbolic forces, for which he invented numerous names and functions, but the essence of which was permeated with the concepts of conflict, and revolutionary change. He was in fact composing manifestoes, the crux of which is contained in his utterances on what he called "Contraries."

Without Contraries there is no progression. Attraction and Repulsion, Reason and Energy, Love and Hate, are necessary to Human existence. From these contraries spring what the religious call Good and Evil. Good is the passive that obeys Reason. Evil is the active springing from Energy. Good is Heaven. Evil is Hell.[23]

Within these few lines are contained Blake's metaphysical, religious, social, moral and political beliefs. He was in fact a dialectical idealist, and the philosopher Hegel would have understood him, though he might not have approved of him. To these Contraries, Blake could have added Innocence and Experience, as he mapped the pilgrimage of man's "soul" from a primal harmony and Eden through a world of terrors, and conflicts, of which his Lamb and his Tyger became preeminent symbols.

> What is the price of Experience? do men buy it for a song?
> Or wisdom for a dance in the street? No. it is bought with the price
> Of all that a man hath, his wife, his children.
> Wisdom is sold in the desolate market where none come to buy,
> And in the wither'd field where the farmer plows for bread in vain.[24]

Blake's is a revolutionary interpretation of Bunyan's Pilgrim's Progress — in which a vision of Jerusalem is to be attained only through a change both outside and within the pilgrim. But such a change cannot be obtained without a reconstitution of the human being himself and his living world and a transvaluation of his values. He must and will recognize that those prevailing today have been imposed upon him by the so-called "religious" — that is, the "establishment," and enforced through institutions: the church, the prison, law, the factory mill, government. All of these have laid their "shackles" on the mind of man and woman. All of these forces are subsumed under the generic Tyranny, which Blake calls "Reason," and which in its actual and transcendental form he gave the name of "Urizen." Opposed to Urizen is inextinguishable Energy — the active principle within humanity, the force for change, for self-realization and self-attainment, the human instinct, which sees more than can be reached by the five senses — perceives an attainable unity of mind and body, of spirit and matter, and his name is "Orc". He is Revolution. He is the enemy of the Passive — of pestilential inaction.

Energy is the only life, and is from the body; and Reason is the bound or outward circumference of Energy... He who desires but act not, breeds pestilence... Active evil is better than passive good...

Urizen is the calculating god — dry-as-dust logic — the sterile god of Order and Submission, who has ruled the world to-date. Orc is of Today — he is America and he is France — and he is also of the Future. Urizen is the divinity of what the righteous have called heaven, the realm of passivity and acceptance; Orc is the divinity of what they have called Hell, the constructive rebel, the true Lucifer, the light-bringer. The great Milton (whom Blake admired, and wished to correct) had laid the Fall to "Man's disobedience." Blake sees the Fall of Man as due to the ascendancy of Tyranny. Sex and the body are holy. Man is holy. Blake's prophetic work is an epic of the restoration of divinity to mankind.

The times were appropriate — times of Revolution: America and France. But England was still in chains.

> I wander thro' each charter'd street,
> Near where the charter'd Thames
>   does flow,
> And mark in every face I meet
> Marks of weakness, marks of woe.
>
> In every cry of every Man,
> In every Infant's cry of fear,
> In every voice, in every ban,
> The mind-forg'd manacles I hear.
>
> How the Chimney-sweeper's cry
> Every black'ning Church appalls;
> And the hapless Soldier's sigh
> Runs in blood down Palace walls.

But most thro' midnight streets
I hear
How the youthful Harlot's curse
Blasts the new born Infant's tear,
And blights with plagues the
Marriage hearse.[25]

Blake was well aware that conditions outside of London were no better. For the great efflorescence of industrialism was already bringing it about that — as one historian puts it — "half the workers in the cotton mills were children; and of the other half, two-thirds were women. Their working day was fifteen hours, and in it they walked twenty miles among machines...The elder Peel's Act of 1802 won a twelve-hour day only for parish children. It was in 1819 before he won a twelve-hour day for free children, and both Acts were for long mere paper acts."[26]

What contemporary industrialism in the factories and mills was like — Blake understood only distantly. His images are rather those of a pre-industrial era. Personally, he was acquainted only with the brick-kilns around London.[27] But his imagination adequately filled the physical lacunae, and his vision is no less frightful and predictive of the ravages of a machine civilization to come.

If, in the figure of the hated Urizen, he assails the philosophy and science of preceding eras, and conjoins Newton and Locke as prime movers in the tyranny of "Reason" (unjustly, it might seem), Blake was thinking rather of the uses made by some of the *philosophes* in extolling the beauty of a mechanized universe and its "Order" — and the need to preserve such a preestablished harmony, and not tamper with the beautiful mechanism. Vulgarized, this view was given wide popularity in Pope's celebrated *Essay on Man*: "Know then thyself, presume not God to scan; the proper study of Mankind is Man" and concluding with "Whatever is, is right." Thus Urizen became nefarious Reason (mathematics, science, mechanics) as well as industrial tyranny, economic exploitation, master of slaves and creator of a slave mentality. Here is Urizen's plan on how to rule mankind:

...And Urizen read in his book of brass in sounding tones:
"Listen, O Daughters, to my voice. Listen to the Words of Wisdom,
So shall you govern over all; let Moral Duty tune your tongue,
But be your hearts harder than the nether millstone...
Compell the poor to live upon a Crust of bread, by soft mild arts.
Smile when they frown, frown when they smile; and when a
    man looks pale
With labour and abstinence, say he looks healthy and happy;
And when his children sicken, let them die; there are enough
Born, even too many, and our Earth will be overrun
Without these arts. If you would make the poor live with temperance,
With pomp give every crust of bread you give; with gracious cunning
Say he smiles if you hear him sigh. If pale, say he is ruddy.
Preach temperance; say he is overgorg'd and drowns his wit
In strong drink, tho' you know that bread and water are all
He can afford. Flatter his wife, pity his children, till we can
Reduce all to our will, as spaniels are taught with art.[28]

This was exactly what Pitt preached to the people in the name of George III, "economy and frugality in the consumption of corn." All controls of prices and of food monopolies, he claimed, would be striking at "the freedom of trade." And he claimed that the "only way to prove a sincere and enlighted regard to the poor," was to guard them from "false and dangerous expectations of enough to eat."[29]

Blake understood the true meaning of "laissez-faire" as propounded by economic liberalism — just as he understood the "scientific" fatalism preached by Thomas Malthus's *Essay on Population*, with reference to restriction of births.

But Urizen is also the Creator of the World! See him in the magnificent color print (one of Blake's most celebrated) as he sets out to fashion the temporal world and leans out of Eternity with compasses in his hand, into the void — the universe "external to mind or intellect." For, acording to Gnostic doctrine, the world was created not by the true, but by a false God. Yet, and fortunately, along with Urizen, there came into being a Contrary, Los ("Soul")

— poetic inspiration, the prophet as poet. Poetic Inspiration unbound and instinctive is the father of Revolution — for Orc is the son of Los. And in the midst of the American Revolution, as described by Blake, Orc and Urizen come face to face — America and Britain — George Washington and George III. Here Urizen appears as "Albion's Angel", forced to hear Orc's prophecy of the victory of democracy in America, and the dreadful words: "For Empire is no more, and now the Lion and Wolf shall cease."

> Art thou not Orc...
> Blasphemous Demon, Antichrist, hater of
>   Dignities,
> Lover of wild rebellion, and transgressor of God's
>   Law,
> Why dost thou come to Angel's eyes in this terrific
>   form?"
> ...I am Orc, wreath'd round the accursed tree:
> The times are ended; shadows pass, the morning
>   'gins to break;
> The fiery joy, that Urizen perverted to ten
>   commands,
> What night he led the starry hosts thro' the wide
>   wilderness,
> That stony law I stamp to dust; and scatter
>   religion abroad
> To the four winds as a torn book, and none shall
>   gather the leaves;
> But they shall rot on desart sands, and consume in
>   bottomless deeps,
> To make the desart blossom, and the deeps shrink
>   to their fountains,
> And to renew the fiery joy, and burst the stony
>   roof;
> That pale religious lechery, seeking Virginity
> May find it in a harlot, and in coarse-clad honesty
> The undefil'd, tho' ravish'd in her cradle night and
>   morn;
> For everything that lives is holy...[30]

It seemed as if the spirit of Revolution were sweeping the whole world — and the ancient world of feudalism were toppling. And so he wrote the first book of *The French Revolution* — meant to extend to seven books — setting forth the history of that great event in simple, unadorned verse, still full of biblical cadences. The book was set in 1791, but never published, for it seems the times had become threatening. Joseph Priestley's house in Birmingham was sacked by a mob; Paine was soon to be threatened with prosecution for the second part of *The Rights of Man*; King Louis XIV of France made an unsuccessful attempt to flee Paris. The Revolution was moving toward a climax. Repression in England became more severe.

And it was in those years that Blake wrote down his great Credo, *The Marriage of Heaven and Hell*, ending it with another manifesto, "A Song of Liberty",

> Albion's coast is sick, silent; the American
>   meadows faint!
> Shadows of Prophecy shiver along by lakes and
>   the rivers,
> and mutter across the ocean: France, rend down
>   thy dungeon!
> Golden Spain, burst the barriers of old Rome!
> Cast thy keys, O Rome, into the deep down falling,
>   even to eternity falling...
> The fire, the fire is falling!...

France had become a Republic... In 1793 England entered the war against France.

He was fervid in his hatred and abomination of War, and he had written:

> The Strongest Poison ever known
> Came from Caesar's Laurel Crown.
> Nought can deform the Human Race
> Like to the Armour's iron brace.[31]

He had raged when he saw the tools and implements of peace turned into "swords, arrows, cannons, mortars" — with the consequent perversion of the minds of their makers. We know that he was opposed to England's war on France and the Revolution. He watched events in England and in France with great anxiety, scarcely able to control his own seditious thoughts. He hailed the temporary peace when it came, and was horrified by the resumption of the war. His wife, Catherine, life-long helpmate and assistant in his artistic labors, no doubt shared his feelings, and may at one time have voiced an enthusiasm for Napoleon Bonaparte.

As the Revolution in France was followed by the Terror, and by the Directory, and was finally crushed by Napoleon's *coup d'état* — he experienced bitter moments. For now it seemed that the giant Orc had been degraded into an all-conquering Napoleon. But for Blake neither France nor Revolution ever died. Orc would rise again. Blake's apocalyptic vision moved the Day of Judgment to the future. Orc was to become Christ — the revolutionary. Not, to be sure, the Jesus of the so-called "religious" — humble, submissive, turning the other cheek.

And he asked and replied:

> Was Jesus born of Virgin Pure
> With narrow Soul and looks demure?...
> Was Jesus gentle, or did he
> Give any marks of Gentility?...
>
> His Seventy Disciples sent
> Against Religion and Government...
>
> And in his hand the Scourge shone bright;
> He scourg'd the Merchant Canaanite
> From out the Temple of his Mind...
>
> Humility is only doubt,
> And does the Sun and Moon put out...

For Jesus hearkened to the voice of God who said to Him:

> If thou humblest thyself, thou humblest me;
> Thou also dwelst in Eternity.
> Thou art a Man, God is no more,
> Thine own Humanity learn to adore...[32]

He was not alone in his time to voice such radical theology. In 1791, the Rev. Mark Wilks, preached a sermon at St. Paul's Chapel, Norwich — the day was July 14! — on the "Origin and Stability of the French Revolution," in which he proclaimed:

Jesus Christ was a Revolutionist; and the Revolution he came to effect was fortold in these words: "He hath sent me to proclaim liberty to the captives, and the opening of the prison to them that are bound."[33]

To the end of his days Blake remained fixed in this belief:

Are not Religion and Politics the Same Thing? Brotherhood is Religion.[34]

And had he not replied to Isaac Watts's "Praise for the Gospel"

> Lord, I ascribe it to my Grace
> And not to Chance, as others do
> That I was born of Christian race
> And not a Heathen or a Jew

with his own "Divine Image":

> ...And all must love the human form,
> In Heathen, Turk, or Jew;
> Where Mercy, Love and Pity dwell
> There God is dwelling too...?

For as he put it, "All deities reside in the human breast."

In the early years of the new century he composed his vision of the Last Judgment, and the Regeneration of Man. But this Judgment Day was no pastoral, with the sheep on one side, and the sinners on the other. We know what Blake thought of the notion of sin, acceptable to the conventionally religious and the established priesthoods. In his prophetic work the sheep are the humble,

oppressed, maltreated, exploited — the real men, women and
children of London, and of the Lancashire factories; the soldiers sent
out to war upon other human beings, misled by their authorities; the
prisoners, the "harlots", the chimneysweepers — in sum, the
proletariat and their dependents. They rise up against the oppressors
to destroy them once and for all. There is no forgiveness here! No
humility! This is in a sense the "final conflict" — a war for the
rehabilitation of all of humanity. The poet speaks with Miltonic
accents:

> ... Numerous as the leaves of autumn, every species
> Flock to the trumpet, mutt'ring over the sides of
>   the grave and crying
> In the fierce wind round heaving rocks and
>   mountains fill'd with groans...
> Many a woful company and many on clouds and
>   waters,
> Fathers and friends, Mothers and Infants, Kings
>   and Warriors,
> Priests and chain'd Captives, met together in a
>   horrible fear;
> And every one of the dead appears as he had liv'd
>   before,
> And all the marks remain of the slave's scourge
>   and tyrant's Crown,
> And the Priest's o'ergorged Abdomen, and of the
>   merchant's thin
> Sinewy deception...
> They shew their wounds: they accuse: they sieze
>   the oppressor; howlings began...
> The cold babe
> Stands in the furious air; he cries: "the children of
>   six thousand years
> Who died in infancy rage furious: a mighty
>   multitude rage furious,
> Naked and pale standing in the expecting air, to
>   be deliver'd.

Rend limb from limb the warrior and tyrant,
     reuniting in pain." ...
Trembling the judge springs from his throne
Hiding his face in the dust beneath the prisoners
     feet and saying:
"Brother of Jesus, what have I done? intreat my
     lord for me;
Perhaps I may be forgiven."
The Prisoner answers: "You scourg'd my father to
     death before my face
While I stood bound with cords and heavy chains.
     Your hipocracy
Shall now avail you nought." So speaking he
     dash'd him with his foot ...

The new liberation is here!

Let the slave, grinding at the mill, run out into the
     field;
Let him look up into the heavens and laugh in the
     bright air.
Let the inchained soul, shut up in darkness and in
     sighing,
Whose face has never seen a smile in thirty weary
     years,
Rise and look out: his chains are loose, his
     dungeon doors are open;
And let his wife and children return from the
     oppressor's scourge ...

The good of all the Land is before you, for Mystery
     is no more ...

Then All the Slaves from every Earth in the wide
     Universe
Sing a New Song ...
And the song they sung was this
Composed by an African black from the little
     Earth of Sotha:

> "Aha! Aha! how came I here so soon in my sweet
> native land?
> How came I here? Methinks I am as I was in my
> youth
> When in my father's house I sat and heard his
> cheering voice.
> Methinks I see his flocks and herds and feel my
> limbs renew'd,
> And Lo, my Brethren in their tents, and their little
> ones around them!"[35]

The vision of the rehabilitation of mankind is concluded with Blake's last prophetic book, *Jerusalem*. His eyes ever fixed on England, he begins with a call to Albion dictated to the poet by the Savior:

"Awake! awake O sleeper of the land of shadows, wake! expand!" — a call to rise from her "soul's disease" — and to hearken to the thunder of oppressed humanity, "the soldier's fife, the Harlot's shriek, " the cries of Scotland's sons at the "Furnaces," and the daughters of Wales at the "looms." Such is England unawakened, such is England in love with War and Desolation, with a population spending "the days of wisdom, in sorrowful drudgery to obtain a scanty pittance of food." Jerusalem is the ultimate reconciliation of mundane contraries — the ultimate harmony that annihilates the dichotomy of mundane struggles (for bread, for life, for humane joys, for the arts). Jerusalem is "in every man" — that is, the potential of its attainment lies within us all, for "Jerusalem is called Liberty among the Children of Albion."

> Why stand we here trembling around
> Calling on God for help, and not ourselves, in
> whom God dwells...?
> Albion is cast forth to the Potter, his Children to
> the Builders
> To build Babylon because they have forsaken
> Jerusalem.

> The Walls of Babylon are the Souls of Men, her
>   Gates the Groans
> Of Nations, her Towers are the miseries of once
>   happy Families,
> Her Streets are paved with Destruction, her
>   Houses built with Death,
> Her Palaces with Hell and the Grave, her
>   Synagogues with Torments of ever-hardening
>   Despair...[36]

Albion — humanity — Albion — England — rose like another
Orc...

> In anger, the wrath of God breaking, bright
>   flaming on all sides around
> His awful limbs; into the Heaven he walked,
>   clothed in flames,
> Loud thund'ring, with broad flashes of flaming
>   lightning and pillars
> Of fire, speaking the Words of Eternity in Human
>   Forms, in direful
> Revolutions of Action and Passion...

His self-division is at an end as he is rejoined by his
"Emanation" — the other self of him, from which he had been
separated — and "Jerusalem" and "Albion" are united, as are all the
self-divided, "alienated" elements of the material as well as the
spiritual world — for self-division is bondage. Selfhood is done
with, and Albion is worthy of the vision of Jesus,

> And Albion knew that it
> Was the Lord, the Universal Humanity; and
>   Albion saw his Form
> A Man, and they conversed as Man with Man in
>   Ages of Eternity.
> And the Divine Appearance was the likeness and
>   similitude of Los...

And thus Humanity (Albion, reunited with Jerusalem) is
consummated in the vision of the Man-God Jesus, who now has also
the likeness of the High Poetic Imagination — the Poet-Prophet.

Alienated humanity is restored to its integrity, having achieved its freedom. Contraries are reconciled — there are no more masters and no more slaves. The separateness of body and mind; action and passion; the senses (sex) and spirit; the self and the unself; the heart and the head — all are now portions of a new harmony, and new synthesis. Now man can turn his best talents and energies not to destruction of self and others, to wars, to exploitation, but awakened in mind and body from the drudgery, brutalization, and enslavement to false institutions, freed from the "mysteries" imposed upon him by his former masters (now gone!), to the highest development of his new Self — a consummation in Art, and Science.

Blake had always believed that "the Arts and Sciences are the Destruction of Tyrannies or Bad Governments", and "Poetry fettered fetters the human race. Nations are destroyed or flourish in proportion as their poetry, painting and music are destroyed or flourish..."[37]

In Jerusalem are then all contraries abolished? Not at all. This very modern question Blake's prescience knows how to answer. The Contraries will subsist, but in a higher form. They will become the contending elements of Debate, of Creation, of the Arts and the Sciences — the war now will be an "intellectual war." Here is Blake:

> ...Urthona rises from the ruinous Walls
> Of his ancient strength to form the gold armour of
>   science
> For intellectual War. The war of swords departed
>   now,
> The dark Religions are departed and sweet Science
>   reigns.

Walter Savage Landor, a poet of distinction, and a later contemporary of Blake, wrote in his Notebook: "Never did a braver or a better man carry the sword of justice." With which judgment there will be few who will disagree.

Although he did not live to see his new Jerusalem built, he had to the very last kept his vow:

> I will not cease from Mental Fight,
> Nor shall my Sword sleep in my hand
> Till we have built Jerusalem
> In England's green and pleasant land.

3.

Blake and his personal Lucifer — Orc — dwelt in comparative obscurity — largely unknown to the world outside, and their terrifying calls to rebellion and resurrection threatened no one. But there was another Lucifer afield, a source of terror as well as exultation, very much a part of this world, whose demoniacal personality, actions, notoriety as well as fame, were to appall conventional society in its mores — at the same time that they amazed, and often inspired, and eventually made him into a legend. This was George Gordon, Lord Byron. Along with Shelley and Keats, Byron belonged to the second, the younger generation of Romantics, who, unlike the first, lived their mature lives not in the presence but in the aftermath of the French Revolution. With the younger poets, the French Revolution represented a gigantic event, but also an "unfinished" work of transformation — whose ideals remained unquenched, to be realized and accomplished in some proximate future. Together with their forerunners, Wordsworth and Coleridge, they represent a galaxy of poetic genius unequalled before in British letters except during the Elizabethan Renaissance, and never to be equalled thereafter.

But such are the paradoxes and vagaries of prejudice, legend, and historic perversion — that, like an incubus, they bear down on reputations — and this is the case with Byron, Shelley and Keats. Even critics of our own day, still in the bonds of Victorian strait-jackets, tend to follow Carlyle's fuliginous admonitions to "close your Byron and open your Goethe." Shelley, as we shall see, was no less a victim of such treatment and varying estimations. Only John Keats, after the virulent obloquies during his own lifetime, gradually inherited respectful acceptance chiefly because he could be misinterpreted as somehow standing "above" quotidian battles and problems — a "sickly" poet who was a premature prophet of a later "aesthetic" movement.

One pathetic characteristic links the three younger poets — their premature extinction. By 1824 they were all dead — Keats at the age of twenty-five; Shelley, scarcely thirty; and Byron at thirty-six. They did not, like Wordsworth and Coleridge, outlive their creative apex. They died at the height, not at the nadir, of their powers, having exhibited an amazing early flowering of genius. The stigma of ostracism or exile was upon them: self-exile in the case of Shelley and Byron; isolation in the case of Keats. They died far from England — Shelley by drowning off the Gulf of Spezia; Byron of a fever in Greece; and Keats of consumption in Rome.

Byron died at Missolonghi in 1824, before he could actually participate on the battlefield in the struggle for Greek liberation. But the "legend" of Byron already had its inception before that date, and was to receive its final contours as a result of the Greek episode. The man and poet whose brow was early branded with the mark of "Cain" was to be crowned with the laurel of "hero." It would be impossible to describe adequately the impact of the Byronic legend and of Byron himself upon the culture of the nineteenth century. The announcement of his death shook the entire Western world. It stunned the elderly Goethe as well as young Pushkin.

The story of this "half-angel" and "half-devil" — of this offspring of a crapulous and wastrel father and an irresponsible, savage-tempered mother; of Byron's clubfoot and his irresistible beauty and magnetism, his personal debaucheries, and his bi-sexual adventures — has found enough assiduous chronicles to satisfy an inextinguishable curiosity, and tickle an inveterate pruriency. Such failings in great men and women tend to allure us, making us kin to them, at least in our thoughts, if not actions. But such derelictions, extensive as they might have been, though they play a part in it, could scarcely account for the persistent hold Byron has exercised on highly intelligent, perceptive and creative spirits up to the present. In the pervading seethings of scandal, one frequently tended to lose sight of a many-sided genius.

We tend to forget, for example, that despite his many vagaries and his self-indulgence, he very early revealed exemplary moral courage, and firm principles. We forget that as a very young man, he stood up in the House of Lords, and in a maiden speech denounced the pernicious proposal to impose a death-penalty on the "machine-wreckers," those impoverished and wretched loom-weavers who vented their rage upon the new machinery that spelled death to their own home-industry. And how many now recall his valiant support of Catholic emancipation and of the Italian *carbonari* in their struggles against Austrian domination? Need we also be reminded that alongside the *Weltschmerz* — the cosmic ache — to be found in *Childe Harold's Pilgrimage*, there are passages of eloquent wrath directed against tyranny, injustice, and British "cant"?

The enigma of Byron is many-leveled. More than any other of his contemporaries he was the great master of narrative poetry, at this time still a strong competitor of the novel. With *Childe Harold* he swept Sir Walter Scott the poet from the contemporary scene. He awoke and found himself famous, and the enchanter of thousands upon thousands of readers. Here he was the poet who spoke most movingly of the age's self-division, the dichotomy of the soul in the transitional post-Napoleonic era — an era of what seemed to be "non-heroism." Sentiment, even sentimentality, lived here side by side with irony, self-derision, mockery — tears and laughter — laughter "so that he might not weep."

An eternal voyager, or — as Shelley called him — "the Pilgrim of Eternity" — he took his readers in his many breath-taking tales, as well as in *Don Juan* and *Childe Harold*, into the Italy of the sad present and the magnificent but now decaying past; as well as into more distant climes; he transposed Goethe's celebrated glorification of Italy, "Kennst du das Land wo die Zitronen blühn," which Mignon recites to Wilhelm Meister, into his own passion for the Near East,

> Know ye the land where the cypress and myrtle
> Are emblems of deeds that are done in their clime,
> Where the rage of the vulture, and the love of the turtle,
> Now melt into sorrow, now madden to crime?[39]

He offered his readers the figures of the romantic outlaw, the Byronic desperado, the defiers of heaven and earth; the sultry and crime-laden Cains; he transported them to the land of minarets and harems — where love was violent, even dangerous, and sometimes blood-laden; he took them where love was also light-hearted, frolicsome, and naughty. He brought his readers the realms of danger, from which they could escape scatheless and breathless, and return in safety to their counting-houses and their sewing. He concentrated all of Romanticiam in his Corsairs, his Laras, his Giaours. But he also knew another side of this Orient — the Orient of reality — the bitter scene of struggle, warfare, the desired prey of France, England, and Russia.

He also shared in one of Romanticism's startling phenomena — Romantic Titanism. But he was no Prometheus. Rather an amalgam of Cain and Lucifer — both principal characters in what he called his "Mystery" play, *Cain*. Through their lips he spoke his defiance of the oppressive powers in heaven and on earth. Both Cain and Lucifer are the "No-sayers" — enemies of submissiveness, complacence, superstition and tradition. Lucifer is Cain's mentor. Cain cannot abide a deity that savors the blood and flesh of living sacrifices and that scorns the fruits of the soil. In his anger he kills Abel. Lucifer, traditionally maligned as the Serpent and perverter of man and woman and as the infernal "tempter," proudly declares:

> I tempt none
> Save with the truth...
> I would have made ye Gods...
>
> Evil and good are things in their own essence,
> And not made good or evil by the giver...

> One good gift has the fatal apple given —
> Your reason: — let it not be over-sway'd
> By tyrannous threat to force you into faith
> 'Gainst all external sense and inward feeling:
> Think and endure, — and form an inner world
> In your own bosom — where the outward fails...

Cain to Abel:

> Thy God loves blood...

and he refuses to live in a "Paradise of Ignorance."

Having been taken by Lucifer to view the universe — and now the possessor of a higher truth — Cain is transformed. He becomes the "outsider" — he has no use for the commonly accepted notion of happiness "which humbles me and mine."

> The dead,
> The immortal, the unbounded, the omnipotent,
> The overpowering mysteries of space —
> The innumerable worlds that were and are —
> Suns, moons, and earths, upon their loud-voiced
>   spheres
> Singing in thunder round me,...have made me
> Unfit for mortal converse...

and, like Byron, he becomes a wanderer and an outcast,

> Eastward from Eden we will take our way...

Here Byron is Lucifer-Cain, triumphant and yet sorrowful. For sorrow seems half of the fallen angel's immortality.

In the other poetic drama, *Manfred*, the hero is a thinly disguised Faustian figure strongly saturated by Byronic pessimism. There is a heavy curse upon his soul (Byron could never forget the accusation of incest with his half-sister Augusta); and he is in search of forgetfulness. He is already old in his youth, "an awful chaos" — consisting of "light and darkness — and mind and dust." In the highest Alps he seeks unattainable answers to his inexplicable searches. Of course, the mountains cannot give him peace nor answers. He dies, but even in his death he is the great defier: "And yet you see I kneel not."

Byron did not possess the intellectual depth and scope of Shelley, nor his wide-ranging poetic imagination, nor his music. Nor did he have the superb sensuous artistry of Keats. But there was one realm in which he was supreme — the realm of Satire. Here he belongs in the company of the very great: Aristophanes, Rabelais, Cervantes, Swift, Heine, Gogol. Here lay his greatest strength, and finest insights. Here were his inexhaustible humor, his irony, his savage but scintillating sarcasm. When he was roused, the lion within him woke, and it was well for the lesser beasts to beware.

Such a one was Robert Southey, erstwhile revolutionary and pantisocrat, now a confirmed Tory, who upon the death of George III composed a *Vision of Judgment*, which he had prefaced with a scorching attack on what he called the "Satanic School" of poetry, of which he regarded Byron as the head. The poem exalts the King as fit to enter heaven and hob-nob with such pure Eternals as George Washington, as well as with John Milton, and the one-time beheaded King Charles I!

Byron, in his turn, proceeded to bury the poet-laureate, and demolish the etherealized late King George. So he wrote his own *Vision of Judgment*. Byron does not fail to recall that the King died in 1820, a time of numerous uprisings in the south of Europe. Of the King's funeral he said:

> It seem'd a mockery of hell to fold
> The rottenness of eighty years in gold.

Now for the heavenly ascent. St. Peter, made aware of an untoward clatter at his gate, is told that George III is dead:

> "...And who *is* George the Third?" replied the apostle:
> "What George? what Third?" "The king of England" said
> The angel. "Well! he won't find kings to jostle

> Him on his way; but does he wear his head;
>> Because the last we saw here had a tussle,
> And ne'er would have got into heaven's good graces,
> Had he not flung his head in all our faces..."

But Satan puts in a prior claim, and offers his evidence:

> He ever warr'd with freedom and the free:
>> Nations as men, home subjects, foreign foes,
> So they that utter'd the word Liberty!
> Found George the Third their first opponent, Whose
> History was ever stain'd as his will be
>> With national and individual woes?

Nor does Robert Southey escape Byron's scorn. He appears as one of the witnesses for the King:

> He had written praises of a regicide;
>> He had written praises of all kings what ever;
> He had written for republics far and wide,
>> And then against them bitterer than ever:
> For pantisocracy he once had cried
>> Aloud, a scheme less moral than 'twas clever;
> Then grew a hearty anti-jacobin —
> Had turn'd his coat — and would have turned his skin.

In a subsequent hubbub, the King succeeds in slipping into Heaven:

> And when the tumult dwindled to a calm,
> I left him practising the hundredth psalm...

Byron never forgot Southey, nor the other "renegades" of the Lake School: Wordsworth and Coleridge. But it was to Southey that he dedicated his greatest single poem — also his longest — *Don Juan*.

In *Don Juan* Byron shows himself as a prime virtuoso. Modulating moods and turns, he is at once serious, comic, satirical, sentimental, scurrilous and bawdy. He is here master of the "ottava rima," the eight-line stanza inherited from the Renaissance Italian poets, whose perfection demands a crackling crescendo, rising to a fortissimo in the last two lines.

To choose Don Juan, the Spanish libertine, for his "unheroic hero," was of course to fly in the face of British decorum, unless one succeeded in moralizing him. Spain invented him; Mozart immortalized him in his heavenly music. Byron took up the challenge.

Byron's hero has little in common with the original Don Juan, except that he is a Spaniard and has numerous amatory adventures. There is no Donna Anna, no Commendatore who will turn into stone-guest and drag the sinner down to Hell; there is no single story-line, except that of wide travel. The incidents and adventures are innumerable. Byron's Don Juan is the converse of Childe Harold; as the latter is introvert, so is the Spaniard extrovert. Whatever there is of melancholy, the sentimental, the reflective, and the satiric-critical is uttered with the poet's own voice. Scabrous and shameless in many places, it is also a paean to a joyous libido. It is a delicious *chronique scandaleuse*, to be read — as many Victorians would do in private (like Trollope's Archdeacon Grantly with his Rabelais) — and to scandalize and malign it in public.

Byron's young Don Juan grows up in the warm clime of Spain, as does the young and married Doña Julia (whose husband is alas! considerably older):

> 'Tis a sad thing, I cannot choose but say,
>   And all the fault of that indecent sun,
> Who cannot leave alone our helpless clay,
>   But will keep baking, broiling, burning on,
> That howsoever people fast and pray,
>   The flesh is frail, and so the soul undone:
> What men call gallantry, and gods adultery,
> Is much more common where the climate's sultry...

Not least delightful and piquant are the author's lively digressions — welcome interludes in the rush of dramatic adventure. Like all such recreant sons, (Julia finds him a tempting morsel), in order to avoid a scandal, Don Juan is sent abroad by his mother. Of his numerous experiences those that have been recalled with undiminished zest are his celebrated shipwreck and his subsequent adventures on the shores of Greece — his liaison with the beautiful Haidée, which is interrupted by her stern parent, the pirate Lambro. Greece offers Byron the occasion for his touching paean to the past glories of that land and a threnody on her present enslavement, "The isles of Greece, the isles of Greece," which are followed immediately by the most delightful, and often malicious digressions: a digression on digressions; a digression on British poets (even Milton does not escape his barb). As the two lovers admire the twilight, the poet's mind turns to the Ave Maria, and the "atheism" imputed to him:

> So kinder casuists are pleased to say,
>   In nameless print — that I have no devotion;
> But set those persons down with me to pray,
>   And you shall see who has the properest notion
> Of getting into heaven the shortest way;
>   My altars are the mountain and the ocean,
> Earth, air, stars, — all that springs from the great Whole,
> Who hath produced, and will receive the soul . . .

And once more he turns and looks into his own soul:

> . . . And if I laugh at any mortal thing,
>   'Tis that I may not weep and if I weep,
> 'Tis that our nature cannot always bring
>   Itself to apathy, for we must steep
> Our hearts first in the depths of Lethe's spring,
>   Ere what we least wish to behold will sleep;
> Thetis baptized her mortal son in Styx;
> A mortal mother would on Lethe fix . . .

Byron cannot steep his bitter memories in the river of forgetfulness — which is better even than the invulnerability Thetis hoped to obtain for Achilles by dipping him in the Styx.

But immediately, he can turn to laughter, as he carries Don Juan and us toward new adventures: the market-place of

Constantinople to be sold as a slave and bought by the Sultan's bride
and brought in woman's clothes into the harem ... But why go on?
Don Juan even gets to England!

And the poet's mind now turns to kings and wars ...

... But never mind: — "God save the king!" and kings!
        For if he don't, I doubt if *men* will longer —
I think I hear a little bird, who sings
        The people by and by will be the stronger ...

Then comes the "tug of war"; 'twill come again,
        I rather doubt; and I would fain say "fie on't;"
If I had not perceived that revolution
Alone can save the earth from hell's pollution ...

For I will teach, if possible, the stones
        To rise against earth's tyrants. Never let it
Be said that we still truckle unto thrones. —
        But ye — our children's children! think how we
Show'd *what things were* before the world was free! ...

And when you hear historians talk of thrones,
        And those who sate upon them, let it be
As now we gaze upon the mammoth's bones,
        And wonder what old world such things could see ...

And I will war, at least in word (and should
        My chance so happen deeds), with all who war
With Thought — and of Thought's foes by far most rude,
        Tyrants and sycophants have been and are.
I know not who may conquer; if I could
        Have such a prescience, it should be no bar
To this plain, sworn, downright detestation
Of every despotism in every nation ...

This was the same man who more than a decade before had stood
up in the House of Lords to defend the Luddite frame-breakers,
and had said:

When a proposal is made to emancipate and relieve, you hesitate, you
deliberate for years, you temporize and tamper with the minds of men; but
a death-bill must be passed off-hand, and without a thought of consequences . . .

He remained true to his word. When the time came he turned his
words into deeds . . .

Taken all in all Byron was the articulate epitome of his times; he
spoke an idiom that was accessible to all; and he could evoke
correspondent echoes in his innumerable readers. It is only when we
view him in his totality, that we can begin to understand the hold he
had on his century. Of the enchantment he exercised through his
personal beauty there could be no question. Whoever looked at him
fell under his sway. His club-foot, that had been his curse, only added
to his attractiveness. He was a fallen, damaged archangel. But he could
be a violent demon — cruel, bitter, raging; scornful and scoffing. But
he could also be generous and kindly. Truly, "an awful chaos."

His appeal was to the high and low. Great geniuses (often
greater than he) found in his works and in his person matter to
fructify their own creations. Goethe saw him as the prime exemplar
of the "modern" — and projected him as Euphorion in the second
part of *Faust*. It was no mean aggregation of men and women who
drew inspiration from him: Pushkin, and Heine, the Polish poet
Mickiewicz; Lamartine, Hugo, Leopardi, the Spaniard Espronceda;
composers like Schumann, Liszt, Berlioz, Tschaikovsky, Verdi;
painters like Delacroix. The operatic settings of his poems and plays
stagger one, if only for numbers. He spoke the tones of the current
"mal du siècle" — the ennui of an unheroic age that almost yearned
for another Napoleon; a time also epitomized by Alfred de Musset's
Confession d'un enfant du siècle. He spoke the age's dualism, its
Weltschmerz, its infinite longings, its own unexercised energies and
unexpressed rebellions, its fret and fever, and its indistinct hopes.
To the insular and cramped he opened vast vistas of hitherto
unpathed wonders of the East. His "heroes" became their surrogates
in their wild adventures, their piracies, their strange loves, their

longings for the "heroic." They shuddered pleasurably at Byron's tainted aura of the sinner; they thrilled at the liberating hero. With the Witch of the Alps, in *Manfred*, they could repeat,

> I know thee for a man of many thoughts,
> And deeds of good and evil, extreme in both,
> Fatal and fated in thy sufferings.

4.

> O for ten years that I may overwhelm
> Myself in poesy; so I may do the deed
> That my own soul has to itself decreed...

Such were the hopes of young John Keats, set down when he was barely twenty-one. He was not to be granted ten years of life more. A little over four years later — in 1821 — he died. Yet, within his brief span, — particularly in those "anni mirabiles" of 1818 and 1819 — he succeeded in achieving a consummate poetic artistry — the equal of the greatest the Romantic movement was destined to produce — small in body, but rich with the weight of his golden genius.

Unlike Wordsworth and Coleridge, and many of the other Romantics in England and on the Continent, Keats left no formal autobiography or chronicle of his poetic growth and credo. But he did leave something equally precious — and in some respects even more revelatory — the incomparable body of letters to his brothers and sister, to his friends, and to his beloved Fanny Brawne — which because of their candor, their informality, their forthrightness and simplicity — convey in a more immediate way the sense of the human being, the struggling poet, in his quest of self-understanding and understanding of life around him and his craft. They are in fact a revelation of the forcing-house of genius — of the deprivations, joys, hauntings, and affections, and not least his confidence in his poetic vocation. His poetic quest is already previsioned in the poem, lines of which have been quoted above, where he continues,

> First the realm I'll pass
> Of Flora and old Pan

that is, the joys of Nature, and pagan sensuous pleasures, and then he asks,

> ...Can I ever bid these joys farewell?

and answers:

> Yes, I must pass them for a nobler life,
> Where I may find the agonies, the strife
> Of human hearts...[40]

He carried within himself contradictions and conflicts out of which he sought to forge a positive self as poet and thinker, as well as human being. He bore the marks of his age, no less than those of his own deprivations. Of the more shattering of these, he was scarcely ever or never to speak. He was orphaned early in life: first when his father, a successful keeper of the 'Swan and Hoop' Livery Stables, was killed in a fall from his horse. John Keats had not yet reached his ninth year. He "lost" his mother twice: when she remarried less than a year later, and moved out of the children's orbit; and, when she returned, again a widow, already a prey to her mortal illness, consumption. She died when Keats was fifteen. He nursed her, but scarcely knew her. And he mentioned her only once; his father never. He sought, and in part found, compensations in his grandmother's house and his school. The liberal master of the school, John Clarke, and his son, Charles Cowden Clarke, were to remain his life-long friends — the latter an unwavering admirer. His guardian, to insure a stable career for him, had him apprenticed to a surgeon, and later transferred to Guy's Hospital, London, as a student and dresser. Though he passed his examinations successfuly, he knew himself unfitted for the profession. His mind roved among the stars... He knew himself a poet. His instrument was the word, and not the lancet. As he told young Clarke, "the other day... during a lecture, there came a sunbeam into the room, and with it a whole troop of creatures floating in the ray; and I was off with them to Oberon and fairyland."[41] "My last operation," he told another friend, Charles Brown, "was the opening of a man's temporal artery. I did it with the utmost nicety, but, reflecting on what passed through my mind at the time, my dexterity seemed a miracle, and I never took up the lancet again."[42]

He was handsome, generous, and affectionate. On his brothers and his sister he lavished a care and solicitude that were almost maternal. And he made friends, whom he kept for a life-time. Chief among them was Leigh Hunt, friend of Shelley, and along with his brother John, editor of *The Examiner*. That radical journal was a thorn in the side of the government and brought imprisonment on the brothers for a slur on the Prince Regent. Young John Keats celebrated Leigh Hunt's release with a sonnet, and the *Examiner* remained an important part of his reading almost to the day of his death.

It is regrettable that posterity remembers little of Leigh Hunt except the unfriendly immortalization of him as a Skimpole in Dickens's *Bleak House*. Dickens, of all men, might have remembered Hunt's history as a liberal at a time when liberalism was not so easily professed as in Victoria's day. He might have remembered, despite Hunt's many foibles — his later accesses of childishness and eccentricity, his vanities — the doughty editor of the *Examiner*, and his espousal of the abolition of slavery, Catholic emancipation, Parliamentary Reform, in an era of bleak reaction chiefly notable for repressive legislation, the Peterloo "massacre", and the profligate court. Himself a son of a prisoner, Dickens might have been more generous toward the prisoner Hunt. An established poet, Hunt became Keats's mentor, whose opinionated direction Keats knew how to manage, and but for whom he might not have met many friends who were to admire, inspire, and encourage him.

There was the ever-loyal Richard Woodhouse, to whose careful ministrations — and note-books — we owe the preservation of many of Keats's poems, and their most useful annotations — an office he filled with passion and veneration, succinctly defined in his own words about the young poet:

"Such a genius . . . has not appeared since Shakespeare and Milton."[43]

There was William Hazlitt, next to Coleridge the most brilliant of the British Romantic critics, painter and essayist, a liberal in politics, and a profound interpreter of Shakespeare. Keats proved an eager student of Hazlitt's ideas, and used them fruitfully in developing his own poetic theory.

Not least important of these friendships and associations (and they included Charles Lamb and Shelley) was that of Benjamin Robert Haydon, a painter of stature. (Keats was to figure in one of his most celebrated monster canvases: *Christ's Entry into Jerusalem*.) Haydon's impact on Keats was to be one of those happy accidents (if there are such!) which in many ways determine a singular aspect of a recipient's psyche. Haydon introduced Keats to the Elgin Marbles in the British Museum...

Haydon brought Keats into a direct contact with the Hellenic revival, in one of its most consummate forms, the friezes of the Parthenon. Keats knew no Greek — and what he knew of Greek mythology and literature he had learned from translations and the Frenchman Lemprière's, *Dictionary*. Here, he was brought bodily face to face with something that transcended all expectancy. The marbles had been appropriated from the Parthenon by Lord Elgin in 1800, and bought by the British Museum in 1816. This was a culminating moment in the earlier history of Greek archaeology — a movement initiated in the mid-eighteenth century by that eccentric German genius, Johann Joachim Winckelmann (whose birthplace Stendhal gave a great French writer his *nom-de-plume*).

Winckelmann's *Geschichte der Kunst des Alterthums (History of Ancient Art)* became the Bible of the neo-Hellenic art movement, and his succinct aphorism concerning the "idealization" within Greek art as "Edle Einfalt, stille Grösse," — "Noble Simplicity, serene Greatness" — became a by-word. His ideas were popularized in England by the Swiss-born artist Henry Fuseli, who introduced them, among others, to his friend William Blake. It is not likely that Keats knew of Winckelmann, though he would no doubt, have, rejoiced in and accepted Winckelmann's tribute to Hellenic art.

Once in England, the Elgin Marbles became the subject of bitter controversy. Their authenticity found a staunch defender in B. R. Haydon. He at once sensed and stressed the importance of these sculptures for the understanding of the Greek spirit, and described his first sight of them, and the profound — almost shattering — impression they made on him. In 1810, as Haydon tells the story, Sir Robert Wilkie

proposed that we should go and see the Elgin Marbles...I had no more notion of what I was to see than of anything I had never heard of, and walked in with the utmost nonchalance...To Park Lane then we went, and after passing through the hall and thence into an open yard, entered a damp, dirty pent-house where lay the marbles ranged within sight and reach...I felt the future, I foretold that they would prove themselves the finest things on earth...I shall never forget the horses' heads — the feet in the metopes! I felt as if a divine truth had blazed inwardly upon my mind and I knew that they would at last rouse the art of Europe from its slumber of darkness...[44]

Seven years later Haydon brought Keats to the British Museum. Keats was stunned.

> My spirit is too weak; mortality
> Weighs heavily on me like unwilling sleep...,

he wrote soon thereafter in a celebrated sonnet. He cannot gather his faculties together: he commingles the feelings of mortality, pain, his sense of fainting in the presence of this survival of "Grecian grandeur."[45]

Here was palpable testimony of a reality that seemed to transcend quotidian realities — a "something" that triumphed over mutability, — a felt perfection that had miraculously come down through the ages to speak eternities! Here was an experience and an element that were henceforth to intermingle with and determine his future creations — from the first line of *Endymion*,

> A thing of beauty is a joy forever

to the unfinished torsos of the epic *Hyperion*.

Might not these marbles be speaking a "truth" that no amount of reasoning and speculation could achieve? Here was the evocation of death and immortality at the same time — and in his heart there was born this "feud" that he would carry within him for the rest of his life. He must hammer out a world-view to satisfy both the man and the poet...

When he turned away from this beauty, there, outside, was the world of daily struggles — the turmoil of another sort of reality. How could he escape those? The circle around Leigh Hunt was a bee-hive of political discussion. 1817 and the years immediately following were rife with disturbing events. Radical journalists like William Hone, editor of *The Reformist's Register* and Thomas Wooler of *The Black Dwarf* were being charged with libel. They were tried and acquitted. Keats rejoiced:

Hone's the publisher's trial, you must find very amusing; and as Englishmen, very encouraging. His *Not Guilty* is a thing, which not to have been, would have dulled still more Liberty's emblazoning... Wooler and Hone have done us an essential service.[46]

He bewailed the absence of a Milton or an Algernon Sidney in the present political life of England. In a long letter written in 1819, he analyzed the current situation in the country, the progress of freedom, until the reaction against the French Revolution set in:

The example of England, and the liberal writers of France and England sowed the seeds of opposition to... tyranny — and it was swelling in the ground till it burst out in the French Revolution. That had an unlucky termination. It put a stop to the rapid progress of free sentiments in England; and gave our court hopes of turning back to the despotism of the 16th century. They have made a handle of this event in every way to undermine our freedom. They spread a horrid superstition against all innovation and improvement. The present struggle in England of the people is to destroy this superstition. What has roused them to do it is their distresses. Perhaps on this account the present distresses of this nation are a fortunate thing — though so horrid in their experience.

There are, he continues, signs of significant change in the temper of the English, as, for example, in the attempted prosecution of the book-seller and publisher Carlile.

For this conduct he I think has had above a dozen indictments issued against him; for which he has found bail to the amount of many thousand pounds. After all they are afraid to prosecute; they are afraid of his defence. It would be published in all the papers over the Empire; they shudder at this. The trials would light a flame they could not extinguish. Do you not think this of great import?

And he cites as another example, the reception which was extended to the political speaker Henry Hunt at what was to become the notorious Peterloo demonstration. Released on bail, he was given triumphal acclaim in London, where a crowd of near 200,000 stood in line to hail him. Keats wrote:

It would take me a whole day and a quire of paper to give you anything like detail...The whole distance from Angel Islington to the Crown and Anchor was lined with multitudes...[48]

Unfortunately, the following May, Henry Hunt was convicted and sentenced to two and a half years' imprisonment.

These sentiments Keats harbored during the critical years of his life, when he was undergoing the agonies of carving out a poetic vocation, forging what he called an "identity"; attending on his dying brother, Tom (also, like his mother a victim of tuberculosis); suffering the venomous attacks of hostile reviewers; and maturing in a preternatural growth from the neophyte verses of *Endymion* toward the golden fruition of the great *Odes* and the *Hyperion* fragments.

When he was completing *Endymion* toward the beginning of 1818, he opened the third book of that poem with a scathing attack on what he called the "present Ministers":

> There are those who lord it o'ever their fellow men
> With most prevailing tinsel: who unpen
> Their baaing vanities, to browse away

> The comfortable green and juicy hay
> From human pastures...
> With not one tinge
> Of sanctuary splendour, not a sight
> Able to face an owl's, they are still dight
> By the blear-nations in empurpled vests,
> And crown, and turbans...

Like others of his generation, he too was tossed on the seas of uncertainties. But of one thing he was sure; Of his vocation as poet; and he was prepared to face all the hardships such a choice would entail. He was a proud young man: "I think I shall be among the English poets after my death."[49]

"I find that I cannot exist without poetry — without eternal poetry — half the day will not do — the whole of it — I began with a little, but habit has made me a Leviathan. — I had become all in a tremble from not having written anything of late."[50]

To be a Poet! "What a thing it is to be in the mouth of Fame." He had his own Pantheon of greatness that included Shakespeare, Milton, and Wordsworth; as well as the Elizabethan Edmund Spenser. Their language was in his ears, to be passionately absorbed. There was also George Chapman's translation of Homer; and Ovid, too, in translation. And not least the vision of ancient Greece...

His first volume of *Poems* had fallen on deaf ears; and he was now about to begin an epic poem, *Endymion*. Here the Elizabethan amatory or erotic shorter epics — literature calls them "epyllions" — stood god-mother to Keats's creation: Shakespeare's *Venus and Adonis*, Christopher Marlowe's *Hero and Leander*; the mythological poetry of Michael Drayton — all products of the sensuous rediscovery of the classical Renaissance. At one with other Romantics, Keats too was swept by their passion for the infinite, the unattainable, so clearly described by Shelley:

> The desire of the moth for the star,
> The night for the morrow,
> The devotion to something afar
> From the sphere of our sorrow...

In Shelley, that unquenchable longing for the Ideal becomes a
"pursuit of death" — the only realm where that ideal can be realized.
For Keats, in whom the immensity of death was an immediate
reality — present or imminent — and, who, knowledgeable as he
was of medicine, no doubt suspected a disposition within himself to
consumption — the conception of dying became a portion of that
sensuality and sensuousness with which he reacted to all aspects of
the outside world — a near-erotic experience. Endymion's passion
for Diana, the Moon, is at once Keats's dream of the unattainable
— the dream of a poetic fulfilment; the delirium of love; the quest of
the answer to the duality within him of the external and the
internal, the world of struggle and failure, and the integration of
that world into a realm of beauty — into Poetry.

In *Endymion*, he put it clearly:

> But this is human life; the war, the deeds,
> The disappointments, the anxiety,
> Imagination's struggles, far and nigh,
> All human; bearing in themselves this good,
> That they are still the air, the subtle food,
> To make us feel existence, and to show
> How quiet death is...

But elsewhere, he depicts life as a subsequent Victorian might have.
He was writing from Teignmouth by the sea:

> I was at home,
> And should have been most happy — but I saw
> Too far into the sea; where every maw
> The greater on the less feeds evermore: —
> But I saw too distinct into the core
> Of an eternal fierce destruction...
> Still do I that most fierce destruction see,
> The shark at the savage prey — the hawk at
>   the pounce,
> The gentle robin, like a pard or ounce,
> Ravening a worm...[51]

This was a "struggle for existence" from which he would fain escape. Out of this world? Such is Endymion's dream. Turn that struggle into poesy; and poesy into beauty, and that beauty into a permanent inheritance for others...

A thing of Beauty is a joy forever...

Endymion itself is uneven, heavily laden with imagery and incident, over-luxuriant in its lavishness — but it contains many beauties, not the least being the unforgettable "Hymn to Pan," of which even Swinburne might have been proud. Endymion's quest ends with the conviction that the "ideal" he is seeking, the Love he wishes to attain, is to be found in this world, and in the human beings around him. In the Indian Maid, he discovers Love, and also his own true self, and is thus made fit for a union with Cynthia, who, in the fanciful transformation which Keats employs, is none other than the Indian Maid.

> O I have been
> Presumptuous against love, against the sky,
> Against all elements, against the tie
> Of mortals each to each, against the blooms
> Of flowers, rush of rivers, and the tombs
> Of heroes gone!...
> There never liv'd a mortal man, who bent
> His appetite beyond his natural sphere,
> But starv'd and died...

The story of the reception of Keats's early works is well-known. Neither Blackwood's *Edinburgh Magazine* nor the *Quarterly Review*, those mighty pillars of conservative opinion, hastened Keats's premature death, as was sometimes believed. With the exception of John Gibson Lockhart, the only truly literary figure, who now remembers critics like the Crokers, the Jeffreys, and the innumerable other criticasters who were ready to pounce on literary works politically or aesthetically anathema to them? But it is not true that the recipients of such invective, derision, and condemnation do not suffer. Keats suffered, but was not defeated. He understood to what extent the attacks on what such critics called the "Cockney School of Poetry" (because based in or near London), were also directed against the poetical and social and political principles of Leigh Hunt, their favorite *bêtes noires*. Keats was caught in the cross-fire, and *Endymion* was thought to be a fit target once more to annihilate that whole school of poetry. The personal attacks on Leigh Hunt defy credibility; but it will suffice to cite a few samples of those directed against our poet:

Mr. Hunt is a small poet, but he is a clever man. Mr. Keats is a still smaller poet, and he is only a boy of pretty abilities, which he has done everything in his power to spoil...

Amiable but infatuate bardling, Mr. John Keats...

Copyist of Mr. Hunt...

and finally,

It is a better and a wiser thing to be a starved apothecary than a starved poet; so back to the shop, Mr. John, back to the plasters, pills, and ointment boxes... But, for Heaven's sake, young Sagrado, be a little more sparing of extenuatives and soporifics in your practice than you have been in your poetry...[52]

Keats was one of the most self-critical of poets; but not to the extent that he became self-annihilating. He well knew the faults of *Endymion*. To the book publisher, Thomas Hessey, he wrote:

Praise or blame has but a momentary effect on the man whose love of beauty in the abstract makes him a severe critic of his own works. My own domestic criticism has given me pain without comparison beyond what Blackwood or the (Edinburgh) Quarterly could possibly inflict, and also when I feel I am right, no external praise can give me such a glow as my own solitary reperception and ratification of what is fine.

As for *Endymion*,

It is as good as I had power to make it — by myself. Had I been nervous about its being a perfect piece, and with that view asked advice, and trembled over every page, it would not have been written; for it is not in my nature to fumble — I will write independently...[53]

He was, in fact, declaring his independence of his models — first from Leigh Hunt; soon even from Wordsworth. At any rate, in his mind he was already planning another epic poem, *Hyperion*, destined to be the testing ground of his achieved maturity ... It was at this very time that he said, "I think I shall be among the English poets after my death."

He also knew that the most pressing problem of his creation now was to clarify and define his own aesthetic — that is, also define its relation to himself and the world...

In studying the making and development of genius it is easier to trace the intellectual or literary sources of his creations than the internal emotional and psychological ones. Every genius has a secret history, which even autobiography — if there is such — fails to unravel. In Keats we have no formal autobiography — no *Dichtung und Wahrheit* — in which forms the early nineteenth century was so prolific. We have, instead, the invaluable scattered, fragmentary personal notations of the letters, which offer us in chronological sequence a special kind of history of his "Bildung" as human being, thinker, and poet. But even in this semi-public search for self-definition, there are intimations and suggestions of problems, the clues of which we can only tentatively find in his finished poems.

We can never know, for example, how his childhood and early manhood had been affected by an alienation from his parents, by the presence of disease both at home and in the hospital in which he served, nor how aware he was — but how could he not be aware? — of the possible latency of sickness within himself. Certainly the anxiety must have been there! To what extent did these represent one aspect of that dualism, of which the other were his sense of his own genius, his irrepressible need to create poetry, his almost pathological sensuous organism and its responses — in other words, the affirmative part of him?

He was painfully aware of his own weaknesses, as he confessed to B. R. Haydon:

Truth is I have a horrid morbidity of temperament which has shown itself
at intervals. It is I have no doubt the greatest enemy and stumbling block I
have to fear...However, every ill has its share of good. This very bane
would at any time enable me to look with an obstinate eye on the Devil
himself...I feel confident I should have been a rebel Angel had the
opportunity been mine...[55]

Himself of a highly erotic nature, this morbidity was carried over
into his attitude toward women. Having gotten over his boyhood
notion of the "ethereal" quality of woman, he now found difficulty
in coming to terms with them in "their reality". In contrast to the
freedom he feels when he is among men, he confesses

...When I am among women I have evil thoughts, malice, spleen. I cannot
speak or be silent. I am full of suspicions and therefore listen to nothing. I
am in a hurry to be gone.

And he adds, significantly,

You must be charitable and put all this perversity to my being disappointed
since boyhood...

and even more significantly,

I must absolutely get over this but how? The only way is to find the root of
evil...For after all I do think better of womankind than to suppose they
care whether Mister John Keats five feet high likes them or not...[56]

He *was* five feet high! One cannot help feeling that he was
rationalizing his withdrawal; at least justifying it to himself, in view
of the attraction women exercised over him. The young man, who,
in viewing one of Benjamin West's paintings, and who disapproved
of it because there was "nothing to be intense upon, no women one
feels mad to kiss," could also write that he would never marry,

...though the most beautiful creature were waiting for me at the end of a
journey or walk. I should not feel — or rather my happiness would not be so
fine, and my Solitude is sublime. Then instead of what I have described,
there is a sublimity to welcome me home. the roaring of the wind is my wife
and the stars through the window pane are my children. The mighty
abstract idea I have of Beauty in all things stifles the more divided and

minute domestic happiness...No sooner am I alone than shapes of epic greatness are stationed around me...I melt into the air with a voluptuousness so delicate that I am content to be alone...[57]

Alas! How could he have foretold that within a few days of writing that letter, perhaps a few weeks, he would fall in love with Fanny Brawne, and later become engaged to her! And that he would be writing those letters aflame with fever and ungovernable transports that would shock the Victorians?

And how remarkable that the first year of that love from the end of 1818 to the end of 1819 should coincide with the fullest flowering of his poet genius!...

It will therefore come as no surprise that his definition of poetry and the poet partake of the character of its propounder. His friends attested to his febrile and intensive sensitiveness to and identification with the phenomena around him, and his incomparable powers of observation. Thus, Joseph Severn, the painter, wrote:

Nothing seemed to escape him, the song of a bird and the undernote of response from covert or hedge, the rustle of some animal, the changing of the green and brown lights and furtive shadow, the motions of the wind...even the features and gestures of passing tramps, the colour of one woman's hair, the smile on one child's face...[58]

Such sensibility he carried over to his personal associations, not without some dangers to himself. For, as he confesses, it leads to an abnegation of the "self" — or what he calls "identity," and generalizing therefrom to the all-inclusive theory that the true poet has no "identity."

When I am in a room with people if I ever am free from speculating on creations of my own brain, then not myself goes home to myself: but the identity of every one in the room begins to press upon me that I am in a very little time annihilated — not only among men; it would be the same in a nursery.

Readers of the poems need not be reminded how this notion of "self-extinction" operates in the frequent images — taking the form of drowsiness, narcosis, death and its erotic equivalents.

It is out of these feelings, and sensuous responses, and others forever hidden from us, that Keats developed the celebrated theory of "negative capability," and of non-identity of the truly great poet. At one pole he places such poets as Wordsworth with their "egotistical sublime" — that is, those speaking with an emphatic "I"! and advancing relentlessly their central philosophies of life; at the other pole the true "poetical character" — Keats is thinking primarily of Shakespeare —

which is a thing per se and stands alone; it is not itself; it has no self — it is everything and nothing. It has no character; it enjoys light and shade; it lives in gusto, be it foul or fair, high or low, rich or poor, mean or elevated. It has as much delight in conceiving an Iago as an Imogen. What shocks the virtuous philosopher, delights the chameleon poet.

Poets of this class relish both the dark and the light side of things, because both end in "speculation" — which for Keats means the imaginative transformation of their experiences into art.

The Poet has no identity, he continues ... It is a wretched thing to confess; but is a very fact that not one word I ever utter can be taken for granted as an opinion growing out of my identical nature — how can it, when I have no nature?[59]

Of course, he had a "nature". Only it was in what he called a state of "siege of contraries." And what contraries! Let us look at the critical year that begins roughly in October 1818, and ends in September, or so, 1819. It embraces one constant dichotomy — that of Life and Death: Life — his meeting with and desperate love for Fanny Brawne around October 1818; Death, his brother Tom's in December. In November he commences work on *Hyperion*. During the first half of the following year he produces that incomparable series of poems which included "The Eve of St. Agnes," and the great Odes: "On the Grecian Urn," "To the Nightingale," "On Melancholy," "To Indolence." Toward the end of 1819 he abandons *Hyperion* altogether, leaving us the two fragments: *Hyperion* and *The Fall of Hyperion*. With this act, one may say Keats's poetic career has come to a close. In December he was unwell, and at the beginning of the following year he had his first ominous hemorrhage...

In the critical year of 1818-1819, of which we have spoken, the struggle for self-integration reflected the additional volcanic upheaval of his almost delirium-like passion for Fanny Brawne. A triadic pattern was now established which included Life-Love-Death. As he wrote to Fanny, in July 1819:

...I have two luxuries to brood over in my walks, your loveliness and the hour of my death. O that I could have possession of them both in the same minute...[60]

Yet at the same time the battle for a self-definition still raged within him, the battle between Certainties and Uncertainties — or, to put it differently, Identify or Non-Identity — a reasoned philosophy or an intuitive one.

He was at one with the great body of Romantics in upholding the antipodal character of Reason and Intuition — Reason and the Poetic Imagination. Spontaneity, insight, intensity, vision, primacy of the intuitive imagination and the ego, the superiority of "feeling" over "theory" — these were among the fundamental tenets that formed the shibboleths of the Romantic "revolt". They might be crying with Goethe, "Gefühl ist alles!" — "Feeling is All!" — or with Wordsworth proclaim the omnipotence of Nature as a teacher, superior to books and colleges, to hair-splitting philosophers or "botanizing" scientists. — They were at one in their faith in the predominant role of the poetic — or artisitic — imagination as the active agent that reconstituted the outside world into an artistic unity, through its intrinsic organizing capacity. The Imagination was the "I" — the fusing or as Coleridge called it the "esemplastic" magician that brought order out of chaos — the alchemist that turned the base metal of external reality into gold...

Many of the Romantics — but not all — held that Science, and Newton in particular, had depoetized or "demythicized" the world. Science was identified with Reason — and the rational or systematic pursuit of knowledge — the rational search for Truth — were thus Satanic instruments destructive of the poetic world. Blake, as we have seen, was a notable example of such assumptions. Analysis destroys the poetry of life.

Keats too fell a prey to such superstition. Newton "had destroyed all the poetry of the rainbow by reducing it to the prismatic." Such, Haydon reports, was the conviction of Charles Lamb and John Keats.[61]

Uttered perhaps in jest at a dinner, this was an opinion seriously held by Keats. He embodied that notion in "Lamia" — a poem in which the "philosopher" Apollonius destroys both Lamia and her lover and husband, the youth Lycius. Penetrating into the true nature of the beautiful woman, in reality a snake and a witch, Apollonius "unweaves the rainbow." And Keats comments:

> There is an awful rainbow in heaven:
> We know her woof, her texture; she is given
> In the dull catalogue of common things.
> Philosophy will clip an angel's wings,
> Conquer all mysteries by rule and line,
> Empty the haunted air, the gnomed mine —
> Unweave a rainbow...[62]

concluding that "But a moment's thought is passion's bell." Keats's is not an evasion of abstract thought. It was an attempted escape from importunate claims thought made on feelings and the persistence of "the weariness, the fever and the fret" in a world "where but to think is to be full of sorrow."[63]

He had said, "I shall never be a reasoner because I do not care to be in the right." No, he would rather trust to the "faery power of unreflecting love." He would not have his love for Fanny Brawne destroyed by the desiccating probings of philosophy ...

To remain in uncertainties! The great "Odes" are the distillations of these "uncertainties". Better remain with acute sensations. Snatch at the moments that feed the sensuous and the sensual — ephemeral as they might be. Translate yourself into the past, where casements open up on infinite landscapes of unlimited possibilities. In the "Eve of St. Agnes" he had given sensations their almost unrestrained scope — would indeed have passed beyond, if his friend Woodhouse had not persuaded him to attenuate the erotic midnight encounter of Porphyro and Madeline, whereas he had wanted to consummate the love-scene. (Such boldness would repel lady-readers!) ... So he had raised the principle of "uncertainty" into his personal categorical imperative —

At once it struck me, what quality was to form a man of achievement, especially in literature and which Shakespeare possessed so enormously — I mean *Negative Capability*, that is when a man is capable of being in uncertainties, mysteries, doubts, without any irritable reaching after fact and reason...[64]

Almost two years later he was reaffirming that principle — identifying himself with it, in speaking of his friend Dilke,

a man who cannot feel he has a personal identity unless he has made up his mind about everything. The only means of strengthening one's intellect is to make up one's mind about nothing — to let the mind be a thoroughfare for all thoughts...[65]

Yet, there is for him at least one certainty:

I am certain of nothing but the holiness of the heart's affections and the truth of the imagination. What the imagination seizes as Beauty, must be Truth — whether it existed before or not ... The imagination may be compared to Adam's dream — he awoke and found truth ... However, that may be, O for a Life of Sensations rather than of Thoughts!

Hence the importance of intensity in Art — "making all disagreeables evaporate." In a world in constant flux, Art translates the momentary and evanescent into the eternity of Beauty. In Art the ephemeral is annulled. The Grecian Urn, the Nightingale, Porphyro and Madeline are "living" testimonies to Art's potency. But omnipotence?

No. The imagination may soar aloft with the Nightingale, be at one with the enchased figures of the Grecian Urn, momentarily savor the overpowering mellowness of Autumn, stand at casements looking out on infinity — alas! there is always the downward pull of the earth...

There is here no soothing of the "wakeful anguish of the soul." There is ever the ache in all pleasures; the pain — no matter how luscious the dainties are to the palate, and the sounds to the ear; and in turning toward the beauties of the past, there is ever the agony of knowing that these "happy pieties" are gone forever. No intoxication as of hemlock or other opiates; no beakers brimming of the "warm South," can avail against the weight of the present...

He struggled valiantly to emerge out of his dark forest of conflicting feelings and thoughts. How was he to assimilate the world outside — the world of sorrows, of unending battles, into his notions of the Poet, and of his Art? He rejects the belief that the world is a "vale of tears" — "from which we are to be redeemed by a certain interposition of God and taken to Heaven."

Gradually — if still somewhat confusedly — he feels himself stepping into the light: Out of the "vale of tears" into the vale of "Soul-making."

"Soul-making" — we may take it — is the achievement of a full and integrated and mature "consciousness."

This is effected by three grand materials acting the one upon the other for a series of years. These three materials are the Intelligence, the human heart (as distinguished from intelligence or mind), and the World of Elemental space, suited for the proper action of Mind and Heart on each other for the purpose of forming the Soul, or Intelligence destined to possess the sense of Identity...I will call the *world* a school instituted for the purpose of teaching little children to read — I will call the *human heart* the horn-book used in that school. Do you not see how necessary a world of pains and troubles is to school an intelligence and make it a Soul? A place where the heart must feel and suffer in a thousand diverse ways! Not merely is the heart a horn-book. It is the mind's experience, it is the teat from which the mind or intelligence sucks its identity...

I began by seeing how man was formed by circumstances — and what are circumstances? — but touchstones of his heart... — and what are the provings of his heart but his fortifiers and alterers of his nature? and what is his altered nature but his soul?[67]

These reflections may serve as tentative "program notes" for Keats's own journey, as he threaded his way toward defining a number of elements of his revised "poetics". Had he been thus far merely a "dreamer" — and was he now finding his way to being a "poet"? What was the difference between the two? Were all those "provings" and "alterations" of his consciousness working toward some sort of "perfectioning" not only in his own vocation, but universally in the world itself? He had felt that there was an advance, or, what he called "the grand march of intellect" in the world — and he cited the superiority of Wordsworth over Milton, in that the former thought more deeply "into the human heart" than Milton, and had felt more deeply the "burden of the mystery." "It proves," he wrote to Reynolds, "that a mighty providence subdues the mightiest minds to the service of the time being, whether it be in human knowledge or religion..."[68] He now felt that the "wealth of poetry is unexhausted and (indeed) inexhaustible."

What achievement it would be to be able to embody all these elements: the idea of progress, the role of the poet, the struggling world in an epic that would make Beauty and its progressive transformations its center; and the poet, as human being living in this world as well as in the world of his imagination, the bearer of the new vision! And to make Sorrow one of the principal elements in this projection of Change! Not as revealing a theatre of stagnation and inertia, but one of constant movement forward. And leave a monument that would amaze like the marbles of the Parthenon!

Greek mythology seemed to lend itself naturally to this idea. Here he found in the wars of the Titans against the Olympians, in the overthrow of old gods and their succession by the new ones the materials that could be assimilated both into his theory of poetry as well as his evolving view of the world. Keats subtracted from that mythology all the elements of goriness, centering both on the grandeur and the tragedy of the principal actors. His was to be the epic of the succession of Beauty by ever greater Beauty — a natural process predestined by Fate, Necessity, and Nature: Saturn succeeded by Jupiter; Hyperion. ancient god of the sun, by Apollo. This necessary course was to be borne in upon the fallen deities.

Young Apollo, the new sun-god, was to be endowed with qualities that will make him superior to his fallen predecessor. Anticipating the later views of Walter Pater and Friedrich Nietzsche, the new god was to be not only the god of light, of joy, of poetry and music, he was also to be the god of pains and sorrows. The joys were to be tinged by a sense of human suffering.

And so, in *Hyperion* (the first of the two fragments), the fallen Oceanus instructs the other defeated deities, and Saturn in particular:

> We fall by course of Nature's law, not force
> Of thunder, or of Jove...
> Thou art not the beginning nor the end...
>
> ...For 'tis the eternal law
> That first in beauty should be first in might;
> Yes, by that law, another race may drive
> Our conquerors to mourn as we do now...
>
> So on our heels a fresh perfection treads...

Apollo, the young and the glorious one, in the throes of a sadness he cannot understand, turns in perplexity to Mnemosyne, Memory, the mother of Poetry:

> Yet I can read
> A wondrous lesson in thy silent face:
> Knowledge enormous makes a God of me,
> Names, deeds, grey legends, dire events, rebellions,
> Majesties, sovran voices, agonies,
> Creations and destroyings, all at once
> Pour into the wide hollows of my brain,
> And deify me, as if some blithe wine
> Or bright elixir peerless I had drunk
> And so become immortal...

It is Keats speaking to himself, as he describes Apollo's anguish of a new birth and the wild commotion that shakes him, calling it a "dying into life." The reader will not fail to note the radical reversal in Keats's thinking Before he had spoken of life into death; and here, of death into life...

Thus ends the fragment called *Hyperion* — unfinished like some piece of recovered Greek statuary.

Dissatisfied, Keats struggled to create a second massive piece, *The Fall of Hyperion*.

He had been reading Dante, and in Carey's translation of the *Inferno* he conned the opening lines:

> In the midway of this our mortal life
> I found me in a gloomy wood, astray
> Gone from the path direct...

Like the great Italian, Keats would now also speak in his own voice. He too was struggling with a cosmic theme — the growth of a soul. He too was struggling to translate a cosmic philosophy into epic poetry — like Milton and Dante. He too was speaking as an "identity":

> Methought I stood where trees of every clime
> Palm, myrtle, oak, and sycamore and beech...

Around him is a "feast of summer fruits," and tasting of them, and drinking of a "transparent juice," he falls into a deep slumber ... On awaking he has his vision ...

He is standing before a sanctuary, amid ruins, and an altar approachable by ascending steps, the mounting of which fills him with anguish, fear and near-death. Almost expiring, he succeds in achieving the first step, and comes back to life. He is climbing toward the sacred heights of poesy, and may, he feels, even be worthy of reaching the top; worthy too of being instructed by the priestess-goddes Moneta — who is Mnemosyne, mother of the Muses. He hears her voice:

> None can usurp this height ...
> But those to whom the miseries of the world
> Are misery, and will not let them rest.
> All else who find a haven in the world,
> Where they may thoughtless sleep away their days,
> If by a chance into this fane they come,
> Rot on the pavement, where thou rotted'st half ...

This is the realm of the "poet," not the "dreamer":

> The poet and the dreamer are distinct,
> Divers, sheer opposite, antipodes.
> The one pours out a balm upon the world,
> The other vexes it ...

You, Keats, are as yet a "dreaming thing," a "fever of thyself":

> What benefit canst thou do, or all thy tribe,
> To the great world?

To be a poet, he must be like those who

> love their fellows even to the death,
> Who feel the giant agony of the world ...

Before revealing to the would-be poet the mystery of the cosmos, the death of the old gods, and the birth of the new, she will disclose her own secret. She lifts her veils. She is the pagan Mater Dolorosa,

mother of sorrows, as well as benign mother of consolations —
sufferer and soother of the "giant agonies of the world" — without
the understanding of which no one can be a true poet:

> ...Then saw I a wan face,
> Not pined by human sorrows, but bright-blanch'd
> By an immortal sickness, which kills not;
> It works a constant change, which happy death
> Can put no end to; deathwards progressing
> To no death was that visage; it had pass'd
> To lily and the snow; and beyond these
> I must not think now, though I saw that face.
> But for her eyes I should have fled away.
> They held me back with a benignant light,
> Soft mitigated by divinest lids,
> Half closed, and visionless entire they seem'd
> Of external things — they saw me not,
> But, in blank splendour, beam'd like the mild moon,
> Who comforts those she sees not, who knows not
> What eyes are upward cast
> I ached to see what thing the hollow brow
> Behind enwombed: what high tragedy
> In the dark secret Chambers of her skull
> Was acting...

Guided by Moneta, he is granted a sight of the majestic, though
dethroned, and woebegone fallen god Saturn, and of the former
sun-god Hyperion, enraged, and not yet ready to accept defeat.

At this point, *The Fall of Hyperion* breaks off. And we are left
with another torso!...

In abandoning *Hyperion*, Keats gave as his reason that "there
were too many Miltonic inversions in it." That is true. But it may be
surmised that Keats felt, in addition, that he had not yet reached that
stage of artistic maturity of thought, of the philosophical idea, that
would make completion possible, so that he might compete with
Milton or Dante. One may also assume that illness and the
anticipation of an early death may have played a part in his decision.
The loss of a fully realized *Hyperion* is irreparable.

But we may be partially consoled by the rich treasures that followed in those shorter models of superb perfection, the "Odes" and the narrative poems, chiefest among them that paean to happy love and ideal beauty, "The Eve of St. Agnes."

He was twenty-four: How many poets had accomplished half as much as he in such a brief life-span?

In February 1820 he suffered his first very serious hemorrhage. "That drop of blood," he said to his friend Brown, "is my death warrant. I must die."[70] In June he had another attack. Advised to seek a more favorable climate, he left England in September, and arrived in Rome on November 15. Here he was in the company of Shelley. He died on February 23, 1821, and was buried in the Protestant Cemetery of Rome.

If I should die, he had written to Fanny Brawne in 1820, I have left no immortal work behind me — nothing to make my friends proud of my memory — but I have loved the principle of beauty in all things, and if I had had time I would have made myself remember'd.[71]

Posterity was to invalidate these despairing words, as well the inscription he had requested for his tombstone: "Here lies one whose name was writ on water." Today he is among the very great poets of all times. Shelley composed his magnificent epitaph in *Adonais*. But one might well add another: Théophile Gautier's tribute to Art:

> Les dieux eux-mêmes meurent
> Mais les vers souverains
>   Demeurent
> Plus fort que les airains.
>
> The gods themselves pass.
> But sovereign verse
>   Remains
> Mightier than brass.[72]

5.

> All things are sold ... even life itself
> And the poor pittance which the law allows
> Of liberty, the fellowship of man,
> Those duties which his heart of human love
> Should urge him to perform instinctively,
> Are bought and sold as in a public mart
> Of undisguising selfishness, that sets
> On each its price, the stamp-mark of her reign.
> Even love is sold; the solace of all woe
> Is turned to deadliest agony ...
> — Shelley, *Queen Mab* —

The vicissitudes of a poet's reputation are rarely so glaringly revealed as in the case of Shelley. Maligned and reprobated as "atheist," apostle of "free love," — a satanic subverter of state, church, and virtue, bludgeoned by the *Quarterly Review* and other journals of power, treated with cushioned condescension by the Victorians, imaged as an "ineffectual angel" by Matthew Arnold; adored and then abjured by Robert Browning — Shelley waited for generations before being accorded the rank of a major poet — and a century before he was to be considered as a thinker too. It took the insight of George Santayana, the scientific understanding of A. N. Whitehead, and the broad intelligence of Bernard Shaw to force an acknowledgment of him as both thinker and poet.

Without doubt, he stands today as a myriad-minded poet, profoundly versed in history, science, philosophy and letters; a thinker who possessed an extraordinary sense of reality; a poet who was able to translate his revolutionary fervor into an eloquence that still makes him one of the most articulate spokesmen of humanity.

There was a singleness of purpose in him — an amazing unity that controlled his ever-enlarging vision with its maturing and varied manifestations. What he was in his earliest philosophic poem, *Queen Mab*, he remained in his last poetic drama, *Hellas*.

Whether William Godwin ruled his thought, or (as happened much later), Plato — he remained a practical visionary, for whom the fate of mankind was a primary concern. Highly sensitive, endowed with a nervous organism that responded with intensity to the world around him, he was from his earliest manhood a part of the sufferings, woes, needs, and joys that made up the existence of human beings no matter where — be it in England, Ireland, Spain, Greece, or Italy. His mind's and his affections' domain was wide, as was the range of his poetic genius. He was capable of speaking in the breath-taking sublimities of *Prometheus Unbound*, addressing himself to the more learned; and he spoke in the common language of the common people, as in his "Song to the Men of England." He was one of the great poetic myth-makers of all times. Yet, his mytho-poetic creations are those — we dare say it — of a "realist."

He was many-sided, and the intellectual heir of many ages. He could translate Goethe's *Faust* and Calderon; he had mastered Greek, Latin, Italian, Hebrew, French. He knew his English poets thoroughly.

But at the center of all his thinking and dreaming was the "unfinished" French Revolution — the great tasks still left for posterity to fulfil.

He was a born rebel. When he was seventeen he read William Godwin's celebrated treatise, *Political Justice*, and he became intoxicated with the gospel of "philosophical anarchism," and its call to eradicate the deleterious and repressive governmental and religious institutions that distorted mankind, so that its true native goodness could achieve frutition, and human beings realize their full potentialities. Godwin's anarchism was "philosophical" — that is, it abhorred violence. The obliteration of repressive institutions would be achieved by the forces of Reason. Shelley adopted that doctrine. Man was a rational creature. Whether high or low in station, all that he required was to be shown the "irrationality" of what was, to be persuaded to abolish it.

For that too was the faith of the eighteenth century French thinkers, who were the bases of both Godwin's and Shelley's thinking: Voltaire with his scepticism, Baron d'Holbach with his staunch materialism, and radical social criticism; Condorcet with his unshakable optimism and his dedication to the ideal of human progress and human perfectibility. In these masters Shelley also found incipient analyses of the class-nature of society, attacks on private property, anticipations of social and political egalitarianism. In England, William Godwin, Mary Wollstonecraft, his wife, Thomas Paine (among others) supplied additional fuel — criticism of the institutions of marriage, advocacy of women's rights, a defense of the French Revolution, and sundry other radical ideas.

Young Shelley proved an enviable disciple. Soon, while at Oxford, he published a pamphlet, "The Necessity of Atheism," and was forthwith expelled, along with his collaborator and friend, Thomas Jefferson Hogg. This occured in March 1811. Shelley was then barely nineteen. In the same year he eloped with and married sixteen-year-old Harriet Westbrook — a precipitate action that was to have tragic consequences for both of them...His father, a baronet, was outraged at his monstrous offspring.

Already he had dedicated himself to the reform of the world. He would be at once pamphleteer, propagandist, activist and poet, — a convinced "liberator".

Wherever there was any sign of repression or resistance — there he was, either in spirit, or in person. What he believed, he would proclaim. That which he proclaimed he would translate into action. With him, theory and practice were one.

On his honeymoon in Ireland, he published an "Address to the Irish People," supporting Catholic Emancipation and Repeal of the Union Act, and shared a speakers' platform with the fiery Irish libertarian, Daniel O'Connell. How far-sighted he was even then is shown by his *Proposasl for an Association* — organization of sectors of the Irish people for the achievement of their political and social ends. (His mentor, Godwin, was afraid of organization and of revolution, and heartily disapproved of his disciple's advocacies!) Back in England, he wrote a "Letter to Lord Ellenborough," who had presided at the trial of the printer Eaton, publisher of Holbach and Paine, and who had him sentenced to prison. Shelley's activities became known to the government, and he was now under "observation."

He was about to venture on his first major philosophical poem — *Queen Mab* — in which he would set forth the body of his thought in the heightened language of poetry, and in mythic form. He was, of course, following in the arduous footsteps of the great philosophical poets of the past and present: Lucretius, Dante, Milton, Goethe, and Wordsworth. He would translate Holbach, Godwin, and others into poetry. But Shelley was a child of the Great Revolution, and his poetry would be philosophical, social, and revolutionary.

Change, Reason, Revolution — the triad represents the rooted belief of Shelley. Their triumph was assured by that law of Nature called "Necessity." Events in the material and spiritual world are bound together by one inexorable tie — the irresistible connecting link of cause and effect. Neither Chance nor destructive Fatality are the rulers of this universe — though these may momentarily prevail (hence doubt and even a shadowy despair). As Reason is one of the offsprings of Necessity, its mandates are equally inevitable and irresistible. Reason will show the world the world's irrationality — the irrationality of its oppressive institutions and laws. Reason will change the hearts and minds of humanity once the veil of ignorance and superstition is lifted, and Truth is borne in upon them. Reason will throw open the prisons of the mind and body. Reason needs no physical adjuvant to make its victorious way. It will even convince the powers that be how irrational their behavior is and how immoral. Violence will disappear. And so will that most horrible oppression of all — War itself...

Queen Mab is a dream vision, composed in 1812. It echoes Godwin's *Political Justice* and other thinkers; yet it is at the same time an extraordinary epitome of Shelley's capacity to amalgamate them and turn them into poetry. Much of the machinery and some of the elaborations are crude at times and immature; and in parts the imitation of other writers' styles is only too evident.

The poem is a Utopian dream, presented to Ianthe's eyes as she is borne aloft in Queen Mab's chariot. To her are revealed the past, the present and the future. The underlying metaphysical idea is that the whole world is a unity — the universe is an interlacing of its many parts mounting from the minutest grain up to "Man's imperial race." "Every atom is sentient in unity and part."

The Past represents a lurid chronicle of oppression and exploitation and superstition. The Present is a panorama of outrages against humanity. In words which must have seemed most daring at the time, Shelley lashes out at King and aristocracy. The King is the "fool/Whom courtiers nickname monarch." The courtiers are "gilded flies" battening upon the miserable mechanic's labor, upon the poor peasant, the "squalid" miner, "leaner than fleshless misery," all of whom labor to "glut" the grandeur of the parasite. "Kings, priests, and statesmen" — using as their excuse "man's evil nature."

> That apology
> Which kings who rule, and cowards who crouch, set up
> For their unnumbered crimes,

foment wars and send thousands to their slaughter.

Perhaps the most eloquent lines are dedicated to the excoriation of "commerce," that is, to use a later phrase, the "cash-nexus". This, more than anything else, has led to the degradation of mankind, to great inequities — a system that corrupts both those who exploit it, and brutalizes and degrades those who are its victims.

All things are sold. "Gold is a living god." Human beings are
being turned into "scarce living pulleys of a dead machine. / Mere
wheels of work and articles of trade / That grace the proud and noisy
pomp of wealth!"

Already, even before the full flowering of the British industrial
system and its triumphant machine economy, Shelley is describing
"alienation" — then current only as a term in Hegel's obscure
writings, and waiting more than thirty years yet for its fullest
elaboration by Karl Marx. Shelley understood how the "harmony
and the happiness of man / Yields to the wealth of nations." He
understood the sequent "deep stagnation of the soul," "the withering
of all passion" — which are the fruit of the "sordid lust of self." He
understood the attractions, cajolements and temptations of gold and
of superstition. He knew well what the brutalization of man meant.

But

> ... the eternal world
> Contains at once the evil and the cure.

For in every heart there is "perfection's germ ... even in the
perversest time." Always there will be one man or woman, compact
of virtue and truth, who will rise to "bind the scorpion falsehood
with a wreath of ever-living flames," and initiate the work of human
regeneration. That liberator will teach humanity to crush religion
and all its minions. He will make them understand the laws of
Nature — the meaning of Necessity:

> Spirit of Nature! all sufficing Power,
> Necessity! thou mother of the world!
> Unlike the God of human error, thou
> Requir'st no prayer or praises ...

Necessity is the universal spirit that guides the world, though to the
untutored mind, Nature all around might appear as a chaos of
"contingency and chance."

But actually,

> No atom of this turbulence fulfils
> A vague and unnecessitated task,
> Or acts but as it must or ought to act.
> Even the minutest molecule of light,
> Fulfils its destined, though invisible work . . .

Shelley is what moderns would call a "mechanical determinist."

Having viewed the horrors and injustices of the contemporary world, Ianthe is now ready for a reviving vision of the Future. "Happiness and science dawn though late upon the world."

> O happy Earth! reality of Heaven!

Once liberated from the oppressor's chains, and now given free play to its instincts, reason and its intelligence, what limitless possibilities for change are now opened to humanity! Changed itself, it will also be enabled to change the face of the world. Young Shelley had once said, "By chemical agency the philosopher . . . may transmute an unfruitful region into a land of exuberant plenty." Such was his acute scientific prevision.[73]

> The habitable earth is full of bliss;
> Those wastes of frozen billows that were hurled
> By everlasting snow-storms round the poles,
> Where matter dared not vegetate or live,
> But ceaseless frost round the vast solitude
> Bound its broad zone of stillness, are unloosed;
> And fragrant zephyrs there from spicy isles
> Ruffle the placid ocean-deep . . .

Science applied by a regenerated rational humanity can indeed transform the earth into a paradise. The human being, now changed, unites within himself Reason and Passion. That is true Love, needing no "fetters of tyrannic law." Love becomes "a sweet bondage which is Freedom's self."

So all contradictions are resolved, and Queen Mab finally adjures the dreamer:

...Bravely bearing on, thy will
Is destined an eternal war to wage
With tyranny and falsehood, and uproot
The germs of misery from the human heart...

Queen Mab was Shelley's Utopian poetic manifesto of 1812-1813.
Subsequent events in the life of the country and abroad, and his own
personal experiences brought him into a closer and more challenging
relation to the realities of his own and the country's situation. On
the personal side, his marriage to Harriet, which was beginning to
sour, came to a disastrous end when he met Mary Godwin, Godwin's
and Mary Wollstonecraft's daughter, in 1814. Enchanted by her
beauty and her brilliant mind, he fell in love with her and she with
him. They eloped. In 1816 Harriet drowned herself in the
Serpentine. Shelley's name, already marked for public reprobation,
now became anathema in the eyes of the respectable public. He was
denied custody of his children by Chancery, Lord Eldon sitting in
judgment. He was England's pariah.

In the world at large, crucial changes had taken place.
Napoleon had fallen. The Congress of Vienna and the Restoration
marked the end of a revolutionary epoch. Absolute monarchy was
once more in the saddle on the Continent. The wretchedness of the
population of France and England became intensified under a new
economic crisis. Repression continued. Yet Shelley felt there were
signs of an awakening opposition; the movement for parliamentary
reform in England was gaining ground; hunger marches became
more aggressive, though subjected to military repressions. Abetted
and inspired by the revolutionary ardor of Mary Godwin, Shelley
composed his second major politico-social poem, *The Revolt of
Islam.*

In *Queen Mab* the "regeneration" of mankind occurred without
any tangible physical struggle on the part of the revolutionaries.
The contradictions of society were resolved in the abstract. There
was no blood shed. Moral suasion served as the major force of

regeneration. But after 1815, with the Counter-Revolution now firmly in control, the whole concept of revolutionary action and counter-action would have to be revised. *The Revolt of Islam* was to be the epic narrative of the immediate past — though in highly idealized form; — the story of the French Revolution, and its aftermath, Napoleon and the Reaction. At its center would be two living beings participating in those historic events, two revolutionaries, man and a woman, Laon and Cythna. For Cythna is the "new" woman (another Mary Godwin) taking her rightful place in the war for freedom. Both Laon and Cythna become revolutionary leaders.

Can man be free, if woman is a slave? Shelley asks in the poem.

The poem was written to rouse the spirit of his contemporaries, when darkened by despair with the collapse of all revolutionary hopes; and to help overcome the "gloom and misanthropy which have become the characteristics of the age in which we live... But mankind appear to me to be emerging from their trance.. "⁷⁴

Through Laon, Shelley once more affirms his faith and mission:

> It must be so — I will arise and waken
>   The multitude, and like a sulphurous hill,
> Which on a sudden from its snows has shaken
>   The swoon of ages, it shall burst and fill
>   The world with cleansing fire: it must, it will —
> It may not be restrained! — and who shall stand
>   Amid the rocking earthquake steadfast still,
> But Laon? on high Freedom's desert land
> A tower whose marble wall the leagued storms withstand!

Cythna too, though at one point in the story imprisoned, never abandons her vision of a new world to come:

> And thus my prison was the populous earth —
>   Where I saw — even as misery dreams of morn
> Before the east has given its glory birth —
>   Religion's pomp made desolate by the scorn

> Of Wisdom's faintest smile, and thrones uptorn,
> And dwellings of mild people interspersed
>   With undivided field of ripening corn,
> And love made free, — a hope which we have nursed
> Even with our blood and tears, — until its glory burst...

Once free, she is the outspoken fiery "liberator" — bringing her words of ardor and hope and revolution to bear upon men and women, urging them to undo the teachings of King and Church; and not be deceived and cajoled by their preachments "that among mankind, the many to the few belong,/By Heaven, and Nature, and Necessity." "This need not be," she cries,

> Dungeons and palaces are transitory —
> High temples fade like vapour — Man alone
> Remains, whose will has power when all beside is gone...

Reaction triumphs, and Laon is burned at the stake, where Cythna joins him. But this is not the end, for one virtuous man in despair stabs himself, to remain a living memory for others, and a goad of conscience. All is not over yet...

> This is the winter of the world...
> The seeds are sleeping in the soil...

England could no longer be Shelley's home. And so, like Byron, he became a self-exile. The period from 1818, when he arrived in Italy, to the time of his drowning in 1822, was also the period of his most exuberant creativeness — the time of *Prometheus Unbound, The Cenci, Hellas, Adonais,* the many exquisite lyrics (among them "Ode to the West Wind," and "The Cloud") and the very considerable body of political verse and prose, including *A Defence of Poetry.*

On the political field, those were turbulent years. It seemed that the promise of *Laon and Cynthia* was about to be fulfilled; that the lethargy and pessimism of the years following 1815 were about to lift. From Spain, from the Kingdom of Naples, from Greece came electrifying news of revolts. Shelley's ear was attuned to all these events, and he greeted them with spirited enthusiasm. For Spain he wrote an "Ode to Liberty" in 1820; for the Kingdom of Naples in revolt he wrote his "Ode to Naples"; the news of uprisings in Greece he greeted with an unfinished poetic drama, *Hellas*. He heard of the Manchester mass-meetings to protest unemployment and hunger, and of their repression by yeoman and military, — the Peterloo "massacre" — and he composed "Song to the Men of England" and "The Masque of Anarchy." Though often troubled in his health, and given to depressions — to which he gave eloquent utterance — his eyes never left the high horizons of world events.

All of his political and social sentiments he was now to voice in the grandest of all his works, the poetic drama *Prometheus Unbound*. Aeschylus had been one of his most cherished Greek poets, and it was almost natural that he would wish to give the latter's *Prometheus Bound* a new meaning and body. The theme of Prometheus had become a popular source of reinterpretation in the late eighteenth century, and was to become even more so in the nineteenth. Goethe, Byron, Beethoven (among others) had utilized it.

Shelley's *Prometheus Unbound* is (aside from the *Prometheus Bound* of Aeschylus) the most superb rendering of the Prometheus legend. Into this poetic drama, Shelley poured all his humane passion. His mytho-poetic powers were here at their height, and he wrought out his ideas in mighty images and in incomparable lyrics and apostrophes. Here he compressed the world's history, as well as the interrelation of Nature and Man. Prometheus the Titan, who had helped Jupiter to his throne, and then found him the tyrant, enemy of mankind, is at once the fire-bringer (figuratively and literally); the teacher of man and man's greatest friend. He is also the liberator of humanity. He is our contemporary. He is the revolutionary, who has been riveted to the Caucasian rock for three thousand years. He is the cosmic martyr. In Aeschylus, Prometheus is finally reconciled with Zeus. For Shelley there could be no such reconciliation. Tyranny is doomed. Tyranny must fall. Prometheus knows the secret which is destined to fell the Tyrant. None of the indescribable tortures to which Jupiter subjects Prometheus can wrest this secret from him — not even the visions of the martyrdom of man from the times of Christ to the French Revolution. For Prometheus knows that the force that is destined to bring about the downfall of Jupiter is none other than Jupiter's offspring, Demogorgon. Demogorgon is Necessity.

In what we may call the Passion of Prometheus all Nature participates. While he is suffering, all natural forces and spirits languish and lament. When he is liberated, all Nature rejoices, and hymns her exultation in exquisite lyrics. These are paeans to humankind. Jupiter — tyranny everywhere — whether embodied in the British Lords Castlereagh, Eldon, Ellenborough, or in the restored Bourbons, or in the Turkish oppressors of Greece — will fall likewise.

Yet Prometheus is compassionate. On the eve of his triumph he even repents of the curse he has pronounced on Jupiter. He would even recall it. For he too — like Shelley — abhors violence and wrath.

Prometheus Unbound may be called a Hymn to Man. Man liberated can become Promethean. With the fall of Jupiter mankind comes into its own. Man becomes conscious of his illimitable powers. Where there are no longer oppressors and exploiters, humanity can begin to master the forces in the world, subjugate them for their own social uses, universalize their power to the advantage of all. What new forces are released within him now! Here now is *Man* not *Men*!

> All things confess his strength. Through the cold mass
> Of marble and of colour his dreams pass:
> Bright threads whence mothers weave the robes their children wear;
> Language is a perpetual Orphic song,
> Which rules with Daedal harmony a throng
> Of thoughts and forms, which else senseless and shapeless were.

> The lightning is his slave; the heaven's utmost deep
> Gives up her stars, and like a flock of sheep
> They pass before his eyes, are numbered, and roll on!
> The tempest is his steed, he strides the air;
> And the abyss shouts from her depth laid bare,
> Heaven, hast thou secrets? Man unveils me; I have none...

Womankind is regenerated:

> And women, too, frank, beautiful, and kind
> As the free heaven which rains fresh light and dew
> On the wide earth, past; gentle radiant forms,
> From custom's evil taint exempt and pure;
> Speaking the wisdom once they could not think;
> Looking emotions once they feared to feel,
> And changed to all which they dare not be,
> Yet being now, made earth like heaven...

And all humanity is now "equal, tribeless, and nationless... the king over himself." Such is the triumph of Prometheus. The dramatic poem ends in that ineffable chorus in which the Earth, the Moon, and Demogorgon, and all spirits proclaim the new-found harmony of the universe.

Though his fantasies roamed far and wide, and circled the globe as it were, Shelley was a realist whose eye penetrated to the core of things. He could define his meanings as clearly as anyone. In "The Mask of Anarchy" he had pungently and mercilessly excoriated the British rulers who had been responsible for the massacre of Peterloo and other outrages. Through the lips of Liberty, he defines the true meaning of Freedom, saving it from the customary vaporings.

> What art thou Freedom? O! could slaves
> Answer from their living graves
> This demand — tyrants would flee
> Like a dream's dim imagery...

> For the labourer thou art bread,
> And a comely table spread
> From his daily labour come
> In a neat and happy home.
>
> Thou art clothes, and fire, and food
> For the trampled multitude —
> No — in countries that are free
> Such starvation cannot be
> As in England now we see

And he continues, Thou art Justice, and Wisdom, and Peace, Love, Science, Poetry and Thought.

Even more practically and precisely he expressed his social thought in a manuscript written around 1820, but not published in his lifetime. A careful reading of "A Philosophical View of Reform" will set at rest the lingering delusion that Shelley was "mad," "hare-brained" and "impractical". It was to be some time before the most pressing issues he set forth were presented with equal clarity and force:

The public right to demand happiness is a principle of nature;
The labouring classes, when they cannot get food for their labour, are impelled to take it by force ...

The propositions, which are the consequences or corollaries of the preceding reasoning, and to which it seems to have conducted us are: —

That the majority of the people of England are destitute and miserable, ill-clothed, ill-fed, ill-educated.

That they know this, and that they are impatient to procure a reform of the cause of this abject and wretched state.

That the cause of this misery is the unequal destribution which, under the form of the national debt, has been surreptitiously made of the products of their labour and the products of their labour of their ancestors; for all property is the produce of labour.

That the cause of that cause is a defect in the government ...

The power which has increased... is the power of the rich. The name and office of the king is merely the mask of this power, and is a kind of stalking-horse used to conceal these "catchers of men", whilst they lay their nets. Monarchy is only the string which ties the robber's bundle...

Labour and skill and the immediate wages of labour and skill is a property of the most sacred and indisputable right, and the foundation of all other property. And the right of a man to property in the exertion of his own bodily and mental faculties, or on the produce and free reward from and for that exertion is the most inalienable of rights...

If the Houses of Parliament obstinately and perpetually refuse to concede any reform to the people, my vote is for universal and equal representation...

In "The Mask of Anarchy" he had adjured the workers of England:

> Men of England, heirs of Glory,
> Heroes of unwritten story,
> Nurslings of one mighty Mother,
> Hopes for her, and one another;
>
> Rise like Lions after slumber
> In unvanquishable number,
> Shake your chains to earth like dew
> Which in sleep had fallen on you —
> Ye are many — they are few.

It was not long — and he would have been inordinately pleased — before the Chartists of England, for whom *Queen Mab* had become a sort of bible, and the German working classes were singing the "Song to the Men of England."

> Men of England, wherefore plough
> For the lords who lay ye low?...

We class Shelley with the great realists of the century not merely by virtue of the statements and sentiments expressed above, but even more emphatically by virtue of those expressed in his symbols, myths, and poetic visions. For the essence of his "realism" — as of

all true realism — consisted in the fact that no matter what the
vehicle of his expression, its form, — the content is ever one that
seeks to penetrate into the central core of social, moral, and political
human relations. He perceived what were the motive forces of
society; he perceived its class-nature, and the specific relations
which resulted from such a structure, and the pressing need for a
revolutionary change. He labored under the insuperable difficulty
that the class that he hoped would liberate itself was neither class-
conscious enough, nor strong enough to wage the struggle in its own
right and on its own behalf. Hence his deceived hopes that the
revolutionary transformation would be achieved without violence,
blood-shed, or war.

That he sometimes despaired is only too evident. For there was
cause for despair, as uprising after uprising was crushed, and the
world seemed doomed to eternal tyranny. But it must not be
forgotten that his many odes to liberty were composed at the very
same time when he was immersed in Platonism. In that spirit he
transplants his visions of regeneration to a Platonic ideal world, into
the realms of immortality, to which death seems at times a welcome
gateway. Hence the poem, "Adonais," commemorating the recently
deceased Keats. But unlike other disenchanted "liberators" of
humanity, he never descended to a vapid cynicism nor to a cosmic
pessimism. Knowing that political and social reaction was still
terribly potent, he could write the noble conclusion to his *Hellas*,
which celebrated the Greek revolution, and while exulting that

> The world's great age, begins anew,
> The golden years return...

and, foretelling,

> Another Athens shall arise,
> And to remoter time
> Bequeath, like sunset to the skies,
> The splendor of its prime...,

he could also conclude *Prometheus Unbound* with counsel for
posterity, in memory of the great Titan-liberator:

> This is the day, which down the void abysm
> At the Earth-born's spell yawns for Heaven's despotism,
> And conquest is dragged captive through the deep:
> Love from its awful throne of patient power
> In the wise heart, from the last giddy hour
> Of dread endurance, from the slippery, steep,
> And narrow verge of crag-like agony, springs
> And folds over the world its healing wings.
>
> Gentleness, Virtue, Wisdom, and Endurance
> These are the seals of that most firm assurance
> Which bars the pit over Destruction's strength;
> And if, with infirm hand, Eternity,
> Mother of many acts and hours, should free
> The serpent that would clasp her with its length;
> These are the spells by which to reassume
> An empire o'er the disentangled doom.
>
> To suffer woes which Hope thinks infinite;
> To forgive wrongs darker than death or night;
> To defy Power, which seems omnipotent;
> To love, and bear; to hope till Hope creates
> From its own wreck the thing it contemplates;
> Neither to change, nor falter, nor repent;
> This, like thy glory, Titan, is to be
> Good, great and joyous, beautiful and free;
> This is alone Life, Joy, Empire, and Victory.

III.

FRANCE — THE FURNACE OF WORLD HISTORY

I.

RETREAT FROM GLORY

I.

RETREAT FROM GLORY

Hatred of France!! Of that France lit by so much
genius and so many virtues! From which have come
so many truths and so many examples! France —
which one cannot see without feeling an affection
which resembles the love of one's country, and
which one cannot leave without the memory of
having lived there, mingling with something deep
and melancholy that almost feels like exile!
— Alessandro Manzoni, 1823 —

France is the dial of Europe. In other countries a
man must hear the hour strike, before he can tell
the time. Here he can read the time of the day. It is
easier to mishear than to misread.
— Ludwig Börne, 1822 —

Victor Hugo relates that when the newly restored Bourbon
King Louis XVIII for the first time appeared in the Faubourg St.
Marceau of Paris, "his entire success consisted in a remark made by a
workman to his companion: That fat man is the government."[1]

The return of the Bourbons and their adherents was not hailed
as an unmixed blessing by all of France. For the peasants and the
middle classes they represented a formidable threat to their well-
being. For it was these two groups that had been the special
beneficiaries of the Revolution through the forced sales of national
lands, and the division of much of it among the peasants. The
middle classes had enriched themselves by the purchase of such

123

lands. The peasants dreaded a possible attempt at a reappropriation of that which they had won. In addition, they were also in mortal fear of the republicans of Paris.

The changes which had been wrought by the Revolution and Napoleon had been vast. They had established the bourgeoisie in power, and along with them a very extensive civil service. The alliance of bourgoisie and bureaucracy was to be of great significance for the future of the country. Between 1817 and 1830 the number of tradesmen in France rose from approximately 800,000 to double that number. In no other country, not even in England (that "nation of shop-keepers"), was the shop-keeper to acquire the symbolic stature he obtained in France. France became the epic land of the bourgeois tradesman, a most fruitful subject for novelist and caricaturist, with his dream of quick enrichment, his leasing out of houses, tenements, flats; and his ambition to qualify for the franchise and become a member of the National Guard.

Along with him, another powerful element came into prominence and influence — the bankers and financiers who had become enriched during the Napoleonic wars through their vast banking enterprises and their purchases of lands. The Rothschilds, the Foulds, the Laffittes, the Pereires — among many others — were destined to play a crucial role in the political and social history of France.

And not least, the peasant-farmer. He differed greatly from his analogue in England. Here, by contrast, the initiation of capitalist farming, the ever larger appropriation of the so-called waste-lands by the owners of large estates, had been reducing the independent farmer to the status of either tenant-farmer or agrarian worker. One might almost say that this was a return to a kind of feudalism, but with a capitalist direction.

In France, the peasant-farmer owned his piece of land, and strove to increase his holdings and improve them. This land-hunger and passionate attachment to the soil were to prove another very critical element in France's future history. The peasant and farmer were to become the bulwarks of conservatism, fiercely opposed to radical Paris and its working classes. Since three-quarters of the country was agrarian, such a struggle was to turn into a kind of unspoken civil war. Strong also was the French farmer's resistance to encroachments on his rights by the absolute authorities. It is a notable fact that in England the independent farmer disappears from literature, except for some nostalgic poetry or idyllic recollections. In France he became the subject of sharp, often harsh, realistic depictions — from the time of Balzac to that of Émile Zola.

We have thus three very cogent sources of instability of the Bourbon Restorations — the lower and upper bourgeoisie, and the peasant farmer. But there were also other forces that were to contribute to unsettlemnt: There were the victims of the "White Terror" which was unloosed upon Republicans and Bonapartists, with it proscriptions, confiscations, and executions. One of the most notable victims of the new purge was Marshal Ney. The Republicans, though persecuted and ostracized, still retained their faith in revolutionary doctrine, and remained loyal to their slogan of an "unfinished revolution."

The fifteen years preceding the outbreak of the Revolution of 1830 may be said to be divided into two phases: the first, the attempted consolidation of the Bourbon absolutism, still along "constitutional" lines guaranteed by the Charter of 1814. After 1820, however, and particularly after 1824 and the accession of Charles X, the growing opposition to the régime produced more and more stringent counter-legislation, and a gradual rescission of the provisions of the Charter.

What were the political alignments in France at this time? On top, there were the King and his entourage, the so-called "Ultras," or ultra-royalists, with their leader, the Comte d' Artois, who was the brother of the King, and around him a sort of secret government of other aristocratic Ultras. Mildy opposed to them were the so-called constitutional monarchists, critical of the excesses of the Ultras, and supported by an impressive sector of the aristocracy, and the well-to-do upper bourgeoisie. Their principal organ was the *Moniteur*. And finally, there was the conglomeration of independents, opposed to the régime, consisting of Republicans, Bonapartists, and Orléanists (followers fo the House of Orléans). Their organ was the *Constitutionnel*.

This leaves out a large section of the urban population, variously organized or disorganized, who were to represent a forceful element in the approaching struggles against the absolute monarchy. For in the hearts of multitudes, the men and women workers, the faith in the French Revolution had never died. It remained strong in the industrial towns like Paris and Lyons, and among the students. But it did not represent merely an "idea". It found concrete expression even in this period of oppression in the number of insurrections — all of them unsuccessful. In memory, they harked back to a people's "heroism," — a period rich and vivid in the journals, pamphlets, and speeches. These multitudes recalled 1793, when France was emerging from chaos, and was achieving revolutionary triumphs that staggered the opposing armies of Europe. They recalled a populace of France, not as Chateaubriand depicted them:

Then out of their hiding places appear all these naked kings, filthy, stupefied by poverty, disfigured and emaciated by their labour, with no virtue save their shamelessness and their pride in their rags.[2]

No, but as they were chanted in their revolutionary songs, songs like the *Ça ira*:

> Sous nos guenilles, nous sommes
> Des courageux travailleurs...
>
> Yes, under our rags,
> We are brave workers,
> Desiring for all of mankind
> Knowledge and a better life...

Historians of recent date have demonstrated to what extent the maligned "rabble" of France had not only been concretely politicalized, but also how widely they read and absorbed the literature of the day. During the Revolution there were such figures as the cook Constance Evrard who was capable of proffering wise and far-reaching political counsel.[3]

And here is Jeanbon St. André, formerly Jacobin member of the Committee of Public Safety, later one of Napoleon's prefects:

Do you know what government was victorious? ... A government of the Convention. A government of passionate Jacobins in red bonnets, wearing rough woollen cloth, wooden shoes, who lived on simple bread and bad beer and went to sleep on mattresses laid on the floor of their meeting halls, when they were too tired to ... deliberate further. That is the kind of men who saved France. I was one of them, gentlemen. And here, as in the apartments of the Emperor which I am about to enter, I glory in the fact.[4]

Among republicans, students, and many others, clandestine organizations were formed, such as the Loges des Amis de la Verité (Lodges of the Friends of Truth), which were soon to broaden under the influence of the Italian Carbonari into the French Charbonneries. It is these groups that mounted insurrections in 1821 and 1822 at Belford, Saumur, La Rochelle, and Colmar. They were speedily and severely repressed. These secret societies of the 1820's drew in many soldiers, lawyers, doctors, journalists, but had little appeal for working-men, and made scant effort to attract them. Even Lafayette became a member of the Charbonnerie. But the working population in the cities was far behind its English brethren in organization and leadership, and was united only in loose fraternal associations, such as the Compagnonnage, a sort of Masonic trade-guild — lacking altogether that class-consciousness which was already animating the British worker.

Yet, all these proved threatening and explosive elements. The government brought forth its most potent armaments — the Law and the Church. Emergency legislation suspended individual freedom;

and the newly instituted courts, the Cours Prévotales, half-military and half-civilian, passed judgment against which there was no appeal.

The Church was recruited to support government measures. In a nation in which anti-clericalism was strong, and in which the Revolution had wrought far-reaching changes in the relationship of Church and State, had secularized a good portion of the country, had dispossessed the clergy of its vast holdings, and had even won over a good number of them, it was not easy to reinstitute the full authority of the Church to subserve political interests. Anti-clericalism had permeated schools and the universities. Now, the government undertook to reactivate religious organizations. Secret religious associations — such as the celebrated Congrégation de la Vierge — partly lay, partly clerical, which had remained underground, came to the fore, profiting also by the support of the most distinguished members of the Ultra aristocracy, such as M. Villèle, and the Prince de Polignac. The school system and the universities were placed under special supervision, jointly secular and clerical; and seminaries for the training of priests were reestablished. Suspect professors in the School of Medicine were expelled, and even such distinguished lecturers of the Collège as Victor Cousin, the philosopher, and Guizot, the historian, were suspended.

Out of a population of about 32 million, only about 90,000 were entitled to vote for Parliament in 1829 — the so-called "pays légal". Louis XVIII had given explicit directions:

The King expects of the electors that they direct all their efforts to keeping from the polls all the enemies of the throne and legitimacy.[5]

Despite that, the voting population was to take its own course. With what results we shall soon see.

There were enough forebodings and signals of dire events to come. In February 1820 the Duc de Berri, son of the Comte d'Artois, was assassinated at the Opéra. The government threw all caution to the wind, rid itself of even moderate Ultras, and commenced a series of severe repressions under the ministry of Villèle. These continued after the accession of the Comte d'Artois to the throne as Charles X, in 1824. Six years later they were destined to seal the doom of the Bourbons.

A relentless Magaera, repressions grew fiercer and more savage as France heard thunders from across her border — uprisings in Piedmont and Naples — uprisings in Spain and Portugal — even uprisings against the Czar of Russia on the part of the so-called Decembrists. In Greece the insurgent forces appeared to be winning against the Turks. It seemed as if the whole fabric of the Restoration were being rent.

In a hurry to forestall similar unrest in France, Louis XVIII during the last years of his reign, and Charles X after his accession in 1824, moved to counter the rising opposition within the country and the significant electoral successes of the liberals with more and more stringent repressive measures. The franchise was more thoroughly restricted, even to the exclusion of licensed tradesmen; the censorship was tightened, and the right of the double vote was extended to a favored few; taxation was made even more oppressive. Not the least ominous actions were the intervention of the French military forces in Spain, under the prodding of the Catholic right; passage of a law against sacrilege; the reestablishment of the law of primogeniture, and the indemnification of former emigrés by means of huge fortunes.

But there were forewarnings of storms to come: For the first time since the days of the seventeenth century French Fronde, barricades were raised in the streets of Paris. This was in the year 1827. Here, a young student of twenty-two, destined for future fame, participated in an unsuccessful uprising. His name was Auguste Blanqui...

Everything that the liberal bourgeoisie cherished was being jeopardized by the actions of the régime. In the ranks of the liberals were to be found some of the best brains of Europe: the banker

Laffitte and General Lafayette; the liberal writer Benjamin Constant and the intrepid scholar Paul-Louis Courier; the poet Béranger and the Catholic royalist, the Comte de Montlosier; and not least, that indestructible Abbé Grégoire, priest of the French Revolution, who had once said, "Kings are in the moral order what monsters are in the physical"; the philosopher Cousin, the historian Guizot; and most surprising of all, old Chateaubriand himself. No less important, behind all of these stood that vast army of the nameless, without whom no significant revolution has ever been won.

II.

DECADE OF THE 1820's
THE GREAT PREPARATION

II.

DECADE OF THE 1820's
THE GREAT PREPARATION

There was an ominous, inchoate restlessness in the air. The young poet Edgar Quinet described it as

a blind impatience to live, a feverish expectancy, a premature ambition to embrace the future, a sort of nervous tension of thought in birth, an unbridled thirst of the soul, following the aridity of the Empire... In the autumn of 1820 I felt... that profound disturbance that was indistinctly, gropingly, darkly exciting the French mind from border to border.[7]

The blight of a lethargy of the spirit, the feeling of ennui, helplessness, impotence that Alfred de Musset was to describe so vividly in his *Confession d'un enfant du siècle* seemed about to lift — that feeling of hopelessness that infected the younger generation, "an ardent, pale, and nervous generation," — produced by anxious mothers during the wars of the Empire; and after the accession of the restored Bourbons, so that

when boys talked of glory, the answer was, "Become priests," and when they talked of hope, of love, of energy and life, it was still, "Become priests."

The dismal sense that all the greatness of France was gone now seemed about to disperse. What was occurring sporadically among the restless masses as well as among the intellectual leaders was also taking place in that most desolated sphere of creation, literature. A new spirit was about to awake.

Unlike England (not to mention other countries), France had produced no great poet after the collapse of the Revolution, during the Empire, and immediately after Waterloo. The only truly poetic

133

genius was extinguished when André Chénier died by the guillotine in 1794, at the age of thirty-one. The only literary writer of stature who spanned the entire period from the Revolution of 1789 up to the Restoration was the prose-poet Chateaubriand, who ruled as an undisputed king, a palmary rhetorician, worshipped by the now advancing young generation, whose innovations he could not but regard with some suspicion and unrest. Despite his variant political allegiances — an admirer, and an official of Napoleon's, then his embittered enemy — he was a bulwark of conservatism.

He was a pre-Byronic romantic, who brought to his many readers a multiplicity of experiences. A journey to America provided him with materials for his depiction of the "noble savage," the American Indian, whose moral superiority and depth of sentiment were to put Frenchmen to shame when contemplating their own corruption. *Atala* became the rage. Chateaubriand was a master at eking out scanty fact with material drawn from his imagination. His *René* was a veiled autobiography, highly idealized, Rousseauistic in its sentimentality, its morbid broodings, its "Weltschmerz." A master of descriptive prose, he could bring to life the roaring of the ocean, no less than the rush of winds through the American primeval forests; he could also poeticize that vagueness of feeling, that "melancholia" that was so precious to the age. He was adept at suggesting rather than presenting eroticism and sentimentalizing that too. His finger was ever on the pulse of the age.

All these elements he brought into play in one of his most influential productions, *Le Génie du Christianisme* (*The Genius of Christianity*), which appeared in 1802, just at the time when Napoleon was about to reestablish the Catholic religion in France. With that book he gave France and the world at large a prose epic of Christendom — with a sensuousness that is almost pagan in its freedom; a lyricism that is more redolent of the vineyard that of the cloister; a passion and exaltation that stood surrogate for high feeling and high thought; and made for an aesthetic rather than credal surrender to faith. "I believe," he said, "because to believe is beautiful."

There is a God. The plants of the valley and the cedars of the mountains bless his name; the insect hums his praise; the elephant salutes him with the rising day; the bird sings his praises among the foliage; the lightning bespeaks his power, and the ocean declares his immensity. Man alone has said, "There is no God."[8]

In an age of arid prose reality, an age of scepticism, such a book was bound to stir the imagination when it contemplated the contemporary torpor of religious sentiment.

With an intrepidity that does more credit to his breath-taking rhetoric than to historical fact, Chateaubriand evoked the poetry, the grandeur, and the might of Christianity:

Of all religions which have ever existed, the Christian religion is the most poetical, the most human, the most favorable to freedom, to art, and to literature... To it the modern world owes everything from agriculture to abstract sciences, from asylums for the unfortunate to churches, built by Michelangelo and ornamented by Raphael... There is nothing more divine than its morality, nothing more beautiful and noble than its dogmas and rites...It favors genius, purifies taste, approves and stimulates the virtuous passion, invigorates thought, provides poets with the noblest themes...[9]

Scarcely ever before had Christianity been made so sensuous, seductive, and attractive to a jaded taste. Sceptics and the devout could find something in the book to satisfy them. Everything from the dogma of the Trinity, the Incarnation, the Redemption, down to the least particle of Nature — everything from the poetry of Dante, the painting, architecture and sculpture of the Middle Ages and the Renaissance — everything from motherhood to music — all of these — in Chateaubriand's resplendent rhetoric — Christendom had endowed with poetry, nobility, majesty, and beauty greater than any other religion had or could have done. Christianity has saved civilization, and has guided it toward perfection.

This was the nepenthean draught poured out by Chateaubriand — deliciously spiced, coming from the hands of a man who was no ascetic, but from a Christian who had traveled the roads of doubt and uncertainty before arriving at this goal — a man who enjoyed the pleasures of the flesh — animal and human — and made of religion a voluptuous feast of sentiment. Had he himself not confessed that he had been converted at his mother's death-bed? "I wept and I believed."

He could boast with justice (as he did in his fascinating *Memoirs*): "Have I not also worked with my hands to restore the fallen steeple of the old Christian basilica?"[10]

The book proved a most welcome and formidable weapon not only in the hands of Napoleon, but later also, when King Louis XVIII ascended the throne of France...

It was in a spirit of adoration and humility that the younger generation approached the master. Such an one was young Victor Hugo, at the age of sixteen, already something of a poet himself, who came to pay homage to the much older man, whom he was soon destined to displace from his seat of eminence...

Who are the members of this generation that is beginning to bloom within this remarkable decade? What great changes they will themselves undergo when challenged by the epochal events of the following decade! Within them is lodged the intellectual future of France — they are the makers of a new literature, a new poetry, a new art. Even those who are already in their thirties will undergo remarkable transformations. The poet Alphonse de Lamartine had already in 1820 published his *Méditations poétiques* — saturated by Byronism. He is thirty. Stendhal is forty when, in 1823, he publishes his epoch-making manifesto of Romanticism: *Racine et Shakespeare*. But his greatest works are still ahead of him. He bridges two ages — that of Napoleon and that of the Revolution of 1830. Others are mere youngsters: Balzac, Delacroix, Michelet, Comte, Thiers, Enfantin — are just over twenty-one. Victor Hugo is not yet eighteen; and George Sand (as she will call herself) is only sixteen. The Abbé Lamennais is one year older than Stendhal, and only yesterday he was speaking with the voice of a royalist and reactionary: "Restore authority and universal order will be born again." Tomorrow he will speak in other, startlingly radical tones. Tomorrow Lamartine, while remaining the poet, will enter upon his political career, which will bring him to high places. Before the decade is over young Hugo will have produced his *Odes et Ballades, Cromwell,* with its iconoclastic Preface, and *Les Orientales.* And what remarkable changes history holds in store for him!

Chateaubriand might well shudder at this agglomeration of poets, novelists, dramatists, historians and political leaders and thinkers in the making.

For France was an unextinguishable hearth. And ever a-glimmer…

III.

WAR OF DOCTRINES
AND THE NATURE OF MAN
UTOPIA AND ANTI-UTOPIA

1.

ANTI-UTOPIA: MAN IS EVIL

1.

ANTI-UTOPIA: MAN IS EVIL

The Restoration had need of powerful propagandists to influence the minds of the various nations, recognizing in the spread of ideas weapons equal to those in their military arsenals, and as necessary as the soldiery. In Vienna, Prince Metternich surrounded himself with a coterie of brilliant and eloquent adherents, skilled with their pens, for a number of them had been — like Friedrich Schlegel — in the forefront of the German Romantic movement.

It was to be expected that France, the lordly land of ideologues, would not fail in producing even more adept defenders of the Old Order. The influence of their conservatism was to extend far and wide. They were at home in the philosophies of the Enlightment, which they abhorred. They had studied Edmund Burke's celebrated attack on the French Revolution, *Reflections on the Revolution in France,* and their hatred of that historic event was compounded by their experiences as émigrés. On their return they were sure to find willing ears and sympathetic hearts leaning their way. This, it must be remembered, is the century when ideas crossed borders as swiftly as armies, when a Russian officer stationed in Paris was likely to pick up a suspect book in some book-stall, or a suspect idea in a fashionable salon. Ideas in the head — as Heine was to say — are not so easily detectable by customs officers or border guards as books. A thought is invisible dynamite.

Joseph de Maistre was by far the most rigorous and brilliant, as well as the most intransigeant of these French émigré ideologues of the Restoration. He was fearless, impressive, and carried his theories to their ultimate conclusion. His psychological analysis of

143

human nature carried convincing force, and he found followers not only in France. Baudelaire was one of his admirers; Tolstoy studied him closely. The careful reader will probably note that a number of his ideas are by no means extinct even in our own day.

DeMaistre contended that Man was a sick animal. Man is not naturally good. He is both moral and corrupt: he is just in his understanding but perverse in his will. He needs must be governed. He is incapable of governing himself and others; and to conceive him as capable of establishing a body politic, such as a republic, is nothing short of criminal nonsense. No more is he capable of creating a constitution. The notion that "constitution is antecedent to government," — advanced by such thinkers as Thomas Paine — is for him a thoroughgoing fallacy.

It is folly to believe that constitutions came into the world apriori, as if the multiplicity of laws could have been assembled and unified by chance. It is obvious that these elements were guided in their disperseness by a hand higher than that of man, "guidée dans leur chute par une main infallible, supérieure à l'homme."[11]

Man can modify everything in the sphere of his activity, but he creates nothing; such is the law — as true of the physical as of the moral world. A man can no doubt plant a seed, raise a tree, perfect it by grafting, and prune it a hundred ways, but he has never imagined that he is capable of making a tree. How then has he imagined that he has the power of making a constitution?[12]

It was the presumptuous Eighteenth Century, that more than any other, in its "rage philosophique" dared undertake an "insurrection against God," and defy the Divine Order. In its arrogance and challenges it even demanded that God remove himself and leave all human guidance to human Reason. What wonder then that such presumption should receive an answer and condign punishment from the Lord himself? In His Wisdom God ordained the French Revolution!

How did God punish this execrable delirium? He punished it the same way
He created light, with one phrase. He said, "So be it!" And the political
world collapsed.[13]

Such was the French Revolution, that "fange sanglante," that
"bloody swamp." For to carry through such a Revolution it was
necessary "to overthrow religion, insult morality, violate every
propriety, and commit every crime."[13]

The French Revolution proved the incapacity of human
Reason to create and develop a viable political state. What, de
Maistre asks, is necessary for the proper education of an ideal
subject?

"Man needs beliefs, not problems."

His cradle should be surrounded by dogmas; and, when his reason awakes,
all his opinions should be given, at least all those relating to his conduct.
Nothing is more vital to him than *Prejudices*. Let us not take this word in
bad part. It does not necessarily signify false ideas, but only, in the strict
sense of the word, any opinions adopted without examination. Now these
kinds of opinions are essential to man; they are the real basis of happiness
and the palladium of empires. Without them, there can be neither religion,
morality, nor government. There should be a state religion just as there is a
state political system; or rather, religion and political dogmas...should
together form a *general* or *national* mind sufficiently strong to repress the
aberrations of the individual reason, which is, of its nature, the mortal
enemy of any association whatever because it gives birth only to divergent
opinions...It can be said in general, that all men are born for monarchy...[14]

It is God who has given governments to people, operating in
two fashions: often as through a slow, plant-like growth; or more
quickly, in confiding power to "rare men, the true Elect."[15] The
masses of people play no real part in political events. They revere
authority and submit to it because it is something sacred — apart
and inviolable. Sovereigns are infallible. When, as in the French
Revolution, the masses rebel, led by blinded leaders, Divine
punishment follows.

If Providence "deletes, it is no doubt in order to rewrite."[16] God scourges in order to teach. His instruments are War and the Executioner.

Yes, the Executioner. In one of his most celebrated single passages, de Maistre writes his eloquent encomium of this instrument of God's justice, "an inexplicable being who has preferred to all the pleasant, lucrative, honest and even honorable jobs ... that of torturing and putting to death his fellow creatures ... For him to exist in the human family a particular decree, a *Fiat* of the creative power is necessary." He is therefore one of God's special creations! With what may appear as particular verve (almost glee) de Maistre describes his labors:

A poisoner, a parricide, or a blasphemer is thrown to him; he seizes him, he stretches him on the ground, he ties him to a horizontal cross, he raises it up; then a dreadful silence falls, and nothing is heard except the crack of bones breaking under the cross bar and the howls of the victim. He unfastens him; he carries him to a wheel; the shattered limbs interweave with the spokes; the head falls ...

And yet, all grandeur, all power, all subordination rests on the executioner: he is the horror and the bond of human association. Remove this incomprehensible agent from the world, and at that very moment order gives way to chaos, thrones topple, and society disappears. God, who is the author of sovereignty, is the author also of chastisement; he has built our world on these two poles; for Jehovah is the master of these two poles, and on these he makes the world turn.[17]

Aside from Revolution itself, there is another mighty enemy, de Maistre, affirms, whom it will be necessary to extirpate before peace can be secure. That is Protestantism — "that fatal ulcer which attaches itself to all sovereignty and gnaws at it without cease; that universal dissolvent."[18] For there is but one religion that can stand and withstand scientific proofs — the Catholic. Just as legitimacy of a throne is theocratically originated and validated by Divine Ordinance, so, standing even above monarchial legitimacy and supremacy is the Roman Catholic Church, and its supreme pontiff, the Pope. He is sovereign and infallible. Infallibility in the spiritual realm, and sovereignty in the temporal are perfectly synonymous terms. The Pope is the ultimate source of European sovereign power, because only through him can secular sovereignty in Europe achieve unity. Thus emerges that European Charter, "without threats, without laws, without warfare, without violence or resistance, proclaimed not on mere paper, nor by voice of the town-crier, but in the hearts of an all-Catholic Europe... Every nation in Europe withdrawn from the Holy See will inevitably be plunged into servitude or revolt."[19]

"Bon chrétien, fidèle sujet." "A good Christian — a loyal subject." De Maistre died in 1821, and he did not live to see the restored French monarchy overthrown in 1830. Though many of his works remained unpublished until after his death, they thereafter became the bibles of Conservatism. Their influence extended as far as Tzarist Russia, and they profoundly affected subsequent Catholic and neo-Catholic movements throughout the century, including that of England. The Russians expunged the papal element, and substituted their own Tsar-Pope, but retained much of the political ideology. De Maistre had been an official emissary to Russia, and had spent many years there. It was in that atmosphere that he indited one of his most influential works, The *St. Petersburg Dialogues*. Thus he amply repaid his hosts.

2.

UTOPIA: MAN IS GOOD

2.

UTOPIA: MAN IS GOOD

Is not this an injust and an unkind public weal,
which giveth great fees and rewards to gentlemen,
as they call them, and to goldsmiths, and to such
others, which be either idle persons, or only
flatterers, and devisers of vain pleasures; and of the
contrary part maketh no gentle provision for poor
plowman, colliers, laborers, carters, ironsmiths,
and carpenters; without whom no commonwealth
can continue?

— Sir Thomas More, *Utopia,* 1516 —

The People: And what work do you do in our
society?
The Superior Class: None. We were not made to
work.
The People: How did you acquire your wealth?
The Superior Class: In taking the trouble to govern
you.
The People: What! Is this what you call governing?
We toil, and you play. We produce and you
squander. We create wealth and you absorb
it . . . Oh, you elegant men, class that is not the
people, go, form your own nation and govern
yourselves.

— Constantin François Volney, 1791 —

1.

That great-souled humanist, Sir Thomas More, coined the word
"Utopia" — meaning "Nowhere" — and described the ideal
commonwealth of the future which he envisioned, wherein the

harsh injustices and inequities he witnessed in his own day would be replaced by a society in which an equitable distribution of the world's goods would abolish both rich and poor, idleness and exploitation; and where those who labored would at last enjoy the fruits of their hands' work. He could hardly have foreseen what a rich succession that "dream" of his would engender, and what hopes of turning Utopia — the Nowhere — into a Eutopia — a "land of felicity."

Just as the French Revolution had proved in many minds to be a dreadful nightmare — God's way of punishing the sins of France — and a dire warning to forestall the recurrence of such an event, so in other minds it generated new hopes for mankind, and filled them with a vision of the future in which humanity could both change itself and change the world around it. The battle-cry of "Liberty, Equality, and Fraternity" was for them no illusory call to anarchy and enslavement, but an injunction to set the world aright. Man was no monster, no "Centaur" — half-beast, half-human, tainted and irreclaimable, a creature ever to be held in check. Rousseau was no dead letter to them. Man was good. The ideas and ideals of the eighteenth-century "philosophes" were not dead, nor their trust in the irresistible powers of Reason to attain truth, nor their faith in Progress. It remained only rightly to understand the true nature of the society in which the human being lived and labored, to illuminate the inexhaustible potentials within him — and to lead him to the point where he realizes the forces within him for changing the conditions around him that cry for change. He had witnessed the world-shaking transformations wrought by the great Revolution, brought about by the actions of his fellow human beings, by his own countrymen. The realm of possibilities still stretched before him. Utopia beckoned. The times seemed ripe as never before. Standing out in an unavoidable glare were the new elements that had come into being: the scientific and technological advances of the time; the creation of new machinery; the emergence of new forces in modern society — the so-called "proletariat," and the strength of the bourgeoisie. What Disraeli was to call the "two nations," — the "haves" and the "have-nots" — were arrayed in opposite ranks, unequal as yet in strength, but as if preparing for battle. The misery of the populations resulting from the many years of war bore eloquent witness to the possible dangers ahead. The poor, if organized, were not a force to be disdained. The gap was widening...

France became the cradle of the new Utopianism — Utopian Socialism. From France it spread across Europe, to America, and as far as Russia. Of the many Utopian writers and preachers, there are two who were the most remarkable: Saint-Simon and Charles Fourier.

Among the extraordinary geniuses of this age, Henri de Rouvroy Saint-Simon stands out as one of the most extraordinary. With justice he has been called a nineteenth-century Faust. He was one of those "prophets of the future," who in the first twenty-five years of the century led the forces dedicated to Progress, founded a "church" dedicated to humanity, and became the prophet of a new "religion." He was destined to influence the thoughts and actions of men and women in many lands. Such diverse figures as Thomas Carlyle and John Stuart Mill in England; Heinrich Heine and the "Young Germany" School; Mazzini, George Sand, Berlioz and Liszt; Russians like Alexander Herzen and young Dostoyevski — to name only a few — at one time or another came under the sway of Saint-Simon or his disciples.

He sounded the trumpet call to the battles for the future:

The imagination of the poets has placed the golden age at the cradle of mankind, amidst the ignorance and brutishness of primitive times. It would be more fitting to relegate the Iron Age to those years. The Golden Age of humanity is not behind us; it is before us. It will be found in the perfection of the social order. Our fathers have not seen it; our children will one day attain it. It is up to us to clear the way for them.[20]

Henri de Rouvroy Saint-Simon was a descendant of that Duc de Saint-Simon, who at the end of the seventeenth and the beginning of the eighteenth centuries wrote a remarkable chronicle of the age, shocking in its revelations, and one of the glories of French literature. The younger Saint-Simon was one of those rare creatures who within one life-time enclose a multitude of careers. He was an encyclopedist, in direct line of the notable "philosophes" of the preceding era, of whom he was a contemporary, for he was born in 1760. But he belongs to the nineteenth century.

When he died in 1825, his variegated life included the experiences of the aristocrat, and those of an adventurer, of a spendthrift and sybarite, soldier, speculator, student and master. His fortunes alternated between fabulous wealth and such poverty that his faithful servant supported him for years. He fought as a soldier for France, and on the side of the American Colonies against the British. He was a republican, yet he speculated in national lands under the French Republic. He was also a prisoner of that state. He possessed one of the most active intelligences of the time; he was voracious of knowledge, prolific in ideas, plans, books. He was a fantast and a prophet. At the age of forty, he attended and organized courses in line with those of the École Polytechnique and the École de Médecine. Like many of his contemporaries, he was a passionate student of physiology, which he regarded as a clue to the understanding and solving of social problems. He was a megalomaniac, and his gods were Charlemagne, Napoleon, Newton, and Francis Bacon. He was also one of those geniuses whose moral and social vision outdistanced his moral actions. He veered with the winds of politics.

Yet there were few contemporaries who saw so clearly what the new century demanded. Though he appropriated ideas generously from others, even from such ultra conservatives as de Maistre and Bonald, in his principal and fundamental ideas he belonged to the new age.

He foresaw that the destiny of the age was allied to Industry and the Industrial Revolution, the machine, its masters and servants. He recognized the anarchy of his day, and proposed measures to overcome it.

Already, in 1802, in his *Letters from Geneva,* Saint-Simon had perceived within the French Revolution and the Terror elements of a class war "not merely between the nobility and the bourgeoisie, but between nobility, the bourgeoisie, and the propertyless masses ... , in the year 1802, a discovery of genius."[21]

In the same *Letters,* Saint-Simon advised the upper classes, if they wished to save the world from anarchy, to make use of the services of *savants,* the "hommes de génie," scientists, artists, inventors as guides and directors of the interests of the nation. He advocated the establishment of a Newtonian Academy, to which all members of society would subscribe and which would subserve all of humanity.

He had a boundless faith in the infinite possibilities of the sciences to solve human problems, particularly those of society. He was living at a time when the science of physiology was beginning to occupy a significant role in the study of the human body — a movement which was later in the century to culminate in the revolutionary discoveries of Claude Bernard. Saint-Simon contended:

The main functions of philosophers, moralists, and metaphysicians is to study the relationship between phenomena that are physical and those called moral. When they become successful in this branch of their work, it should be called physiology.[22]

He sought to discover a universal law that would serve to establish a science of humanity. What was needed for such a venture was a new encyclopedia — a new "synthesis," embracing all of knowledge, including history, unifying them under one principle or law that would hold for the moral as well as the physical sciences. That would be the Science of Man. Biology would be its key and center, and the new science emerging would be historical and evolutionary. It would exhibit history as a process, subject to inexorable laws.

He claimed to have discovered one such law of history, the law of "alternativity." Organized systems, he claimed, — society itself — are succeeded by systems of transition. Synthesis succeeds analysis, and analysis succeeds synthesis. His followers were to rename such periods of history the "organic" and the "critical." But within each period that is "synthetic," there is already, at its peak, what Saint-Simon calls the "germ of dissolution."[23]

Such is the process of history. Such is the history of all institutions.

Such too the history and fate of Christianity. The reign of Christianity is over. The reign of "positive" (i.e. scientific) ideas is here. The transcendental morality of Christianity has been superseded by a new morality, a "terrestrial morality."

The era of positive ideas is beginning. One can no longer give morals any other motives but those of palpable, certain and present interests. This is the spirit of the age. This is the great step forward which civilization is about to make..., the establishment of terrestrial and positive morality.[24]

He was already anticipating what his disciple Auguste Comte, the future founder of "Sociology," was to proclaim with his "Positivism."

"Politics," Saint-Simon said, "is the science of production... Everything by means of industry. Everything for it.[25]

Among his many projects he was also proposing what today would be called a "technocracy." He called for a class of specialists, whom he named "industriels" — bankers, manufacturers, merchants, and technicians, to direct the interests of the country, to replace the hordes of "idlers," and he addresses these "industriels":

I propose to free you from the supremacy exercised over you by the courtiers, the idlers, the nobles, by the phrase-makers.[26]

He had the boldness to attack the royal family and its hangers-on, as well as a whole body of bureaucrats who surrounded the Bourbon rulers, and sucked the nation's life-blood. His celebrated Parable of Parasitism brought on him the charge of insulting the court, and a trial, as well as a vindication. What would happen, he asked, if society were to lose her leaders of productive industry, her scientists, her savants, her artists and writers? She would then lose her vital forces. But suppose, instead, she were to lose, on the same day

Monsieur, the brother of the King, Monsieur, the Duke of Angoulême... all the great officers of the crown, all the ministers of state... all the... cardinals, archbishops... all the judges... and, in addition to these the ten thousand richest landowners among those who live as nobles...

Of course, he adds with half-concealed irony, the French, being kind-hearted, would be afflicted, for "they are a good people," but the loss would not result in any political evil for the State, since, Saint-Simon adds, every one of these could be most easily replaced.[27]

Though Saint-Simon was laying the foundation stones of what later became known as "technocracy" — an authoritarianism of a scientific and financial élite — he was deeply aware of the plight of the lower classes. He was far from advocating, or even understanding the class-struggle, though he did perceive the class nature of society. And he was revolted by the patent immorality of the upper classes and their exploitation of those below them:

Society today is truly topsy-turvy... The nation has admitted as a fundamental principle that the poor should be generous towards the rich, and that as a consequence the less well-off should deprive themselves daily of their necessities in order to swell the surplus of big owners... Ignorance, superstition, idleness and love of sumptuous pleasure are the characteristics of the supreme chiefs of society, and the capable, economical and hard-working are employed only as subordinates and instruments... A horde of parasites... without producing anything, want to consume, — frauds, that is to say, thieves. The workers thus see themselves deprived of the enjoyment of the fruits of their labor, which is the aim of their labor...[28]

Of course, he was addressing himself to the upper sectors of society — the bourgeoisie, the intellectuals, the élite — even princes and kings, in the hope of converting them to his principles.

His last testament — and in some resepects his most eloquent statement — is contained in *Le Nouveau Christianisme — The New Christianity,* "Dialogues between a Conservative and an Innovator." It was composed in 1825, the year of his death. It is a fervent call for the reorganization of Christianity in the light of the social needs of the times. It is revolutionary, and radical, and was to prove one of his most influential works, anticipating and sparking the even more radical demands of the Abbé Lamennais, after 1830.

If Christianity, Saint-Simon urges, is to fulfil the Christian principle of the all-embracing brotherhood of mankind, it is incumbent upon our society to do so "in a way that would be most advantageous for the greatest number of people" — that is, to ameliorate "as promptly and as completely as possible, the moral, and physical existence of the most numerous class." For the Christian Church today, as represented by its clergy, is "most diametrically opposed to the divine principle of divine morality."

There is, he continues, a new religion that will include all of humanity. The failure of Christianity in the past was not only that of the Roman Catholic Church, but of the Protestant as well. Luther, too, had failed to focus on earthly felicity and on the amelioration of the lot of the common man.

However, today the realms of possiblity have been infinitely extended, especially as concerns the interest of the disinherited poor.

"Now that the dimensions of our planet our known," it is possible for "the industrialists, the artists, and the men of learning to draw up a general plan of work that would make the territorial possessions of mankind as productive and as rewarding as possible in all respects."

And he addresses forceful words to the princes of the various realms:

Princes. What is the nature, what is the character, in the eyes of God and of Christians, of the power that you exercise? . . . You call yourselves Christians, yet you continue to base your power upon physical force, so that you are still only the successors of Caesar, and you forget that the true Christians propose, as the final outcome of their efforts, to annihilate completely the power of the sword, the power of Caesar, which, by its very nature is provisional . . . Listen to the voice of God which speaks through my lips, and become good Christians once more, and stop looking upon armies, noblemen, heretical clergies, and perverse judges as your principal sources of sustenance. United under the banner of Christianity, you will be able to accomplish all the duties that this banner imposes upon the powerful; remember that it commands them to employ all their forces in advancing as rapidly as possible the social well-being of the poor.[29]

Thus spoke one of the most erratic, and yet one of the most highly endowed and seminal geniuses of the new century. Like his thoughts, his life and feelings soared now in the realms of prognostic fantasies of human felicity, and now sank in despair, which at one point brought him to the brink of suicide. Megalomania and practical wisdom — a self-involved Messianism, combined with clear insights into the state of his society — these were all parts of the man. He radiated an influence that extended far and wide. There is therefore something symbolic in the reported meeting of Saint-Simon with one of the future Russian revolutionary Decembrists — one of the noblest and most valiant of that group — Michael Lunin. It was in the salon of Madame Lydie Rogers. Saint-Simon is reputed to have remarked:

Giants will return. Not giants in stature, but giants in the power of reasoning. Machines will replace the arms of men. The seven-league boots of the fairy tale are ordered for humanity of the great captain of the army of workers. Industry is the only politics of peace, because peace is the only politics of nations, even if governments continue for a while longer to make us grasp the full odiousness of their present methods by the odiousness of their results.[30]

And there is another profound symbolism in the death-bed words to his disciples Rodrigues, Bailly, and Halévy:

Our business is well in hand...The pear is ripe. You must pluck it... Forty-eight hours after the appearance of our next publication, we shall be a party.[31]

For, immediately after his death and interment, *Le Producteur*, the organ of the Saint-Simonians was founded, and the "new religion of humanity," dedicated to carrying out the work of the founder of the "physiology of the human species," was established.

The poet Béranger sang:

J'ai vu Saint-Simon le prophète,
Riche d'abord, puis endetté....

I have seen Saint-Simon, the prophet,
Now in riches, now deep in debt,
Who remade society from the ground up,
Full of the labors he had commenced —
In old age he still stretched out his arms,
Sure of embracing the Thought
That would save Mankind....[32]

2.

Charles Fourier, who survived Saint-Simon by twelve years, and whose productive life parallels that of Saint-Simon, remains one of those Utopians, who, unspectacular by comparison with the Faustian count, live mostly in their imaginary visions and their dreams of the future. Outwardly he led an almost humdrum life — a small bourgeois clerk in clothing houses in Marseilles, Rouen, and Lyon, during the last years of his life residing in Paris. He was the son of a substantial draper of Besançon — a city that was also the birthplace of Victor Hugo and Proudhon. Impoverished during the Revolution, he found means to support himself by trade, and was thus enabled to devote himself to thinking and writing about the regeneration of mankind. It is said that when he lived in Paris, he would come home every noon in expectation of the arrival of some capitalist who would be ready to support and finance his reformatory system. He composed his works with the regularity of a machine, not even aware of the meanness of his surroundings. He never married. He strove to live with the dignity and the serenity of a philosopher.[33]

His writings appeared almost at the same time as those of Saint-Simon. The first of these, *La Théorie des Quatre Mouvements,* was published in 1808, and the last, *Le Nouveau Monde Industriel* and *La Fausse Industrie* between 1829 and 1837, the year of his death.

Even more than Saint-Simon, Fourier exhibits a dichotomy. He hovers between insights of extraordinary genius, foreshadowing important later discoveries in psychology and sociology — and most far-fetched and fantastic interpretations of natural phenomena and their relation to mankind and society. It is true that, as M. Gide remarks, what he predicted has in some measure come to pass

— fantasy has in our day become reality; but the specifics of his previsions, and the recommended instruments for their attainment, which he proposed, too often have a most bizarre character.

Let us take him at what, in his day, appeared most extravagant. He is speaking of the future of communication, and its lightning-like rapidity. What shall we say of the following, now that stations are being established in outer space, and satellite communication is a reality?

A certain vessel leaving London arrives in China today; tomorrow the planet Mars having been advised of the arrivals and movements of ships by the astronomers of Asia, will transmit the list to the astronomers of London.[34]

Many great geniuses say and do ridiculous things in their lifetime. Fourier published them. But he was also possessed of a refreshing humor, and brilliant satirical gifts, and could mingle laughter with seriousness, as Engels had occasion to point out.[35]

Unlike Saint-Simon he is not carried away by the achievements of contemporary society — whether industrial or scientific. He is appalled by the intensification of indigence amidst this so-called "progress", and what he called the "opposition of two kinds of interest, collective and individual." "Homo homini lupus" in our civilization. "Every man a wolf toward others."

Every person engaged in an industry is at war with the mass, and malevolent toward it from personal interest. A physician wishes his fellow-citizens good, genuine cases of fevers, and an attorney good lawsuits in every family. An architect has need of a good conflagration which should reduce a quarter of the city to ashes, and a glazier desires a good hail-storm which should break all the panes of glass. A tailor, a shoemaker, wishes the public to use only poorly dyed stuffs and shoes, made of bad leather, so that a triple amount may be consumed, for the benefit of their trade; that is the refrain...It is thus that in civilized industry every individual is in intentional war against the mass; a necessary result of an anti-associative industry, or an inverted world.[36]

Such is Fourier's picture of a society that is "morcelée" — fragmented, and which, as he puts it, creates the elements of happiness, but not happiness itself; a society which has brought forth a staggering disproportion between riches and poverty, so that poverty has become the "offspring of abundance." Nor have the rich themselves won happiness for themselves.

Furthermore, such a society has produced many non-productive elements. Such are the "parasites" — and we find them in the home (that is in women, children and servants), and even more glaringly in the armies of the military, in the fiscal offices, among manufacturers, traders — "agents of positive destructions," as well as "agents of negative creation."[37]

One by one, Fourier examines the deleterious and depraving uses made by society of science, etc., in adultering and corrupting its own products and productions in the interest and to the advantage of the few. The trader has become an "industrial corsair," living "at the expense of the manufacturer and producer."[38]

And the results of "free competiton"? Civilization has been metamorphosed into an "industrial" and "mercantile feudalism," through "federative companies" — our present monopolies — such, for example, as the British East India Company.

No less deleterious are the effects of such a system upon agriculture and our natural resources. He sounds the modern note of ecological despoliation and destruction. Away, he cries, away with the picturesque descriptions of rustic bliss! Look at our agricultural workers! Look at the anarchy of production!

What then is the answer?

Like so many thinkers of his day, Fourier fixes his sights on the world at large, on fundamental and general principles governing Nature and Man. His speculations cover the past and the present, and look to the future. He has the nineteenth-century passion for "synthesis," a predilection for systematization. He marks out the stages of historic change through five periods, culminating in our present "civilization." Such a civilization reveals monopolistic, imperialist aspects — concentration on the one hand, and fragmentation on the other — one that "raises every vice practised by barbarism in a simple way, into a complex, ambiguous, hypocritical mode of existence."[39]

Yet, there is another stage ahead of us — the highest — that which Fourier calls "garantisé," — the passage from "neo-feudalism" of the industrial and commercial present, to the achievement and organization of the "régime sociétaire."

Now, to transform society into a "social régime," we must begin with the individual. To understand the individual we must look to his psychology. From an analysis of the mind of man will flow the economic consequences. Modern psychology will invest Fourier's system with a new terminology, but a great deal of the essence will remain. Fourier centers upon what he calls the "passions" — the feelings, affects, desires, instincts of human beings, all of which he regards as "good." What is the relation of these "passions" to society? Why are they, or seem to be, at war with it? Describing himself with a modicum of humility as another Newton, Fourier poses the theory of "attraction" as applied to modern man and his social system. He draws a contrast between "duties" and "passions."

All these philosophical whims called duties have no relation whatever to Nature; they proceed from men, Attraction proceeds from God: now, if we desire to know the designs of God, we must study Attraction. Nature only, without any regard to duty, which varies with every age, while the nature of the passions has been and will remain invariable among all nations.

Morality, as understood today is the

mortal enemy of passional attraction. Morality teaches man to be at war with himself, to resist the passions, to repress them to believe that God was incapable of organizing our souls, our passions wisely.[40]

Hence the common notion that passional attractions constitute "vices" and must be resisted. That is because today society views the passions from an egotistical point of view, from the standpoint of the individual, as being ego-centered. Under such circumstances it stands to reason that they can entice us to evil.

But the passions, harmonized through the law of attraction, can be made the instruments of the greatest good. This can be achieved only within a new social order. The passions, when socially directed, are the very strongest guarantees of internal individual harmony, of the free development of individuality, as well as of social harmony.

It would serve little purpose to detail here Fourier's elaborate system of the passions, except momentarily to stop on those society has labeled as "vice" — in Fourier's system, the so-called "distributive" passions. For Fourier these possess the "property of forming ... the mainspring of social harmony." Among these is one he fancifully names the "cabalist," that of intrigue, rivalry, or competition; another, the "composite," harmonizes the allurements of the senses and the soul; a third one, called the "butterfly" passion, is the need for change and variety. These can be made productive only when solidarity of humanity is achieved, in an association of men and women that combines capital, labor, and talent. Such a community is the "Phalanstery," consisting of some 1,500 persons, of whom seven-eighths should be cultivators and manufacturers, i.e., workmen; the remainder "capitalists, scholars, and artists."[41]

Work will no longer be a curse, for it will be made attractive, and fitted to the abilities and capacities of the worker. Above all, it will be varied, The distribution of the total product of such an enterprise will allot 5/12ths to labor, 4/12ths to capital, and 3/12ths to talent. A minimum of the necessary subsistence would be allotted and guaranteed to all members, irrespective of their labor.

Eventually there will be — as Fourier envisions — six million of
these phalanges or communes on the face of the earth, having a
center in an earth congress. This would not be an egalitarian society,
but ruled and directed (without force, of cource) by a series of
authorities, reaching all the way to the supreme "Omniarch."

In the face of such prospective felicity and harmony, Fourier
himself is carried away. The inhabitants of such communes "would
grow angry at the word 'impossible'." Labor would become a sport
(today we would say a "game").

Such will be the athletes who will take the place of our mercenary and
languid workmen and who will succeed in making ambrosia and nectar
grow upon a soil which yields only briars and tares to the feeble hand of the
civilized.[42]

Fourier is not for revolution; nor does he preach a class-
struggle. What need of these? There would be a "unity of interest"
in such Association, and all antagonisms would disappear along
with the drudgery of labor, for even the rich would now want to
share in such work. Envy would disappear, as would all idlers or
poor. "The enjoyment of graduated ease" of the poor will make the
rich happy too.[43]

Fourier is especially emphatic on the emancipation of woman.

Social advances, and change of periods are brought about by virtue of the
progress of women towards liberty, and the decadences of the social order are
brought about by virtue of the decrease of liberty of women...The
extension of privileges to women is the general principle of all social progress.[44]

In a barbarous age men found it necessary to "brutalize"
women so that they could be sold or shut up in harems; in "civilized"
periods it is necessary to "stupefy" them so as to make them fit for
philosophical dogmas, the servitude of marriage, and the debasement
of falling into the power of a husband whose character "will perhaps
be the opposite of theirs."

What is their existence today? They live by privation, even in industry, where man has invaded everything down to the petty occupation of sewing and the pen, while women are being seen drudging at the painful labor of the field . . . What, then, are the means of subsistence of women without a fortune: The distaff or it may be their charms, if they possess any. Yes, prostitution, more or less veiled, is their sole resource.

Yet, "woman, in a state of liberty will excel man in all functions of the mind and body, which are not attributed to physical force."[45]

Civilized marriage is no less a perpetration of brutality upon the best instincts of woman, when it relies on the chance coupling of husband and wife "devoid of any illusion of the mind and the heart." It is a bitter paradox that modern society, which extends freedom to cheat and manipulate, denies the freedom to love.

Such is Fourier's dream. Such the Phalanstery, in which each member would purchase shares, but those with the smallest number of shares would be allotted the highest interest. Capitalist, worker, intellectual would all work together and live in harmony.

Fourier saw himself as the prophet of this new world to come — and, in his own words, lifting "the veil of thought previously impenetrable." He saw himself as the discoverer of "the calculus of universal destinies . . ," of the "fundamental system which regulates the laws of all the past, the present and future movement."[46]

We today are so thoroughly penetrated by the notion of an intrinsic "aggressive" or war-like constitution of the human being, that the vision of a possible "harmony" strikes us as naive, and innumerable ideological handbooks are available to make us accept the doctrine of a laicized "original sin," — i.e., Man is evil, and a wolf! Life in contemporary society certainly lends credence and support to such thinking. But why should the concept of "harmony" be any more or any less "naive" than the concept of eternal warfare? And whom does such a "war" concept profit most?

It is against this "original sin" that the Utopians — and Fourier — are at war. True, among the many seminal ideas that he propounded, there are others that must strike us as ludicrous. Let us, if we so wish, laugh heartily at his fantasies — such as that of the aurora borealis, covering the earth, spreading heat and light, and melting ice-caps! Let us laugh at the vision of a citric boreal acid emanating from the sea that would gradually turn the ocean into a lemonade! Shall we laugh at his dream of a world with thirty-seven million poets, and an equal number of geometricans and dramatists, and six hundred thousand palaces in place of disgusting hovels?

But also, let us remember him for his common sense, his brilliant dissection of the social system, of business cycles, his penetrating analysis of the anarchy of so-called "overproduction" — his treatment of the "passions"; and the tragedy resulting from frustration and repression under the modern industrial system; his respect for the dignity and intellect of woman, and, not least for his immitigable faith that mankind was capable of rebuilding the world.

Once more let us turn to the poet Béranger:

> Fourier nous dit: sors de la fange,
> Peuple en proie aux deceptions!

> Fourier said to us: Rise from the slime,
> You who have been the slaves of lies!

IV.

VICTOR HUGO AND THE TRIUMPH
OF ROMANTICISM

IV.

VICTOR HUGO AND THE TRIUMPH
OF ROMANTICISM

> The Spirit of the Time growing slowly and quietly
> ripe for the new form it is to assume looses one
> fragment after another of the structure of the
> previous world. That it is tottering to a fall is
> indicated only by symptoms here and there. Frivolity
> and again ennui, which are spreading in the
> established order of things, the undefined foreboding
> of something unknown — all these are hints
> foretelling that there is something approaching.
> This gradual crumbling to pieces, which did not
> alter the general look and aspect of the whole, is
> interrupted by the sunrise which, in a flash and at a
> single stroke, brings to view the form and structure
> of a new world.
> — Hegel, *The Phenomenology of Mind* —

> The public waits, and minds are in motion. Literature
> is on the eve of an Eighteenth Brumaire. But
> Heaven only knows where the Bonaparte is!
> — *Le Globe* —

On the evening of February 25, 1830, at seven, the curtain rose at
the Comédie Française on *Hernani,* a play by Victor Hugo. In
the historic tumult which then took place, and in the vividness of
the subsequent descriptions given by contemporaries, the true
meaning of the event has been frequently lost. The evening, it is
true, mingled cheers and boos, whistles and hurrahs, approbation
and disapprobation. Insults countered insults — and in the turmoil,
we may be sure, a number of spoken lines went unheard.

171

It was not that here Romanticism was celebrating its triumph in France. That was, in a certain sense, true. But Romanticism had already triumphed. The overwhelming significance of the occasion lay in the fact that the stronghold of literary conservatism — the great Théatre Français — had finally been breached with tremendous éclat. The way to this victory had been prepared by Alexandre Dumas's *Henri III et son cour* and Alfred de Vigny's new version of Shakespeare's *Othello*. But Hugo's victory represented a kind of final confirmation. It was the consummation of a movement that had been in the making for some years, whose programs and manifestoes were now regarded as finally vindicated. The true significance of *Hernani* lay in the fact that it was the overt presentation and acknowledgment of the politicalization of literature and of a new aesthetic.

The audiences that attended the theatre that evening came not so much to see and hear a play, as to participate in a political event. The theatre was the political arena. While on the surface the struggle over *Hernani* appeared as one concerned over literary forms, underneath it was actually a vivid representation of the seething spirit of Paris and France in the last years of the Bourbon Restoration. Only a few months separated February 1830 from the "three glorious days" of July — the July Revolution of 1830.

And now, that which the Saint-Simonian journal *Le Globe* had asked was answered. There was a Bonaparte at hand to lead another coup-d'état — this time in the realm of letters. He had powerful forces in opposition; but also a sturdy band of recruits in his own right. At the moment of *Hernani,* he was twenty-eight years old. In appearance he was acclaimed as handsome as a god. Like France herself, he stood at serious cross-roads. Like his hero Hernani, he too could have exclaimed, "Je suis une force qui va!" "C'est un demon redoutable, te dis-je que le mien!" He felt that he was an irresistible force — inhabited by a formidable demon...

Who but the possessor of an irresistible force and a demonic drive would have attracted to himself an aggregation of such prestige, including such older poets as Alfred de Vigny and Alphonse de Lamartine? As well as the noted writer, librarian of the Arsenal, Charles Nodier? And that unmentionable coterie of younger men and women, some of them mere youths, but already bearing the anticipatory blazon of fame: Gérard de Nerval, Petrus Borel, Honoré Balzac, and Hector Berlioz the composer? And the promising critic and poet, Sainte-Beuve; and youngest of all of them, Alfred de Musset and Théophile Gautier?

What was there about this young poet, Victor Hugo, that imposed itself upon those who came in contact with him? Théophile Gautier describes him as he was then, with his monumental brow, and his "superhuman beauty." His chestnut hair was long, and his eyes, piercing like an eagle's (the epithet will attach itself to him for a long time to come); his face was pale, and fastidiously shaved. "One would scarcely believe that this perfect gentleman was the chief of a band of long-haired and bearded terrors of the smooth-shaved bourgeois."[47]

He was a child of his age — and within him were the divisions of his time: divisions that ran through the family, the country, and — one might add — the world: political, psychological, social, personal. He was the child born in an armed camp. His father was a soldier, a soldier of the Revolution; later a fervent Bonapartist, eventually becoming a general. His mother, a simple woman, remained a royalist and a legitimist. Victor Hugo was born at Besançon, and his father took care to remind him that he was conceived in the mountains,

...not on the Pindus, but on one of the highest peaks of the Vosges, in the course of a journey from Lunéville to Besançon. You seem to be conscious of that almost aërial origin. Your Muse, so far as I can see, shows herself to be consistently sublime.[48]

But it was not of the glories of the poet that the father dreamed for his son. A practical soldier and administrator he was somewhat suspicious of aërial flights...

Personal and family cleavages ran deep in the Hugo family: the marital unhappiness of Victor's parents, their frequent separations forced the children to reside now with the father, now with the mother — now in Naples or Madrid, now in Paris; and finally with the mother alone. Under his mother's and her lover's influence, the boy, already precocious and a near-genius, became royalist, legitimist, and devout. Engraved on his memory were the impressions derived from the many journeys, the most forceful of them being those in Spain, whence his father was forcefully expelled with the fall of the Napoleonic régime in 1813.

It was a miracle that the acclaim the youthful poet received — including the approval of the royal house — did not undo him as a creator. "Chateaubriand, or nothing," was his battle-cry. The age yearned for heroes to emulate, and in letters there was none to equal myriad-minded Chateaubriand and his aureate prose-poetry. There is a story that the older writer had proclaimed the youth an "enfant sublime."[49] A few years later, the battle-cry of the young poet will be "Napoleon or nothing!"

The currents of ideas that played upon him in his early years were those that played such a profound role in determining the character of European literature — those emanating from Germany: sentimentalism touched by medievalism, and those elements which Madame de Staël's *De l'Allemagne,* written under the influence of Weimar and the critical school of Friedrich and August Wilhelm von Schlegel, had named characteristically Nordic or Germanic: the sad, brooding, philosophical spirit — the German "soul"; the longing for the "infinite" — the "beyond" — and the Wertherian *Weltschmerz.* Of the English influences the most prominent were those of Shakespeare, Byron, and Sir Walter Scott.

In France, as we have seen, the poetic spirit had run dry, except for André Chénier. But there were new poetic stirrings, and among Hugo's elders none was more influential than Alphonse de Lamartine, whose notable volume of verse, *Méditations poétiques et réligieuses,* brought out in 1820, may be said to mark one of the turning points in the history of French Romanticism. It was a kind of poetry tending to soothe the mind and the soul — at once gentle and rebellious, devout and almost blasphemous, always personal. Its love poetry was a mingling of the sacred and profane, a poetry of despair (Lamartine had lost his mistress Mme. Charles through death). His nature poetry celebrated the southern lakes. The spirit of Byron hovered over all of it, and Lamartine remained hopeful of some kind of religious conversion on the part of the English poet. At this time Lamartine was strong for royalism, and he was severe on the French Revolution and the unbelief of his times. He, too, was to change radically in politics as well as in his poetry, and he was to become a force in France's history.

But at the moment the tide was with the young — the brash, eager band of poets, painters and musicians, who regarded their elders as "ancients," and who talked incessantly, danced and drank, and at times wrote poems, painted, and composed.

With Wordsworth they might have chanted, "Bliss was it in that dawn to be alive." And to be young and have talent (perhaps even genius!) must have been heaven. It seemed to them they were bearing the future of Art in their hands — and perhaps in the Arts lay also the secret of the future of France?

Those were days of happiness for the young artists. The coterie, calling itself the "cénacle de la Muse française," would meet at the home of Charles Nodier, and then, when the latter was appointed librarian at the Arsenal, they would gather in those spacious quarters — a stately place — which the traditional reverence of the French for culture has preserved to this very day. Nodier, forty-four years old, a talented writer, an accomplished linguist, a lover of the fanciful and the fantastic, especially fond of German literature, and a gifted poet and story-teller in his own right, presided. There were beautiful and gifted women there too, like Sophie Gay, and her daughter Delphine (in love with and loved by Alfred de Vigny), and Madame Victor Hugo, and lovely Marie Nodier. Such days, especially the Sundays, Alfred de Musset recalled with warmth, and addresing Nodier,

> Lorsque, rassemblés sous ton aile
> Paternelle
> Échappés des nos pensions
> Nous dansions
> Gai comme l'oiseau sur le branche...
> Quelqu'un récitait quelque chose
> Vers ou prose....

Yes, assembled under your paternal wing, Charles Nodier, we danced and listened to a reading of some poem or piece of prose (perhaps my own too?). It was exhilarating.

Newly discovered lands of many riches lay before them — treasures of the past rediscovered; treasures of the present brought from so many parts of the world. Théophile Gautier exulted:

What a wonderful time! Walter Scott was in the very flower of his success; we were initiated into the mysteries of Goethe's *Faust*..., we discovered Shakespeare... and the poems of Lord Byron. ... We discovered the East, which had not yet become banal. How young, new, vari-colored, intoxicating, how full of zest it all was! ... In the armies of Romanticism as in the army of Italy everything was young![50]

And at the center stood Hugo. The Hugo household in the rue Vaugirard had become a sort of shrine, sanctified by the romantic imagination of its votaries. There was the Madonna-like vision, Adèle, whom Hugo had married in 1823, with her little daughter at her breast. There was the ravishing figure of the poet. Father, husband, and poet — all seemed in their eyes the realization of romantic perfection...

Young Hugo had matured rapidly as a poet with his *Odes* of 1822, his *Nouvelles Odes* of 1824. The 1826 collection of *Odes et Ballades* was hailed in *Le Globe* by a young medical student turned critic — Sainte-Beuve — with raptures that extolled the purity, chastity and sanctity of the love the poet was describing. A subsequent meeting of the poet and this critic was to have unpredictable complications for the whole Hugo family — for Sainte-Beuve fell in love with Madame Hugo...

Victor Hugo was changing rapidly. He had drawn closer to his Bonapartist father, and become a strong Bonapartist himself, so that when he felt that a number of Napoleon's marshals had been insulted at a reception of the Austrian embassy, he wrote a fervent glorification of the Emperor, "Ode à la Colonne de Place Vendôme." At the same time he was completing a formidable drama around Cromwell, and writing a preface for it destined to become a notable manifesto of the French Romantic movement.

The figure of Cromwell loomed large in the minds of French historians of this time. For those of conservative persuasion Cromwell stood forth as a warning of what a civil war, like that of England, could effect, and what dire results flowed from a violation of the divine right of kings. For moderate liberals the history of the English Civil War and the Compromise of 1688, that established a limited monarchy, represented an ideal toward which France should strive. There were numerous works on the subject of the Protector, historical as well as dramatic. Young Balzac himself essayed a drama on this theme.

Politically, Hugo, though still wavering, was inclined to favor a reformed monarchy. In 1827 it was evident that the French régime was in trouble, so that the figure of Cromwell offered a ready analogy. He could be seen as another Louis XVI, or as a Robespierre. Or even as a Napoleon! About this time Hugo had written a poem about Napoleon entitled "Lui." Here he had asked, "Tu domine notre âge; ange ou démon, qu'importe?" "You dominate our age.

Angel or devil — what matter?" And here was Cromwell, a leader, a magnetic personality, hitherto dedicated to the cause of people's liberties. Now he was aspiring to a monarch's crown! Hugo introduced the person of John Milton as a spokesman for democracy, and through him Hugo utters his own warning challenge to an irresponsible autocracy. Milton reminds Cromwell of the latter's glorious past, and warns him of the pitfalls of kingship and recalls to him the fate of King Charles I:

> You wish to be king, Cromwell, and in your heart of hearts
> You've said: It is for my sake my people have conquered . . .
> Ah, cast off
> This mummer's sceptre, this mask of kingship!
> Be the Cromwell you were! Hold the world in balance.
> Let a free people hold sway over nation —
> But you — be not monarch over them! Save our liberties . . .
> Be more than king. Return to your ancient heights.
> One word sufficed to bring light to the world —
> Be Cromwell again — when Milton speaks the word . . .[51]

> Sois plus que roi. Remonte a ta hauteur première,
> Il n'a fallu qu'un mot pour créer la lumière . . .
> Toi, rediviens Cromwell á la voix de Milton!

Cromwell came to birth: a long, cumbrous and diffuse creation, too large to be staged, marked by frequently moving eloquence, even greatness. It conveyed its powerful impression: absolute power was no longer sacred; and through its excesses it is condemned to destruction.

The Preface to *Cromwell* supplied its aesthetic counterpart: a manifesto of literary Romanticism.

Let us speak boldly. The time for it has come, and it would be strange, if, in this age, liberty, like light, should penetrate everywhere, except to the one place where freedom is most natural, the domain of the mind. Let us take the hammer to theories, poetics, and their systems. Let us throw down that old plasterwork that conceals the façade of art! There are neither rules nor models other than the general laws of nature, which soar above the whole field of art, and the special laws which result from the conditions of existence appropriate to each subject...

Thus Hugo set out to slay the "classical Goliaths." It will be remarked that in this program, France comes as a belated proponent of a libertarian Romanticism. England and Germany had already defined in their own ways the nature of such freedoms, and the character of the art that was or would soon emerge as Romantic.

But in France, still deeply entrenched in "classicism" — such a pronouncement marked a formal declaration of war on the part of its most militant poet and dramatist. It also clarified the division between the prior "romanticism" of nostalgia, vagary of feeling, that nestled in absolutism and medievalism, and that newer "romanticism" which, coming at this particular time, was assuming profoundly political tones. To demolish — or try to demolish — the traditional theatre in France, was, in effect, to try to level the stronghold of autocracy. To deny the validity of "classical" rules and laws was tantamount to a revolution... The *Preface* is a declaration of independence in favor of modern poetry and art.

We would declare for a free, outspoken, sincere verse which dares say everything without prudery, expresses its meaning without seeking for words; which passes naturally from comedy to tragedy, from the sublime to the grotesque..., lyric, epic, dramatic, at need; capable of running through the whole gamut of poetry, of skipping from high notes to low, from the most exalted to the most trivial ideas, from the most extravagant to the most solemn...

With a boldness which dares play havoc with historical accuracy — with an eagle's flight and eyes — Hugo surveys the whole history of poetic art, which in his view, exhibits a "triadic" pattern (the triad will dominate Europe's thinking for many years to come) from the primitive "Ode" to the Greek epic, and finally, in our modern times, coming to full fruition in the drama. The drama is the distinguishing contribution of this third epoch of poetry, "the literature of the present day." "Civilization begins by singing its dreams, then narrates its doings, and lastly, sets about describing what it thinks." The Germans would have described this last stage as the "self-awareness of the ego." Modern poetry is the mingling of the Sublime and the Grotesque. "Darkness and light, the grotesque and the sublime, the body and the soul, the beast and the intellect" — all these are to be the essence of modern art. This fusion of opposites finds its consummation in "the god of the stage" — Shakespeare.

Here, too, at this canonization of Shakespeare, France was a belated arrival. "Spät kommt ihr, doch ihr kommt," as the German poet once said. "You come late, but you have come." The struggle to domesticate Shakespeare in France had, in truth, been a hard one, though he had had stalwart apologists, such as Charles Nodier as early as 1801. In 1821 the historian Guizot reinterpreted Shakespeare for the French, contrasting his work with the traditional classical theatre. In Shakespeare he saw a reflection of English history — and in his age a naive liberty and absence of a "despotisme savant" — the despotism of a cultured élite. Shakespeare's comic characters were influenced by the presence of the lower classes, and exhibited the latter's strength at that time. By contrast, the French classical theatre mirrored a hierarchical society, an organized absolute power, an upper class that made of the theatre a playground. Hence came its loss of popular appeal. Thus the drama reflected the separation of the people from poetry, and the separation of poetry from the government. "Government and poetry must exist for all." Shakespeare must be taken as an exemplar because in him we recognize "the generality of interests, sentiments, conditions, which for us today constitute our human scene."[52]

In a similar vein, but more trenchantly, the writer who called himself Stendhal published, in 1823, *Racine et Shakespeare.* He attacked Racine as a "craven courtier"; accused him of a pompousness fitted for the enjoyment of the "snobbish court of Louis XIV." An age as stirring as that which had witnessed the French Revolution, the Republic, and the Empire demanded a fresh kind of drama. Shakespeare was more akin to such an age. His drama was filled with action, and his characters were true human beings. Unjust as Stendhal was to Racine and his great art, he was calling for a devotion to Nature rather than to starched classical rules. His epigrammatic distinction between Romanticism and Classicism is fresh even today.

Romanticism is the art of presenting to the people literary works which, in view of the existing state of customs and beliefs, afford them the utmost pleasure. Classicism, on the contrary, presents the literature that used to give the utmost pleasure to our great-grandfathers.

The change in the literary climate may be gauged by the difference in the reception given English acting companies in the early 1820's and toward the end of that decade. In the first instance the English actors were whistled off the boards. In 1827 the Abbot-Kemble troupe performed at the Odéon and at the Théatre Italien; and their tour was so successful that they remained in France until July 1828. Alexandre Dumas attended a performance of *Hamlet,* with Charles Kemble and Harriet Smithson in the principal roles.

The impression it made on me far exceeded my expectations. Kemble was wonderful, and Miss Smithson divine as Ophelia. Only then did I realize what drama could do, and from the ruins of my past efforts, which this revelation brought about, I realized what we needed to create a new world. For the first time I had seen real passion on the stage, inspiring men and women of real flesh and blood.[53]

There was another young genius in these audiences, and for him the experience was even more fateful. Hector Berlioz, aged 25, saw Harriet Smithson act, and fell in love with her. This drama will be described later. As for Shakespeare, Berlioz wrote,

I could... gauge the great absurdity of the ideas Voltaire had spread in France about Shakespeare.., and the pitiable narrowness of our old poetics, decreed by pedagogues and obscurantist monks. I saw, I understood, and felt that I was alive, and that I must 'arise and walk'.[54]

Molière and La Fontaine, Berlioz was to remark later, are "rich continents, but Shakespeare is an entire world." Humanity has much to be grateful for in that encounter of Shakespeare and Berlioz, for Shakespeare did indeed become a "world" for the composer that he was to explore far and wide, and whose riches he would mine, and in turn transmute.

Victor Hugo, too, was to be preoccupied with Shakespeare for a long time to come...

Let us return to February 1830 and *Hernani*. Preliminary skirmishes had already taken place in the reviews, and there were expected troubles from the censors. Hadn't they some time before barred a production of Victor Hugo's *Marion Delorme?* And wasn't there some to-do by the actors during rehearsals? What, one asks, were all the fuss and preparations — as if two armies were to be engaged in a vital battle? Was it the rumors afloat that in *Hernani* classical French prosody, the stately rhymed hexameter, was to be ravished publicly? That the pure vocabulary of classical tragedy was to be debased to the language of the streets? That the sacred three unities were to be disemboweled?

Actually *Hernani,* as a play, bridged two eras. Thematically, it harked back to the classical drama of Corneille. Here was a cloak and dagger plot, replete with the aura of Spanish "honor" — reminding one of Corneille's *Le Cid*; with nobleman and king battling for the love of a noblewoman. But to complete the melodrama, it also introduces the suicide of three of its principal characters...

The curtain is about to be rung up. There are the three knocks. We are in Saragossa, Spain, around the year 1519; and here is the bedchamber of Lady Doña Sol. Doña Sol's maid, alone, hears a knocking at a secret door of the chamber.

> Serait-ce déjà lui? C'es bien à l'escalier
> Dérobé. Vite, ouvrons.

Already the audience is aware of some strangeness in these lines. These are not the classical lines of Corneille or Racine, the rhymed alexandrines as they were called, each brought to a stop at the end of a line. No, these are not the lines of *Le Cid:*

> O rage! ô désespoir! ô vieillesse ennemie!
> N'ai-je donc tant vécu que pour cette infamie?

Or of *Phèdre:*

> Le dessein en est pris; je pars, cher Théramène,
> Et quitte le séjour de l'aimable Trézène.

No, in *Hernani* the "escalier" is split off from "dérobé." And the middle pause, the caesura, is sure to disappear.

But it is not the lover Doña Sol is expecting who appears. It is not Hernani, but Don Carlos — Charles, King of Spain, who is in love with Doña Sol. A bribe persuades the maid to hide him in a closet.

What opening of a drama could be more tempting to an excited audience? A castle (that of Ruy Gomez, uncle to Doña Sol), night, an awaited lover, a dangerous and powerful rival — all together in one place! And not least, the fact that Doña Sol is the betrothed of Ruy Gomez, at the command of the King!

Hernani arrives. He is an outlaw, whose father had been sent to the scaffold by the present King's father. He is proscribed, and waiting to avenge himself on the son of his oppressor. The lovers plan to escape the next day, but alas! from his hiding place Don Carlos overhears all. He has his own plans.

The play is full of "honor." Honor outraged: that of Ruy Gomez — outraged by the King and by Hernani. Honor pledged: Hernani's word given to Ruy Gomez for saving his life from the King — a pledge of his life to be redeemed at the moment Ruy Gomez calls for its redemption. At the center, a King, lecherous, absolute, treacherous, ambitious of being crowned Holy Roman Emperor. And add a conspiracy to assassinate him!

That a play, encumbered with so much of the faded panoply of improbable fantasy and melodrama, a play that shifted between uneasy bombast and truly eloquent lyricism and grandeur, should have made history, speaks volumes for the sad state of the theatre in France at the time. But the grandeur remains, and the tinsel may well be forgotten, or reserved, as it was to be, for the operatic stage.

It is hard for one generation to relive the aesthetic experiences of another, and often there is cause for wonder at the excitement generated at another time. But we have the testimony of a young contemporary, set down immediately after the first performance. He is speaking of the fourth act, in which Don Carlos appears at the tomb of Charlemagne.

This fourth act is the most powerful reverberation of Hugo's genius. A thunderous applause broke out at that overflow of feeling .... One single cry of frenzied enthusiasm broke from all the throats ... All rose up as one, and not a single person left ...[55]

The audience of that time heard things we no longer hear, caught overtones and allusions, hints; was swayed by the entire atmosphere of the evening, the excitement, the anticipation of bravos and boos; and the sense of participating in an epochal event. The play spoke to the times, to the moment; of that, there could be no doubt. Take, for example, the scene just referred to, that in the tomb of Charlemagne — where the conspirators are assembled to assassinate the King, who expects soon to be elected head of the Holy Roman Empire. The celebrated soliloquy of Charles needs no apologists even today. It represents a turning point in the drama, for here the monarch speaks of the nature of kingship, its responsibilities and trials. We may be sure that the audience caught many an oblique allusion, and applied it to the ruler of France in 1830, whose throne was being shaken.

The King of Spain is awaiting the three cannon volleys that will announce that he has been elected. He addresses Charlemagne, and reflects on the nature of power bequeathed by that Emperor, the

Europe that he left, a building having two men at its summit, Emperor and Pope. What a grand "Idea" come to a flowering! In almost Hegelian terms he sees that "Idea" emanating from God, taking hold of mankind, "realizing" — so to speak — itself in response to the needs of the time, and embodying itself in Man, in society and its organs, in Emperor and Pope. How to seize and understand that "Idea"!

This is not Charles speaking. This is Napoleon!

And what of the people that is to be governed?

> Rois! regardez en bas!
> — Ah! le people! — ocean! — onde sans cesse émue!....

> Kings! look down below!
> — Ah! the people! — an ocean! — wave upon wave!
> Wherein nothing is cast but it perturbs the whole!
> The surge that breaks the throne, and rocks the tomb!
> A glass in which kings rarely look but ill,
> Alas! gazing at times into these gloomy waters,
> What numberless empires lie in their depths,
> Great wreckage of vessels, stirred by ebb and flow....[56]

Elected head of the Holy Roman Empire, Charles V forgives the conspirators, and bestows Doña Sol upon Hernani. The nuptials are celebrated at Saragossa, and Doña Sol and Hernani are about to retire. There is a beautiful lyric interchange between them reminiscent of Shakespeare;

> Doña Sol:
> Regarde. Plus de feux, plus de bruit. Tout se tait.
> La lune tout à l'heure a l'horizon montait;
> Tandis que tu parlais, sa lumière qui tremble
> Et ta voix, toutes deux m'allaient au coeur ensemble,
> Je me sentais joyeuse et calme, ô mon amant,
> Et j'aurais bien voulu mourir en ce moment!

See, there's no light, nor noise, All is still.
Even as you spoke, the moon has risen,
Her trembling light and your dear voice together
Have reached my heart, and I so joyful, calm,
Beloved! At such a moment seemed it rich to die!

Hernani:
Ah! qui n'oublierait tout à cette voix celeste?
Ta parole est un chant ou rien d'humain ne reste.
Et, comme voyageur, sur un fleuve emporté,
Qui glisse sur les eaux par un beau soir d'été
Et voit fuir sous ses yeux mille plaines fleuries,
Ma pensée entraînée erre en tes rêveries!

And who would not forget all, hearing your celestial voice?
Your speech is like a song with nothing human mingled;
And like to one who travels down a stream,
Gliding on a summer's eve, sees pass before his eyes
A thousand flowered plains, so too my thoughts are drawn
Into your reveries![57]

Just when the lovers are at the height of their bliss, catastrophe overtakes them. The sound of a horn is heard: That is the agreed-on signal, portending that Ruy Gomez has come to demand a redemption of the pledge — Hernani's life. Hernani will, of course, respond; Doña Sol will, of course, refuse to survive him, and with Ruy Gomez's suicide, the stage is witness to a Shakespeare holocaust...

But Hugo was victorious. The play ran for forty-five nights, and the poet earned 27,000 francs.

It is not by his plays that Hugo's fame has been kept alive. They have survived mostly by virtue of Verdi's genius, as have so many other librettos.

Victor Hugo was primarily a poet. One might say *the* poet — though indefatigable as a writer in other media —like the novel, the drama, political essays, not to mention innumerable letters. Before long, he was also to take a personal part in political life. The vastness of his production is dumbfounding. He appeared endowed with inexhaustible energy. Only twenty-eight years old in 1830, he had already made his mark in poetry, prose narrative, and poetic drama. As we shall see, his energies and his productiveness expanded with the years. But one of the most striking characteristics of the young poet even now was his capacity to change, to respond to the changing times.

Like the others, he too was swept into the mainstream of the intellectual movements of the time, drawing his inspiration from innumerable sources. Of course, Byron and Napoleon stood at the central points of his creations. His emergent liberalization of political thought sharpened his awareness of the liberation movements in other countries — in Greece especially. The Orient was embodied for him in Greece and Spain. He had never been to the East (unlike Byron), but Spain became its surrogate.

Car l'Espagne, he stated in the Preface to his *Orientales*, c'est encore l'Orient; l'Espagne est à demie africaine, l'Afrique est à demi asiatique.

Of course, the more mundane purposes that involved the major powers in the struggles of the Near East — and Greece in particular — and joined them in their crusade to destroy the power of the Turks totally escaped the idealistic vision of the poets, with their eyes fixed on the achievement of Greece's liberation. Their feelings might well have been summarized by the German poet Wilhelm Müller when he said,

> Ohne die Freiheit, was wärest du Hellas,
> Ohne dich, Hellas, was wäre die Welt?

Without Freedom what would you be, Hellas? And without you, Hellas, what would the world be?

The great powers, Russia, England, and France, intervening in the Near East, succeeded in annihilating the Egyptian navy at the battle of Navarino, in 1827. In 1829 Greece was constituted as an "independent" monarchy. Russia gained significant new territory and influence in the Near East. "Independent" Greece was given a Bavarian prince for monarch.

But to the poetic imagination that struggle was another inspiring evidence of freedom's forward movement. The Near East came close to them. Napoleon's invasion of Egypt at the end of the preceding century, the discovery of the Rosetta stone, and the decipherment of its hieroglyphics by Champollion added incalculable dimensions to history and Orientology, no less important than the rediscovery of Hellenic Greece.

Hugo's poems, *Les Orientales*, published in 1829, fused all these elements — the Byronic, the wild and beautiful, violent and cruel Orient, and the Greek wars of liberation.

The fecundity of Hugo's imagination and his technical virtuosity had never before been better revealed. The critic Sainte-Beuve had opened his eyes to the radical metrical experiments of the French Renaissance poets Ronsard and Du Bellay; the brilliant philologist Claude Charles Fauriel had made him acquainted with Greek folk poetry. With a mastery that had already become legendary Hugo now played the full diapason of sound, the full spectrum of mystery and passion — sometimes with intoxicated abandon.

A number of the *Orientales* are specifically political in content. These celebrate the heroic exploits of Canaris, the naval hero; they mourn the Greek failure at Missolonghi, whose defense aroused the wonder of the world; they depict the horror of the bloody retribution meted out to captured Greek prisoners by the Turkish rulers (the severed heads which were exposed at the seraglio speak out in the voices of the heroes); they hail the part such Frenchmen as Colonel Fabvier and the French armies had played in the war,

En Grèce adieu, vous tous! il faut partir...;

and hail the victory at Navarino that turned the mourning songs into chants of triumph,

Qu'on change cette plainte en joyeuse fanfare!
Une rumeur surgit de l'Isthme jusqu'au Phare...

O change this song of woe to joy!
A rumor rises from the Isthmus to Pharos...
Greece is free, and in his grave
Byron hails Navarino![58]

The non-political poems epitomize Oriental Romanticism. There is a pirate song, there is the battle-cry of the Mufti, a captive's lament, a fetching "Sara bathing," there are evocations of Spain, and Granada in particular; a version of Mazeppa in the Byronic vein, and — perhaps most famous of all — "Les Djinns" — "the Jinnies," (Mohammedan haunting spirits) — a kind of symphonic poem describing the approach, the mounting terror, prayer to the prophet, and departure of the evil spirits — rendered almost musically from a piano, to a crescendo, a fortissimo and finally a decrescendo, — a piece of virtuoso execution.

The beginning:

Murs, ville
Et port,
Asile
De mort
Mer grise
Ou brise
La brise,
Tout dort

— later rising to a fortissimo climax:

Cris de l'enfer! voix qui hurle et qui pleure!
L'horrible essaim poussé par l'aquilon,
Sans doute, ô ciel! s'abat sur ma demeure...

Walls, city
Port
Asylum
of death

> Gray sea
> Where breeze
> Enfolds,
> All sleeps

and

> Cries of hell! voice that howls and weeps!
> Horrible swarm, driven by blasts,
> Surely oh heavens, they are pouncing on my home...

The book of poems is completed by "Lui" — dedicated to the glory of Napoleon, conqueror of the world, of the East, a Mohammed of the West. Hugo is obsessed by the man. Did he already see himself as the Bonaparte of literature?

IV.

GERMANY — THE DISSEVERED SELF

I.

"FREEDOM," "LIBERATION," AND DISENCHANTMENT

I.

"FREEDOM," "LIBERATION,"
AND DISENCHANTMENT

> In Germany, every time three persons express the
> same opinion, panic immediately seizes the thirty-
> four princes and the ninety ministers upon whom
> the Lord has bestowed the country. They dream of
> associations, conspiracies, revolutions, and subver-
> sions, and they arm themselves with all the powers
> at their command to dissolve this dangerous trinity.
> — Ludwig Börne —

When Napoleon's armies crossed the Rhine, in what then seemed
an irresistible sweep, they brought down not only the Holy Roman
Empire — which had been a fiction for centuries — but also the
walls and fortresses of German medievalism and feudalism. Thirty-
six petty states with their miniscule rulers — the so-called
"Duodezfürsttum" — steeped in outworn traditions and usages,
laboring under the medieval privileges of a landed aristocracy,
served by a torpid and complaisant clergy, were suddenly shaken
from their slumbers. Princelings found themselves dispossessed of
their realms. In 1809 even the two most powerful of these states
— Austria and Prussia — lay prostrate before the French victors,
Feudalism was abolished; the right of citizenship was extended to
all, even to Jews; ghettoes were brought down, land was redistributed
and legal and religious equality was established.

   To expel Napoleon and the French it was necessary to rally all
Germans, especially the citizens of Prussia, with national slogans
and battle-cries, as well as promises of reform. In the name of

195

Freedom, the war was christened "Freiheitskrieg" — "War for Freedom." King Frederick William III — generous of promises — offered the prospect of extensive reforms, and his more honest counsellors, liberals, proposed the abolition of feudal prerogatives, the drafting of a constitution, and the establishment of a parliament. But even while these hopes were being held out to those who were to bleed and die for "freedom," the die-hard possessors of property and power were already hatching plans for the annulment of the yet unattained changes. On five occasions the King promised a constitution; on five occasions he broke his promises...

Came 1815 and Waterloo. Legitimacy, once more in the saddle, began its work of undoing the Napoleonic transformations. Now that victory was in their hands, the King of Prussia, along with his brother-rulers, showed their true faces. Down with the old slogan of a "Freiheitskrieg"! No! This had been a "Befreiungskrieg" — a war to free the fatherland from a foreign oppressor! Once more the Jewish ghetto was established in many places, and the Jews relegated to their medieval status of pariahs. The feudal chains which had bound the peasantry before Napoleon were now reforged.

Prussia, fattened by the absorption of Saxony, Pomerania, and the Rhine Provinces, stood, alongside of Austria, at the head of the new German Confederation. Whatever diets were established — whether Federal or local — were so tramelled in their powers of action, that they became the instruments of the nobility and the agrarian landed interests.

Unfortunately for the rest of the population, there was no sizable middle class to claim its share of rights and recognition. Unlike England and France, Germany had had no bourgeois revolution. This was to form an important element in what was to constitute the tragedy of Germany. The other element was the substitution of "Einheit" — Unity — for "Freiheit" — democratic freedom. The German struggle for Unity was to supersede the struggle for Freedom.

Great was the disenchantment of the liberal German patriots — especially among the intellectuals, the writers, and the university circles. But protests proved ineffectual in the increasingly repressive atmosphere that followed 1815. Notable university professors were dismissed or suspended from their posts, especially after the passage of the stringent Carlsbad Decrees of 1819. Among the victims were such personalities as the patriotic poet and historian Arndt; the philosopher-theologian Schleiermacher; the distinguished biblical scholar de Wette; and even the great Alexander von Humboldt himself, one of the principal founders of the University of Berlin.

Among the conservative circles, and especially the student bodies, anti-French feeling compounded by a virulent anti-Semitism turned into a frenzied chauvinism. Political philosophers of the Romantic period had already prepared the ideology of Pan-Germanism; and the resurrection of the Holy Roman Empire — modeled on a fictive medieval ante-type — was to mark the new "Unity." Student and other intellectual aggregations took the lead in their various associations, the Burschenschaften, Turnvereins, and Tischgesellschaften to foster such sentiments. "Freedom" now came to mean the freedom to restore the old, old Germany, even down to its hierarchical various "orders" — the nobility, the clerisy, and the "people." At the head stood the Monarch ... At least such was the dream ...

But there were also more pragmatic engines with which to insure the stability of the restored order — the police, the military, and the censorship. Spies were sent out to audition university lectures, and it is a misfortune that we do not have records of what such auditors made of Hegel's phenomenological flights ... In addition, there were effective prisons to underscore positive warnings.

But what was true of Prussia and Austria, and many of the other German states, could not be said of the Rhenish provinces, which, more than any other sector of Germany, had been influenced by the French Revolution, the Napoleonic invasions and reforms, and French ideas. It is here that in times to come German liberalism and radicalism were to find their most fertile soil.

II.

ROMANTICISM:
THE FRAGMENTED SELF

II.

ROMANTICISM:
THE FRAGMENTED SELF

1.

Mensch werden ist eine Kunst.
Becoming human is an art.
— Novalis —

It is only in the context of the German fragmentation — political, social, and intellectual — the momentary cosmopolitanism of the Napoleonic era, and the subsequent relapse into the separate narrow provincialisms of the several states, that German Romanticism acquires meaning. The humiliations and abasement that the crushing defeats of 1806 and 1809 inflicted on the mind and body before both could be roused to the national fervor of opposition and final destruction of the French armies brought about a state of mind in the more articulate portion of the population that the Germans, so rich in terminological inventiveness, termed the "German Misère." "Zerrissenheit" — dismemberment of the Ego — became the mark of that and subsequent generations. And after Waterloo and the Restoration, when the so-called "Liberation" had been achieved, and the Old Order restored, and political activity became once more circumscribed and delimited and its expression legally constricted — the German mentality was forced into an inward direction, and the Ego into internalizing its activity.

The period of German Romanticism, which extends, roughly, from 1790 to 1830, is rich in genius, near-genius, and multiform talent. The mere volume of its productivity is amazing. In poetry, story, philosophy, scholarship, science, drama, and music prodigies are accomplished. In at least two fields — music and philosophy —

201

German preeminence is unquestioned. Börne could say bitterly, "Among all other nations, the Germans have done the most philosophizing. That is because they have lived least."[1] This is partly an unjust statement. Germans philosophized and "lived". But they lived as they philosophized; their bodies and minds bore the marks of the numerous prison houses — their German states — and where the body was chained, the mind soared. "Gedanken sind frei," thus goes an old German folk-poem, "Thoughts are free."

German Romanticism is, in a way, a continuation of that "Sturm und Drang" — Storm and Stress — which in the 1770's expressed the inner tensions of the time — a prerevolutionary insurrection in literature in such works as Goethe's *Werther* and *Götz von Berlichingen,* and Schiller's *Robbers.* But German Romanticism of our period — post-revolutionary and post-Napoleonic — more clearly manifests itself in a turbulence that finds no outlet in political activity of a radical kind — and with an unprecedented explosiveness expresses itself in flight, fantasy, dream, nightmare, death-longing — eruptions in personal life, disruptions within. It is no wonder then that in its manifestations it probes into the "unconscious" and the "subconscious" — and lays the foundations for such psychological revolutions as were to culminate in the work of Sigmund Freud.

It was the Germans who coined the term "Doppelgänger" — the "Double" — for the disjointed "other" self — projected outside, and living another's life. He is the "Other", the alter-ego, emerging out of the suppressed and repressed internal personality that supplements the unreality, the impoverished existence of its creator. He is our released "free" agent, often also the truthful mirror of our distorted self ...

If, as has been suggested before, one central aspect that united all Romanticisms is the concept of "Freedom," we are now in a position to observe how "Freedom" manifests itself under the special conditions of a specific historic reality. German Romanticism is Freedom internalized, translated into an absolutism and supreme authority of the "I" — the Ego. It differentiates itself from the Romanticism of other lands in its determined pattern of a belief in the all-sufficiency of that Ego to create its own world transcending the world of external realities, and in its proclamation of the right to its own freedom in all aspects of its life, feelings, passions, actions. The full freedom of the "I" replaces the full freedom of the "We". The outside world is our creation, which we can transform through the genius of our personal imagination. That is, we can create our own ideal world.

The call to a national unity to oppose and finally crush Napoleonic dominance, and the ensuing war of liberation, represented a short-lived suspension of the feelings of "Misère" and abjectness. Philosophers rallied to the cause, and like Fichte, helped animate the spirit of resistance and national dignity and pride; poets like Arndt turned out fiery patriotic exhortations; folk-poetry collections and history served to recall a more heroic past — and promises and programs of reform gave the spirit more practical incitements. Once the Old Order returned, post-Napoleonic Romanticism carried on the "program" of its predecessors, only with greater intensity and even more hectic waywardness. All in all, German Romanticism remained *one,* and from the first developed that paradoxical dualism that was to be of such moment for the future ideology of Germany. Side by side with its "anarchism" of the Ego, it also developed the philosophy of a "Machtstaat" — the political philosophy of the absolute state. One might epitomize the course of German Romanticism through two of its earliest figures: Friedrich von Hardenberg, who wrote under the name of Novalis. He died before he was thirty — one of the most gifted, though unfulfilled, of all Romantic poets, who alongside of his transcendental visions, his longings for the infinite, his "Blue Flower," that symbol of poetic consummation, also composed a highly idealistic politico-philosophic-theocratic program for the restoration of European unity in the image of a medieval Germanic body politic. His work is titled *Christenheit oder Europa — Christendom or Europe.* The other figure is that of Friedrich Schlegel — arch-priest of Romanticism, author of a nihilistic erotic novel, *Lucinde,* proclamation of freedom of the flesh and the soul, who almost at the same time was developing his political theory of the absolute state and absolute monarchy. He lived long enough to cap his career by turning Catholic (alongside of his wife, Dorothea), and ended as one of Metternich's most eloquent adjutants in Vienna. Thus the "Zerrissenheit" of the once nihilistic and turbulent and insurgent Ego found a haven of restoration in submission to absolute authority — both religious and secular.

There were, however, others for whom there was no such secure harbor. The extraordinary dramatic genius, Heinrich von Kleist, the disenchanted patriot, when scarcely past thirty, took his own life and that of his beloved in 1811.

Such paradoxes, contradictions, not to mention tragedies, mark the vortex that is Romanticism. Yet, they should not prevent us from recognizing the remarkable intellectual activity that characterized the various groups which foregathered in Berlin, Jena, or Heidelberg. These were hot-houses of debate — of high talk and low — where genius and talent discoursed, defying the happenings of the outside world, an élite association, enclaves of light in the midst of a surrounding desolation...

If, now we were more closely to define the various aspects of "Freedom" — as the Romantics expressed it — we might say its four-fold character consists in upholding the doctrine, originated by the philosopher Fichte, of the "world-positing, the world-creating Ego," in other words, what we might term "Flight from Necessity," independence of an external world of cause and effect, of the "non-Ego." Secondly, in a "Flight from Reality," — Germans call it "Weltflucht," moderns an "internal emigration." Thirdly, "Sehnung" — "Yearning" or "Longing" — a deliberate escape into Chaos, Sickness, and Death. And finally, "Flight into Submission."

We have said that the Romantics "lived" philosophy. No other nation, no other group of writers and artists, was so thoroughly affected and permeated — even if in a distorted form — by its philosophers, in this case by the transcendental idealists, particularly Fichte.

Observe yourself, Fichte preached. Turn your eyes away from all that surrounds you, and toward your inner self. That is the first command that philosophy directs towards it disciple ...

He who is conscious of his self-sufficiency and independence from all that is around him and outside of him — and one becomes that only if one makes oneself independent of that through oneself — needs no things in support of his own Self, and cannot use them, for they undo his own self-sufficiency and turn it into pure appearance. The "I" — the Ego — he possesses, and which interests him, disssolves his faith in things; he believes in his self-sufficiency out of inclination; he seizes it with emotion. His faith in himself is unmediated.[2]

It was upon such ideas as these that the Romantics seized with avidity. The unremitting upheavals from the time of the French Revolution to 1815, the carnage and the misery of those years and thereafter; the restrictive provincialism of the Restoration and the inhibition of political activity all made the exaltation of the autonomous Ego a welcome surrogate.

The Romantics, if they reacted with vehemence against the rationalist Enlightenment and the "Humanitäts-Ideal" of the eighteenth century, also found themselves challenged by the dominating figure of the indestructible Goethe. Here their ambiguous relationship becomes most evident: they could not deny his greatness, and his paramount preeminence in practically all spheres of creativeness. They owed an immeasurable debt to his earlier works, to the Sturm and Drang dramas, and to *Faust;* yet they stood in opposition to that overwhelming calm grandeur of the overshadowing Olympian, who seemed to soar above time and circumstance. And later, in the time of the national revival, no less than in the dark times of the Napoleonic triumphs, they resented that divine indifference to the historic events around him, that almost made

him companion to a Napoleon; they resented his immersion in his
scientific studies (and sometimes justly so) — for the bloody battle
of Jena interested him only in so far as it gave him and his disciples
favorable occasions for the study of bones and bone structures! Yet,
they were enslaved to him also. His dramatic works and his
Wilhelm Meister became the archetypal sources of their own
numerous and less notable imitations. Thus, Novalis hoped to outdo
Wilhelm Meister with his own fragmentary novel, *Heinrich von
Ofterdingen;* and Heinrich von Kleist to topple Goliath with his
own dramas. Goethe, though he did not altogether reject them,
regarded German Romanticism as "sick," contrasting it with a "healthy"
Greek "classicism." Actually no Romantic outdid the Romanticism
of Goethe, as he revealed it in the second part of *Faust,* which was
completed shortly before his death in 1832.

Yet, in another respect they were (like other Romantics
elsewhere, but not to the same degree) enslaved by Goethe. The
figure of *Faust* (as portrayed in the first part of that drama) invited
an imitation of that cosmic ambition at supreme self-cultivation and
self-development of one's personality — to make of one's life a work
of art — that worked so disastrously in the inflation of the Ego, not
only in the hey-day of Romanticism, but also thereafter. A Titanism
pervades the Romantics — both the greater and the lesser ones, as if
there were nothing they could not absorb or consummate. They
would all be Fausts in their comprehension of the inner and outer
workings of the world, but their Mephistopheles is internalized. He
is within them. He is the "Other."

2.

There is one Romantic who would have accepted the charge of "sickness" or "sickliness" as a mark of distinction. That is Novalis — Friedrich von Hardenberg — who, perhaps more than any other of the school, epitomizes what was best and what truly morbid and fragmented in the movement. For it was he who wrote:

Life is a disease of the Spirit...Could man but begin to love sickness and suffering, he would perhaps in their arms experience the most delicious rapture and feel the thrill of the highest positive pleasure...Does not all that is best begin in illness?...[3]

One of the pioneers of German Romanticism, he lived a brief life from 1772 to 1801, and died of tuberculosis. He was a scion of an aristocratic family, the Hardenbergs, and one of the very few Romantics who had practical experience in the work-a-day world. He was a student of science, particularly expert in geology, and was an auditor (Assessor) of government salt mines in Saxony. Inordinately avid of learning, his passions extended far and wide; and his numerous fragments dedicated to philosophy, poetry, and science give a partial indication of a genius that might have developed into an outstanding poet and thinker had he not been cut off so soon. All his work is tinged with a deeply religious sentiment, the fruit of his early training in the faith of the Moravian Brethren, the so-called Herrnhuter — a pietism that laid great stress on a simple and intense devotion to an inward spiritual life, based on good conduct rather than on theological doctrine. Into his metaphysical system he also absorbed Spinoza, Fichte, and the seventeenth century shoemaker-mystic Jakob Böhme.

But among the Romantics, Novalis stands out as one of the very few literary figures who did not disdain to be employed professionally. His knowledge of the mining industry — salt and ironworks — brought him close to physical nature in a very tangible form, and with the underground reality of the men who labored in the mines. The world of rocks, and ores, and salt, he fused with his observations of other natural phenomena and sought to integrate

them into a wider perception of and a search for an understanding of
the "ultimate" nature of the cosmos. As for Böhme, so for Novalis
too, Nature was a series of "signatures," a vast cosmic "metaphor," a
series of "hieroglyphics," he hoped throughout his brief life to
decipher, and merge with his own personal experiences as poet and
human being. In the same way he sought a key to the meaning of
Life and Death, and behind those, of a Beyond...

No one would have guessed from his punctilious attendance
upon his professional duties the inner feverish excitement —
almost ecstasy — with which he looked upon the world and
"through" it. Not least strange was his love-relation to Sophie von
Kühn...She was twelve years old when he came to know her, and
became engaged to her; she was fifteen when she died. Her life, and
her death in particular, were at first shattering, then a transmuting
experience. She became an apotheosis of erotic Love, no less than
of Religion. It seemed as if this profound experience proved
the precipitating agent which enabled him to blend Life, Death,
Immortality, Love and Christ, and the great vocation of Poetry
into one unit. Creatively what followed were the *Hymns to the
Night,* the *Spiritual Songs,* the unfinished novel, *Heinrich von
Ofterdingen,* and the politico-religious tract, *Christenheit
oder Europa.*

In the first three of these poetic works are to be found all the
elements of Romanticism that speak of a transcendence of the
physical world, and the quest of the "Infinite." Dreams, visions,
anticipations, foreshadowings, unending signatures and symbols
that express the unceasing quest to lift the veil of Isis — conquer the
obstructions and open the eyes to "the landscapes of invisible
worlds." "Nothing." Novalis wrote, "is more attainable by the Spirit
than the Infinite...The world is a universal trope of Spirit, its
symbolic image." "Man is a Metaphor."[4]

His is a world of Night, Dreams, Death, and Awakening. Even
our most confused dreams, he contended, are partial rents in the veil
of the Unknown. Night and Death are entrance gates to Infinity.

> Gelobt sei uns die ewge Nacht,
> Gelobt der ewige Schlummer...

> Praised be eternal Night,
> Praised eternal slumber...

We are wearied of our wandering, and long for our Father's home...

> Im Tode ward das ewge Leben kund,
> Du bist der Tod und machst uns erst gesund...

> In Death eternal life was manifest,
> Thou art Death, restoring us to health...[5]

Life is sickness, Death is health!... "Leben ist der Anfang des Todes. Das Leben ist um des Todes willen."

Life is the beginning of Death. Life exists for the sake of Death. Life is a disease of the Spirit...Does not that which is best begin in illness?[6]

Scientific concepts reenforce his images of Death.

We spring like an electric spark into the other world. There is an increase of capacity. Death is transformation, displacement of the principle of individuality, an entering into a new, more permanent, more potent combination.[7]

The dichotomies of the world — internal and external — could be resolved only in Death and in the realm of the Ideal. In *Heinrich von Ofterdingen* Novalis set himself the objective of outdoing and annulling Goethe's *Wilhelm Meister,* by transforming Goethe's more or less realistic novel of self-education and self-development by means of what he called "magical idealism." The protagonist of Novalis's novel is a medieval Minnesinger, and his quest is the "Blue Flower," symbol of ideal unity of inner and outer worlds, a quest that was to lead him to the attainment of full poetic insight and mastery that would finally lift the veil of Isis. For Novalis, the poet is seer, philosopher, magus, scientist — the prophet. Heinrich wanders through the world that is half-fantasy, dream, foreboding and anticipation, and half reality. Like Dante, Novalis has his own

Beatrice, the deceased Sophie von Kühn, whose presence pervades
the pilgrimage toward the realm of the ideal. In his wanderings,
Heinrich von Ofterdingen comes to know men and women of blood
and flesh, in varieties of professions such as commerce and mining,
as well as thinkers and men of action. He also encounters a living
love (as did Novalis), who in no way overshadows Sophie's image.
He enters a mine and sees miners at work. Though in his life
Novalis was well acquainted with and had made note of the pitiful
condition of those who worked underground, after descending into
the mines, he cannot refrain from chanting the happy life of the
miner, whom he glorifies as the utterly dedicated and selfless
"artist." For the miner is the "lord of the world." He understands
the structure of the rock-formations — their secrets — for he is in
touch with the ancient past that is revealed to him down below. For
him, all the "craggy palaces open their treasures" — whether these
be gold or diamonds:

> He guides the golden streams
> Into the King's own house,
> And decks his diadems,
> With precious jewels...

Unconcerned about his own needs, "he rejoices in his poverty". He
is king of the mountains, while down below,

> Let others strive and perish
> To get them goods and wealth,
> The miner in the mountains,
> Is the happy lord of the world...

> Sie mögen sich erwürgen
> Am Fuss um Gut und Geld,
> Er bleibt auf den Gebürgen
> Der frohe Herr der Welt.[8]

Novalis died before completing *Heinrich von Ofterdingen*. The
scanty notes that are left us give us too few clues as to what happened
when Heinrich attained the "Blue Flower," and touched Infinity...

Novalis brought the same kind of "romanticizing" to his political-theocratic thinking in *Christenheit oder Europa*. Though composed in 1799, it was not published until 1826; but the essay was well-known among his Romantic colleagues, and of considerable influence. Novalis — like many of the others — had travelled far from his early admiration of the French Revolution. In this essay, he envisions Europe united under a revivified Christendom and a renovated Catholicism, with a Church that would supersede dissident Protestantism, and ultimately embrace the entire world. In such a movement of rehabilitation, Germany would take a leading part. The secular powers of Europe, hitherto involved in bitter internecine struggles, would cement this new brotherhood of man; the supremacy of the State would harmonize with the mandates of the Ego — individual and community would be reconciled...

Only religion, he wrote, can once more awaken Europe, and offer people security, install Christendom with all her renewed splendor, visibly revealed in her ancient, peace-making office, here on earth.[9]

Shall not then, he asks, Protestantism finally cease, and make way for a new, enduring Church? The age of unbelief, of triumphant worldliness is nearing an end. Anarchy is the creative womb of religion. Once more we shall witness

those resplendent times when Europe was indeed a Christian land, when a single Christianity dwelt in the world, and united all within one communal interest — doing so without itself possessing worldly means.[10]

Such was Novalis's dream of a restored world-unity, which he saw had been embodied in the unity of a medieval Europe under one Church. It was a dream which like many such dreams would find practical exponents in this Romantic age, divest it of its romanticizing elements, and lay the foundations for an absolute Machtstaat — a "power-state" His own dear friend, Friedrich Schlegel, would play an important role in such a redefinition, but he would have strong collaborators, endowed with greater political realism...But alas! they would hardly realize or wish to realize Novalis's dream of bringing about "the holy times of eternal peace"!...

3.

In those early days of German Romanticism nothing seemed impossible. Had not Novalis written:

Is not the entire cosmos within us? We do not know the full depths of our Spirit. The secret path leads toward our inward. Within us, and nowhere else, lies Eternity with all its worlds, the Past and the Future. The outer world is a world of shadows, and casts her shadow into the realms of light . . .[11]

Such sentiments and their like were the heady potions the Romantics quaffed. They were powerful enough to inflate the Ego, and stimulate a sense of Titanism. It was such feelings that animated one of the most brilliant of those Romantics — Friedrich Schlegel, one of the most gifted and at the same time unfulfilled near-geniuses of the time. Along with his brother, August Wilhelm von Schlegel, he defined what may be called the aesthetic "Weltanschauung" — the "world-view" — of German Romanticism. Their lectures were widely attended, and enthusiastically received. It is hard for us to conceive how strongly and fervently Romanticism and its hierophants had penetrated into the lives of the universities and the university towns. Whether in Berlin, or Jena, or Heidelberg, the air was filled with talk of the lectures of Fichte, or Schelling, or the theologian Schleiermacher, of Friedrich and August Wilhelm Schlegel. No such Romantic fever took hold of Oxford or Cambridge, or the Sorbonne . . . What he lacked in consecutive literary and philosophical achievement, Friedrich Schlegel supplied in the dynamism of his magnetic personality, and his fragmentary utterances, which like his brother's, ranged far and wide over the field of world literature. In his own exaggerated way, Novalis paid tribute to Friedrich Schlegel:

. . . You have received a rare destiny from God. It is possible I never shall see your like again. In my eyes you are the High Priest of Eleusis. Through you I have learned to know Heaven and Hell — through you I have tasted the Tree of Knowledge . . .[12]

Friedrich Schlegel had, like many others, begun as a fervent admirer of the French Revolution. Though he soon turned away, he did not abandon a kind of emotional and intellectual anarchism which glorified absolute freedom of the personality. The first law of universal poetry, he asserted "is that the arbitrariness of the poet does not suffer any law above itself." Individualism and the cult of the personality were the centers of his existence, and he extolled "the free-ranging spirit," — "der freischwebende Geist," — "Willkür" — "arbitrariness," the law of lawlessness ... He was for a wilful and deliberate courting of "Chaos" as the creative womb of genius, and he asserted his "indubitable right of disorder." But, of course, such "disorder" was not to mean political or social agitation, which would also entail leaving the inner world, and going out to others, coming in contact with that which he abhorred, the common, the vulgar, the "rabble." The revolution which he advocated was altogether internal — a revolution of the "élite." But even such a revolution could horrify. For Friedrich Schlegel composed a novel, *Lucinde*.

Whoever has not experienced it, wrote Varnhagen von Ense some time after its publication, can scarcely conceive the ferment that took place in Berlin, how all conceptions, attitudes, views and judgments were shocked and enraged and shaken. *Lucinde* alone seemed to undermine all prevailing ideas. Celebrites ... were totally demolished by it, and its unflinching audacity penetrated more and more deeply ... [13]

A rescript of the Elector of Hanover in 1800 warned that Friedrich Schlegel's presence in Göttingen, should he propose to visit there, would not be tolerated.[14]

What was this very "dangerous" book that so aroused the public? It was a manual of "free" love — a declaration of independence of the emotional life, as embodied in the perfect physical and spiritual union of man and woman. After a stormy amatory and unsatisfactory apprenticeship, Julius, the hero, finds the consummate partner, and writes his prose "Song of Songs." In real life, Lucinde was none other than the celebrated Dorothea, daughter of the great Moses Mendelssohn, wife of a man by the name of Veit, whom she divorced in favor of Friedrich, and for whose sake she became a convert to Protestantism. Years later she was to follow her husband into Catholicism — a consummation of spiritual "freedom" ("Freigeisterei") and religious versatility her father, who was the eminent prophet of Jewish enlightenment, would scarcely have approved. In true romantic fashion, the sexual and the spiritual are given a fuliginous metaphysical turn, so that the realms of the immediate and the infinite are brought into close contact. In the consummation of the true love experience the present and the eternal embrace too. For,

Love is not merely the serene desire of the infinite; it is also the sacred enjoyment of a beautiful present... It is not only a commingling, a transition from the mortal to the immortal, but also the perfect unity of both...

To Lucinde, Julius describes what he has learned from her:

You have taught me the Infinity of the human spirit, and I have comprehended through you the meaning of marriage and life, and the glory of all things... When one loves the way we do, human nature returns to its original godliness... [15]

He, who had hitherto felt himself unskilled in love, and incapable of it, now finds that this love not only enables him to become the true artist he has always hoped to be (in the novel the hero is a painter, as is Lucinde), but also led him — in the true tradition of Goethe — to make his life a work of art. For the first time he achieves inward and outward unity. Opposites are reconciled, and the "riddle of his existence has been solved."

In his attacks on conventional marriage, Friedrich Schlegel was voicing the sentiments of a good number of the women of the times, who sought emancipation from the slavery of a marriage decreed by a parent, and enforced by the state — marriage of convenience and not of love. In one of his "Fragments," Friedrich Schlegel speaks out boldly — and for some of his readers altogether too boldly — against that kind of enslavement:

Almost all marriages are concubinage, marriages, so to speak, of the "left hand," or better, provisional attempts, and distant approximation to a true marriage, whose true nature exists not according to the paradoxes of this system or that, but in the spiritual and secular right of several persons becoming one ... Hence, free choice, which also should have the right to speak out, when the question arises as to whether an individual wishes to be something for himself, or only a portion of a communal personality, should as little as possible be restricted. And one cannot see what fundamental objections can be raised against *a mariage à la quatre* ... That which people call a happy marriage is to Love what a correct poem is to an improvised song ... [16]

The same Titanism of the Spirit, that notion of infinite Universality, of all-inclusiveness, he also applied to his definition of Romantic Poetry. It partakes of that dream of unity in the aesthetic world which was to be achieved in the reincarnation of a political medieval unitarian structure.

Romantic poetry is a progressive universal poetry. Its mission is not merely to reunite all separate genres of poetry and to put poetry in touch with philosophy and rhetoric. It will, and should, now mingle and now amalgamate poetry and prose, genius and criticism, the poetry of art and the poetry of nature, render poetry living and social and life and society poetic ... Romantic poetry alone can, like the epic, become a mirror of the entire surrounding world, a picture of its age. And yet, it too can soar, free from all real and ideal interests, on the wings of poetic reflection, midway between the work and the artist. It can even potentialize this reflection and multiply it as in an endless series of mirrors ... Other types of poetry are complete and can now be entirely analyzed. The Romantic type of poetry is still becoming; indeed, its peculiarity is that it is always becoming and that it can never be completed ... [17]

Undoubtedly, a gallant and noble program! Who was there capable of fulfilling the call for a poetry that would be a mirror "of the entire surrounding world, a picture of the age"? One like Friedrich Schlegel himself, who had said that the Poet had more important tasks than to tell us "how one lived in boredom in London when this was the fashion" — or one who would, like the prolific

Wilhelm Tieck, write, "When have Greatness and Beauty so
degraded themselves as to be useful"?[18] or the dramatist Zacharias
Werner, "Should and need that which is Better, forgetting its goal
and might, share the lower rabble's lower sorrows"?[19]

Was there anyone among all the Romantics who, gazing
outside of his enchanted circles, was aware that the labor conditions
in some parts of the German states were such that after 1800 the
working week was extended by 40% — the working day from 12 to
14 hours and more, that children under nine worked up to fourteen
hours a day? Or even anticipate that it would take a half-century
before the employment of children under twelve would be prohibited
in Germany?

Yet one should not underestimate the truly magnificent
contributions that the aesthetic theories that Friedrich and A.W.
Schlegel made in enlarging the vision of Europe, and deepening its
understanding of literature and art. They reinterpreted the Hellenic
world; they reestablished the great contributions of Spain; of
medieval France and the northern countries; of medieval art. Other
nations were to profit immeasurably from their achievements:
Coleridge and Carlyle in England; Victor Hugo in France. Nor can
one forget the profound impact of German transcendental idealism
on the rest of Europe, and even America.

Nor in treating of the ethereal character of these Romantic
circles, their "Weltflucht" — flights from reality — should one
forget the more practical and immediate interests that the remarkable
group of women who joined and surrounded them brought into the
struggles for woman's emancipation. The circles in Berlin were
presided over by women of rare intellectual distinction, mostly
Jewish, — Rahel Levin (later Rahel Varnhagen von Ense),
Henriette Herz, Dorothea Schlegel, by the last of whom even the
anti-Semetic philosopher Fichte was so taken that he wrote,

Praise of a Jewess may sound strange from my lips. But this woman has taken from me the belief that out of that nation nothing good could ever come. She has uncommonly great spirit and knowledge, little or no outward glamor, an utter absence of pretence, and a thoroughly good heart. One learns finally to love her, and that with one's whole heart...[20]

For these women were much more conscious than men of the social implications of their subordinate status, and it was a pity that in the constricted atmosphere of the Romantic circles they found so little room for activity in behalf of other women...

4

Goethe has said, "In der Beschränkung zeigt sich erst der Meister"
— "The true master shows himself in his delimitations." The
German Romantics, in their hunger for "transcendence," had little
use for delimitations. In their quest of the "infinite," they also
glorified and vaunted (among other things) "Chaos" and "Abgrund" —
the "Abyss." One of Wilhelm Tieck's anarchic characters cries out:
"Welcome, though desolate, delightful Chaos! Thou makest me
great and free!" And Friedrich Schlegel likewise: "In the rapture of
destructions the spirit of Divine Creation first manifests itself."
Friedrich Hölderlin speaks of the "wonderful longing for the Abyss."[21]

In no other German Romantic of this period are the wastes of
"Chaos" and the depths of the "Abyss" so tragically and passionately
exhibited as in Heinrich von Kleist. If there is any one figure that can
be said to represent German Romanticism in its most creative as well
as its most shattering aspects — it is Kleist — one of the most gifted
of German dramatists, and one of the few truly great playwrights of
this period. Few other Romantics bore within themselves such
searing marks of irreconcilable self-division, of internal disorder, of
the seeds of self-destruction. None other was so thoroughly undone
by his times.

He was a stricken genius of a stricken world. All his life long he
tried to reconcile the creative poet and the Prussian military officer
— the man of feeling with the Prussian citizen. He struggled
incessantly to harmonize the ideal of freedom and selfhood with
that of subordination and order. Within him the anarch fought
against the rigid discipline of the soldier, the poetic creator against
rigid authority.

The Romantic School had its various coteries, circles — in Jena,
Heidelberg, Berlin. Kleist formally belonged to none of them,
although he was on friendly terms with a number of their adherents.

They in turn treated him somewhat condescendingly. He was a preeminent outsider. Few of his contemporaries had so little to show of worldly success in their lifetime; very few of them, indeed, were to obtain that posthumous glory and reputation that fell to Kleist's lot. But no genius can live by a posthumous resurrection; and Kleist knew and felt all the bitterness of neglect. He was fortunate, however, in friends, men and women, who cherished him, and acknowledged his genius; but these were not among the potentates who control public opinion, theatres, and the press.

He brought a hectic life to a shockingly dramatic end. In 1811, at the age of thirty-four, he committed suicide by the Wannsee, just outside of Potsdam, along with a married woman who was dying of cancer.

Heinrich von Kleist was born in 1777 in Frankfurt-an-der-Oder, in eastern Prussia, and was descended of a long line of soldiers and Junkers. He was almost naturally destined for the army. He served for nine years, and took part in a number of military campaigns. In 1799 he resigned from the army to devote himself to the study of science. He had come to abhor the army and army discipline. In a letter to his tutor, he wrote:

I considered the officers as so many drill-sergeants; the soldiers as so many slaves; and when the entire regiment performed, it all seemed like a living monument of tyranny ... At such moments, I had the wish to leave a calling in which two thoroughly opposed principles suffered martyrdom: I was ever in doubt whether I should behave as a human being or as an officer ...[22]

His connections with the Court were close enough to have opened a career for him in the civil service; but he was no more willing to subject himself to bureaucratic discipline and routine. Time and again he would be offered employment, accept it, and after a short time withdraw. Such conduct, coming hard on his resignation from the army, was not looked upon with favor among government circles. In his own very supercilious and rebellious manner, he noted that on one occasion, in 1800, the King of Prussia had shown himself highly displeased with him.

Well, he wrote to his half-sister Ulrike, if he doesn't need me, then I need him even less. For it wouldn't be hard for me to find another King, but for him it wouldn't be so easy to find other subjects.[23]

What then was he fitted for? He was aware that he had a brilliant mind; he was aware that he had talents. He felt he needed time for self-development and study. He was fascinated by science and philosophy. But his university career was as desultory as his government employments. On another side, society was making its own demands upon him. If he wished to marry and establish a household, he would have to find some fitting and gainful employment. Here too was the rub! He became engaged to a young woman, Wilhelmine von Zenge. Her family, of course, would not hear of marriage until he had proved that he could support her adequately.

His was an attractive and engaging personality. People who got to know him came to love him, though frequently puzzled by his highly-charged, febrile character — while acknowledging his gifts. Women were drawn to him. He was forthright, a person of high integrity, who spoke from the heart. But he did not always know how to control his feelings. How could they know that he harbored a secret none around him, or after him, would ever resolve?

Before settling down to study and prepare for a "career," he undertook a journey to Würzburg to attend to his health. Whatever the illness, it apparently had wrought serious damage to his state of mind. There can be little doubt now that it was connected with a pathological fear that he was sexually impotent. Whatever the sources of that anxiety — whether youthful masturbation, venereal disease, or a passing homosexual episode — the fact remains that he thought himself incapable of entering upon a marital relation until he was cured. In Würzburg he believed himself restored to health. He also felt that he was regaining faith in himself and in his intellectual capacities. But the fact remains that he was never destined to achieve a permanent relation with any woman, though he loved many, and was beloved. To the end of his days he dreamt of wife, children, family life, but the only children (as he would call them) he created were the offspring of his brain, not of his loins. And these too would reveal all the marks of a problematical origin...

However, his physical restoration did not save him from an impending mental crisis. Though his academic training was highly sporadic, he had an insatiable appetite for learning. He was an auto-didact — a self-taught intellect — driven to find a stable philosophy of life and a key to the understanding of the world and of himself. His ambition was no less than to get at "ultimate Truth." In the world in which he was living, when, as we have seen, philosophy was not only in the air, but also a part of one's thinking, and even more significantly, of one's living — Kleist's Titanism, the feeling that he could achieve that kind of ultimate knowledge was itself a form of morbid passion, a sign of profounder internal tensions likely to break out in a major crisis. He was living in an age when German philosophers were reconstructing and constructing world-systems — years that produced Kant, Fichte, Schelling, and Hegel! In Kleist's case that morbid "Titanism" was — so he believed — to be shattered on the rocks of Kantianism. He concluded that Kant had shown that we can never apprehend ultimate reality — "das Ding an sich" —"the Thing in Itself"; that it was the human mind that gave form to the outer world, that supplied the "forms" of experience — Space, Time, and causal relations; that the world we apprehend was merely the world of phenomena, of things as they appear to us; but that the real, the so-called "noumenal" world was unknowable, and would forever remain hidden from human penetration. All knowledge was purely tentative. For Kleist, such a conclusion precipitated a mental and moral cataclysm. Whether it was or was not the reading of Kant that produced it does not matter. Individuals are, as a rule, not "shattered" by this or that book, this or that philosophical idea, unless they are already predisposed — "ripe" — for such a revolution. The seeds of unsettlement were already within Kleist's mind. It required only the right moment, the right impulses from within to bring them to full fruition. We have seen how the German Romantics tended in their ego-centrism to measure themselves against greatness — say, that of Goethe. For Kleist it was the inner conviction that he, Heinrich von Kleist, was at sea on the ocean of knowledge and understanding, with no harbor in sight. With the disappearance of the possibility of attaining to ultimate Truth, all basis of morality, ethics — all meanings as well — are destroyed. "Ignoramus — ignorabimus." We are left in Chaos. Using a Kantian image, Kleist describes his state of mind to his betrothed, Wilhelmine:

I will speak as clearly as I can. If all human beings had green eyeglasses instead of eyes, they would see all objects as green, and they would never be able to decide if their eyes were showing them the things as they are, or something that has been added to them, belonging not to themselves but to the eyes. And so it is with our understanding. We cannot be certain that that which we call the Truth is really such, or only an appearance. If the latter, then the Truth we have been gathering ceases to exist when we die, and all our attempts to preserve something that would follow us into the grave are useless...Since this conviction dawned upon me..., I have not touched a book...And I am obsessed by this one thought: Your sole, your loftiest goal is gone...And now you have no other...[23]

His immediate impulse was to flee. He would go to Paris...

At this critical moment — as at many others to come — his half-sister, Ulrike, stood at his side. She was the administrator of the Kleist estate, and time and again she came to his rescue when he was in need. But more than that, now she was ready to accompany him to Paris. In July they reached the French capital. Here his soul was revolted by what he considered the immorality and degradation of the French; and his German patriotism burned fiercely. The chaos within him would not yield to order, even in the changed climate. He felt himself heading for destruction. To Wilhelmine he wrote:

On this trip I sometimes felt that I was proceeding toward my precipice . . . And I have often struggled with the thought whether it were not my duty to leave you, to separate you from one who is clearly hurtling toward his abyss . . .[24]

He was toying with the idea of Death. Life, he contended in the same letter to Wilhelmine, was precious solely when one was capable of contemning it. "Only he can use it for lofty purposes, who can cast it away freely and cheerfully." He wishes to die a glorious death (the soldier within him awoke once more), if only he can have achieved "three things: a child, a beautiful poem, and a great deed. For life, after all, has nothing more sublime to offer than that one can throw it off sublimely."[25]

Disappointed with Paris, he turned toward Switzerland. A confirmed worshipper of Rousseau, he now dreamt of a bucolic existence, of a life simple and unencumbered by the wear and tear of the outer world. He would make Switzerland his new fatherland. He dispatched his new hopes to Wilhelmine. And she, more realistic and conventional than he, declined to abandon title, home, and family for the great simplicities of a farming life. In her reply we can already hear the muffled tolling bells of an impending end to their relationship. Kleist rented a house on an island of the Aar in Switzerland.

He had already found his vocation — that of dramatist. How extraordinary! Despite all the turmmoil, spiritual and physical, his incessant wanderings, the ravaging sense of having lost an intellectual foothold in the world — of having lost science as a life's guide — he was finding his own voice as a creative artist! In Paris he had conceived the idea of a tragedy, eventually to be called *Die Familie Schroffenstein* — a traditional "Gothic" knightly play of feuds, revenges, castles, and overhanging "curses" — a play not without talent considering his novitiate. More maturely, he was also at work on another tragedy, *Robert Guiscard* — also on a medieval theme — a work that was to haunt him for the rest of his life, and which he was never to complete. The fragment that has survived shows an amazing advance in poetic and dramatic skill. In addition he was planning his masterly comedy, *Der zerbrochene Krug — The Broken Jug* — stimulated by a print he saw in Berne. Here in Switzerland he found a group of congenial friends — among them the relatives of the celebrated German poet Christoph Martin Wieland. When, somewhat later, he came to know the aged poet himself, the latter paid the younger man a tribute the like of which few neophytes have encountered. Kleist read a portion of his *Guiscard* to him, and Wieland was overcome with amazement. Wieland later recalled the moment:

If the spirits of Aeschylus, Sophocles and Shakespeare had combined to create a tragedy, the result might have been what Kleist's *Death of Guiscard* would have been, if the entire work equalled those portions which he recited to me. From that moment I was convinced that Kleist was born to fill the great gap in our contemporary literature which, in my opinion, not even Goethe or Schiller had been able to fill, and you can imagine how eagerly I pressed him to complete this work.[26]

"It was the proudest moment in my life," Kleist wrote to Wieland five years later. Alas and alack! If only the words of the wise could be translated into mundane currency, say, of a theatrical production, or even the immediate approbation and acceptance of contemporaries! But the prevailing theatre of Berlin was a desert waste, populated by the vapid plays of an Iffland or a Kotzebue. Only in Goethe's Weimar was there a theatre that was likely to experiment with significant new drama; but that too failed to appreciate the coming of fresh genius like that of Kleist. But Kleist was far from over-awed by Goethe — the Titanic ruler of Weimar's culture. Kleist had a dose of Titanism himself! "Ich will ihm den Kranz der Stirne reissen!" he was reported to have said. "I will tear the laurel from his brow!"[27] Yet what insecurities and uncertainties lay hidden within that aggressive pride! Once more he returned to Germany, where his *Schroffenstein* was published in 1803 to modest acclaim. Yet he was haunted by *Guiscard*. Driven by a manic ambition, he now rejoiced, now despaired of the work. Once again he went to Paris. Here, in a fit of despondency, he burned whatever he had written of *Guiscard*. The fragment that survives shows a mature hand, its theme is the heroic "soldier" — in this case the eleventh century Norman conqueror Robert Guiscard. He is besieging Byzantium in his irresistible sweep, but at the gates of that great city — his supreme goal — his army is laid low by a pestilence that more than decimates it. The leader himself is stricken, but he must not show himself as vulnerable and destructible; and so he dissembles. The only scene left us shows him facing a host of petitioners who plead that he return to Italy with the maimed hosts. The scene is strongly reminiscent of *Oedipus Rex*, but also deeply colored by Kleist's own personality and his hunger for a "glorious death."

The soldier in him was still fully alive. He was a Prussian and a patriot. That passionate extremism which was so great an element of his character he exhibited in his hatred of Napoleon and the French. It knew no bounds, intensified as it became by his sense of Prussia's humiliation and moral dismemberment. The measure of his desperation can be gathered from his madcap plan to join the French army, which was then planning an invasion of England! Fortunately, German authorities refused him this permission, and he was forced to return to Germany. Once more he sought government employment, and indulgent superiors found him a place in an economic department of the government. But before that he was forced to listen to a sharp reproof administered by the King's *Generaladjutant*, Kökeritz:[28]

You have abandoned the army; you have turned your back on government service; you have roamed in foreign parts; you have thought of settling in Switzerland; you have been composing *vershes;* you've tried to join the French army...

All of which was true.

But he, in turn, burned with an uncontrollable rage that the King of Prussia was so reluctant to join Austria and Russia against Napoleon. In 1806 came the great débacle of Jena. Napoleon seemed more invincible than ever. Kleist once more turned away from government work.

It would be useless to follow every one of his footsteps during the succeeding years: his six-months' imprisonment by the French on the suspicion that he was a German spy; his removal for a time to Dresden, where he established a journal with the political scientist Adam Müller, which failed after a year. He was waiting, waiting for the day when Prussia would awaken from her lethargy, and the King would join Austria in an all-out campaign against the French. But in 1809 Austria herself was crushed at Wagram. For Kleist the agony and shame of these defeats and the pusilanimity of the Prussian King were climaxed by the latter's alliance with Napoleon, who was preparing to invade Russia. He felt degraded as a Prussian soldier and as a German.

Yet such is the miracle of the creative genius, that during the last six years of his life, in spite of all the anguish he had been experiencing, Kleist produced six dramatic works, two volumes of short stories; a novel (now lost); edited two reviews, and was planning a third!

Artistic creation demands an ordering of materials, and Kleist was shaping Chaos, the "Abyss," and Death — shaping Disorder into Order. If one were to try to define Kleist's *Weltanschauung* as it manifests itself in all of his literary work, one could with justice say that it consists of a moral nihilism that carried to a Kleistian excess must finally give way, even create, Law and Order. For him, human nature no less than all of the natural world remained incomprehensible. Within the human being himself were to be found forces — terrible as well as benign — whose actions must remain a mystery to us. Already, in his earliest tragedy, *Schroffenstein,* he uttered, through the lips of one of his characters, a conviction that was to remain with him to the end:

> Do I seem like a riddle to you?
> Take comfort: God is such to me.

And almost at the same time he expressed that sentiment more fully to Wilhelmine:

Truly, when you consider that we require a whole lifetime in order to learn how to live, that even in death we have no notion of what Heaven demands of us; when there is no one who knows what is the purpose of his existence, and his own goals; when human reason is inadequate to bring to us an understanding of oneself, of the soul, of life, and of the things around us; when for centuries now there has been doubt as to the meaning of Right, can God demand responsibility from such creatures? Let them not say there is an inner voice that secretly but clearly whispers to us: This is Right. The very same voice that calls upon the Christian to forgive his enemies, calls upon the New Zealander to roast him and eat him amid prayers ... And, after all, what is Evil, absolute Evil? ...[29]

What others might consider a World Order is in fact World Disorder. Time and again, Kleist speaks of the "fragile constitution of the world" — "die gebrechliche Einrichtung der Welt" — the "assault" that the human being is subjected to by some indeterminate fatality. Nature too is the slave of Chance. But within the human being an incessant dualism is at work — within him is a war between feelings and the need for order. None understood better than Kleist to what lengths excesses of feelings could lead (he himself was prone to rages that expressed themselves in shocking scurrilities!); none felt more in need of controls. Yet human feelings are the only means of challenging tyranny and injustice. They are mankind's most precious possession. It is significant that Kleist found the embodiment of such feelings most effectively represented by women, in each case faced by the "Verwirrungen" — the confusions — of a confusing world: in Alcmena, of the *Amphitryon* play, in the Marquise of O**; in Käthchen of Heilbronn; in Eva Rull of the *Broken Jug;* just as he probed the full terror of a cataclysmic passion in the character of Penthesilea.

Utter nihilism of feeling, particularly when translated into action, must bring about the destruction of the world, even if actuated by the noblest of motives. It creates the need for a counter-force: Authority, the Law, the State. Thus is Chaos turned into Order.

Nowhere in Kleist is the dualism and its resolution more clearly manifested than in two of his later works: the short-story, *Michael Kohlhaas,* and the drama, *Der Prinz von Homburg.* They are products of the period of political agitation, when the poet's patriotic fever was at its height. He had before this been principally concerned with internal psychological phenomena, hardly touching (with the possible exception of the comedy, *The Broken Jug*) on the conflict between human beings and society. In *Michael Kohlhaas* and the *Prince of Homburg* the conflict becomes explicit.

Michael Kohlhaas is based on a seventeenth century historical chronicle. Kleist retells the story in a deliberately dry chronicle style, and the contrast between the bloody events narrated and the literary manner produces a particularly striking effect, because of the seeming detachment of the writer. Michael Kohlhaas is an upright, judicious, and well-to-do horsedealer, living at the time of Luther and the Protestant Reformation, who comes into conflict with what Kleist terms the "shatterable order of the world." He is the victim of a wanton and arbitrary act of tyranny on the part of a Saxon Junker aristocrat, Wenzel von Tronka. Without provocation or justification, the latter has confiscated Kohlhaas's two horses — on a fictitious pretext — and has abused both the groom and the animals, and maltreated them. Kohlhaas seeks legal redress, and appeals to the Elector of Brandenburg; but all his efforts are frustrated, and his complaints ignored through the chicanery of the Elector's subordinates — actually allies of the house of Tronka. The usually patient and sober Kohlhaas is at his wits' end. He decides to take justice into his own hands. He sells his possessions, determined on leaving the country. "I cannot remain in a land where I am not protected in my rights. Better be a dog than a man, if I am to be trodden underfoot," he exclaims. He gathers his servants around him, collects arms, and sets out to hunt the malefactor, Tronka, wherever he might be. In his savage pursuit, he calls upon all those he suspects of harboring Tronka to surrender him or suffer the consequences; and when foiled, he proceeds to lay waste town and country-side. In his mind he has become the avenging archangel Michael, destined to restore justice to the world and "create a new order." His guerilla band grows to a hundred — and the entire land is terrified. For, as Kohlhaas puts it, he is now responsible to no earthly lord, only to God.

At this juncture, Martin Luther intervenes, and in order to bring Kohlhaas to his senses, promises to appeal directly to the Elector, and obtains an amnesty for him. Kohlhaas allows himself to be persuaded. However, in the course of the succeeding negotiations, he is tricked by the Saxon authorities, is accused of fomenting a new conspiracy, is arrested and transported to Berlin. He is condemned to die. The Elector has been by-passed; a higher authority has been invoked. The evil done to Kohlhaas is redressed: he is given back his two horses, now restored and in good condition. Junker Tronka is sentenced to imprisonment. Kohlhaas accepts the final verdict as just, and is beheaded. Thus Kleist's "fragmented" and "fragmentable" world order is repaired, especially since the Elector of Brandenburg immediately following the execution confers knighthood on the two young sons of the executed avenger! Order is restored. Justice has been vindicated, the Law justified.

It is curious and ironic that Kleist did not perceive that the injustices perpetrated on human beings — like Michael Kohlhaas — stemmed not from some incomprehensible fatality, transcendent and uncontrollable, but from human beings, made of flesh and blood and bones, but, unlike Michael Kohlhaas, endowed with absolute power over life and death. The poet Kleist is outraged by this manifestation of wilful tyranny and identifies with Kohlhaas. The Prussian officer in him demands a disciplined submission to the State. Kleist, having unloosed chaos, must have order.

In an even stronger sense, this dualism is revealed in Kleist's most powerful and moving drama, *Der Prinz von Homburg*. The play marks the culmination of that poet's tragic attempt at achieving popular recognition and acceptance as dramatist and political spokesman for his time. It is no wonder that he believed that an ironic fatality governed all his life's activities. In 1808, he had composed a patriotic drama — *Die Hermannsschlacht* — *The Battle of Arminius* — meant explicitly to rouse the Prussians to renewed resistance against Napoleon, at the moment when Austria was preparing for another campaign. The victory of the Germanic hero Arminius over the Romans in the Teutoburg Forest in A.D. 6 seemed particularly appropriate now, since it had been achieved as a result of Arminius's skill in uniting other Germanic tribes to war against the Roman general Varus — a victory that was so overwhelming that it remained for Germany an unforgettable memorial. It is also immortalized by Augustus Caesar's despairing cry of "Varus, give me back my legions!" Through Arminius, Kleist is shouting: "Hass ist mein Amt, und meine Tugend Rache" — "Hatred is my province, and revenge my virtue." Further to rouse his compatriots, Kleist was composing perfervid war poems. Both the poems and the play fell on deaf ears. The play did not achieve production until many years after Kleist's death.

Der Prinz von Homburg had an even more disastrous history. Being a glorification of the Prussian house of Brandenburg, it was also composed with an eye to the Queen, a descendant of the eponymous hero of the play — a celebrated military leader in the Thirty Years' War against Sweden. Unfortunately, the drama incurred the disfavor of the Court, and was not only barred from the Prussian stage, but did not even see the light of publication during the playwright's lifetime. The failure of *Der Prinz* was followed by another mortal body-blow. In 1811, the King of Prussia signed a treaty of alliance with Napoleon. It did not need much more utterly to destroy Kleist. "Germany! Fatherland! Who will save thee now?" It is Kleist crying out through one of his dramatic characters. His own and Germany's fate seemed conjoined.

There was good reason for the royal court, the military, and the Junker aristocracy to have taken umbrage at *The Prince of Homburg*. For in the principal character Kleist was creating not a "hero" of military tradition, in the rigid Prussian sense, but a heroic "anti-hero" — perhaps the outstanding of that kind in German drama. Instead of the fully disciplined ideal soldier — say, like the one celebrated in the song, "Der gute Kamerad," who cannot even grasp the hand of his fallen comrade, for he must load his musket — Kleist had created an officer of the highest rank, commander of a cavalry division, who in a moment of great trial breaks down. A strange character indeed, this prince, an unbalanced character, living an ambiguous life. He is a dreamer. He dwells in two worlds: the world of arms and an inner world, the world of the somnabulist! He is indeed "umnachtet" — "night-shrouded."

In the realms of German Romanticism "Mesmerism" and its associated manifestations: hypnotism, magnetism, somnabulism — and what we today term extra-sensory perception, previsionary trances, catalepsy and other psychic phenomena — were followed with intense passion. One of the most celebrated treatises of the time was G.H. von Schubert's *Ansichten von der Nachtseite der Naturwissenschaften* — *Notions concerning the Occult Aspects of the Natural Sciences*. Kleist was particularly receptive to these ideas, which only reenforced his own natural predisposition to day-dreaming, absent-mindedness, self-immersion (already observed and noted down by the poet Wieland). Personal contact with Schubert himself in Dresden strengthened such preoccupation. That interest is clearly manifested in the fascinating play, *Käthchen von Heilbronn,* composed in 1808, no less than in the later play of the *Prince of Homburg.*

In *The Prince of Homburg* the clash between the two worlds — that of the dream and that of external realities — society — assumed its most pregnant form. This is truly a "dream-play" — for it opens with a dream and ends with one. The two worlds confront each other — both incomprehensible. In the realm of his inner world, in the dream, the individual can isolate himself from the onslaughts of a hostile outside, and create a life more favorable to his being. Such is the Prince's world, as we see him in the opening of the play. On the eve of a critical military engagement he is discovered by the Elector and his entourage asleep and dreaming. The dream is lyrical, for it takes place in a garden, where the Prince has taken refuge. The dream represents the "feeling" portion of the man, his inner "truth" and reality. The Prince is winding a laurel wreath for himself in anticipation of certain victory. The astonished Elector takes the wreath from the hands of the sleeper, winds his own golden chain around it; and in turn gives it to his niece, Princess Natalie, with whom the Prince is in love. As the latter reaches out for it, the Princess retreats, and the Prince snatches one of her gloves. The amazed spectators withdraw, and the Elector sets the stage of future action and catastrophe, with the words:

> Back into Nothingness, Herr Prinz von Homburg,
> Into Nothingness, into Nothingness! On the field of battle
> We'll meet again, if it please you, sir;
> In dreams such things are never achieved![30]

The "Leitmotiv" has been established. For the dreamer, the lover, the soldier, on awakening, continues his distracted state — a waking somnabulism, and puzzles over the origin of the glove he holds in his hand. When the Commander-in-Chief reads the order of battle, the Prince is only half-present, especially when he discovers that the glove belongs to Natalie. It is this half-waking, this half-sleeping state, the "poetic" element within him that brings on the near tragedy. He only half-hears the order enjoining him and his mounted cavalry from entering into action until a specific order was to be given on the field of battle. The Prince is impulsive, rash, a Hotspur, and has often before acted with impermissible precipitation. And now, too, in disobedience of the order, he rushes into battle prematurely, and is victorious. But he is guilty of a dereliction and is condemned to death by the Elector. The dream is shattered. The Prince knows himself beloved by the Elector, and cannot believe that he must pay with his life. Had he not won a glorious victory?

Then he sees the grave being dug for him. He who had faced death a hundred times cannot face death now! He breaks down. His inner collapse is complete. The "nothingness" the Elector had mocked turns into a reality — a spiritual and moral Chaos. With abject misery, he pleads with the wife of the Elector and with Natalie to intercede for him:

> On my way here I saw the grave
> By the light of the torches — it was open,
> The grave that tomorrow is to hold my corpse.
> Dear Aunt! these eyes of mine that gaze on you
> Tomorrow will be darkened, and this breast
> Pierced by the murderous lead.
> Windows on the market-place already bespoken
> Will look opon this dismal scene,
> And I, whose eyes were fixed on the future,
> Looking toward the peaks of life as to a fairy-land,
> Am to be penned between two narrow boards,
> And on my chest a stone that reads: *He Was!*[31]

Both Natalie and the Elector's wife are distraught by the Prince's abject state, and Natalie undertakes to plead with the Elector. Against the Elector's adamant insistence on the inexorable laws of war, military discipline, the claims of the fatherland, she pleads the cause of the heart, of feeling, and urges mercy as the noblest Jewel of Order. The Elector yields: If the Prince, he says, believes that the sentence is unjust, he will be set free. Let him only say so!

But the Prince has come to himself. He sees the verdict as justified; he will submit to it and die. Others, too, fearing the impact of an execution on the morale of the army, have added their pleas to those of Natalie. The Prince is saved, but he is to be brought back to life through another dream scene. He is awaiting the end in his

prison cell, and is taken, his eyes bound, back into the garden. Here
Natalie and the others await him. As his eyes are unbound, he is
crowned and hailed as victor. The Prince wonders: Is this a dream?
Outside, the armies are readying for the final assault on the Swedes.
The cry resounds, "Death to all the enemies of Brandenburg!"

Once more Order has triumphed. Justice and Law have both
been vindicated, as well as the Prussian military code. The
supremacy of the State has been affirmed. The House of Brandenburg
has been extolled. The political Kleist has triumphed over Kleist the
poet, the dreamer. For since 1807, he had come under the
conservative influence of Adam Müller, a brilliant if unscrupulous
champion of reaction, a vigorous opponent of Prussian reforms
advocated by Hardenberg and Stein, but a very persuasive political
propagandist. In most of his own political sentiments Kleist found
himself at one with Müller

Yet the *poet* within him was saying, "No!" Despite all
acceptance of supreme authority and law, Kleist is still pleading for
and extolling the promptings of the heart. The Prince and Natalie
— not too mention the old and tried General Kottwitz — are the
representatives of the dominion of feelings as opposed to the
hard-headed and tradition-bound ethos of the Elector. They are the
advocates of the rights of the "inner" human being, with all his
ambiguities and confusions. They are the "poets" and their language
in the play is lyrical. The Prince is sensitive to nature. The Elector
and the other soldiers speak the brusque, bluff, and almost colloquial
lanquage of the army. Kleist's is the language of realism — far
removed from the rhetorical excesses of the older German drama.

But the most astonishing and incisive element of the play is
Kleist's treatment of the "heroic." In the eyes of the Court and the
military the Prince has shown himself a coward; and his behavior is
a betrayal of true Prussian army tradition. Nor could they
understand the inner workings of the Prince's soul — the ambivalences, the dream-world, what the Elector calls "nothingness",

but which for Kleist represent the essential man. What had these to
do with a soldier? The realm of what we today call the "unconscious"
was a realm of danger to an established order. The Court barred the
production of the play from all Berlin stages for some time to come.
Even after Kleist's death, the edict continued, and Heine remarked:

Let Berlin lieutenants-of-the guard mock and call it cowardice that the
Prince of Homburg recoils at the sight of his open grave. Heinrich von
Kleist had as great courage as his large-chested, tightly-corseted colleagues,
and he has ... proved it. All robust beings love life ...[32]

In his daring probings into the "Nachtside" — the nocturnal
aspects of the human psyche — no other Romantic — not even
E.T.A. Hoffman — approached Kleist for intensity and insight.
Two of his somewhat earlier plays, *Penthesilea* and *Das Käthchen
von Heilbronn* represent Kleist's immersion into the a-rational
workings of the human heart and mind. Modern psychology will
regard these two dramas as illuminating and previsionary
illustrations of extreme aspects of the love-hate relationship and
sadism (as in *Penthesilea*); and of masochism and dream-psychology
(as in *Käthchen*). That, like his other plays, but in a profounder
sense, these were self-revelations, Kleist was only too well aware. In
a letter to the actress, Henriette Hendel-Schutz, he wrote:

All that you say about *Penthesilea* has touched me indescribably and deeply.
It is true, my inmost being is to be found in it. And you have grasped that
fact like a seer — all the pain and the splendor of my soul. I am now curious
to know what you will say about *Käthchen von Heilbronn*, for the latter is
the antithesis of *Penthesilea* — her other pole — a creature as powerful
through total submission, as the other is through action.[33]

Could anything have been more explicit and illuminating as a
key to his entire creation and being? In venturing upon a subject
drawn from classical antiquity, Kleist was treading upon ground
sacred to the humanist circles of Weimar, challenging Goethe's
proprietary classicism. *Penthesilea* outraged Goethe. He saw in the
play a peversion of the Greek ideal of "noble simplicity, and

serene greatness" (as defined by Winckelmann); and since he
regarded the Romantic movement as an extended "sickness," he
found all evidence of diseased creation in this play. It was neither
noble, nor simple; and certainly it was not serene. Never inured to
rejection (and who is?), Kleist found this one of the most galling
experiences of his life. Goethe recognized Kleist's talent. He had
even produced the *Broken Jug* at Weimar, where it did not meet with
favor. But *Penthesilea* defied all the canons of tragedy — especially
"classical" tragedy. It had dared to descend into the nether world of
the Geek psyche, and was even more frenzied and savage than the
Bacchae of Euripides.

Penthesilea, Queen of the Amazons, warrior-woman of great
beauty, deep feeling, and unquestioned valor, has set out with her
army of women against the Greeks, on the fields of Troy. They are to
vanquish and bring back male warriors to repopulate the country.
Contrary to divine edict that requires each Amazon to "choose whom
the gods present in battle," Penthesilea has already fixed on the great
Achilles, and upon seeing him, falls madly in love with him, and
proposes to conquer him by force of arms. But Achilles in his turn has
fallen in love with her. In battle he triumphs over her, but she, on
recovering from the contest, is made to believe that she is the victor.
When the truth comes home to her, she is overcome by a maniacal
rage. She must kill the man she loves. Achilles, on the other hand,
conceives a stratagem of feigned submission to her, and sends her a
challenge. He will offer no resistance and allow himself to be taken
captive. Penthesilea takes the challenge seriously, and in her blind
fury, destroys the defenseless hero. In her madness she cries out;

> Set all the hounds upon him! With firebrands
> Whip up the elephants, to tread him down!
> With scythe-armed chariots dash against him!
> Mow down the lushness of his glorious limbs!...

> And now amidst her pack of hounds she rages,
> Her lips foam-flecked, she calls them her own sisters.
> They howl, and like a furious Maenad she herself,
> Dancer-like flies over fields with stretched bow,
> Incites the dogs, and breathing death and blood,
> She calls on them to hunt the fairest game
> That ever roamed o'er this fair earth . . . [34]

She not only kills Achilles, but mutilates his body. When she recovers her sanity, she cannot believe that she has committed the outrage, and disabused, she kills herself. Kleist himself spoke of Penthesilea as "really having eaten" Achilles out of love! Tenderness and brutality, Eros and Mars — that is Penthiselea, "half-fury and half-grace" (so Achilles describes her). In her, Kleist has extended the dimensions of Romantic nocturnalism, and the "Umnachtung" — the benighting of the rational mind — so that it plunges down, deep down into the abyss, even down to anthropophagy!

In *Käthchen von Heilbronn*, night also prevails — night figurative and literal. Here it takes the form of dreams and obsessional masochism. Here too occurs what the Germans call "Doppelschlaf" — the "double" sleep — dreams by two separate individuals that overlap in a kind of collusive telepathy. Käthchen, the fifteen-year old daughter of a Heilbronn armorer, has dreamt of a Graf vom Strahl, a knight she has never seen before and with whom she has fallen in love. When he actually turns up to have his armor repaired, she falls to the ground in a swoon. Thereafter she leaves home and follows him, utterly possessed, sleeping in stables, oblivious of his rejection. Vom Strahl, too, has a dream of some unattainable daughter of an Emperor, and in his dream he sees himself entering Käthchen's chamber. What might have become a serious drama of social conflict and implications, Kleist, however, turns into a fairy tale. (Poor Kleist hungered for popular acceptance!) The all-suffering, pathetic, lovely girl finally wins her man — she is discovered to be the illegitimate daughter of the Emperor!

Again the social order has been vindicated, but at what cost to art!
Later playwrights struggle with similar themes in which an
outraged establishment is threatened by an unacceptable relationship
between king or noble and a lower-class "outsider," as in Grillparzer's
The Jewess of Toledo and Friedrich Hebbel's *Agnes Bernauer*. But
here the nature of the social conflict is made clear, and proper
measures are taken to eliminate the threat. In each case the woman
is murdered. In Kleist's play, however, the knight, though in love
with the girl, cannot think of marrying her, so concious is he of his
social status. For all the distressing hocus-pocus in the drama, there
are moments when Kleist the poet triumphs, especially in his
depiction of the sterling character of Käthchen, who despite her
pathological fixation emerges as a charming, even enchanting
personality. She is far from simple-minded, and forms a striking foil
to the crass, sometimes grossly heartless vom Strahl, who is not
above taking the whip to her. The dream sequences are impressive,
especially one in which the knight surprises Käthchen asleep in a
stable, and converses with her in her dream-state. (By this time he is
deeply in love.)

Strahl: My dear Käthchen!
Käthchen: My noble Lord...
Strahl: You are very fond of me, aren't you?
K: Of course, very much...
S: But I —— what do you think — I'm not ——
K: Oh, you scamp!
S: What?! Scamp?! I hope —
K: Go Away! You're in love, yes in love — like any young girl!
S (to himself): Strong as a tower — so firm in her belief. I will play along.
      Käthchen, if it's as you say ——
K: What is your pleasure my Lord?
S: Tell me — what is going to happen?
K: And what do *you* think can happen?
S: Have you thought about it?
K: Of course...
S: What do you mean?

K: Come Easter, you will marry me.

S(suppressing a laugh): So? Marry? Really? I'm not so sure...
    Look here Käthchen, who told you that?

K: Marian, my maid. She saw it in the lead she cast for me on
    New Year's Eve.

S: And she foretold —

K: A great handsome knight would marry me.

S: And you believe — just like that — that it's me?

K: Yes, honored Lord... You came to me at midnight
    Just the way you are now,
    To greet me lovingly as your bride...
    (She wakes up.) Oh my God! Lord of my life! What's happened to me?

S(to himself): What seemed a dream to me was only the bare truth...[35]

Der Prinz Von Homburg was Kleist's final testament. Only for him there was to be no rehabilitation, no gracious reprieve from death. He felt himself betrayed by the King of Prussia — all his patriotic efforts could now be termed treasonous; for had not the King joined hands with Napoleon? His literary career was a shambles — what had he to show? His pathological frenzy rises to a harrowing climax as he becomes obsessed with the idea of death. Only he is afraid to die alone! He must find a companion. Henriette Vogel — a married woman who is mortally ill — is willing to join him. With appalling military precision he plans the double suicide, and on November 21, 1811, by the Wannsee, outside Potsdam, he shoots her and himself.... He had finally found the "abyss deep enough" for himself and his companion. The King of Prussia crowned Kleist's death with an order suppressing further discussion of the event lest the "perverted views" of the deceased poet and officer and their diffusion should nullify "all efforts to elevate the religious and moral sentiments of the population."[36]

When, many years later, Heinrich von Kleist was finally "resurrected," he became the revered symbol of "Prusianism" and of the authoritarian *Machtstaat — absolute state-power.*

Kleist opens the windows for us upon a whole vista of internal and external "Verwirrungen," confusions and contradictions, ambivalences and ambiguities that characterize German Romanticism, and also the German conciouness of his own day and thereafter. The two contradictory impulses — one hurtling toward "chaos" and the "abyss," toward self-destruction and destruction of the cosmos, the eradication of conciousness in the name of some "absolute" — call it a "Götterdämmerung"; — the other, Authority and Power to counter the ultimate collapse of the cosmos — are ever present within him. On the one hand nihilism of the emotions — apotheosis of the "Self"; on the other, apotheosis of the State. Friedrich Schlegel was to find a safe harbor in his peregrinations from a cosmic solipsism to submission to the absolutism of Church and State. For Kleist there was no quietus, save in Death.

5.

When the grand sorcerer of Weimar unleashed his two demonic figures of Dr. Faust and Mephistopheles upon the world, he could scarcely have realized that he was projecting a paradigmatic history not only of one individual German "soul", but actually also of Germany herself. For from Goethe's *Faust* to, say, Thomas Mann's *Dr. Faustus,* the great parable of the divided soul, or of the "two souls" — to echo Faust's own cry of "Zwei Seelen" — came, in the eyes of many, to stand for the shattering, sometimes frightening image of two forces — call them Heaven and Hell — that made unresolvable claims upon man's life, thoughts and actions. Absorbed into the Romantic psyche, they became the "Doppelgänger", the "Double," symbol of human self-division. For Germans, living during the Napoleonic supremacy, the element of the satanic could easily be identified with the figure of the mighty conqueror, even becoming identified with an inscrutable fatality. For until the French disasters of 1812, he was the *One* — an irresistible force, playing fast and loose with nations, states, and — of course — human beings. Was this not, in fact, a struggle between Light and Darkness, God and Satan, a cosmic struggle that more minutely reflected in every man's and woman's individual soul? For the essence of that power was Mystery. And the human soul too was mysterious.

Thus Faust and Mephisto became internalized within the microcosm of the German romantic world. Every human being carried his own little Satan within himself. His vivid imagination was all too easily stimulated by anxieties, having a realistic basis (chaos without, and chaos within) — and all too readily became the prey of frightful dreams, even hallucinations. Within, there was this leering, menacing, mocking, cajoling and beckoning specter, an inescapable companion. Later in the century other lands too would succumb, and Ivan Karamazov (like Dostoyevski himself) would have interminable colloquies with a descendant of Goethe's

Mephistopheles, and would finally be converted (like so many German Romantics) to the need and acceptance of submission to an eternal Law, embodied in the absolutism of Church and State...

Yet there were Romantics within Germany not attached to any of the enclosed coteries or *cénacles* of Jena, Heidelberg, or Berlin, whose inner turmoils and diremptions did not lead them toward a political or religious authoritarianism. They, too, struggled to overcome the chaos of self-division. For they, too, had their inner "Doppelgänger." If they found no resolution to their dismemberment, they were more than others of their contemporaries aware of the world around them, and the human beings within that world, and their own presence as members of a fragmented social order. They were the critical "outsiders." They were, like the others, "fantasts" — but their fantasies uncovered, at times, sterner immediate social realities; they even came close to uncovering the nature of their "other" self.

One of these was Adelbert von Chamisso. The name itself betrays a kind of duality: it is that of a man born a Frenchman, become a Prussian by a forced adoption. Chamisso was a French aristocrat who was dispossessed of land and home at the time of the French Revolution; who as an émigré, reluctantly, accepted service in the Prussian army. He was an aristocrat with strong democratic leanings; a Prussian who loved France, and worshipped Napoleon — a man belonging to two countries and yet to neither! That such realities could lead to an inner self-division is obvious. Chamisso only too clearly recognized this fatality, and expressed it poignantly in a poem, "Die Erscheinung" — "The Apparition" — and in his celebrated story, *Peter Schlemihl.*

In the poem the writer returns home late one night, and finds his own "self" standing at his reading desk. They challenge each other's right to being the true "He" — and each agrees to substantiate his claim. "Let us know," says the "other" — the Doppelgänger — "who you are." The Poet commences:

"I am a man whose only aim and thought
Were towards the Good, the Beautiful, the True;
Who never sacrificed on strange gods' altars,
Nor ever pandered to worldly empty fashions;
Disowned and spurned — disdaining pain and sorrow,
I wandered far, and dreaming held the smoke
To be some glowing flame, but on awaking
Upheld what I deemed right. Canst say the same?"

And he, with grating, wild, and scornful laughter:
"I'm not the man you boast yourself to be —
All different I from all that you are vaunting:
I am a coward, liar, falsifying wretch —
O thou, the misunderstood, heroic in thy sorrows —
Which of us two is he who knows himself best?
Or limned himself in this true colors?
Which of us two shall forfeit his own Self?
Come near me if you dare, and I will go!"

I gazed with horror upon that terrifying form:
"Thou art the one! Remain, let me vanish!"
Into the night I sped — to weep and weep.

If this is Chamisso's judgment upon himself, it is eminently unfair, passionate as is the self-reproach. For he was a noble-souled person, having little in common with many of the world-evading Romantics. His feelings for others — particularly the lowly and the wretched — were deep. They are revealed not only in his own social verses, but even more clearly in his translations of the Frenchman Béranger's popular songs and ballads. He was one of the very few German poets of this time whose heart and admiration went out to the unfortunate Russian Decembrists — the makers of the "first" Russian revolution, many of whom perished by hanging, or were exiled to Siberia.[37] He hated Prussian autocracy, and looked forward to the dismemberment of the old order. Aside from his literary attainments, he also achieved an extraordinary reputation as a natural scientist and was elected to the Prussian Academy. Today he is remembered principally for his incomparable parable, the satirico-serious *Peter Schlemihl*.

Here, the Faustian theme is given a new twist. Peter Schlemihl sells not his impalpable soul to the Devil, but his shadow, and in return receives a miraculous sack from which he can draw an inexhaustible store of gold coins. But what respectable person does not own a shadow? Peter Schlemihl soon discovers that he is a pariah — all that come to see him in daylight are, at first, startled, then horrified, and avoid him. He is the alienated being who does not conform to the customary in society — a monster, no less! Whatever gratification he may obtain from his immense wealth is poisoned by a corresponding loss of that he most desires — companionship and woman's love. The girl who is unselfishly in love with him must sacrifice herself to the practical tyranny of her father. He is left with only one companion, his servant Bendel, who accepts his master's alienation, and even offers always to accompany him, and stand with him in such a way that none will notice there is no shadow. Bendel's shadow will serve for both. In utter despair, Schlemihl awaits the day when the Devil would return. He will ask to have his shadow restored. When the Devil offers to return the shadow, but demands Schlemihl's soul after his death, Schlemihl rebells. He casts the magic pouch from him. He will live without a shadow — alone if necessary. Leaving all behind him, he now wanders all over the world, and becomes immersed in the study of sciences — aided in his worldwide wandering by an accidental purchase of seven-league boots. Unrecognized, he returns to his hometown, where he finds that Bendel had used the fortune he had left with him to establish a hospital in Schlemihl's name. He sees Mina, the woman who loved him and whom he loved. He departs, leaving them a note:"Your old friend too is doing better now than ever before; and if he is atoning, it is an atonement of reconciliation."

Whatever autobiography Chamisso infused into the story — and how could he avoid touching on his homelessness and his self-division? — became merged with the larger intent and meaning of the parable. To Madame de Staël he had once complained that he was "a Frenchman in Germany, a German in France, a Catholic among Protestants, a Protestant among Catholics, a Jacobin among aristocrats, a nobleman among democrats." Had he not also sold his shadow by accepting service as a Prussian officer? But the larger implication of that sale becomes evident: Schlemihl sold his shadow for gold. Thus, he had sacrificed — sundered apart — the integrity of his personality, sundered the total human being within, and severed it from its social responsibilities and participation. He had sold his share in society.

But the satire is more complex. In fact it is double-edged. For society too becomes its target. One sees how society flocks around Schlemihl, now become the multi-millionaire, eager for his largesses! They even take him for the Prussian King, traveling incognito! Yet, how bound they are by convention, and ready to ostracize the person who departs from the traditional norm! And how they worship money! In the early days of his poverty, Schlemihl is instructed by the wealthy man whom he has approached with a letter of introduction: "Whoever is not the possessor of at least a million is — you must excuse the expression   a villain!" And humble Peter Schlemihl exclaims with passion, "Oh, how true!" The moral, enunciated at the conclusion of the story, is — in Chamisso's words — "Would you live among people, then you must first of all learn to venerate your shadow, then money. However, would you live within yourself and for your better self — then you need no advice." In other words, be like others, and worship gold. Else, withdraw and live your own life according to your inner commands. Chamisso was fortunate enough to be able to do so. He received reparation for the loss of his properties and was able to continue his dedication to science and poetry. He lived long enough to see European aristocracy shaken by the Paris July Revolution of 1830, and to witness the emergence of a new school of German poets and novelists — Young Germany — writing under the banner of Saint-Simonism and deeply involved in the political and social scene. Peter Schlemihl was to affect a score of writers, and the Yiddish-Hebraic name of the hero (the etymology is still very doubtful) standing for a luckless, calamity-prone incompetent, was taken over into European speech. Not the least considerable variant of the theme of the shadowless person is that used by Richard Strauss in *Die Frau ohne Schatten*.

6.

Hegel, greatest philosopher of the Romantic era, thus describes the character of the period, the fragmentation of the individual, and his consequent "alienation":

This is the prose of the world, as it appears both to our conciousness and to that of other people, a finite world, one of mutability, of relativization, a world under the rule of necessity which the individual is unable to escape. For the individual being is caught in a contradiction in which he sees himself as a sealed unity, while being all the while dependent on other people . . .[38]

"The prose of the world." Hegel is describing what we may well call a "collective consciousness" of the age — a strained, torn, dissevered conciousness laboring under the burdensome realities of wars, invasions, and personal and collective dislocations. The individual becomes a "sealed" unity, isolated, seeking to escape from the putative grip of "Necessity" — darkened by the feeling of helplessness, seeing no other forces to counter it. In such times, the disposition to seek refuge in fantasy, mysticism, dreams, and elements of the "unconscious" becomes prevalent. As the earlier Romantic dream of the "blue flower" — the ideal perfection resolving human dichotomies to be found in some transcendental realm — begins to fade, "Necessity" acquires the terrifying form of some imponderable, inscrutable dark force. The ethereal dissolves in the face of the "prose" — say, like the practical machinery of Metternich's authoritarianism. Fantasy faces reality — and turns into a nightmare.

Such is the world depicted by the most gifted story-teller of Romanticism — E.T.A. Hoffmann.

"A horrifying cry of anguish in twenty volumes," Heinrich Heine called Hoffmann's works. He was contrasting Novalis with Hoffmann and added,

(Novalis) with his idealistic images is always soaring in the blue empyrean. Hoffman, on the other hand, despite all his bizarre distortions, always clings to earthly realities.[39]

It is this very impingement of reality on horror, and horror on reality, that represents the essence of Hoffmann's half-hallucinatory and half-realistic personal and artistic experience.

Who was this "lively little man," as Heine saw him at the Café Royal in Berlin in the year 1822 (the last year of Hoffmann's life), "his facial muscles in constant play, gesticulating in a droll, even uncanny fashion"? Who was this multi-gifted man whose stories were to fascinate and influence such geniuses as Balzac, Dostoyevski, and Edgar Allen Poe, as well as composers? Who was this man who in the course of his forty-six years of life was musician, composer, conductor, stage-designer, painter, caricaturist, practising jurist — and the egregious story-teller?

Against his personal background — one that even today defies credibility — the wonder of his achievements grows even more startling. He was the child of a broken marriage, restricted within a neurotic household of unbalanced women and relatives. The tenant living above them was the deranged mother of the future playwright Zacharias Werner, who believed herself another Mary, and her son another Christ, and whose shrieks mingled strangely with the chamber music more or less competently performed in the child's household . . .

He became a student of law, and a portion of his life was spent on legal and judicial matters — an activity he detested. His true passion went out to music — his first love. He played a number of instruments, conducted, and composed innumerable works of all kinds, among them the first of the German Romantic operas — *Undine*. Here he was soon to be overshadowed by the greater genius of Carl Maria von Weber. In pursuit of his theatrical, operatic and musical profession he was forced to wander from city to city, now in and now out of a job — subjected like so many of his contemporaries to the vicissitudes imposed by history — and frequently leading an existence bordering on poverty. A critic of fine perception, he fought the battles of Beethoven, Gluck, and Mozart — and against the all-too trivial taste of contemporary audiences. He found himself as a story-teller in 1808, with the publication of *Ritter*

Gluck and thereafter poured out story after story as prolifically as he had music. But his own internal life remained a storm-tossed ocean. Here, Heine has truly remarked concerning one aspect of Hoffmann's life,[40]

Hoffmann...saw only spectres around him... He was a magician who turned human beings into beasts, and these at times into Prussian state-councillors. He could evoke the dead out of their graves, but life itself rejected him like a sorry spook. This he felt; he felt that he had become a spectre himself. All of nature appeared to him like some badly-cut mirror, in which he saw his own death-mask thousand-fold distorted...

What of the other part of him, the part that produced an incredible amount of work — and also made of him an exemplary jurist, winning the approval of his superiors?

Is it any wonder that to solace a wracked soul he resorted to the amenities of the tavern — ever more and more immoderately?

Yet for all this, he preserved an inner integrity of character, a strong liberalism of the mind, and a steady sense of justice. Toward the end of his life he had more than one occasion to prove these in practice. And he had life-long friends, dearly devoted to him and admiring of him, two of whom became his biographers. Not the least of Hoffmann's qualities was his gift of humor and satire. His pictorial caricatures frequently brought on him considerable trouble and unpleasantness, and his outspoken judicial honesty even threats of prosecution.

In few other writers of the time is the conflict between fantasy and reality brought into such sharp focus, or into such glaring juxtaposition. He was particularly tormented by the realization of the hazardous place and role of the artist — in this case the musician — in the changing society of his day. The age of aristocratic patronage was fast going, and Hoffmann saw the precariousness he was facing vis-à-vis the new patrons — the bourgeoisie, with its own particular demands, tastes, and moral codes. In these, the "Philistines," he saw the *bêtes noires* — enemies of light, of culture — worshippers of material gods. But such Philistinism was not restricted to the middle classes. The petty courts of Germany were not immune to it; their rulers and courtiers, their ladies and gentlemen, arrogant and pretentious, appeared little inclined to honor the true artist, or great musical works. They too looked upon the artist with condescension, if not with indulgent contempt. They saw in him the eccentric, the frenzied devotée of some strange ideal and idea, and often thought him something of a madman. Yet, he had to live, to keep body and soul together; hence the constant conflict between the inexorable claims of his art, and the harassing demands of a quotidian existence.

To the Romantic view of the artist as prophet, sage, visionary, Hoffmann opposed the conviction that in fact the artist *was* something of a madman, not in the conventional clinical sense, but in his eccentricities, devout idealism, and obsession with his vocation. These represented threats to the established order — the "prose of the world." For actually the artist's insanity was a higher sort of sanity. His hallucinations, mental aberrations, his personal behavior patterns represented a critical response to a society full of hypocritical pretense, dedicated to and engaged in sordid thoughts and occcupations. In such a world, we are all mad. The difference between the artist and the rest of us, one of Hoffmann's characters explains as follows:

There are certain people, whom nature, or some special destiny, has deprived of a covering envelope under which we others carry on our madness unseen. They are like those thin-skinned insects who give the effect of malformation, since we see the play of their muscular movements. Actually everthing in them conjoins to work normally. What in us remains thought, in them becomes action.[41]

The artist is, according to Hoffmann, one of those "ambiguous" characters who are to haunt not only his pages, but much later those of Thomas Mann. Thus, Frau Councillor at a small ducal court chides the composer, Johannes Kreisler (Hoffmann's alter ego):

You, with your fantastic exultation, with this heart-searing irony will always arouse unrest and confusion — and instill total dissonance in all conventional relations as they now exist.[42]

Obsessions were at the center of Hoffmann's own life, as they were of his literary creations and characters. That such obsessions often verged on insanity none was more aware than he himself. In his own person he often contended with what he believed the inroads of madness. Whether as a result of his immoderate drinking, or mental derangement, he often saw his own "Double," sometimes multiplied. In a number of his stories, obsession takes the form of unquestionable insanity. Thus, in *Mademoiselle Scudéry,* the artist-jeweler Cardillac cannot resist a possessive passion for his precious masterpieces, and reclaims them by murdering his clients. In another tale, that of *Ritter Gluck,* an obsessed musician imagines himself to be the great composer Gluck, and the creator of that genius's masterpeices, which are revealed as blank pages. Another individual is possessed by a driving genius to create the perfect violin. There are other "artists" whose productions never leave their deranged brain. Powers they cannot control seem to move them. Demonic forces reside within them, as they do in the outside world. "Alas, Brother Medardus, thus the Devil walks the earth without cease, and offers human beings his elixirs!"

The "Double" within us and often manifesting himself outside of us will often lead to destruction. Did not Hoffmann himself see his own creations, coming to life as he lay asleep, so that he had to be roused and reassured by his ever-patient wife?

Such a monstrous "Double" is the monk Medardus, in Hoffmann's most celebrated horror-story, *The Devil's Elixirs.* Medardus is tempted to drink of the forbidden potion within a flask possessed by the monastery, with which Satan once tried to tempt Christ. At once, fantastic evil powers are released within him that drive him to commit the most monstrous crimes. At one point he even sees his own "Double" being led to execution — a scene the greatest of French composers, Hector Berlioz, was to remember, when he came to write his *Symphonie Fantastique*.[43]

Dwelling as he did in a world of weird, eerie distortions — he could yet dream also of a fanciful, beautiful no-man's land of realized fantasies and dreams. He created his own Märchen-world — a fairy-tale realm, in which youth might somehow fulfil the wishes a crass, material-ridden universe denies him. Thus, in the story of the *Golden Pot,* the bleak and frequently terrifying every-day reality — the buckram-stiff world of conventions and petty bureaucrats and frozen councillors' law-books and account-books — disappears and is dissolved as portals of magic realms open upon youth, life, and love ... Alas! how different from Hoffmann's true beliefs, or his sad experiences, where his own passion for his beautiful young student Julia Marc was to remain utterly unfilfilled, as an ambitious, worldly, parent placed her on the marriage mart, and auctioned her off to a well-to-do businessman, forever to be lost, but to be resurrected and immortalized in the Julia of Johannes Kreisler's dreams!

Yet, he never lost his sense of humor, often mischievously satiric. Into his masterpiece, *Kater Murr* — *Tomcat Murr* — Hoffmann infused not only his own love-sentiments, but also the best of his humor and his seriousness — comedy and satire, bitterness and laughter. Here the two worlds — the world of the artist — the composer — and the world of quotidian brute interests, whether aristocratic or bourgeois — world and "anti-world" meet. Hoffmann has created his own favorite bestiary. In this instance it is a tomcat and the petty ducal court that stand on one side. They are the world of prose. The world of high imagination, fantasy, and artistic rebellion stands on the other. Tomcat Murr is no ordinary animal. He has pretensions to being a writer, and actually composes both in prose and verse. He is in fact at this moment writing a sort of autobiography, and is using one of his master's books as a source of blotting papers. These get interspersed with Murr's production, and through an oversight appear in the printed volume, along with Murr's own matter. So, side by side, in alternating sections, we have Murr's and Johannes Kreisler's careers.

Tomcat Murr is the bourgeois Philistine, *par excellence*. He knows what is best for him, and how to turn everything to his own greatest advantage. He is the true philosopher of successful self-interest. He is a moralist, too. Having by chance rediscovered his own mother, who is in a bad way and deplorably emaciated, Murr gives way to a phil-maternal impulse, and plans to bring her a left-over herring-head. But alas! on his way to the roof-attic with the tid-bit in his mouth and good intentions in his heart, his evil genius prevails, and he eats it himself! And he reflects thus: "Who can measure the fickleness in the human breast of those who wander by moonlight? Why did not Fate seal up in our hearts the wild play of our passions? Why must we, frail reeds, bow before the storms of life? Oh, unfriendly Destiny! Oh Appetite, thy name is Tomcat! Like another pious Aeneas, I climbed to the roof, with the herring-head in my mouth, and I was about to enter through the attic window. But alas! I fell into a strange state..." In him also two souls strove for mastery, and the true Murr prevailed, and greed triumphed! The Philistine soul had won out!

Johannes Kreisler dwells in another world. Over against him stand the banality, the smugness, the acquisitiveness — unfortunately to be found also in the upper strata of society. Kreisler's presence at the little court of Prince Irenäus, *the papier-mâché* autocrat, introduces a disturbing element. Here he is a tutor — in fact, as actually was the case, a "servant" — who pits his self-respect and pride against those superior in rank, for whom he seems to have little respect. His music sets up extraordinary responses and turmoils in some of his more sympathetic hearers, creates dangerous emotional climates that threaten to annul distinctions of place. Kreisler is a rebel, and his friend tries to explain him to a member of the court:

Kreisler doesn't wear your colors; he does not understand your language; the chair you bid him sit on, so that he may be seated below you, is too small for him, too narrow. You cannot regard him as your equal, and that angers you. He refuses to recognize as eternal the contracts you have established defining the nature of life; indeed, he believes that a vicious sort of vanity, in which you are caught up prevents you from seeing life as it really is ... The spirit of true love resides within him, but how can it warm a heart eternally frozen, in which there never was the spark to stir the flame?[44]

For Kreisler — like every artist, according to Hoffmann, — is an "eccentric" — and,

In a certain sense every eccentric is mad, and seems all the more so, the more zealously he strives to ignite the external, dull, dead life of those around him with his own inner and glowing creations.[45]

Did Kreisler really end up insane? We do not know. Hoffmann never completed the long novel, but it is likely that he did go mad.

Hoffmann, his creator, retained his sanity — though through his excesses he destroyed his body. His wit, his critical faculties grew more pungent with age; his integrity of character remained unshaken. Like Kreisler, he too desired — though he was no political radical — to fire what he called the "cold, motionless prose of life" into a consciousness of itself. Against his will, he was forced, in the days of the severe reaction after 1815, to plunge into the political arena. As a jurist, he was appointed to a commission which was to inquire into the outbreaks of what was being called "demagogy" — the mild expression of discontent and questioning on the part of a few students and writers, mostly directed against the repressive measure of the Carlsbad Resolutions of 1819. A word, a gesture was enough to send the authorities into a fit. Arrests were numerous, and the restrictive activities of the police became so excessive, that Hoffmann was led to protest, and intervene. In doing so he was defying the highest authorities, — even the King of Prussia. Additionally, he expressed himself in print, in one of his brightest and sharpest satires, *Master Flea,* where he caricatured the Minister of Police. The book was confiscated, the questionable passages were expunged by the censor, and Hoffmann himself was subjected to painful interrogations. Had he not been seriously ill at the time, there is little doubt that he would have suffered some major reprisal.

In 1822, the year of Hoffmann's death, Heinrich Heine paid him a lasting tribute. He was commenting on the truly realistic elements to be found in his fantasies — no matter how eerie they might appear on the surface:

Just as the giant Antaeus remained strong and invincible so long as he touched Mother Earth with his feet, and, as soon as Hercules raised him from the ground, forfeited all his vigor, so too the Poet remains strong and mighty as long as he remains on the ground of reality, and is powerless the moment he rapturously soars into the blue air.

And commenting on the assertion that Hoffmann's writings (as well as those of other Romantics) were the products of fever and sickness, Heine contended:

But have we, who are not altogether blessed with good health the right to such observations? And particularly now, when literature seems like one huge hospital? Or, is it possible that Poetry is a human sickness — like the pearl, the sickly matter of which the poor oyster is suffering?[46]

7.

In the tragic chronicle of German romantic genius — image of the disarray no less than the greatness of this era — none can claim greater title to inclusion than the poet Friedrich Hölderlin. In one of his most vivid poetic images, Hölderlin describes the nature and function of the poet: Just as the lightning bolt of Jupiter fructified Semele, so that she gave birth to Bacchus, "the holy one," so it behooves the poet to stand with open heart and hands, bare-headed, to receive the Father's bolt, and offer of his heavenly gift to the people of the land. "Since we are pure," he adds, "the lightning will not sear our hearts."

Of the purity of his heart, and of the devotion to his poetic mission there can be no doubt. But the lightning-bolts, if not of Jupiter, of other less gracious divinities, seared him as they did few others of his contemporaries.

He may be said to have lived two lives and experienced two deaths. One half of that life he lived as a creative — though generally disregarded — poet; the other half was encased in the prison of his ruined mind — his long-enduring insanity.

Like a number of his contemporaries, he was an "outsider." He belonged to none of the Romantic *cénacles,* nor to that other coterie of Olympians, who were centered in Weimar. But he felt himself closest to Friedrich Schiller, and altogether removed from Goethe. Actually he was like some isolated watchtower or lighthouse looking out on far-stretching and tumultuous seas, constantly battered by storms.

He was born in 1770 — the same year as Beethoven, Hegel, and Wordsworth, and died in 1843, thirty-six years or so after his mental breakdown.

His life was connected with the river Neckar, and its enchanting country-side, and the three towns of Lauffen, Nürtingen, and Tübingen. In Lauffen he was born; in Nürtingen his mother soon thereafter settled; and in Tübingen he was educated and there he spent his final years. Only two other cities played an equally memorable role in his life: Frankfurt, where he experienced the ecstasy and tragedy of his love for "Diotima," and Jena — where he was brought close to the Weimar circle and the philosopher Fichte.

He was twice orphaned: in Lauffen, at the age of five, when his father, then overseer of the local monastery, died; in Nürtingen, when he was ten, and lost his stepfather, mayor of that town, to whom he was deeply attached. Destined almost from birth for a theological and clerical career, Hölderlin was entered after a preparatory period at religious schools in the then celebrated theological institute of Tübingen, the "Stift." To his mother it appeared that he would now be on his way to a secured life, since church-offices were state-supported. Few young men were so lucky in their school-mates as Hölderlin was at the "Stift." Among his fellow-students were Schelling and Hegel. It is not hard to imagine what stimulus such an association was to afford him: three minds, alert, active, and already touched by genius.

However, it was not long before serious doubts about his clerical vocation began to assail young Hölderlin. The school and its students were not shut off from the outside world, nor its mighty historic and cultural events. Hölderlin was drawn toward poetry — and his great presiding god was Friedrich Schiller. Very soon he was to make a critical decision. But in the meantime he studied, talked a great deal, argued philosophy and theology, and looked out on the world around him.

In 1789 that world was shaken by a revolution in France. Hölderlin was then nineteen. In the "Stift" — as in the rest of the country — the upheaval in France aroused exultation and horror. Hegel, Schelling, and Hölderlin — among others at the seminary — followed the course of the Revolution with breathless interest and sympathy. What mighty portents these appeared in a world frozen in absolutism, rigidity, and ossified custom! All over the country the young joined in new associations in the name of the Rights of Man. Royal and ducal thrones were shaken — not least that in petty dukedom of Württemberg, a notoriously despotic one. Legend has it that at the Tübingen seminary students celebrated the French Revolution around a "Tree of Liberty." Such celebrations were taking place all over — either publicly or in secret. "Bliss was it in that dawn to be alive," Wordsworth had written. We may be sure that the young theologians gave the event a religious aura, as expansive visions of a new day rose before their enthralled eyes. Hegel too saw a "Kingdom of God" in the offing, and in an early poem, figuratively joined Hölderlin and Schelling in

> A league which no oath ever sealed,
> To live a life of free truth,
> And never to acquiesce in any law
> That fetters mind and feelings . . .[47]

The political fervor of a number of these seminarians knew no bounds. In their student albums and keepsakes they inscribed the names of France's revolutionary heroes, among them even the name of Saint-Just!

Young Hölderlin was not far behind. That which he called the "warning flame of Spirit of the Age" — "die mahnende Flamme des Zeitgeists" — had touched him too. As the idea of becoming a local pastor grew more and more repugnant, (he hesitated to reveal his feelings to his beloved mother for a long time) — all the more the idea of turning poet lured him. But now the "Zeitgeist" spoke of immediate heroic happenings — of revolution, of change, of freedom; and the young poet responded. With characteristic youthful exuberance he now clamors for action, and in his verses he is ready to "break our unhappy lyres, and *do* what the artist dreamt of." His worshipped Rousseau and Schiller are now conjoined in his mind with the revolution in France. Soon, so he hopes, the flames will engulf the German lands and transform them. In 1793 he completed his studies at the seminary, and received the title of "Magister." He had chosen his vocation — that of poet.

He knew he was embarking on a world of uncertainties, abandoning prospects of security, at least for the time being. The alternative choices before him were scanty — a place as some minor goverment official, for which he felt himself unsuited; or that of tutor in some well-to-do or noble family. The latter was a post many young, ambitious, and brilliant scholars were forced to enter on, with hopes of eventual improvement and attainment of such professions as writers, editors, lecturers, and university professors. But being a tutor in some household generally entailed humiliations such as fell to the lot of servants. The "Sturm and Drang" dramatist Reinhold Lenz had already given that occupation its classic formulation in a tragedy, *The Tutor,* which, almost two centuries later, Bertolt Brecht was to adapt in order to describe the character of the German mind.

Yet, as he left Tübingen, Hölderlin was aglow with high hopes and even higher ambitions. He had thrown off the shackles of theology, and he likewise saw the shackles that were binding Germany in despotism falling apart under the impact of revolutionary forces.

> The people slumbered, but Fate
> Saw to it that they not fall
> Into a deep sleep, and so there arose
> The implacable, the fearful son
> Of Nature, the ancient Spirit of Unrest.
> He moved like fire that in the heart of the Earth
> Seethes, shaking the ripening pear-tree,
> And the ancient cities; tearing the mountains,
> And hurling oak-trees and rocks from their heights...[48]

He was not afraid of "destruction," for, as he put it, "aus der Zerstörung wird der Lenz geboren" — "from destruction rises the new Spring."[49] Nor was he timid as he foretold "a Fatherland reclaimed from the hands of robbers," by whom he meant the local German princelings.[50]

His outbursts knew no bounds. He saw the superstition of "Infinity," by which he meant the seemingly infinite powers of tyranny, dispersed by "Finitude," and he adjured his fellow-Germans,

> Brothers, will the hour tarry?
> Brothers, mindful of the thousand slaves,
> Of our grandsons born to shame,
> Of the hopes our monarchs cherish,
> Of the goods our soul can joy in,
> Of the gods' ancestral might,
> Brothers, for the sake of Love,
> Kings of Finitude, awake![51]

As he was about to enter on his first tutorship in the household of Frau Charlotte von Kalb in the summer of 1793, he wrote to his brother:

My concern now is not the individual human being, but mankind itself. I love the generation of the coming century. For this is my profoundest hope, the belief which upholds me and keeps me active: that our grandchildren will be better than we, that Freedom will at last have arrived, and virtue more easily prosper in Freedom's holy light than in the frosty zones of despotism. We are living at a time when everything is working toward a better day... Dear, dear brother! that goal — culture, the improvement of mankind... that goal, I know, is alive within you too...[52]

Charlotte von Kalb — a friend of Friedrich Schiller — was a remarkable woman in an age of remarkable women — a brilliant intellect, and she was generously concerned to advance young Hölderlin's career. This relationship brought him close to the intellectual leaders of Jena and Weimar. Unfortunately, his young charge proved to be an intractable pupil, and Hölderlin's first venture was a failure. Despite this, Frau von Kalb did not abate her solicitude for the young poet.

At Jena, Hölderlin attended the brilliant, frequently inflammatory, lectures of Fichte, then still in his radical phase. The university itself was one of the more turbulent ones, and some of its student associations extremely militant. With such an advocate as Frau von Kalb, Hölderlin found easy access to Schiller, who was soon to publish a fragment of the young poet's *Hyperion* in the influential journal, *Thalia.* The presence of greatness around him — one thinks of Goethe, Schiller, Wilhelm von Humboldt, and Fichte, among others — did not overwhelm Hölderlin. His critical as well as his poetic faculties ripened quickly. He deepened his knowledge of Greek letters, history, and culture, but even here he was not swept into the neo-Hellenic cult that now, after Goethe's return from Italy, was rapidly becoming a "tyranny." Greek enthusiast that he was, he had his own views of the meaning of the Greek ideal for the modern world, as he was soon to show in his *Hyperion* and the fragments of his *Empedocles* drama. For a moment he toyed with the idea of a possible lectureship or professorship in Greek subjects, in order to escape the slavery of tutoring. He was greatly heartened in seeing his work appearing in journals, and was looking forward — with Schiller's help — to having a book published by the eminent firm of Cotta. But the prospects of emancipation proved illusory...

Personally, Hölderlin was unusually attractive (one of his friends spoke of hims as a young "Apollo"); he was a loving and loveable person — a fact attested by his life-long friendships. A select few truly understood, admired and valued his blossoming genius, and foresaw greatness for him. It was one such admirer who proposed him as tutor in the household of the Frankfurt family of the Gontards, thus, unwittingly, setting the stage for one of the most critical, turbulent, ecstatic and tragic moments in the lives of two beings. Friedrich Hölderlin, who entered upon his new duties early in 1796, was not aware that the published fragment of his *Hyperion* was already in the hands of Susette Gontard, the young wife of his future employer. A woman of great beauty, intelligence, and sensitiveness, a lover of music and poetry, she was two years older than the tutor, and the mother of four children. At the age of seventeen she had entered upon the then customary marriage of convenience with the rich merchant Gontard, a marriage, in which, at least on her part, love had played a small role. The interests of husband and wife differed widely, and it was almost inevitable that she and Hölderlin were soon to be drawn together in mutual sympathies. They were both musical; Susette played the piano, and he the flute; they both loved poetry, and they fell in love. The boy whom he was to tutor became deeply attached to him. Thus was created a circle sharply defined, and in its atmosphere sharply contrasting with that prevailing in the household, its master and friends. For the rich and well-satisfied bourgeois the tutor was but another servant. Fortunately, the warmth and understanding of that inner circle compensated for the humiliations the thin-skinned poet felt all too deeply — the feeling, as he put it, of being a "fifth wheel" of that resplendent social equipage; like servants, a necessary evil. The woman whom he was to immortalize as "Diotima" — the wise instructress of Socrates — saved him from despair, gave him new life, intensified his sense of a poetic vocation, and marked out a new era and a new universe for him. She came to symbolize not only the grandeur of love, but the sympathies of Nature and the world at large, and helped him to integrate and synthesize his poetical and cultural *Weltanschauung*.

If he idealized her, there was in her a great deal worthy of idealization — a solidity of intellectual and moral conviction, and a dedication. In Hölderlin she had at last found someone who understood her and her needs, and to whom she could give all the depth of an affection hitherto untapped and denied her, and receive in turn one equally boundless. She was frankness herself, as her marvelously beautiful letters to him written after their separation testify — with their integrity and inner wholeness. Her presence relieved what he called the "smart of servitude." A few months after assuming his post, he wrote to his friend, Neuffer:

There is one Being in this world with whom my spirit can and will dwell for thousands of years, and see how school-boyish all our thinking and understanding must appear when confronted with Nature. Charm and loftiness, serenity and life, spirit and feeling, and form, make for a transcendent unity in this Being. You may well believe me when I say that only rarely can such a Being even be imagined, and hardly ever found in this world. You know the state of mind I was in, how repugnant all common objects had become. You know how I lived without faith, how niggardly I had become with my feelings, how wretched I felt. Could I have become as I am now, joyful like an eagle, if this *One* Being had not appeared, strengthened, rejoiced and glorified me with her luminous Spring? It is impossible to think of her in mortal terms...I can write no more.[53]

All that she meant to him, both at the time and later, he embodied in his poems, as for example, in "Diotima."

> Come now, Rapture of Heavenly Muse! Allay for me,
> You who once reconciled elements, the Chaos of this Age!
> Assuage the raging battle with Heaven's music of peace,
> Until in the mortal heart that which is severed unites;
> Until the pristine nature of Man, serenely grand and noble,
> Rises mighty and calm from out this seething age.
> Return to the needy hearts of the people, oh living Beauty,
> Return to the hospitable board, return to the temples.
> For Diotima lives like the tender flower in winter,
> Rich in her innate spirit, she too seeks the sun.
> But the sun of the spirit, the lovelier world has gone down,
> And in the frosty night only hurricanes war.

As the bond between Hölderlin and Susette became closer and closer, the unresolvable situation moved toward catastrophe. He was forced to leave the Gontard establishment, and both he and Susette were broken-hearted, and spiritually undone. The lovers were obliged to resort to momentary secret meetings, during which they had barely time to exchange letters. Hers have fortunately survived — his — except for a few fragments — were destroyed. It is not too much to say that so far as Susette was concerned, her life ended in the autumn of 1796, though she lived on for six more years. He too was shattered. And once more he was adrift. Isaak von Sinclair, his closest friend and supporter, sheltered him in nearby Homburg for a while. Then the wandering recommenced. He was tutor again — now in Switzerland, and finally in Bordeaux. From this French city he returned to Germany in 1802, mentally broken. Thereafter, until the complete breakdown in 1806, there was intermittent subsidence of insanity, when he could still compose poems and translations from the Greek.

Those eight years, from 1796 to 1804, were the years of his most fruitful creation — the realization of the self-conscious and self-assertive poetic genius. Here, the role of his "Diotima" cannot be underestimated. He completed *Hyperion*, numerous poems — among them some of his greatest. Her presence is evident in the fragments of the drama, *Empedocles*. "Diotima" came to represent his maturest view of the Hellenic past. She was *the* harmony — the living harmony — that Hellas had once embodied and the earnest of that harmony still to be born when the true nature of the Greek spirit would once more be truthfully and clearly revealed and absorbed — a Greece not of buried monuments and rediscovered sculptures, the past of antiquarians. It was a past that spoke to the present and the future — destined, he hoped, to shape them. It was a past that embodied the concept of human freedom, as well as of a liberated and resuscitated Greek nation. In that way Greece was to stand as symbol for all of Europe, even of the world — an activating force in the creation of a new human harmony.

Ironically too, it must be remembered that these ideas were cast during a time when little enough of harmony prevailed in the European world — a world of almost unintermittent warfare, here and there punctuated by a truce or peace, in which, at any moment — as actually happened — one was forced to shift one's living quarters and goods at the approach of enemy forces. Amidst these hectic movements, Hölderlin remained the close observer of contemporary history. Despite the shocks caused by the Terror in France, he still looked to that nation to bring political and social salvation to the rest of the world. The Gontard family and its tutor were on a flight to Cassel in 1796, and Hölderlin wrote to his brother:

You, dear brother, cannot but feel strengthened in spirit by the proximity
of so staggering a drama as is presented by the giant steps of the
Republicans. It is certainly easier to hear of the Greek thunder-clubs that
thousands of years ago hurled the Persians from Attica across the
Hellespont down to barbarous Susa, than such an implacable thunderstorm
passing over one's own house...[54]

He still looked to the German states — and particularly to his
own small Duchy of Württemberg — to rise up against their own
oppressors. There is an early version of a poem, "Die Schlacht,"
—"The Battle" — which critics have called his "Marseillaise," and
in which he expressed this sentiment:

> Oh Battle for the Fatherland!
> Flaming glow of early dawn!
> At last the German wakens with the sun,
> Young with victorious life...
>
> No longer a child, he,
> For those miscalling themselves Fathers
> Are thieves who have ravished the infant from his cradle,
> And betrayed his innocent heart,
> And turned him into a household beast of burden...[55]

The two larger works of this period between 1796 and 1800,
Hyperion and *Empedocles,* are both political testaments. *Hyperion,*
a prose-poetical novel in letter-form, was conceived before his
meeting with Susette Gontard, but it acquired its fully rounded
character under her influence. Its two volumes were published 1797
and 1799 respectively. The scenes of the *Empedocles* drama — all
fragments — were not published during Hölderlin's lifetime. It is
likely that the first version of what is called *The Death of
Empedocles* might have been deemed too radical for publication at
the moment. Though both works have Greece as their background,
they point directly or indirectly at contemporary Germany. In both,
the language — whether of prose or poetry — is highly charged; and
in both cases, whether through the lips of the modern Greek youth
Hyperion, or the ancient Graeco-Sicilian sage Empedocles, it is
Hölderlin who is speaking.

Hyperion is not just another Werther. If he is, like Goethe's hero, at odds with himself and the world, he is also at odds with his country, aghast at its infantilism and its "incurable corruption." But Hyperion is also inspired by the certainty that there is divinity in mankind — the "God within us" — and by trust in a world-sustaining harmony, evidences of which he has already discovered in the life, polity, and art of the ancient Greeks. He meets the Greek maiden Diotima, and in her presence and in her person he is given an actual embodiment of his vision: the reality of harmony and beauty. He longs for action. The outbreak of the Russo-Turkish war of 1770 fills him with new hope — the liberation of Greece. Now, he believes, is the moment that promises to restore what he calls "the sacred theocracy of the beautiful within a free state." He will be one of the agents of that restoration. He takes leave of Diotima, and becomes the leader of a band of patriots, and in the first days of the war, is able to obtain three victories against the Turks. But very soon he becomes disenchanted, when his followers, instead of living up to their alleged high purposes, turn to plunder and worse, and are soon scattered to the four winds. Yet, not utterly despairing, Hyperion joins the Russian forces and is wounded in an engagement. On his sick-bed he renounces all further participation in the conflict. He will go away with Diotima, but she, in his absence, has pined away and died. In search of peace and renewed strength, Hyperion undertakes a journey to the European continent, and comes to Germany. Here, he is appalled by what he observes. In a letter to his friend Bellarmin he writes:

And so, I arrived among the Germans . . . Barbarians from times immemorial, whom industry and science, and even religion have made yet more barbarous, profoundly incapable of any divine emotion, vitiated to the marrow for the delight of the holy Graces . . . I can think of no people more self-divided than the Germans. You see artisans, but no people; thinkers, but no people; priests, but no people . . . Isn't this like a battle-field where hacked-off hands and arms and other limbs lie in pieces on top of each other, while the spilled life's blood oozes into the sand? . . . [56]

Such is Germany, a land in which poets and artists live like strangers in their own house; like Ulysses, who sat at his door in the garb of a beggar, while the brazen suitors within asked, "Who has sent us this vagabond?"

Such were Hölderlin's sentiments as he looked around him. He was not writing *in vacuo,* or out of some excess of gall. This was the moment of Prussia's and Austria's defeats and humiliations at the hands of the French, the time of the Congress of Rastatt, meeting between 1797 and 1799 — an interval of comparative peace-making. Hölderlin's friend, Isaak von Sinclair, a minor official at the court of Hesse-Homburg, politically a radical strongly inoculated with French revolutionary ideas and hopeful of seeing a democratic government established in the Rhenish provinces, had taken Hölderlin along to Rastatt to witness the political drama taking place there. What they saw was a cock-pit — German fighting German, greedy to redistribute possessions each to his own advantage, intent on robbing the weaker neighbor, or appropriating this or that ecclesiastical property. This was indeed a travesty of the Holy Roman Empire in all its inglorious death-throes.

Hyperion has before him the dark reality of the present, and he would have lapsed into absolute despair were it not for the ideal he envisions and hopes would be soon realized — irradiated by the Greece of the past — the full flowering of total man and total woman. Ancient Hellas, in Hölderlin's eyes, stood for Freedom; though like so many others he tends to forget that it was a polity built upon slave labor.

The human being is a god as soon as he attains humanity. And being a god — he is beautiful...Religion is the love of beauty...It is out of this beauty of mind and spirit that inevitably was born the spirit of freedom.[57]

Hölderlin's Hellenic worship was not a retrogade dream of the restoration of a lost antiquity, but a dream of a future in which Hellenism becomes a symbol — an indispensable element in the

creation of a new world. So that even in the darkness of the present
— one of chaos, destruction, the appalling poverty of spirit among
Germans — he is able to build his new palace of hope:

The darling of Time, the youngest, fairest daughter of Time, the New
Church will arise out of these defiled, antiquated forms, when the awakened
sense of the divine brings to man his divinity, and to his heart its beautiful
youth once more. When — I cannot foretell, for I can barely surmise it; but
that it will come — of that I am sure — very sure. Death is a messenger of
Life, and that we now lie asleep in our infirmaries proves that we shall soon
awaken to health. Then, only then, shall we BE; then will the spirit's true
elements have been found!...[58]

For him the essence of life was conflict. Opposition, he held,
was good for the Spirit — as he states in one of his very beautiful
images: "The heart's surge would not foam up so beautifully, and
become Spirit, did not the ancient, mute cliff of Fate stand opposing
it." Like William Blake and Hegel he recognized the immanent
presence of "contraries." In 1797 he wrote to a despairing friend,
who had returned from France crushed by the post-revolutionary
events:

I have one source of consolation, in that every ferment and dissolution
necessarily leads either toward destruction or to fresh organization. There
is no such thing as destruction *per se*. One may safely assert that our world
today never looked so variegated as now. It is a variety of contradictions and
contrasts of the old and the new; malignity and passion; egoism in sheep's
skin; egoism in wolf's skin; superstition and unbelief... I believe in a future
revolution of convictions and ideas which will put to shame all that has been.[59]

So Hyperion too reflects that the "dissonances of the world"
are like lovers' quarrels. "Reconciliation is in the midst of strife, and
all that is parted finds one another again."

It is out of this feeling of constant destruction and renewal that
the drama on the subject of Empedocles took shape between 1797
and 1800. The figure of and the traditions surrounding the
pre-Socratic Graeco-Sicilian philosopher of the fifth century B.C.

must have proved particularly attractive to our poet at this time, both
from a philosophical as well as political point of view. Here was an
almost legendary thinker reputed to have been not only a poet and
philosopher, but also a highly creative physician and natural scientist,
endowed with almost superhuman wisdom and knowledge. Empedocles
was a descendant of a noble family that was renowned for its
democratic views — which Empedocles himself shared. Legend
attributed to him a sort of divinity, and surrounded his death with a
preter-natural aura: he was believed to have cast himself into the
mouth of Aetna to prove his god-like nature. Having aroused the
disfavor of the authorities and the populace by his radical utterances,
he was said to have suffered exile. What remains of his philosophical
and scientific fragments must have proved fruitful to Hölderlin,
especially, Empedocles's notion that Nature was the theater of
incessant warfare between two "divinities," Love and Discord —
manifested in all her domains, plant, animal and human. So far as
present history was concerned, the town of Agrigentum could easily
stand for Germany, and Empedocles himself as a symbolic figure, a
Spirit — or as Hölderlin puts it — "the appointed one, who kills and
reanimates, in whom and through whom a world dissolves and
renews itself. Man, too, feeling so fatally the decline of his country,
could at the same time anticipate a new life."[60]

The planned drama was never brought to completion. There are
fragmentary scenes of various versions, which in the course of
composition reflect the poet's changing moods. The earlier portions
glow with the prospects of an overturn of the ruling powers —
particularly in the Duchy of Württemberg, where his close friend,
von Sinclair, was a prime agitator for reform. At this stage
Empedocles stands for rebellion. In the first of the fragments, *The
Death of Empedocles,* the philosopher is accused by the religious and
secular authorities of Agrigentum of stirring up the populace against
law, custom, religion and the state. The Archon, magistrate of the
city, describes the pernicious influences exercised by Empedocles:

> Like to him, the people are drunk,
> They heed neither law, nor urgent tasks,
> Nor judges. Customs are overthrown,
> Like once powerful shores by some warring
> And incomprehensible tide.
> The days are turned into wild festivals . . .[61]

The Priest is no less rabid against this Promethean, who like other seers and light-bringers deem themselves favorites of the gods because they have glimpsed immortality and now presume to bring their visions to the people. They undermine the foundations of society, and force the priesthood to severe countermeasures:

> Hence we bind up the eyes of men
> That not too gladly they feed on light,
> For never must that which is divine
> Be present to their eyes . . .[62]

Empedocles is anti-royalist. When the citizens offer him the crown, he not only declines the honor, but reproves them:

> No longer is this the time of Kings . . .
> Shame be yours
> That you still yearn for Kings.
> You are too old for that.
> In your fathers' time
> It would have been a different thing . . .
> Nothing will help you now unless you
>   help yourselves.
> You have offered me a crown,
> Take instead the holiest that is within me . . .

Implored to give them counsel, Empedocles urges them to break with the past:

> Long have you thirsted for the unwonted;
> As from a sickened body the spirit
> Of Agrigentum longs to leave the ancient ways.
> Dare! Dare do it! That which you have gotten,
>   inherited,

Learned from your fathers' lips —
Of Law handed down, and ancient Custom,
And all the names of gods of yore,
Boldly forget! And like to new-born babes,
Rise up and turn your eyes to godly Nature . . .
When in your hearts you yearn for deeds,
And for your own fair world, then join hands,
Once more, and speak the Word:
Divide the wealth you own, and share
      beloved ones,
Both deeds and glory — like true Dioscuri.
Let each of you be like the others . . .
Then, oh then, ye Genii, habitants of ever-
      changing Nature,
Then, cheerful spirits, will a people free
Call you to festive boards — hospitable and pious;
For lovingly do mortals give of their best,
Once their souls are freed of slavery's chain . . . [63]

Empedocles traces for them the "great lines of the Future" — a life proceeding "in its irresistible course of fulfilment" toward a new world. The primal days of a new restoration — which Hölderlin calls the "days of Saturn" — will come back, and with them universal peace. Then, Empedocles adds, will it be time to think of the past and return to the tales of the forefathers . . .

Hölderlin was not the only one of the Germans hopeful of a radical change in the political and social life of the country. The philosopher Fichte, writing in May 1799, also looked to the French to bring about radical reforms:

I am as certain as I can be that if the French do not achieve overwhelming power in Germany, at least in a significant section thereof, and bring about a change — within a few years no person known to have entertained liberal thoughts will be safe. [64]

Such hopes were soon to be shattered. The ascendancy of Napoleon Bonaparte through the *coup-d'état* of November 1799, the outbreak of new wars, the reluctance of French generals to encourage revolutionary agitation in the German provinces sounded the tocsin of the French Revolution. Isaak von Sinclair and a number of his coadjutors were soon to suffer severe persecution.

For Hölderlin, too, these events brought their share of distresses. He was foot-loose again — once more the reluctant tutor, and a wanderer. Between January and April 1801 he was in Switzerland; between January and June 1802 he was in Bordeaux, France, whence he returned to Germany in a terrifying state of emotional and mental disarray. The intervening years had been among his most creative ones; and even the harrowing interim between 1802 and 1804 was not without sufficient remissions, allowing for a considerable body of extraordinary poetry. Susette Gontard died in 1802. Her passionately confessed love had undoubtedly been the generative element in his maturation, and the cement that held him together, despite all the pains of physical separation. To what extent her death was to prove a critical element in his ultimate mental disintegration is of course a matter of speculation. That it was such an element — perhaps the chiefest among all others — cannot be doubted ... Anyway, after the separation, he was resolved, "Leben will ich denn auch!" — "Yes, I too will live!" — for "he who has thus loved, follows, must follow the path to the Gods." Such was his conclusion to the poem, written around 1800, "Menon's Lament for Diotima."

He would live and create, though he would never forget. True to his innermost principle — disintegration and integration — he strove at this turning-point to reorder his personal life as well as his thinking, to find a way of again synthesizing his existence and his *Weltanschauung*. Shaken — if not shattered — he voices his doubts and uncertainties in the last fragments of *Empedocles,* in which the philosopher now passes judgment on himself. Was it Hölderlin himself speaking? The Greek thinker condemns himself as a "sinner" against man and God; in his self-proclaimed arrogance of near-godhood, he believes he has never truly "loved" mankind. It is time for him to go. He is living in an age of dissolution, and in an hour of the "departing God of his people." He is the vessel of the passing of the Old, and of the old Gods.

> Where a land must die out, Spirit chooses
> One man at the end, whose swan-song
> Intones the last of life.[65]

As the prospects for immediate radical changes in Germany faded, Hölderlin sought for a new synthesis. It was, in fact, a strange, striking and a daring one. He created a metaphysical Utopia to replace the more earthly one that he once hoped would arise under the influence of the French. His eyes now turn toward Germany, though he is under no illusions about her present state or her readiness to create a new order. Nevertheless, he trusts to the future. German topography now takes a prominent place in his Hymns and Odes — among the richest creations of the last period of his mental health. These and other elements are now integrated into his new Utopia, which we may with justice call "the return of the gods."

Unlike Schiller's Greek gods, who have departed never to come back again, Hölderlin's have retreated to the upper regions, *but they will return*. They will reappear when Germany sheds her pettiness, apathy, her blindness, her preoccupation with a self-centered, sordid, meaningless existence — when she recognizes that her true destiny is that of becoming an "unarmed" leader of Europe's regeneration.

> But alas! our generation wanders in darkness,
> Dwelling forever in Orcus — strangers to things divine;
> Chained to their own crafts, and in the roaring workshops
> Each hears only himself, and without cease and painfully
> The savages toil with mighty arms, but ever and ever
> Unfruitful, like the Furies, remains the labor of the poor . . .[66]

And, addressing his Fatherland, Hölderlin cries out in anguish,

> Wo ist dein Delos, wo dein Olympia?

> Where is thy Delos, where thy Olympia
> That we may all join in the supreme feast?[67]

The gods have withdrawn from us because we are unworthy of their presence. In the empyrean where they abide, they await the reformation that must come from within us. These are Greek gods, but how different from the all-powerful, all self-sufficient, indifferent gods of myth, history and tradition! For all their immortality and inviolability they are lonesome beings, for they need humanity to complete them. They need human beings endowed with feelings, who suffer and rejoice.

> Their own immortality suffices for the Gods,
> And if the Heavenly Ones lack any thing
> It is heroes and human beings
> And mortals.
> For since the Immortals feel nothing in
>   themselves,
> Another, if such things may be uttered,
> Must sympathize and feel in their stead.[68]

Humanity is central to Hölderlin's thinking. The gods need mankind just as much as mankind needs gods. The new Utopia Hölderlin presupposes is one of reconcilement of all elements in nature and man — and that reconcilement also postulates one of Christianity and Paganism. With amazing daring Hölderlin now integrates Christianity and the Hellenic pantheon. Christ is "brother of Heracles," and symbolically also brother of all the Greek gods and goddesses. He is brother of Bacchus no less than Apollo. An amazing new theodicy now emerges, startlingly proclaimed in one of his sublime poems, "Bread and Wine". The instruments of the Christian Mass are joined with those of paganism in a universal sacrament, as Christ is joined to Bacchus and Apollo, god of the sun.

> Brot is der Erde Frucht, doch ists vom
>   Lichte gesegnet...

> Bread is the fruit of the earth, but it is blessed
>   by Light,
> And from the thundering God comes the
>   gladness of wine;

> Hence they make us think of the heavenly
>   ones, who once
> Were here and will come back in seemly
>   times.
> That is why we hymn the wine-god in earnest,
> And not light-mindedly conceived are the
>   ancient's praises sung...[69]

Christ is the embodied annunciation of the imminent Coming of the Great Reconciler — the over-all god of gods — pagan and Christian. (Hölderlin sometimes speaks of him as "Father Aether.")

> But meantime comes as torchbearer the Son
> Of the Highest, the Syrian, down among
>   the shadows,
> The blessed wise men see it; a smile from
>   the imprisoned
> Soul lights up, thawing the eye with light.
> In the arms of the earth, more gently the
>   Titan sleeps and dreams,
> And even the envious one, Cerberus, drinks
>   and sleeps.[70]

This is the proclaimer of the ultimate brotherhood — of the ethereal *Agapé* — the holy feast and revelry that will celebrate the union of humanity in the presence of Bacchus, Venus, Heracles, Apollo, Saturn; in the presence too of Christ, and — let us add, according to Hölderlin — of the Madonna! Spirit and Nature live side by side — for Hölderlin was not at one with the transcendentalists that subsumed all existence under Spirit. He loved Nature, and natural objects — just as he loved mankind. Hence he spoke of the poet's vocation:

> Are you not kin to all the living?
> Does not Fate herself nourish you to serve? ...
> We, the people's poets, gladly wander
> Where life breathes around us and seethes,
> Joyful and gracious to all —
> Trusting all. Else, how could we sing
> To them the God who is their own?[71]

Alas! neither within him nor without were the dissonances to be resolved ... He was thirty-six years old when his inner light was quenched. Then came the darkness, now and then penetrated by a moment's lucidity: — in a few touching poems, among them an only poetic reminiscence of his Diotima; in a few letters. In 1806 he was declared incurable, and thereafter lived in Tübingen, overlooking his beloved Neckar, tended by the carpenter Zimmer and his wife, to both of whom posterity owes a monument for their devotion. He was visited now and then by fellow-poets and friends, whose record of these visits is heart-rending. The schizophrenic poet now signs his work with the name of "Scardanelli," and bows formally to his visitors, addressing them with nobiliar titles. Devoted admirers began to collect his poems, and soon were to publish a first collection. But he himself is of another world, now and then lighting up, as when he hears that Greece is again astir. He might have been writing about himself in anticipation, when he celebrates Ganymede,

> Spring comes. And every thing in its way
> Flowers. But he is far away — no longer here.
> He has lost his way: For the Genii are kindly,
> Only with the heavenly ones does he now
>   commune...[72]

"Sunt lacrimae rerum," Virgil once wrote. "There are tears for misfortune." But for such a misfortune and such a sight as the poet presented in those long years there are feelings that are "too deep for tears."

8.

Music ... is the most Romantic of all the arts — one might even say it is the only genuinely Romantic art, for its subject is the Eternal. It was Orpheus's lyre which opened the gates of Orcus. Music unfolds before man a new, unknown kingdom, a world which has nothing in common with the world of sensuous reality around us, and in which we leave behind all precise emotions in order to surrender ourselves to an ineffable yearning ... Beethoven's music moves the levers that open the floodgates of fear, of terror, of horror, of pain and arouses that longing for the eternal which is the essence of Romanticism. He is thus a pure Romantic composer.

Thus E.T.A. Hoffmann.[73] In music German Romanticism finds its most perfect fulfilment, Here it achieved world preeminence. Despite fluctuations in other realms of culture, political and social upheavals, the dominance of German Romantic music persisted throughout the century. The power of Romanticism might slacken, become enfeebled in other spheres, and even seem to have totally died out — but for Germany, Romanticism was to persist in its most powerful embodiment — music.

For the Romantic, music came to represent the very essence of Romanticism. It was a fulfilment of that irrepressible search for "transcendence" — a quest for the resolution of the dichotomies between the limited ego and Infinity — for liberation from the burdens of quotidian existence. In the undefinable language of music, the German Romantic imagined he could finally achieve an ideal "Weltflucht" — an escape from the world. In music, limitations were shattered, and another world was restored. The symphony, the string quartet, the lyric Lied, even the opera, these were gateways into those mysteries of the world and of nature denied to science, reason, or mere worldly experience. Music opened the portals of salvation and became "eine Erlösungsreligion." Music assuaged the longing for Infinity — the "Unendlichkeitssehnsucht." For Heinrich von Kleist — to cite one example — music represented the algebraic formula for all the arts, and he hoped to find in counterpoint the most important revelations as to the very nature and essence of Poetry.[74]

But it was left to Arthur Schopenhauer — a contemporary of Hoffmann and Beethoven, neglected in his own day — to establish music as the supreme art, integrate it into his metaphysic, and finally make it into a fundamental part of German ideology and the German "collective consciousness." In no other country was music to play such a vital role in the life and thought of a people. Schopenhauer's ideas were to achieve musical body in Richard Wagner and his tonal "metaphysic." The arc that encompasses Beethoven at one point, and Wagner at another, describes not only a polarity of two musical geniuses, but may be said, symbolically, and practically, to typify the history of Germany from Napoleon to Bismarck, from the French Revolution to the triumphs of Prussian imperialism. In music, the course might be said to run from the affirmative heroism of Beethoven's *Fidelio* to the mortuary dusks of Siegfried and the *Götterdämmerung* . . .

German philosophers of the transcendental school had sought to enshrine "Reason" or "Idea" as the Absolute, and Nature and the human consciousness as parts of a universal rational process tending toward the Ideal. For Schopenhauer, on the contrary, it is the Irrational or the A-rational that is the motive power in man and nature. He names it the "Will," a transcendent force that permeates the universe, manifesting itself in the drives and conflicts of human life as tragic potencies inevitably leading to defeats. Mistaking themselves as free agents, human beings ignorantly engage in this warfare, without recognizing that they are merely acting out the urgencies of a completely indifferent fatality. Only to the artist and the philosopher is it given to understand what it is that is at work, and to rise above such conflicts, and withdraw into a Nirvana — the realm of contemplation and compassion. Art is a means as well as an expression of such withdrawal — and, of all the arts, it is music that comes closest to the Absolute. For music is the art most free of particularities and material dependence such as other arts are subject to. The latter need words, or clay, or the outside world. Music needs none of them. Here, and here only, the individual attains "freedom" — a partial freedom, it must be admitted — but freedom none the less from the particularities of life itself. Here he participates not in any individual sorrow, terror, and ecstasy, but becomes immersed in "universality" — universal Sorrow, Terror, Ecstasy. He becomes self-less; his individuality has disappeared. Here he has come closest to understanding the nature of the "Will" — or the universal Life-Process. As another philosopher phrased it,

In the aesthetic liberation from Being — i.e., from suffering which Art achieves in those moments of aesthetic enjoyment, we are like the slave who forgets his chains, or like the warrior no longer in the presence of his overpowering opponent, not because he has overcome him, but becaue he has fled from him, and in the next moment may be overtaken by him.[75]

We have become detached from the world. True, such a detachment is only temporary, for we are soon drawn back into the clutches of the "Will," and are — in Schopenhauer's words — merely keeping "the Sabbath of penal servitude of willing." But ineffable revelations are opened for us — timeless and infinite, such as no other art can offer. We are no longer concerned with Action, but with Contemplation — with "will-less perception." Thus, with its "universal language of the heart," which, in Hoffmann's words, is likened to "the language of angels," music is deemed to proffer a kind of knowledge of the mysteries of the world unapprehensible by other more mundane means.

One need not labor the point as to the validity of such thinking, or the fact that music was a special experience offering satisfactions, sensuous and emotional, differing in kind from those insights into the nature of the universe offered by reason, experiment and scientific investigation. For the Romantics and their successors music was an experience that corresponded to the needs and the temper of the times, offering an escape from the physical and moral havoc, as well as the disappointments and disenchantments following the collapse of Utopian revolutionary hopes and the subsequent Napoleonic failure to fulfil democratic aspirations. No less bitter was the awakening of Germans from the intoxication of the war of "Liberation" into the desolating dawn of the Restoration. One need only instance Hölderlin, Fichte, Hegel — among many others — as exemplars of such disenchantments.

And Beethoven himself was no exception. He too had shared in the veneration for Napoleon — the hero that had broken European feudalism, and whose Code seemed like a beacon light for the future of Germany. But Napoleon had had himself crowned Emperor, and had even, in 1802, signed a Concordat with the Pope. When a publisher approached Beethoven with the idea of composing a sonata in honor of Napoleon and Revolution, the composer was enraged.

Has the devil got hold of you all, Gentlemen, he wrote, that you should suggest that I should compose such a sonata. Well, perhaps at the time of the Revolutionary fever — such a thing might have been possible, but now, when everything is trying to slip back into the old rut, now that Bonaparte has concluded his Condordat with the Pope — to write a sonata of that kind...By good Heavens, such a sonata — in these newly developing Christian times — Ho ho — there you must leave me out — you won't get anything from me...[76]

It is a mark of E.T.A. Hoffmann's critical perceptions that he set Ludwig van Beethoven at the center of Romanticism and as the very apogee of that movement. Romanticism had, from Friedrich Schlegel on, aspired to a Titanism — but had achieved it — if at all — in intention rather than fulfilment. But here, in Beethoven, it seemed Romanticism had actually found its fulfilment — here was a "heroic" Titanism concretely embodying itself in works that could well challenge that of other titans of the age — like Goethe and Napoleon. Napoleon's heroism might now appear tarnished, but Beethoven's belief in heroism was to remain unshaken. His *Eroica* symphony might not bear the name of Napoleon in its final dedication, but the work remains, none the less, a personal testament to tragic heroism — registering defiance, sorrow, hope; his overtures (really anticipants of the symphonic poems of later composers) remain paeans to heroic humanism — in man and woman; and, not least, *Fidelio,* the opera and its various overtures, triumphant exaltations of heroic womanhood and jubilation at the defeat of tyranny. Such too the affirmative Credo that resounds through the Ninth Symphony — a mighty choral, vocal, and symphonic celebration of the power of Joy as an instrument in forging human brotherhood. All in all — great secular Credos...

This was the "public" Beethoven — speaking to the world in world-embracing ideas. There was the other "I" — the Beethoven who spoke from the inner self, who, in Hoffmann's words, opened "the floodgates of fear, of terror, of pain..."

What would Hoffmann not have given to live long enough to hear the last five quartets of Beethoven! Alas! he died in 1822, three years before Beethoven completed the first of them. Nowhere else is the tragic titanism of the "I" more searingly and triumphantly revealed than in these proclamations of the suffering and defiant Self, struggling mightily to impose order on the chaos of feelings, seeking new ways to express the seemingly unutterable pangs and inner tragedy of his existence, to express the war within himself and with the world, struggling to break through traditional moulds and shape new ones to satisfy the incessant queries within him, and evoke the answers, straining and shaping new complexities to define existence. How to translate the inner agonies already evident in his heart-searing Heiligenstadt Testament — where the loss of hearing seems to him an earnest of approaching death? And yet how to cry out his defiances! How to give voice to the other agonies — those of frustrated love, of loneliness, of bitterness, and at times, of humiliations — and even, finally, of resignation, and then rise up, phoenix-like, from the tumult of internal frenzies to shape chaos into organized wonders! His utterances have been called dialogues — indeed, so they are: great dialogues with himself, with the world at large, and not least with what he believed to be Fate, Necessity, or God. Such is the second movement of the mightiest of his piano concertos — the Fourth; such the "dialogues" of the Ninth Symphony; and, most penetrating, the last quartets, as that in F-major, with its expressed query and answer: "Muss es sein? Es muss sein!" — such, too, the A-minor quartet with its indication in the slow movement of being a "Holy Song of Thanksgiving by a Convalescent to the Divinity, in the Lydian Mode."

What other Romantics strove for — and only partially achieved — Beethoven successfully consummated — the breaking through of older forms, reshaping traditional classical idioms in order fully to express himself, express the violent sweeps of his titanic ego. He created music that seemed to want to transcend itself, to be more than music, to test, challenge to defy the limitations of his medium, and even of his own genius, but also the capabilities of future performers. Four movements no longer suffice to enclose either the quartet or the symphony. The Quartet in C-sharp minor exhibits those "pressures toward discontinuity," and yet turns all to "perfect coherence and profound integration." Here Beethoven uses "six distinct main keys, thirty-one changes of tempo, . . . a variety of textures and a diversity of forms within movements — fugue, suite, recitative, variation, scherzo, aria, and sonata form."[77] The last piano sonatas tax the extreme potentialities of the instrument, and subject seemingly intractable material to sublime cohesion. It is as if Beethoven were saying, "Here I stand. So muss es sein!" A Prometheus striving to contain Infinity . . .

Such is German Romanticism's self-realization in music. In the field of letters — manifold as its achievements — it could never produce a great prose or poetic epic — a great novel to rival that of England or France. Such a creation demands a national and popular cohesiveness, a consciousness of unity, a sense of kinship with the larger world outside its national boundaries, a society expressing new forces at work, and a feeling for principal contemporary intellectual, aesthetic, moral, and political currents. Not that there was any lack of novels, sometimes the work of extremely talented writers. But the scope of their work was narrow, and practically all of them reflected the predominant influence or were imitations of Goethe's *Wilhelm Meister*. France and England, having shaped an altogether different sort of history, had brought forth the modern European novel, or were well on their way. Where there is no encompassing breadth of common endeavor and aspiration, where the population is fragmented, and without a unifying center such as the British and French bourgeoisie possessed — the novel remains a purely parochial creation. Beethoven's Utopianism celebrated the brotherhood of man — but such a brotherhood of interests and feelings was far from present in the atomized German states. As a matter of fact, the German novel was to wait until the mid-century before producing a masterpiece of international stature, and — paradoxically — that was to be the work of a Swiss writer — Gottfried Keller's *Der grüne Heinrich*.

9.

It was in the short-story, the novelette, the fairy-tale, the folk-tale, and, preeminently, in the lyric and the folk-song that German Romanticism could celebrate some of its major successes. And here its prime achievement was the German *Lied* — the fusion of poetry and music. German Romantics proved worthy inheritors of the movement of "rediscovery" of ancient songs, lyrics and ballads, inititiated in England and Scotland in the eighteenth century, and later carried on in Germany by Herder and Arnim and Brentano, the latter two the authors of *Des Knaben Wunderhorn,* a collection of popular poetry (somewhat modernized by them). These proved magical sources of inspiration to original composition by other poets. Folk-song was to play a significant part in movements of national liberation, particularly in Austria, that multi-national state.

Just as E.T.A. Hoffmann tried to define the Romantic view of music and of Beethoven, so Josef von Eichendorff, one of the eminent lyric poets of that era, attempted to characterize the meaning of Lyric and Lied for his contemporaries.

The lyric is of all poetic forms the most subjective; it does not derive from a deed or act performed, as does the epic, and not from the deed or act in the process of performance, as does the drama, but from the special and deeper basis of both: the inner man. The lyric is concerned with mood, and not with the external manifestations of mood. Just as the epic is the poetry of the past, of the saga and traditional heroic legend, so the Lyric is essentially the poetry of the present, for it is directed toward the individual, and as such is therefore restless and changeable as the times. Roused and borne on the waves of the times, an invisible and mysterious Aeolian harp, played upon by ever varying gusts, and capable of a wonderful infinite modulation, the lyric is by its very nature musical, and singable, and its proper organ is the Lied.[78]

The fusion of music and lyric, music and ballad, is another of the prime achievements of German and Austrian Romanticism. Goethe had already provided composers with his

wonderful lyrical and ballad productions, but he was to wait for
Romantic composers (whom he scarcely appreciated) to give them
commensurate musical settings. The Romantic realization of the
Lied, and the popular response to it, once more underlines the
characteristic temper of the times, the "Zeitgeist."

It is enough to name a few of the century's composers who set
the Lied to see to what extent they succeeded in internationalizing
the poetic productions they were setting. Schubert, Schumann,
Brahms, Hugo Wolf, Richard Strauss and Gustav Mahler immediately
come to mind. Of the poets, the world at large knows Heinrich
Heine, but how many — outside Germany — would have recognized
the names of Josef von Eichendorff, or Eduard Mörike — had these
not been transmitted in musical settings?

In the *Lied,* the German "Zeitgeist" finds a most characteristic
expression. Here, when it is at its greatest, the fusion of tone and
word is like the welding together of body and soul — the body, the
word; and the soul, music, into irrefragable totality. It is here that
the German Romantic spirit can feel thoroughly at home. Here it
could contract its insatiable longings for "infinity" within apprehensible
bounds, translate and transmute the small but universal commonplaces
of life into enchanting fantasies, and leave the workaday world
behind. Here, as Eichendorff declared, "Stimmung" — "Mood" —
takes over. Here the homelessness of the spirit can find rest; here
the flight from the world, "Weltflucht," transports the wandering
student, poet, or musician, with his wanderer's staff in hand, into
mysterious regions — for "wandering" is, as Eichendorff remarks, a
grace extended by the Lord God himself to the German soul. There
is the forest where he can enjoy isolation — "Waldeinsamkeit"
— and listen to "das deutsche Waldesrauschen" — "German forest
murmurs." Here he can dream the "eternal dream of the far" — joy
in hearing the hunter's horn, evoke in his mind ancient times with
their castles and their romantic inhabitants. Here he can celebrate
"eternal Sundays" — "den ewigen Sonntag." Here he can indulge
his soul in joyance at love won, or in sorrow at love lost. And not
least he can savor the bitter-sweet taste of a death-urge — German
"Todeslust."...

These are all themes taken from Eichendorff's poetry — but they are common to the entire stock of Lieder and Ballads of the Romantic and post-Romantic period, with certain unimportant variants. Something like a veil of Nirvana-forgetfulness irradiates the distance. But the reality is always there, inexorable, and its prerogatives are inescapable. So too, for Eichendorff. Joseph Freiherr von Eichendorff was a Catholic aristocrat, who lived from 1788 to 1857, and his life thus embraced some of the most startling and violent upheavals Europe had ever experienced: the French Revolution, Napoleon, the Revolutions of 1830 and 1848. Unlike many of his contemporaries, he needed no conversion to the principles of the Restoration, which even he found insufficient. The dualism so characteristic of Romanticism is present in him too: the yearning for an escape — as we have seen; and, on the other hand, a persistent haunting sense of the horror of the times. Take, as an instance of the first aspect, the beautiful lyric, "Mondnacht," known throughout the world in Robert Schumann's superlative setting:

> Es war, als hätt der Himmel
> Die Erde still geküsst,
> Dass sie im Blütenschimmer
> Von ihm nun träumen müsst...

The following prosaic rendering cannot reconstruct the music of the words, but only render their sense:

> It was as if the sky
> Had kissed the earth to sleep,
> So that in her blossom's lustre
> She could only dream of him.
>
> A breeze swept through the fields,
> The grasses sway in the still,
> The forests rustle gently,
> The night is starry bright.
>
> And my soul spread her wings,
> As far as they could reach,
> And flew through silent regions,
> As if she were heaven-bound.

Here is the longed for home, the home in Heaven. But there is the other side. In another poem he laments,

> O könnt ich mich niederlegen
> Weit in den tiefsten Wald...
>
> Oh, could I but lay me down
> Far in the deepest wood...

and (he continues), with his ancestral sword at his head, lie there and forget "these stupid times," with their meaningless doings and goings, and dream of ancient glories and honor, and of the olden knightly feats. For, he cries out, we are living in a land of Philistines and hucksters, and in a time when even love is bought and sold in the market-places. For this poet there is a Utopia, but it lies, not in the future, but in the past, in the Middle Ages. Only a return to those days and those beliefs can bring regeneration to a debased humanity. Here only is mankind's true "home." "The great idea of Romanticism," he wrote, "is homesickness, longing for a lost home — that is to say, for the Universal Catholic Church." The task and hope of such reconstruction lie in the hands of the nobility.

In every stage of civilization there will be aristocrats, no matter how they are called, raised up above the masses in order to give them guidance. For the nobility..., by virtue of its imperishable nature, is the ideal element of society; its task is chivalrously to preserve everything of magnitude, nobility, and beauty... and to mediate between the ever-changing new and the ever-remaining, by which means only the two can survive...[79]

Thus, Eichendorff's flight into forest-solitudes ended in Metternich's ideological heaven... It is therefore not surprising to learn that he considered the French Revolution nothing but the work of vagabonds, adventurers, and scoundrels, selfishly out to plunder and destroy, while mouthing high-sounding demagogy. The result: tyranny and misery for mankind...

If the German Lied is the crowning height of lyrical Romanticism, its greatest glory is Franz Schubert — the true founder of the modern Lied. Upon that indescribable Austrian genius, who composed masterpieces like "Der Erlköning" and "Gretchen am Spinnrade" at the age of seventeen, and who at the time of his premature death at the age of thirty-one had created over six hundred songs, numerous symphonies, chamber works, cantatas and piano works, superlatives have been heaped that hardly begin to do justice to his accomplishments and stature. Nor can any posthumous lamentation compensate for the hardships Schubert encountered in his life, his failure to obtain adequate recognition, or even adequate publication. A number of his major works were only discovered posthumously. Musical Vienna was not altogether the composer's heaven it was reputed to be!

It would be useless to try to encompass the quality of such a genius, even in the more limited domain of the Song. The great poets, as well as lesser ones, were made his tributaries — for Schubert ranged far and wide, even in the last year of his life discovering and setting Heine's poems, which had just then appeared. The virtuosity and mastery which marked his earliest masterpieces are only deepened and extended in the course of his maturation, but not excelled so far as perfection is concerned — particularly in the precocious successful fusion of the pianistic and the vocal lines. In the sustained perfection of that interlinkage — the fusion of autonomy and subordination — each of these parts intertwining with the other — Schubert would have no superior. His art was sophisticated enough to do more than justice to Goethe's complex poetry; and simple enough in its master-sophistication to achieve elsewhere the transformation of the Art-song into true folk-song. *Die schöne Müllerin* and *Die Winterreise* — Wilhelm Müller's two lyrical cycles — superbly exhibit Schubert's sense of the advantages of the simplest kind of text as a necessary prerequisite for the particular art he was to perfect. The traditional German folk-poetry had a directness and simplicity, a closeness to the speech of the people, and an economy of sentiment that was of paramount importance when German poets came to assimilate it into their own domain. Eichendorff and Heinrich Heine knew, of course, how to create the new "folk-song" which, soon became a portion of the nation's lyrical treasury. One need merely think of Eichendorff's "Das zerbrochene Ringlein" and Heine's "Die Lorelei."

For Schubert the two cycles written by Wilhelm Müller offered the very material he needed for such a conversion. Their seeming unsophistication, their language and images of popular origin, Schubert was able to transmute into that simplicity which is the highest kind of sophistication. He thus created the new "art-folk-song." In these he attained both universality and particularity: the homely and traditional themes of all folk-poetry — love lost, love won, domestic sorrows, death, even suicide — ecstasy and gloom. All these now acquire a character of "finality." The young miller who drowns himself, the wanderer who likewise has lost his love and is ridden by the death-wish are integrated into the simplicities of nature around them — the brook and the forest become persons to commune with, almost endowed with human sympathies; they are parts of the tragedy, as are, symbolically, the organ-grinder, the crow, the guidepost. If the spirit of the grave-yard hovers over these poems and songs, these are Romanticism's most beautiful requiems.

The insatiable Romantic in search of more grandiose satisfactions than those of the Lied, could find them in the "palaces of impossibilities" — Romantic opera. Here, too, Germany achieved supremacy. The enchanter, Carl Maria von Weber, was a master who could turn impossible and faulty librettos, and he had his share to contend with, into almost credible realities. He could satisfy the yearning for the supernatural shudder with the magic of the *Freischütz;* the longing for the Orient in *Abu Hassan;* the exoticism of gipsy life with *Preziosa;* evoke the opulence of medieval chivalry in *Euryanthe,* and restore fairy-lore and fairy-land in *Oberon.* Inexhaustible wonderlands of sound could conjure up at once the demonic evil spirit of Samael, no less than the lure of the forest, the hunter's joy, love — never losing that affinity to the folk song and other German folk-elements; yet also supplying a richness of tone-coloring and musico-psychological thematic subtlety that naturally brings his work close to that of Richard Wagner.

10.

> I know two wonderful languages by means of which
> the Creator has vouchsafed to human beings the
> capacity to grasp and understand heavenly things in
> all their potency. They enter into our inner self
> through altogether different channels than words.
> In some miraculous way, all at once they succeed in
> moving our entire being, penetrating into every
> nerve and cell of our body. One of these languages
> only the Lord speaks. The other is spoken by a few
> chosen beings whom He has anointed. The first of
> these languages is Nature. The other is Art.
> — Wilhelm H. Wackenroder,
> *Herzensergiessungen,* 1797 —

The vast stretch of time and history that bridges the fall of Rome
and the first "reawakening" — the Renaissance — was looked upon
by the Enlightenment of the eighteenth century as a time of
darkness. The poet Alexander Pope scornfully referred to it as the
"Gothic night." But now, under the new historic impulses, of which
national self-consciousness was so great a part, Romantics converted
this derogation and contempt into glorification, as the great cultural
monuments of the Middle Ages, such as the Nordic hero-sagas,
Dante's *Divine Comedy,* and other immense troves of the medieval
creations were "rediscovered" and reinterpreted. Not the least
amazing of these were those most "Gothic" of all medieval
productions — the great cathedrals and churches. Only recently
regarded as strange and confused conglomerations, irregular and
intricate, and corresponding to none of the neo-classical requirements
of order and regularity, self-restraint and coherence, they were now
seen with new eyes as masterworks of high organization and
artistry. "Gothicism" — the adoration of things medieval — was

soon triumphant. Young Goethe as early as 1772 celebrated the
"organic" structure of the Strassburg Cathedral, a "romantic"
enthusiasm he was soon to modify (if not retract) under the
influence of the neo-classical Hellenic revival, set in motion by
Winckelmann. The still uncompleted but equally magnificent cathedral
at Cologne became symbolic for all such constructions still surviving
from the "dark" days. In Germany the reconstruction and completion
of the Cologne Cathedral was assimilated into the movement of
national unity, and Germany was claimed as the archetypal cradle of
all Gothic architecture. Here were found valuable reenforcements
for that political and religious medievalism that was to be of great
moment for the history of the nineteenth century. What astonishing
proofs these were of native creations — fit to be set beside those of
Greece and Rome, if not above them! Art was now drawn into an
ideological struggle against the dominance of Goethe and the
infection of pagan Hellenism — German national sentiment
against cosmopolitanism...

Painting, too, was brought into the fray. Medieval and early
Renaissanc art of the painter was now rescued from the miasmatic
reputation or disrepute of being "naive", "untutored". The "primitives"
now came into their own. Like the Gothic cathedrals these too
reflected their makers — spirits guided by a deeply-felt religious
inspiration, and humility, a modesty and reserve and a fervent
transport sharply in contrast to the senuousness of Greek art.

In the hectic, fever-charged days of German Romanticism, an
aesthetic conversion sometimes paralleled a religious one; the path
led from a worship of Hellenic art to the worship of what was soon
to be called "Christian" art; as it led — Friedrich Schlegel is a notable
instance — from Protestantism to Roman Catholicism; from
Goethe and Hellenism to the Renaissance religious painters...

Just as the eighteenth century neo-Hellenic revival had its
"bible" — Johann Joachim Winckelmann's imposing *History of
Ancient Art,* so now, too, in 1797, there appeared a slender book

destined to have, if not an equal, yet a profound influence on the religious-aesthetic thinking of the period. It was characteristically entitled *Heart-Effusions of an Art-loving Monastic (Herzensergiessungen eines kunstliebenden Klosterbruders)*. These were, indeed, outpourings of a passionate, sensitive and high-strung spirit, inebriated by his ecstatic discovery of the great Reformation artist Albrecht Dürer of Nürnberg, and the outstanding religious painters of the Italian Renaissance. In a strange commingling of contraries, the Protestant Dürer and the Catholic Raphael join Wackenroder's pantheon, both now bathed in a medieval Catholic light, and both anointed high-priests of Christian art.

The end of the eighteenth and the beginning of the nineteenth century had been a bleak, sterile period in German art. French classicism dominated the art-academies, including that of Vienna. Literature, criticism, music had made prodigious strides during this period, but painting had lagged far behind. Wackenroder's book was a call for a regeneration of German art, a restoration to the level of Dürer's day and that of Raphael. The means of regeneration was to be by way of religion. Art was to be a religion, and the artist its priest. Religious paintings, as well as the Gothic cathedrals were sacramental experiences on the part of their creators, who in their devotion to their work had practised *Kunstfrömmigkeit* — a rapt and religious devoutness. For art was a miracle, and the process of creation a sacred mystery. The making of a work of art was a sacramental dedication, a form of prayer. Christian art — religious art — was the highest fulfilment of the artist's vocation. God speaks in Nature, the artist in his creations. As one aesthetician put it, in Art "Man feels God within him." Both God and the artist express that which is ineffable. Naive piety, child-like simplicity and reverence, the "heart" — these are the prerequisites for artistic creation, whose meaning and worth cannot be penetrated by mere intellect. The artist works with unconscious capability. For the viewer of art too is reserved a sacramental role. We are filled, says

Wackenroder, "with a religious shudder at the sight of these great blessed saints of art." The edification and inspiration we feel is such as "to cleanse the heart and mind through high thinking" — a purification that no system of morality or religious philosophy can produce. Such art offers us an access to Infinity. Ludwig Tieck compares the mood effected by Gothic architecture as almost that of music. It is the "divine" within us that responds.[80]

The book fired Friedrich Schlegel, who echoed Wackenroder's sentiments when he viewed the works of art Napoleon had pillaged and brought to Paris. His brother, A. W. von Schlegel, celebrated the "Union of Church and the Arts" in a poem. By others, the contrast between Christian and pagan art was sharpened. "Cologne is Bethlehem," another writer protested. "There is no other salvation, and no other name that can bring blessedness."[81]

The grandeur of Gothic architecture brought Friedrich Schlegel to sad reflections on the present state of Germany and the Germans. "When one looks at these objects, one cannot help recalling the sort of people those Germans were — a people still possessed of a future."[82]

The aura of the religious was extended to cover even landscape painting. Germans were called upon to found a new school of landscape painting that would depict the "state of the soul" ("Seelenzustand"), and present symbolic representations of its "infinity." The painter Philipp Otto Runge even gave symbolic interpretations of color, in which he identified blue with the God the Father, red with the Paraclete, Jesus Christ the Intercessor; and yellow, with fire.

Gradually, too, the magic world of the Pre-Renaissance painters came into view, eventually to revolutionize the aesthetic life of the century. The new kings were Fra Angelico and Giotto — among others; — the equals, it was contended, if not the superiors of Raphael and Michelangelo.

Acting on the passionate ideas and sentiments of Wackenroder, Friedrich Schlegel and other Romantic thinkers, a small band of German painters decided to bring the priesthood of the artist into actual being. In 1810 they retired to a convent in Rome to devote themselves to painting in the true spirit of a sacred vocation, and to live accordingly. In imitation of the Nazarites of the Old Testament (Samson, it will be remembered was one), they grew long hair and beards as signs of their dedication to their high calling, and called themselves "Nazarenes." They declared their independence from traditional academies of art and from subservient obeisance to French classicism. Under the leadership of Friedrich Overbeck they proposed to create a new school of art that would raise German art from its degradation. Overbeck, who was soon converted to Roman Catholicism, was joined by other talented painters, among them Peter Cornelius. The school and its followers produced numerous vast canvases, some celebrating historical events, others more particularly concerned with biblical subjects. Overbeck's "Christ's Entry into Jerusalem" was one such prime model. But their most lasting achievement consisted in the rehabilitation of fresco painting.

As for the Nazarenes, the group in Rome soon fell apart and its adherents were widely dispersed. There was something pathetic about this well-meaning and idealistic enclave of artists who illustrated German "Weltflucht" so concretely, seeking both artistic and spiritual regeneration, and the regeneration of their faraway Germany through a return to the work and spirit of the older religious painters. This was a part of the hopeless dream that Novalis had dreamt — of a reconstitution of the "wholeness" of life through a revival of the spirit and body of the Holy Roman Empire. It was Eichendorff's dream, too. And this at a time when Napoleon's armies were writing the death-warrant of an already crumbling institution!

Yet, if the Nazarenes did not produce world-celebrities — though a number of their coterie like Overbeck and Cornelius were craftsmen of undeniable talent — their ideas lived on, and, by that strange paradox, which is history, achieved an unpredictable influence. In England, especially, through the intermediacy of the French art-historian F. de Rio, the Nazarene ideal found a fertile soil. Here amidst the stir created by the Oxford Movement, with its efforts of regenerating the Church of England, and its offspring, the neo-Catholic revolt, spear-headed by John Henry Newman, the Gothic ideal appeared as a timely auxiliar.

No less influential were the Nazarene ideas in the birth and formation of the English Pre-Raphaelite Movement of the mid-century, headed by the Rossettis. It was one of their "Brotherhood" who came across Rio's *La Poésie Chrétienne,* a direct descendant of Wackenroder and the "Christian art-aesthetic." This was John Ruskin, then at work on his revolutionary book, *Modern Painters.* Rio had revealed to him the miracles of Cimabuè, Giotto, Fra Angelico and Masaccio — a momentous experience, and a revelation. As Ruskin later confessed in his autobiography, "Perceiving thus what a blind bat and puppy I had been, all through Italy, I determined that at least I must see Pisa and Florence again before writing another word of *Modern Painters.*"[83]

The consequence of Ruskin's transformation not only for aesthetics, but also for the whole complex of social thought in England can only be indicated in a sentence. Under the influence of Carlyle, under the impact of Gothic art, Ruskin's "medievalism" became a vehicle for a critique of contemporary art as well as contemporary society. It led to such questions: "What are the elements of a society productive of such an art as that of the Gothic cathedrals and the pre-Renaissance and Renaissance painters?" And: "What sort of art are we producing today, and why?" The answers were to be far-reaching. They found voice in such poets, artists and thinkers as William Morris and Bernard Shaw. They also threw a light on reasons for the failure of the Nazarenes, and such allied movements. Far from their own embattled native land, ensconced in a convent in Rome, they could only fugitively ask such questions. The answers lay far, far beyond the Holy City...

11.

German Romanticism had no Saint-Simon, no Fourier, no Robert Owen to chart the way to a revolutionary future. Germany had had no bourgeois revolution. She was in the infant stage of industrialism, her middle class was weak, and her working-classes even weaker. A peasantry, though legally liberated from serfdom, did not break the bonds of servitude that chained them to the Junkers. Germany was not a single nation — but a collection of atoms. Romantic poets and philosophers dreamt of a "unity" — and they looked to the Middle Ages for their exemplar, and thought they had found it in the Holy Roman Empire. Such a dream had no relation to past or present historic realities. However, there were hard-headed politicians, political thinkers, and statesmen who were forging a future for Germany with weapons that would discipline the subterranean forces of the "abyss" and create a viable state in modern terms. The secret would lie in the attainment of absolute power by the state. Whatever regenerative forces had been loosed during the Napoleonic era and the wars of "Liberation" would be tamed, brought under control and utilized in the period of the Restoration. The new state that they envisaged would preserve absolutism and elements of feudalism, but it would be a "modern" state, capable of vying with other modern states, particularly England.

Unlike Saint-Simon and other Utopians, German Romantic political thinkers saw the "golden age" of mankind as lying not in the future, but in the past. If only it could be brought back! Thus Josef Görres one of the most prominent of these thinkers:

What a wonderful time, this, the Middle Ages! Lovingly, and life-intoxicated, the earth glowed for the people, who, though not yet strong of voice, had nothing of the outworn, of the sickly about them. All was full of fresh juices; all pulses beat, all sources overflowed, all was alive, even if to an excess... It behooves us no longer to boggle at what the Middle Ages have achieved, but to ask our forefathers that they may not withhold from us — in our days of degradation — their spirit, and that they refresh us in our hour of need with the good and the beautiful which they have brought forth...What we need is not to transform the old in our own image, but that we form ourselves in accordance with the old, that we collect our forces out of the confusion in which we are floundering.[84]

It was natural, that along with that "dream" would also come a glorification of the feudal state of serfdom, and its beautiful "relation of man to man" and the mutual affection of all![85]

But at the center of German Romantic political thinking stood the State. The State, according to Adam Müller (who exercised a deep influence on Kleist, among others), represents

the intimate integration of the totality of physical and spiritual needs of the entire physical and spiritual life — internal and external — of the nation, and results in a comprehensive, energetic, and infinitely dynamic living entity.[86]

The State is viewed as the integrative element involving all interests within its confines — whether those of the nobility, or the newly risen commercial class with its demand for a free market and freedom from restrictions. The State embodies "eternal" elements: the nobility, the clergy, the merchant class, the farmer — all organized in so-called corporations, or "Stände," with the family as the basic unit, itself a state in embryo. Thus there can be no thought of "self-interest" and no "free competition." The State is an organism, like the human body, in which each member is subordinated to the whole.

At the center of the State is the "Volk" — the folk, the people,

a sublime community of a long line of past, now living and future generations ...of which every generation, and in every generation every individual authenticates the common bond...What an immortal and beautiful community manifests itself to the eye and mind through a common speech, common customs and laws, and in a thousand blessed institutions,

all culminating in "one immortal family...the ruling family," and in the mature head of this family, the King, a force tending "for the reconciliation of all contending forces."[87]

It stands to reason that within such a state all science and thought must be subordinate to a higher authority, that of Religion, without which it becomes an "empty phantom." Science must become a "rampart of sacred beliefs."[88]

In such a state it becomes clear — according to the same Müller — Jews "should not receive political rights, because their eyes are turned toward Jerusalem and the Temple." As for indifferent Jews, their religion is self-interest, they know nothing of patriotism, "reciprocity of service or sacrifice," and do not belong within the German "folk-community."[89]

The State has divine sanction, as Adam Müller asserted, for Christ died not only for Man but also for the State.[90]

12.

Romantic nihilism and pessimism find their most mordant, corrosive, and trenchant expression in a pseudonymous series of sketches — *Nachtwachen — Nightwatches* — by a writer who called himself "Bonaventura." Whoever he was, and the authorship is still a matter of controversy, his work is actually a most thoroughgoing satire directed against Romanticism, but its targets are not only Romantic thought, the Romantic way of life, and Romantic illusions, but also optimistic visions of a rational world-order, and the human capacity to apprehend it. The imaginary speaker is the night-watchman of the town, who with bugle and voice proclaims the hours of the night. The town is both microcosm and macrocosm. As watchman he has a thorough knowledge of its inhabitants, particularly their darker side. Like another Jonathan Swift he is outraged by the hypocrisy, narrow-mindedness, fanaticism of the community; the cruelty, arrogance and emptiness of those in power, and the pretentiousness of those who build world-philosophies. He sees the starving poet in the garret (eventually a suicide), suffering from the neglect of an age of sheer "prose." He sees the free-thinker in his last moments of life, badgered by a persistent priest. He is also acquainted with the local insane asylum. Here he comes across one of the inmates who believes himself to be God, the World-Creator, holding the world in his hand:

It's a strange thing, he says, speaking as God, that I'm holding in my hand, and when from minute to minute — which they call centuries — I regard it through my magnifying glass, things on this little ball I am holding seem to get crazier and crazier . . . That sun-speck, crawling on its face, calls itself Man . . .

The tiny spark of godliness infused into this little "speck" has driven Man mad, and he has reached the point of thinking himself God, and building transcendental philosophical systems, in which he gazes at himself with admiration! I should have seen, the "God" continues, that the spark of divinity would only lead to trouble, for the tiny creature does not know whither to turn. Bored on earth, imagine what his lot would be in eternity!

What shall I do? ... Utterly destroy him? That would pain me, for the dust speck likes to dream of immortality, and believes that because he dreams, it must exist ... Perhaps the best thing would be to wait until I can fix the Day of Judgment when I have a better idea of what to do...[91]

But the nightwatchman, in his own person, decides to anticipate God and his Last Judgment. In a sudden access of wilfulness, instead of announcing the time, he trumpets the immediate advent of Judgment Day! This was the last hour of the (eighteenth) century:

Oh, you should have seen what a pushing, thrusting and jostling there was among these poor mortals, and how the nobility ran to and fro, and sought to range themselves in order before the Lord God. A multitude of justices and other wolves were ready to fall out of their skins, and in desperation, tried to change themselves into sheep, while with burning anxiety and eagerness they offered widows and orphans large pensions, rescinded unjust judgments, and promised to refund the stolen sums with which they had beggared the poor devils, as soon as Judgment Day was over. Many a blood-sucker and vampire denounced himself as worthy of hanging and decapitation ... The state's proudest man stood humbly and almost cringing, with his crown in hand and deferred precedence to a ragamuffin, because he thought human equality was imminent...[92]

"Bonaventura's" and the watchman's reflections end appropriately in a graveyard. Here, the watchman lifts the lid of his father's coffin and discovers a worm. Hamlet-like he addresses an apostrophe to the insect:

Kings feed on the marrow of the land, and you feed on the King himself... On how many brains of how many kings and princes have you fattened, obese parasite, to have arrived at this state of corpulence? How many philosophers have you retrieved from their idealist philosophies and brought back to this, your realism? You are an incontrovertible proof of the usefulness of Ideas, for you have been nourished by the wisdom of ever so many heads! ... Human heads, and now the home of a worm! ... Microcosms that once housed that which was great and glorious, that which was horrifying and frightful — creators of temples and gods, Inquisitions, and devils! ...

As he touches his father's body, it turns to dust.

I fling this handful of dust into the air — and what remains is — NOTHINGNESS![93]

13.

To the south of the disparate German states — spreading far and wide — was Austria. Its heart and center was Vienna. Napoleon had come and gone — Napoleon who had brought such shame upon the Austrian empire and had almost signed its doom as a great power. And now, after 1815, it seemed as if the glories of the old Holy Roman Empire had been restored. Good Emperor Franz I could look with satisfaction upon the territories under his sway, extending from the tip of Italy to the borders of Turkey, Russia, and Germany. There they lay sprawled before him — Italy, Poland, Hungary, Bohemia, Dalmatia, Illyria! What miracle kept it all together, and was to keep it so for many years to come?

Viennese have an indulgent expression, "Schlamperei," which stands for a kind of slackness, even slovenliness, an idealized easy-going "let it be" attitude. The Emperor gave it classic formulation, "Let us sleep upon it." Was it "Schlamperei" that kept this multiform congeries of nationalities in cohesion? Hardly. For alongside that tendency, there was the Argus with a hundred eyes, situated in the Ballhausplatz. Metternich and his cohorts, keeping watch on the world. There were the racial and nationalist animosities that held the provinces at each other's throats. There was the lure of Vienna and its opulent court to buy favors and subordination of clergies and noble houses; and not least, a Chinese Wall to keep out unwelcome ideas, books, persons, and a surveillance that cleansed universities of suspect scholars (such as the great theologian Bolzano). There were also troops stationed in various parts of the empire — Polish soldiers in Austria, Hungarians in Italy. And in Vienna itself the very knowledgeable Police President, Count Sedlnitzky.

To compensate for these somewhat disturbing discomforts there were the distractions — the spice of life — offered to the Viennese: Music, Theatre, Love...

The great city of Vienna was a riot of nationalities, national costumes, national colors. Here North and South, East and West mingled in apparently festive cohesion and fraternity. In this whirligig, one lost sight of the fact that, though feudalism had been officially abolished, Austria had remained a semi-feudal state; labor-rent was still being paid to landlords; the industrial and economic condition of the country was still backward, and its development inhibited by restrictions on innovation and modernization. There was no strong middle class to assert itself. But the country had its "good father" in the Emperor, who would take good care of all. Stagnation and inertia were raised to the rank of high principle and policy. "Let it be — let it simmer" was the proverbial expression.

"Let it be" — so long as the reigning deities of Austrian culture — music, theatre and love prevailed.

Vienna was the home of musical genius. No other city could rival it. Franz Haydn had lived here till his death in 1809; Beethoven to 1827, and Schubert from 1808 to the end of his life in 1828. At the majestic Court Opera (the Hofoper) there were the masterworks of Carl Maria von Weber. Elsewhere, innumerable theatres presented comedies and the Viennese favorite *Singspiel,* the musical drama. And for the great majority, the fever-inspiriting aphrodisiac of the Viennese Waltz...

Thus was engendered the mythical Vienna, city of the "blue Danube," of "Wiener Blut," to be echoed down the century, even as the twilight of the Empire was fast approaching: "Wien, Wien, nur du allein" — "Vienna, Vienna, only thou alone shalt ever remain the city of my dreams"...

The "city of dreams" contained, in addition to the gaieties of the streets, of the dance-halls, and the wine-cellars — the passions and agonies of Beethoven and Schubert, and the soul's divisions of Austria's greatest playwright, Franz Grillparzer, and its tragic poet, Nikolaus Lenau.[94]

It was in the comic and musical theatre that the make-believe world found its most satisfying representation. Here was a land of succulent fairy-tale and magical fantasy, seasoned with delightfully witty ballads, and catchy tunes.

Its supreme magician was Ferdinand Raimund. His engaging ballad-operas, the *Singspiel*, epitomized an important side of the Viennese temper of this period. Raimund, a former pastry-cook, who had been vending his wares in the upper regions of the Burgtheater, had developed a passion for the theatre, not unusual in a city where the coachman would advise you of the evening's performance at the opera. In time, he became one of Vienna's most gifted comedians, as well as one of its most successful playwrights. He knew his Vienna, and his wit, the characters he created, his songs, along with his masterly use of the Viennese dialect, made him the mirror and rage of the city. He became the creator of Vienna's most popular songs.

Vienna is a baroque city — dense with baroque churches and palaces. The gorgeous intricacy and heaviness of the baroque — one must remember the Habsburgs had a Spanish background — affect the mind deeply, urging it to ponder the transitoriness of human life, and reminding it of ever-present death and divine judgment. The Austrian *Singspiel* is baroque transcendency humanized by a benignant smile, and mildly reprobative of the follies and foibles of mortals. *The Magic Flute* of Mozart may be said to have stood godfather to the Singspiel, its magnificent sublimity reduced to the homely realism of characters and local color. The *Singspiel* transformed metaphysical Necessity and Fatality into virtues — with indulgent admonitions. Ferdinand Raimund is the master of the serio-comic baroque.

Was there not a further paradox in the fact that in his own life this arch-comedian was subject to fits of melancholia that finally led to his suicide, when he became convinced that he had been bitten by a mad dog? This was the "tragic comedian" who kept his audience roaring with laughter and delighting in his songs...

The baroque impinges in his plays in the form of the medieval *contemptus mundi* — disparagement of the world — especially of earthly riches. Here semi-allegorical figures battle for human souls, often of the simpler and humbler kind. Here are the old morality plays, but with song and humor, and recognizable individuals. A peasant is corrupted by acquiring an unexpected fortune. He lives the selfish life of a self-indulgent millionaire. The allegorical figure of Youth apprises him that he is leaving him; age and sickness beset him. Soon all Vienna was singing, along with Youth,

> Brüderlein fein, Brüderlein fein,
> Musst mir nicht böse sein...
> Geld kann vieles in der Welt,
> Jugend kauft man nicht mit Geld...

Money can do a great deal, but it cannot buy youth. *Vanitas vanitatum!* And the chastened wastrel, turned happy peasant once more, chants:

> Wie lange steht's denn noch an,
> Bist auch ein Aschenmann!
> Ein Aschen! Ein Aschen![95]

Fair warning to the audience: You too may be dustman soon, and cry, Dustman! Ashes!... We are puppets of the Goddess Fortune, now she raises us, and now abases us. "All laughter spent," the audience goes home, chastened, instructed, and reconciled. In the end all will be well. A misanthrope — in another play — sees himself as he really is, when the fairy King of the Alps impersonates him, and thus reforms him. The moral remains the same,

> So dreht die Welt sich immer fort,
> Und bleibt doch stets an einem Ort...[96]

The world turns and turns, and yet stays in the same place.

Two years before his self-inflicted death in 1836, Raimund achieved his greatest success with the ballad-opera, *Der Verschwender — The Spendthrift*. A fairy in love with a mortal, Flottwell, bestows

unlimited wealth upon him, which the youth proceeds to squander.
Once more all will turn out well. The allegorical figure of a Beggar
— an ominous warning voice — strides across the scene, finally
reimbursing an impoverished Flottwell with the alms the latter had
once extended to him. The philosophical carpenter of the play
— once Flottwell's valet — strikes the keynote of the drama — and
of Raimund's central idea — in the song of resignation and complaisance,
that all of Vienna was soon to echo:

> Da streiten sich die Leut' herum,
> Oft um den Wert des Glücks,
> Der Eine heisst den Andern dumm,
> Am End weiss keiner nix...
>
> Das Schicksal setzt den Hobel an,
> Und hobelt alles gleich...

We fuss and fret over fortune's worth, envying this or that man's
good luck, thinking that even the poorest is too rich — and all to
what end? Fate comes along, and sets the carpenter's plane a-going,
and levels us all alike...

Such a philosophy of quiescence and acquiescence conformed
well with the official policies of the monarchy, especially so far as
the subject nationalities were concerned. German was the official
and dominant language in the various provinces and states, and it
was policy to encourage national cultures and national languages
among Hungarians, Poles, and Czechs, and other Slavs, as little as
possible. German Romanticism provided Metternich with skilful,
brilliant auxiliaries in the persons of Friedrich Schlegel, Adam
Müller, and Friedrich Gentz, adroit propagandists of absolutism and
the status-quo. At the same time — and this is another of history's
paradoxes — German Romanticism was instrumental in stirring up
and advancing the nationalistic sentiments of the subject states
through its passionate interest in native folk-lore, folk-song, and in
the historic past. Herder's *Stimmen der Völker* — the epochal
collection of national folk-poetry of many nations, and subsequent

German anthologies proved of profound importance, in Poland Hungary and Bohemia, in rousing local nationalisms and patriotism, and incipient movements of national independence.

As for the German part of Austria, few could have imagined at this time that the façade of seeming contentment and resignation, of geniality and self-indulgence covered a "simmering" foreboding of storms to come. Few would have thought that not only the Hungarian, the Pole, the Czech, but even the Viennese himself might drop the mask of "Gemütlichkeit" — genial amenity — raise a clenched fist, and even mount a barricade — like those unspeakable French!...

V.

"SKELETON OF A TITANIC FORM"
THE ITALY OF GIACOMO LEOPARDI
AND ALESSANDRO MANZONI

THE ITALY OF GIACOMO LEOPARDI
AND ALESSANDRO MANZONI

1.

O patria mia, vedo le mura e gli archi
E le colonne e i simulacri e l'erme
Torri degli avi nostri
Ma la gloria non vedo,
Non vedo il lauro...

O Fatherland, I see your walls and arches
And your columns, statues and altars,
The towers of our ancestors,
But your glory I do not see,
I do not see your laurels...
— Giacomo Leopardi, "All' Italia" —

...And we pass
The skeleton of her Titanic form,
Wrecks of another world whose ashes are still warm.
— Byron, *Childe Harold's Pilgrimage* —

Italy — a geographical expression.
— Metternich —

Italy? Which Italy? The Italy of Chateaubriand — "nostalgia of the desert"? Or the Italy of the poets, painters, historians, dreamers — the land of Goethe's Mignon? The land of Gibbon's majestic procession? The land of Byron's tears and Shelley's exultations?

Or is it the post-Napoleonic reality — the Italy that was a perpetual *memento mori*?

309

For the real Italy of 1815 was a collection of fragments held together by force — mostly exercised by Austria. The southern portion was ruled by a restored Bourbon; the Papal States by the restored Pius VII, who also brought back with him the Inquisition, the Index, and feudalism. The only seemingly independent state was that of Piedmont, governed by Victor Emmanuel I, and like the other Italian states dependent for their rulers' survival on Austria. A multitude of lesser minions, tied to the apron-strings of Austria, held sway over such duchies as Parma, Modena or Tuscany. Unlike the German states, Italy did not even possess a common language, the dialects of the south being incomprehensible to the north, and those of the north to the south. Italy was a poor country, the greater part of it agrarian, and — especially in the south — subject to frequent famines. Only half her land was cultivable. The north was richer in productive land, but an infant industrially. Italy's total production was insufficient to feed her population. But she possessed gorgeous palaces, many of them decaying, that contrasted dramatically with the misery of the surrounding countryside and its population. A traditional "aristocracy," politically impotent, lived in ostentatious luxury, profiting from its local authority to lord it over dependents — insolent and proud and displaying a philistine contempt for the professional, the workingman, and the peasant.

The Italians had suffered under the rule of the French. Under the Directorate they had sung a bitter song as they watched the strutting French invader:

> Liberté, Egalité, Fraternité,
> I Francesi in carozza, e noi a pie ...

The French in their carriages, and we Italians on foot ... They had also smarted under the Napoleonic Empire, which bled their wealth and their youth, and they rejoiced in Napoleon's fall, only to find their new rulers a far more bitter curse.

The Austrians were everywhere — they ruled Lombardy, Venice, Parma, and other duchies; and where they were not, there were the Bourbons. Disenchanted liberals began nostalgically recalling Napoleon's reforms, the Code Civile, natural rights, civic equality — and in their imagination conjured up the glories of the French Emperor, whose widow now reigned over the tiny duchy of Parma, and whose son was kept a hostage in Vienna. What puny reminders these of the greater splendors of the past!

But even amidst the ashes of defeat and despair there were glimmerings of light. Among the nobility, among members of middle-class professions, the literati, and even among workingmen and soldiers, the traditions of liberalism and constitutionalism spread by the French Revolution, and, not least, memories of a great Italian past, served to spark disaffection, dissidence, and even occasional insurrections. Secret societies had sprung up, such as the Federati, the Guelfia, the Italici, and most important, the Carbonari of the south. These kept alive the hope of a democratic revival, and of a unified Italy. These Italian "charcoal-burners" — inheritors of the French Charbonnerie — showed an astonishing growth, and represented a threat to the Austrians and the Bourbons. Farther north, Florence and Milan exhibited an intellectual ferment that portended trouble. The Utopianism of the Carbonari took fire. It spread to the Papal States, in the region of Macerata, not far from the home of Giacomo Leopardi, where an insurrection broke out in 1817, followed by a Carbonari congress in Bologna. Though quickly suppressed, such a rising served notice of others still to come.

Of greater consequence was the popular revolt in Naples, in 1820, directed against Ferdinand IV. This was, in fact, a counterpart of that taking place in Spain, against Ferdinand VII, not long before. Ferdinand IV of the two Sicilies was brought to heel, and in his panic promised his people a constitution, an act he soon recanted. He called for aid; and with the assistance of his Austrian allies, crushed the insurrection led by General Guglielmo Pepe, with the time-honored consequences of executions, imprisonments, and flight of survivors. A similar fate befell the uprising in Piedmont, which led to the abdication of Victor Emmanuel I, but was betrayed by its alleged ally, Prince Charles Albert. On April 8, 1821, the insurrectionary forces were totally defeated at Novara. In Milan, a center of Lombard dissidence and Carbonari strength, a number of distinguished implicated leaders — men and women — were arrested, some of them to be confined in the dreaded Bohemian prison of Spielberg.

Amidst these defeats and betrayals — some, alas!, also by Italians — it is no wonder that a mood of despair descended, scarcely assuaged by memories of recent heroisms.

It is out of this sorrow, still fringed by an irrepressible hope, that Italy's greatest poet of the age composed a hymn to his country that was to hearten Italians for many decades to come. O patria mia, Leopardi wrote in his poem, "All' Italia" —

> ... vedo le mura e gli archi ...
> Ma la gloria non vedo ...

2.

In Giacomo Leopardi, Alessandro Manzoni, and Silvio Pellico the sad drama — nay, tragedy — of Italy in the post-Napoleonic years is unfolded. Leopardi's *Canti,* Manzoni's novel, *I Promessi Sposi,* and Silvio Pellico's chronicle of imprisonment, *Le mie Prigioni* recount the bitterness of those seemingly unending days . . .

Leopardi's "All' Italia" was practically the first patriotic hymn addressed to Italy since the days of Petrarch. Along with its companion piece, "Sopra il monumento di Dante," with its similar hortative reproachful theme: the shame of Italy, and invocation to a new heroism, it set the country afire. The poems appeared in Florence in 1819.

They were the productions of a twenty-year old unknown, who lived in the secluded and unimportant town of Recanati, in the Marches. Like Byron, whom he admired, but not uncritically, Leopardi awoke and found himself famous. The Abate Pietro Giordani, friend and mentor, a liberal of extraordinary sensitiveness, was roused to the point of ecstasy. "Oh, Giacomino," he wrote from Milan, "what greatness is yours already . . . Your songs are running through this town like a wildfire. Everyone wants them, everyone is overwhelmed by them. I've never seen (never, never), neither poetry nor prose, nor anything of talent, so greatly admired and lauded. They speak of you as of a miracle . . . What great an honor you will be to poor Italy, and of what great benefit . . ."[1]

If the poem, "All' Italia," is at times magniloquent, it underscored the anguish and disorder, as well as the nascent hope of the times. "L'armi, qua l'armi, io solo combatterò . . ." "Arms, arms, give me arms! I alone will fight, and fall alone," Leopardi wrote, in rhetorical fervor. The companion poem on Dante evoked, with equal force, the glories of the Italian past, and mourned the abased present. Like Byron before him, Leopardi deplored the neglect of and indifference to their great poets, Dante and Petrarch, on the part of

Italians. In another connection, Leopardi related the poetical stagnation of his country to the absence of a truly political life and of a sense of nationality — a land "without activity, without industry, without... the spirit or habit of society..."[2]

But such moments of rebellious fire and resentment of his country's plight flared but briefly. The unextinguished hearth of his genius burned — and burned on to the end of his life; but in actuality it consumed both itself and him.

Leopardi is Italy's poet of cosmic despair — despair of himself as well as of the world around him.

It almost seemed as if four fatalities stood in conjunction at his birth — those of family, time, place, and character. There was the fatality of family: a family of the lesser aristocracy, in which both parents, Count Monaldo Leopardi and his wife clung with frightful tenacity to prestige, class and faith. The mother was an inordinately capable manager of the daily affairs of an estate almost brought to ruin by her improvident husband, but she was also a woman of fanatical temper — conservative, proud, devout, and eternally concerned with the felicities of death and dying. Leopardi has left us a portrait of her that is at once horrifying and cruel, unsparing in its detachment, but undoubtedly true; a picture of an obsessional character who did not even spare her own children, whose near-fatal illness roused in her a feeling of joy. "She considered beauty a true misfortune, and seeing her children ugly or deformed she thanked God for it..."[3]

The Count was a petty tyrant, shackled, like his wife, by tradition and pride. He was authoritarian and absolute. Amazed at his boy's precocity, he already saw in him a future priest pursuing an alluring career, with untold possibilities. How his heart must have rejoiced when he saw young Leopardi shutting himself in the splended library — the Count's gift to the town that never used it — poring over tomes upon tomes of theology, history, Greek and Roman classics, and already when a mere boy beginning to master

Latin, Greek, and even Hebrew! Here Giacomo spent all his time from the age of ten to seventeen — a strange figure bent over books, dressed in a black cassock! Were it not for the other children of the family, this would have been a household of the loveless and the unloved.

Is it any wonder that young Leopardi fell under the two-fold spell of father and mother — and even developed their mental proclivities — particularly, what the Middle Ages termed "contemptus mundi" — "contempt for the world." What shall one make of the boy as he composed an "Appressamento della Morte" — "The Approach of Death," a celebration of early death, and a vision of the world as utterly without worth? Already in these verses he used terms of opprobrium, which many years later and under much changed circumstances of life and thought, he will reuse! Here he is at eighteen:

> See how sad and hard
> Is your life on earth . . .
> Slime and excrement . . .[4]

It is hard to say whether it was as a consequence of those excruciating years of study, or an earlier predisposition to disease — but when Leopardi emerged from these studies he was a physical cripple, a hunchback. The town's urchins laughed at him; older citizens looked upon him with open-mouthed amazement. But other, equally serious changes had taken possession of him — a mental revolution, which his father blamed on his tutor Giordani, but which must have anteceded that association. Though a frigid and careful paternal parsimony kept the young man tightly manacled at home, it could not keep him manacled in thoughts. The shock came when Leopardi began writing poems — like "All' Italia." The boy in the black cassock would never be a priest! . . .

The character of his mother's feeling towards her son's defection may be gauged from an anecdote related by one of the poet's admirers, who, some years after Leopardi's death, visited the

Palazzo Leopardi, and seeing a portrait of the poet, remarked, "May the woman who bore you be blessed." "Lifting her eyes to heaven, she exclaimed, 'God forgive him!' "[5]

Such was the doom of family, where only his brother and one sister — themselves prisoners too — offered sympathy and a measure of understanding.

Doom of time and place...How to satisfy those longings for sympathetic intellectual companionship that would bring the joys of conversation and exchanges to this genius, who was now not only a poet, but already a highly reputable philologist. He saw himself as "a house suspended in the air, held by rope to a star," but alas! also a "pearl in a dung-heap." Doomed to die in his "savage native city."

> Né me diceva il cor che l'età verde
> Sarei dannato a consumare in quest
> Natio borgo selvaggio, intra un gente
> Zotica, vil...
>
> For my heart never told me my green age
> Was doomed to waste away here
> In this barbarous town where I was born,
> Among abject and boorish people...[6]

The doom of time — his own times and his sense of aging. Like Byron he felt old before his years:

My spirit, he wrote when he was twenty-seven, has not only used up its youth, but has advanced a long way into old age, from which one cannot turn back, so that I consider that my life may be considered nearly over, nothing being left to complete it but death.[7]

He felt excluded from life and from the love of woman. Conscious of the horror of his presence, he yet sought for the love of woman, "the woman who cannot be found." Fanatically he enshrined her in his fantasies; then, disappointed, he recoiled with disgust into his own dream-world. He alternated between adoration of lofty womanhood of his own class, and a romantic devotion to the more accessible — that is, to his fancy — and younger "Silvias" and "Nerinas." When he became a celebrity, society women courted him, more intent on adding him to their bric-à-brac drawing rooms than in true appreciation of his genius and his emotional needs.

He was more fortunate in his male friendships. He found appreciation in many quarters, notably in the Abbate Giordani (anathema to his parents), and in later years in the devoted companionship of Ranieri. Distinguished scholars and historians, such as Bunsen and Niebuhr, valued Leopardi's learning, and would have been happy to help him, had he agreed to wear the cassock, or even a token clerical garb, which a post in the papal entourage entailed. But he refused.

Partial liberation came to him through the generosity of many admirers; publishers solicited scholarly editions of Latin classics; others invited him to Milan, Bologna, Florence. Visits to these cities offered him intermittent moments of happiness.

Though he often spoke of death, his many literary projects in prose and verse, and his actual productions, belied that "half-love." For his true salvation lay in creating, in setting down his thoughts and feelings in the inimitable poems of the Canti, not many in number, but unquestionable gems; in his delightful dialogues, satirical in tone and in the manner of Lucian: the *Operette Morali*; and in the thousands of pages of his *Zibaldone* (the *Medley*) — filled with ideas, thoughts, reminiscences, aphorisms, and what-not, some trivial, others wise and perceptive and original.

The doom of times: yes, they were out of joint. Italy, as he complained, was crushed under a barbarian heel. But he found few points of sympathy with those who would combat the evil. Thus in Florence, in the midst of the mental stir, the excitement being created there by some of the foremost members of the intelligentsia — those who were voicing their liberal and democratic ideas in the journal, *L'Antologia,* and who wished to make literature a vehicle for needed political and social reforms, Leopardi felt himself isolated and alienated. His contempt extended to the whole age —

> Di questa età superba
> Che di vote speranze si nutrice...[8]

— that proud age, that fed on empty hopes and was absorbed in trivial things, hostile to "virtue" — a motley crew of men who scorned high thinking, "I, your worthy disparager trample under foot."[8]

For at heart Leopardi was a Manichaean. He regarded the world as the theatre of an unequal struggle between Light and Darkness, Good and Evil, in which the greatest blessing lay in liberation by death. And so he addresses Ahriman, the Persian god of Evil and Darkness, the ever-vanquishing Destroyer:

> Re delle cose, autor del mondo, arcana
> Malvagità, sommo potere e somma
> Intelligenza, eterno
> Dator de' mali e reggitor de moto

Ahriman, King of all things, author of the world, mysterious maleficence! Supreme Power and Supreme Intelligence, eternal giver of Evil and Prime Mover...

If ever a boon was asked of Ahriman, grant that I may not live beyond my thirty-fifth year. All my life I have been your chief preacher, the apostle of your religion. Grant me one boon. I do not ask for what the world calls gifts: not for riches nor love, the only thing worth living for. I ask for what is considered the greatest of evils, Death. I cannot, live any longer.[9]

Had Leopardi read Byron's *Manfred,* which appeared in 1817? We do not know. But there are undeniable resemblances (Byronic ideas appear and reappear throughout Leopardi's works), for in Byron's drama Arimanes too is the great Destroyer, beneath whose footsteps "the volcanos rise":

> His shadow is the Pestilence...
> To him War offers daily sacrifice;
> To him Death pays his tribute; Life is his
> With all its infinite agonies...[10]

It is in this spirit that Leopardi could write,

What is life? The journey of a sick cripple, who with a heavy burden on his back, climbs over steep mountains and through desolate, exhausting and arduous lands, in the snow, the frost, the rain, the wind, under the blazing sun, for many days, without ever resting by day or night, in order to reach a certain precipice or ditch, into which he must fall.[11]

He felt himself the proclaimer of Truth — what he called, "the unhappy Truth." Nature is not the kindly mother of Man. She is a step-mother. Where Byron posited a "omnipotent Tyrant" whom heroic man can defy, Leopardi knows no such adversary. The young man in the black cassock, ensconced in the Leopardi library, has travelled a great distance now. He has destroyed Spirit, and set in its place Matter — cold, indifferent, unfeeling Matter. Matter is the central and basic reality; it is out of Matter that what we tend to call Spirit (or Thought) arises; Matter "that is all, all we know and conceive, and all we can know and conceive." Nature is a constant process of production and destruction, and against her there is no appeal. The process is continuous. Where then is God?

This being the necessary consequence of the present order of things, does not give a great idea of the intellect of whoever is or was the author of this order.[12]

There is no "hidden" God. There is no God. There is no guilt in Man. Guilt, if any, is in Nature — in the world "order" or "disorder." What is left for mankind? For beings like himself, Leopardi would answer, the Truth. For those who need them — there are "illusions." Not illusions that pervert mankind, corrupt and abase them — no! But those that "generate noble thoughts and actions. Those brave, magnanimous, virtuous and useful to the general or the private good; those imaginings which, though vain, are fair and happy, and give worth to life…."[13] Here Leopardi appears to be anticipating the later psychological theories of "sublimation."

But was he himself free of illusions? Hardly. At least one persisted throughout his life — that of winning the love of a woman. Again and again disappointed, he finally wrote his heart's epitaph:

Or poserai per sempre,
Stanco mio cor. Perì l'inganno estremo,
Ch'eterno io mi credei. Perì...

Be still tired heart.
Rest forever. Gone is the last illusion
I thought eternal. Gone...
Life is boredom and bitterness;
Beyond that is Nothingness. The world is a swamp.
Let this be your last despair...
Fate has allotted to human kind
Nothing but death. And now, scorn
Yourself, Nature, and that brute Power
Which, hidden, commands our common doom,
And the infinite vanity of all that is.[14]

He was a brilliant, savage satirist. Toward the end of his life he vented his rage against the unfortunate participants in the catastrophic uprising of Naples in the 1820's. Using the pseudo-Homeric mock-heroic poem, "The Battle of the Frogs and Mice," as a model, and the traditional Italian stanza, the ottava rime, favored for such satires, he poured scorn in his "Paralipomeni della Batrachiomachia" on all the belligerents: the Neapolitans are the "mice"; the Papal subjects the "frogs," and the Austrians, the "crabs." His bitterest sarcasm is directed against the liberals; in his eyes they are helpless as well as incompetent; pretentious and full of boasts. Metternich and Francis I of Austria do not escape his derision. Brilliant as is Leopardi's performance, it is saddening because in its utter hopelessness it does not even take note of a significant contemporary event — namely the Revolution of 1830 which had just broken out in France and Belgium. For Leopardi, all hope of his country's and mankind's regeneration was gone. This, one of his very last works, was dictated in portions to his dear friend Ranieri. The poet was then blind, and could no longer read; he could barely write...

Toward the end of his life he settled in Naples, on the outskirts of Mount Vesuvius. Here he was tended by Ranieri, and the latter's sister.

Their devotion knew no limits. Here he dictated his reflections on
Nature and Man — Fatality and Doom. The magnificent poem, "La
Ginestra" — "The Flowering Broom," — is in fact his obituary — as
well as mankind's. It has two principal characters — the volcano
Vesuvius and the plant. It opens and ends with apostrophes to the
flowering plant.

> Qui su l'arida schiena
> Del formidabil monte
> Sterminator Vesevo,
> La qual null'altro arbor nè fiore ...

> Here upon the arid shoulder
> Of the formidable mountain,
> Vesuvius the destroyer,
> Cheered by no other tree or flower,
> You scatter your lonely shrubs,
> O fragrant broom,
> Contented with the parched wastes ...

But soon a cosmic irony intervenes

> Dipinte in queste rive
> Son dall' umana gente
> Le magnifiche sorti e progressive ...

Let man come and gaze upon these slopes, for here "depicted on these
cliffs is the magnificent and progressive destiny of mankind." See here
mirrored our "proud and foolish century." See here the handiwork of
"impious Nature." Let those given to illusions bask in the warmth of
optimism. The man who loves the Truth will assign the guilt for this
destructiveness where it properly belongs — not to mankind, not to
puny man, but to her who is the "mother in bringing us forth, but a
stepmother in will." Sitting on these slopes, the poet had contemplated
the starry skies, with their infinitude of constellations; thinking on the
illimitable vastness of the empyrean — comparing all these with
miniscule man, self-conceived "master, lord, and end of all creation."
Suddenly out of the "thundering womb" of the volcano came a night

and day of ashes, molten lava, pumice, stones, metal, and burning sand, shooting up to the very skies. And all is over, just like a ripened apple falling to the ground and crushing a whole colony of ants! The fury of such an avalanche is graphically depicted in the very sounds of Leopardi's verses:

> ...cosí d'alto piombando
> dall' utero tonante
> scagliata al ciel profondo,
> di ceneri e di pomici e di
> sassi
> notte e ruina...
> furiosa tra l'erba
> di liquefatti massi
> e di metalli e di'infocata arena
> scendendo immensa piena...

Nature has no more care or regard for the human being than for the innocent ant... Yet man presumes to boast eternity... And there, eighteen-hundred years ago lay Pompei, and now resurrected — a once buried skeleton.

The poet then turns once more to the flowering broom:

> E tu, lenta ginestra che di selve odorate
> Queste campagne dispogliate adorni...

> And you, slow, flowering broom
> Who with your fragrant copses
> Grace these wasted arid lands,
> You, too, will fall a prey
> To the cruel power of subterranean fire...
> And you will bend your blameless head,
> Beneath the mortal weight,
> Unresisting,
> A head not bowing
> In cowardly supplication,
> Nor raised in insane pride toward the stars,
> But wiser, and less infirm than man,
> You do not ween your feeble kind immortal,
> By Fate or by yourself.

Few poets of this period have equalled Leopardi in the poetic evocation of the "anguish of existence," or in such a moving testament of pessimistic nihilism. Of course, he is not free of contradictions. Nature, Chance, or Fatality are now viewed as impassive, neutral agents of destruction; now they take on the shape of Ahriman — god of darkness and evil. Now it is Matter in motion; now a stepmother. Like so many romantics, he extends his own weaknesses — physical and mental — to cover the cosmos. He universalizes his unhappy ego. Yet he typifies the Romantic who is anchorless in a turbulent sea — unable to find a glimmer of shore in chaotic times; bringing to his visions the inheritance of an unhappy home, an enfeebled body, and an unhappy land.

The wilderness of such a self is not easily breached; and there seemed to be few to give him the love he wanted and needed, or help him attain a measure of equilibrium of body and soul. At least, he believed he could find no one. The world was a never extinguishable Vesuvius — a "sterminatore" — the "exterminator," something that John Ruskin too felt in looking on that volcano, in whom he discerned,

if not the personality of an Evil Spirit, at all events the permitted symbol of evil unredeemed... visible Hell. If thus in the natural, how else in the spiritual world?[15]

Giacomo Leopardi died in Naples on June 14, 1837. All his life long he had been in poor health, and he developed a series of complicated ailments affecting his eyes, his lungs and his heart. He died at a time when cholera was raging in southern Italy. On the very morning of his death, he managed to dictate the last six lines of his last poem, "The Setting of the Moon."

How incredulous he would have been had someone told him that he would one day — not too far of — be hailed as Italy's greatest poet of the century! Though his numerous prose works reveal a brilliant, but often perverse, intellect; an acidulous satirical gift; and his autobiographic writings a gripping intensity — it is as the poet of the "Canti" that he can claim literary primacy. Unlike the poetry of many other European Romantics, Leopardi's is marked by a classical restraint, a sparse and controlled rhetoric, an avoidance of exaggerated emotionalism that calls to mind the reserved eloquence of Lucretius, with whose *Concerning the Nature of Things* Leopardi's works have more than casual affinities.

In his most accomplished poems, admirably controlled, Leopardi's lyrics rarely forfeit their lyrical and musical qualities, whether in the unrhymed or rhymed "canzone." At such times they must be read aloud in the original, for here the Italian limpidity cannot be adequately rendered in another idiom. Take, for example, the autobiographical "Le ricordanze" — "Memories."

> Vaghe stelle dell'Orsa, io non credea
> Tornare ancor per uso a contemplarvi
> Sul paterno giardino scintillanti,
> E ragionar con voi dalle finestre
> Di questo albergo ove abitai fanciullo,
> E dell gioie mie vidi la fine...
> Delle sere io solea passar gran parte
> Mirando il cielo, ed ascoltando il canto
> Della rana rimota alla campagna!
> E la lucciola errava appo le siepi
> E in su l'aiuole...

> O you bright stars of the Bear, I did not think
> That I should return once more as I used to,
> And gaze upon you glittering
> Above my father's garden, or converse with you
> From the windows of this house, where as a boy,
> I lived, and saw the end of happiness...
> Passing the greater part of eve
> Watching the sky, listening to the far-off song
> Of the frogs in the open fields!
> The firefly wandered about the hedgerows
> And above the flowerbeds...

The poem brings to mind another one, written by an Englishman, some thirty years before — Wordsworth's "Tintern Abbey." Here too the poet visits a scene of the past — not, like Leopardi, his paternal home, but the river Wye, along with his sister Dorothy, and reflects on his past and present feelings. Both poems are marked by simplicity of language — "the language of common speech" and profound introspection. But what a gulf separates the thought of the two poets! Wordsworth looks back upon his past experience with joy, sees in his younger sister his former youthful self, feels the joy of nature reflected in his own instinctual rapture and thoughtless exultation, and contrasts those reactions with his present ones — when he has drawn the lessons of Nature into himself and looks upon her with expanded wisdom and profit for human relations. For Leopardi, the recollections serve only to accentuate his present state of mind and heart, and represent in his own words, a "funereo canto" — "a song of death."

That central theme of Leopardi's thought is reiterated in his other poems, particlarly in the "Night Song of a Nomadic Shepherd in Asia," where the musical element of the poem is reinforced by the masterly rhyme scheme:

> Cha fai tu, luna, in ciel? dimmi, che fai,
> Silenziosa luna?
> Sorgi la sera, e vai,
> Contemplando i deserti; indi ti posi.
> Ancor non sei tu paga
> Di riandare i sempiterni calli?
> Ancor non prendi a schivo, ancor sei vaga
> Di mirar quest valli?
> Somiglia all tua vita
> La vita del pastore...

> What are you doing Moon in the sky? Tell me,
> Silent Moon?
> You rise at eve, and go
> Gazing upon the deserts, and then you rest.

Are you not weary yet,
Ever moving through these ceaseles paths?
Are you not sated yet; still desirous
Of gazing upon these valleys?
Like yours
Is the shepherd's life...

Here too is a song of mourning, as the shepherd reviews his own hard life, winding toward a weary, hopeless old age. Watching the moon, he asks, "What am I?" In your motions, as in our lives, "uso alcuno, alcun frutto indovinar non so" — "I can divine no purpose, no fruit."

Such then is Leopardi. His is the passionate cry of the enslaved "ego" sounding forth the time-old theme of "Vanitas vanitatum." His is the enslaved soul never able to free itself from the incubus of past and present afflictions.

He could not utter a "De profundis Te clamavi" — for there was no god to whom he could appeal for succor. Wrapped in his own nihilistic pessimism, he could not have anticipated the honors that would be laid up for him by succeeding generations. For them he was not the prophet of despairs, of desolation, but the poet of a renascent Italy — a poet of the Risorgimento. In 1848, on the eve of another great revolution against the Bourbons, Neapolitans fought for liberation, and recited his poems. During the revolution, volunteers passed through his native Recanati, as if on a pilgrimage to some shrine. The noted Italian patriot, Luigi Settembrini, (Thomas Mann's figure of the same name in *The Magic Mountain* travesties this noble being) recalled in later years

the days of our youth, when the Austrian police was at our heels, and we created in our books a world in which we found life and liberty... All the world, that excitement, those unfettered plans, those dreams, was represented by Leopardi in those *Canzoni*... The words were a real flame; we repeated them and they were repeated at their death by those who died for our country.[16]

3.

O giornate del nostro rescatto!
O dolente per sempre colui
Che de lunghe, dall labbro d'altrui
Como un uomo straniero, le udrà,
Che, a' suoi figli narrandole un giorno,
Dovrà dir sospirando, 'io no c'era'...

O days of our deliverance!
Forever grieved he
Who hears it from afar, from another's lips,
Like a stranger,
And who one day, telling it to his son,
Will sigh, 'I was not there.'...

The poem, "Marzo, 1821" was composed by Alessandro Manzoni of Milan when he foresaw the triumph of the Constitutionalists of Piedmont as they were about to cross the Ticino, to crush the Austrians. The victory, alas, fell not to the Italians, but to the Austrians, and Manzoni did not publish the poem until 1848. But he did follow it immediately with a historical tragedy, *Adelchi,* set in eighth century Italy, in which he described the destruction of the Lombard kingdom at the hands of Charlemagne, and thus indirectly voiced his despair at what had taken place in 1821. He was, in one way, more fortunate than Leopardi, for he lived to a ripe old age, and when he died in 1873, the dreams of the Italian Risorgimento had been realized, and the Italian nation had become a reality.

Alessandro Manzoni in the early years of the century was part of that group of Italian liberals who had founded the progressive review, *Il Conciliatore,* in 1817, and included such forward-looking intellectuals as Silvio Pellico and Count Federigo Confalonieri, who were to pay heavily for their activities. Though not involved in their conspiratorial agitation, Manzoni was with them in spirit, and was crushed by the catastrophies that beset their cause.

Manzoni was the scion of a prominent aristocratic family. On his mother's side he was descended from Cesare Beccaria, the distinguished legal philosopher; on his father's, from a long line of feudal lords. His mother, after a separation from her husband, settled in Paris, where young Manzoni spent five years. Here he was brought into contact with a notable group of *philosophes* — successors of the great enlighteners of the eighteenth century. In those early years of the new century, from 1805 to 1810, the young man eagerly absorbed their liberal social, political, and religious ideas. Though a Catholic, he became strongly anti-clerical, and wrote poetic glorifications of the Goddess Liberty. He was one of the adoring followers of the revolutionary priest, the Abbé Grégoire. After his marriage to a Swiss Calvinist, he gradually veered, and very soon was reconverted. His wife too joined the Catholic Church. Manzoni, now fired by new fervor, composed the *Inni Sacri* — sacred hymns celebrating the Resurrection, the Virgin, and the Passion. Under the spiritual direction of a Monsignor Tosi he composed a defense of the Catholic Church against the published attacks of Count Sismondi. Paris drew him again and again, and he was perilously poised between his erstwhile liberalism and his old mentors, and his renewed fealty to Roman Catholicism. That dualism was to remain with him to the end of his life, as he hovered between a political liberalism and a strict religious conservatism. It was the political liberal who vows to see the Austrian "stranger" expelled from Lombardy, in the poem "Marzo, 1821." It is the divided man, who, upon hearing of the death of Napoleon at Saint Helena, and who, though he once abhorred the cruel conqueror, cannot forget the man who unified the Italian states, and now in the elegy, "Il cinque Marzo" lets him ascend to Heaven.

Manzoni was poet, dramatist and historian, but for the world he remains the creator of one masterpiece, a novel, *I Promessi Sposi* — *The Betrothed* — that was destined to occupy a single place in the life and history of Italy, for like its author it came to be venerated as a monument to the Risorgimento. With this work Manzoni's purely literary activity came to an end. *I Promessi Sposi* was published between 1825 and 1827, and was composed in the local Lombard dialect. Its success in Italy and abroad was immediate. In its final form, in 1840, the dialect gave way to the more literary Tuscan. It is in this version that it is known and read throughout the world. Both Goethe and Lamartine hailed it as an extraordinary achievement.

Sir Walter Scott had succeeded in establishing the historical novel as a formidable literary *genre,* and its influence spread far and wide in the nineteenth century. It became the surrogate for the poetic epic, and was to culminate in the greatest of all such works, Tolstoy's *War and Peace.* The historical novel also played a prominent role — along with folk-poetry — in various movements of national revival and national liberation. Manzoni's novel became the "epic" of the Italian Risorgimento, the national rebirth.

For Manzoni could not, of course, write a historical novel dealing with his own times. The censor and the Austrian police would have made short shrift of both author and his work. Manzoni was a conscientious and learned historian. He had no need to distort history. Italy of the seventeenth century, particularly that portion under Spanish domination, offered a sufficient store of war, tyranny, misery, ravage and destruction as well as of heroism, charity, benevolence and self-sacrifice to alert the astute reader to certain startling parellelisms with his own times. And famine and the plague — as many centuries well knew — were no respecters of time or place. As for wars — well, when was there a century without them? Thus, in many respects, the seventeenth and the nineteenth century were akin.

The Betrothed is remarkable in that, unlike other historical novels, it has no outstanding hero or heroine — no conquerors, kings, queens, generals, or adventurers. It is a novel of "unheroic" heroes, engaged not in mighty enterprises, but in preserving their existence, their love, and their relationship to their families. Its two principal characters are drawn from the ranks of the "anonymous" — from the mass that "has no name," — "volgo, che nome non ha" — a silk-weaver of the town of Lecco, and his betrothed, a peasant girl — Renzo Tramaglino and Lucia Mondella. They belong to the respectable little folk of the village. All they ask for is a peaceful existence, marriage, a family, and steady employment. Yet they find ranged against them forces of oppression and persecution — local potentates who with their attendant "bravos," hired ruffians, can easily terrorize the population, and subject it to their will. Supported by the lower echelons of public servants, subservient to them, and indifferent to their social responsibilities, they are able to twist the law to suit themselves. In Lecco they find such a lackey in the lawyer. And they hold sway also over the local curé, the abate Don Abbondio. Don Rodrigo is such a tyrant, feared, and avoided. It is he who brings potential tragedy upon the lovers, for he is greedy to possess Lucia himself and through his ruffians brings pressure upon the curé to prevent their marriage. Aided by the counsel and intervention of a dedicated priest, the Capuchin Friar Cristoforo, Renzo and Lucia are enabled to flee from Lecco, Renzo heading for Milan, while Lucia finds refuge in a convent in Monza.

Manzoni's deep-seated feeling is with the people of the countryside — the peasants and the small artisans. It is fused with a love of the native region that finds voice in his warm descriptions of the landscape around Lecco. It is Manzoni who expresses Lucia's sorrow on parting from her village, translating it into moving lines:

> Addio, monti sorgenti dall'acque, ed elevati al cielo...
> Farewell, you mountains rising up from the waters to the sky,
> you rugged peaks, so familiar to those who have grown up
> among you, and so deeply imprinted on their minds, like the
> faces of our own kin; and you streams, whose rushing sounds
> we learned to distinguish like the voices in our home...

> Farewell, house where I was born, where I sat, with my
> secret thoughts, learning to divine from the foot-steps of
> the passers-by one tread awaited with a mysterious terror . . .[17]

Here she speaks the feelings of all peasants, afflicted by
visitations different from those of Lucia, but painful none the less
— those forced out of their homes by the soldiery, by warfare, or by
sheer hunger and deprivation . . . For Manzoni, though an aristocrat,
and of a family of considerable affluence, unlike Leopardi, had
occasion to observe and study the world around him. He knew the
peasantry of Lombardy, as well as the life of the silk-weavers. Nor
had he completely forgotten the lessons of his Paris associations.
His reconversion — no doubt sincere — did not utterly blunt his
critical perception of the Church. On Don Abbiondo he looses his
masterly irony, which that self-seeker well deserves. On the other
hand, such figures as Friar Cristoforo and Cardinal Federigo
Borromeo (the latter a historical figure), idealized as they are in
their humility, self-denial, and true benevolence, were none the less
meant to stand as examples to their less worthy brethren. Friar
Cristoforo, no abate Abbiondo, dares confront Don Rodrigo in his
castle and castigate him — for which defiance he is removed by Don
Rodrigo's machinations from his convent to far-off Rimini.

Against the power of active evil the simple folk in Manzoni's
novel have only few weapons — quiet acceptance, unspoken
resentment, and native common sense and astuteness. But sometimes
they speak — and speak out. Lucia's mother, for example, the simple
peasant woman, dares express herself to Cardinal Borromeo about
the abate's perfidious conduct:

It would be a good thing, she says to him, if all priests were like your Grace,
and sided with the poor people, and weren't so eager to get them into
trouble so as to save their own skins . . . If our abate had only done his duty,
things would have been much different . . . You are not of that company that
think the poor are always in the wrong . . .[18]

She is not blind to the waywardness of Justice. "Contro i poveri c'è sempre giustizia" — "against poverty justice always stands ready to act." Now listen to Don Rodrigo speaking about the victims he was persecuting:

La giustizia? Poh la giustizia! Justice — A fig for justice! And Milan! Who is there in Milan who gives a care for them? Who listens to them? Who knows they exist?...They belong to no one![19]

Nor is Renzo himself always the submissive spirit, the passive onlooker of his own and other people's plight. In escaping from Don Rodrigo's clutches, he finally arrives in Milan, at the very moment when bread-riots have broken out. The bakeries are being ransacked, their proprietors threatened, and the city commissioner's house is being besieged. On entering the city, Renzo had picked up a few loaves of bread lying on the ground, ignorant as yet of why they were there. He soon finds out. He stuffs them in his pockets, and watches the proceedings as a neutral spectator, but he is soon caught up in the general fever. His sympathies are with the hungry, for he has frequently witnessed hunger in his countryside. The riots were the aftermath of poor harvests and the rising price of bread. Though Manzoni is not a proponent of "mob" violence, he too knows the meaning of poor harvests, war, and back-breaking taxation for the peasantry and the city-folk. The chapter on the riots, is like that on the plague, a most vivid depiction of the impact of starvation in one case, and of a pestilence in the other on a mass of seemingly helpless persons, no less than an indirect critique of administrative bungling, if not indifference.

Pursuing his flight and eager to reach the border so as to find safety in the Venetian republic, Renzo leaves Milan, and is accosted by a friendly person — actually a policy spy. He accompanies him to an inn, where Renzo hopes to lodge for the night. Under the influence of the wine which Renzo imbibes immoderately, and the proddings of the *agent-provocateur,* he becomes talkative. He had already inadvisedly produced his loaves of bread, and thus aroused the attention of the other inn visitants. But now, he becomes indiscreet. His zeal gets the best of him, and the rebel, so long held in restraint, becomes vocal. He almost reveals the name of his persecutor, but restraints himself in time. But when the landlord presses upon him a paper in order to register his name and his origin, the shrewd peasant in him balks. He will sign no document. And why? Because those who ask him to sign documents, he says in his own quaint way,

keep them in their own hands, and so the words they say fly away and disappear. But the words of people, poor devils like ourselves, they listen to carefully, and in the twinkling of an eye, they catch them in mid-air with their pens and pin them down to paper, and use them when they choose.[20]

This scene is as rich in humor as it is fraught with peril for poor Renzo. He has not forgotten the incident he has just witnessed in Milan , and carried away by his fervor, he exclaims, "Vivi giustizie! pane! Ah, ecco le parole giuste!" "Long live justice! Long live Bread! Ah, these are true words, believe me!" He has fallen into the spy's trap...

He is arrested the following morning, but through a fortunate intervention on the part of sympathetic pedestrians, he is enabled to escape his captor. He reaches the safety of the Venetian republic. In the meantime, Lucia has been kidnapped out of the convent in Monza, and brought into the stronghold of one of Don Rodrigo's friends — a malefactor so notorious for his machinations that he is known only by the terrible name of the *Unnamed One*. Here a miraculous event takes place — nothing less than a spontaneous conversion. The sight of innocent Lucia — now in his grasp — ready to be turned over to Don Rodrigo, sets the Unnamed One's conscience afire, transforms him into a repentant sinner! Lucia is saved! And conveyed to Milan. Here, Renzo, on his way back finds her. Milan is now a desolate city — swept by the bubonic plague. The population, decimated, is frantic and in a panic. The stricken are piled into a lazaretto, whose condition defies description. The thousands of dead are buried in mass graves. As in all such situations, rumors fly — suspicions of organized poisonings, witchcraft, foreign conspiracies sweep the city.

In the Milan lazaretto Renzo finds his beloved — she had been stricken, but has recovered. Here too is the good Friar Cristoforo, a ministering angel. And not least, Don Rodrigo, a victim of the plague — now on his death-bed.

With one grand malefactor expunged, another, even grander converted, and with the kindly intervention of the benevolent Cardinal Federigo Borromeo, the lovers are happily united and joined in a long-delayed matrimony.

Even a bare recital of the events exposes a number of capital flaws — the worst being the incredible sudden conversion, altogether unprepared in the story. The book is also marred by a number of digressions — mostly historical, which Manzoni believed to be a necessary foundation for his fictitious narrative. These detract from but do not undo the otherwise magnificent achievement on Manzoni's part. It is rich in its brilliant description of natural scenery as well as of the cities; rich too in its portraits of many characters and their surroundings — rich too in satire and irony; but richest in its warm humanity. The little folk stand out graphically in their simplicities, their integrity, their directness, their folk-wisdom: the hardhitting Perpetua, abate Abbondio's housekeeper, with her sharp tongue, and her sharp realism; the level-headed but courageous Agnese, Lucia's mother; Renzo — the all-suffering but by no means defeated victim; Lucia — but one could go on. Inanimate "characters" take on life: the landscape and Milan — the bread-riots and the plague achieve an almost separate human existence.

The ending constitutes an idyllic quietus. One would wish for another conclusion. For all their vicissitudes and their peregrinations, for all their sufferings at the hands of villainous lords, the two lovers seem not to have undergone any perceptible change of character, nor any kind of development. Events flow over them — but they do not struggle against the flood. They seem never to have awakened from their pristine simplicities. Tenderly drawn, they are and remain children. For a moment only Renzo is roused to anger at the "order" of this world. Thereafter he relapses into the passiveness and patient submissiveness enjoined upon him by the two benevolent priests.

The married couple settles down to a peaceful domesticity, he to his weaving and she to her household chores. Renzo "signs off" — as we say today — with the following reflections, expressed to Lucia:

Ha imparato... a non mettermi nè tumulti... I've learned not to get mixed up in riots. I've learned not to make speeches in the streets; I've learned not to raise my elbow too high. I've learned not to hold door-knockers in my hand too long, when there are hot-headed people around...

These all refer to specific incidents that got him into trouble.

When Lucia, justly aroused, objects:

What about me? What do you think I have learned?... I never went looking for troubles. They came looking for me!,

Renzo consoles her with this concluding thought:

Troubles often come to us because we bring them on ourselves; and not even the most innocent and careful conduct can keep them away from us. When they come, whether through our fault or not — trust in God can lighten them and render them useful in improving our lives.

This conclusion, Manzoni adds, "though reached by poor people, has seemed so just to us, we thought of putting it down here, as the gist of the whole tale — 'come il sugo di tutta la storia'."

These ambiguities — both of Manzoni's character and of the novel — shocked many of his contemporaries. They could scarcely believe that the man who, in "Marzo, 1821," had adjured his fellow-Italians to go forth and drive the Austrian "strangers" from their soil, would now preach such quietism.

To write and publish in 1827, in the darkest and most ferocious time of reaction, when the priests are in command, the Austrians were terrorizing Venetia and Lombardy and tyrants were up in arms everywhere, a book which praised priests and friars, and advised patience, submission, and pardon, meant (Manzoni certainly didn't want this, but it is the necessary consequence of the book) to advise submission to slavery, the negation of patriotism and of every generous sentiment.

Thus, Luigi Settembrini.[21]

Leopardi's father wrote him that the Jesuits in Rome were recommending I Promessi Sposi to their penitents. Leopardi himself wrote as follows:

The fact that Manzoni has chosen for the setting of his novel one of the most wretched and servile periods of Italian history must hide many reasons, and deep ones too. But they certainly don't appear, and what seems instead to come out of his account is the deplorable conclusion that one must not complain of the present, as Italians have been much worse off at other times, and the Austrians are pure gold compared to the Spaniards.[22]

Yet for all these criticisms, this is an unforgettable book — with its world of oppressors and oppressed, its constant emphasis on the perversion of justice — particularly in the case of the poor; its brilliant depictions of village and city, and, most of all, for its being the Italian epic of the "gente di nessuno" — "people of nothing" — the nobodies of society.

Though with this novel Manzoni's purely literary career came to an end, he long remained a symbol, and his novel continued to be regarded as a national monument, having established a standard of literary language, free of pretension and artificiality, and close to the speech of the people — a fresh, robust, colloquial speech, and projecting a historic experience close to the hearts of the Italian people. The Milanese would boast that they had two greatnesses, the Duomo and the Man,

> Un tempio e un uomo
> Manzoni ed il Duomo.[23]

And Verdi, who was to compose the moving *Manzoni Requiem* on the first anniversary of that writer's death, recalled the impression Manzoni made on him in 1868.

What can I say of Manzoni? How to describe the extraordinary indefinable sensation the presence of that saint, as you call him, produced in me? I would have gone down on my knee before him if we were allowed to worship men. They say it is wrong to do it and it may be; although we raise up on altars to many who have neither the talent nor virtue of Manzoni and indeed are rascals.[24]

4.

Because he was on the periphery of the active liberal movement in Lombardy, Manzoni escaped the punishment that was meted out by the Austrian government to many of his friends and associates. He was not among those apprehended by the Austrian police in connection with the events of 1815 and 1820. Those arrested were, in a number of instances, first condemned to death, but had their sentences commuted to long imprisonment. Among these was Silvio Pellico.

Pellico has given us the most immediate and personal document of these times — an account of his ten years' imprisonment, eight of them in the terrible fortress of Spielberg, in Bohemia, in the vicinity of Brünn. *Le mie Prigioni — My Prions —* was published two years after Pellico's release in 1830, and the book was soon in everyone's hands.

As the editor of *Il Conciliatore,* he had been under suspicion for some time; but now, as a member of a secret society, he was arrested on October 13, 1820, and sentenced to death. The sentence was commuted. In 1822 he was transferred to Spielberg. The severity of the treatment to which political prisoners were then subjected — isolation, chains, insufficient and inadequate food and medical care, resulted in frequent illness, and deaths. The torments were occasionally relieved by striking examples of kindness, even sympathy on the part of a number of the jailers. Some relief was also afforded by the proximity of other politicals, and the infrequent opportunitites for exchanges. Pellico himself witnessed the death of a few of his fellow-prisoners. He was finally pardoned on August 1, 1830. While on his way home, and stopping in Vienna, he heard with joy of the "three glorious days" of the Paris Revolution of 1830. In visiting the imperial grounds of Schoenbrunn, he met with an interesting experience, not devoid of irony:

While we were in the magnificent avenues of Schoenbrunn, Pellico relates, the Emperor passed and my guard made us withdraw, for the sight of our emaciated persons might sadden him.[25]

It was *Le mie Prigioni* that, more than other Italian literary works of that time, brought home the searing experiences of the heroic pioneers of the Italian Risorgimento. His was the testament of all those brave spirits who had dared to defy Austrian autocracy, and face the consequences.

For Pellico, release from imprisonment was also the end of his political activities. Like Manzoni's Renzo, he retired to devote himself to religion and charity. Although the author of numerous works, including tragedies, it was only *Le mie Prigioni* that has survived.

"Ah!" he concluded his prison narrative, "delle passate sciagure ..." Ah! for my past misfortunes and sufferings, as well as for the good or evil yet reserved for me, may the Providence of God be blessed; of God who renders all men, and all things, however opposite to intentions of the actors, the wonderful instruments which he directs to the greatest and best purposes.[26]

VI.

THE AGONY OF SPAIN
AND FRANCISCO GOYA

VI.

THE AGONY OF SPAIN
AND FRANCISCO GOYA

1.

On November 7, 1823, Colonel Rafael del Nuñex Riego was hanged in Madrid. Condemned by the Fiscal — the courts — to death, he was to be executed in exemplary fashion: He was to be beheaded, and his body was to be quartered, each part to be distributed to an appropriate district of Spain. Subsequent mercy altered this punishment to a public hanging.

This tragic death reverberated throughout Europe. Wilhelm Müller, poet of "Die Winterreise" and "Die schöne Müllerin," author of poems dedicated to the struggles in Greece, wrote a hymn to the memory of the Spanish martyr:

> Muse! Muse! heran!
> Schaudere nicht zurück
> Vor dem hölzernen Thore der Schmach,
> An dessen Balkon
> Schwebet der Held ...

> Muse, my Muse, approach!
> Do not recoil
> Before the wooden gate of shame
> On whose balcony
> Your hero is swinging ...

> Hero of Freedom,
> Shamefully murdered!
> But Freedom — who can murder her?
> From the strangled throat

343

Of your corpse
She cried aloud to Heaven:
"Justice!"
And with muffled wails to the Depths:
"Vengeance!"

With Riego's death, what had proved the first challenge to and revolt against the Holy Alliance came to an end. Echoes of the execution and the uprisings in Spain, which had begun in Cadiz in 1820, found almost immediate response in Naples, in the same year, and even in far-off Russia, in 1825.

To live in dreams of by-gone glories and greatness is the unenviable privilege of senescence, harmless, perhaps, in individuals, but fatal to nations and their rulers. Spain had once been mistress of half the world, holding both the Old and the New World as fiefs. Such past greatness lived on in the minds and dreams of subsequent kings of Spain even in the days of decay and stagnation. Spain, at the end of the eighteenth and the beginning of the nineteenth, was in such a state. Spaniards still behaved, as Lord Wellington put it, "as if Europe were at their feet."[1] Here was a royal court so utterly corrupt and degenerate as to become a byword to the people for treachery and shame. The Queen, mother of Ferdinand, the future king, was openly the mistress of her favorite, Manuel Godoy, and the mother of his children, while her husband, King Charles IV, was the complacent and depraved admirer of his wife's lover. It can come as no surprise then, that the outbreak of the French Revolution and the emergence of Napoleon should have been regarded in many quarters as prophecies of national salvation. An uprising in 1808 toppled Charles IV and his queen. Napoleon in turn toppled King Ferdinand VII, and placed the crown on the head of his own brother, Joseph Bonaparte.

The new king of Spain, though he might have harbored serious intentions of liberalizing the government of Spain, soon found that he was on hostile territory. The country was determined on his expulsion, if not destruction. The uprisings of 1808 against the French found their immortal memorials in the painted canvases of Francisco Goya. A liberalized Cortes — the Parliament — convened in Cadiz, and promulgated the celebrated "Constitution of 1812." Democratic hopes ran high. The new constitution reaffirmed a great many of Napoleon's reforms: for he had suppresseed three quarters of the religious houses, abolished the tribunal of the Inquisition, feudal rights, seigneural courts of justice, and provincial customs duties. The constitution also attempted to limit the prerogatives of the monarchy, subordinate it to the Cortes and its ministers, and provide for freedom of the press, though not of religion. The clergy was to be excluded from a share in legislation, the Inquisition was to be suppressed, and church lands secularized. The "Constitution of 1812" became the battle-cry of freedom for liberal Spaniards, and remained their battle-cry thereafter.

But the doom of Napoleon's power in Spain was already sealed in 1808. The resistance of Spaniards to the French occupation, the victories of Wellington in the Peninsular Wars, and Napoleon's defeat at Leipzig brought down the curtain. Spain and Portugal had all along been nothing but pawns in the contest between Napoleon and the British, and the final triumph belonged to Britain...

And so, in March 1814, Ferdinand VII returned from his exile in Valençay. Weak, stupid, and cruel as he was, he was also perfidious. On his return he repudiated his promise to sustain the new constitution. He restored the Inquisition, as well as the prerogatives of the Church, and embarked on a persecution of the "liberales" — as all those in opposition were now called. The South American colonies were in revolt, and Ferdinand set about regaining them.

It was this enterprise that sparked the Revolution of 1820.

Rafael de Nuñez Riego was thirty-six years old in 1820. As a soldier he had fought against the French, and after 1808 he had been imprisoned in France. He escaped, made his way to England, and then was sent back by the English to Spain in 1814. He became commandant of the battalion which was about to be sent to South America to reconquer the colonies for Spain, and reenforce the Spanish army of General Murillo.

On New Year's Day, 1820, Riego and his fellow-commander Quiroga headed a revolt of officers and men against King Ferdinand. They raised the banner of revolution in the Andalusian villages of Cabezas de San Juan. Riego issued a "pronunciamento" — a proclamation — to the army: he declared himself for the Constitution of 1812. Within the army there had already been brewing a strong discontent reflecting that in the country at large, for Spain was facing imminent bankruptcy, and it was to avert this that the King was sending his expedition to South America to recover, along with the colonies, its trade and rich resources. The grievances of the army against the government were further aggravated by the feeling that they, who had fought to restore King Ferdinand, were being pushed aside in favor of sycophants and undeserving place-seekers. Many of the members of the army had been imbued with liberal ideas; there were Freemasons among them. Riego, while in France, had also absorbed revolutionary notions. Such was the weakness of the monarchy of Spain that Ferdinand VII was forced to capitulate, and swear allegiance to the Constitution. Until 1823, he was virtually a prisoner of the Cortes.

Spain's Revolution of 1820 was to be crushed by a foreign force — that of France. Under pressure from the Holy Alliance, from the "Ultras" — the ultra-conservatives of France, both lay and clerical — King Louis XVIII of France sent abroad the "Ten Thousand Sons of St. Louis," as they were called, under the leadership of the Duc d'Angoulême. The French army entered Spain on April 7, 1823. Spanish resistance was short-lived. King Ferdinand VII was liberated and restored. The recriminations against and executions of the rebels were so bloody as even to horrify the French Duke.

Riego and his followers tried to continue a hopeless struggle, and took refuge in the mountain regions of Jaen, and thereafter in the Sierra Morena. He was captured on September 15, 1823, brought to Madrid, and after being shamefully maltreated, condemned to death, and hanged. The Duke of Angoulême wrote to the French minister. "This country will relapse into its old absolutism."[2] France was to remember for a long time this expedition in which French blood had been shed to restore a corrupt absolutism. France would echo the poet Béranger's prophecy:

> À la fin de la campagne,
> Nous s'irons tous étonnés
> Qu'en enchaínant l'Espagne,
> Nous nous s'irons enchaínés.

> At the end of the campaign,
> We'll be surprised to see
> How in enslaving Spain,
> We've enslaved ourselves.[3]

2.

Spain had no poet of the stature of Byron or Leopardi adequately to voice her anguish, abasement, woes, and resentments. But she did have her laureate spokesman in the master-painter and etcher, Francisco Goya. On canvas and in his etchings and drawings, he has given us all of Spain — darkness and light, tragedy and savage comedy; as court-painter the official though decaying grandeur of kings, queens, state councillors, of the beautiful Duchess of Alba with whom he was in love — the once proud and arrogant Spain, once a world-conqueror. In his etchings and drawings he has also given us the other Spain — the Spain of terror, hatred, nightmare specters, griefs and sorrows.

In 1823, the year Riego was executed and the incipient revolution brought to an end, Francisco Goya was already in his seventies. His life's work was practically over. He had five more years to live. He had served four kings — three of them Spanish Bourbons, and one a Bonaparte. In his lifetime he had witnessed more than a man cares to see — too much perhaps. Almost thirty years before, he had undergone a severe crisis; he had contracted syphilis and for a time he was paralyzed. For the rest of his life he was deaf.

He had lived through the expectant years of the French Revolution, and though he was no revolutionary himself, he had moved in circles in which the ideas of the French Enlightenment and Revolution were rampant. He was the friend of playwrights and politicians whose thoughts were turned toward a more generous future, and who were hopeful of proximate changes. There were the two Moratíns, Nicolas Fernández and Leandro, both innovators in poetry and drama. There was also the brilliant satirist and political liberal, translator of Rousseau's *Social Contract,* Gaspar Melchior de Jovellanos. There was the poet Yriarte; and not least the violent opponent of the Inquisition, the poet Meléndez Valdés. To them was applied the pejorative title of "afrancesados" — the "Frenchified ones" — for they sympathized with French ideas and the Napoleonic reforms. It is not unlikely that the elder Moratín's scorching, corrosive, and realistic study of city life — the *Arte de las Putas* —*The Art of the Prostitute* — which was a kind of poetic *vade mecum* through the brothel quarters of Madrid, of which the inhabitants are treated with sympahy and humor, took hold of Goya when he came to engrave his own terrifying visions. Moratín's book was banned by the Inquisition. The outraged author asked: Was what he had written any worse than the depictions of the bloodshed atrocities of a Herod, or those of War? Leandro Moratín, one of Goya's closest friends and associates, was the author of satirical and topical dramas, as well as of a treatise on witches and witchcraft. Goya shared his hatred of the Inquisition and its abominations. The sparse documents which have come down cannot decisively prove the interdependence of the two men, but the parallels are too striking to leave much doubt.[4]

Whatever the relationship, the etched world of Goya's *Caprichos* is the world of those men, too: the two Spains — the Spain of oppressive silences, of inertia, of world-weariness; and the Spain of smoldering and erruptive volcanoes.

Critics early began to remark on the presence of two Goyas — Goya, the public painter of notable personalities, muralist of churches, Goya the court-painter; and the other Goya, the more personal, intimate, the etcher of private visions. They generally associate a significant change in his style with his personal crisis of 1792, when feeling himself close to death, he began creating his "Cabinet Pictures of Various Popular Diversions." In presenting them, Goya remarked that these were "observations for which there is no place in commissioned works, since the latter afford no scope for caprice and invention."[5] It is here that we come upon such subjects as the "Procession of the Flagellants," "The Trial before the Inquisition," and "The Madhouse."

Goya had announced a series of eighty etchings entitled "Caprichos" for sale in February 1799, but he withdrew them from public distribution. Why? What was he afraid of? The announcement of the proposed sale reads as follows:

The author, persuaded that the criticism of human errors and vices (however dependent it may seem upon eloquence and poetry) may also be the object of painting, has chosen among the manifold extravagances common to all civilian society, and the prejudices and snares sanctioned by habit, ignorance, or self-interest, those themes for his work which he has deemed apt in furnishing material for ridicule and at the same time exercising his inventive imagination.[6]

Goya's patron, the Minister of Finance, Saavedra, had just fallen into official disfavor. Was Goya afraid of falling a prey to the Inquisition? Would he, too, be joined to the procession of penitents condemned by that court, and march to his doom, crowned with the peaked cap, the "corozado" of the condemned sinner?

At any rate, these "Caprichos" are a chronicle of the times. Those words eloquent poets might have set are here made graphic visions. They can be dated between 1796 and 1798. Here staged before us are all the social vices, "the ferocious abnormalities," — here is the laying-bare of the "irrational base in the most customary and typical manners of contemporary society."[7]

"The Dream of Reason produces Monsters." This is the way Goya himself entitles one of these etchings. A man is asleep at a table. Around him and above him hover his dreams, not of love, pity, kindness. At his feet is a cat; above him owls and bats. These nightmare visions, whose laconic descriptions barely suggest the secrets of the inner man, were they Goya's attempts at preserving his reason through a controlled creation? Or was it Spain he was portraying? Or both himself and Spain? We do not know. What would we not give for those lost letters, diaries, and confessions made to friends? Why, even in his majestic large paintings, he had dared to cast a critical eye on the court! Take, for example, the celebrated portrait, "Family of Charles IV," with its fat King, its repulsive Queen, and other figures, as they stand contrasted with the nobility in the forms of the Prince of Parma and the Infanta!...

He is beset by ferocious demons. Cryptic, sybilline notations veiled inward meanings: they are cryptograms of an inner consciousness and an "unconscious." "Nadie se conoce" — "No one knows himself" — is one of the superscriptions. He seems to be on his guard. Jovellanos, dear friend and patron, man of letters, and high in public office, liberal thinker and agrarian reformer, and also poet and satirist, fell into disgrace in 1798. One of the Moratíns complained bitterly of the sad state of contemporary letters in a land where thought was suspect:

Believe me, he wrote to Juan Forner, the time in which we are now living is not a favorable one for us. If we follow the main stream, and speak the language of the credulous, our foreign friends laugh at us and even at home they find us foolish. And if we try to dissipate the fatal errors of those who do not know, the Sainted and General Inquisition will apply her customary remedies."[8]

The nightmare horrors of Satanism and witchcraft, still frightful obsessions in those days, are here too, in Goya's picture of the Aquelarre — the Goat's Meadow, meeting place of Satan and his cohorts.

Gluttony, vengeance, vice, innocence betrayed, plight of the wretched peasant, corruption of monk and friar, lechery for sale, a prostitute haled off to jail — prisoners, aristocrats, paupers — an entire gallery of debasement, despoliation, betrayal and misery! Was this Goya's *roman à clef?* His contemporaries thought so, and read into these productions semblances of important personages of the day...

But whether directly personal or not, these visions seemed to say: This is the "testimonio solido de la verdad" — "the solid testimony of truth."

History was being made and unmade. At Bayonne, across the border, in 1808, Napoleon was deposing one king after another. In Madrid, his general, and brother-in-law, Joachim Murat, was meeting with a frenzied hatred on the part of the Spanish populace. In May of that year, in the Plaza Major, took place a set-to between Spaniards and the French troops, which was followed by a massacre of insurgent prisoners on the Prado. Goya was a witness, and was never to forget what he saw. Some years later he set down these memories in two of his most formidable canvases: "Street Fighting near the Puerta de Sol," and "The Repression of the Uprising of the Third of May."

Now the outside world was very much with him — a dark and bloody world that succeeded the accession of Joseph Bonaparte to the uneasy throne of Spain — the war of the "guerrilleros" against the French: massacres on both sides. There was 1811, the "año del hambre," "Year of the Great Hunger." This massive onslaught of horrors beat upon the artist's consciousness, bringing on a maddening fury, outrage, pity, revulsion, a kind of creative madness that grew into the eighty-five engravings later generations would call "The Disasters of War." His own times neither saw nor knew of them. They did not come to light until 1863.

In these engravings, Goya's hatred of war and its carnages explodes in a bitter violence and graphic reality hitherto unknown to European art. Goya himself called these productions "The Fatal Consequences of a Bloody War." He spares neither Spaniard nor Frenchman. Rape, pillage, ever-present death, corpses piled high — these are elements common to both sides. The captions are at times ironic, at times commiserative: "Were you born for this?," "This I Saw," "Barbarians," and so on, till the sight is staggered and recoils — unbearable for us, as it must have been for the artist. An inferno of human animalism, these and succeeding works constitute, in the vivid words of one of Goya's biographers, an "audit of hate."9

Joseph Bonaparte's days of kingship were numbered. Wellington was advancing, and the French were withdrawing. Among those in retreat was General Hugo, Victor Hugo's father.

But Goya kept on dreaming of "Divina Libertad" and of a "Divina Razon" — "Divine Liberty and Divine Reason" — both apparently lost in the infernal chaos of the times. With the return of Ferdinand VII to the throne of Spain, the land once again began moving — back into a medieval past...

In 1819 Goya bought a house in Madrid, the "Quinta del Sordo" — "the House of the Deaf Man" — and began decorating it with his "pinturas negras," — "black paintings" — a series of private hallucinations bordering on madness. Here we see the devouring rapacity of Time and Nature, here Saturn is feeding on his own children. This is a stampede of horrors. What better commentary on them than Goya's own panel in his study, by some critics thought to be an unfinished work depicting a vast nothingness: A little dog is peering over the ledge of a rock...

Nada. Nothingness.

More productive than ever, he began working on new engravings, "Disparates" — Stupidities — Follies...

During the repressions following the failure of Riego's insurrection, he went into hiding with his good friend Don José y Latro, like another John Milton at the time of another Restoration...

He ended his days in France, in the city of Bordeaux. He had been given permission to go abroad for his health. Here were to be found numerous Spanish refugees, among them Leandro Moratín. Goya even visited Paris. He returned to Madrid for a brief stay, and then was back again in Bordeaux, where he died in 1828.

He belongs with the Titans of all times.

VII.

RUSSIA — "THE FIRST REVOLUTION" AND ALEXANDER PUSHKIN

NOTE: In our transliteration from the Russian, "zh" is to be pronounced like the French "j" in "bon jour"; "kh" like the "ch" in the German "ach!"

RUSSIA — "THE FIRST REVOLUTION" AND ALEXANDER PUSHKIN

1.

> In casting our eyes over the immensity of this monarchy, unique in the world, our mind is overwhelmed. Never did Rome equal her in grandeur ... A people which through its worth and courage has succeeded in becoming master of a ninth part of the world, which has discovered regions hitherto unknown..., and has illumined them with the torch of the true faith, solely through its example.
> — N. M. Karamzin —

After 1815 the victorious Russian army and its officers began returning to their motherland. Among the returning officers was one, Dmitri Yakushkin, who described what he saw on arriving:

From France we returned to Russia by the sea. The First Division of the Guard landed at Oranienbaum and listened to the *Te Deum* performed by the Archpriest Derzhavin. During the prayer the police were mercilessly beating the people who attempted to draw nearer to the lined-up troops. This made upon us the first unfavorable impression when we returned to our homeland...Finally the Emperor appeared, accompanied by the Guard, on a fine sorrel horse, with an unsheathed sword, which he was ready to lower before the Empress. We looked with delight at him. But at that very moment, almost under his horse, a peasant crossed the street. The Emperor spurred his horse and rushed with the unsheathed sword toward the running peasant. The police attacked him with their clubs. We did not believe our own eyes and turned away, ashamed for our beloved Tsar. That

357

was my first disappointment in him; involuntarily I recalled a cat transformed into a Beauty, who, however, was unable to see a mouse without leaping upon it.[1]

Yakushkin was only one of many such officers who were being faced by the startling contrasts between their experiences in Western Europe and in their own country. There, even despite the strict surveillance of the authorities, they had been exposed to the fresh currents of thought — to the ideas of Saint-Simon, Bentham, Condorcet, Adam Smith, and had no doubt visited in numerous salons where a great deal of philosophical and moral discussion was carried on. And had not one of them, Michael Lunin, been in the very presence of Saint-Simon himself? Ideas, as we know, do not recognize national boundaries, whether physical, intellectual or emotional. They found warm reception and a readiness in many of the Russian officers. It was therefore not surprising if they were bringing back in their heads some startling notions of reform.

And what were they to find now that they had come back to Russia? A dreary repetition of that which they had witnessed before leaving, and which their parents and grandparents had witnessed before them — a land steeped in medievalism, with millions upon millions of miserable and ignorant serfs and peasants — this after the searing sacrifices the Russians had brought in order to defeat Napoleon and the French!

They had counted on the Tsar, Alexander I. In his earlier youth he had been reported as harboring liberal, even dangerous ideas of reform. He had dreamt of being a liberator, of emancipating the serfs, of creating a Constitution for his people. But now, victorious and omnipotent, he seemed more than ever in the hands of scheming ministers and counsellors — intolerant, bigoted, and reactionary. There was the cruel but notoriously efficient Count Alexei Andreyevich Arakcheyev — closest of all to the Tsar; there was the mystical and fanatic Prince Golitsin, head of the Holy Synod; there was the obscurantist educator, Count Michael Magnitsky, who saw "the Prince of Darkness coming visibly closer," and the "godless university professors distilling atrocious poison ... for our unhappy youth," and who proceeded to weed out the poisonous plants at the university of Kazan, as did his colleague Dmitri Runich at the university of St. Petersburg.[2]

Whatever hopes liberals had nursed were shattered when Count Michael Speransky, who was deputy Minister of Justice, and had been laboring to reform the structure of the administration and improve the educational system, was dismissed from office and practically exiled. Not least of the national distresses was a financial crisis that created a deficit of almost 350 million rubles. The censorship had grown more restrictive and severe.

Orthodoxy, Autocracy, and Nationalism sat enthroned —while the Holy Synod was constantly preaching the saintliness and duty of obedience.

Many of the returning officers had become Freemasons, and were aware of the uprisings that had taken place in Italy and Spain, and were taking place in Greece. They were appalled by the provincialism and the abysmal state of intellectual life in the two great cities, St. Petersburg and Moscow. They found their discontents mirrored in students, teachers, writers and other members of the intelligentsia, but undirected in their energies because of a lack of leadership.

While in Western Europe, a number of these officers had become acquainted with the conspiratorial methods of the Italian Carbonari. They began organizing their own Russian secret societies under the leadership of distinguished figures such as Prince Sergei Trubetskoy, and in turn succeeded in recruiting other prominent personalities. Soon they crystallized into two principal groups, one in the northern part of Russia, the other in the south. The northern group was the more cautious, more conservative — though liberal enough to look for its models of reform to England and the U.S.A. They proposed the creation of a constitutional monarchy, with a bicameral legislature, the abolition of serfdom, but with guarantees to landowners. Their proclamations have the sound of their American and French predecessors:

The Russian people are free and independent, and consequently are not, and cannot be, the property of any individual or family... The source of supreme power is the people, who have the exclusive right to make fundamental laws for themselves...[3]

The program of the southern group was far more radical and revolutionary. It was devised by Pavel Pestel, and was in essence republican, and demanded the abolition of all class privileges and titles, of immunities from taxation (the special prerogative of the upper classes), and of serfdom. Land was to come under state possession, and was to be allotted to the peasants.

The land is common property of the human race and not of private persons, and therefore cannot be divided among a few men. As soon as there exists even a single person who does not possess any land, the will of God and the law of nature are totally violated and the natural rights eliminated by force and tyrannical government.[4]

More clearly than any of the other agitators, Pestel recognized the new social relations within European societies consequent on the rise of an aristocracy of wealth.

It seemed to me that the essence of the present century consisted in the struggle between the masses and the aristocracy of various kinds, the aristocracy of wealth as well as hereditary. I judged that these aristocracies would finally become more powerful than the Monarch, as in England, and that they were essentially the main obstacle to national welfare and could be eliminated only under a republican form of government.[5]

He had been assured of the superiority of the republican form of government on hearing reports of the growth and prosperity of the United States. He felt that government by one person which was hereditary inevitably ended in despotism.

Among the members of the northern group such radical ideas and proposals met with alarm, especially Pestel's advocacy of terrorism, and even regicide — for which would be recruited a *garde perdu*, a kind of "suicide squad," ready to risk all and dare all in an assassination. For Pestel was determined not to repeat the mistake made by the Spaniard Riego, when he liberated Ferdinand VII, and soon found himself betrayed by that ruler. It was important, Pestel held, to eliminate the royal family and destroy the myth of legitimacy. Among the prospective revolutionaries enthusiasm ran high. Their blood was boiling. The poet Kondraty Ryleev, close friend of Alexander Pushkin, was more sober:

I foresee there will be no success, but an upheaval is necessary, for it will awaken Russia, and we, with our failure, will teach others.

And Prince Odeevsky,

We shall die, oh, how gloriously we shall die![6]

Both of these prophecies were to be fulfilled — too well, too soon, and too tragically...

While the members of these secret societies were debating, consulting, agreeing or disagreeing, History, with the customary prerogative of unpredictability, moved and precipitated the conspirators into action.

Tsar Alexander I died suddenly at Taganrog, in southern Russia, on November 19, 1825.

Not having any children, Alexander should by rights have been succeeded by his oldest brother, Constantine. But the latter had renounced his right to the throne after marrying the Polish Countess Grudzińska, a Catholic. Nicholas was therefore next in line. Such indeed had been the intention and wish of Alexander, as expressed in a secret manifesto declaring Nicholas heir-apparent. Who was to be Tsar now? The confusion was abetted by the action of Nicholas in taking the oath of allegiance to Constantine, and ordering it to be administered throughout the empire. But alarming rumors were reaching him concerning army conspiracies in the north and the south, and so he finally determined to have himself proclaimed emperor on December 14, 1825.

For the revolutionaries the moment of action had arrived. They had previously set the date of revolution for 1826, but now there could be no waiting. Ill prepared, poorly organized, caught without warnings, the leadership of the north could muster only three thousand troops in Petersburg, to assemble on the Senate Square, to demonstrate their refusal to take the oath of allegiance to Nicholas. (Hence the name Decembrist from the name of the month of revolution.) Against them stood a government army three times their size. A large crowd of citizens gathered to witness the ceremony. What might have happened had the revolutionary action been carried out is problematical, but at the crucual moment its leaders, either through loss of nerve or desperation, betrayed their followers, and the troops remained standing, a "standing revolution" — leaderless. The most despicable of the traitors was Prince Trubetskoy, who had been charged with the command of all the troops in the Square, and who ran away and sought refuge in the Austrian embassy. Later, after his arrest, he presented Nicholas with a list of the members of the Society of the North.

After preliminary parleyings between the insurrectionists and the government had failed, government troops were ordered to fire, and the insurrectionists fled in disorder. Many soldiers and civilians were killed.

This was the end of the northern conspiracy.

That in the south experienced no different fate. Pestel was arrested on December 13; a southern insurrectionary army, directed by Sergei Muravyov-Apostol, fought bravely but was defeated by government troops at Pologi, on January 3, 1826.

And thus ended the "First Russian Revolution."

This was a revolt of any army élite — an extraordinary group, intelligent, and endowed with political awareness — but unable to draw to themselves a large segment of the army for lack of adequate propaganda and instruction in the goals they were seeking to achieve. Additionally, they had failed to establish an adequate base within the rest of the population, particularly the discontented and rebellious serfs, for fear of a social revolution and a civil war. They aspired to achieve a revolution by substituting the rule of an army élite for the monarchy, and thereafter "handing down" a new form of government.

Whatever the ultimate reasons for the débacle — and historians have been debating the question for more than a century — there can be no doubt as to its tragic consequence for the participants and for Russia.

Five hundred and twenty-nine persons were brought to trial, of whom more than one hundred and twenty were declared guilty as being the most responsible leaders. Pestel, Sergei Muravyov-Apostol, Ryleev, Kakhovsky, and Bestuzhev-Riumin were condemned to be quartered, and a large number to be decapitated or exiled. However, in a prearranged mercy — Nicholas was a fine actor! — the Tsar modified the sentence. Five leaders were to be hanged, the remainder were to be exiled to Siberia for varying terms, thirty-one of these for life.

A horrified population waited for word of commutation of the death sentences, since officially the death penalty did not exist in Russia. On July 13, 1826, the five men were hanged. One hundred and twenty-six were sent to Siberia.

Not many of the accused behaved as shamelessly as Prince Trubetskoy, when he went on his knees before Nicholas and abjectly implored that his life be spared — offering full information and confession. However, there were others, like the Decembrist Yakushkin who, when summoned by the Tsar, stood his ground.

Nicholas: . . . Why then do you answer me nothing?
Yakushkin: What do you wish of me, Sovereign?
Nicholas: I think I speak to you plainly enough; if you do not wish to ruin
     your family and to be treated as a swine you must confess to everything.
Yakushkin: I gave my word of honor to name no one . . . Still whatever I
     knew about myself, I have said to his Excellency (General Laveshav).

Nicholas: What has "his Excellency" and your contemptible "word of
    honor" to do with it?
Yakushkin: Sovereign, I can name no one.
Nicholas: Put him in chains so that he cannot move.[7]

Nor were the wives of the condemned less heroic than the
men. Many of them followed their husbands to Siberia, and
continued by their side for years.

In 1856, on his accession to the throne, Alexander II decreed an
amnesty for the surviving Decembrist exiles. About twenty-five of
these were still alive. Some preferred to remain in Siberia as their
only home. A few returned.

The heroic lessons of the Decembrist movement and of the
Decembrists were taken to heart by posterity, many of whom called
themselves "Sons of the Decembrists." Their influence extended
throughout the century. Far from ending the struggle against
autocracy, the work of the Decembrists marked only the beginning
of such efforts. As one of their worthy "descendants," Alexander
Herzen, expressed it,

The heritage we received from the Decembrists was the awakened feeling
of human dignity, the striving for independence, the hatred of slavery, and
respect for Western Europe and for the Revolution, the faith in the
possibility of an upheaval in Russia, the passionate desire to take part in it.

And Russia's foremost poet, Alexander Pushkin, who had been a
close friend of the executed poet Ryleev, wrote this tribute to the
Decembrists, not published until after Pushkin's death:

> In the depths of the Siberian mines,
> Keep alive your proud patience;
> Not in vain were your grievous toils,
> And the high reaches of your thoughts.
> Hope, true sister of affliction,
> Shall rouse strength and joy
> In this subterranean gloom.
> The hour you are awaiting will come...

Through gloomy bolts, love and friendship
Will reach you, as in your prison burrow
Does my free voice. The heavy chains
Will fall, prisons crash,
And Freedom will greet you at the door,
And your brothers restore to you your sword.

2.

> No, I shall not utterly die. In my lyre
> My soul shall outlive my dust, secure from stain —
> And I shall be famed, as long as one poet only
> Remains alive in this our world.
>
> Long shall I remain endeared to the people,
> For noble thoughts struck on my lyre,
> For exalting Freedom in this age without pity,
> And asking mercy for the fallen.
> — Pushkin, "Exegi Monumentum" 1836 —

On February 8, 1837, in the late afternoon, a duel took place between Baron George d'Anthès and Alexander Pushkin, near the Black River, outside St. Petersburg. Two days later Pushkin lay dead. He was then in his thirty-seventh year. The tragedy did not consist only in the fact that the life of a genius was thus snuffed out, but also that the death and its antecedent events brought out glaringly the conflicts, tensions, and drama that characterized the Russia of Alexander I and Nicholas I, the era of the Napoleonic wars and of the "Holy Alliance" — and wove them into a tragic pattern that constituted the life, the poetical genius, and the extinction of the poet.

For young as he was at the time of his death, Pushkin, like Lord Byron, set his stamp upon his time, so that his younger contemporary, the critic Vissarion Belinsky, was well justified in speaking of it as the "Pushkin era." Another contemporary, destined to become one of Russia's preeminent novelists, Nikolai Gogol, was equally emphatic in testifying to the meaning of Pushkin. "With him," he wrote on hearing of the calamity, "all the greatest joy of my life is gone. I undertook nothing without his advice . . . God! My present work, inspired by him, his creation — but I can't go on. Time and again I have taken up my pen, but it always fell from my hands."[8]

The last seven years of Pushkin's life had been inaugurated with a burst of productiveness unmatched by any of his preceding creative periods, but they also began with that strange infatuation that carried the seeds of the fatality that was eventually to destroy him. He had wooed and won one of Moscow's dazzling beauties, the eighteen-year old Natalia Goncharova.

In the midst of his courtship, and in anticipation of a new life, he had withdrawn to his family's estate at Boldino, away from the hectic social whirl of St. Petersburg, and the fretful negotiations with his future bride's family in Moscow. At Boldino he had completed his major life's work, the narrative poem *Eugene Onegin,* which had been seven years in the making; numerous shorter works, several "little tragedies," and five prose tales. Not least, he had finally secured official permission to publish his tragedy, *Boris Godunov,* which had been completed five years before — the Tsar's gracious offering toward Pushkin's approaching nuptials. Was it really possible that the years of storm and stress were over? So it seemed. Tsar Nicholas, self-appointed censor and adviser of the poet, appeared more kindly disposed toward him than ever. Pushkin was thirty years old and already the acknowledged prince of Russian letters.

He was a genius with obsessions. When he was composing, he was obsessed, crouching on floors or on tables, or over his desk, with hundreds of slips of paper filled with writing, oblivious of everything and everyone around. The outside world was obliterated, internalized, and transformed. Yet his poetic frenzy was disciplined; disciplined "crystallization," it might be called. The poetic clay was being carefully shaped with firm and masterly hand — a process so different from the inner and outer life he had been leading.

It was at this time, when his creations were reaching their full tide, that he composed a short poem, "The Demons." This was a confessional self-revelation, veiled with the traditional Romantic elements of the supernatural, but actually an exploration of his inner soul. The Russian ballad stanza (a verse-form popularized all over Europe by the German poet, Bürger's "Lenore,") conveys all the eeriness and terror:

The poet is driving through a blizzard.

> Mchatsya tuchi, vyatsya tuchi;
> Nevidimkoyu luna
> Osvieshchayet sneg letutchyi;
> Mutno nebo, noch mutna...

"Clouds scurry, clouds whirl — an invisible moon lights up the flying snow ... I drive on, in the open plain; the sleigh-bells ring out, but despite oneself there is terror, terror all around in these unknown vastnesses." The driver is blinded by the snow, he loses his way, and cries out that it is a demon who is driving the sleigh, plunging it hither and thither. But the traveller sees not one, but many demons surrounding the sleigh. "In the unbounded emptiness the demons circle in swarms, and their pitiful shrieks and howls tear my heart..."[9]

Unfortunately, it was not only imaginary demons that Pushkin had to contend with in his life. He too was a child of his generation — living in a strife-torn world, growing to manhood and poetic maturity in the time of the Restoration, in a land that was to become the principal bulwark of reaction and repression. Culturally, it was France that held ultimate sway over the upper classes and the gentry; and French was the language of fashionable interchange, while Russian was reserved for communication with servant, serf, and lowly office-holder. Native Russian literature leaned heavily on that of eighteenth and seventeenth century France. Tutors were imported, mostly from France and Germany, less frequently from England. Literature, that is the writing of poems, stories, dramas, was considered something of an avocation, not yet a serious profession deserving of independent respect and reward. But France,

once a revered teacher (recall Catherine the Great and her
patronage of the French Encyclopedists!), had turned into an ogre, a
country that had spread the plagues of democracy and revolution
throughout the world. A country to be carefully watched.

It was into this whirlpool, where past, present and an obscure
future struggled, that young Alexander Pushkin was thrust. His
genius destined him for prime laureateship, for the vocation of
refashioning the literature of the land. But his whole creative life
was hedged in with such restraints and external obstacles as to
embitter practically all his years. He was truly a child of the century,
for he was born in 1799, and he reflects its passion, searchings,
weaknesses, and strengths, no less than its frustrations. That within
his brief career he could leave such an impressive body of superb
creations is one more testimony to the stubborn heroism of genius.

He fought to assert the supremacy of the poet's vocation, like
so many Romantics — and its superiority over official rank and
status. But he was also boastful of his family tree, which he felt to be
quite lofty. In a savage poem, entitled "My Pedigree," he heaps scorn
on the parvenu aristocracy recently created by the Tsar, on their
lowly origins, and proudly declares, "I am simply a Russian petty
bourgeois." But actually he boasted of his descent from an African
prince, who became the favorite of Peter the Great, as well as of
kinship with the ancient family of the Pushkins, notable heroes and
soldiers — who had achieved high station long before the arriviste
aristocracy that was deriding him. "I am descended from ancient
boyars." The demon of pedigree kept on rankling and rankling. He
felt he had to prove himself the equal of those upstart nobles — he
felt the need to defy them, to provoke them, even incite them, by
adopting their code of "honor." Throughout his life he was engaged
either in challenging to or fighting duels.

Actually, the social and economic position of his family had
been in the process of decay for years, their property reduced to two
estates in disrepair, and the ownership of a few hundred serfs, then

euphemistically referred to as "souls." His father was improvident and miserly, his mother tyrannical and hateful toward her son. He was physically unpreposessing, proud, obstinate, and resentful. He was not even spared the savagery meted out by landowners to their serfs and servants. He was the "little monkey" and he never forgot or forgave these humiliations. Yet the family was educated, highly literate, and the library at home contained numerous French books — philosophical as well as licentious. The boy devoured both kinds. Voltaire became his passion, and the scabrous *Pucelle d'Orléans* among his favorite reading.

He was precocious. His poetic talent was recognized while he was still very young, which is not always the fate of young poets. He was admitted to the very exclusive imperial Lycée, just then established by Tsar Alexander I at Tsarskoye Selo, and his promising poetic productions were acclaimed not only by his fellow-students, but also by the patriarch of poetry, the venerable G. R. Derzhavin, and by the younger, even more celebrated poet and translator, V. A. Zhukovsky. Before long, the latter was lauding Pushkin not merely as an equal, but as his superior. Yet Pushkin ranked low as a student at the Lycée, and upon graduation, was assigned an inferior position in the office of the foreign ministry — in fact, the lowest rank as "Collegiate Secretary."

He was eighteen years old, and made friends easily. A number of them at the Lycée were to make their mark in the history of Russia. He was also befriended by his elders, the poet Zhukovsky, the historian Karamzin, and Prince Viazemsky. At Tsarskoye Selo he had come in contact with military officers stationed there, and he occasionally joined them in their favorite dissipations: brothels, actresses, drinking, and gambling. But he also participated in their more serious occupations, literary and political discussions, the latter often of a dangerous character. A number of the officers were already members of secret societies. Bacchus and Venus took their not inconsiderable toll of Pushkin's physical being, while Philosophy and Politics ministered to his mind. His friends, young and older, looked to him for great things. Zhukovsky had written to Prince Viazemsky: "We must all unite to help this future giant grow up. He will outstrip us all."[10]

Many years later, Pushkin paid tribute to his early patrons in verses he intended to, but did not include in the published version of *Eugene Onegin.*

Oh, the triumph of my innocent days! Your dream is sweet to my soul... The world welcomed me with a smile... Old Derzhavin noticed me on the brink of his grave and blessed me... The guardian of Russian life [Karamzin], leaving his scrolls, would listen to me and caress my timid Muse, and you, deeply inspired poet of everything that is beautiful, you of virginal hearts [Zhukovsky], was it not you who, carried away by sympathy, held out a hand to me and summoned me to pure fame?[11]

He was not deeply interested in his official duties, which were light; but he was involved in writing poetry, and, of course, in social life, dissipations, and politics. In St. Petersburg, his circle of friends and acquaintances had widened considerably, and he became an assiduous visitant in fashionable salons, literary groups, and in the theatre. He came to know more and more members of secret organizations, such, for example as the Union of Welfare, and they, in turn admired him and loved his poetry, but were wary of him. His fiery temperament, his indiscretions, and his undisciplined life represented risks which precluded a more intimate participation in their activities. His close friend Pushchin was profoundly disturbed:

My first thought, he wrote in his *Recollections,* was to confide in Pushkin. In his way, he was fighting for the same things as we — verbally, in writing, poetry and prose... I am fairly certain, I would have taken him with me from the start, because of my great friendship for him. Later, when I thought of putting my plan into action, I could no longer bring myself to tell a secret that was not mine alone, and one whose ill-judged disclosure could have jeopardized so much. The instability of his impulsive personality and his associations with untrustworthy people held me back. It was natural that Pushkin should notice a change in my behavior and begin to suspect I was hiding something from him... I reassured him by telling him that he was doing good work for the cause, outside all the secret societies.[12]

No one of them could have denied that Pushkin was courageous. In poems, in epigrams, circulated from hand to hand, presumably of anonymous authorship, his temerity knew no bounds. His barbed shafts aimed high, and his targets were not insignificant. They included one of the Tsar's highest — and most detested — officials, Arakcheev; the Archimandrite Photius; Prince Golitsyn, minister of education, and even the Tsar himself. Among his longer poems, the "Ode to Freedom," "The Village," and "The Dagger," evoked extraordinary response and amazement. The "Ode to Freedom," which he wrote in 1817, has all the bravado and dash of an inflamed student. It daringly recalls the fate of Louis XVI, and the assassination of Tsar Paul I — an event which brought Alexander I to the throne.

> I will sing the freedom of the world,
> And strike down iniquity sitting on the throne . . .
> Tyrants of the world tremble!
> And you, fallen slaves, take heart and hear.
> Arise!

It concludes with a pointed admonition:

> Learn now, oh Tsars,
> Neither rewards nor punishments,
> Neither daggers nor altars,
> Are your true safeguards;
> Bow your heads beneath the trusty canopy of Law;
> And the Liberty and Peace of your people
> Shall prove your strongest fortress . . .

And preceding these lines, a reminder aimed directly at Tsar Alexander himself:

> Rulers, remember: It is Law that bestows throne
> and crown upon you,
> Not nature, You stand above the people,
> But high above you stands Eternal Law.

This was daring enough. But even more daring was "The Village." Here Pushkin touches on the most pressing of Russia's problems — serfdom. The poem tells of a visit by the poet to a village (actually his family's estate at Mikhailovskoe). He is tired of the fever and pressures of St. Petersburg, and on arrival rejoices in the peace of the countryside. But

> Alas! one dreadful thought clouds my soul:
> Amid these ripening cornfields and mountains,
> Humanity's friend with sadness views
> The murderous shame of dull oppression.
> Here savage masters, destroyers of the people,
> By fate elected — with tyrant rods
> Usurp their labor, time, and goods,
> Blind to their tears, and deaf to their groans...
>
> Oh! If my voice knew how to stir the heart!
> Why deep within me does this fever burn
> Fruitless, and power of speech denied me?
> Shall I ever, friends, see a people freed,
> And slavery end, by will of Tsar?
> And over a fatherland, enlightened by freedom,
> A beautiful dawn burst at last?

At his boldest he does not shy from aiming at Tsar and throne. In the poem, "Noel," he comes close to *lèse majesté*. Tsar Alexander is depicted as returning from a Congress at Aachen, where in conjunction with Prussia and Austria, he has been assuring the "peace and tranquillity" of Europe. He arrives at a Russian peasant hut, in which he finds Mary and the Child Jesus. He makes all sorts of liberal promises — had he not already promised Poland and even Russia constitutions?

> The Child leaps up in his cradle.
> "Really? Is it truly so?"
> And to him his Mother: "Hush-a-bye, Baby,
> Close your eyes and sleep,
> Now that you've heard
> Tsar-Father's fairy tales..."

Such poems were spread by word of mouth throughout St. Petersburg. Adherents of the secret societies knew them by heart. Pushkin, unlike their members, still believed in a gracious Tsar,

whose desire it was to solve Russia's many problems. The future
Decembrists felt altogether differently. The poet-soldier Kondratyi
Ryleev was a republican, and for the overthrow of Tsardom. He was
the author of a celebrated revolutionary poem:

> How the Blacksmith
> Comes to the Shop.
> Glory!
> The Blacksmith carries
> Three knives.
> Glory!
> The first is for the Boyars, for the great ones,
> Glory!
> The second for the Priests, for the Monks,
> Glory!
> And the third knife
> For the Tsar.
> Glory![13]

Such thoughts were far from Pushkin's mind, though in a later
poem, "The Dagger," he was to come quite close to them. Those of
his friends who were influential at the Court, like the conservative
Karamzin and Zhukovsky, much as they liked Pushkin, were
appalled by his poetic utterances, whose authorship was no secret.
The axe came down soon enough...

His fate might have been worse. He was exiled — but not to
Siberia, as he and his friends had feared. He was "transferred" to the
south of Russia, more than one thousand miles away from St.
Petersburg, to Ekaterinoslav, and placed in charge of the administrator
of the southern colonies, General I. N. Insov. In his way, Pushkin
was lucky. He would be away, it was true, from the centers of
Russian culture, from society, friendships, and debauchery. But he
was destined to find compensations; in fact, new and profound
sources of poetic inspiration. A gracious Tsar had placed him in the
hands of an indulgent and liberal-minded superior, who was a
Freemason, and who knew how to value the man and poet in

Pushkin. Pushkin did not suspect that the south of Russia, the Caucasus and the Crimea, would open new doors of his imagination, enlarge his poetic vision, advance his creative energies and productions. On May 18, 1820, he left St. Petersburg. A few weeks before, he had completed his first major poetic work, the fairy tale *Ruslan and Ludmila,* which appeared in the summer of 1820. Pushkin, though not materially enriched, became a celebrity...

He had been nourished on folk-tales and folk-lore from childhood. The nurses of his household, in reality mother-surrogates during those difficult early days, knew how to tell stories. They also gave him the affection denied him by his own parents. He was to immortalize both Uliana, his nurse, and Arina Rodiovnovna, his sister's nurse, in his poems. *Ruslan and Ludmila* is a fairy-tale that satisfied both sophisticated and the unsophisticated readers and listeners — the story of a wicked magician who ravishes away a beautiful bride on her wedding night; and of a bold hero, who goes in search of her, has innumerable adventures, not the least being that he single-handedly routs an enemy besieging the city of Kiev. For the sophisticated, there was the story, in fluent verses, simple and direct, spiced with a tongue-in-cheek humor — for Pushkin was satirizing, and here in fact parodying a poetic and far-fetched fairy tale of his patron and mentor, Zhukovsky (who, generous man that he was, forgave him), and other Romantic vagaries. The heroine performs no less fantastic feats than her hero, for she manages to gain possession of the magician's cap of invisibility, while Ruslan strips him of his magic powers. Pushkin, speaking for himself, reflects on the dangers of magic:

> Ya kazden den, vostav ot sna,
> Blagodaryu serdechno boga...

> Every day, on awakening from sleep,
> I give heart-felt thanks to God
> That in our days magicians have grown scarce,
> And — honor and glory to them! —
> Our marriages are no longer threatened!...

Some years later, Pushkin added a delicious prologue:

> By curving shore a green oak,
> And on that oak a golden chain,
> And day and night a learned cat
> Walks round and round on that chain;
> When to the right — he sings a song —
> When to the left — he tells a tale...
>
> And I was there; I drank the mead,
> I saw that oak by the sea,
> And it was to me this wise cat
> Told those many stories...

Who would have imagined from these light-hearted, sprightly and fanciful verses that the poet's heart was oppressed, that "exiled" from civilization, he identified himself with another poet-exile, Roman Ovid, sent by an implacable emperor to spend long years at Tomi, by the mouth of the Danube?

Pushkin tried to make the best of it. He transplanted his cosmopolitan life to the Caucasus, the Crimea, and elsewhere; he made new friends who ministered to his restlessness by taking him on their excursions, or having him as their guest. He roamed the countryside; he explored, he made love, but he also absorbed a great deal of what he saw, and turned it into poetry. There was the Raevsky family, with their beautiful girls, who tried to teach him English, for they were lovers of Byron's works, and they hoped he would become better acquainted with that poet. But Pushkin never took to English. He read Byron in the diluted and commonplace prose translations of two Frenchmen, Pichot and de Salle. But even through this obscuring medium he penetrated into the British poet's thought, and found him an inexhaustible source of poetic inspiration. Was not his life like that of Byron? Was he not also a "pilgrim"? And was not the nature he saw around him like that which Byron loved: the sea, the mountains, the Orient, the primitive, the mysterious? And was he not like Byron filled with wild loves? And, in his own more restricted way, also an apostle of Freedom? He was living in the shadow of Byron's *Cosair, Lara, Childe Harold*. And here in the south he was close to the revolutionary uprising in Greece, in the presence of Greek leaders of the liberation movement — like the Ypsilantis, and the recruits being mustered for a war with Turkey. The news reaching him from Spain roused him too, for there a similar uprising was taking place.

A strange picture, he wrote. Two great peoples, who fell long ago into a contemnable insignificance, are arising from their ashes at the same time, and rejuvenated are appearing on the political arena of the world.[14]

In a constant delirium he roamed this exotic world, now with Cossacks visiting unfriendly Circassian territory, now skirting the magic shores of the Black Sea, moving from Orient to Europe, visiting Tartar villages, hearing Georgian songs, seeing ancient ruins, following Insov, when that superior was transferred to Kishinev.

If the authorities who had removed him from St. Petersburg hoped to immunize him from subversive influences, and cure him of infection by revolutionary thought, they were soon to be undeceived. In a sealed letter they had sent General Insov about Pushkin, along with praise for some of the "highest beauties of design and execution" to be found in his poems, they particularly named his "Ode to Freedom" as "revealing dangerous principles from that contemporary school, or perhaps it would be better to say, from that anarchical system which people maliciously call a system of the rights of man, of freedom, and of independence of people...Mr. Pushkin will reform, if only we may believe his tears and promises," and, provided with good examples, may eventually turn out to be a "fine servant of the government, or, at least, writer of the first rank."[15]

Ironically enough, it was here in the south of Russia that he found himself in the very hotbed of revolutionary talk. It was here that he met future Decembrists like Pestel, Davidov, Yakushkin, and General Orlov. Like their northern colleagues, they too were unsure about Pushkin's general reliability as a conspirator; they did not invite him to join their secret organization. But in spirit, he felt himself to be one of them, and used his poetry as his weapon. It was at this time that he composed "The Dagger" — a paean to heroic assassins like Charlotte Corday, Karl Sand (the murderer of Kotzebue), and Brutus.

> Hephaestus, god of Lemnos, forged you
> For the hands of immortal Nemesis,
> Thou silent guardian of freedom, Avenger Dagger,
> Last judge of offence and shame!
>
> Where Thunderer Zeus is silent, and sword of Justice sleeps,
> Thou art the maker of hopes and damnations,
> Thou hidest under the thrones of monarchs,
> And in the folds of festive robes...

And he added an apostrophe to Karl Sand:

> Oh noble and just man, by fate elected,
> Sand! your life was forfeit to the block,
> But the sacred voice of your virtue
> Speaks even within your ashes.
>
> And eternal shade, you wander through German lands,
> Solemn threat to despots and their strength,
> Your dagger burns with a quenchless fire
> On your triumphant tombstone — nameless, uninscribed.

In his notes on history, he remarked that "only a fearful cataclysm could destroy the deep-rooted slavery which exists in Russia," and that "our political freedom is inseparable from the emancipation of the peasants." He compared his own efforts in behalf of Russian literature and language to the political aims of the revolutionaries:

Only a revolutionary like M. Orlov or Pestel can love Russia, in the same way as only a writer can love language. Everything must be created in this Russia and in this Russian language.[16]

If he thought himself completely secure, he was mistaken. What he said in social gatherings, what he wrote in his letters was noted, we may be sure, and duly reported to the proper quarters. He longed for St. Petersburg, and despite all the activity around him, even involving him, he felt terribly bored, bored with the narrow provincialism of Kishinev; even bored with his innumerable amours. Only when he was writing did he feel at peace with himself.

He had composed two poetic narratives in the style of Byron's oriental tales — "The Prisoner of the Caucasus" and "The Fountain of Bakhchisaray," both poems of ardent passions. In one, a Circassian maid falls in love with a Russian prisoner, helps him to escape, and for love of him drowns herself. In the second, the passion of an Oriental potentate for a Christian captive arouses the Tartar's former favorite to a fit of jealousy, which eventually leads to the death of both women.

But it was not only tragic incidents which occupied him. He could be sardonic, satiric, even scurrilous. The *Gabriliad* is an erotic parody of the fall of Adam and Eve, the Virgin Birth and the Annunciation. Voltaire's *Pucelle d'Orléans* is very much to the fore in this sacrilegious work. The Virgin Mary is possessed in turn by Satan, the angel Gabriel, and even God himself! Pushkin, of course, did not put his name to the poem. His friends were delighted with it; others were outraged. The Minister of Police, Count Benckendorff, was duly apprised of this "rebellious poem which carries the torch of revolt among all the classes of the population and attacks the sanctity of faith, the indispensable bridle of all peoples, especially the Russians, with the dangerous and treacherous weapons of sarcasm."[17]

Pushkin's influential friends in St. Petersburg finally succeeded in persuading the government to transfer the unhappy poet, but not, as he hoped, to the capital, but to Odessa, a cosmopolitan city, a bustling port, with a thriving cultural life, and live theatres. The city also contained a considerable number of Poles, among them notable aristocratic families, boasting beautiful as well as amorous ladies. Among them was Carolina Sobiańska, who looked with favor upon Pushkin, as she was also to favor Poland's Adam Mickiewicz. Pushkin was not slow in joining the gaieties and temptations of Odessa. He went to the theatre, ate, drank, gambled, made love, wrote love poems, and was even beginning to profit from his published works. There was a proverbial fly in the Odessa ointment — namely Count Vorontsov, his present superior, vice-regent of the Bessarabian region, who treated Pushkin as an insignificant subordinate, had little use for poetry, and even less for Pushkin's talents. The friction between them was not lessened by the presence of the Countess Vorontsov, who was very attractive and to whom Pushkin began paying court. She too proved amenable to his poetry and other persuasions . . .

Pushkin combined strong amatory propensities — never fully satisfied — with an equally strong anti-connubial bias. Like Balzac, he felt the need to conquer; and the more highly-placed and seemingly inaccessible the prey, the more eager and breathless the pursuit. He was physically unattractive, and he knew it. But he had flaming eyes, eloquence, and genius. Women were drawn to him, many out of sincere affection, even love; others because he was something of a celebrity. His own amatory experiences and his knowledge of society had filled him with a pathological fear of cuckoldry. Yet, when he himself was passionately involved, and allowed himself an untrammeled flow of feeling, he was a true lover, and his poetry expressed with candor and deep emotion what he really experienced. But the cynical side of him was always awake, keeping a watchful eye on his stormier half. He was extremely sensitive, easily alert to humiliations — whether real or imagined. In the case of Count Vorontsov the humiliations were real, only the antagonists were unevenly matched: Pushkin the subordinate — armed with bitter epigrams — and Vorontsov armed with full authority. Vorontsov would have been glad to get rid of the gadfly, and in 1824 succeeded in sending Pushkin to Kherson to investigate a locust plague in that district.

But events were moving toward an inevitable crisis.

How could Vorontsov — crude Philistine that he was — know that the contemned underling, despite insults and vexations, was in those very years of 1823 and 1824 creating poetic works that the world would hail as masterpieces — a dramatic idyl, *The Gipsies,* and the first two chapters of *Eugene Onegin,* and that the name of Vorontsov, governor of Bessarabia, would be totally forgotten, had he not made life miserable for Russia's greatest poet?

Pushkin returned from his mission to the locusts, furious, determined to resign. This was the boldest step he had ever taken in his life — one bound to offend not only Count Vorontsov, but the highest circles in St. Petersburg.

Another circumstance served to aggravate his culpability in the eyes of the authorities. He had written a letter, presumably to Count Viazemsky, which found its way into the hands of the police, and in turn was transmitted upward.

While reading Shakespeare and the Bible, Pushkin wrote, the Holy Spirit is sometimes in my heart, but I prefer Goethe and Shakespeare. You want to know what I am doing: I am writing various strophes of a romantic poem, and I am taking lessons in pure atheism. There is here an Englishman, a deaf philosopher, the only wise atheist whom I have ever met. He has written a thousand pages in order to prove *qu'il ne peut exister d'être intelligent Créateur et régulateur* — destroying, by the way, the feeble arguments for the immortality of the soul. The system is not so comforting as is usually imagined, but unfortunately, it is more plausible than any other.[15]

This letter, and his resignation, were enough to fill the cup of transgressions. Minister Nesselrode wrote to Count Vorontsov:

His Majesty has commanded me, as a legal punishment to strike his name off the list of civil servants in the Ministry of Foreign Affairs for bad behavior; however, His Majesty does not agree to leaving him entirely without surveillance, on the ground that, making use of his independent position, he will, without doubt, spread more and more of those harmful ideas which he holds, and he will compel the authorities to employ the most severe measures against him. In order to avoid, if possible, such consequences, the emperor thinks that he cannot be kept under control in retirement, and hence he finds it necessary to send him to the estate of his parents in the Pskov government, under the surveillance of the local authorities. Your Excellency will not delay in reporting this decision to Pushkin, which he must act on punctually, proceeding to Pskov without delay, once having been provided with traveling money.[19]

On July 25, 1824, Pushkin left Odessa for his family's estate at Mikhailovskoe. His parents knew nothing of what had occurred, and Pushkin, aware that his own relation to his folks was anything but friendly, expected the worst.

He bade farewell to the South, which despite the tribulations and humiliations he had experienced, had given him so much that was to make him into a mature poet. He was already possessed of a wide audience. He had learned to mould word, sound, and image in ways unheard of before him in Russian poetry. He had left St. Petersburg an apprentice poet; he was now filled with a sense of accomplishment, and a feeling of confidence in his poetic future. The other future was of course more uncertain. A younger generation hailed him as the sovereign Russian poet, the creator of a new literature, and their spokesman. His *Fountain of Bakhchisarai* had won wide acclaim, and Vyazemski had written a brilliant introduction to the work. He was bringing back with him a magnificent "dramatic" idyl, *The Gipsies,* and two cantos of *Eugene Onegin,* an epic narrative poem, which, he felt, would fulfil his youthful boast that he would achieve immortal fame. He had learned a great deal from the literary masters of European literature, Goethe, Schiller, Byron, and his Russian predecessors. He knew that he could now stand on his own feet. His veneration for Byron never slackened, but he could judge him objectively yet with reverence: a titanic figure, whose presence was ever with him. Byron's death in April 1824 moved him deeply, as it had the rest of the world.

Pushkin must have shocked and astonished the illiterate local priest (who had not even heard of the British poet) by ordering "an evening mass for the peace of his soul." In a beautiful farewell "To the Sea" he evoked the spirit of Napoleon, and also commemorates Byron," another ruler of our thoughts," like the sea, "mighty, deep, and dark." The first two cantos of *Eugene Onegin* still reflect the impress of Byron's brilliant *Don Juan*. It was hard to shed the Byronic mantle. Byron, unlike Shakespeare, was not "myriad-minded," but he was many-faceted. In him a passionate sentimentalism clashed with a sense of reality; one portion of his self sought the unattainable infinite, the other looked with critical irony both upon himself and the world, and masked tears in laughter. Pushkin's problem would be to move from the ego-centrism of Byron, for whom all heroes of his mind's creation mirrored himself, to that stage where he could objectify his own created figures, diversify them, and make them the mirrors of a variegated world. In the seven years it would take to complete *Eugene Onegin* Pushkin would undergo many changes, and his poem, too, would show a profound growth.

But at this point, the Byronic yearning for a life of individual "freedom" was still with him, a life close to Nature, to "natural" man (so much a portion of Romanticism), and a humanity free of the dross of civilization.

Such an ideal Pushkin celebrates in *The Gipsies*. These are the happy primitives, who, despite poverty and insecurity, live a natural and wise life. Aleko, a civilized and unhappy Russian, the "modern" man, believes he can find salvation, peace, and comfort for his *Weltschmerz* by joining a caravan of Bessarabian gipsies. He too is seeking "freedom." Like a Byronic hero he is "pursued by the law." He falls in love and is loved by the gipsy girl, Zemphira, beautiful, wild, and unpredictable. She is the daughter of the "Old Man," who is the epitome of natural wisdom. Aleko joins the gipsy band, becomes the exhibitor of a dancing bear, part of the entertainment that provides for the gipsies' subsistence. But unrest gnaws at him. Two years pass, and Aleko discovers that Zemphira had fallen in love with another man. In a rage, Aleko kills the girl and her lover. The gipsies do not comprehend such violence. They tell him to leave, for they insist he understands neither their life, nor the meaning of Freedom. Had he not denied to others the freedom he had sought for himself? The poet concludes with reflections on Fatality, Chance, and Passion, that only too well reveal Pushkin's own ambiguous feelings. For even the seemingly happy gipsies are not excempt from misfortune. "Everywhere there are fatal passions" and "from the Fates there is no defense."

The Old Man, father of the murdered girl, thus instructs Aleko:

> Leave us, proud man!
> We are wild; we have no laws.
> We do not torture, we do not kill —
> We have no need of blood and groans.
> But with a murderer we will not live.
> You were not born for this wild life,
> For you want freedom only for yourself . . .

Both Ryleev and Viazemsky took exception to the poem, especially to Pushkin's treatment of Aleko. The "unheroic" hero of the tale appeared to them to clash with the dignity of literature, and their own political attachments. That Aleko should become a bear-trainer and pass a hat around before a gaping crowd was surely unbecoming! Pushkin should at least have made him a blacksmith . . .

For the last time, looking out on the Black Sea, and wondering about his future, Pushkin exclaimed:

> Fly, ship, carry me to far borders
> On the menacing whims of the treacherous seas,
> But only not to the sad shores
> Of my foggy, native land . . .

In August 1824, he was back in Mikhailovskoe, under the surveillance of Von Aderkas, the governor of the department, and whatever other surrogates were available — in this instance, Pushkin's father.

What visitors could he expect to come and see him, now that a *cordon sanitaire* had been established around him? His letters, and those of his friends, he knew, would be opened, his movements would be carefully observed and recorded. He dreamt of escaping abroad. He wrote feverish letters to his friends, appealed to the Tsar, pleading a serious illness, an "aneurism" - - but all he got was permission to go to Pskov for treatment. At home his father badgered him, and sometimes even provoked scenes of violence. Pushkin took refuge in neighborhood diversions, with families well provided with young women. In his own drab household he found time to solace himself with a young serf-girl, and soon fathered a child. That was one side of his life in "exile."

There was another. For once he withdrew to his own somewhat dismal quarters, he became a different person. The worldly, amorous libertine had only to shut the door of his chamber to turn into a magician! There, sprawled in strange postures, he bent over his manuscripts. Here his sorcerer's powers were unrestrainable. By the end of 1826, he could boast that he had composed six cantos of *Eugene Onegin*, the tragedy *Boris Godunov*, and numerous lesser works.

His friends had been appalled by this "exile" and feared for his career as poet. Prince Vyazemski called it an "assassination" and a *"coup de grâce."* How could the Tsar fear the words of a poet, and who ever heard of a poet endangering the safety of a society?[20]

Yet, wonder of wonders! there were friends daring enough to come and see him. There was Ivan Pushchin, whose appearance filled the poet with joy, not unmixed with tears. Pushkin read aloud from his works, especially *The Gipsies*. The visit did not escape supervision, for a neighboring monk "dropped in" for a while, to the poet's embarrassment. Later Pushchin reported: "We had a presentiment that we were drinking together for the last time."[21] With others, like Baron Delvig, he relived his schooldays at the Lycée. Soon, he hoped, he would escape; surely something was likely to happen to change this life of his he could not bear. Surely, once again he would be reading his works in the salons of Moscow and Petersburg!

Then, suddenly, history intervened. On December 1, 1825 Tsar Alexander died. No news could have been more gratifying to the poet. There followed the confused interregnum, until Nicholas was to take the oath on December 25. Pushkin determined to go to St. Petersburg, even without official permission. He started on the way, and, according to tradition, being superstitious, he turned back on encountering a hare and a monk — both evil omens. Actually, one may guess, he was deterred by a feverish anxiety. Had he gone to St. Petersburg, and to the home of Ryleev, and arrived there on the 24th of the month, he could have come upon a meeting of the leaders of the Union of the North — the group that was planning an uprising for the following day. The Decembrist revolt failed, and then came the executions and exiles. In Mikhailovskoe the news caused an indescribable panic. Though Pushkin could not have been suspected of having participated in the planned *coup d'état*, he was known to have been on very friendly terms with many of the conspirators. And now, what would happen to him? He was alone, isolated; he besought his friends for news, and hastened to destroy a number of incriminating papers, including his autobiography. He appealed to Zhukovsky to intercede with the Tsar for permission to return to St. Petersburg, promising to keep his opinions to himself and not to enter "into an insane conflict with the established and necessary order." Zhukovsky's reply was unexpectedly harsh. "Of course you are not implicated; but your poems have been found among the papers of the accused, "adding, that so far as "order and principles" were concerned, Zhukovksy hated "every disgusting thing" Pushkin had ever written, and urged him to stay on in the country and await further developments. But an impatient and terrified Pushkin could not wait, and addressed his own petition to the Tsar through Von Aderkas, governor of the Pskov province, pleading his "aneurism," and his undermined health, and asking to be allowed to go to Moscow or abroad. He also promised never to become a member of any secret society, and denied knowledge of any secret society in the past.[22]

Difficult as was his present situation, he tried to ease it through innumerable flirtations and liaisons in the neighborhood, around the circle of the delightful Osipov family, with the adorable but persuasive Anna Kern, and such other women as gracious divinities might send his way. All the time he was hopeful that Tsar Nicholas would be merciful toward the accused Decembrists, but the announcement of the sentences meted out to them came as a shattering blow. Pestel, Ryleev, Michael Bestuzhev-Ryumin, Kakhovsky, and Muravyev-Apostol were hanged. More than a hundred others were to be deported! Only yesterday, it seemed, he had chatted with many of them!

He was a survivor. In "Arion," a poem written years later, modeled on one of Horace's famous odes, he was to describe his feelings at the time. He imagines himself in a boat, with others. All seems calm and carefree. Suddenly a gust of wind arises and sweeps both helmsman and sailor to their death.

> Only I, mysterious singer,
> Cast ashore by the storm,
> Chant my hymns of yore
> And dry my damp garments
> In the sun, at the foot of a rock ...

He would never forget. For his exiled friends he composed verses in secret, and had them secretly transmitted. For himself he reserved the heavy debt of guilt, remorse, and future atonement, made doubly bitter by the accommodations with the reigning Tsar to whom he was now subjecting himself. Underneath his usual exterior garb he would wear a figurative hairshirt — and his penitential psalms would be his poems — frequently anonymous — that would remain unpublished during his lifetime, filled with bitter excoriations of tyranny.

Suddenly in September 1826 an unpredictable event took place. Pushkin was summoned to Moscow, to appear before the Tsar himself, "not in the position of a prisoner." The Tsar of all the Russias wished to speak in person to the man of whom he had heard such strange tales, but whose reputation as a poet was incontestable. Reliable tradition has it that during his momentous interview Pushkin was candid, and in a confessional and penitential mood. He admitted knowing the conspirators personally, and, that but for the grace of God, he could have been with them in Senate Square on the fateful day of the revolt. The Tsar proved gracious. From this day on, he said, he would be Pushkin's own censor, and all would be forgiven. Leading the poet from his study, he is reputed to have addressed the courtiers: "Gentlemen, here is the new Pushkin. Let us forget the old." Whatever the exact details of the meeting, two matters were definitely settled: The Tsar would take Pushkin under his wing, and would be the poet's future censor...

Actually, it turned out, Pushkin was to be blessed with four censors: the Tsar, the Tsar's minister of police Count Benckendorff, the government censorship board, and the ever watchful policemen and postal authorities. At that moment of triumph, he did not anticipate that he had bound himself to the imperial leash, seemingly slack at times, but ready to be drawn in sharply at the slightest evidence of waywardness. For the moment, Pushkin was happy. What absolute monarch had ever, since the days of Augustus Caesar, shown such solicitude for and interest in a poet?

So he basked in the Tsar's grace, in the prospect of revisiting Moscow and once more seeing, as he wrote in *Eugene Onegin,*

... the ancient cupolas.., dazzling white walls, shining like fire with their golden crucifixes. Ah, brothers! how happy I was when I caught a glimpse of the churches, the towers, the gardens, the palaces of my old city! How often, during the absence decreed by a wandering destiny, have I dreamt of you, Moscow! What magic in that name!... How many things it says to the Russian heart![23]

Was the bear really tamed, ready to be exhibited like Aleko's docile animal in the great marketplaces of the world? Count Benckendorff, the Tsar's appointed intermediary, was no fool, and he knew his victim better than the victim knew him. From now on every minor transgression, every lapse would meet with warning or reproof. Past sins would rise up to trouble the present. A poem on the French poet André Chénier he had written in 1825 had reappeared in private circulation with the compromising title of "December 14"; and the embarrassing *Gabriliad* as well, for both of which he was called to task. The Tsar did not like *Boris Godunov,* and suggested that it be turned into a historical novel on the style of Sir Walter Scott. When Pushkin ventured to read that play privately at a gathering, he was immediately reproved for not having applied for prior permission. These readings met with overwhelming enthusiasm on the part of his hearers; at one of them Adam Mickiewicz was present. But what good did they do if he could not publish the play, or have it staged? There was some, if insufficient balm, in that Pushkin was allowed to return to St. Petersburg, where he could indulge in gambling, making love, and other foibles — from which he would recuperate by occasional visits to Mikhailovskoe. On one such occasion he encountered a living ghost from the past: He came face to face with Küchelbecker, Decembrist and poet, under guard as he was being transferred from one fortress to another... What bitter memories this meeting was bound to stir up!

At times he must have felt like a baited animal. What poisonous resentment was being distilled within him! It found partial outlet in his poems, such as "The Prophet."

> Like a corpse I lay in the desert,
> And the voice of God called out to me:
> Arise, prophet, and see, and hear...
> Set the hearts of men on fire with the sword...

But he expunged these lines:

> Arise, arise, prophet of Russia,
> Put on the vestments of shame,
> Go with a halter around your neck,
> And appear before the vile assassin.[24]

The "poison" within him found an even more forceful expression in one of his most savage poems, "The Upas Tree." The mythical antiar tree oozes poison from its bark, and spreads fetid and pestilential death around it. It is to this tree that "one man" sends "another man." The messenger is to bring back the pitchy mass, of course, at the expense of his own life. With it the "Prince" will be enabled to anoint the darts with which to destroy neighboring enemies. Pushkin altered the original "Tsar" to the more vague "Prince."

His most devastating attack on absolutism was to come some years later, in 1833, in the consummate poetic narrative, *The Bronze Horseman.*

In April 1828, Russia declared war on Turkey. Pushkin saw in this event a means of salvation. He would join the army, he would make contact with General Paskevich, play truant, and go south — which he proceeded to do. He was with the victorious Russian army when it entered Erzerum. At the end of September 1829, he was back in Moscow.

Before leaving for the war, he had engaged in another, equally hazardous undertaking. He had sued for the hand of Natalia Goncharova, whose father was *non compos mentis* as a result of a fall, a man whose estate was in decay, and whose fortunes were then at a very low ebb. The prospective mother-in-law was bent on selling her daughter at a high price — and Pushkin was engaged in bickering for her like any tradesman. Natalia was naive, and — not in love. Pushkin was dazzled by her youth and beauty. There is no greater tragedy than that which follows the self-entrapment of an individual who is passion's fool, and knows himself such. In May 1830 he wrote:

My fate is decided. I am to be married. She whom I loved for two whole years, whom my eyes at first sight sought out everywhere, and with whom a meeting seemed bliss, my God, she is almost mine! The expectation of a decisive answer was the most painful feeling of my life. The expectation of the last lingering card, remorse of conscience, the dream before a duel — all this in comparison signifies nothing...I am to be married, that is, I sacrifice my independence, my carefree, whimsical independence, my luxurious habits, my aimless wanderings, solitude and inconstancy.[25]

It is with such feelings that Pushkin was entering upon his most momentous life-experience!

His father assigned to him the estate at Boldino, with its two hundred "souls," worth 4000 rubles a year. It was a sorry place, run-down and depressing. But following the hectic courtship and the excitement of the betrothal, it proved a gratifying and restful retreat in the fall of 1830. Cholera prevailed there as in other parts of Russia, and he was cut off from Moscow where his betrothed lived. A quarantine prevented him from rejoining her before the end of the year.

Don Juan was to be married! Pushkin had drawn up a list of his amatory conquests, many real, some imaginary, which he conned with all the glee of a Leporello. Like another of Don Giovanni's victims, his heart went beating, "Vorrei, e non vorrei" — eternally debating Yes and No. But the die was cast. He had no hesitation, however, when it came to sitting down and composing poetry. Boldino's seclusion was propitious to creation. He had recently completed a long historical poem, "Poltava," on the subject of the legendary figure of Mazeppa. It had met with scant approval. Now he would show the world! Some years before, when he had finished writing *Boris Godunov,* he exclaimed, "I feel that my soul is fully developed. I can create."[26] It was in this spirit that he settled down. Urania was kindly disposed. Prospero waved his magic wand, and was master of the world of imagination. A seven-years' task of intermittent labor was over. *Eugene Onegin* was completed. He noted the date: October 7, 1830...

Unlike so many of his literary contemporaries in other lands, Pushkin has left us no autobiography in verse or prose. We have no depiction of "the growth of the poet's mind." Whatever auto-biographical material he had set down in stray notes in the early twenties, he had destroyed in the wake of the Decembrist collapse. His fascinating and numerous letters do, however, offer a number of clues to his intellectual and artistic development.

In its own way, *Eugene Onegin* — having taken such a long time in the making — may be said to be a cursive mirror of Pushkin's growth and process of self-realization. Commenced in 1823 as an offspring of Byron's *Don Juan* and his humorous tale, *Beppo,* Pushkin's work is in its initial chapters brilliantly ironic, self-mocking, parodistic, and — derivative. Gradually the poem begins to achieve its own independence, and becomes a novel in verse: the characters become less ego-images, and more clearly objectified. What might have become merely another amalgam of the Childe Harold-Don Juan themes, travelogue spiced with adventures, endless digressions and ironic asides in the poet's own person, turns into a drama of contemporary life, built around three distinct central characters: Eugene Onegin, Tatiana Larin, and Vladimir Lensky. They are representatives of Russian upper-class society of the early twenties of the nineteenth century.

This was no longer the exotic Orient, the world of Circassian beauties and romantic captives. This was the reality of Moscow and Petersburg, of the Russian countryside, the mansions, estates, farms; here we have the alternation of the seasons; rooms with samovars, gossip, chatter, noise, balls and soirées, filled with the commonplaces of every-day life; young women in search of suitable husbands, bachelors in search of wealthy heiresses...

Concurrently, a certain stylistic luxuriance had given way to a disciplined control and mastery, a restraint amounting almost to understatement. The Romantic "overflow of powerful feeling" is now channelled, held in bounds by the fourteen-line stanza, with its

intricate and amazing rhyme-scheme, yet diverse in its rhythmic
and musical patterns, moulded to the situations: now matter-of-fact
as in a local drama, now responding to the deeper currents of feeling
and thought. For all the irony, satire, mockery — the central theme
is serious and even sad: consonant with the tragic incongruities that
beset human beings caught up in the web of social behaviors and
attitudes, in codes of life imposed upon them in contravention of
their better feelings; beings either too impotent or not sufficiently
mature or wise to resist them, and expose them as fraudulent and
destructive.

There is an additional character in the poem — the Poet in *sua
propria persona* — whom we encounter in Onegin's company on
two occasions: once in St. Petersburg, and another time in Odessa;
one who wanders in the Byronic manner through the whole work,
commenting on many matters, frequently on himself. But the "I" of
the poet never dominates the scene, as does the ego of Byron's
egocentric heroes.

The poem begins in the year 1819. Young Eugene Onegin is
twenty-four years old. His recently deceased father had brought his
estate to ruin, but Onegin has fallen heir to his uncle's wealth and
lands. Eugene is the typical upper-class dilettante — he has a
smattering of all kinds of knowledge, but no knowledge; he is a beau
and a gad-about, has gone through various schools of amours; his
life has been the usual round of balls, soirées, theatre, gambling. But
now he has reached the point of satiation. He is bored, restless,
cynical. Our Poet was drawn to Onegin. The two wander along the
Neva river and talk... A Byronic *Weltschmerz* — a "cosmic" pain
— gnaws at both of them...

> Kto zhyl i misleel, to nye mozhet
> V dushe nye prezeerat lyudei

> He who has lived and thought, cannot
> But despise humanity in his heart...

They are both alike: weary of the world's conventions and vanities.

> Ya bil ozloblen, on ugrium...
>
> I was embittered; he morose...
> In both the heart's flame was dead...

And what awaited them was nothing but Fortune's and men's spite "in the very morn" of their days.

On his estate, Eugene is bored. He despises his Philistine neighbors; and to lighten his ennui, he even attempts to introduce some liberal reforms, such as reducing the quit-rent his peasants have been accustomed to pay him. The peasants were grateful, but his neighbors agreed that Eugene was a dangerous radical.

But how to pass the time? Fortunately, there is a new arrival in the vicinity, Vladimir Lensky, nineteen years old, just returned from his stay at the university of Göttingen. He is an orphan, gentle, filled with enthusiasms, emotional; he has brought back from Germany vague philosophic and poetical ideals, à la Schiller and Goethe, dreams of "freedom," a fiery eloquence, and long hair. For him the world is full of wonders, for he is something of a poet. He is rich and handsome, and a very eligible bachelor. But he too cannot stand the local gentry, and their banalities. "Sheer idleness, that customary bond of friendship" brings Lensky and Eugene together.

Young Lensky is in love with a neighboring girl, Olga Larin, whom he hopes to marry very soon. Eugene yields to a momentary whim, agrees to visit the Larin family with Lensky, meets Olga's older sister Tatiana.

Tatiana Larin, though not so beautiful as her sister, is altogether different from her in temperament. She is wild, melancholy, shy — a stranger to her own family. She is a dreamer, and lives a good part of her life in books, such as those of Rousseau and Samuel Richardson. The sight of Eugene inflames her. Here, she feels, is a person who might have stepped from the pages of romances she had been reading. Something previously unknown takes hold of her — the mystery and terror of a passion she cannot control. She cannot sleep, and must speak to her nurse:

> Nurse, tell me about your old days.
> Were you ever in love then?

> Raskazhi mne, niania,
> Pro vashi starye goda:
> Byla ti vliublena togda?

Tatiana, like so many of her class, lives in total ignorance of the former life of her servants. Her nurse is amused:

> Oh, my Tania! We never heard of love in those days!

She describes how serfs and peasants married. She herself was only thirteen, and the boy not much older. They were brought together by a marriage broker, and then she was thrust into a strange family. What had love to do with it? But Tania is in love. She loses her head, and writes the celebrated letter to Onegin, a letter in which all the pent-up feelings of the young girl have been suddenly released, and dare to confront the unpredicted and unpredictable:

> Ya kvam pishu — chevo zhe bole?
> Shto ya mogu yescho skazat?
> Teper, ya znayu, vvashei vole
> Menia presreniem nakazat...

> I write you... What else could I do?
> Yours is the power to punish me with scorn,
> But no! I know you will pity my lot,
> And not cast me off...

Pushkin remarks in an aside, that Tania cannot spell Russian correctly, and therefore writes in French.

Tania is pitting her deepest and best feelings against those of a man who is suspicious and even derisive of them, a man she does not know. He does not respond by letter, but when they meet again, he instructs her, as if she were a sentimental child. But he is forthright:

he tells her he is not fitted for marriage, and that he could only bring
her unhappiness. He cannot retrieve his early illusions. But, he adds,
she will love again; this infatuation will pass. Onegin is good-
natured, and honorable (for he could easily have seduced Tania!). All
he lacks is understanding!

Tatiana is deeply wounded; but persists in her obsession. She
has a dream with images of fright: she is wandering in a snow, she
comes to a dreadful chasm, she is pursued by a bear who carries her
to a hut in which there are horrible, monstrous figures. Onegin is
there too, their lofty lord and master. He carries the exhausted girl
to a bench, and leans her head on his shoulder. Lensky and Olga
enter, and, of all things, Onegin kills Lensky with a knife.

All of Tatiana's virginal eroticism and fears are obviously
symbolized in the dream, which is also a prefiguration of the actual
tragedy about to be enacted.

At the celebration of Tatiana's birthday, Onegin flirts outrageously
with Olga, arouses Lensky's rage, and is challenged by him to a duel.
Onegin, though he is as contemptuous of life as he is of feelings, is
not enough of a contemner of the prevailing "code of honor" to
refuse to fight and face the derision of his class as a coward. They
fight. And Lensky falls. Onegin leaves home, and wanders abroad. In
Odessa he meets our Poet. On returning to Petersburg, he once
again sees Tatiana at a soirée. She is married to an imposing general,
and utterly changed. The young girl he once knew is now a beautiful,
self-possessed lady of wealth and station. This time it is Onegin who
falls desperately in love with her. In a masterly scene, when they
are alone, she confesses that her love has persisted even to the
present, but that she would never be his.

> A schastye bilo tak vozmozhno,
> Tak bleezko! . . .

> Yet happiness was so possible,
> So close . . . But now my fate
> Is already sealed . . .
> I married. Leave me, I beg you.

I know in your heart
Is pride and true honor.
I love you (why dissemble?),
But I am married to another,
And I shall be true to him forever.

Thus, a narrative poem, or novel in verse, that began in a lightsome mood, as if just another ironic and amusing tale of adventure, gradually changed into a drama of wasted lives. The mirror that Pushkin turned on the world around him proceeded to focus more and more sharply on the reality as he saw it then — the real world of upper class society in an absolute state, founded on feudal relations. The characters live, as it were, in an insulated chamber, though they are basically decent, honest, and well-meaning. Tatiana yields to her mother's insistence that she marry a person of rank and wealth, whom she does not love. Did it ever occur to her that she was parodying and living the experience

though more horrifying — of her own serf-nurse? Yet, Tatiana is the only character in the work who "matures." She has indeed, loved, and loved truly. And she still loves. Now she understands Onegin, and knows that he cannot truly love. She is as genuine now as she had been as a girl. She accepts the reality of a loveless marriage and rejects a reckless liaison.

Poor young Lensky, too, has few roots in reality. He is full of good sentiments, but they are vague and insubstantial; he is filled with a nebulous and sentimental "Schwärmerei" — and his poetry is equally insubstantial. But he is very young, and Onegin should have recognized his immaturity, and his own reckless conduct. Onegin, too, is a victim of and slave to the mores and corrosion of his serf-based society and its dehumanization. So that the prerogative of "honor" — even to the point of killing or being killed — takes precedence over the human values of love and friendship. The mask that society has imposed has become the true face.

Onegin is the "superfluous man" — a character that is to appear frequently in subsequent Russian literature — too clear-sighted to accept the world as it is; too weak to break with it. His refuge is negation, irony, cynicism, self-immunization from feeling. Action dissipates in frivolity, philosophy in an élite nihilism.

Yet Pushkin actually planned another ending than that of cynical inactivity for Onegin. For himself, it was to be a partial atonement; for Onegin, positive action. A tenth chapter of *Eugene Onegin* was to bring Onegin in contact with future Decembrists, perhaps even involve him in the Decembrist conspiracy. A manuscript notation in one of his short stories indicated that in October 1830 "was burned X Canto."[27] How much of that chapter had actually been completed we shall never know. Pushkin apparently read a number of stanzas of this section to Viazemsky in December of that year, and their contents were known to others. What is left is a cryptogrammatic set of fragmentary lines, later easily deciphered, that speak derisively of Tsar Alexander I, mention uprisings in Naples, Spain, and Greece; the Tsar's growing repressions, and meetings of the Decembrists in St. Petersburg in 1819, at the homes of Nikita Muravyev and Ilya Dolgoruki. Here

> Lunin, a friend of Mars, Bacchus and Venus,
> Daringly proposed his resolute measures,
> And swept by inspiration — muttered...
> Pushkin read his Noels,
> Melancholy Yakushkin, it seemed,
> Silently unsheathed a regicidal dagger;
> Seeing Russia in the world,
> In her, pursuing his ideal.
> To them the lame Turgenev hearkened,
> And abhorring the lash of slavery,
> Foresaw in this throng of nobles
> The liberators of the peasants.[28]

Pushkin wisely never made Onegin into a Decembrist, for Onegin had neither the firmness, the political conviction, nor the idealism necessary for such absolute commitment.

But that Pushkin should have, as late as 1830, been haunted by his memories of Decembrism is a striking indication of his ambivalence. Here he was on the eve of his marriage. The Tsar was looking more graciously upon him, and was soon to honor him with a court office, grant him access to the state archives, extend generous loans to him, since Pushkin's needs always exceeded his means, no matter how extensive these might be . . .

Eugene Onegin appeared in its completed form (parts had been published separately before) in 1833. There were few who recognized the historic significance of this novel in verse. Many were puzzled by it; others dismayed. They remembered the Pushkin who had composed *The Gipsies* or *The Prisoner of the Caucasus*, or *Ruslan and Ludmila,* and they deplored Pushkin's departure from an exotic romanticism. It took the next generation, the so-called "generation of the 40's," to set a true value on the poem and the poet. Its standard-bearer, the critic Vissarion Belinsky, hailed Pushkin as the initiator of a new era in the literature of Russia. For Belinsky, Pushkin was *the* poet of Russia *par excellence*. He drew particular attention to the social factors that played a crucial role in the lives and fortunes of Onegin, Tatiana, and Lensky. As the representative of the "newer" generation of social thinkers, Belinsky was repelled by Tatiana's marital constancy to a husband she did not love:

Eternal fidelity, he wrote, *to whom* and *in what?* Fidelity to relations which are a desecration to feeling and to the chasteness of feminity, for there are certain relations, which, unsanctified by love, are supremely immoral.[29]

True, Tatiana was not as yet the "new" Russian woman. But Belinsky failed to observe that in her mature stage she saw and understood Onegin; she knew that in him the mask had become the man.

Pushkin had written the first of the great modern Russian novels. The conclusion of the poem is prophetic. For here nothing really happens. Each of the two principal characters goes his or her own way. There is no romantic coming-together in a passionate fulfilment or in a "Liebestod" . . .

Early in January 1831 Pushkin at last saw his historical tragedy, *Boris Godunov*, off the press. He had waited six years for this work, which, he confessed, he "loved best of all," to see the light. Conceived in 1824, and completed the following year, its subject was deemed too inflammatory in the light of the times, and the combined influences of the Tsar, Benckendorff, and the critic Bulgarin succeeded in imposing a quietus upon it. The few voices of admirers of the play could not drown out the overpowering disapproval and disfavor of those on high. There were some who declared that Pushkin was in "utter, utter decline," that he was merely an imitator of Victor Hugo's *Cromwell*, and that the play, written in unrhymed pentameter, was not poetry. The ravens of tradition croaked their cacophanies here in Russia, as they had done elsewhere in Europe, and not without success. The play was not destined to come on to the boards of theatre until long after Pushkin's death. Its gradual recognition as a revolutionary moment in Russia's dramatic history was to mount in succeeding generations, but the world at large was to discover its true greatness only when it was transformed into Russia's majestic operatic work by the musical genius of Modeste Mousssorgsky.

Many outside influences played upon *Boris Godunov,* as they had upon other historical plays of the period in Europe. Shakespeare and his histories have, indeed, a major role. In an indirect way, Walter Scott's novels also played their part. But of all of Pushkin's contemporaries and predecessors (aside from Shakespeare), it was Friedrich Schiller who had written the most impressive and massive historical tragedy, *Wallenstein,* in which not only the protagonist, but also the populace, i.e., the armies, play a significant role. Schiller, who was historian, playwright and philosopher, was deeply concerned with the "philosophy of history." Pushkin had lived in the close proximity of the conservative historian Karamzin, the foremost interpreter of Russia's past, and it was from him that Pushkin drew immediate materials for his play, but the interpretation of the historic events was Pushkin's own.

Like the other writers of his era, Pushkin was a sharp critic and opponent of the neo-classical drama. With him as with the others, it was Shakespeare who served as the most formidable element of the anti-classical Romantic armory. Pushkin, unlike Victor Hugo and Stendhal, did not publish a manifesto defining the new aims of the Romantics, but in practice he was reviving the informal chronicle structure of Shakespeare's histories. His verse form was the Shakespearean pentameter line. Like Shakespeare he chose as his subject a critical period of history, the struggle of the feudal baronage against the rising monarchy, in which the populace, too, would have a considerable place. Shakespeare had taken as a central theme the struggles of the houses of York and Lancaster, and brought them to a resolution in the establishment of the Tudor absolutism. So Pushkin chose one instance out of the tempestuous epoch of Russian history called the "Times of Troubles" — the series of usurpations that bridged the dynasties of Rurik and Romanov — the emergence and temporary triumph of the false Dmitri, a pretender to the throne occupied by Boris Godunov. A year before his death in 1805, Schiller had commenced a tragedy on the subject of the false Dmitri, of which he only completed a few fragments.

In a draft of a preface to *Boris Godunov,* written in 1828, Pushkin stated:

Firmly believing that the obsolete forms of our theatre demand reform, I ordered my Tragedy according to the system of our Father Shakespeare... Voluntarily disclaiming the benefits offered by a form of art justified by experience and confined by habit, I tried to compensate for their lack, of which I was sensible, by the true representation of the people of the period, and of the development of historical characters and events, in short, I wrote a truly Romantic tragedy.[30]

It was clear to him that the character and the form of the neo-classical drama of Corneille and Racine and their imitators reflected the ethos and limitations of an upper-class society:

Why then, he asked, have we no popular tragedy?...Could our tragedy, modeled on Racine's tragedies, shed its aristocratic habits? How could it pass from the measured, haughty and decorous dialogue to the rude frankness of popular passion, to the free judgments of the market-place? How could it shed its servile tone? . . . Where would it learn the dialect which is understood by the people? What are the passions of this people, of what nature are the sinews of its heart? . . . Insurmountable obstacles rise up in its path — and in order to set up its stage, it will have to change and overthrow the customs, manners and ideas of centuries.[31]

In another note he had defined the aim of tragedy: "Man and the people. The fate of Man, the fate of the people," and the special qualities required of a dramatist, such as "philosophy, impartiality, the political acumen of a historian, insight, a lively imagination. No prejudices or preconceived ideas. *Freedom*."[32] For him there would be no false theatrical effects, no romantic pathos. The language would be high or low — but always the speech of the people.

Though filled with echoes of Shakespeare's chronicle plays, particularly *Richard III, Henry IV,* and *Henry V*, Pushkin's tragedy succeeds in displaying an integrity of its own, and is infused with a deep sense of the Russian background, history, and character. Pushkin's achievement becomes all the more striking in view of the fact that, as in his reading of Byron, he was forced to penetrate into the meaning of Shakespeare through the glutinous medium of inadequate translations.

The twenty-four scenes of *Boris Godunov* (there are no act subdivisions) move with kaleisdoscopic speed and economy. The dramatic action commences with the accession of Boris Godunov to the throne of the Tsars in 1598, on the death of the reigning Fyodor, elder son of Ivan the Terrible. Dmitri, the heir to the throne had been murdered in 1591, a crime which Pushkin along with a number of historians attributed to Boris Godunov, but which recent historical research has been inclined to question. Tsar Fyodor, a weak and mystical character, has allowed the reins of power to slip into the hands of Boris, his brother-in-law, and the latter knows how to draw all the advantages from that action. The Boyar nobility, whose prestige and powers had been shorn by the Tsars, see in Boris the possibility of regaining their former status and influence, and Boris, wiser than they, pretends a reluctance to accept the crown, and insists on the approval of the

Russian people. Once on the throne, he proves as intransigeant toward the nobility as his predecessors. It is at this point that a Pretender to the throne makes his appearance, the false Dmitri, who claims to be the true son of Ivan. Actually, he is a young monk of seventeen, Grigori Otrepyev, who, with the connivance of the Poles, and with the acclaim of many Russians, now threatens the powerful Boris. The discontent and the dissident rally to his banner. Boris dies suddenly in 1605, and the victorious Dmitri is crowned in the same year. A year later the false Dmitri is assassinated, civil war follows, a new pretender comes along, unrest continues, until in 1613, Michael Romanov is elected Tsar and establishes the Romanov dynasty in Russia.

With this bare and seemingly limited scheme, Pushkin succeeded in giving a brilliant picture of disturbed times, the wrestling for power, the instability and opportunism of the nobility. This is what the sharp-witted little monk in the Chudov monastery recognizes at a critical moment. He makes his way to Poland, where he obtains the support of the Polish nobility, and falls in love with Marina, daughter of the Governor of Sambor. There is a highly memorable and dramatic moment in the scene between the false Dmitri and Marina, in which the human element that craves love for its own sake leads him to confess his true origin, only to meet Marina's scorn and threats of exposure. For Marina's sole ambition is to be a Tsar's wife. Here Grigori rises to heights, as he enlarges before her his own historic role:

> Surely you do not think I fear you!
> That they will believe a Polish girl
> Rather than Russia's Tsarevich?
> Know, neither King, nor Pope, nor magnates
> Care whether my words are true or not.
> What care they if I am Dmitri or another?
> I am their pretext for their wars and strife.
> That is all they need. And as for you, rebellious one,
> They know well how to silence. Believe me.
> Farewell.

In this utterance, Marina recognizes the signs of a true Tsarevich!
She will be his. She will be with him. One after another, members of
the nobility — loyal and honest once — join the winning side...
  And what of the people?
  They are the passive mass. How can these dynastic changes
matter to them? They are brought in to sustain the pleas of the
boyars and the clergy, in order to "persuade" Boris to accept the
crown.

> The People (on their knees groaning and wailing):
> Have pity on us, Father! Be our ruler!
> Be our Father! and our Tsar!
>
> First Man: Why are they wailing?
>
> Second Man: How should we know? It's the boyars' business,
> Not for the likes of us.

In the quiet of the secluded cloister of Chudov, the saintly scribe
Pimen, chronicler of Russia's great past, instructs young Grigori in
the vicissitudes of the powerful Tsars, recalls the peaceful days of
Fyodor, and concludes:

> Oh, horrible, never yet experienced woe!
> We have angered God, and sinned.
> We have taken for our ruler a Tsar's assassin!

The Boyars soon become aware that they have exchanged
Tsarist thongs for scorpions:

> Have we any assurances for our poor lives?
> Each day disgrace awaits us: Siberia, cloister,
> Dungeon or chains; and then, in some wasteland,
> Starvation or the noose...

Espionage, tale-bearing, informing are the order of the day.
Nemesis broods not only over them but over Boris himself, as he
learns that a Dmitri, as if returned from the grave, is on his way:

Ukh, tiazhelo!... Dai i dukh perevedu...

Ah! how grievous... Let me draw breath.
I felt my blood rush to my face
And heavily drain away. So that is why
For thirteen years on end I've always dreamed
Of the murdered child! Yes, yes! It is that!
Now I understand. But who is he —
That fearful enemy? Who is against me?
An empty name — a shadow...
Can shadows tear the purple from me,
Or sounds disinherit my children?
I am mad! What have I to fear?
Blow on this phantom, and it is no more!...

But the phantom will not disappear. At the critical moment Boris
feels death approaching, and in solemn words adjures his son on his
duties and policies when he becomes Tsar:

Umirayu.
Obnimensia, proshchai, moy sin, seichas
Ti tsarstovat nachnios...

I am dying.
Let us embrace. Farewell, my son. Now
You begin to reign. God! oh God!
Soon I shall stand before Thee,
And have not time to shrive my soul.
Yet I feel, my son, that you are dearer
Than is salvation to my soul. So be it!
I was born a subject, and it is meet
That in obscurity I die a subject.
Yet I attained to sovereign heights.
How? Do not ask. Enough, that you are innocent.
You reign by right, and I, I alone
Am answerable for all to God...

Useless counsel, useless remorse! The Pretender is taking Moscow,
and the once loyal followers of Boris, pledged to Boris's son Fyodor,
are forsaking him. Soon young Fyodor will be no more, and the line
of the Godunovs will be extinct. Grigori Otrepyev, the new Dmitri,
will be crowned.

The imperial censorship of Nicholas ruled that the populace in the play not be allowed to hail the new Tsar with the shout of "Long live Tsar Dmitri Ivanovich!" Instead, it decreed a solemn substitution.

> Good people! Maria Godunova and her son Fyodor have taken
> poison. We have seen their dead bodies.
>   (The people are silent with horror.)
> Why are you silent? Cry, "Long live Tsar Dmitri Ivanovich!"

It has been remarked that in forcing Pushkin to alter the conclusion, the authorities had done him and his work an unforeseen but great service dramatically. For the silence of the people is eloquently ominous...

It is not surprising that Tsar Nicholas, Count Benckendorff and their henchmen looked with unease upon the play when it was presented to them in Moscow in 1826. Pushkin himself must have been aware — as he wrote four years later to Benckendorff — that certain passages might give umbrage, as if reflecting on some disturbing current happenings of the time. Such passages were duly expunged...

From their point of view, the censors were not to blame. The memory of the assassination of Tsar Paul, with the acquiescence, if not the connivance, of his successor, the future Alexander I, was still fresh. The Decembrist uprising in 1825 was even fresher. Under such circumstances, a dramatic work that dealt with a successful usurpation by an upstart, with the cooperation of the nobility and the passive acceptance of the people, would certainly not conduce to quieting auditors.

But now in 1831, there was no such concern at the court. Pushkin had been well taken in hand. His marriage in March of that year would seal his dependence on the Court, which would be more strongly confirmed by sinecures and other emoluments. The beautiful Natalia Pushkin would be entertained lavishly, and kept socially occupied in Petersburg and neighboring Tsarskoye Selo — winter and summer residences of the imperial family. Under so many watchful and solicitous eyes the unpredictable poet could be kept in check. A commission to write the life of Peter the Great would hold him in the archives. If only the poet would learn to be grateful!...

Pushkin was now giving numerous hostages to fortune. Married to a woman whose extravagance matched his own; soon, the head of a family that included a growing number of children, himself leading a divided life, now living in Boldino, where he could write, now in St. Petersburg where he was caught up in society, he seemed to be whirling in a vortex of activities that threatened to swallow him. While away from his wife, he filled letters with admonitions, warning her against flirtations; against extravagance; reminding her that she was a married woman and a mother...

He had never felt more creative. He was preparing a comprehensive history of the Pugachev Rebellion, for which he would have to go to Orenberg and Kazan. In the meantime, he retired in 1833 to Boldino, and here he completed his most important single poem after *Eugene Onegin* — *The Bronze Horseman.*

The idea for this amazing work he owed to Adam Mickiewicz. His relation to the Polish poet, once very friendly, had by this time become soured. For at the outbreak of the uprising of Warsaw, Pushkin had given vent to bitter excoriation of the Poles. Upon the fall of Warsaw, Pushkin along with Zhukovksy published anti-Polish poems of extraordinary vehemence. Among them Pushkin's own "To the Slanderers of Russia" was so rabid as to appall his own friends, such as Vyazemski and A. I. Turgenev. Mickiewicz, on his side, replied with a scornful castigation of time-servers, recalling true lovers of liberty like the Decembrists.

In his dramatic poem, *The Forefathers,* Mickiewicz had written about Russia, described St. Petersburg, and Falconet's celebrated heroic statue of Peter the Great, which overlooked the Neva.

Pushkin too was writing about St. Petersburg, and the statue of Peter the Great. But the "hero" of the poem is not so much the great Tsar as a very "unheroic" character — a "little" man, an expendable human being. He is significantly named Eugene. Two mighty forces are counterposed against him: Peter the Great, embodied in the equestrian stone, and the river Neva at a time of a catastrophic inundation in 1824.

Eugene is a humble government clerk, though (like Pushkin) of noble descent. He is a person of moderate ambitions: all he hopes for is a home, to be married soon to Parasha, a widow's daughter living across the river; gradual advancement in his profession and — not much more. About his "hero", Pushkin said,

I maintain that I had the right to choose my neighbor as the hero of my humble tale, though he is not a warrior or second-class Don Juan, nor a demon — not even a gipsy; but simply a citizen of our capital, of the kind we meet everywhere in thousands; and not distinguished in our society by wit or good looks, but just quite mild and simple, and furthermore a solid sort of young chap.[33]

The statue of Peter the Great speaks of a mighty Tsardom, of Peter, who had tamed the sea, and had raised up the city which is named after him out of the marshes. How powerful he looms as he gazes across the Neva!

> Terrible he was in the encircling gloom!
> What thought sat in his brow!
> What strength concealed within him!
> And in that steed what fire!
> Where are you galloping, proud steed,
> And where will you plant your hoofs?
> O mighty master of Fate!
> Was it not thus, aloft on the brink of the abyss,
> You reined up Russia with your iron curb?
>
> O moshchnii vlastelni sudbi!
> Nye tak li ti nad samoi bezdnoi
> Na viscote, uzdoi zhleznoi
> Rossiu podnyali na dibi?

Eugene retires to his poor chamber, to dream of Parasha, and of his future . . . Meanwhile the wind is rising. If the weather turns bad, he will not see his beloved for two or three days. The winds grow stronger, and the Neva overflows her banks, and threatens to bring destruction to the city. Eugene perches himself astride one of the two lions standing before a mansion, and watches the seething waters as they swirl with all sorts of débris. He fixes his gaze on the distance . . . What is happening to Parasha and her mother? The waters lap the feet of the lions . . .

> Around him is water and nothing else!
> And with its back turned to him,
> On unshakable eminence
> Over the turbulent Neva,
> Stands the image on his bronze horse
> With arm outstretched.
>
> Nad vozmushchennoyu Nevoyu
> Stoit sprostertoyu rukoyu
> Kumir na bronzovom kone.

Finally the waters begin to subside, and Eugene succeeds in hiring a boatman to carry him accross. But the simple hut and its inhabitants are gone, and not a trace of them remains. Eugene loses his mind. He wanders around the city, distraught, disheveled, altogether indifferent to his appearance or his whereabouts — a waif. And suddenly, one night, he finds himself at the mansion with the two lions, and there, too, is the statue! Now it all comes back to him. He clenches his hands, and trembling with rage, whispers, "Very well, you builder of marvels! You just wait!" And he runs off. But close behind him he hears the galloping hoof of the pursuing statue. Thus all night. Thereafter he avoids seeing or meeting the Bronze Horseman. And then one day, the flood drives a ramshackle little house on to a deserted island. There it is discovered one day, and on its threshold the body of our madman . . .

The Bronze Horseman was not cleared for publication during Pushkin's lifetime. The censors must have suspected an implied criticism of Tsarist rule, or perhaps a reflection on the great Peter.

Whatever the passionate feelings that were bursting within him, Pushkin subdued with a masterful appearance of control, though horror and madness must have been his — not unlike those of the Eugene of his recent poem. Was he not also the sport of Tsar and Fate? And what a contrast he unfolds, when he displays his love for St. Petersburg in the passionate apostrophe,

> Liubliu tebia, Petra tvorenie,
> Liubliu tvoyi strogii, stroinyi vid...

> I love you, city of Peter's creation,
> I love your stern, harmonious look,
> The majestic flow of the Neva...

and describes the end of Eugene's life and madness:

> By the threshold the madman was found;
> On that very spot they buried his old corpse
> Out of charity, for the sake of the Lord...

Pushkin's catastrophe was equally inevitable. The Bronze Horseman not only pursued him, but eventually overtook him. Or, to put it more accurately, Pushkin allowed himself to be overtaken. Now it was he, Pushkin, who was the little man, Eugene; now he was Lensky. And as if he were preparing his own script, he found a surrogate for the role of the murderer, Eugene Onegin. It was, in real life, the handsome Alsatian rake, Horse Guard lieutenant Baron George d'Anthès, adopted son of Baron Louis van Heeckeren, Dutch minister to Russia. Natalia, young, dazzlingly beautiful, adored and admired, simple and unsophisticated, caught up in the enticing net of glamour and gaiety, in the enchantment of court-life, danced, and flirted, and won hearts: and d'Anthès was gallant, an aristocrat, rich. She was married as a matter of harsh expediency, and to a man she did not love, whom she did not understand, and whose genius she could never begin to appreciate. Though she was never unfaithful to her husband, she was not above responding to such adoration as d'Anthès pretended to offer.

Refined upper-class Russian society watched the spectacle of flirtation with breathless interest, sometimes with amusement, and not infrequently with glee. Pushkin, always sensitive to even imagined affronts, now felt his feelings abraded to an insufferable intensity. He had made many enemies, who would rejoice in his downfall. He had written epigrams and poems that touched many a raw spot in very high places. Recently he had been attacking such figures as Minister Uvarov, one of Benckendorff's principal associates; and he had aimed his shafts at other notabilities, at their peculiar sexual predilections, their cupidity, their baseness, in words that in this day would have resulted in more than one suit for libel. He had also recently been humiliated by the Tsar himself who had named him, a mature man, and Russia's outstanding poet, to the post of the Tsar's "Kammerjunker" — gentleman of the chamber — an office generally assigned to very young men, and carrying with it vexatious official ceremonies. Additionally, his personal correspondence, even that with Natalia, was being opened by the police, and its contents forwarded to the Tsar. Heavier and heavier grew his gambling debts, and his other expenses. As the d'Anthès courtship of Natalia intensified, tongues wagged, faces leered and smirked. Natalia did little to alleviate the heart-sickening jealousy of her husband.

No internal storms, nor pending external ones, could deter him from literary work. Pushkin found time to embark on an important journalistic project, *The Contemporary,* the first issue of which appeared in April 1836. It included his own "little tragedy," *The Avaricious Knight,* and his *Journey to Erzerum.* It also introduced to the world a promising young writer, Nikolai Gogol, whose celebrated story, *The Nose,* appeared in the third issue. Pushkin's own magnificent novelette, *The Captain's Daughter,* followed in the fourth. By this time Pushkin had already demonstrated an astonishing versatility in various literary domains: the short story, history, drama, the lyric, epic and ballad, the fairy tale.

Only his very close friends knew what was going on inside him. Prince Viazemsky reports one incident:

In the winter of 1836-1837, I happened to walk along the Nevsky Prospect with Natalia Pushkin, her sister Catherine Goncharov, and young Heeckeren (i.e., d' Anthès). At that moment Pushkin rushed past us like a whirlwind. He did not look back and immediately vanished in a crowd of people on the pavement. The expression on his face was terrifying. For me it was the first sign of the coming storm.[34]

The storm did break. It was prepared in the form of a "jest" perpetrated by a coterie of nobles, in a letter circulated by hand to various recipients. In it "Monsieur Alexandre Pouchkine" was unanimously nominated "coadjutor of the Grand Master of the Order of Cuckolds, and Historiographer of the Order." The letter was transmitted to Pushkin and his friends in November 1836. Whoever was the prime mover of the "jest," it is now certain that Baron von Heeckeren had a hand in it, Prince Dolgorukov, another unsavory character, was the writer of the epistle, and d'Anthès the abettor.

Pushkin challenged d'Anthès. But for the time being matters were settled and the challenge withdrawn when d'Anthès proposed to Natalia's sister, Ekaterina Goncharova (whom he eventually married). But he continued his ardent pursuit of Natalia, and on one occasion came near compromising her seriously. Pushkin was sure that Heeckeren was inciting his adopted son, and wrote him an insulting letter, calling him "pimp," and his "bastard son" a syphilitic. D'Anthès accepted the challenge in his father's name, since diplomatic status prevented the latter from involvement in a duel.

What is most astonishing in all this affair is the apparent indifference of the highest authorities. They did little to keep the affair from leading to the inevitable clash, and ultimate tragedy. A word from the Tsar, or from Benckendorff, and d'Anthès would have been "persuaded" to cease and desist, and Heeckeren silenced. But Benckendorff was notoriously hostile to Pushkin, and kept aloof. Before the duel, Pushkin appeared immoderately calm, even exultant. Poor thrall of honor! He was vindicating name, ancestry, and intellectual primacy — like some ancient knight-at-arms!

Pushkin was brought home fatally wounded. While on his death-bed, he received a message from the Tsar adjuring him to die like a Christian.

A shocked Russia paid her last tribute to the poet. To avoid demonstrations, his body was quietly transferred to the Svyatogorsk monastery for burial near Milkhailovskoe. Only one publication dared print an obituary, for which its editor was severely taken to task...

D'Anthès was ordered deported. Heeckeren was recalled to his country. D'Anthès returned to France, where he became a pillar of legitimism, rose to be a Senator, and almost fought a duel with the critic Sainte-Beuve. Natalia remarried and survived to 1863.

For Russia Pushkin came to be the symbol of the poet-martyr. He was her first major national poet whose verses were learned by heart, and recited year after year. He was Russia's first poet to achieve international celebrity. He was to be the source of inspiration and influence extending from Lermontov on to Gogol, Belinsky, Nekrasov, Dostoevsky, Tolstoy and beyond. From his works the Russian national school of music drew its rich materials. Russian opera was shaped by Pushkin's poems, plays, and stories. Paradoxically, it was the Russian composers who may be said to have brought Pushkin to the consciousness of the world at large. One thinks immediately of Glinka's *Ruslan and Ludmila;* Tschaikovsky's *Eugene Onegin* and *The Queen of Spades;* Moussorgsky's *Boris Godunov;* Rimsky-Korsakov's *Golden Cockerel* and *Tsar Saltan;* Rachmaninov's *Aleko,* and Stravinsky's *Mavra* — all of which stem from Pushkin.

The twenty-three year old poet, and soldier, Mikhail Lermontov, Pushkin's poetic successor and worshipper, expressed his outrage in a lament that infuriated Pushkin's detractors. Writing soon after the poet's death, he called the killing a murder.

The Poet dead! — the thrall of honor,
He fell besmirched by slanderers' hands...
You greedy servitors that crowd around the throne,
Hangmen of freedom, genius and fame!
Who hide beneath the canopy of Law,
While right and justice silently condone!
You minions of depravity — remember that a Court,
God's Court, awaits you with its judgment stern,
A court, no lackey to the tinkling sound of gold...
Not all the black blood in your veins
Will wash away the Poet's righteous blood.[35]

Pushkin is the mirror of Russia: her lover, her critic, a beacon light in a great darkness. Above all, her uncontested Poet-Laureate:

I zabyvayu mir — i vsladkoi tishinye
Ya sladko usyplion moim voobrazheniem,
I probuzhdayetsa poeziya vo mne:
Dusha stesniaetsa liricheskim volneniem...

I forget the world — and in the sweet silence
I am sweetly lulled by my imagination,
And poetry awakens within me:
My soul is seized by a lyrical glow,
And stirs, and murmurs, and seeks as in a dream
To liberate itself at last in freedom of expression —
And now come toward me invisible throngs of guests,
Old acquaintances, children of my fancy.

And thoughts swirl boldly in my head,
And light rhymes run to meet them,
And fingers crave a pen, and pen paper,
And instantly the lines flow freely,
Thus a ship slumbers motionless on still waters;
But see! — sailors suddenly begin to stir,
Race up and down the rigging, the sails swell,
Filled with wind — and the huge bulk moves,
And cleaves the waves.

It sails. Where then shall we sail to?[36]

Part Two

THE RISING TIDE
1830-1848

I.

FRANCE — 1830
PARIS ON THE BARRICADES

PARIS — JULY 1830

> There are great things which are not the work of
> one human being, but of a people. The pyramids of
> Egypt are anonymous: such too the Days of July.
>   — Victor Hugo, *Journal* November 1830 —

> The old world is melting into nothingness, the old
> doctrines are snuffed out. In the midst of seeming
> disorder, of confused effort, one can even catch
> glimpse of a new organization for the world. The
> religion of the future casts its first gleams over
> mankind waiting in expectancy, and over all its
> future destinies.
>   — The Abbé Lamennais —

While Hugo, Delacroix, Gautier and their legionnaires were fighting the battle of Romanticism versus Classicism, Shakespeare versus Racine, an even more serious battle was being waged in the political arena, which represented a most formidable challenge to the future of the French nation.

It has often been said that whom the gods wish to destroy, they first make mad. But we may also add, they make them blind, so that they walk toward the abyss with all the assurance of sleep-walkers. Such indeed was the way of the Bourbon régime. Aware of the rising discontent within the country, it moved steadily to meet the crisis with more and more intense measures of repression. Having already alienated the bourgeoisie and the peasantry, not to mention the workers, by the restitution of most of the properties of the emigrés, as well as close to a billion francs; having passed laws

419

making sacrilege a capital offense, attacked schools and universities and made them subsidiary to the Church; the extreme Right, the so-called "Ultras," prepared for the complete annulment of the Charter. Having previously failed with the ministries of Villèle and Martignac, Charles X now turned to the Duc de Polignac, and made him minister-president; and to Marshal Bourmont, whose military career had been notable for a series of treasons, and made him minister of war.

Jules de Polignac, who entered upon his critical office in November 1829, was both stupid and an Ultra. He dreamt that the country could be returned to a total absolutism.

It may be difficult, he said, but it is not impossible for us to return some day to a system which incorporates aristocratic principles and closes the door of the Chamber of Deputies to mediocre men driven by turbulent and revolutionary passions.[1]

Anyone else, more alert, would have read the signs of the time, or overheard some disturbing rumors. There was, after all, the incredible success of the Opposition in the elections. This was the first time, since 1814, that the government had failed to win. It was reported that Polignac, in addition to being a religious as well as a political fanatic, was subject to spells and superstitious visions. Facts stared him in the face. In the Chamber of Deputies, 221 members were petitioning for the removal of the ministry, seemingly unconcerned about the King's threats.

Of Charles X it used to be said that he differed from Louis XVIII: "Nous avions un rois sans jambes avec une tête; maintenant nous avons des jambes sans tête." "We had a king without legs," (Louis was gouty), "but with a head. Now we have a king with legs, but no head."[2]

The King's appointments were nothing less than a declaration of war upon the Charter, that is, war upon the French people. Armand Carrel, militant editor of *Le National,* author of a *History of the Counter-Revolution in England under Charles II* (as a soldier, he had dared fight on the side of Spain against France), now asked, "Who is most likely to play the role of William of Orange?"

Other signs were no less ominous. France was suffering a profound economic crisis, which had been lasting five years. The crisis originated in England in 1825, and spread to other countries. There were serious business failures in France, notably those of Chaptal and Creusot. Other industries were also in trouble; there were numerous bank failures, and the usual scourge of poor crops. The price of wheat rose 40% above that in 1815, and 60% by 1829. The price of bread rocketed to 125%. Wages fell between 30 and 40%. Food riots occurred frequently, 90 cases being reported in 1820. The cry rose that the "King and the Jesuits" were responsible for these troubles. Hand-lettered posters became prominent: "Vive Napoleon!" "War to the death on Charles X and the priests who want to starve us to death!" "March to the Tuileries and demand bread and work!" The commissioner of police in the Faubourg Saint-Antoine reported:

The approach of winter frightens the people with good reason . . . Soon the father of a family will not earn enough to buy bread, and how can he provide for clothing for his children and payment of rent?[3]

The mounting crisis was felt all over the country. In Lyon alone, in 1826, there were 11,000 looms standing idle. In Paris 3000 construction workers were jobless.

The temper of the people, at least that portion that was entitled to vote, may be gauged from the parliamentary elections. In 1824 a majority of rightists were voted in. In 1827 and 1830 it was the left that was in the majority. The opposition to the régime could boast of men of brain and talent, who sometimes formed themselves into associations, such as *Aide-toi; le ciel t'aidera* ("Help yourself, and Heaven will help you"), with the avowed purpose of agitating for a change of the ministry. Among them were such figures as Guizot, Thiers, Carrel, Mignet, and many other intellectuals of distinction, who aspired to a place in the government. In no other country, it may be said at once, were writers and artists so closely involved with politics, and statesmen and politicians so closely in touch with writers and artists. The spirit of republicanism was aflame again, and not even the threat of imprisonment could deter bold journalists, such as the heroic Paul-Louis Courier, or poets like Béranger, from unveiling the truth about the state of the country. For Frenchmen, the French Revolution of 1789 was still a fact. Hymns in praise of the King were frequently countered by those in praise of liberty.

Important actors stood in the wings, watching the drama being enacted with more than casual interest. Prime among these was Louis-Philippe, the duke of Orléans, cousin of the present King of France. He had the shrewdness of an accomplished and experienced business man, and the flexibility and agility of an acrobat. He had managed always to land on his feet, no matter how difficult the somersault. He was the son of Louis Philippe Joseph, duke of Orléans, the Philip "Égalité" who had voted for the execution of Louis XVI, and was himself executed in 1793. His son, when it served his purposes, also called himself "Égalité"; on other occasions he was known as the duc de Chartres. He had been a soldier in the armies of the Republic, then had conspired against the Republic, had gone to America, and on returnig to Europe had found Napoleon in the saddle. After a sojourn in England, he made his way to Palermo, where he wooed and married the daughter of King Ferdinand IV. That royal family of Bourbons despised and detested the house of Orléans, but they compromised; for, as his prospective mother-in-law put it, "My daughter is 28 years old and despairs of getting married."[4]

Upon the Restoration, he returned to France, became reconciled to King Louis XVIII, and received back a good portion of his former estates as well as a high army rank. He was now enormously wealthy. He was worth in the neighborhood of fifty million dollars.

It was no secret that the affluent members of the liberal
Opposition looked with favor upon him. So far as business acumen
was concerned, he could well stand comparison with any of them.
The very influential banker Jacques Laffitte took to him. Laffitte's
money was subsidizing *Le National,* which was edited by Thiers and
Carrel.

Louis-Philippe bided his time. On May 31, 1830, he gave a gala
reception in honor of his visiting in-laws, the King and Queen of
Naples. King Charles X of France graced the occasion with his
presence. The crowd that gathered at the Palais Royale — Louis-
Philippe's residence — showed its enthusiasm for the host; but was
much less demonstrative toward the French king. A clever observer
commented on this occasion:

It's a celebration well in keeping with Naples. We are dancing on a volcano.[5]

The shrewdest politician of that day (and probably of any other
time), Charles-Maurice de Talleyrand, remarked on June 11, 1830:
"The decisive moment is approaching. I see neither compass, nor
pilot, and nothing here to stop the shipwreck."[6]

On July 25, 1830 came the notorious Ordinances of Charles X.
They were published in the *Moniteur* the following day. They
provided for a strict censorship of the press. All publications were to
be subject to government approval and authorization, renewable at
three months' intervals. The Chamber of Deputies was to be
dissolved, and the membership of the Lower House to be reduced to
258. Only those would be eligible to run who paid a direct tax of 1000
francs.

Alexandre Dumas wrote in his *Recollections:*

I had booked a seat on the mail coach for Marseilles, packed my luggage, and
was about to set out at five the next evening, when at eight in the morning,
Achille Comte burst into my room and cried, "Have you heard the news?
The Ordinances are announced in the *Moniteur.* Are you still going to
Algiers?" "I'm not such a fool," I replied. "We'll see stranger events here
than there." I called to my servant. "Joseph, go to my gun-makers and fetch
me my double-barreled gun and two hundred twenty-caliber bullets."[7]

Exaggeration, perhaps. But similar sentiments were unquestionably in the hearts of hundreds of Parisians. While the deputies were paralyzed, and only a few seemed to know what to do, the people of Paris streamed out into the streets, many of them gathering around the Palais Royale.

The date: July 27, 1830.

The people shouted, "Charte!"

They were met by mounted cavalry. Who fired the first shot? We shall never know. There were a number of people killed and wounded. Crowds began moving toward the Louvre, the rue Saint-Honoré, the Place de la Bourse... But the King was at Saint-Cloud. Business as usual: Dinner, whist...

At the theatre of the Porte Saint-Martin in Paris a performance is interrupted. They are bringing in a wounded comrade...

On Tuesday, July 27, a number of liberal papers continue to appear, such as the *Globe,* organ of the Saint-Simonians; the *National,* and *Le Temps.* Police swoop down and confiscate the presses.

On Wednesday, July 28, barricades are raised. Carriages and wagons are overturned, barrels are filled with paving stones. The tricolor is displayed. Crowds now swarm around and take possession of the Arsenal, repository of arms.

"Ce n'est pas une émeute; c'est une révolution," Marmont, major-general of the guard, reported to the King. This was no mere uprising. Paris was readied for a stage of siege. The royal army was alerted. Eight thousand men began descending upon the Paris insurgents. The Revolution was on. As always, the students of the École Polytechnique were in the lead. At Saint-Cloud, the King no doubt heard echoes of a cannonade. Counseled to enter into negotiations, he is said to have replied:

No. It does not befit me to treat with subjects who are in a state of rebellion. Let them put down their arms, and they will soon see the fruits of my kindness.[8]

Thursday, July 29. What a strange assortment — these revolutionaries! What a dramatic study in contrasts! A bizarre pell-mell — a student walking side by side a worker, a national guardsman, and a tramp...

The royalist soldiers were poorly supplied. They were hungry, and their morale began to sag. The insurgents attacked the Louvre. A young boy is at their head, and opens the gates. He is wounded. The Swiss guard flees and the insurgents capture the Tuileries. Paris is in the hands of the Revolution.

Alexandre Dumas recollecting:

I do not know who said it — perhaps I myself... The Revolution of 1830 was the last rifle shot of Waterloo. This is a great truth. When I arrived at the Pont de la Révolution, I stopped dumbfounded, I thought I was seeing things and rubbed my eyes. For there the tricolor floated above the Notre Dame... I leaned against the parapet, my arms outstretched, my eyes fixed, and filled with tears.[9]

And the poet Alfred de Vigny:

Not one prince has made his appearance. The poor decent soldiers of the guard have been abandoned, and left without orders, witout bread now for two days, pursued, pursued, and fighting all the time. Oh Civil War!...[10]

Now it was time for the bankers to step in. Laffitte took over direction of the Revolution. At the Hôtel Laffitte in the rue Artois there were meetings and negotiations. The new makers of France were here: Guizot, Périer, Sebastiani. All was being arranged properly. General Lafayette was to lead the people. A provisional government was to be set up. Laffitte, speaking for the others, declared that Charles X and his régime were close to collapse. The Republicans, he insisted, did not have the country behind them, and they would not fight against Laffitte and Lafayette. It was essential to proclaim the Duc d'Orléans king at once. He was to appear in a citizen costume — look democratic; wear a grey hat and umbrella. It was expedient to issue a Manifesto and emphasize that the Duc d'Orléans was devoted to the cause of the Revolution; he had never fought against France, and he was wearing the tricolor. The return of Charles X to Paris would only mean shedding the blood of the people. The Duc d'Orléans awaits the wishes of the people of France, for it is from their hands he desires to receive the crown of France.

In such a manner was the republican dream terminated...

Saturday, July 31. Carrying the colors, which, in his own words, the people of France "have reclaimed, and which I have carried a long time," Louis-Philippe entered the city, and assured Frenchmen that the Chamber would be convoked, and a Charte promulgated.

It needed only the presence, the panoply, and the blessing of Lafayette to establish the new order. Aged, cynical Chateaubriand reported:

He hands the Duc d'Orléans the tricolor, advances to the balcony of the Hôtel de Ville, and embraces the Prince in sight of the stupefied crowd, while the latter was waving the national flag. The republican kiss of Lafayette made a king. Strange consequence of the whole life of the Hero of Two Worlds![11]

At the beginning of August Charles X abdicated in favor of his grandson Henri V, and then rushed off, like so many of his predecessors, to England. At the same time, Louis-Philippe addressed the two Chambers, amidst cries of "Vive Orléans, vive la Liberté!" The Chamber of Deputies declared the throne vacant, and Bérard proposed: "de proclamer immédiatement Roi des Français, le prince lieutenant-géneral, Philippe d'Orléans."

The republicans were afflicted. The deputies marched to the Palais Royale with an amended constitution, and the offer of kingship. The crowds sang the "Marseillaise" and "La Parisienne" — the latter composed by Casimir Delavigne and set to music by Auber. Strange irony! While Paris was surrendering a good slice of her liberties into the hands of the Laffittes and the Casimir Périers, and a millionaire king, they also chanted the words of "La Parisienne"!

> Peuple français, peuple de braves,
> La liberté ouvre ses bras.
> On nous disait, "Soyez esclaves"
> Nous avons dit, "Soyons soldats."
>
> People of France, gallant people,
> Liberty is opening her arms,
> They used to tell us, "Be slaves,"
> But we said, "Let us be soldiers."
> Suddenly Paris, her memory astir,
> Found her glorious voice again:
> > Forward let us march
> > Against their cannons,
> > Meet their fire, meet their steel,
> > And rush to victory...

The new King was crowned on August 9.

The "three days of glory," July 27, 28, and 29, were to remain fixed in the memories and hearts of the French for decades to come. Berlioz was a witness, and he exulted:

The spendid order that reigned during these magical three days is maintained and confirmed; no looting, no lawlessness of any kind. The people have been sublime.[12]

Even Chateaubriand was forced to admit that these "three days" which had shone over France had matured the destinies of her people more than a century could have done.

But what was even more significant, to some terribly disturbing, was the conviction that the Revolution could not have been won without the support of the populace of Paris and other cities of France, and that it had become a force with which to reckon in the future.

The eminent historian Michelet celebrated the youthful energies that had gone into the making of those "three days," working concurrently with other forces:

In that brilliant morning of July the young heart was not intimidated by its vast hope, its powerful electricity, that superhuman enterprise . . . Hundreds of springs hitherto inert and heavy moved independently, moved of themselves, found their place in the ensemble . . . That immense movement was set in motion under my eyes . . .[13]

France had once more become the center of the world.

The poet Théodore de Banville chanted:

> Dis nous, mil-huit-cent-trente,
> Époque fulgurante,
> Tes rêves, tes ardeurs,
> Et tes splendeurs . . .
>
> Tell us, oh Eighteen-thirty,
> Resplendent epoch,
> Your dreams, your ardors,
> And your glories . . .
>
> Eighteen-hundred and thirty,
> Dawn that still dazzles me —
> Promises of destiny,
> And laughter of the morning . . .

Word of the "Trois glorieuses" traveled all over Europe; inflamed hearts, and terrified. Once more France had affirmed her historical mission to speak for the enchained world. All eyes were turned on Paris.

On the Baltic coast, a young German poet, already famous, Heinrich Heine, heard the news and exclaimed:

Lafayette, the Tricolor, the Marseillaise! . . . I know what I must do . . . I am the son of the Revolution and I take up the charmed weapons upon which my mother has breathed her magic blessing . . . Dear friends, in Paris the cock has crowed . . . Yes, everywhere, in all countries men will quickly grasp the meaning of these three July days and recognize in them the victory of their own interests and celebrate.[14]

In the large Aula, the lecture hall of the University of Berlin, the distinguished Professor Boeckh was lecturing on the fine arts. A student, Karl Gutzkow, soon to become a literary light, is in the audience:

The thunder of the cannon from the barricades of Paris echoes into the hall. Boeckh was lecturing on the fine arts, but no one was thinking of these brilliant formulations and his classic speech. Hegel entered and announced the names of the winners of the scientific competition of the Academy, but no one heard him, except those who had participated... No, all I wanted to know was how many had been wounded in Paris. Were the barricades still there?... Was the archbishop's palace smoking, or was Charles X bewailing the loss of his throne? Would Lafayette create a monarchy or a republic?... Learning lay far behind us. History confronted us...[15]

In Paris M. Laffitte, the eminent banker, could with justice celebrate his triumph. "The patriots and I — or rather, I and the patriots," he said, "we worked hard and without respite for the triumph of the duc d'Orléans."[16]

And with admirable candor he announced. "C'est maintenant le régne des banquiers." "Now the bankers will take over."

Thus was consummated the second great revolution in France!

The young Englishman, John Stuart Mill, was in Paris at this time. He rejoiced at the downfall of the Bourbon régime, and was enraged by the aftermath of the Revolution. As for the revolutionaries, he wrote,

They had but one idea, that of fighting for their legal rights, and the observance of the legal rights of others, followed as an immediate corollary... These men, the ignorant, despised, and long-abused people shrunk from all unnecessary carnage — the moment resistance ceased, that moment they abstained from assault — they took equal care of the soldier who had opposed and of the citizen who had aided them... But then the *educated* and the *rich*... came upon the stage... eager for place and careless of public interest.[17]

II.

1830 AND THE ARTIST

Stendhal:
"Le Rouge et le Noir"

Berlioz:
"Symphonie Fantastique"

Delacroix:
The Painter and Romanticism

1

NOVEMBER 1830
STENDHAL: "LE ROUGE ET LE NOIR"

> Near the salt mine of Salzburg, a leafless branch
> falls into the depths of one of the mines. Two or
> three months later it is found with its tiniest twigs,
> no bigger than a titmouse, entirely covered with an
> infinity of sparkling diamonds. One can no longer
> recognize the original branch.
> What I call *crystallization* is the operation of
> the mind that draws from everything around it the
> discovery that the beloved object has new perfection.
> — Stendhal: "De l'Amour" —

While firing was going on nearby, Henry Beyle, better known as Stendhal, sat in his room in the Hôtel de Valois, 71, rue de Richelieu. He was reading Napoleon's *Mémorial de Saint-Helène*, a book the hero of his forthcoming novel would pore over again and again. Now and then Stendhal jotted a note in the margin of the book: "Fusillade, platoon firing while I read this page, 1.15 p.m....."

He had looked forward to this event, had anticipated it, and expected it; though now, at the age of forty-seven, he felt little inclined to mount a barricade. As it was, the firing would seriously interfere with the publication of his new book, *Le Rouge et le Noir*, for the printers, who were among the vanguard of the July Revolution, used the type-lead for making bullets. *Le Rouge et le Noir* appeared in November 1830.

Stendhal did venture forth during one of the three July days, and somewhat later wrote about his reactions in a letter to his friend Sutton Sharpe:

Fully to enjoy the spectacle of this great Revolution, you would have to saunter along the boulevard. (By the way, there are no trees any more from the rue de Choiseul to the Hôtel Saint-Phar, where you and I stayed for a few days on arriving from London.)... The more you are removed from the *great week*... the more astonishing it appears to me. It is like the effect produced by colossal statues, by Mont Blanc, which is more sublime... twenty leagues from Geneva than seen from its base... A unique spectacle; for a hundred men without stockings or vest, there was, on July 28, one who was well dressed. The mob proved heroic, and full of the noblest generosity after the battle.[18]

He was not accustomed to speak in symbols, but he might very well have used the symbol of "crystallization" to describe his own person, character, and talents at this moment. He was a late-comer to the novel. His first one, *Armance,* had appeared just three years before, and fallen foul of friends and critics. He had dealt with a delicate subject, the sexual impotence of his principal character, his love for a beautiful woman, and his ultimate suicide. The novel was enigmatic, for Stendhal was far from forthright in it, and his readers were puzzled.

But this second novel, *Le Rouge et le Noir,* showed a brilliant crystallization; the branch did indeed flower. Was Stendhal aware that he had written one of the century's masterpieces? Certainly, his contemporaries and his immediate posterity were not...

To the group of younger Romantics he was almost a stranger. A bare few knew of him as the author of biographies of composers and painters, of travel books, and of an analysis of love, *De l'Amour,* too brilliantly cold and analytical to attract them. Stendhal's roots were in the eighteenth century, and his feelings for the Romantic cénacles, and for Victor Hugo, in particular, slightly frigid. His private journals and confessions would have shocked his contemporaries with their self-revelations and introspective self-searchings; fortunately they did not appear in print until long after his death. He had four life-long passions: Napoleon, women, Italy, and the music of Mozart and Cimarosa.

To most of the fashionable salons of the day he was a stranger, a relict of another century, notable for a ready, sardonic wit, and for a series of variegated fascinating life-experiences. He was known as a Bonapartist, and even as a kind of republican after the ancient pattern, who was at his best when in the company of a select few.

He felt more Italian than French. A Ulysses, he had wandered far and wide — even as far as Russia — and seen much. Finally he had come back to Paris in 1821, bruised in purse and in the heart, for he was in the habit of constantly falling in love, and all too frequently with unhappy consequences. As his *De l'Amour* proved, he was, like so many philosophical experts in that field, more successful in theory than in practice. As a matter of fact, it was his latest unfortunate and unsatisfactory involvement that led him to write that book.

He despised the English and hated England. But he adored Shakespeare, about whom he wrote a notable defense, *Racine et Shakespeare,* which had aroused considerable attention. He had met and known Lord Byron, and become friendly with him, having seen him for the first time at the opera in Milan in 1816. Who was there who would not listen to such experiences? Other connections he would confess more privately — his friendship with Silvio Pellico, whom he admired; and his contacts with other Carbonari of Italy; as he would his frank opinions of the régime of Charles X of France, which were none too flattering.

An unsettled wanderer all his life long, he had also been many things besides being a writer. "At different times in his life he was a soldier, an administrator, a clerk in a wholesale grocery,...a traveling salesman,...a consul, a tutor..."[19]

Of all his life's experiences (aside from his amours), certainly those most fascinating to his hearers must have been Stendhal's days when he was with Napoleon in Russia, participating in the advance as well as the retreat of the French armies. Stendhal had begun as a very young soldier, and had ended as an official of the

Empire. At first sight, as a young soldier, he had fallen in love with Italy, and particularly with the city of Milan, and was drawn back again and again with a constancy he was not to manifest in other amours. He had also been an army official in Germany, had gone to Vienna, had seen Napoleon at the crest of his fortunes. While in Germany, he had come across the name of a small town, Stendal, the birthplace of the great renovator of Greek studies, Johann Joachim Winckelmann: and, a passionate devoté of pseudonyms, M. Beyle adopted the name of the town, and henceforth called himself Stendhal.

His native town, Grenoble, where he was born in 1783, was associated in his mind with much that he hated, and little that he loved. He immortalized her adversely as Verrières in *Le Rouge et le Noir*. He hated his father, to whom he refers time and again as the "bastard" in his letters; but he was in love with his mother, who died when he was very young. His father was a tyrant, and the son became a rebel. His father ruled with an iron hand; and he was tight-fisted when it came to money-matters. Young Beyle was always to be haunted by memories of the beautiful country-side around Grenoble. He early showed an extraordinary talent for mathematics, and won entrance into the École Polytechnique of Paris. He was fortunate in having influential relatives, the family of Noël Daru and his sons, and it was their influence that in a large measure determined his official career. He never enrolled in the École Polytechnique...

He was a mathematician, and he sought, in establishing for himself a philosophy of life, to found it upon what he believed to be the inexorable certainty of traditional mathematics. One wonders what he might have said had he gotten wind of the work of one of the greatest mathematical geniuses of his day, Nicolas Lobachevsky, one of the founders of non-Euclidian geometry! He naturally turned to that body of philosophers of the eighteenth and early nineteenth century who were freest of abstract metaphysical thought. These were the "ideologues," a group of thinkers who founded their thinking on the sensationalist principles of John Locke, and attempted to develop a science of psychology, morality, education, and politics on the basis of mechanism, materialism, and sensualism. Stendhal was most profoundly attracted to the works of Destutt de Tracy (whom he got to know personally), who left unfinished a massive work composed in the first decade of the nineteenth century, and a more compact abstract entitled *Elements of Ideology*, which was published in 1817-1818. Stendhal was also acquainted with the works of other ideologues of the period, like Gabriel Mably, the eighteenth century socialist; Condillac, the psychologist; Helvetius, Condorcet, and the Englishmen Malthus, Adam Smith, William Godwin, and Jeremy Bentham. To these he added other "gods" — Voltaire and Rousseau.

Out of this amalgam he tried to "crystallize" a view of nature and man, directed toward a true discovery of the springs of human behavior and actions, and to a predetermination of their future possibilities. For him too "to think was to feel." Sound judgment, logic, observation and cool analysis — relentless and disinterested exploration — were the instruments; and the goal was happiness, which, though it might be based on utilitarian self-interest, was equivalent to "virtue," for it involved the greatest good to the greatest number. The ideal was to approximate in thinking the clarity and certainty of the mathematical sciences, to eschew obscurity and mysticism; always to come back to the fundamentals — that all our knowledge is rooted in sensation or perception, and their derivatives, memory, judgment, and will. But Stendhal's mind was no simple mechanism that could be reduced to some very elementary fundamental proposition. His "ideology" all too frequently was seduced by and at war with the great enemy — passion, unpredictable and mysterious! And, as he came to acknowledge, there were always secrets of the soul, unknown to their masters, recessed motivations and impulses. To pry into those, to uncover them — here was a fertile ground for the psychologist and the novelist... Here, indeed, is to be found the great paradox that is Stendhal — an eighteenth century thinker, with insights and anticipations that could only be properly understood in the twentieth!...

He was in England during the tense period of 1817-1818, and he witnessed the wretchedness of the working population and the strikes in Manchester in 1818. He predicted a revolution! He was not a Saint-Simonian, for unlike them, he foresaw that this brand of Utopian socialism with its faith in the "industriels," the moneyed bourgeoisie, was bound to fail. For a time, he even looked to the American republic for an answer to his and the world's problems, but he was repelled by what he believed was the pursuit of the dollar, and the incubus of "ennui," "Un seul mot exprime toute la civilisation de l'Amérique, ce mot est *dollars*." "A single word expresses all the civilization of America — *dollars*."[20]

With the same thoroughness, objectivity, and planning he was to bring to his work as commissary of the Grand Army of Napoleon, or as military administrator in Brunswick, he set about examining himself. The documents: journals, diaries, notes, composed as self-explorations, unpublished in his lifetime, are a mine of information and speculation in psychological self-analysis, and were to become an alluring Circe to what was to be known as psychoanalysis.

1815 brought an end to his political career. His father's death left him a competence, but from now on he would have to live by his pen, until some new mighty upheaval would bring him back into the great world of politics... So far as his political and social ideas were concerned, the period of the Restoration still found him a dyed-in-the-wool Bonapartist, a republican, a friend of the Carbonari, and the intransigeant foe of the Reaction. "An array of bayonets or of guillotines can no more stop an opinion than a bagful of louis-d'or can stop the gout."[21]

He loved to punctuate his letters and notes with an English that is enchantingly maladroit. Writing from Rome in 1820, at a low-tide of liberalism, he expresses his anger at the multitude of priests and stupid noblemen he sees around him. "Je suis devenu very cool sur la politique. All Europe shall have the liberty in 1850, mais pas avant. Voilà mon calmant." Poor enough balm!

He was suspect to the police of Milan, and in 1818 he was expelled from that city. Here is the report of Baron Torresani, chief of police, dated January 29, 1818:

Henry Beyle is known as the author of an ill-famed work entitled *Rome, Naples and Florence,* by de Stendhal. In this work not only did he unfold the most pernicious political ideas, but he also compromised the reputation of numerous persons residing in these provinces by his calumnious statements, and even had the insolence to hold forth in the most damnable manner against the Austrian Government... Let me add respectfully that Beyle, during his stay of several years in Milan, made himself known as the enemy of religion, an immoral man, and dangerous to royalty, in such a degree that it is incomprehensible that my predecessors should have tolerated his presence so long... especially in view of the fact that he maintained close connections with our most notorious liberals.[22]

So here he was, back in Paris, his small inheritance exhausted, his journalistic work for a British periodical come to a halt, concocting pot-boilers like the *Promenades dans Rome,* his hopes of government office very low indeed, watching the "imbecile Bourbons" — as he called them — heading for a crisis, and — most important — completing a novel that would epitomize France in the decade before 1830.

In his *Confessions of a Child of His Age,* which appeared in 1836, Alfred de Musset's description of the generation that was born during the Napoleonic Wars, and survived into the decades of the Restoration would have been well understood by Stendhal, and might almost serve as a superscription for *Le Rouge et le Noir.*

For fifteen years they had dreamt of the snows of Moscow and the sun on the Pyramids...When these children spoke of glory, they were told, "Become Priests!" When they spoke of ambition, "Become Priests!" Of hope, of love, of power, of life, "Become Priests!"[23]

In Stendhal's novel Red is the symbol of military glory — now vanished; of the Napoleonic era; and Black, of the priesthood. Had the Napoleonic dream vanished? Not quite. It hovers in the consciousness of the century as myth, and potential reality. It is the antitoxin to the poison of "ennui" — the sickness of an "unheroic" age. It becomes the guiding-star out of the banality, out of the sordid commonplaces of life. It is still a theme to conjure with, to rouse feelings, to stir political visions. In the mantle of the Napoleon Bonaparte that was, a lesser Napoleon will rise to power and become another Emperor...

In *Le Rouge et le Noir,* the young protagonist of the novel — let us not call him hero, or even anti-hero — Julien Sorel, dreams Napoleon. When we meet him for the first time, this son of a well-to-do peasant, owner of a saw-mill, is perched high up, buried in the *Memorials of Saint Helena,* at the very moment when his whole future is being decided for him. For he is about to leave his brutish father and brothers, and join the household of the Mayor of Verrière, M. de Rênal, as tutor to his children. Some time before, a Bonapartist army surgeon had stayed with the Sorel family, and imbued the young boy with the Napoleonic fever. Julien, by virtue of his quick brain and his scholarship, will no doubt be destined for the church. He is a promising lad, and very handsome.

The provincial town of Verrières (read Rouen, Paris, France!) is ruled by three powerful autocrats — public opinion, convention, and money. "Rapporter du revenu" — bringing in the "dough" — is the first principle. The personal embodiments of these powers are the mayor, an aggressive, acquisitive and dominating conservative; and his rival, M. Valenod, superintendent of the workhouse. M. de Rênal, Julien's employer, is obsesed by a fear of liberals, whom he sees under every bed. Mme de Rênal, who is thirty years old, lovely, naive, and uninstructed in the ways of life and love (she had been brought up in a convent), is a devoted and submissive wife. She had brought her husband a considerable dowry, and she has expectations of an even greater fortune. She is highly sensitive; and being married to an insensitive man, has assumed that all men were like him. Julien is different from any other men she has ever met. He is proud and a "plebeian in revolt." He has talent, energy, and a prodigious memory that can reproduce the entire New Testament in Latin. For the first time Mme de Rênal discovers the meaning of passion.

Young Sorel soon finds out that there is another force in town even more powerful than the secular authorities, the Church. That new knowledge determines his choice of career. Whether he feels a vocation or not, this, he decides, is the only path open to a young man of talent hungering for rapid advancement and influence. Julien Sorel hopes to become the Napoleon of the Church of France! He is, as the French would say today, "enragé." To achieve his goal, in the face of an aggressive, hypocritical and brutal society, he will use the skill and strategies of an army general. He will apply a similar strategy to his own life, his behavior, and his relations to others. He will outmaneuver M. de Rênal. He will win Mme de Rênal's favors. He will avenge himself on the world as it is constituted today, a world built on vanity and hypocrisy. He too will be a hypocrite. He will be Napoleon, Don Juan and Tartuffe — all in one! "I must become a priest!" he says to himself.

Alas! how often the unpredictable intrudes itself on the best-laid plans! — that is, the unpredictable that is both within us and without us. It is a tragic irony that Julien, almost at the summit of his ambitions, should be brought low by the actions of a priest; as well as by the unpredictable within himself — a sudden eruption of an uncalculated passion and rage!

The education of Julien Sorel is painful. He discovers all too soon that being a priest is not enough — and that being a good priest is often a serious hazard. In at least two instances he finds that a powerful patron is more powerful than a dedicated priest. Integrity — Horace the poet to the contrary — needs other weapons than itself, and sometimes poisonous ones are more effective! . . .

Through the influence of the rector of the seminary, Julien advances in life, and becomes secretary to the Marquis de la Mole in Paris. Here he comes into contact with the aristocratic society of the Restoration. Here, also, he finds all the primal elements of Verrières translated into more lavish vacuity and boredom. Here he finds parvenu climbing, intrigue, scandal-mongering; royalism without heart or fervor or dignity; hypocrisy and fear — but alas! no real thought, or ideas. The Marquis is a man of intelligence, power, and insight, though also a hide-bound aristocrat and royalist. He recognizes Julien's capacities. The exceptional character in the family is Mlle Mathilde de la Mole, who has both beauty and brains, and is ill at ease in an atmosphere she feels as totally devoid of "heroism" and personality. She recognizes that Julien is a "man" — she senses the potential heroic qualities in him, but she is hampered by the chains of upbringing, status, and fortune. She longs for an age of chivalry, and worships a forebear who at one time had been executed and whose mistress cut off his head and thenceforth cherished it! She struggles against the voice of reason but finally gives in. She becomes pregnant, but insists on marrying Julien, and actually obtains the reluctant consent of her father.

How often does a slight error play into the hands of Nemesis! At Julien's suggestion, the Marquis de la Mole makes inquiries about him from Mme de Rênal; and Mme de Rênal, now in a state of repentance (as she believes), writes a letter at the dictation of her young and malicious confessor. The Marquis withdraws his consent to the marriage, and Julien in a moment of irrepressible fury, rushes off to Verrières and there in the church shoots Mme de Rênal. She is wounded, but not fatally. Julien, however, is resolved to die, though besought to change his mind by the two women who love him. Now he knows that it is Mme de Rênal that he really loves and has always loved, and she, in turn, avows her love for him. His martyrdom and execution by the guillotine kill her. Mathilde de la Mole fulfils her dream — and carries off Julien's severed head and buries it in a cave...

It is scarcely to be wondered at that *Le Rouge et le Noir* should have failed of finding a sympathetic readership in 1830. To ears still bewitched by the sonorous rhetoric of *Hernani,* and the mellifluous extravagance of Romantic poetry and its exoticism, the severe, almost surgeon-like detachment of Stendhal must have come as something frightfully disconcerting. It had little of the surges of Lamartine's poetry, its vagueness, its dreamy associative imagery, and its *Weltschmerz.* Nor did it have the élan, the fantastic afflatus of Balzac's magical tales. More than any other production of the time, it was a sharp, almost clinical dissection of a "sick" age — and of human beings caught up in the post-Napoleonic decade of "unheroism." And for all its apparent objectivity, it was also a study of frustrated and defeated passions.

It is not merely Jules Sorel who suffers catastrophic defeat. It is also the others, persons of passionate probity and a sense of justice who are brought down. Mme de Rênal is a pure, simple, wonderfully sympathetic being, but in no position to combat the brutishness of a husband, rigid conventions, or her own awakened ego. She is like so many other women of the time, a piece of chattel, bought and sold on the marriage mart. But things are no better in the more aristocratic circles of the de la Moles. Mathilde de la Mole is also for sale. She is a more critical being than Mme de Rênal, and she is outraged by the society around her. Within her too there burns a "secret fire," but where is she to find the tinder to make it flare up? Or the person to do it? And so, she takes refuge in some far-fetched worship of past heroism. If it appears in her vicinity in the person of the Spanish

Count Altamira, who is proscribed in his own country for his liberal activities (there is a price on his head), she is scarcely able truly to understand the realities actuating him. And so, seeing him at a ball, she muses to herself: "I can see nothing conferring honor on a man except a sentence of death...It's the only thing that can't be bought." Julien too is deeply impressed by Count Altamira's personality and integrity...

For others, it is easier to compromise. Even the courageous rector Father Picard exhibits cracks in his integrity, as he warns Julien against being too outspoken in the presence of the Marquise de la Mole on the subject of royalty. "They are KINGS," he says, "and that gives them an imprescriptible right to respect from lowborn creatures such as you and me. We are priests, however, for she will take you as such; by virtue of this office, she regards us as a species of upper man-servant necessary to her salvation."[24]

But there are also the utterly incorruptible — such as the timber merchant Fouqué, a friend of Julien's who remains unshaken and loyal to the end.

Julien is destroyed not only by the society in which he strives to rise, but also by his own inner self. The mathematical schemes he concocts in his plans to win victories over men and women, and society; the rigorous dedication to "hypocrisy," to "playing a part" which he tries to perfect in the seminary; his devotion to cunning — all of these break down in a moment of unsuspected passion. For Julien is a dreamer! He had been dreaming when on the verge of entering the household of the Rênals, as he stands on a great rock, looking at the flaming August sky:

...The cicadas were chirruping in the meadow below the rock. When they fell silent, all around him was still. At his feet he saw twenty leagues of country. Now and then he caught sight of a sparrow-hawk, taking off from the large rocks overhead, silently describing immense circles. Julien's eye mechanically followed the bird of prey. He was struck by its tranquil, powerful movements. He envied such strength; he envied such isolation. This was Napoleon's destiny. Would it one day be his?[25]

Here, in one magnificent symbol, is contained the essence of the book: To be a bird of prey (a marvelous one at that!) and to be a dreamer at the same time — what an irony! And what seeds of catastrophe! He is a "plebeian" who wishes to soar, but now and then his plebeianism betrays him, as when he is moved by the singing and the voices of prisoners confined in M. Valnode's workhouse. He is only too aware of the emptiness of the society to which he aspires. "Yet these people," he thinks to himself, "are the forlorn hope of the party which has the Marquis as one of its leaders." Julien abides by his own principle: "Chacun pour soi dans ce desert d'égoïsme qu'on appelle la vie." "Each man for himself in this desert of egoism men call life." To which principle he adds a schooling in the perfection of hypocrisy. But what of those hidden springs within him?

It is these hidden springs of human behavior that Stendhal has set out to uncover — motives concealed from the mover, feelings and urges that are masked. Stendhal's unparalleled achievement lies in the subtle self-revelations of his principal characters, the inner dialogue or monologue, anticipatory of the later "stream of consciousness." These are processes of self-discovery or self-deception, efforts to reconcile contradictory feelings; they are the self-division of the soul. They are brilliantly carried out in the moving reflections of Mme de Rênal as she discovers the frightful elements of passion hitherto concealed; in Julien's constant pre-occupation with divining the motives of others with whom he is at "war," and in attempting to outmaneuver them, and thus preserve and save his "ego"; in Mathilde's self-division vis-à-vis her peasant lover turned hero and martyr. And finally in Julien's self-discovery at the end of the book, a tragic commentary on the emptiness of the goal he has set himself. His calculated egoism cannot stand comparison with the social and utilitarian principles of happiness developed by Count Altamira, who is facing death in a humanitarian cause. It is a "heroic" egoism, not the egoism of the sparrow-hawk. Julien finally recognizes himself as a plebeian engaged in a class war. And he addresses the jury:

Messieurs, je n'ai point l'honneur d'appartenir â votre classe...

Messieurs, I have not the honor of belonging to the same class as yourselves. You see in me a peasant in revolt against the lowliness of his lot.[26]

The insecurity and fears of the Ultra-royalists are reflected in the words of the Marquis de la Mole, uttered in Julien's presence:

In fifty years' time there will be nothing in Europe but Presidents of Republics and not a single King. And with these four letters KING the priest and the gentleman too will disappear. I see nothing but candidates paying court to the unwashed majorities.[27]

Stendhal's style of writing is consonant with his surgical probings. He has none of the rhetoric of Romanticism, the ornate eloquence of Chateaubriand, the high theatricality of *Hernani*. The forthrightness of the prose matches the objectivity of his analysis of the soul. Scarcely ever is there a description of nature, scarcely even a long descriptive passage.

It is only in the very last portion of the book that the author intervenes, sometimes very directly, in politicalizing his theme, and even indicating the nature of his own theory of the novel. It is certainly Stendhal as well as Julien that is speaking when they reflect on the "true" priest:

Ce bon prêtre nous parlerait de Dieu. Mais quel Dieu?...

This good priest would speak to us of God. But what God? Not the God of the Bible, a petty despot, cruel and thirsting for vengeance... but the God of Voltaire, just, kind, infinite...[28]

It is, again, Stendhal who is speaking through Julien, when the latter realizes that even in prison he cannot rid himself of hypocrisy, though here he is alone: "Oh, our Nineteenth Century!" Julien-Stendhal exclaims...

Seemingly undismayed by public indifference, Stendhal continued writing the imposing successors to *Le Rouge et le Noir,* like *La Chartreuse de Parme* and the unfortunately uncompleted *Lucien Leuwen.*

Stendhal himself came to terms with the new government of Louis-Philippe. He accepted public office. As for his later career and the novels, we shall come back to them in a later chapter...[29]

2

DECEMBER 1830 — "SYMPHONIE FANTASTIQUE" HECTOR BERLIOZ AND THE POETS

> Grenoble, 16 September, 1828. Come as soon as you can...We will read *Hamlet* and *Faust* together. Shakespeare and Goethe, the mute confidants of my life, oh! come. No one here understands this passion of genius...The day before yesterday, in a carriage, I set the Ballad of the King of Thule in Gothic style. I will give it you to put into your *Faust*, if you have one.

This is Hector Berlioz, age 25, writing to his friend, Humbert Ferrand. Years later, in his *Memoirs,* he recalled that early enthusiasm, which was to remain his life-long possession:

I must record as one of the most remarkable incidents of my life, the impression at once strange and profound, which the first reading of Goethe's *Faust* in the translation of Gérard de Nerval made on me. The wonderful book fascinated me from the very first, I could not leave it. I read it without a stop, at table, at the theatre, in the street everywhere.[30]

Shakespeare, Byron, and Goethe's *Faust!* What Romantic but came under their spell! Nerval's translation of *Faust,* partly in prose, partly in verse, was not the first to appear in France, but it proved the most popular and the most influential. It was published in the remarkable year 1827 — the year of the Preface to *Cromwell,* of Delacroix's celebrated painting, *Sardanapalus*, and of Berlioz's own cantata *The Death of Orpheus.*

Great as was the impact of Byron, that of Goethe's *Faust* was equally great, but more lasting. From Byron's *Manfred* on to Thomas Mann's *Doctor Faustus,* and beyond, the Faustian Man towers colossus-like over the imagination of Europe. For the world at large, *Faust* meant the first part of that drama. Goethe completed the second part shortly before his death in 1832.

It is not surprising that *Faust* should have exercised such a potent attraction for and influence on the Romantics. Setting aside its intrinsic poetic qualities, and its dramatic elements, there was in addition one aspect that stood out: its essentially "Romantic" elements. Paradox and irony that Goethe — the avowed enemy of Romanticism and of the Romantics — should have composed one of the most "Romantic" works of the period, and, if we also consider the second part, set the stage for the future development of numerous anti- or non-classical movements in literature and art such as Expressionism and even the Theatre of the Absurd. For the Romantics and their successors were to see in the figure of Faust the embodiment of the illimitable aspirations of modern man toward an attainment of universal knowledge and experience, the proud affirmer of an Ego with infinite possibilities; at the same time, a titanic figure who exposed the inherent and fatal dualism of Man himself — revealing the "two souls" — "zwei Seelen" — that rive him apart, one drawing him down — toward the earthly (sometimes the too earthly), and the other, upward, the transcendental. The Faustian man acknowledges no boundaries to his wishes, recognizes no barriers to their fulfilment. That dualism is reenforced by the other major and absolutely necessary figure of the drama — Mephistopheles: personified negation, criticism, cynicism, pitiless observation and penetration of unconscious motives, who sees all too clearly how kin are Faust's ideal strivings and sheer animalism. He is the censor of Faust's psyche, the merciless judge of that dark side of him that indulges itself in carnal play with the innocent Gretchen, and the obscene routs of the Walpurgisnacht — the Witches' Sabbath...

Not least, Faust was the promulgator of the cult of the self, of the personality, of the development of one's individuality, no matter at what or whose expense: to know all, to be all, to master all — even the profoundest secrets of Nature...

It is hard to imagine what young Hector Berlioz would have experienced had he been able to read that drama in the original, especially the sublime lyrical passages, the simple ballads, the music, say, of the Prologue in Heaven. But he saw and understood a great deal even if through the misted glass of Nerval's version.

Out of that adoration came the early *Eight Scenes of Faust;* the *Symphonie Fantastique* of 1830, and much later *The Damnation of Faust.* Alongside of *Faust,* there were, of course, many other elements that flowed into the making of Berlioz's musical compositions, for like other Romantic composers, he exhibits in the largest measure the fusion of literature and music, the appropriation of literary themes and subjects, characteristic also of the pictorial arts — just as, somewhat later, poetry will appropriate music and painting in the Symbolist and Impressionist movements. No less important an aspect of Berlioz's creation is the element of musical autobiography — self-revelation. And finally, the Romantic pre-occupations with extraordinary psychic experiences — such as we have already remarked — the nocturnal side — "die Nachtseite" of the human soul.

Berlioz's *Symphonie Fantastique* may be said to be one of those capital works that mark and epitomize Romanticism. It was first revealed to its audiences at the Conservatoire on the evening of December 5, 1830 — and joins Victor Hugo's *Hernani* and Stendhal's *Le Rouge et le Noir* in establishing that year as the "annus mirabilis" of genius.

Berlioz's *Symphonie Fantastique* is an autobiography. Not in its specific details as much as in the general atmosphere and its success in projecting the vicissitudes, tribulations, disturbances, and agitations within an artist's mind. It is a generalized portrayal — though we may be sure that Berlioz's own unhappy passion for the beautiful actress, Harriet Smithson, the accesses of distraction, bordering on insanity, the frenzy of love as well as other horrors played a significant part in its creation.

I was just going to begin my great symphony *(Episodes in the Life of an Artist),* Berlioz wrote in February 1830, to depict the course of this infernal love of mine ... [31]

A link is established between auditor and the composition in performance by means of a "program" — so as to enable the auditor to identify with the varying moods and experiences of the "artist" under the influence of extraordinary psychological and physical tensions and agitations. To help him better to associate with these processes, Berlioz also utilizes a musical connecting device, the "idée fixe," (later in the century it will be called the "leit-motiv"), the melodic theme that stands for the Beloved, and which is varied with the changing moods of the lover in such an astoundingly skilful way as to constitute, in brief, an epitome of his living experience. Here is born the "symphonic poem" — which at the same time brought into music a full psychography. Romanticism consummates itself in this "programmatic" self-revelation, already, of course, anticipated in Beethoven's last Quartets, and in the German Lied.

Here is Berlioz's programmatic introduction to his symphonic poem:

A young musician of morbid sensibility and ardent imagination poisons himself with opium in an access of amorous despair. The dose of narcotic, not strong enough to kill him, plunges him into a deep sleep, accompanied by strange visions, during which his sensations, sentiments and recollections take the form, in his sick brain, of musical thoughts and images. The beloved woman herself becomes for him a melody and like a fixed idea which he finds and hears everywhere.

We are carried musically through the artist's dreams and passions, and encounter the first of the "idées fixes" — a tender and agonizing theme. Then we are at the Ball, thereafter in the Country, then along with him in the March to the Scaffold. He dreams he has murdered his beloved. And finaly we join him at a Witches' Sabbath, a nightmare horror, that is puncutated by parody and distortion of the Beloved's theme and of the "Dies Irae."

The modernity of Berlioz's genius stands revealed. There is the "idée fixe" and its variations; there is the special preoccupation with the morbid consciousness, and its reflection in dreams, and the inducement of such dreams through opium.

Here German soul-searching has taken over and triumphed. The nocturnal aspects of the human soul which they had studied and were studying, the interconnections of Mesmerism and animal magnetism, hypnotic trances, somnabulism, these were the provinces of those who styled themselves "Romantic physicists." G. H. von Schubert had composed a most influential treatise, *The Symbolism of the Dream*, and J. W. Ritter had been particularly concerned with the "unconscious," or that which he called "passive consciousness, the Involuntary."

Many things, he wrote, can only be explained in this way: friendship, love.., the power of imagination... All our actions are a kind of somnambulism, i.e., answers to questions, and it is we who interrogate. Each one carries in him his somnabulist, of whom he is himself the magnetist... God in the heart. This phenomenon is absolutely somnabulistic. The waking state has no memory of it.[32]

In France, Gérard de Nerval (who became unbalanced and finally hanged himself) was deeply interested in Swedenborg, Illuminism, and the hermetic books of the Cabbala. He drew a great many of his own fantastic ideas from the Germans, and in a number of stories dealt with specific states of insanity.

How do I know, he wrote, if this alleged infirmity may be the symptom of a more energetic activity, of a more complete organization, and if nature in exalting all the faculties did not render them for perceiving the unknown?[33]

But by far the most influential role was that of E.T.A. Hoffmann. His popularity in France was such that by 1830 his complete works appeared in translation in twelve volumes. In England Carlyle became Hoffmann's translator. It is most likely that so far as the *Symphonie Fantastique* was concerned, Hoffmann supplied the *Doppelgänger* motive in the "March to the Scaffold." In Hoffmann's celebrated *The Devil's Elixirs* the protagonist of the novel sees his own other Ego being carted off to execution.

Finally, it is undoubtedly certain that the idea of the opium dream came by way of the Englishman Thomas De Quincey's *Confessions of an English Opium-Eater.* It was published in 1822, and was translated into French by Alfred de Musset, as well as by others. Originally it was written as a defense by that wayward English Romantic against an accusation made by Coleridge that DeQuincey's indulgence in opium was the action of "an adventurous voluptuary, angling in all streams for a variety of pleasures," whereas his own indulgence was "the one sole therapeutic source available against his particular malady." This pathetic duel is of little interest to us, except that it was a case of a very black pot accusing the black kettle; for Coleridge, despite well-diffused stories to the contrary, for one reason or another, remained an addict to the end of his life. De Quincey had begun taking opium during his days at Oxford, in 1804, in order to alleviate his rheumatic pains.

"Opium! dread agent of unimaginable pleasure and pain!..." De Quincey's apostrophe to opium oscillates between exultation and elevation on the one hand and deep depression on the other. The exultation was to enchant later poets, especially the Symbolists:

O just, subtle, all-conquering opium! that to the hearts of rich and poor alike, for the wounds that will never heal, and for the pangs of grief that 'tempt the spirit to rebel,' bringest assuaging balm: eloquent opium!... Thou buildest upon the bosom of darkness, and out of the fantastic imagery of the brain, cities and temples beyond the art of Phidias and Praxiteles... Thou only givest these gifts to man; and thou hast the keys of Paradise, O just, subtle, and mighty opium!...[34]

And on the other side, the tyranny of bad dreams:

...Upon the rocking waters of the ocean the human face began to reveal itself; the sea appeared paved with innumerable faces, upturned to the heavens; faces, imploring, wrathful, despairing; faces that surged by the thousands, by myriads, by generations...Over every form, and threat, and punishment, and dim sightless incarceration, brooded a killing sense of eternity and infinity...Ugly birds, or snakes, or crocodiles...gigantic vermin.

It is out of such strands, adding the body of genius to them, that the imagination of Berlioz created the unforgettable fantasies of the *Symphonie Fantastique.* The torments he had undergone are vividly depicted in his letters and *Memoirs.* Now these personal tribulations were brought to a climax by his utter despair over Harriet Smithson, rumors of her infidelities, and his own sense of rejection. Berlioz proceeded to replace her with a beautiful young pianist, Camille Moke, an act of desperate rebound doomed to end in a catastrophe. The idea of murder was never far from his mind, and the "March to the Scaffold" was nothing if not a projection of his feelings. Yet, for all that, here he was with a musical triumph. Someone had said to Fétis, the music critic, that Berlioz was possessed of a devil. And Berlioz proudly reported Fétis's reply, "The devil may possess his body, but by Jove! a god possesses his head."[35]

On December 7, he wrote,

I had a wild success. The *Symphonie Fantastique* was received with shouts and acclamation; they had to repeat the March to the Scaffold, and the Witches' Sabbath was quite overwhelming in its Satanic effect.[36]

Additionally, he had won the Prix de Rome, the same year! Assured of the pension which accompanied the prize, and of the hand of Camille — "my marriage is fixed for Easter of 1832," — he set off for Italy at the beginning of 1831. Poor, poor Berlioz! How was he to know that his *via crucis* was only beginning! His spirits were high, and with justice. He had brought to music something fresh — a richness of orchestral effects, a mastery of color and mood; he had invented the psychological tone-poem. And he had made new friends. Franz Liszt had been there at the performance, and had acclaimed the work. Thus began a great friendship with the Hungarian genius, who was to be one of the most dedicated and devoted of Berlioz's protagonists. Berlioz, in turn, introduced Liszt to Goethe's *Faust*. And he was to have no inconsiderable influence on Liszt's musical creations...

Berlioz had scored yet another triumph, a triumph over his stubborn and almost inflexible father, the physician, Dr. Berlioz, who had been insisting all along that Berlioz become a physician too. He had tried to obey, but the first contacts with the dissecting rooms of the École de Médecine in Paris had made him jump out of the window in disgust. He had returned to the school, but his heart was elsewhere: at the opera, in concert halls, with Beethoven and Gluck...In 1824, he had written to his father — an artist's declaration of independence:

I am voluntarily driven towards a magnificent career (no other epithet can be applied to the career of an artist) and I am not in the least heading for perdition...I think, indeed, I am convinced that I will attain distinction in music; everything points that way from outside, and from within the voice of nature is stronger than the most rigorous dictates of reason I have every conceivable chance in my favor if you will back me...This is the way I think, the way I am, and nothing in the world will change me. You could cut off my allowance or force me to leave Paris, but I do not believe you will want to make me lose the best years of my life.[37]

His father periodically cut off his allowance; then relented, and finally gave in. Berlioz was at times penniless, but he knew what he wanted, and there was no stopping him. His mother had been even more firmly opposed to his musical career; her religious feelings were outraged by what she conceived to be the immoral influences inherent in theatrical and operatic life.

Berlioz was obsessed. He triumphed over the great Cherubini, autocrat of the Conservatoire, and gained admission and performances. He fought against the dogged traditionalists of musical Paris, and raised the banner of Gluck, Carl Maria von Weber, and Beethoven; and he could not tolerate the sacrileges perpetrated on the works of his revered masters. He had discoverd the new heavens of Beethoven's last quartets. He organized "purists" like himself, and publicly corrected deflections from the original scores of Gluck and Weber. His literary tastes were very wide: Scott, Byron, Thomas Moore, Shakespeare, Goethe, Virgil, Gautier. He was of those who supported the Greek war of independence by composing a cantata, *La Révolution grecque.*

He was completing the score of *The Death of Sardanapalus,* inspired by a famous painting by Delacroix, when the July Revolution erupted. He went out into the streets:

I shall never forget the aspect of Paris during those memorable days. The wild bravado of the gamins, the enthusiasm of the men, the frenzy of the public women, the mournful resignation of the Swiss and the Royal guard, the singular pride the workers exhibited, when, being masters of the city, they refrained from pillage...And the music, and the songs, and the raucous voices resounded in the streets — to have an idea of these, one had to be there![38]

How surprised and delighted he was when he heard the crowds singing a war-song of his own setting — a poem of Thomas Moore's, "Forget not our wounded comrades"! How he rejoiced when he led them in the singing of the *Marseillaise,* which he was soon to arrange for two choruses and a large orchestra, and which he was to dedicate to the hymn's poet, Roget de Lisle...

Was it at this time that he became interested in the Saint-Simonians? A few months after he arrived in Rome he wrote to the Saint-Simonian Charles Duveyrier in July 1831:

I read with avidity a number of issues of the *Globe,* which someone lent me recently and my last doubts have been completely removed. In all that concerns the political reorganization of society I am convinced that the plan of Saint-Simon is the only true and complete one, but I must tell you that my ideas have not varied in the least in all that concerns the supernatural. God, the soul, an afterlife, etc., I do not think this need be an obstacle to my joining my hopes and efforts to yours for the betterment of the most numerous and poorer class, for the natural ordering of talents and for the destruction of any kind of privilege, which, hidden like vermin in the folds of the social body, has up to now paralyzed all efforts which attempt to remedy it. Write to me about this: I will reply to you at once to let you know my ideas about the way in which I can be used musically in the great work when I return to Paris.[39]

During his absence in Italy, Camille Moke jilted him in favor of the materially more substantial M. Pleyel, of the celebrated firm of piano makers. With murder in his heart, Berlioz set off for France; fortunately, his fury abated, and he became reconciled to his fate. As for the tantalizing Harriet Smithson (to anticipate somewhat), he did finally marry her in 1833, despite her lack of dower or property, and the fact that her career as actress was in notable decline. Now his two passions coalesced — Shakespeare's Ophelia was his. But the marriage was not untroubled. The years following his return to France were particularly difficult for Berlioz, harried as he was by financial difficulties, which he sought to ease by employment as a musical journalist. Harriet's career as actress was practically over; and the birth of a son further aggravated the domestic situation. The couple separated in 1840. But there were other sources of harassment, bitterness, and frustration — the hardships of making his way as a composer. His opera, *Benvenuto Cellini*, was hissed off the stage by an audience utterly devoted to the theatrical and pompous style of Meyerbeer — king of the Opera. An equally dismal fate befell, in 1846, the performances of the great "dramatic legend," *The Damnation of Faust*, a work of which he had been dreaming all his life, which he hoped would prove to the world that he was "the musical colossus." The dream turned into a nightmare. The twelve performances of that work were given, as Berlioz himself complained, "before half-empty houses," and cost Berlioz himself a small fortune.

It would be useless to expatiate on the state of theatrical and operatic life of Paris — the machinations, cliques, political favoritism, artistic and other prejudices, and, not least, traditionalism that wrought havoc with a true artist's career — particularly of one who was also an innovator.

But there were also successes. *Romeo and Juliet,* "a symphony for chorus, solo voices, and orchestra," was acclaimed, and young Richard Wagner, ten years Berlioz's junior, took note of that revolutionary work and was enchanted. If genius is in part obsession, Berlioz was certainly one of the most obsessed. He remained firm in that declaration of independence he had pronounced to his father. No tribulations, no obstacles could stem the flow of his creations. Embittered often by the indifference of his fellow-countrymen, he continued nevertheless, as his ambitions, and his scope widened. His Romantic titanism demanded expanded frontiers, ever larger forces, orchestral and vocal, to fulfil his demands of the "new" music. Ever surer of his massive orchestral sense and power, he employed more than four hundred musicians and singers for his epochal *Requiem.* His phenomenally successful effects were abetted by the technological advances in the making and perfecting of wind-instruments. (Advances in piano manufactures were keeping equal pace.) The performance of the *Requiem* at the Invalides was an astounding achievement, and a source of great satisfaction to the composer. His reputation as composer and conductor outside of France grew year by year. Franz Liszt, who learned much from Berlioz, a major artist himself and composer, but also a most generous soul, had recognized Berlioz's genius almost immediately, proclaimed it widely, and what was even more important, produced his *Benvenuto Cellini* and other works at Weimar. Schumann was no less an admirer. Writing in 1848, Berlioz said with bitterness, "During the last seven years I have lived solely from what my works and concerts have earned me in foreign lands. Without Germany, Bohemia, Hungary, and especially Russia, I should have starved in France over and over again...No, I have nothing to do in France, except cultivate the friendships that are dear to me..."[40]

If he tended to exaggerate his trials, the fact remains that the bulk of his grievances had true foundations. But he had a coterie of friends and admirers — almost the whole of the Romantic School! And Niccolò Paganini, in tribute to Berlioz's *Harold in Italy* made him a gift of 20,000 francs, to which he later added another 10,000. He, who could not win the field held by Rossini, Meyerbeer, and later, Offenbach, was fortunate in the admiration and understanding of such personalities as Schumann, Liszt, and Wagner, who not only recognized his true genius, but also the revolutionary nature of his innovations. They saw in *Romeo and Juliet* a kind of new "choral" symphony, a symphony of disparate parts, yet subtly connected by the unifying tie of the leit-motiv. Critics even traced the connection between the love-theme of Berlioz's masterpiece and that of *Tristan und Isolde*. He was never at a loss for musical ideas; they sometimes came tumbling at such a speed he had to devise a sort of musical shorthand for himself. He had many talents: he was one of the most prolific musical journalists of the century; he was autobiographer; he was the author of an epoch-making theoretical work on orchestration. He was his own librettist: partially in *The Damnation of Faust* (the other being Goethe), and fully in the massive operatic work, *Les Troyens*. It was this production, designed to last five hours in performance, that embittered his last years. Completed in 1858, it saw the light at the Théatre Lyrique in November 1863, cut in half; even the second part being also truncated. The book was based on Virgil's *Aeneid* — the poem he had studied when a boy, and which he never ceased to worship. The two parts deal respectively with the capture of Troy and with the love of Dido and Aeneas. Here, in this swansong, Berlioz's lyrical vein flowed as never before. But even this mutilated version fell on almost deaf ears. For Berlioz Paris had not changed. Many years were to elapse before *Les Troyens* was restored in its fullness and granduer to the operatic stage of France. By that time Berlioz was dead. He had survived Harriet, and his second wife, Maria Recio, and most tragically, his own son. He died in 1868. To encourage him, when in his moments of despair, Daussoigne-Méhul, his friend, had once written him:

All honor, then, to the men of genius who have enlarged our horizons. So forge ahead, Berlioz, and do for our nephews what others did for us. Music was not born yesterday, and art is boundless... Courage! Germany awaits you, and France will perhaps honor your fame in 1964. Does this not suffice for a man of spirit?[41]

3

EUGÈNE DELACROIX:
THE PAINTER AND ROMANTICISM

Les artistes sont les plus heureux des hommes...

Artists are the luckiest human beings. I've said this
to you many times, and I am today more convinced
than ever. This is what I mean by the good fortune I
ascribe to them: They are those who above all others
succeed in filling, to a certain point, the frightful
void in the hearts of man, which, in my opinion, is to
Happiness what shadows are to the sun.
— Eugène Delacroix to Pierrèt, 1819 —

We are in the Salon 1831 looking at the large painting by Eugène
Delacroix, "Le 28 Juillet: La Liberté Guidant le Peuple."

We see her — Freedom — standing in a Phrygian bonnet,
brandishing the tricolor, proscribed since 1815, a strong woman,
with powerful breasts, dark-skinned, with fiery eyes. She exults in
the cries of the people, the combat, the roll of drums, the scent of
powder, the booming bells. All around her, as she stands on the
barricade, there are bodies. She is leading the Parisians to an
immortal combat. To the left of her stands a young urchin; to the
right a student — Delacroix himself? — in a top-hat and a gun in his
hand.

This is allegory and realism, altogether reminiscent of and as
powerful as Goya's "Uprising of the Third of May." A painting to
commemorate the fallen of the July days of 1830. There is irony
here: The Revolution is over. Louis-Philippe is on the throne. The
painting itself was to have a strange history. After being exhibited

in the Salon of 1831, it was hung for a brief while in the Luxembourg, and then stored away by the artist during the reign of Louis-Philippe. It was to remain in hiding until 1848.

Four years before, Delacroix had along with other Romantics, including Berlioz, been overpowered by the performances of the English Shakespearean troupe at the Odéon. Miss Harriet Smithson was a member of the company, and she had triumphed as Ophelia. It was then that Berlioz became infatuated with her. On Wednesday, September 1827, Delacroix wrote to Victor Hugo:

Well, well! Total invasion! Hamlet raises his hideous head. Othello readies his murderous dagger, and subverts the good police of the drama. Who knows what else? King Lear is about to pluck out his eyes in the presence of the French public. It would benefit the dignity of the Academy to declare all such importations incompatible with public morality. Adieu to good taste. In any case, you must provide yourself with a hefty cuirass underneath your coat. Beware of the classical daggers...[42]

Delacroix's adoration of Shakespeare dated from his boyhood. Then he had loved the historical tragedies, and had even attempted a fragmentary translation of *Richard III*. In 1822 he painted himself in the black costume of Hamlet — *mal du siècle* personified.

As a painter, he had flamed across the sky like another young Victor Hugo, who was his junior by four years. Delacroix was twenty-four when he completed the epic painting "Dante et Virgile aux Enfers," arousing the fury of conservative painters who swore by the classicist Jacques Louis David. But he was vigorously supported by the artist Antoine Jean Gros, a member of the salon jury. He had learned a great deal from his fellow-artist Théodore Géricault's "The Raft of Medusa," but no less from his idols Rubens and Michelangelo. In the history of Romanticism, Géricault's painting constituted a sort of revolutionary manifesto of painting. Delacroix had taken lines from Dante's Canto VIII to depict the fury and torments of the unfortunate inhabitants of Hell, one of whom is trying to climb into the boat carrying the two poets. The angered Virgil fends him off:

Allora stese al legno ambo le mani;
per che 'l maestro accorto lo sospinse,
dicendo: 'Via costâ con li altri cani!'

Then he reached out to the boat with both his arms,
On which, the Master, wary, thrust him off,
Saying, Away there with the other dogs!'

It was believed — and there is no reason to doubt the report — that Eugène Delacroix was the son of Talleyrand — that extraordinary combination of salamander, phoenix, and Mephistopheles in European political history. Delacroix's legal father had been an important official in the government, but both his parents were now dead.

Certainly, his true paternity never stood in his way. As a matter of fact it helped him greatly. The young journalist, Adolphe Thiers, already on the scent of political preferment, wrote an adulatory article on Delacroix in the *Constitutionnel*, and the government bought the painting.

At first he became one of the excited Romantics, and shared their aims and interests. He attended the early cénacles at the Nodiers and met the numerous talents and some of the geniuses: Hugo among them. Until 1831 he was an ardent follower of their programs and principles. He, too, was passionate for Shakespeare, Byron, and Goethe's *Faust* — though even these loyalties became somewhat attenuated in his later life. In 1823, he had an additional world-shaking revelation. He saw the paintings of the Englishman John Constable, then being exhibited at the Louvre: "The Hay Wain," "A Lock on the Stour," and "A View near London." A new vision of the uses and nature of color and light dawned on him — as profound a revolution as that produced by the literary masters and equal to that resulting from his visit to Morocco some years later.

A confirmed Bonapartist all his life long, he possessed the Napoleonic complex, the titanic urges of the Romantics. He was certain of his goal, and would allow no one to inhibit him. He was

attacked for his "barbarous execution," his "fanaticism of the ugly."
He was described as a "sick man under deliriums," but he persisted
in his own way. Urged by one of the officials in charge of the arts to
change his style, or forfeit the chance of commissions, he replied
that he would adhere to his own manner, "though the earth and the
stars were on the other side."[43]

He had Herculean ambitions and plans. "In the matter of
Composition, I have enough for two lifetimes; and as for projects of
all kinds, I have enough for four hundred years."[44] The extraordinary
individual, he insisted, has his own special way of seeing things.
"The world will not stop me from seeing things in my own
fashion."[45] Rules are for those who have the kind of talent that can
be acquired. There is nothing so transient as rules. Everything is a fit
subject for the artist — the subject is you yourself. The true
primitives — these are the original talents.[46]

Was he a Romantic? In later years he would repudiate the
ascription, though with a reservation:

If by Romanticism is meant the free display of my personal impressions
and my repugnance for the types invariably admired in the schools, and for
academic formulas, I must confess that not only am I a Romantic, but that I
was so even at fifteen: I already preferred Prud'hon and Gros to Guérin and
Girodet...[47]

Like another Faust, he wailed: "Oh! is it Fate — to desire ceaselessly
the expansion of myself, of the spirit that is myself, lodged in a vile
clay vessel!"[48]

His dedication to his art, and his almost superhuman activity
and productiveness are not unlike those of Balzac or Goethe. But he
did not possess the sensuality or sexuality of either of these men. His
personal comportment was one of reserve, and his associates
ascribed his "aristocratic" detachment to his origins. But Gautier
divined in him a "savage beauty" — almost that of a wild animal,
with "feline eyes" — masking the fierceness within with a "smile
full of urbanity." For he was the painter of "somnolent tigers and
ungovernable mares, of massacres and battles, of hells and orgies, of
funeral ceremonies."

In the painting, "Les Massacres de Scio" — "The Massacres of Chios" — exhibited in the Salon of 1824, in which he pays tribute to the heroic stand of the Greeks against the Turks, he mingles Orient and Greece. Blood, violence, brutality, murder are here. One group is awaiting doom, or dying already. Another, that of the victorious Turks, is triumphant. And all this contrasts violently with the blue, serene sky and the roseate clouds! Indifferent Nature? one asks. It was this work that his teacher Gros condemned: "C'est la massacre de la peinture." While painting it, Delacroix was like some inebriate; and he addresses the art of the painter: "Oh silent strength that speaks at first only to the eye, but which prevails over and seizes all the faculties of the soul . . . If I am not moved like a serpent in the power of a pythoness, I am cold . . . All the good things I've made have been done this way."

"The Massacres of Chios" was bought by the government and deposited in the Luxembourg.

He was the poets' painter, as Berlioz (whom unfortunately he did not appreciate) was the poets' composer. Byron inspired the painting of *Marino Faliero;* his poetic drama, *Sardanapalus*, Delacroix's "Death of Sardanapalus"; later *Don Juan* was to elicit "The Drawing of the Lots in the Boat." With equal fervor he produced illustrations of Shakespeare, Scott, and Goethe's *Faust*. For the benefit of Greek patriots he painted in 1826 "Greece Lamenting on the Ruins of Missolonghi." His "Death of Sardanapalus" created a scandal, which he never got over. Here, Sardanapalus, the last king of Assyria, hopelessly besieged by Arbaces, orders the destruction of his palace by fire, as well as the slaughter of all his attendants and concubines. A veritable orgy of death and destruction! A warrior plunges a jewel-crusted yatagan in the breast of a slave-woman. A monumental bacchanal of the macabre! It was this painting that some years later was to enchant Baudelaire.

But Ingres and classicism carried the day in the exposition of 1827, which proved disastrous for Delacroix. "No more canvases sold, no more orders for five years," he lamented.[50]

But he was irrepressible. He designed the costumes for Hugo's *Amy Robsart;* he attended a reading of that poet's *Marion Delorme,* the play that was refused performance. He was of the company of Balzac, Vigny, Dumas, Musset, and Sainte-Beuve. His most profound literary admiration, however, went to Stendhal, whom he regarded as writing the best French of the age, and whose company and wit he enjoyed at all times. They had at least one god in common — Mozart. For Balzac, whose furious energies and inexhaustible creativeness Delacroix should have found attractive, he had little respect, though Balzac adored Delacroix's work.

Delacroix was not a revolutionary, not even a republican, and in the course of years would become increasingly conservative. But now, the July days of 1830 carried him away. He did not mount the barricades, but his heart was overjoyed at the sight of the tricolor floating once again over Notre Dame. Dumas's account of Delacroix in those days is amusing. Referring to the painting, "Liberty Guiding the People," he wrote,

People have said that the man holding the blunderbuss to the right of FREEDOM was a portrait of the painter himself. From that it is an easy step to claiming that he fought like the devil. Also there was the rumor that Delacroix was a fervent republican. Poor, dear Delacroix! We spent our life together agreeeing on art, but sworn enemies in politics...When I met Delacroix on July 27, on one side of the Pont d'Arcole, he pointed to some men, whom one sees only on days of revolution, who were sharpening, one a sabre, the other a foil. I vouch that Delacroix was badly frightened, and showed his fear in very direct ways. But when Delacroix saw the tricolor floating over Notre Dame, when he recognized — the fanatic Bonapartist that he was, with a father who became prefect of two of the most important cities of France under the Empire, and a brother who rose to be a general, and had been wounded five or six times, and another brother who was killed at Friedland — when this fanatic Empire worshipper recognized the Imperial standard — oh, Heavens, he could not contain himself! Enthusiasm replaced fright, and now he glorified the people who a moment before had filled him with terror.[51]

Whether this story is true or not, so far as Delacroix was concerned, his life, his career, his painting, and his thinking were about to take a most critical turn. As a result of the French victory over Algiers, Africa became open to French colonial expansion. In the subsequent negotiations, Delacroix accompanied the Comte de Morny on his visit to the Sultan of Morocco.

A world that he had already entered but only in imagination, through Victor Hugo's *Orientales,* was now a reality for him. But Hugo's Orient was a composite thing — half-Spain, half-Orient. In the preface to his volume of poems, Hugo had written prophetically,

...For Empires as for Letters, before long, perhaps, the Orient will be called upon to play a role in the West. The European status quo, already worm-eaten and cracked, is already breaking up in the face of Constantinople. Our whole continent is leaning toward the East.

Delacroix returned from the Orient with fresh ideas and subjects that he was to utilize for the rest of his life. As for ideas, he had made a new discovery. He had found a Nirvana. Not Saint-Simon, not Fourier were to be his guides henceforth. For him the Orient — North Africa — came to represent the answer to the problems spawned by a contemporary decadent Europe. He became anti-Romantic (at least in his utterances), and politically and socially ultra-conservative. Among the Moors of Morocco he had found a prevalence of "habit and custom." "The Moor gives thanks to God for his poor food and his poor clothing. He is very happy to have these." As for women, he was particularly impressed by their subjection and submission, for, as he remarked, "Women are in need of restraint in these times... They have too great authority."

He carried these ideas into his assessment of contemporary France, when he returned in June 1832. On June 5 and 6, on the occasion of the funeral of the republican General Lamarque, there was an outbreak of violence in Paris. "Go to the Barbary states," Delacroix advised his fellow-citizens," and there learn patience and philosophy."

More and more deeply, he became a cultural pessimist. Progress, scientific and technological advances were illusions. No social or political movement can ameliorate the lot of mankind. "All progress necessarily leads not to greater progress, but to the negation of progress, back to the point of departure."[52]

In the Orient, he claimed, he had found "true antiquity" — not the antiquity extolled by the pseudo-classicists, but an antiquity still alive and vigorous. This new classicism Delacroix would now impose upon his newly discovered Orientalism.

In the name of his discoveries, he was now to repudiate his earlier divinities — Byron, no less than Goethe, the latter of whom was now charged with "meanness and affectation," and even Shakespeare was found to be "bombastic and turgid." The French Romantics — "c'est l'école de l'amour malade" — "a school of sick love. Unreal, false."[53]

The Romantics' dreams of changing the world — they too are sheer delusions. "The Hugos and the Berlioz...those pretended reformers...with the blind confidence of their generation, and that which came before them...can they not see that progress...in good as well as in evil, has today brought us to the brink of any abyss, into which it can well fall and make room for a total barbarism...?"[54]

Make your railroads and your telegraphs! Traverse in a twinkling of an eye lands and seas! Direct the passions as they do the aërostats! Abolish all the bad passions, which have not lost their detestable empire over the heart, despite the liberal and fraternal maxims of the age!...Come to Barbary, there you will see the true naturalness, which is always disguised in our own country.[55]

Did Delacroix not see that the Orientalism he was espousing was of the very essence of Romanticism? Was it not the ancient myth of the "noble savage," "the simple man and woman," "Nature's noble children" that the eighteenth and nineteenth century had created, and then imperially exploited, degraded, and doomed to destruction?

But what he drew from Morocco — that which was to be permanently fixed for the future — was not his primitive vision as reduced to an ideology of civilizaton, but the masterpieces he was destined to produce, long after he had left Africa. He was the first modern painter to have gone to that part of the Orient, and to bring it back in masterly visual terms. This was again his contribution to Romanticism.

He was caught in his inescapable dualism. There was the ivory tower, of which Baudelaire spoke, which enclosed him and his soul away from the sight of onlookers and priers. There was the outward man, who could conceal all that went on inside him with that aristocratic bearing and reserve that belied the inward turmoils. But what of that other part, that time and again manifested itself in his painting, and sketches, described by Baudelaire as "a volcanic crater concealed behind a bouquet of flowers"?[56]

At least one side of that dualism was clearly divined by Baudelaire when he comes to speak of the "morality" of Delacroix's works:

The morality of his works, if one may permit oneself to speak of morality in painting, also bears the marks of a visible Molochism. Everything in his work is desolation, massacres, conflagration. Everything bears testimony to the eternal and incorrigible barbarism of man...A terrifying hymn in honor of Fatality and irremediable suffering...[57]

Another aspect of that dualism is reflected in his self-dedication to paintings on Biblical themes. It is not likely that Delacroix had heard of or could have been influenced by the German school of the "Nazarenes" — another offshoot of Romantic medievalism.

There is a figure in French literature whom Eugène Delacroix closely resembles in his psychic configuration. That is Gustave Flaubert. There is the same feverish dedication to art, the same deceptive anti-Romanticism which actually cloaks the deep romanticism of the disenchanted heart. There is the parallel passion for the Orient, and its "naturalness"; the same condemnation of modern ideas of progress and social amelioration; the same withdrawal from a complete involvement with women; there is the peripatetic sexuality without a fixed compass point; there is in both a suspicion — perhaps a fear — of direct personal outpouring; and there is the transference of the affections to a mother-figure, or as in Flaubert to an actual mother. There is a retreat into the ivory tower — away from the outside world. For Delacroix there was the inimitable, eternally faithful mistress-maid, Jennye LeGuillou, a true child of nature, with the touching relationship of the guardian-mother toward the guarded son — an honor to the painter and a glorification of devotion that might well have come straight out of Flaubert's moving story, *The Simple Heart*.

Once more, Baudelaire has well defined the ever-present Romantic in Delacroix:

The imagination of Delacroix! Never afraid to scale the difficult heights of religion! The Heavens belong to him as does Hell, war, Olympus, and the sensual delights. Here is the very type of the painter-poet![58]

III.

FRANCE: 1831-1848

Honoré de Balzac
And The Quest of The Absolute

George Sand
And The Quest of The Self

Stendhal: Journey's End
"La Chartreuse de Parme"

1

HONORÉ DE BALZAC
AND THE QUEST OF THE ABSOLUTE:
MAGIC, REALITY AND THE EPIC OF MAMMON

> Now that the human mind has established celestial physics, and terrestrial physics — whether mechanical or chemical — organic physics, vegetable and animal — it remains for it to complete the scientific system of observation by founding *social physics*.
> — Auguste Comte,
> *Cours de Philosophie Positive* I, 1830 —

> He dissects man, studies the interplay of passions, examines each fibre, analyzes the entire organism. Like a surgeon, he feels neither shame nor disgust when he plunges his hands into the wounds of humanity. His only concern is with truth, and he exhibits our heart to us on the operating table. Modern science has presented him with the instrument of analysis — experimental method. He proceeds like our chemists and our mathematicians.
> — Zola on Balzac, 1866 —

In 1830 appeared the first volume of a work that with its successors was destined to exercise a major influence on the thought and actions of the century. It was entitled *Cours de Philosophie Positive,* and was written by an erstwhile adherent and disciple of Count Saint-Simon, Auguste Comte. Though Comte's theories and conclusions were to be fiercely debated, criticized, approved, confuted, or religiously sustained, they were to retain a very significant role, for they embodied perceptive insights into the needs and character of the age.

473

His term "Positivism" was to stamp the age in its reassessment of the place and destiny of science as the key to the solution of many of humanity's problems; and his coinage of the term "Sociology" was to mark the recognition of the necessary relationship that must be established between Science and Society. He embedded in his own and succeeding generations the hope and ambition that the study of society could be as great a scientific undertaking and adventure as that of physics or chemistry, and the understanding that critical for such a study was Biology, and particularly its evolutionary theory.

He is at one with the age in what we call the "passion for synthesis," the attempt to find in all aspects of human culture and history an all-embracing unity and law. In that he was heir of the Encyclopedists of the preceding century, as well as a contemporary counterpart of Goethe and Hegel, and unknowingly of the German *Naturphilosophen,* Fichte and Schelling. But he shows the impress of his age's scientific thinking in his rejection and renunciation of what his foremost disciple, Émile Littré, called a preoccupation with "the infinite and the absolute" — of metaphysical speculation and concern with "ultimates." What he called the "positive" stage in human history has now been reached, "when the human intelligence recognizes the impossibility of obtaining absolute notions and renounces the search for the origin and the destiny of the universe..., and applies itself solely to the discovery, by means of combined reason and observation, of its effective laws, that is, their invariable relations of succession and similarity,"[1] — in other words, the immutable laws of Nature. Science is at the center of his system, but not science for its own sake, but as an instrument of social advancement, as a cure for antagonisms and chaos, and as a means of enabling human beings to live for others, through achievement of "Order" and "Progress."

He would not have been a child of his century if he too had not envisioned the process of history as taking place as a "triadic" scheme — historic phenomena as involving a sequence of "threes"

— what we may call the secularization of the Trinity. Comte's triadic passion manifests itself in the historic process as three stages through which mankind has passed in developing and expanding its consciousness of the world: the theological stage, reflected in man's belief in gods and spirits; the metaphysical, when phenomena and events are understood and interpreted in terms of abstractions; and finally the positive, or scientific stage, when humanity is enabled to utilize science, that is, observation and experiment, and thus arrives at a position to "see, so as to foresee," and foresee so as to act. In Comte's words, "Science, d'où prévoyance; prévoyance, d'où action." The history of science too, in his view, follows a predetermined course in an order of complexity, from mathematics to biology, now to be completed by the most complex element, sociology.

If there is something almost touching in this faith in schematization, so self-assured and proud, and in this belief in the powers of science — at least to our generation — let us not forget the palmary achievements of science and scientists of that period, an achievement equal to that of any age. Yet, another element in this striking glorification of science — of even greater interest to our own age — was the prevalent idea in that period that science was moving toward a great "unitary" discovery — that grand prospect of uncovering a single element or law that would give us some ultimate key to the understanding and the mastery of Nature, and thus serve in the understanding and advancement of the interests of Mankind in general.

It seemed, then, that the scientific investigations and discoveries were flowing into one major stream — toward the same goal or destination. For in the year in which Comte's first volume of the *Cours* appeared — 1830 — Charles Lyell published the first volume of the epoch-making *Principles of Geology,* which found almost immediate sympathetic response. In the following year, a young man set off on an expedition aboard *The Beagle* — Charles Darwin. And toward the end of that decade, as he would later recall, the latter set down in his notebook "facts in relation to the Origin of Species, about which I had long reflected."[2] The great Cuvier, who had made such notable contributions to comparative anatomy and the study of fossils was still alive and active. The Swedish chemist, Berzelius, had recently shown how close was the relation of electricity and the chemical elements with their positive and negative charges, and had determined with the greatest accuracy the atomic weights or equivalent combining weights of the elements. Was it sheer accident or coincidence that in the period between 1837 and 1844 a number of eminent scientists, such as C. F. Mohr, William Grove, Michael Faraday, and Justus Liebig, each in his own way, was on the road to determining that all world phenomena might very well be manifestations of a single force, "one which could appear in electrical, thermal, dynamic, and many other forms, but which could never in all its transformations be created or destroyed"?[3]

So that a chemical process could be converted into an electrical one, and vice versa, magnetism could produce motion, and motion could produce electricity!

And as for the human body, had not notable physiologists like Xavier Bichat and François Magendie, one a vitalist, and the other a materialist, shown how closely the human body and its functioning were determined by physics and chemistry? And it was within this very decade of the 1830's that Theodor Schwann and Mathis Jakob Schleiden were to prove the cellular theory and the cellular origin of the most highly developed tissues in the body of man and of plants.

Finally, were not the laws of the conservation of energy, and of the convertibility of energy sign-posts pointing inevitably toward the discovery of the *unitary* principle that allied all of nature? If such correlations could be established in the physical sciences, what possibilities were not open to the biological sciences? Might not biology, or, for the moment physiology, really be the clue to the understanding of society itself? Comte had awarded biology the prime role in advancing a science of society.

François Vincent Raspail, the "Poor Man's Doctor," scientist in his own right, fighter on the barricades in 1830, one of the "Fifteen" tried by the government in 1831-1832, prisoner in the Sainte-Pélagie (what great names are associated with that edifice!) and again prisoner after the Revolution of 1848, was a proud apostle of science. (How many walking along the Boulevard named after him even know anything of the man!) He wrote,

> To Science, without which all is madness,
> To Science, the only religion of the future;
> Whose goal is God,
> Whose temple is the Universe,
> Whose cult is the study of Nature,
> Whose practice is kindness to all...[4]

It was inevitable that the "passion for synthesis" and the search for a "unitary" principle in life, as well as the other mighty currents of the age: scientific, social, political and moral, should eventually converge to become essential elements of that literary form that would henceforth dominate the nineteenth century — the novel. To watch Honoré Balzac's life and work, to observe the emergence of that vast structure that was designed to give his age a picture of its social and moral anatomy, is also to enter upon the conflicts and contradictions of the period, its ambiguities and dualism. It is, to use a favorite image of Balzac himself, to be present in the laboratory of some great scientist and observe his experiments, breathlessly following his failures and his successes.

It is a commonplace, but one deserving repetition, to state that fiction is autobiography, and autobiography fiction. "Dichtung und Wahrheit" — Poetry and Truth — intertwine in our own lives, in our self-expression, in our very gestures. We stand revealed in our falsehood no less than in our integrities. The fact that outstanding works of fiction are able to project many characters that are differentiated, the fact that the novelist can project himself into many psyches, does not in the least conceal *the* one thread — the subtle emergence of the "I" of the writer — that is autobiography. This holds true of the drama too. And this is eminently true of Balzac's 563 characters that appear in his novels, presenting varieties of types and occupations, many of them unforgettable for their individuality.

If Balzac was not the Prometheus M. André Maurois imagines him, he was something of a titan-Faust, a giant in strength as in weaknesses, a human being wrestling with superhuman efforts to transcend, to break the bounds of mortality both in his own individual life as in the massive opus he accomplished. As he surcharged his own person — body and mind — with that excess of energy that was bound in the end to destroy him, so he does with many of the children of his imagination.

Had he lived in another age, he would have been burnt as an alchemist-magician, for that was what he imagined himself to be in his own day. A coeval of the new century — he was born in 1799 — he poured into his crucibles and alembics the part of the scientific knowledge that he was master of, and intermingled it with elements of mystical illuminism, and pseudo-science that he drew from such diverse sources as Swedenborg, Mesmer, Gall the phrenologist, Lavater the physiognomist, and the Cabbalism of the Middle Ages. Like Faust, he saw Nature as One; and like Faust he hungered to find out what it was that held it together. Two souls struggled within him: one; the Romantic self, aspired to the spirituality of "angels"; the other, more earthly, the Realist self, drawing him down to the earth.

He identified with two titans of the age. Thinking of Napoleon, he said, "Ce qui'il n'a pas achevé par l'epée, je l'accomplirai par la plume" — "That which he could not accomplish with the sword, I will accomplish with my pen." The other demi-god was Beethoven, though Balzac's acquaintance with his music was scanty. But he saw in Beethoven titantic greatness, heroic strivings, grand achievements.

He was voracious. He wanted many things: physical, spiritual, intellectual. And that was to constitute the never-ending drama of his life. Critical as he was of his own times — of the rage for "money" and of "place" — he was as much bound up with both as any of his own insatiable characters. A savage indicter of the ethics of the Exchange — the Bourse — he was himself an avid speculator, and might have made a successful career of it, had he been able to devote himself full-time. But he had too much else to live for: love, the fleshpots, and not least — writing. He knew himself a genius, and no one could tell him otherwise. When in his early writing days he submitted a play on Cromwell to a critic, who scornfully exclaimed, "Anything but literature!" — he knew better than the critic. He had the capacity of taking risks — so necessary to genius. And he also knew that luck was a function of character. If hack-work was the entrance-gate to letters and fortune, he would do hack-work, a merciless occupation, which, in his case, he covered with an anonymity. For a time he was forced to become a law-clerk, and he learned what he could about litigants and litigation, the law, and the courts of law. For his pot-boilers, produced by the innumerable "factories" that peddled their sensationalism to a waiting public, he imitated, borrowed, took with a free hand; and the so-called "Gothic" novels of horror, such as those of Mrs. Radcliffe, "Monk" Lewis, Maturin and E.T.A. Hoffmann served him as models. But his eyes were already fixed toward a higher heaven. There was one star there toward whom he aspired — the magician of the North — Sir Walter Scott, whose magnificent and broad fictional canvases of historical subjects he would emulate, hopeful also of matching their financial success. To eke out his income as hack, he turned to journalism, a field now expanding with breath-taking rapidity. Fashion, humor, satire, politics, and not least scandal — what did not the reading public of the day crave and consume! The great moguls of journalism had already appeared — such as Émile de Girardin, founder of *Le Voleur* and *La Mode*, among others, and husband of the beautiful and popular Delphine Gay, whose salon would soon be open to him...

"Ah! but a man's reach should exceed his grasp." Balzac would have understood Browning's word. Everything in excess — enough is not enough! He became the proprietor of a printing establishment, and lost large sums, his own as well as his family's and his friends'. His lavish tastes, even when he was living in a garret, knew no bounds, and throughout his life his debts kept mounting in proportion to his fabulous self-indulgence, and despite his ever-waxing income. Playing hide-and-seek with his creditors became as much a part of his life as sitting at his table for fifteen hours on end, trying to meet some unrealistic deadline. He had an unlimited capacity for work and adventure — at least he believed so in his more mystical moments. One would imagine he thought he could annul the law of the conservation of energy.

He was far from handsome: gap-toothed, and gauche in his manners (women would in due time improve him); but he managed to attract persons of various ranks with his fiery eyes and his inspired way of speaking.

Women took to him. In 1819, his family moved to Villeparisis, not far from Paris. Here he came in contact with the family of the Bernys, particularly Madame de Berny, then in her forties. She was born in Versailles, and her god-parents were King Louis XVI and Marie Antoinette, for her mother had been one of the ladies of the royal court. She was unhappily married, and she brought to the young tutor of her children all the pent-up affection of a frustrated wife. In 1822 they became lovers. She gave the young Balzac a kind of devotion and understanding and a physical passion that despite all the vicissitudes of his career, and his amatory wanderings, lasted to the end of her life. She had greatness of heart, and she dedicated to him the superiority that a woman in love possesses over man — the capacity of unlimited giving and feeling. At her death she had her love-letters destroyed, but whatever is left of that correspondence is among the most moving in all of Balzacian biography. She was the mother he had never known (he had never forgiven his own mother for preferring her illegitimate son Henri to himself); she was at the same time lover, critic, guardian and guide. She was in Balzac's words, "the heart that created him." She was the "Dilecta" to whom he dedicated his work. She never for a moment doubted his genius, and she worshipped it.

She was also his great teacher in the wor'·ings of a woman's heart and soul. His feminine readers used to remark on the subtlety with which he often depicted womanhood. As his fame grew, they sought him out. The more aristocratic among them introduced him into upper-class salons. The Paris of the lower and the middle classes he had gotten to know pretty well already.

Success came. Not with the publication, as he had expected, of the first novel signed "Honoré Balzac," and entitled *Le Dernier Chouan,* but with an anonymous work, *La Physiologie du Mariage. The Last Chouan,* the story of a counter-revolutionary uprising in the Vendée, in northern France, and the attempt of soldiers of the Revolution, under the command of a dedicated republican, Hulot, to suppress it, fell flat. In its original version, it was strongly republican in sentiment, but Balzac was soon to change its tone, and adapt it to his revised political notions.

It was a bold thing for a young man of thirty to undertake a Physiology of Love — actually the work had been begun some years before — but "Physiology" was in the air, and was being applied to many forms of life and human activity. The most celebrated of these was Brillat-Savarin's *Physiology of Taste.* Balzac had a notable predecessor in his analysis of love in Stendhal's *De l'Amour,* published in 1822. Balzac's full title ran, *The Physiology of Marriage, or Meditations of an Eclectic-Philosophical Nature on Conjugal Happiness and Unhappiness, by a Young Bachelor.* Actually despite its high-sounding title and pretensions, it was scarcely a manual of marriage, but rather a study of physical relations, and the management of a conjugal household, as well as of the varieties of adultery manifested in upper class society. Additionally it was a handbook for

husbands on how to manage their wives in a milieu in which there
were "three million burning pasions" that could "feed on four
hundred thousand women . . . What husband could now sleep peacefully
beside his young and beautiful wife, knowing that there were at least
three bachelors on the prowl?" "Marriage is a combat to the death
before which the partners each ask the blessing of heaven, for to love
forever is the most fool-hardy of enterprises. The battle is long in
commencing, and victory . . . is to the most adroit."[5] With coolness,
Balzac analyzes the incidence of marital hazards according to the
husband's occupation, placing among the most vulnerable bankers,
who are forced to be away from home for long periods. In order to
hold a woman, the man must be instructed in the secrets of the art of
love, for marriage is a science. Woman is a lyre, who does not yield
her secret except to the skilful player. Woman is what man makes
her. "Le lit est tout mariage," "The bed is all of marriage." He who
can rule a woman, can govern a nation. Nor are the economic factors
to be contemned. Marriage is the primary source of property.

Yet, like Stendhal, Balzac would reform the status of woman by
giving her a saner sort of education. He would also abolish the dowry,
and emancipate her from the bond of virginity! Brazenly, he adds
that his book is not intended for the lower orders of society, the lower
tradesmen, farmers, factory workers, farm-workers, for whom the
"life of the spirit, the benefits of education, the delicious tumults of
the heart are an inaccessible paradise," but only for persons of
"leisure, for those who have the time and the mind to love, for the
rich who have appropriate passions, and for the intelligentsia which
has obtained a monopoly of chimaeras."[6]

In this brief and pointed irony-tipped passage Balzac has
involved the problem of marriage in the structure of that portion of
society to which he was addressing himself. That he has deliberately
avoided speaking of love as such is itself a damning sentence passed
upon the character of upper-class marriage.

He wished to shock, and he succeeded. The book achieved a resounding *succès de scandale.* Many women saw in the book a vindication of the rights of women. Others, like Zulma Carraud (when the authorship became public knowledge) wrote passionately to Balzac, and expressed their outrage at this libel on feminine virtue.

But he was famous...

1830 was to be an epochal year for him as it was to be for France. With the keen scent of a wolf-hound, he sensed the directions of the literary winds. It was a time for "Actualité" — "Topicality" —things of the time, manners, every-day life, household life, marriage and love. Who better than he could write of the private life of Parisians? He knew the city up and down, practically every nook and corner of Paris...

Dimly, he was beginning to envision even vaster possibilities — a boundless prospect opened before him that in a few years was to include the lives, the mores, the thoughts of the world around him: Paris, the provinces, society and its various strata; philosophical ideas that were maturing within him. He would give all these a visible garment of reality!

Scenes from Private Life, the first set of such stories, appeared in 1830, and was successful. Here he brought to life the shop of a linen-draper and his family, and already we see manifested something of the spirit of the age — the acquisitive hunger for money. Higher up — in another of the stories — we have the reverse of the coin, an upper class family of pensioners living off the largesses granted by Louis XVIII — parasitism and snobbery...

When his next volume appears, it will be not under the name of Honoré Balzac, as in *The Chousans* and *Scenes from Private Life,* but as by Honoré de Balzac. And in that little particle lies a drama, as it marks a turning point in Balzac's life.

For he was descended from a simple, sturdy farmer family of the Tarn district of southern France. His own father was the son of a hard-bitten peasant. He had made his way to Paris, and had gradually risen by dint of his talents and dedication to a responsible post in the office of army supplies. Transferred to Tours, where Honoré was born, he had even become deputy mayor. In the accepted sense of the word, there was no "noble blood" in the family, but the itch for titles and pedigreee was strong throughout the middle classes of France. Young Balzac was not immune. In the light of all that was happening in the country, why not give himself the "de" too? Was he not noble by virtue of his genius? He was sure of it as he wrote a startling story *La Peau de Chagrin, The Wild Ass's Skin.* It appeared in 1831, "by Honoré de Balzac."

For he was climbing rapidly, into high society, into aristocratic women's beds. The Duchess d'Abrantès wrote to him, and he became her lover, and helped her with her Mémoirs, in which there was much to tell. She in turn introduced him to ancient Madame Récamier and her salon at the Abbaye-aux-Boix, where that famous relict of another era along with that other glory, Chateaubriand — both apparently immortal — received the homage of younger generations. It was here that one day young Balzac was honored by being requested to read his most recent work, *La Peau de Chagrin.* In the eyes of the fastidious and sophisticated *grand monde* he was a kind of parvenu wonder, stoutish already, "dressed like a butcher," in a white waist-coat, not altogether at ease, but "bright-eyed," and on the whole, "impressive." And this was the prodigy that had written the scandalous *Physiologie?*

So he was being drawn more and more into the upper circle of legitimists and royalists. A genius, he was likely to prove a useful auxiliar to their reactionary cause. What a change from the Balzac of other days!

As a very young man he had been, in the words of one of his biographers, "liberal in politics, positivist in philosophy, and anarchist in his sociology."[7] In those days the radiance of an idealized Napoleon illumined all his thoughts. What an age that was then!, "when the word of the fatherland reechoed in the wide hearts of all," as he put it. "I understood the nobleness of existence, I wished for a life ... of usefulness to my like, ... not dead and fled, but one palpitating with feelings ... Oh! Napoleon, Napoleon! ... Caesar at the age of twenty-two, Cromwell at thirty ... A man — all thought and all action ... all arbitrariness, and all justice! A true king!"[8]

In those younger days he was excited by the election of the radical Abbé Grégoire to the Chamber of Deputies. In religion he was a sceptic, almost a deist. His political radicalism terrified the publisher of his pot-boiler, *Jean-Louis,* who asked him to delete such phrases as "Long live Liberty!," "the People," "Despotism," — that smacked of "chaleur séditieuse" — "seditious heat." Balzac did not yield. He kept on injecting into those early works attacks on the *ancien régime,* and he even allowed himself to exult over the taking of the Bastille!

It was a marvelous sight — the arrival of that mass of people at the gates of the Bastille ..., and how that prolonged shout, "Liberty!" penetrated even into its cells![9]

Yet, and this is the paradox (wasn't Balzac himself all paradox?), he could almost at the same time, between 1824 and 1826, produce three serious works of a very conservative character, anonymously: *A Treatise on Prayer, The Right of Primogeniture,* and an *Impartial History of the Jesuits.* And practically at the same moment, foresee an approaching struggle between the rich and the poor — "a perpetual struggle," in which the rich, no matter how well entrenched, must in the end yield ground.[10]

Was he a bundle of contradictions? So much he admitted himself: "I contain in my five feet and two inches every inconsistency, every contrast possible." And no doubt speaking about himself and his literary projects:

Does this kaleidoscope arise out of what Chance has implanted in the souls of those who aim to depict all the affections of the human heart, all the feelings, so that by the power of their imagination they may feel all that they are painting?[11]

Would that also be his way of secretly justifying his waywardness politically and socially, and the attractions rank and caste were to have for him? But even these ambiguities do not obstruct his clarity of vision. He is aware that society was on the point of a critical upheaval. He is writing about the year 1830:

This year, that began with the *Physiologie du Mariage* ... ended with *Le Rouge et le Noir,* productions of a sinister and cold philosophy ..., productions that embody the spirit of the age, and the corpse-like smell of a society in dissolution ...[12]

Where was he during those "glorious" July days? He was spending them in the company of Madame de Berny in Touraine. "Six hundred francs income on the banks of the Loire," he meditated, "That's virtue, happiness. life."

He has little love for the July Monarchy. He calls it a régime of old men — a "gerontocratie." He is disgusted with the government's refusal to intervene in the revolutions of Belgium, Poland, and Italy! He agitates for freedom of the press, and a revision of the electoral laws, while he defends and upholds the hereditry peerage, which the new government is abolishing. "Nous sommes une démocratie des riches," he writes in *La Mode.* But he sees no hope in the parties of the "left," the parties of equality and republicanism; and once a mild partisan of the Saint-Simonians, he now holds them up to ridicule. At the same time, he is flirting with the idea of running as a candidate for election to the Assembly. He is beside himself when he considers the place-seeking hordes around Louis-Philippe, those "fashionables who were wounded by bullets through their valets' waistocats" — living on the unearned honors of participation on the barricades of July.

Do I not see every day bankrupts, counterfeiters, thieves — all treated with honor? Why does the good society recoil before a murderer?[13]

La Peau de Chagrin — *The Wild Ass's Skin* — appeared in August 1831, and caused a stir. With this book Balzac was definitely launched ...

La Peau de Chagrin is a "philosophic" tale, and constitutes Balzac's own mythology of magic power. All his life long, Balzac would be speculating on the mysteries and secrets of life; all his life long he would be in search of a magic talisman. Was it prescience or singular knowledge of his own self, already awakened, that prompted him to create a story of a magic skin, almost predictive of his own end?

Magic is the effectuating of a desired goal or objective through the power of a wish — an overleaping of Nature's nexus of cause and effect, and to speak figuratively, an attempt to vault to heaven, without the interposition of Jacob's ladder... For Balzac it is the distension of the romantic Ego to the bursting point. The secret talisman will solve his problem of the Will and the Power to Do —"Vouloir" and "Pouvoir." Will it also bring "Savoir" — Wisdom?

"A great passion," he wrote, "is as rare as a masterpiece."[14] Passions will be at the center not only of Balzac's thoughts, but of a number of his most compelling works. In their diverse manifestations they will fill his most magnificent pages. But what are the limits of passion? And, when passion becomes obsession — may it not turn into madness? This is the core of the "philosophic" tales such as the Peau de Chagrin, the strongly autobiographical Louis Lambert, and the tragic stories of monomanic obsession, The Quest of the Absolute, Gambara, and The Unknown Masterpiece.

The Wild Ass's Skin is, in its way, a previsionary epitome of Balzacian ideas. It is part fantasy, part what is called realism — it is in reality a fusion of both, for the fantasy itself has the strong undercurrent of a realistic idea closely bound up with Balzac's view of life, nature, and the human being. It does, of course, utilize the traditional "supernatural" apparatus employed with consummate artistry by E.T.A. Hoffman, then at the height of his popularity in France. And peripherally, it is related to Goethe's Faust. But aside from that, the rest is Balzac, Balzac self-revealed, Balzac and the France of his day, Balzac and the conflict of Will and Passion.

The protagonist of *The Wild Ass's Skin* is young Raphaël de Valentin, a youth of twenty-five (some five years younger than Balzac himself), whose aristocratic family has suffered a disastrous fall in fortune. He is at the end of his tether. He is a gifted thinker and writer, and in his garret had been working on a philosophic treatise characteristically (for Balzac) entitled *A Theory of the Will*. The landlady, from whom he had rented his mean abode, has a lovely daughter, Pauline, who falls in love with him, and who, at a great sacrifice, supplements his meagre resources with her own secret contributions.

In his garret, Raphaël can indulge his fantasy and his philosophy. In the world outside he needs money. Raphaël too is a child of the century — Raphaël as a boy living in the days of Napoleonic glory, but now let loose on the world, almost penniless, thrust upon the "unheroic" age where the banalities of everyday life have replaced the dreams of war and glory. He is not prepared or trained for the new society that has come into being. Nor is he willing to bend to the actualities of life. Hence, he is given to suicidal thoughts. A dandy, bon-vivant and adventurer by name of Rastignac converts him to a philosophy of "dissipation," founded upon a metaphysical basis of the merits of "excess." In such a "philosophy," "debauch" is moralized into one of the great obsessive passions, a carnal transfiguration of the imperative "Enough is not Enough!" The heightened eloquence which Rastignac brings to bear upon his hearer is totally persuasive. In those tones there is the unmistakable sound of Balzac's own voice:

Debauch, says Rastignac, is as surely an art as poetry, and demands brave spirits. In order to penetrate its mysteries, to savor all its beauties, a person must apply himself conscientiously...Formidable obstacles hedge in the great pleasures of man, not its single enjoyments, but their system, which establishes as habitual the most uncommon sensations, concentrates them, fertilizes them into a dramatic life, demanding an exorbitant and prompt expenditure of vital forces...After all, war is the debauch of blood, as politics is the debauch of self-interest. All excesses are blood-brothers...These social enormities draw us on like an abyss...Excess is, in short, for the body what the mystical joys are to the soul. Intoxication steeps you in dreams whose fantasies are as strange as those of the ecstatics...[15]

Alas! that such attractive joys should also be subject to the cruel exigencies of the market place. The resources that are drawn on are not only the body and the soul, but also cash. And even Love, as Raphaël discovers, when Rastignac introduces him to the fabulously beautiful and fabulously wealthy, and fabulously mysterious Countess Foedora, also craves and demands money. And so Raphaël adds to his debauches that of gambling. He loses, and finally, with only twenty francs left in his pocket, he plans to end his life . . . He will throw himself into the Seine. On his way there, he wanders into the shop of a strange, ancient antiquarian, a Moses-like figure, and becomes fascinated by the skin of a wild ass, inscribed with a mysterious Sanscrit motto. Raphaël who is learned, deciphers the inscription, which offers the possessor of the skin fulfilment of all his wishes, but with the proviso that with each wish the skin will shrink and the owner's life correspondingly contract. The old man offers him the gift of the skin, which so many before him have refused; but Raphaël accepts it. He utters his first wish: to participate in an orgy such as has never been seen, in the "pleasures of heaven and earth, in a last embrace of death"; in "ancient priapic dissipations," and "triple kisses" and the company of young talents and beautiful women. And lo! no sooner has he left the antiquarian's shop with the skin in his possession, than he encounters friends who carry him off to the mansion of the millionaire Taillefer, who is celebrating the founding of a new journal, in which Raphaël is expected to participate. And so, young Faust has signed a compact with his Mephistopheles and is on his way to the Brocken, to take part in a Balzacian Walpurgisnacht. The orgy exceeds all of Raphaël's expectations — it lasts on and on, and combines super-Lucullan foods, wines, with beautiful women, feverish conversations, revealing in the end the anarchy and cynicism prevailing at the time. "And so they drained the chalice filled up with science, carbonic acid gas, perfumes, poetry, and incredulity." Thereafter Raphaël continues to exploit the miracles of the skin. It works! He falls heir to a fantastic fortune. But the skin shrinks . . . Now Raphaël, as the Marquis de Valentin, is left with his agonies — his life-span diminishes with every wish. Paradox and irony! To have everything at one's command, but not to dare to wish! To live a living death — or to give up living, and live only to die! Each wish becomes in fact a suicidal act. He has given up writing his book on the Will, for the will within him is already dead. At the theatre, a mysterious beautiful being sits by him — it is Pauline, now rich (her father has returned with an appropriately large fortune), enchantingly appareled. She has been in love with him all the time. and he, in turn, knows that he is in love with her. He looks to science for help. but even science knows no way of extending the surface of the skin. Utterly defeated, and weakening in body, Raphaël decides to retire from life, from Pauline, and live out his last hours alone. But when Pauline reappears, he yields to a moment of passion and makes a wish — his last...

Such is Balzac's brief epic of egotism. Egotism is writ large in Raphaël's character, the society which he frequents, in the absence of a useful goal or aim in life, in his relation to poor Pauline, in his pursuit of the vanities of life. So, too, is the Countess Foedora, ravishingly beautiful, enormously rich, but cold-blooded and self-seeking, the very embodiment of self-interest. Raphaël learns something toward the end of his life about the world he has been worshipping, when, confined in a sanitarium, he meets with all that calculating indifference that he himself had practised heretofore. Too late, he realizes, as he looks around him at the other aristocratic habitués of the institution, that

that little world was obeying, without being aware, perhaps, the great law that dominates high society, whose implacable morality Raphaël had come to understand. A glance backward showed it to him as a perfect type — embodied in Foedora. He could no more elicit more sympathy for his physical ills here, than for his heart's ills at her side. The world of fashion banishes from its bosom those who are unfortunate, just as the man in good health banishes from his body the principles of illness. The world hates those who suffer and are unfortunate, treating them as carriers of disease, and never hesitates when it comes to choosing — them or vice. Vice is a luxury ... Whoever suffers in body or soul, is in want of money or power, is a pariah ... Thus the world honors misfortune — it either kills it, or drives it away, abases it, or chastises it ...[16]

Raphaël de Valentin is hurt and angry. But does he really understand? The skin has given him unlimited power — but with each attempt to use it, his vitality decreased. Power for what? That is the central question even for Balzac. Is it for that which the banker Taillefer celebrates during the orgy, after Raphaël has become heir to millions?

Bravo! Taillefer exclaimed. You understand your fortune; It confers the privilege of being impertinent. You are one of us! Gentlemen, let us drink to the power of gold. M. Valentin, six times a millionaire, has become a power. He is a king, he can do everything, he is above everything, like all the rich. From now on, the notion that "all Frenchmen are equal before the law" is a lie inscribed at the head of our Constitutional Charter. He is not going to obey the law, the law is going to obey him. There are neither scaffolds nor executioners for millionaires!![17]

Could the new power of a new aristocracy — the aristocracy of the Bourse — have been expressed more clearly or more blatantly? To the last assertion in Taillefer's apostrophe, Raphaël merely retorts, "They are their own executioners."

Raphaël remains, as M. Michel Carrouges has well remarked, "a human monad," "without doors" to the outside world.[18] Ibsen would have said that he is shut up in his "barrel of selfhood." Is Raphaël in fact not his own executioner? In accepting the talisman, was he not affirming the transcendence of the Ego, and a defiance of the laws of Nature — of natural Necessity?[19]

It is not surprising that Balzac, himself a creature of fierce passions, a "driven" man, with a voracious appetite for a life of physical as well as intellectual enjoyments, an indefatigable writer, bon-vivant, lover, collector of art-objects and a speculator, should have been much concerned with the limits of drives or passions, and the point where one or another of them turns to monomania, transcends

the limits, and brings on disaster of mind and body. What, Balzac
was asking, is the relation of Will, Passion, Thought and Action?
Was it true that "thought, augmented by the transient power of
passion..., necessarily turns into poison within the human being,"
as he speculated in the Introduction to his *Philosophical Studies* of
1834? He must himself have felt the terror of insanity, as passion,
will, and thought clashed within him. Certainly his preoccupation
with monomania and monomaniacs at this time indicates the extent
of his involvement. A year after *La Peau de Chagrin,* he published
another "philosophical study," *Louis Lambert,* a thinly disguised
autobiography — highly idealized. His imaginary protagonist is a
youthful prodigy, at odds with the world — a highly speculative
nature. He, too, is seeking for the "core that would unify all Nature
and Life." He must find the way to the "inscrutable phenomena of
the origin of thought." He is writing a treatise on the Will. To him
Mind and Thought are the quintessential products of Will, and
Volition and Idea, themselves products of Mind, constitute Action.
Will, he believes, can be imparted to material objects, for in his view
Will is a material constitution, such as fluid, similar to an electric
current, which in its eternal transformations constitutes the basic
motive power of existence. Mesmerism or animal magnetism,
somnabulism, dreams, and other visionary phenomena are but so
many aspects of one central element. Louis Lambert is a "voyant," a
"see-er" who believes that the concentrated forces of his Will can in
time discover the unifying principles of both human and supra-
human experiences. He belongs with the thinkers of his age so
greatly concerned with transformation within Nature, the relation
of the organic to the inorganic. And he reflects:

When we consider that the line where flesh ends and the nail begins
contains the invisible and inexplicable mystery of the constant transformation
of fluid into horn, we must confess that nothing is impossible in the
marvelous modifications of human tissue.[20]

Comparative anatomy has shown the basic interrelations of Nature — the ascendancy toward the creation of Man. But need Man be the end? May he not be the means to something higher? "Why must God perish if matter can be proved to think?" And could not Mind then, in its autonomy, become paramount, roam freely throughout the universe, into the past, the present, and the future?

Carried away into such dizzying heights of thought, Lambert himself becomes disembodied mind. And there lay the poison! Passionate search has strung the Mind beyond the breaking point, and he has lost all touch with Reality. On the eve of his marriage to a brilliant young woman — partly Jewish — Louis Lambert goes totally out of his mind, and attempts to castrate himself. He lapses into a form of catalepsy. In his attempted utter divorcement of spirit and flesh, "he may have regarded the joys of marriage as an obstacle to the perfection of his self and his flight towards spiritual worlds."[21]

Balzac did not go mad, but he did manage to shorten his life by his physical and mental excesses. Nature, as he suggested in *The Wild Ass's Skin* limits the amount of vital energy possessed by the human being, and its expenditure is as closely determined as one's resources in a bank. Thus for example, speaking to Théophile Gautier, Balzac intimated that the novelist must live "in a most absolute state of chastity... True chastity, he insisted, develops the powers of the mind to its highest degree, and yields to those who practice it unknown faculties and potentialities..."[22]

Louis Lambert had attempted the impossible. Lambert believed that "from your own bed to the frontiers of the universe there are but two steps, Will and Faith."

Balzac was fascinated by monomania and insanity — and often surrounds these states with the mantle of near-heroism. Despite the ravages on themselves these monomaniacs perpetrate, they often disrupt or destroy the lives of those around them. Such is the Flemish burgher Balthasar Claës, in *The Quest of the Absolute*, who is in search of the ultimate element in chemistry that will be the key to all other elements and hence to Nature itself. He wishes to go beyond the work of the great chemist Berzelius, and discover the "53d element" — the ultimate . . . If "light, heat, electricity, galvanism, and magnetism are all different effects of one and the same cause," may there not be "one unknown principle" which in different dosages might produce these diverse effects?

The tragic musician Gambara, in the story of the same name, also dreams of an ultimate principle — this time in music — the creation of a "new" musical form beyond that attained hitherto, and altogether new musical instruments. In words, which will sound astonishingly modern and predictive, he states his beliefs and his dream:

Music obeys the laws of physics and mathematics. The laws of physics are little known; those of mathematics more so, and since we have started to study their relations, harmony came into being, to which we owe Haydn, Mozart, Beethoven and Rossini . . . Now, if a knowledge of the mathematical laws had given us these four musicians, to what height might we not attain if we could discover the physical laws by virtue of which . . . we could succeed in storing up in greater or lesser quantity, according to the required proportions, a certain ethereal substance diffused in the air, which gives us music as it gives light, the phenomena of vegetation as well as animal life? . . . These new laws would arm the composer with new powers by offering him instruments superior to those now used, and possibly with a grandeur of harmony greater than that which prevails in music today.[23]

Gambara is a strange character, a composer who produces sublime music only when he is drunk. Sober, he can offer nothing but meaningless cacophanies. He has invented his own instrument, the Panharmonicon. "Just as soon as he became sober his reason was dethroned — he was again the maniac."

There are other characters in Balzac's stories who attempt to go "beyond the limits of human nature" — "au delà des bornes de la nature humaine" — and eventually break down catastrophically.

Balzac's own efforts and insatiable ambition to frame a working metaphysic of existence, and to establish an ultimate unitary principle, bordered on just such an excess. How far he was ready to proceed with this illusion can be judged by the story *Séraphita,* in which he sought to give his spiritualist philosophy a narrative coherence. Here he created the androgynous Séraphita-Séraphitùs — the original unitary man-woman figure favored by the medieval Cabbalists. An angelic spirit, she can transcend her sex: she is a man to the woman Minna, and woman to the man Wilfrid. She is the embodiment of a wisdom far beyond that attainable through reason or science. At sixteen she has the mentality of a super-metaphysician. She is thoroughly imbued with the thoughts of God and otherwordliness. She is transcendent intuition, and can instruct mankind in the arduous process of the ascent to Heaven. Her perceptions embrace both immediacy and infinity.

As a statement of final principles, as well as a venture into mystical Cabbalism and Swedenborgianism, *Séraphita* was bound to be a failure. The role of mystic ill becomes Balzac, nor the kind of spirituality and purity with which he endows Séraphita-Séraphitùs. He was too much a man of this world. But it offers interesting clues to Balzac's own duality. In creating an androgynous figure, he was symbolically annihilating human sexuality, and symbolically performing the operation which Louis Lambert attempted physically. Had he not always dreamt of the possibility of the transformation of matter into free-roving Mind — an ascendancy toward God — perhaps even the annihilation of God himself? In an almost blasphemous depiction of Séraphita's ascent to Heaven (the Christian parallel comes to mind immediately) the "voyant" Balzac creates his own unattainable spiritual apotheosis — and confirms its failure...Louis Lambert, his own *alter-ego,* had dreamt of the spiritual "angel" within each human being — the better part of him that begins its true life upon separation from the body after death. And Louis Lambert ended as a madman. Balzac would avoid that extremity. Luckily, he was too much a creature of the flesh.

In August 1831, he wrote to Montalambert,

La Peau de Chagrin is the formula of human life, an abstraction of individualities . . . It is therefore the starting point of my work. Thereafter there will be grouped in accordance with their separate nuances, individualities, particular existences, from the humblest to the King, even to the Priest, the uppermost term of our society. In these tableaux, I will observe the effects of Thought on Life . . .[24]

He was too much the giant Antaeus. He needed to touch the earth to realize the full strength of his genius. In his mind the germ of the future massive *Human Comedy* was already taking root. He was never one to recoil from labor — labors of observation, organization, crystallization, formulation, the gathering of detail upon detail, and the sifting out of the essential. These were merely the hard preliminaries — sheer mechanical tasks. But oh! the vitalizing breath, that, like the Lord's, would infuse life into the human dust, and make an Adam. Here was Balzac's chaos, out of which to create a living world. Here he was like God. The writer, he stated in the Preface to the second edition of *Père Goriot,* "partakes along with God of the fatigues and pleasures of coordinating worlds." (Having identified themselves with priests, prophets, and seers, it was but a step for the nineteenth century to identify the writer with God. Flaubert will soon follow suit.)

It was in 1834 that Balzac formulated the scope of his vast projected work — some portions of which had already appeared — the great "synthesis" to which he was some years later to give the name of *The Human Comedy.* But between 1830 and 1834 a number of events took place which were not only to affect his personal life, but would also prove turning points in his entire outlook.

While Séraphita might be making her spectacular mystic ascent to Heaven, Balzac too was mounting — climbing the social scale with meteoric speed. He was recognized as a celebrity, and his presence was thought an asset to many a salon. He who had once almost starved in a garret was now brought to the Faubourg Saint-Germain, the preserve of aristocratic legitimists, who still dreamt of a Bourbon restoration, only being divided in their loyalties as between Charles X and his son, whom they dubbed "Henri V." From their Olympian salons they looked with contempt upon the parvenu barons of the Bourse; and with even greater disdain upon the "épicier" — the shopkeeper; and with horror and anxiety upon the vast and heterogeneous mass of artisans, ordinary laborers, servants, students, who represented an ever-present threat to all of them.

Balzac aspired to have a duchess as a mistress, and circumstances now favored him. The Duc de Fitz-James, descended by ancestral bastardy from no one lesser than King James II of England and Arabella Churchill, and one of the principal legitimists of the July Monarchy, had a niece, the Marquise de Castries, whose own personal life and career were multi-faceted. Unfortunately for Balzac, he was to encounter a Rock of Gibraltar in the face of his amatory advances. In a state of delirium, he did not heed the warning of Madame de Berny, nor of Zulma Carraud, against the temptations — social, political, and emotional — of the Faubourg Saint-Germain. His flesh was aflame, as were his social ambitions, and at the moment, he was commuting among Madame de Berny, Zulma Carraud, the Duchesse d'Abrantès; and hopefully the Marquise de Castries. If he did not as yet obtain a perfect score, the *ci-devant* law-clerk and penurious literary hack, now turned a literary celebrity, could well boast — to use a modern term — of a sizeable batting average...

And already the seeds of another — even more fantastic love-affair — were germinating. One day, he received a letter (now unfortunately lost, but capable of reconstruction) that had been posted from far-off Odessa on February 28, 1832. It was signed mysteriously "L'Étrangère," and gently reproached Balzac for falling away, in *La Peau de Chagrin,* from that delicacy toward woman he had displayed in his other stories, and urging him to return to the high mission with which heaven had charged him. M. de Balzac replied with a notice in the *Gazette de France*, April 2, 1832:

M. de B. is in receipt of the letter addressed to him on February 28, and regrets that it is impossible for him to reply, and if his wishes are not of a nature to be exposed publicly, he hopes his silence will be understood.[25]

Soon a lively correspondence ensued (unfortunately only two of her letters have survived), and "the Stranger," even before she finally identified herself, began revealing her soul's craving for understanding and her own passionate appreciation of his genius. "Your genius is sublime; but it must become divine." "You are a luminous meteor."[26] Her resolution to remain "the stranger all her life long" soon broke down.

She was Countess Eveline Hanska, born Rzewuska, wife of Count Wenceslas Hanski, a man considerably older, and owner of a vast estate with three thousand "souls," as well as a castle in Wierzchownia in the Ukraine. She was thirty-three years old. In October 1833 they met for the first time in Neuchâtel; in December at a second meeting they consummated their love. And now all they had to do was to wait for the husband to die. Circumstances (almost masquerading as Nemesis) strung out the affair for years, and finally ended it in marriage, but with a drastic proviso prefigured in *The Wild Ass's Skin.* In March 1850, after waiting for a long time for the Tsar to sanction the union, Balzac and Madame Hanska became man and wife. On August 18 of the same year, Balzac died...

But in the interim they corresponded, rejoiced, and waited. And thus was born the story of *Séraphita* — Eva Hanska's literary avatar. The interim was a time of rapture. To his sister Balzac wrote about the meeting at Neuchâtel, describing Madame Hanska, detailing her beautiful black hair, her soft skin, and not least her "colossal

wealth." "I was drunk with love." At the same time he mentions a
baby — presumably his — that he expects of another donor, Marie-
Louise-Françoise Du Fresnay...[27]

Between 1830 and 1832 he crystallized his political ultra-
conservative views. To the distressed Zulma Carraud, he confided
his political credo:

France should have a constitutional monarchy, should have a hereditary
royal family, a Chamber of Deputies exceptionally powerful, who would
represent property, with all possible guarantees, heredity and privileges...,
then a second elective assembly representing all the interests of the
intermediate mass, who separate the high social strata from what I call the
people. The great body of laws should tend to enlighten the people as much
as possible, the people who have nothing, the workers, the proletarians,
etc. in order for them to become as comfortable as the intermediate mass.
But the people must also be kept under the most powerful yoke...The
largest freedom to the leisured classes, for they have something to
conserve, everything to lose...[28]

"Kings," he believed, "are essential to the life of our old
Europe." In the spring of 1832 he accepted the invitation of Fitz-
James and the editor, Laurentie, to collaborate on the royalist-
legitimist newspaper, Le Rénovateur. Balzac announced his conversion
to Legitimism and Catholicism in an essay, "Sur la situation du parti
royale." Only a legitimate royalty can preserve a balance in a society
where wealth and intellect are unequal. Religion, the most powerful
instrument in inducing the population to accept suffering and
poverty, can provide the most adequate symbols and examples of
patience by exhibiting Christ and the Virgin. Only two years before
he had been critical of the Catholic Church, and had hailed the first
issue of Lamennais's L'Avenir for contending that a new society
needs a new priesthood. Now, he was even prepared to run for
election to the Chamber with conservative support.

But he had not lost sight of the great plan of creating novels
that would serve as the anatomy of French society. In a letter to
Madame Hanska, October 26, 1834, he explains his project:

I believe that by 1838 the three sections of this gigantic work will be, if not entirely completed, at least superimposed so that one will be able to judge it as a whole. The *Études de moeurs* will depict all the social effects without the omission of any situation in life, no physiognomy, no character of man or woman, no way of living, no calling, no social level, no part of France, nor any facet of childhood, old age, middle-age, politics, justice, or war... So then the second layer will be the *Études philosophiques,* for after the effects, come the causes... I shall show the *why* of the sentiments, the *what* of life... After having surveyed society in order to describe it, I shall now survey it to judge it... Then after the effects and the causes, comes the *Études analytiques,* of which the *Physiology of Marriage* is a part, because after the effects and the causes the principles must be sought... Thus Man, Society and Mankind will be described, judged, and analyzed without repetition, in a work which will be like the Thousand and One Nights of the west... Having composed the poem, the exposition of an entire system, I shall make it a science in an *Essai sur les forces humaines.*[29]

As he saw it then, the gigantic project would consist of twenty-four volumes of the *Études de moeurs,* fifteen of the *Études philosophiques,* and nine of the *Études analytiques* — forty-eight in all! If it was a schedule not destined to be fully realized, what was finally realized represents no less a miracle. No one before him, not even Sir Walter Scott, had projected such a structure, or in that way.

But the impossible was already in the making. By 1834 Balzac had completed thirty or so stories and novels (not including those wretched pot-boilers!); by 1840 he will have practically doubled that number, among them not a few of his masterpieces.

Was Balzac thinking of the great palacontologist Cuvier (his contemporary), when he called his project a "poem"? For in *La Peau de Chagrin* he had asked,

Is not Cuvier the greatest poet of our century? Lord Byron had been able to reproduce certain of our moral conflicts through words, but our immortal naturalist has reconstructed worlds from a few bleached bones...[30]

Balzac's work, too, was to be a natural history. He will be society's "Physiologist." He too will be working on an "organism," its various parts and details to be interrelated, the various filaments of actions, thought, experiences, aspirations, ambitions will be intertwined into a vast fluid tapestry that will fix the Present, and at the same time represent it as a process in rapid Change. So, we shall view men and women as they rise and fall, appear and reappear in the course of the many narratives, thus establishing a kind of "unitary" leit-motiv. This is Balzac's "roman fleuve." So far as time is concerned, the "flow" of interrelations will cover the period from the French Revolution to 1846. In space, it will cover the immensity of Paris, the provinces of France, and even other countries. In point of characters and occupations, ranks and offices it will offer the whole abundance which society offers from the high aristocracy to the courtesan, the peasant, the servant.

Protean Balzac was indeed a tripartite being. Part of him was the "alchemist" — the seeker after the philosopher's stone that would unlock the secrets of nature, find the mystical and mysterious ultimate unit. Part of him was the "practical" politician — not statesman — who after 1830 sought to find the best government that would bring about a "unitary" harmony to the nation, and thought he would find it in a constitutional and legitimist monarchy. Balzac became a Carlist —that is a follower of those who agitated for a succession of the dynasty of Charles X. The third part of him was that of the "man of the world," the journalist, the viveur, who lived not in dreams but in contemplation and examination of the world as it was around him.

Here, in his own society, he was destined to find that "unitary" principle he had been seeking in the universe: process, movement, change...Here he was to fulfil his mission of artist which he defined as "saisir les rapports les plus éloignés" — to "seize upon the most far-removed connections" — discover cause and effect where others had merely seen accident, contingency, diversity. Above all, he set himself the artist's goal of being "the apostle of Truth."[31] To bring together into focus such historical periods as the French Revolution, Napoleon, the Restoration, and the July

Monarchy, and represent them in process and development culminating
in the France of his day — that was a task no novelist before him had
attempted. It marks another epoch in the development not only of
the novel, but also of "realism" — the first stage of which had been
initiated by the English novelists of the eighteenth century and by
Sir Walter Scott. Only two other French thinkers of his time had
attempted to "synthesize" the historical process in parallel ways, as
describable moments in history, as progressive steps — Saint-
Simon and Auguste Comte. For Balzac, in addition, the sciences of
biology and physiology were happy auxiliars.

It is significant that *Hernani* and the first of the new "realistic"
stories of Balzac — the foundation stones of the "Human Comedy"
to be — appeared in the same year, 1830. Yet how different the two
works, one, *Hernani*, aesthetically radical, but still deeply rooted in
the "romantic" element of exoticism, of strangeness, of the
"unreal," while Balzac's project was already intent on uncovering
the mainsprings of his society through an appropriation of the
whole world around him! ...

The Revolution of 1830 had dissipated the "mal du siècle" of a
generation that had hungered for glory and honor but had instead
found a desert; but it also initiated a "mal du siècle" — the sobriety
or, one might say, the "hangover" after the inebriation of the
"glorious" days of July. The republicans were disenchanted and
deceived; the proletariat that had bled, had been deceived; the
liberals — deceived — and the royalists and legitimists — horrified.
But what had actually come into being?

In Balzac's eyes a new religion, with its grand temple — the
Bourse, the Exchange. In place of a political charter of rights, an
unacknowledged new Charter — "la Charte d'égoism," "the Charter
of Egotism," with its new poetry and poets — the poetry and the
poets of the "strong-box."

Such a "poet" is Jean-Esther Gobseck in one of the *Scenes from
Private Life* published already in 1830, and in a way a prelusion to all
of Balzac's subsequent work. Gobseck is partly Jewish, and has about

him the aura of the Wandering Jew, so greatly favored by the
Romantics. He is a Napoleonic money-lender. He is a philosopher.
He is the observer of vanities, adulteries, hapless love-affairs — of
society high and low. He has been everywhere, has seen everything,
and knows everyone. He is Mammon. We see him through the eyes
of an indigent law-student, destined to rise as head-clerk and
advocate. We hear him as he instructs the younger man in the ways
of life:

What is life, he says, but a machine set in motion by money? ... We are the
Casuists of the Paris Bourse, a kind of Inquisition weighing and analyzing
the most insignificant actions of every man of any fortune, and our
forecasts are infallible ... There are ten of us in Paris, unknown kings, and
arbiters of your destinies ... Nothing is hidden from me ... I am rich
enough to buy the consciences of those who control the actions of ministers,
from their office boys to their mistresses. Isn't that power? ... Do you
imagine that the only poets in the world are those who have their verses
printed?[32]

Morality, behavior, mores, Gobseck insists — these are all
relative — conventions adapted to the time and the climate. The
only permanent element in life is "the instinct of self-interest." And
the only "concrete reality invariable enough to be worth caring
about — Gold." The battle between the rich and the poor is
everywhere, and is inevitable. It is better to exploit than be
exploited. Thus, Gobseck parades the human passions before him
with the calm of a god. The young man watches and listens with
amazement.

The little wizened old man had grown great. He had been metamorphosed
under my eyes into a fantastic symbol. I had witnessed the power of gold
personified. Life, mankind, filled me with horror. Was everything then
determined by money?

But Gobseck is not without feelings. He contrasts the needs of a
poor seamstress with the luxury and dissipations of the Countess
who has recourse to him for help. "I like to leave mud on a rich
man's carpet. It isn't petty malice. I like to make them feel the touch
of the claws of necessity."

One has the feeling that Balzac is here creating a half-Mephistophelean, half-Avenging Angel of modern society. The strong individualism of Balzac cannot withhold admiration from great "passions" — wherever they might occur, even in their more horrifying manifestations. Denuded of their "magical" properties, the Gobsecks reappear in more glaringly human forms, flesh and blood votaries of Mammon. Their witches' sabbaths are no longer on the heights of the Brocken, but in the money-marts of Europe; the "magical" properties of their gold is now infused into the veins and arteries of modern society, and new bonds are established, and old ones irreparably broken. The nexus of "cash" has replaced the filiations of brotherhood, family, friendship. The coronet of empire and glory has descended upon this new Power; it has its own armies and generals, but no national frontiers. Its allies are in many lands. Its battlefields will be piled with its own kind of victims. Woe to the defeated!

The new "infusion" permeates the country no less than the city, the provinces no less than Paris. Let us, along with Balzac, migrate from Paris to the town of Saumur. Here it is the successful vintner, Félix Grandet, who embodies the inexorable poetry and drama of uninhibited accumulation, of appropriation, of skilful manipulations, outwitting others less adroit than himself, profiting by every advantage, even death, "like an alchemist in the midst of his crucibles," or "like the incarnation of the one god who yet finds worshippers in modern times." His is the Romanticism of the new era — accumulation for its own sake, the magnetism of Power. A successful vintner, he outwits all the other vintners; a successful hoarder of gold, he knows the best ways of buying and selling it. In that irresistible and irrepressible aggrandizement, all human beings around him are turned into viable instruments, but instruments destined for destruction. Thus, he brings tragedy upon his own family, his daughter, Eugénie Grandet, and his wife. Balzac's *Eugénie Grandet* is a book of the heart's desiccation. Eugénie, a sensitive, and even a heroic figure, prospective heiress to a fortune, becomes a pawn in the game. Like so many women of the times, she has become a valuable "property." She is for sale, and there are buyers. Her own feelings, her own affections must play no part in the transaction.

The young girl ... like some rare bird, the innocent victim of its high value, [is] tracked down and snared by specious pretenses of friendship ... Taken altogether, it was a sorry comedy that was being played in the old gray-painted parlor, by the dim light of two candles. Was it not, however, a drama of all time, played out everywhere all over the world, but here reduced to its simple expression?[33]

Grandet's town of Saumur is but a microcosm of the world at large. The charter of egotism has replaced the Ten Commandments. In the new wars now being waged, there is little room for the honorable, the good, or the weak. And woe to those who would remain uncorrupted! "Tell me what you have, and I'll tell you what you're thinking."[34] Your morality, your ethics, your ideas will reflect what you possess.

In Tours, for instance, the exemplary priest, the Abbé Birotteau, becomes the victim of the town's machinations by ambitious women, no less than by ambitious priests. Envy, frustrated hopes, greed, competition, the efforts of the organized "Congregation" — the established religious powers — all these converge to bring destruction upon him.[35]

The watchword of the society and their battle cry is: "Parvenir! Parvenir à tout prix!" "To succeed, succeed at all costs!"[36] "Chacun pour soi, chacun chez soi" — one of Balzac's upright characters is speaking. " 'Everyone for himself, everyone by himself,' these two terrible phrases, along with 'What's in it for me?' represent the trinitarian wisdom of the bourgeois, and the small proprietor."[37]

If the provinces are the microcosm, then Paris is the macrocosm. The "Human Comedy" had not yet taken its title from Dante's poem, but already Balzac is inviting us to descend with him into Hell, which is his Paris.

One of those sights in which most horror is to be met with is, surely, the general aspect of the Parisian populace — a people terrible to behold, gaunt, yellow, tawny, Paris — is it not a vast field incessantly agitated by a storm of interests, beneath which are whirled along a crop of human beings, who are, more often than not, reaped by Death, only to be born again as pinched as ever, men whose contorted and twisted faces ooze at every pore the spirit, the desires, the poisons with which their brains are impregnated; not so much faces, as masks, masks of weakness, masks of strength, masks of wretchedness, masks of joy, masks of hypocrisy — all alike worn, all stamped with indelible signs of a panting cupidity? What is that they are after? Gold or pleasure?... A few words will suffice to justify physiologically the almost infernal hue of Parisian faces, for it is not merely in jest that Paris has been called a hell. Take the word for the truth. There all is smoke, and fire, all gleams, boils, flames, evaporates, dies out, lights up again, sparkles crackles, and is consumed.[38]

Harsh? Perhaps. Even if to some onlookers Paris might have appeared more like Purgatory, and to others like Heaven itself, all of the three regions are clouded by fumes, which it will be Balzac's object to describe in detail.

The circle of vision narrows down on one little world of Paris — say, the boarding house in a mean quarter of the Left Bank — one run by a Madame Vauquer..., the scene of *Père Goriot*.

It is a shabby place, except for certain rooms reserved for slightly more prosperous clients; a place patronized by decayed middle-class persons, students, and a few day-boarders — a place filled with the ever-present musty smell of the kitchen. We are in the year 1819. As the drama moves into action, astounding scenes will be played out here. We meet the three principal characters, the twenty-one year old Eugène de Rastignac, an impoverished son of a Southern aristocratic family, now in Paris to study law and make his fortune; the imposing Vautrin, man of mystery, bewigged and with dyed moustaches, presumably a "retired merchant"; and "Father Goriot," a man of 69, formerly a grain merchant, and once a well-to-do tenant of the Vauquer groundfloor, but now removed to a dismal room on the second floor — also a man of mystery, and for a long time the butt of the other boarders' jests. For he is in the habit of receiving visits from two fashionable ladies, suspected of being his mistresses. A cast of minor characters rounds out the *dramatis personae* of the household.

In this world in a nutshell, a place of "poverty without poetry," fates are shaped that will make and unmake human beings. Here it is that young Rastignac will receive a schooling in worldly wisdom no other institution could have given him. Old Goriot will teach him about relations of children and parents, as well as about self-interest and social aspirations that dominate souls. Vautrin will show him the way to success, which lies in taking advantage of the weaknesses and vanities current in the world. It is he who has read on Rastignac's forehead the fateful watchwords of "Parvenir! Parvenir!" The world of fashion, to which Goriot's daughters aspire, will teach him the rest. Rastignac will prove a good pupil.

An inexorable process of dehumanization, of alienation is perceptible everywhere. Goriot is a monomaniac — his daughters are everything — and they in turn driven by their own passions, drain him of practically all possessions that he has left. They have made "successful" marriages, that is, one to a millionaire banker, the other to a Count, but are unhappy, and each has her lover. Rastignac, under Vautrin's pragmatic education, learns only too quickly; he becomes a master in the ethic of calculation, courts the lovely young Victorine (also a denizen of the Vauquer establishment), whose prospective millions he hopes to inherit, once her brother is put out of the way. At the same time he pursues Goriot's daughter, Delphine, the Countess, and is about to become her lover! . . . In the lower echelons of the establishment others are planning to betray Vautrin, suspected of being an escaped convict, into the hands of the police as soon as they can discover the brand-mark on his chest.

Vautrin! There is scarcely a character in *Le Père Goriot* that has his dimension. Escaped convict, leader of the Society of Ten Thousand, he is the grand-anarch of society. He is Balzac's *Machtmensch*, the Strong Man, who though a criminal, also incriminates all of society. He has read the heart of the world; he is the materialization of Providence. Vautrin is the transcendent victim and destroyer. He too is a Mephistopheles — Mephisto to Rastignac's quotidian Faust. He opens the gates of success for the young nineteenth century Faust not with his infernal magic, but with his simple instructions adapted to Balzac's modern world. He leaps upon intentions before their owner is conscious of them. He is the psychologist of the unconscious. He is not Goethe's "Geist der stets verneint" — the spirit that always denies. No. He is the affirmative spirit, always master of himself even if in chains. Always master of circumstances. "There are only two courses to take, " he says, "either blind obedience or open revolt. I obey nothing." His cynicism is the light of truth focussed on a cynical world. He rallies young Rastignac on his ambition to study law and thus acquire wealth and power. That, he states, "takes a long time."

Do you know, he continues, how a man makes his way in this world? Either by the splendor of genius, or by the adroitness of corruption ... Honesty is of no use. Men yield to the power of genius ... An honest man is the common enemy; but who do you think an honest man is? In Paris it is the man who holds his tongue and keeps his profits to himself. I am not talking of those poor slaves who are always toiling without receiving any reward for their labors and whom I call the confraternity of the poor of God ...[39]

He instructs him in the fundamentals of the reigning character of Law.

Those who drive through the mud in carriages are called honest, but those who go on foot with bespattered boots are called rascals. If you have the ill luck to appropriate the slightest article belonging to somebody else you are exhibited on the square of the Palais de Justice as a curiosity; but if you steal a million, you are labelled as a rarity in the salon. Yet you pay thirty millions to the law and the police for upholding this system of morality!

And as for opinions,

... Care no more for your opinions than you do for words ... When you are asked for them, sell them ... There is no such thing as principle: emergency is everything; there are no laws, but only circumstances ...

Vautrin's prime exemplar is Talleyrand — whom Balzac also admired greatly.

But are Vautrin's preachments those of a criminal and a villain? Just listen to the beautiful noblewoman, the Comtesse de Beauséant — a highly sensitive, imaginative, and deep-feeling human being:

I tell you, Monsieur de Rastignac, you must treat the world as it deserves. You wish to succeed, and I will help you. You must sound the depths of feminine corruption, and gauge the extent of the miserable vanity of men... The colder your calculations, the more effectual they will be. Strike without mercy and you will be feared. Think of men and women only as post-horses that you are willing to work to death at every stage provided that you reach the goal of your desires...[40]

Let us, with Balzac, emerge from the Maison Vauquer and make our way into the world of the shop-keeper, say, that of César Birotteau, successful apothecary and perfumer of the rue Saint-Honoré, producer of the widely celebrated cosmetics known as Birotteau's "Double-Purpose Sultana Cream" and "Pink Lotion" — miraculous discoveries "approved by the Institute." Like so many of his métier, he too is caught up in the fever of financial speculation and expansion, and falling victim to fraud, double-dealing and charlatanism, is brought to bankruptcy. But the story ends happily. He is rescued by his family, good friends, and in particular by a former young assistant. This is a kind of pastoral idyl, transplanted into the jungle of cities. The simple shop-keeper cannot compete with the new cormorants of the money-market — the dealers in Capital and Credit. He too is instructed in the mysteries of the "new Cabbala" by a minion of the manipulators. "You must be prepared to clip the public, and clip it properly. Speculation, that's the big game."

Speculation? Birotteau asks, what's that? Business on an abstract plane... a kind of manipulation that will remain a mystery for some ten years more, according to Nucingen, who's the Napoleon of finance. In Speculation, a man deals only in sum totals; and does things in a big way. He skims the cream off the profits before they even exist and divides great hopes into parcels. In short, it's a new Cabbala.[41]

Birotteau in his simplicity cannot be aware of the new forces that are at work. As he sits cringing and waiting in the anteroom of a banker, hoping to have a loan renewed, is he aware that there before him sits a new god, immobile, and stern — Inexorable Destiny or Fate. He is the primitive man, dying in the end an "honorable" death, having made restoration to his creditors. Here is ancient chivalry in a middle-class bosom. "A martyr," Balzac concludes, "to integrity in business, one worthy of being decorated with the palm of eternal life." ...

Let us ascend to another circle — that of high finance, and enter the *Maison Nucingen*. Baron Nucingen, the "elephant of finance," is the husband of Delphine, daughter of old Goriot. Here we are in the presence of "the omnipotence, omniscience, and universal applicability of money." Nucingen's "house" had risen to power — like the House of Rothschild — during the first two decades of the nineteenth century. Here the financial operations have a vast compass, including the issuing of deposit certificates in stocks, calling in loans, interests in numerous enterprises. Here banking has become a "kind of statecraft," and the banker "a conquering general making sacrifices on a tremendous scale to gain ends that no one perceives."

Here is Nucingen's career after 1815:

Nucingen grasped an idea ... that capital is power only when you are very much richer than other people. In his own mind, he was jealous of the Rothschilds. He had five millions of francs, he wanted ten. He knew a way to make thirty million with ten, while with five he could only make fifteen. So he made up his mind to operate a third suspension of payment. About that time, the great man hit on the idea of indemnifying his creditors with paper of purely fictitious value and keeping their coin. On the market, a great idea of this sort is not expressed imprecisely this cut-and-dried way ...

The fever of speculation spread like a plague through all social classes.

In a very short time, says one of the characters, you will see the aristocracy, the Court, and public men descend into speculation in serried columns; you will see that their claws are longer, their morality more crooked than ours, while they don't have our good points ... Do you know the moral of it all? Our age is no better than we are ...[42]

Mammon is King. Soon he will be Emperor. Balzac saw himself as the "scientific" analyst of society. Could he also be its surgeon: Cut out the abscess and restore the patient? With what remedies, and where to find them? In the Faubourg Saint-Germain, in that antiquated and isolated stronghold of ultra-royalism and Bourbonism? When he brings the same acuity and analysis to this upper circle that he had been bringing to the ascending bourgeoisie, it was only too clear that there was a canker pervading that world too. In this period of great changes, when the aristocracy might have asserted its authority, power, and prestige, what does Balzac find? The denizens of these upper regions live on "historical memories." Instead of taking lessons from the British aristocracy, who knew how to adjust to realities and still retain power over the country, here were persons torn by greed, divided among themselves, out of touch with their time and its intellectual achievements, detesting the arts and the sciences — turned into an oligarchy, that, instead of devoting themselves to their estates, sold them in order to gamble on the Stock Exchange. What remedies could these people offer? Is it that proposed by the Duchess of Langeais — more religion?

Religion ... is a bond uniting all the conservative principles which enable the rich to live in tranquillity. Religion and the rights of property are intimately connected. It is certainly a finer thing to lead a nation by ideas of morality than by fear of the scaffold, as in the time of the Terror — the one method by which your odious Revolution could enforce obedience. The priest and the king — that means you and me, and the Princess, my neighbor — in a word the interests of all honest people personified ...

To which assertion, the sober-minded M. de Montriveau, replies:

If that is how your Court and your Government think, I am sorry for you... Political Protestantism has gained an ascendancy over people's minds... Revolution will rise again, terrible in strength, and strike but a single blow. It will not be the Revolution that will go into exile; she is the very soil of France. Men die, but people's interests do not die...[43]

In looking on the French aristocracy, Balzac experiences both anger and sorrow. Through the lips of the Duchess de Maufrigneuse, as she berates the members of her class, we can hear Balzac's voice:

Will you never stop wanting to live in the fifteenth century, while we're already in the nineteenth? There is no longer a noblesse among us, there is only an aristocracy.[44]

What is happening in the country parallels the city. The aristocracy is selling off the land to the land-hungry peasants. Their magnificent chateaux are falling into a state of disrepair. Both fall prey to the cormorant money-lenders — the small-town usurers. How would you bring God and Religion to the peasant, who is now too well aware of where God is hidden? The Abbé Brosette, in the powerful novel, *The Peasants,* is asking the peasant-farmer Fourchon whether he is raising his grandson in the fear of the Lord:

Oh, no, not at all. I don't tell him to be afraid of God, but of human beings... I tell him, little one, beware of prisons! From there it's straight to the scaffold. Don't steal, but let them give it to you. Stealing leads to murder, and murder invokes human justice. Beware of the razor-blade of Justice, which guards the sleep of the rich from the sleeplessness of the poor. Learn to read. Once you've learned something, you'll find a way to pile up money, so that the law will have nothing against you, just like handsome M. Gaubertin. Wisdom lies in attaching yourself, and then there'll always be some pickings...[45]

In this bleakness of an age in which Balzac saw so much that boded ill for the future of civilization and culture as well as humanity, he found some solace in a Utopian dream. The physician

Benassis rehabilitates a decaying village near Grenoble, and succeeds in converting it into a flourishing productive agrarian commune, with a successful home industry — a self-contained, self-sustaining small commonwealth...[46]

How this small co-operative community was to survive — an enclave within a rapidly changing national economy, in a world of competition, in a world of advancing industry — was something Balzac does not tell us. Dr. Benassis fills the role of a benevolent despot, under whose direction Utopia comes into being. No Utopian dream village could disguise Balzac's realistic fears for the future, and despondency over the present. The prospect that the triumph of the moneyed bourgeoisie might in itself only be an earnest of the potential triumph of the "people" — that is, the lower classes and the dispossessed — could not allay his apprehensions. For, in the very book that depicts the founding of an ideal commune under a benevolent leader, more profound anxieties are given voice.

... The victory over the monarchical system, obtained by the middle classes with a view to extending the number of the privileged class, will produce its natural effect — the people will triumph in turn over the middle classes. If this trouble comes to pass, the indiscriminate right of suffrage bestowed upon the massses will be a dangerous weapon in their hands. The man who votes criticizes. An authority that is called in question is no longer an authority.

So far as the "poor and suffering classes" are concerned, the interlocutor adds,

Though I admire the sublime patience and resignation with which they tread the path of toil, I must pronounce them to be unfit to take part in government. The proletariat seem to me to be the minors of a nation, and ought to remain in a condition of tutelage...[47]

The elegiac note sounds more portentously in what might well be taken as one of Balzac's most penetrating novels, *Lost Illusions*. Here we are faced with the voluntary corruption — in fact, self-corruption — of a powerful literary talent, that of Lucien Rubempré.

Lucien, a native of the provincial town of Angoulème, is sucked into the journalistic maëlstron of Paris, succumbs, and sells himself. In his ascent, he becomes an advocate and associate of the royalists, abandons his friends of former days, and even betrays them.

His range of betrayals becomes ever wider, including his own mistress; and so, in the end, as he has betrayed others, his new friends betray him. There are here, as in others of Balzac's works, characters of integrity, self-respect, and dedication to their principles. There is the writer d'Arthez (Balzac's *alter-ego*); here we find the republican Michel Chrestien — both d'Arthez and Chrestien are Saint-Simonian socialists; there is the unshakable physician Blanchon, and the incorruptible painter Brideau (Balzac had the Christian Socialist Buchez in mind, as well as Delacroix the painter). Here is also the dedicated printer of Angoulème, David Séchard.

We have a picture of two kinds of moralities: the negotiable and the non-negotiable. Lucien represents negotiable morality, as his scruples give way one by one.

Daniel d'Arthez represents the non-negotiable variety. He instructs Lucien in the meaning of true greatness:

One can only become great at a price, Daniel said to him in his gentle voice. The works of genius are watered with tears. Talent is a mortal creature, that has, like other living beings, a childhood subject to maladies ... Whoever wishes to rise above the common run of men must be prepared to fight a battle and not retreat at the first difficulty. A great writer is nothing less than a martyr who does not die.[48]

Lost Illusions was completed in 1843. Balzac was at the crest of his productivity and fortunes. Two years before, in 1841, he had signed a contract for the publication of his complete works under the title of *La Comédie Humaine*. On November 10, 1841, Count Wenceslas Hanski died. The way to marriage which now seemed open was unfortunately to be strewn with many pitfalls and obstacles — an eight years' wait...

For the new edition of his works Balzac prepared a Preface, which was both a Manifesto and a Credo — a statement of the nature of the novel he had brought into being. This was a "program" constructed aposteriori, for the ideas and materials had been there fomed all along. The title *Comédie Humaine* was suggested to Balzac by a friend. The principal ideas that the individual components of the series were to illustrate and illumine, epitomize the thought of the early nineteenth century. Man is a part of Nature, man and animal are related. Society resembles Nature: there are social species as there are zoological ones. The biologist Buffon had attempted in one work to encompass zoology; could not the same be done for society? But the social world is Nature plus Society. The social world is always in the process of change; human nature is infinitely variable, and Chance is the greatest of novelists. It is French society that is the historian, and I, Balzac, am merely her secretary.

In marshalling an inventory of vices and virtues, in assembling the principal facts about the passions, in painting characters, in choosing the principal events of a Society, in composing the type by uniting the principal traits of a number of homogeneous characters, it is possible that I shall eventually achieve a history forgotten by so many historians — a history of the mores of a society.[49]

He had set out to "surprise the hidden sense within this immense assemblage of persons," and discover principles behind this "moteur social" — "the driving force." Man is a product of Society.

Man is neither good or bad. He is born with instincts and aptitudes. Society, far from depraving him, as Rousseau insisted, perfects him, makes him better. But interest also develops his evil inclinations. Christianity, above all, Catholicism, being, as I said in *Le Médecin de Campagne,* a complete system for repressing the depraved tendencies of man, is the greatest element of the Social Order . . . Christianity has given birth to modern man, and will preserve him. Hence no doubt arises as to the principle of monarchy. Catholicism and Royalty are twin principles.[50]

The immense scope of a plan which at once embraces the history and a critique of Society, an analysis of its ills, and a discussion of its principles, gives me the right, I believe, to name the work *La Comédie Humaine.* Is not this ambitious? Is it not just? This is what the public will decide when the work is completed.[51]

If he was not destined fully to complete that immense project, he succeeded in writing and publishing ninety or so individual stories and novels. Add to these the innumerable pot-boilers, the many contributions to the journals, and — not least — the letters, and the miracle of Balzac emerges more clearly than ever.

Not the least significant sector of the *Comédie Humaine* is that devoted to women, and the frequently subtle understanding of their problems it manifests. His own special discovery is the "woman of thirty," — but he is no less concerned with the young girl brought to the marriage market as a piece of chattel to be sold to the highest bidder. He is sensitve to woman's heroism, and it is only necessary here — out of the vast gallery — to recall Mme Hulot, Cousine Bette, Eugénie Grandet, and the dedicated and self-sacrificing servants of the families. He is also a master at depicting alienation and dehumanization of woman — a victim of social pressures and ambitions — all of them symbolic of that hardening of the heart associated with the hunger for advancement and rank.

But the magnificent insights he brought to bear upon women, the bourgeoisie, the aristocracy in this period of breath-taking changes failed him when he came to the treatment of the proletariat as a class. For the unfranchised and unpossessing lower classes as class he had little sympathy or understanding. He who recounted with warmth and sympathy how he was used to follow a working-class couple, eavesdrop on their conversation, identify himself with their poverty and other wants, failed to see those same human beings *en massse* as anything but a source of terror, a threat, and a kind of bestiary. They were the "homme-masse" to be controlled, guided by an upper élite, an infallible monarchy, an infallible church. "Infallibility was the making of Napoleon. He would have been a god if he had not failed the world with the sound of his fall at Waterloo."[53] The working people manifested their heroism as a class in the French Revolution, no less than in the July Revolution of 1830. Despite alleged excesses, as we have seen, they were not a "mob." Balzac allows them a grudging tribute as he contemplates the betrayal of the 1830 Revolution on the part of the bourgeois. Even in defeat, the working population carried off the victory — a moral victory, it is true.

Only under the soiled shirt can one still encounter patriotism; and that is the downfall of France. The July Revolution is the voluntary defeat of those who through name, wealth and talent belong to the upper Ten Thousand. The self sacrificing masses have carried off the victory over the rich intellectual strata, who have an aversion to self-sacrifice.[54]

The times were astir with working-class agitation and action. It was a time when out of a population of thirty-two million inhabitants, over twenty-two million lived on an income of something between six and eight sous *per diem*. When the Lyon textile workers revolted against their abysmally wretched conditions, and then were ruthlessly repressed, they recriminated by "oiling" their productions to increase their weight, and hence their wages, since they were paid by the kilo. In Balzac's eyes they were "corrupt," and that was because they did not have religion. A scathing diatribe against their chicanery, but only a passing word of sympathy for their plight. And what of those hundreds who had been shot down... Not a word...

2

GEORGE SAND
AND THE QUEST OF THE SELF

> The hour of agony and revolt passed for George
> Sand as it passed for Goethe, as it passes away for
> their readers likewise. It passes away and does not
> return; yet those who, amid the agitations, more or
> less a story of their youth, betook themselves to the
> early works of George Sand, may in later life cease
> to read them, indeed, but they can no more forget
> them than they can forget *Werther*. George Sand
> speaks somewhere of her "days with Corinne."
> Days of *Valentine*, many of us in like manner say,
> — days of *Valentine*, days of *Lélia*, days never to
> return! They are gone, we shall read the books no
> more, and yet how ineffaceable is their impression!
> How the sentences from George Sand's works of
> that period still linger in our memory and haunt the
> ear with their cadences! Grandiose and moving,
> they come, these cadences, like the sighing of the
> wind through the forest, like the breaking of the
> waves on the seashore...
> — Matthew Arnold, "George Sand" —

Strange are the vicissitudes of history! Who would have imagined that
one hundred years after her death, George Sand would rise again — in
a miraculous resurrection of fame and readership, once more to assert
her place in the history of human thought! It was only yesterday that
one could scarcely have found anyone who had read any of her
hundred or so writings. One or two readers might have come across *La
Mare au Diable*, or *La Petite Fadette*, perhaps even *Consuelo*. The rest
of her works reposed in the obscurities of libraries.

518

Now she has become a part of contemporary history. The struggle for equal rights for women found in her a pioneer worthy of reestablishment. Numerous biographies, reprints of her books, televised drama testify to a renewed interest, unfortunately not untinged by tha aura of scandal that has cast her true achievements into a shadow.

In her day, she was a presence and a force that extended far beyond her literary achievement, and it is sometimes difficult for another generation to understand the reasons for such an influence, far removed as it is from the immediacy and the needs of a past era. These were no second-rate minds that were drawn to her in friendship and admiration; or, where they were far removed from her geographically, were stirred and affected by her published utterances and her personality.

A visitor to the George Sand chateau of Nohant (and the place runs the danger of being or becoming a shrine!) cannot but be impressed when he enters the spacious dining room, where the table is set as if for expected guests, with appropriate place-cards (of course, the chronology has to be violated). Here one finds the names of Balzac, Flaubert, Turgenev, Liszt, Chopin, Madame d'Agoult, and other notable contemporaries — persons diverse in character and outlook, differing even from those of George Sand herself, but symbolically united by the magic of her presence!

Like Byron, she was read far and wide. Matthew Arnold considered her a worthy successor to Goethe. George Eliot was deeply impressed by her. For German writers she represented a powerful force for emancipation. To the Russians, she was a priestess. That formidable anarchist, Michael Bakunin, said of her that she was "not only a poetess, but a prophet who has a revelation to offer, Here is an apostolic religious nature."[1] Dostoyevski spoke of her with reverent admiration.

She had, of course, against her armies of detractors, but their number and vehemence were themselves strong indices of the impact she had produced.

It is unfortunate, but perhaps all too natural, that the "chronique scandaleuse" of her personal life should have overshadowed so much of her achievement as writer and thinker. What in a man would be regarded and privately envied as a triumphant sexuality, was adjudged in her, a woman, as inordinate debauchery, or at least impermissible libertinism. Even today she is touted as a "notorious" woman. Of course, it was not so much her love-life that presumably shocked and amazed, as her inflexible frankness and honesty with which she proclaimed her right to her independence, and defied the hypocrisy of the world at large. What is often forgotten is that she fought a hard battle to vindicate her right as a professional author, journalist, and publicist, as well as novelist; set an example of undeviating self-discipline in these pursuits, and won for herself, though a woman, an outstanding place in the world of letters. But such achievement was never at the expense of her own self-development, which reflected the various humanitarian currents of the age, and absorbed them into her own works. More than once she battled the editorial censorship of her employers — and won. She associated with the great spirits of the times as an equal, and they, on their part, treasured her friendship and her intellect. Which is not to say that she was not a complex personality, even a problematic one...

She was born in 1804, and so was also a "child of the century," the coeval of all the greatness that was then in France. Like her contemporaries, she went through a course of intellectual, moral and spiritual crises, and was brought abreast of the social changes and political convulsions of the times. In her were mingled divergent social and genetic strains, and varieties of profound early experiences sufficient to cause more than partial disturbance in a growing child. On her father's side, she could trace her descent from Maurice de Saxe, celebrated "maréchal de France." Her mother was a plebeian *grisette,* of Paris, who, as a camp-follower became the mistress, later the wife of Maurice Dupin, a dashing officer, and the son of Aurore de Saxe, George Sand's grandmother. Illegitimacy running high in that strain (grandmother too was illegitimate), Aurore de Saxe became related to three kings of France, Louis XVI, Louis XVIII, and Charles X! Aurore Dupin (she was not yet George Sand) was brought up by her grandmother, who severed her for a time from her mother, after the premature death of her son Maurice, and placed young Aurore in an English convent in Paris. The young girl thus fused a dour Catholic education with a passion for Rousseau, and a precocious non-conformity that had been part of the attractiveness of her father. Her own rebellion began early. Her grandmother, who had wanted a male heir, called her "Maurice," and Aurore was dressed as a boy, and roamed the purlieus of Nohant, and the adjoining town of La Châtre, to the scandal of the neighborhood. For the rest of her life George Sand was to love God, Rousseau, and remain a non-conformist.

But the most incisive lesson she derived from her own unfortunate marriage to Casimir Dudevant. Young, virginal, romantic as she was, at the same time strong-willed, intellectual, and sharp-witted, she found in her arranged union a work-a-day commonplace husband — a husband of the times — moderately intelligent, crude, occasionally even brutal. Here were all the "commonplaces" and none of the ecstasies she had anticipated of love. She withdrew into herself, and he avenged himself by his own excursions, and invectives against his wife that he imprudently committed to paper — and which she discovered.

Soon a mother of two children, Maurice (how that name haunted the family!) and a girl, Solange, she defied tradition, challenged fate, and resolved on an independent career in letters. That meant Paris. She would eke out the temporary monetary settlement with her own earnings by the pen. For any young person this would have proved a hazard, for a young woman it was an act of defiance directed at the whole world . . . At the same time she was about to fashion a new declaration of independence — of the new womanhood.

To understand fully what Aurore Dudevant was facing, let us take a look at Balzac, and his views of woman, marriage, and love. He had interpreted the plight of the young girl, brought up for marriage, exposed for marital auction with perhaps the enticements of a dowry (if not good looks), by a family angling for titles and place, or for greater wealth — and the inevitable consequences of a loveless union, and its disenchantments: adulteries, resignations, and pinings. But even Balzac, penetrating as he was, was too deeply bound up with the traditional view of woman and woman's role to escape the shackles of conventional morality and his own masterful personality. "The destiny of woman," he wrote, "and her sole glory is to make the heart of a man beat faster." Such was the "métier de femme," — the art and mystery and mission of womanhood. "Woman," he wrote to the Duchess d'Abrantès, "is never so touching and so beautiful as when she abdicates all sovereignty, and always bows to the will of a master."[2] He admired the character of Klärchen, in Goethe's *Egmont,* for "bending with astonishing suppleness to the pleasures and wishes of him whom nature has made her master."[3]

Of course, this attitude of "renunciation of all governance and the practice of humility before a master" was very attractive to most men. Church and Law sanctioned and enforced it. In law, unless carefully circumscribed, both the woman and what she possessed became the property of the husband. But for all that attitude, Balzac clearly saw to what extent the customary education of a young girl of the upper classes almost necessarily led to a moral and spiritual crisis, so that an escape from the bonds of domestic or convent servitude into marriage seemed the only salvation, no matter who the future husband!

Here is Balzac, describing the upbringing of the two daughters of the Comte de Granville at the hands of their mother:

They were brought up by a pious but narrow-minded woman, 'imbued with a high principle,' as the classic phrase has it, who conceived herself to have performed the whole duty of a mother when her girls arrived at the door of matrimony without having traveled beyond the domestic circle embraced by the maternal eyes. Up to that time they had never been to a play. A Paris church was their nearest approach to a theatre... Their lessons were kept within the limits imposed by confessors... Never were girls handed over to their husbands more pure and virgin...

The education bore its inevitable result. Religion, imposed as a yoke and presented under its harshest aspect, wearied these innocent young hearts with a discipline adapted for hardened sinners. It repressed their feelings, and, though striking deep root, could create no affection. The two Maries had no alternative but to sink into imbecility or to long for independence. Independence meant marriage, and to this they looked as soon as they began to see something of the world and could exchange a few ideas...[4]

But beyond a deep sympathy for young girls, injured wives, exploited heiresses, frustrated virgins, and cheated brides, Balzac's otherwise far-ranging perceptions would not operate. He adored the Christian resignation of unfortunate wives, and pitied the poor victims. "Royaliste enragé" that he was, with his strong belief in the efficacy of the Church supporting a monarchial status quo, how could he envisage a radical alteration in the status of woman?

In the light of such views advanced by one of the foremost novelists of the day, where could the future "George Sand" turn for enlightenment and support — where was to be found the most advanced thinking on the subject of woman? Obviously, it was among the Utopian Saint-Simonians. They were the most zealous propagandists of the equality of woman, and of her liberation from the bonds of enforced love. Of course, they startled contemporaries by their advocacy of the "rehabilitation of the flesh," their assault on the Judaeo-Christian view of sexuality and the senses, by their insistence on man's and woman's freedom to love, and their attacks on the double standard of morality. Even more important was their effort to link the emancipation of both men and women to a proposed reconstruction of society.

It was into a turbulent Paris that Madame Dudevant ventured when she arrived in January 1831, to embark on her literary career. The effect of the Revolution of July had not yet worn off, nor had the echoes of the Romantic literary "revolution" quite died out. The world was still astir, and Paris was full of geniuses! Aurore Dudevant began her public journalistic career writing for *Le Figaro,* and soon became associated with the *Revue des deux Mondes,* now under the editorship of the redoubtable François Buloz. Henceforth, she was to divide her time between Paris and Nohant. At first she collaborated with her lover, the handsome, nineteen-year old law student and would-be author, Jules Sandeau. Together they signed their articles "J. Sandeau." When they wrote a novel, not a very good one, *Rose et Blanche,* they signed it "Jules Sand." But by herself she had already written her own novel, and when it appeared on May 9, 1832, it bore the signature "Georges Sand." (Later she would change it to George.) The book was entitled *Indiana,* and with it George Sand became famous...

She was not backward in proclaiming her political and social ideas, nor her judgment of the new July Monarchy. She was, she stated, a convinced republican.

I abhor tyranny. I contemn despite myself the unhappy Charles X. I execrate Polignac, the imbecile, the coward, the inhuman. But I am not disposed at all to burn incense before today's idols... Are our old institutions, that are worn-out and decayed, suitable for a young and generous generation that is rising?... I believe we should have a republic... with a more generous constitution, more advantageous to the last classes of society, less exploitable by the ambitious, an order of things, finally, that will last after us... If only I were a man...[5]

Not long after the publication of *Indiana,* insurrections broke out. She was outraged by the atrocities committed by both sides, which she witnessed from her window and balcony overlooking the Seine, in the company of a terrified Solange. But she was even more incensed at the action of King Louis-Philippe, who had ordered that doctors and surgeons reveal the whereabouts of all wounded. Everything new seemed to horrify her — monarchy, republic, human beings. She felt in no mood to be writing novels...[6]

But she could not resist the writing urge. *Indiana* was soon followed by *Valentine,* and in 1833 by *Lélia* — three novels that embodied George Sand's credo: the right of woman to her own individuality, the sacredness of that ego. Marred though these were by romantic extravagance and improbabilities, each of them, and *Lélia* above all, contains remarkable insights not only into the problems and mind of the author, but also into the problems of the individual — particularly woman — in the face of a self-centered society.

Each of the three novels is touched with the pathos and tragedy of frustration. Death concludes the struggles of the protagonists of the two latter works, and even the first of these, *Indiana,* might have ended in a double suicide, had not George Sand changed her mind and removed her two characters to an isolated spot outside of France.

The principal character of *Indiana,* Madame Delmare, is the unhappy Creole wife of the much older and unsympathetic Colonel Delmare. She believes she has found in the young de Ramière the lover her heart craves. Unfortunately she discovers in him all the true stigmata of the age — selfishness, self-seeking, and moral cowardice. For him, woman is merely a field for adventuring, a stepping-stone toward his personal advancement. Indiana's courage and integrity are wasted on him. Her disenchantment is shattering, but she is saved ultimately in finding a selfless love.

Valentine, the heroine of the second novel, is no less noble, no less courageous, no less idealistic than Madame Delmare. She is to be married to an unfeeling aristocratic adventurer, but she falls in love with a man far below her in rank — the nephew of a well-to-do farmer. She marries as commanded, but yields to her passion for her lover, Benedict, and in the end both she and he die. Valentine is the "new" woman. In the three generations of her aristocratic family are reflected three divergent *Weltanschauungen* — three different life-attitudes: in the grandmother, the hedonism and scepticism of the ancien régime and the Empire; in her widowed mother, the Countess, the coldness and egotism of the Restoration; and finally, in Valentine, the frustrated impulses of emancipation from class-prejudice. She is the offspring of Rousseau and Saint-Simon.

Sand had set herself the task of countering the cynicism of the times, the hopelessness so prevalent, by depicting characters who possess principles, nobility of character, integrity, and above all, are prepared to struggle for self-realization, no matter what the risks. In the welter of selfishness, she would show that not all hearts were corrupt and venal, and that there was a realm of possibilities open to them. If she tended to idealize her good characters, sometimes beyond probability, she was really objectifying her own aspirations. Yet, she is at times able to project scenes of startling truth and credibility. How could any reader in her day have failed to respond to that opening scene in *Indiana*, which reveals husband, wife, and guest in front of a fireplace, and in a few pages discloses the full horror of a family life in which the husband is the embodiment of masculine tyranny and the wife of utter feminine helplessness, even hopelessness? How often had such scenes been reenacted in hundreds of French households?

How many must have identified with Madame Delmare, when, after her soul-shattering disenchantment and her near-suicide, she returns to her husband and declares:

I know I am your slave, and you are the master. This country's law has made you my master. You can chain my body, manacle my arms, govern my actions. You have the strongest right on your side, and society will confirm it. But you have no power over my will.

Or, when she replies to the man she loves, who repudiates her, and cynically advises her to seek the comforts of religion:

Do not exhort me to think of God, whose duty it is to move the hearts of sinners. As for me, I have a faith that is greater than yours. Your god is the God of men, he is the King, the founder and stay of your race. Mine is the God of the Universe, the Creator and support of all creatures. Your God has done everything for you alone. Mine has created all human beings, one for the other. You men believe yourselves to be masters of the world. I believe you are only tyrants ... No, Raymond, you do not know God. You believe in nothing ... One day God will come down and liberate ... not only woman, but all slaves ... In submitting, I am not submitting to the will of God, but to the will of man...[7]

Sand is too much the Rousseauist not to draw a sharp contrast between what she believes to be the futile, empty and wasteful life of the chateau and the decent occupations of the farm, as in *Valentine*. For her, the idyl of rustic existence is still a reality, and the Berrichon countryside around Nohant forms a striking background for the drama enacted in hut and palace.

She is a Romantic who defines love in thoroughly Romantic terms. Love is something beyond calculation or reason; it is of divine origin, outside the will of the human being. Once it has entered the heart of the one chosen being nothing in the world can destroy it.

It is doubtful whether George Sand had ever read the fiery *Vindication of the Rights of Women* written by Mary Shelley's mother, Mary Wollstonecraft, and published in 1792, or her husband, William Godwin's daring *Inquiry Concerning Political Justice* of the following-year — both declarations of the natural right of free love, and biting criticisms of enforced matrimony. But she certainly knew the two novels of Madame de Staël, *Delphine* and *Corinne*, both manifestoes of womanhood at war with conventional society. These along with Rousseau had been an essential element in George Sand's early education. Both books were self-revelations.

George Sand's novels, too, are self-revelations. By far the most candid and astonishing confessional by a woman — *Lélia* — gave rise to a whole avalanche of puzzlement, questioning, and suspicion — as well as probings and interpretations.

A tract, rather than a novel, it is a remarkable psychological document, and offers to a modern psychologist a most challenging excursion into soul-exploration. It was no less challenging in the less psychologically oriented time in which it was produced. Behind the abstractions that stand for characters in this story, behind the fanciful and semi-allegorical adventures it depicts, there is the drama of a soul — that of George Sand — in an agonizing struggle for self-knowledge. She herself described *Lélia* as "not a book, but a cry of pain, or a bad dream."[8]

Lélia is a dual person. She is Lélia and she is also Pulchérie, her sister, a courtesan. As Lélia, she is pure spirit, superbly beautiful, wise, but cold — devoid of the feeling of love, as human beings understand it; for the love to which she aspires is preternatural, never to be satisfied. It is the abstraction that George Sand built up — to define one part of herself. As Lélia she has three admirers, each attached to her in his own way: the young Romantic poet Sténio, who loves her with a passion which has no bounds, a love that breaks like wave upon wave against the rock of her aloofness. Lélia pities him, but cannot give him the love he craves. Then there is Trenmor, the detached admirer, the stoic who stands aside. He has lived and suffered, he had committed a crime, and has atoned for it. Finally, there is the priest Magnus, who loves her with a diabolic, carnal passion that will eventually lead him to strangle her. The Lélia of the trans-terrestrial aspiration — intellect rather than passion — represents the male element within her, as the world viewed it — the element that dominates and subdues, without being subdued itself. Pulchérie is the courtesan, the affirmer of the senses, of life — the other side of Lélia — flesh, rather than spirit. In another sense, revealed lucidly in an earlier experience of the two sisters, she is the feminine love of the male Lélia. Such bisexuality is also a part of George Sand's self-revelation. It is Magnus who recognizes the dualism inherent in Lélia. To Sténio he says:

Listen, listen . . . there were two Lélias . . . I saw her, double and complete, woman and idea, hope and reality, body and soul, gift and promise . . . I saw her just as she emerged from the bosom of God: Beauty — that is the say, temptation; hope — that is to say, a trial; kindness — that is to say, falsehood.[9]

Strange contradictions multiply. On the one hand, George Sand is a strong defender of monogamy. But she lets Pulchérie utter the following radical sentiment about man and woman:

These two beings, so similar and dissimilar at the same time, are made so that there is always present hatred in the love that exists between them... Union of man and woman should be a transitory one in the designs of Providence; everything runs counter to their association, and change is one of the necessities of their nature.[10]

"Oh misery and servitude of woman!" Lélia exclaims. And Pulchérie comments:

Under what a mountain of ignominies and injustices must she accustom herself... to be lover, courtesan, and mother — three conditions of the destiny of woman, from which no woman escapes, whether she sells herself in the market-place of prostitution or by means of a marriage contract... [11]

It was a book bound to excite and shock. Thackeray, for example, thought *Lélia*

a wonderful book, indeed, gorgeous in eloquence, and rich in magnificent poetry; a regular topsyturvyfication of morality, a thieves' and prostitutes' apotheosis.[12]

It is perhaps unfortunate that George Sand's prospective lovers did not read this manual, or perhaps did not read it carefully enough. They might have learned a great deal, and perhaps saved themselves hazards and storms, even heart-aches. They might also have missed some of the ecstasies and marvels of a companionship with a woman of extraordinary, though dangerous, endowments. No other woman of the times stood as self-revealed as George Sand. She was as passionate physically as she was emotionally. In her own words she burnt with a "fire" that "devoured her entrails."[13] Sometimes it devoured others.

It was at this point in 1833 that Alfred de Musset came upon the scene...

Alfred de Musset was precocious, and always remained a precocious boy — a genius that never grew up fully — one that could not be at home in a world that frustrated his personal yearnings and appetites. He was like the last sigh of a belated Romanticism. His sensitive and morbid ego was destined always to fall upon the "thorns of life." The creator of some of the most exquisite and nostalgic poetry, he throve on *Weltschmerz.* His works are delicate cameos — small in compass, but superb in craftsmanship. His name has always been associated with the veiled autobiography, *Confession d'un enfant du siécle,* as depicting the physical and moral sickness of the age, of an enervated generation born during the wars of the Empire, cast upon the drab world of the Restoration, and growing up with an utter incapacity to understand or cope with the rapidly changing times, and its new social, political, and moral demands. He was one of those earlier *poètes maudits* — "damned poets" — like Gérard de Nerval, whom the curse of life eventually brought to naught. Nerval, an extraordinarily gifted writer and translator, hanged himself. Musset committed his own moral and physical suicide through dissipations. He was born in 1810, and died in 1857, and after 1840 he practically ceased writing. But even within this limited compass he succeeded in creating imperishable and tender comedies, fantasies of a spirit that could laugh and weep at the same time, always mirroring the conflict within him between dream and reality.

Even in his early teens he was already a habitué of the Romantic cénacles, and at home in the portentous company of Hugo, Vigny, Lamartine, Sainte-Beuve, and Nodier. Madame Victor Hugo was enchanted by this "charming boy, with slender figure and flaxen hair, clear and steady eyes, wide nostrils and vermilion lips, rosy face..." He had fled the study of law, and soon, like Berlioz, he was to escape medicine, and turn to — what? He could also paint agreeably. But the intoxication of poetry was irresistible. Before him he had the greatness of Goethe and Schiller, Shakespeare, and above all, Byron and André Chénier. At twenty he was already hailed as a poet for his *Contes d'Espagne et d'Italie,* and though he had never been in Spain or Italy, he thrilled with his vicarious and delicious exoticism, his fancied debaucheries, pseudo-Byronism — love, adventure, and sneers. In a cynical poem, "Rolla," he mocks himself and his century. Prematurely aged, he is already an unbeliever, living in a world already grown old,

> Je ne crois pas, o Christ! à ta parole sainte:
> Je suis venu trop tard dans un monde trop vieux ...

"We old men, born yesterday, who will rejuvenate us?" We are living in an age hostile to the arts, when the "artist is merchant, and art a trade." He will have no mingling of poetry and politics.

Politics follows action, literature follows thought ... If thought would be something in her own right, she must separate herself from all action; if literature wishes to exist, she must break openly with politics ... A poet may speak about himself, about his friends, the wines he drinks, the mistress he would have, the weather, about the living and the dead, the wise and the foolish, but he may not engage in politics ...[13]

And he reaffirmed this sentiment in verse:

> Que de gens aujourd'hui chantent la liberté ...
> Je n'ai chanté ni la paix ni la guerre ...

> Let the people chant Liberty today,
> As they chanted King and Napoleon,
> I have never sung peace or war,
> If they're deceived, what care I?
> Love is all — love and life in the sun.[14]

He laughs at the dreams of the Utopian socialists, at Fourier and Fourierism, with their "humanitarian coach," and their ideal world of "cabbages and turnips," a world that will be spick and span "like a porringer."

Musset's "Rolla" appeared in Buloz's *Revue des deux Mondes* on August 15, 1833. George Sand was a frequent contributor to that journal. Not long thereafter, Buloz invited a number of his collaborators to a dinner at "Les Trois Frères Provençaux," a celebrated restaurant in the Palais-Royal. Here it was that Musset and George Sand met. Soon they became lovers.

He was emotionally very much of a child, and she, overpoweringly, the mother. He was possessive and jealous, and she independent and often critical of him. He worked in spasms, sometimes not at all, and she had her irrefragable routine, from which she could and would not be diverted. He was all Self. She had broken through the shell of self, and was growing up with the century. He was a gifted "child" and she already had a complicated past, and knew herself too well. He was prone to debaucheries, and sometimes hankered after other flesh, less dominating. He was spendthrift of time and money. She lived in greater part by her earnings as a writer. He was prone to seizures, even hallucinations. He had the visions of a *Doppelgänger*. One such episode had interrupted their ardors when they were at Fontainebleau.

Their sojourn in Venice brought their relationship to a tragic climax. It is easy for outsiders to pass judgment on the marital or other love relations around them. Was the relation between George Sand and Musset, as some critics believed, that of a fragile but tainted angel and a beautiful demon? In Venice, the sick and unpredictable Musset paid a heavy price for his local debaucheries in attacks of *delirium tremens* that duplicated but more intensely his previous experiences. George Sand nursed him as well as she could, but the drama of love was over. The entrance of Dr. Pagello on the scene was a belated *coup-de-grâce*.

Painful and shattering as was that love-experience, on Musset's side it proved the source of a poetic rebirth. The best and most moving of Musset's poetry flowed from these springs of sorrow and disenchantment. The hauntings of his love for George Sand, and the bitterness of that love were never to leave him. But some poets need despair.

> Rien ne nous rend si grands qu'une grande douleur . . .
> Les plus désespérés sont les chants les plus beaux . . .

"Nothing makes us so great as a great sorrow . . . The sweetest songs are those that sing the greatest woe . . . The poet is like a pelican that feeds its young with his own blood . . ."

This is from the series of poems called "Nights" — poems of recollection. In "La Nuit de Mai," (quoted above) the Muse urges him to resume his lyre, even though he sings his imperishable grief. In the "Nuit d'Août" he announces to the Muse he will sing again: "Open your arms, I am about to sing." Muse, what matters life or death? "Heart, swelling with bitterness, make thee a flower to bloom. Love and thou shalt be reborn. Having suffered, more suffering behooves thee. Having once loved, one must love without cease..."

> Aime, et tu renaîtras; fais-toi fleur pour éclorer;
> Après avoir souffert, il faut souffrir encore;
> Il faut aimer sans cesse, après avoir aimé...

Bitterness returns with past memories in "La Nuit d'Octobre." "To ripen, the harvest needs the dew; to live and feel, Man has need of tears... But now farewell hatred." Musset vows forgiveness, and with the morning's rebirth of nature, "we go to be reborn again with her." "Nous allons renaître avec elle."

His plays, inimitably kept alive by the Comédie Française to this day, are like subtly spoken pantomimes, spoken ballets, having the delicate charm of a wistful dream — something far-off, yet touched by tenderness and sadness. *On ne badine pas avec l'amour, Fantasio, Carmosine, Lorenzaccio* — are Musset at his tenderest, and most fanciful — with his sprightly and winsome maidens, and his love-lorn jesters — somber reality sometimes mingling with the flights of fantasy and the improbable.

But what was always with him was the ineradicable sorrow, compressed immortally in verses, set unforgettably by Franz Liszt:

> J'ai perdu ma force et ma vie,
> Et mes amis et ma gaieté;
> J'ai perdu jusqu'à la fierté
> Qui faisait croire à mon génie...
>
> Dieu parle, il faut qu'on lui réponde.
> Le seul bien qui me reste au monde
> Est d'avoir quelquefois pleuré.

"I have lost my strength, my life; my friends and my high spirits, and my pride that made me believe in my genius ..., and the only good that has been left me here on earth is to have wept now and then...[15]

While the lovers were in Venice, the world had not stood still. The year 1834 was once again a year of upheaval. There were uprisings in Lyon, followed by similar ones in other cities of France, including Paris. These were repressed with severe violence, and followed with legislation intended to extinguish the last embers of republicanism in France. In Paris, the unprovoked massacre of innocents in the rue Transnonin aroused horror. Over two thousand suspects were arrested. The Chamber of Peers was constituted as the court to try the cases against the state. Such measures had the support of Thiers and Guizot. Army contingents were raised to 360,000; the law against possession of arms was further strengthened, and liberal newspapers, like *La Tribune,* were suppressed, and its editor, Armand Marrast, was forced to flee. In October 1833 the *Tribune* had issued a manifesto calling for universal suffrage, a public system of education, organization of state credit, a more equitable distribution of labor, the right to association and other liberal measures. Even more fiery appeals were issued by the *National,* which spoke for the republican left. "Down with all privileges, even those of birth! Down with the monopoly of wealth! Down with human exploitation ... The greatest revolutions are not political revolutions. When they are not accompanied by social revolutions, they are almost useless. Authority changes hands, but the nation remains the same."[16]

Membership in radical societies, such as the *Amis du Peuple,* had been growing in Paris and the provinces. General discontent resulted in the explosions of 1834.

George Sand returned to Paris in October 1834. One might say that with that year commenced a new phase in her political and social thought. Her circle of friendships was enlarged when she came to know Franz Liszt, Heinrich Heine, and Berlioz. Delacroix was painting her portrait.

And not the least important was the Abbé de Lamennais.

On April 30, 1834 appeared a brief book entitled *Paroles d'un Croyant — The Words of a Believer* — written by a French priest, the Abbé Félicité Robert de Lamennais. It proved to be an intellectual and moral bombshell. A confession and a credo, it climaxed a career that contained within itself one of the most astounding examples of a spiritual transformation, if not revolution. Lamennais had begun his clerical career as an ultramontane conservative defender of the Roman Catholic Church, with an essay, published in 1817, entitled "On Indifference in the Matter of Religion," — which denounced toleration, private judgment; calling upon ecclesiastical authorities to regenerate France under the supremacy of the Pope — an essay that could not have been outdone in its extreme conservatism by either a Bonald or a de Maistre. Lamennais looked to the Pope, and not to any lay ruler, to bring about a kind of "theocratic democracy" that would in some way be responsive to the needs of the vast majority of the population of Europe, and work toward an amelioration of their miserable condition. But he found little or no support either from Rome or from the clergy in general.

For some years before 1830, he had watched with apprehension the rising tide of misery in the country, and the volcanic eruption that was in the making. The Revolution of July 1830 confirmed him in the major decision of his life. A few days before the publication of his *Paroles,* he had written to his closest friend, Benoit d'Azy:

What is going on in France and Europe, the abominable system of despotism which is developing everywhere with odious shamelessness, so revolts me that it has seemed to me that in this situation silence would be almost as infamous on my part as direct approval. Consequently, I have resolved at all costs, to save my conscience and my honor, by protesting with the force that I possess. The *Paroles d'un Croyant* is therefore being published. Whatever happens matters little. My own comfort of mind comes before everything. I prefer storms without to storms within.[17]

All the disappointment, all the disenchantment of his previous life are contained in this utterance. He had tried and tried again to bring others to his views and his prevision of a crisis. He had appealed to all Catholics: "Catholics, let us understand it well — we must save our faith, and we will save it through liberty."[18]

Fired by the Revolution of July, and with the cooperation of such ecclesiastics as Montalambert and Lacordaire, and with the support of Victor Hugo, Lamartine and the poet Alfred de Vigny, he had founded in October 1830 the journal, *L'Avenir — The Future* — in which was proclaimed the sovereignty of the people, which rejected the "divine" right of kingship, pressed for liberty of conscience, of education, of the press and of association; supported the national struggles of Belgium, Poland, and Ireland. He was still looking to the Pope to lead this radical crusade which would also regenerate the Church. He even undertook a pilgrimage to Rome in order to convince the Pope. Alas! he was met with coldness. The Pope issued an encyclical, *Mirari vos,* which though it did not mention Lamennais, condemned all his liberal ideas, calling them doctrines subversive both of Church and State. The journal soon ended its career.

The *Paroles d'un Croyant* was Lamennais's declaration of independence not only on behalf of himself but also of all people of Europe, at a time of serious upheavals and discontents. It found eager ears and hearts. In Paris, 64,000 men and women were without stable employment. In Lille, in 1834, 34,000 cotton workers lived on charity. In Lyon occurred one of the bloodiest uprisings by silk-workers in 1831; and another by weavers in 1834 — both crushed amidst horrifying bloodshed.

Lamennais's language in the *Paroles* was that of the Prophets of the Old Testament. Anger, pity, apologue and exhortation speak for liberty of conscience and the equality of human beings, the fraternity of nations. Pierre Leroux called the book the "Marseillaise of Christianity," others, the "Apocalypse of Satan." As if coals of fire were on his tongue, Lamennais prophesies a day of wrath:

Be ye ready, for the time approaches. On that day there will be great terrors and cries such as have never been heard before since the Deluge. Kings will howl on their thrones; they will hold firmly to their crowns, but try as they might, the wind will bear them away, and they will be swept away with them. The rich and powerful will come forth naked out of their palaces, fearful of being buried in their ruins. They will wander on the highways asking rags of the peasants to cover their nakedness, and a piece of bread to still their hunger, and I know not if they will be given it . . . Men will look at each other . . . and they will say, We do not know ourselves or the others . . . We did not know what Man is, but know it now . . . Everyone will possess without fear that which is his and will not desire more, for that which is for each will be for all, and all will possess God who includes all the goods.[19]

But it was not merely apocalyptic visions that Lamennais was offering. His eyes were fixed on the present world. He sees the world astir, in England, in Spain, Portugal, and Italy. He recalls Silvio Pellico and his imprisonment. (How little did Lamennais suspect that he was to inhabit a prison himself in the near future!) He ranges as far as Russia and Poland. He has scorn for Pope Gregory XVI and his pact with the Tsar. He warns against the falsifiers of liberty, the misusers of the great word:

Do not be deceived by false words. There are those who will try to persuade you that you are indeed free, because they have inscribed on a piece of paper the word Liberty, and have posted it on all the street-corners. Liberty is not a poster to be read on a street-corner. It is a living power that one feels within oneself, and around oneself, the protecting genius of the hearth, the guarantee of social rights, and the first of these rights. Beware of those who say Liberty, Liberty, and who destroy it with their works. Is it you who choose those to govern you, who command, Do this or Do not do this? Who assign your goods, your industry, your labor? And if it isn't you, how then are you free?[20]

Is it any wonder that Prince Metternich called Lamennais a madman, and regretted that "the practice of burning heretics and their works has been abandoned"?[21]

Henceforward, the People replace Church and State, the People are considered sole legitimate authority, sole legislators, sovereign. He was soon to urge abolition of monopolies and division of capital. In his book, *Modern Slavery*, he almost advances to a revolutionary position, sounding like an anticipation of the "Internationale."[22]

People, People, O awake at last! Rise slaves and rend your chains; no longer suffer them to debase in you the name of Man! Would you, that one day, bruised by the fetters of your bequeathing, your children should say, Our fathers were more cowardly than Roman slaves? There was no Spartacus among them![22]

He brought his criticism of contemporary society to a dramatic climax in 1840 with his arraignment of the régime of Louis-Philippe in *Le Pays et le Gouvernement — The Country and the State* — a summation of all the pent-up grievances of the day. For that book he was condemned to a year's imprisonment and a fine of 2000 francs. Isolated by the Church, by the authorities, by the ruling powers, he remained the inflexible priest of the people to the end. He could never be silenced...

His influence ranged far and wide. Notable personalities, no less than the general population were moved by the magnetism of the man and the eloquence of his words. To take just one example for the present, Franz Liszt.

That great-hearted genius — virtuoso of the piano, virtuoso composer, himself a personified legend, aroused by the "three days" of July 1830 set about composing a revolutionary symphony, which he never completed, though portions of it he was to utilize in a later symphonic poem, "Heroïde Funèbre." In 1833 he sought out Lamennais in order to obtain religious instruction from him. The

Paroles as well as their author overwhelmed him. That man, Liszt was to write later, "consecrated with his lips of fire and his pen of iron Liberty and Equality, those two great dogmas of Humanity."[23] Like Lamennais, Liszt, too, was aroused by the uprising at Lyon, and composed a stirring march-like piece which he prefaced with the battle cry of the Lyonnese workers, "Vivre en travaillant ou mourir en combattant" — "To live and work, or die fighting." He dedicated this piece to Lamennais, and it was to him that he also dedicated an instrumental psalm, "Psalm 130, *De Profundis,*" which he left unfinished.[24]

It was at a private recital of Liszt's that George Sand met Lamennais, and not long thereafter she became his disciple, and he her personal "confessor." She, who was now so responsive to the urgencies of the time, how could she fail to be impressed by that heroic figure?

As for the other radical currents of those days, Socialist and Saint-Simonist, from these too she drew refreshing nourishment. Count Saint-Simon had left a precious Testament for posterity, the *New Christianity,* which was soon to become the "Bible" of a new "Church." There were now hundreds of converts, for the movement was spreading far and wide. A surrogate new "religion," it also now had its priesthood; and converts and adherents as well as curious visitants, flocking to its meetings throughout France, and even beyond the French borders. In Paris they assembled in the Salle Taitbout, in the street of the same name. The most striking aspect for visitors was both the notable number of women present, and the respect accorded them in the meetings. For the Saint-Simonist gospel spoke of the equality of the sexes as well as the "rehabilitation of the flesh." Its sermons presented a new vision of a new world, free of oppression and exploitation, in which all of society, including the princes, the financial moguls, the industrialists, intellectuals, and, of course, workers, would participate in equality of direction. Soon the movement would prove its sincerity by setting out on a serious search for a woman "priestess" to sit by the side of her male counterparts . . .

All of George Sand's thoughts and feelings were now sharpened and brought into focus by two memorable events — the trial of the leaders of the April insurrections of 1834, which opened on May 5, 1835 — the so-called "Procès monstre" — and her meeting with the radical barrister and defense lawyer, Michel de Bourges.

Rarely had a trial brought out so many partisans eager to speak for and defend the accused. Spokesmen for the 121 accused "ring-leaders" included such older republicans as Buonarroti, and defenders like Barbès, Blanqui, Carnot, Comte, Jules Favre, and Lamennais. It was an unprecedented exhibition, for the accused were to face a court that consisted exclusively of 164 Peers, who refused to admit to the defense anyone but bona-fide barristers. Forty-three of the accused declined to appear, and the sessions were marked by stormy exchanges, disorders, and adjournments. The integrity of the proceedings, already undermined by the shameless violation of the Charter as to a trial by one's peers — was futher tainted by the presence of the presiding judge, one Pasquier, a notorious turn-coat and opportunist. The trials were marked by moving pleas on the part of the defending attorneys, not the least distinguished of these for logic and passionate eloquence being Michel de Bourges. But the verdicts were a foregone conclusion. When the sessions were ended in January 1836, there were numerous convictions, imprisonments, and deportations, though a number of those attainted managed to escape the country.

The leadership of republicanism had been decapitated. An unsuccessful attempt on the life of Louis-Philippe by the Corsican Fieschi gave the government the pretext for aggravating repressive legislation and arbitrariness. The press, in particular, was subjected to additional restrictions and burdens, so that all critical and liberal journalism was practically destroyed. To utter anything against the King was declared a crime, and as one historian put it, "a régime that had been born of an insurrection was now declared to be inviolable and immortal."[25]

The trials served further to advance the "education" of George Sand. She had now come to know the liberal notabilities like the socialist Pierre Leroux, Barbès, Arago, Carrel. Most important of all was Michel de Bourges, who had a long history of radical activity and had in his time suffered imprisonment. Their friendship soon ripened into intimacy. She was not one to be easily converted to socialist doctrines, but the events of 1834 and 1835 — the heavy political reaction, the imprisonment and the forced exile of so many of her fellow-countrymen and women gave her no rest. She was no longer the Lélia of 1833. She invoked the names of Jesus, Washington and Franklin, and Saint-Simon as she declared her new adherence. And so she wrote to Michel de Bourges,

Let us go forward, no matter what the subtle colors of your banner, so long as your companies march ever along the road that leads to the ultimate republic...I am but a poor drummer boy, but take me with you.[26]

And she exulted (with reservations!):

Republic, dawn of justice and equality, divine Utopia, sun of a future — chimerical perhaps — hail![27]

How far she had travelled may be seen by comparing her with Balzac, who at the very moment that the "Procès monstre" was taking place, was in Vienna, in the company of Madame Hanska, paying court to Prince Metternich, along with the latter's masculine and feminine entourage, and articulately professing himself a "royaliste enragé" with such fervor that he even astonished Princess Mélanie de Metternich![28]

George Sand now proceeded to revise *Lélia*. The new version bristles with improbabilities, not the least being the remarkable conversions of her characters. Trenmor becomes a Carbonari leader. Lélia herself retires to a convent, and eventually her radical ideas of Christianity and the Church bring about her downfall. She dies in the end a kind of Promethean figure, grief-stricken at the continuing woes of mankind. Her alter-ego, Pulchérie rises from her courtesan's bed in which a young spoiled bon-vivant is still sleeping, to apostrophize the world on the subject of class differences, on misery, on poverty — and finally achieves a crashing fortissimo in a revolutionary exhortation to the wretched of the earth:

And you, vassal, victim, wearing rags — slave, worker, look at him — look at me, pale, dishevelled, desolate — look closely at both of us ... A young man, rich and handsome, who pays the price of love of a woman, and a lost woman, who contemns him and his money! These are beings you serve, you fear, you respect ... Gather up your tools, these heavy chains of your prisonhouse, and strike, crush these parasites who eat your bread, usurp your place in the sun! Kill that man sleeping there, cradled in his egoism. Kill that woman too who weeps, and cannot escape from vice![29]

Into her novels and stories she now shapes her new Utopianism, a composite of Pierre Leroux's mystical socialism, Michel de Bourge's radical republicanism, portions of Saint-Simonian doctrine — to create a kind of social theodicy in which God, Christianity, and the religion of humanity find a place. Though she might be in favor of theories advocating a more equitable distribution of the world's goods, she bridles at any suggestion that would annul the rights of private property. In her treatment of the woman question, her novels now are more concerned with the nefarious impact of class-distinctions on love and marriage, and the attempt of one or another member of the upper class or lower classes to break through the barriers. Now proponents of justice and equality become more outspoken and articulate, and frequently they are drawn from the lower sectors of society. Again and again, they are women.

In proportion as her own consciousness of the various social and political problems expanded to embrace a wider range, she attempted to project that widening on to the characters in her books, transport the process of "education" into the lives other than hers. Her range of characters grew. She read Louis Blanc's celebrated *L'Organisation du travail*, which was published in 1839, and which advocated the establishment of "social workshops" on a cooperative basis. She was making herself more aware of social movements among workers. Her interests embraced the craft of the artisan, the workers on farms, the peasant. She became fascinated with the Compagnonnage, the association of wandering artisans and craftsmen — an anticipation of the later more formal trade-unions.

Thus, in the novel *Mauprat*, a descendant of a dissolute aristocratic family is "educated" to become a good human being through the love of an idealistic woman, and through the ideas of a Rousseauistic rustic philosopher who, though uneducated, speaks a natural wisdom and humanity. This simple bearer of the Truth, symbolically named Patience, brings the gospel of a future brotherhood to both Bernard Mauprat and his beloved, Edmée.

The people are worth more than the nobility, because the nobility crush them, and because they suffer. But they will not suffer always — perhaps. The time may come — you may as well know it: ... The poor will have suffered enough: They will turn upon the rich, chateaux will fall, and estates will be divided. I shall not live to see this, but you will. There will be ten cottages in place of this park, and ten families will live upon its revenue. There will no longer be valets, or masters, or peasants, or seigneurs. There will be noblemen who will make a great outcry, and will yield only to force ... There will be others who will yield generously ... The wicked will be swept away by the wind of the Lord.[30]

The novel had a great impact throughout Europe. To take only one instance, the German radical poet and novelist, Georg Weerth, ecords the way in which the book affected the heroine of one of his stories, written in the 1840's.

The book that Bertha was reading, a large, beautiful edition of George Sand's powerful novel *Mauprat,* about which we can only think with a thrill of exhilaration, and recall it with the feeling as if we were hearing the distant rustle of the Varenne woods ... The strange content of this story, the truly poetic fervor and grand artistic power with which the great Frenchwoman knows how to endow everything she touches, brought the heart of this vivid, easily moved girl to a stage of the most feverish excitement.[31]

When she turns to the artisan class — as in *Le Compagnon du Tour de France*, she selects a master carpenter to speak for himself and for her. In the figure of Pierre Huguenin, son of a master carpenter, she depicts a person of rare distinction — a man who is proud of his calling, harbors a sterling loyalty to his fellow-craftsmen of the Compagnonnage, and has a dedicated sense of class. He is in love with and beloved by the granddaughter of the Marquis de Villepreux, a Carbonaro, who merely pays lip-service to liberal principles. There is pride and dignity in the way he unmasks the hypocritical pretensions of the Marquis, "a great seigneur" — so Pierre reflects — rich and powerful, grown up and old amid social struggles, spanning the republic and the courts, and yet not having "one fixed belief, one victorious sentiment, one efficacious desire, not even one generous hope!" There is pride and dignity as well as courage in the way Yseult de Villepreux avows her love for Pierre to her father:

You have told me a thousand times that you have enough confidence in my judgment and my self-respect to allow me to make my own choice of a husband. When a number of marriages of interest and ambition were proposed to me, you seconded my refusal, and you said you preferred to see me married to a decent working-man than to one of those insolent and base nobles who slandered your political character and abased themselves before your money ... Here is the man I would take for my husband, if you will bless and ratify my choice.[32]

In *Mauprat*, the rustic Patience had, at the beginning of the narrative, been affronted by the still arrogant Bernard Mauprat, and his talk of "canaille" — the "rabble."

"Canaille!" (he retorts) ... Who talks of canaille here? I myself belong to the canaille. It is my life, and I shall know how to make it respected.[33]

So, too, Pierre associates himself with the "rabble."

Remove their stains, repair their evil, and you will see that vile horde has come from the bowels of the Lord just as you have ... There are not two sorts of people, but only one. Those who work in your houses, smiling, quiet, well-dressed are the same as those raging at your doors, incensed, sullen and covered with rags ... No, no. These miserable ones are not of an inferior station to mine, they are my brothers, and their wretchedness makes me blush for my comforts ... So long as there are human beings covered with the leprosy of want, I say that you have achieved nothing with your conspiracies, your bourgeois charters, and a change of cockade.[34]

Pierre, in the author's words, "would merely have to say one word, swear one oath, and all these lands, this chateau, and this beautiful park ... would be his." But he persists in being loyal to his craft and class, and rejects the alluring offer.

Such material proved too hot for Buloz to print in his *Revue des Deux Mondes*, and George Sand had to turn elsewhere to effect publication of the book. She refused to alter the text. When it finally appeared in December 1840, it aroused a furor. But furors were no new things in her life ...

We now go back to the year 1836, and to two letters.

George Sand to Heinrich Heine, Paris, December 13, 1836. Dear Cousin (this was Sand's way of addressing the poet): If you can spare this evening from nine to midnight, come, and you will find us at Chopin's ... There will be a small gathering, very intimate and very well arranged. Be of our company if you love us. Yours G.[35]

Frédéric Chopin to Joseph Brzowski, Paris, December 13, 1836.

I am having a few friends here today, among them Mme Sand. Moreover Liszt is to play and Nourrit will sing.[36]

It must have been a jolly evening. This was probably the second time that George Sand and Chopin were meeting. The company was no doubt exhilarating. Two of the century's most eminent pianists and composers, an outstanding tenor, a great German poet, and France's most controversial novelist. There was of course music, and conversation, no doubt peppered by the presence of a number of patriotic Poles. There was also Madame d'Agoult, the beloved of Franz Liszt, a very remarkable woman, also a writer.

For, it must be remembered, that if George Sand was the preeminent advocate of women's rights, there were other women in France, less distinguished perhaps in the arts, but no less militant and active in defense of women's as well as popular rights, and national causes. Such was the Princess Cristina Belgiojoso-Trivulzio, scion of a militantly political family, whose members included Italian liberals and associates of secret societies in Italy. She was herself an Italian patriot, and in 1848 participated in the Italian movement of liberation. In Paris, her salon was frequented by Heine, Bellini, Rossini, Liszt and other celebrities. She was a historian of the House of Savoy. During the Revolutions of 1848 she exhibited extraordinary moral and physical courage.[37]

As was the case with George Sand, the involvement of the Countess Marie d'Agoult with Franz Liszt has tended to minimize in the eyes of the public her stature as writer, thinker, and historian. She was a descendant of the notable Frankfurt banking family of the Bethmanns; she was the daughter of the Comte de Flavigny, and the wife of the Comte d'Agoult — a person lapped in the opulence of an aristocratic environment. She combined the culture of two nations, France and Germany (she had seen Goethe when she was a child) and she was a person of wide education. She was one of the first to introduce the work of Emerson into France, and a passionate lover of music. Her political education kept pace with her interests in letters and art. Under the pseudonym of "Daniel Stern" (the masculine name would make her work more acceptable!) she published a number of political articles, pamphlets, essays and books. Her crowning achievement was an outstanding history of the Revolution of 1848 — one of the very best of contemporary treatments of the subject.

She was married — in accordance with the dictates of family and caste — to a man she did not love, who was twenty years older than herself, and who shared few of her interests.

When that musical meteor — Franz Liszt — streaked across
the European horizon and dazzled the world both as person and
musician — she fell in love with him. She defied convention, class
and family, and since divorce was unobtainable, she chose to follow
her impulses, and left her husband and her children. Public opinion
was particularly outraged in that she chose to unite herself with a
person of a lower rank, even though one of the most exceptional
men of the times. What might have been forgiven among equals,
was unforgivable here. Liszt himself had been rejected as a suitor of
an aristocratic French young woman he loved, because he was a
mere "pianist." A similar fate had befallen Frédéric Chopin in the
case of a Polish aristocratic family. In such salons they were
"entertainers."[38]

Frédéric Chopin was some six years younger than George Sand,
and he had come to Paris in 1831. He had left Poland just before the
outbreak of the uprising against Russia the year before. Little did he
suspect that he was never to return there. He was a prodigy as
virtuoso and composer; he ravished Vienna when he performed
there, and in Paris too he won adulation. The great house of
Rothschild opened its doors to him, paid him generously for
teaching piano to members of the family, and through its prestige
assured him a wide clientele in other high-placed households. He
had already before his arrival in Paris composed two concerti, and
numerous shorter pieces, one of which had elicited from Schumann
the celebrated *accolade,* "Hats off, gentlemen — a genius!"

He was slight, fragile as a reed, intense, and stormy, and already
afflicted with a pulmonary ailment, a family failing. The story goes
that at first Chopin did not take to George Sand. The child-like
genius — later her "little child" — appealed to her — she could be
mother, lover, and mistress. By the spring of 1837 she was inviting
him, Liszt and Madame d'Agoult down to Nohant. She was sure that
in time she would cure Chopin of the heart-ache of a failed
engagement to a Polish girl, because of parental opposition. He was

sickly, and she would tend him. He was a genius, and she would foster him. He was a Romantic in love and inclined to idealize it, and to shy away from its physical aspect. She would amend that too. Little did she suspect at the beginning of their relation that a good portion of it would consist in nursing a sick patient. There were to be storms, ecstasies, contests, quarrels. The fact that one of them had two children who had been growing up in an unconventional household did not help the matter.

One is sometimes likely to forget — when passing judgment on one or the other member of the alliance — that whether at Nohant, or in Paris, or even in Mallorca (where he was constantly unwell), Chopin composed some of his most inspired works, and George Sand kept adhering to her own rigorous schedule of work and producing regularly. Chopin was nerve-wracked and constantly agonized by fear of death.

But there were the great hours of joy and love. And good company. What exhilaration when guests came down to Nohant — always generously open to them! Liszt, and Madame d'Agoult, and writers, and thinkers, and artists — what good talk and controversy, improvised plays put on, puppet theatre, and what not! But above all — music! Now Liszt is at the piano:

From that window, Sand wrote, float sounds which the whole world would give its soul to hear. And there are none to be jealous of them, except the nightingales. What an artist! Sublime when great matters are toward, and ever superior even in the trivial. When Franz plays the piano, the burden is lifted from my heart. All my agonies turn to poetry ... Above all, he sets the chord of generosity vibrating. He touches, too, the note of anger, so that it sounds almost in unison with the beat of fever in my blood. But never the note of hatred.[39]

There is song too — when the superb soprano Pauline Viardot comes down with her writer husband Louis. She, too, is many-sided, for she composes and writes. She is a superlative performer, but particularly enchanting in her Spanish songs. Pauline is the sister of an even greater celebrity, María Malibran. Pauline will be the heroine of George Sand's novels, particularly *Consuelo;* and the life-long beloved of Ivan Turgenev...

At other times, it is Chopin who is playing.

He is at the piano (it is George Sand writing), and does not notice that people are listening to him. He improvises, as if at random... Our eyes are gradually filled with soft hues which correspond to the sweet modulations captured by our sense of hearing... We dream of a summer night, we expect the nightingale. A sublime song rises up...[40]

When George Sand and Frédéric Chopin broke up in 1847, France herself was moving toward a very great storm. When the Revolution came in the following year, she was not one to stand aloof...

3

STENDHAL — JOURNEY'S END: "LA CHARTREUSE DE PARME"

> La logique de la passion est pressante.
> The logic of passion is insistent.
> — Stendhal —

I am standing this morning, October 16th, 1832, by San Pietro in Montorio on the Janiculum Hill in Rome, in magnificent sunshine. A few small white clouds, borne on a barely perceptible sirocco wind, were floating above Monte Albano, a delicious warmth filled the air and I was happy to be alive ... The whole of ancient and modern Rome from the ancient Appian Way with its ruined tombs and acqueducts to the magnificent garden of the Pincio built by the French, lies spread before me. There is no place like this in the world, I mused, and against my will, ancient Rome prevailed over modern Rome ... On Monte Albano, to the left of the convent, I could see the fields of Hannibal. What a magnificent view! ... Ah! in three months I shall be fifty; can that really be so? 1783, '93, 1803 — I'm reckoning on my fingers — and 1833 makes fifty. Is it really possible? ... After all, I said to myself, I haven't spent my life too badly ...spent it? Oh, that's to say, chance has not inflicted too many misfortunes on me, for have I, in fact, had any control at all over my life? ...[1]

The consul to Civita Vecchia was tired — tired of his official duties, and a humdrum life; yes, even tired of Rome and Italy, and longing to return to Paris and spend the rest of his life in some garret — so he thought — with time and security to complete the many projects he had in mind. He had left Paris in 1830, when the July government finally appointed him consul to Trieste. Here he had a brief stay, for Metternich vetoed the choice. The Austrian police had not forgotten Stendhal's previous record of liberalism, nor the fact that underneath that pseudonym was concealed a "M. Henri

Beyle." So, the following year he was transferred to Civita Vecchia, the port of entry to the Papal States, about forty miles outside of Rome. He was fated to fill this post almost to the end of his life.

The quotidian duties of consulship bored him to death, as did life in Civita Vecchia; but he fulfilled his responsibilities conscientiously, as his innumerable reports to his French superiors testify. He was aware that he was living on the government of France, the "Budget," as he called it, but it was better than starving, and he absented himself frequently enough in order to find spare felicities in travel. But living on the good graces of the state also made for an ambiguous literary existence. He was a voluntary prisoner, subjected to self-censorship; and that made him something of a Doppelgänger — an author of public writings, and also a writer of secret, private ones; the former destined for proximate publication, the latter — he hoped — for the eyes of posterity. It is out of that trove of secret "confessions," intermittently recovered and published after his death, that we obtain complementary insights into the man, half-concealed in his novels and other works.

When he was away from Paris, he felt he was living on "the fringes of barbarism." Paris was an "open window on life." With what reluctance he would drag himself back to Civita Vecchia! On one of these journeys down the Rhone river, in December 1833, he met Alfred de Musset and George Sand, then off to Italy. Stendhal admired Musset, and loved his poetry, but he did not take to George Sand, and disliked her person. She, on her part, was none too well disposed toward him. Of this meeting, Musset has left us a delicious memento in the form of some humorous drawings.

No matter what his mood, Stendhal's pen never rested. He was at work on his autobiographies, such as *Souvenirs d'égotisme,* and the even more remarkable *Vie d'Henri Brulard,* in addition to a very long novel — never to be completed — later known as *Lucien Leuwen.* He was reading old Italian chronicles, which he would refashion into his own *Chroniques italiennes.* He was also proposing marriage, and being rejected. And, worst of all, he was beginning to feel his age. His health was giving way. He would have to return to Paris...

He obtained a leave, and in May 1836 he was there again — and in his own vital element.

In 1837 he moved to the rue Caumartin, No. 8, and it was here that he accomplished that miracle of authorship — *La Chartreuse de Parme* — dictated or written down by himself in fifty-two days between November 4 and December 26, 1838. In his own peculiar English he celebrated the completion of the novel:

The Chart made 4 november 1838-26 décembre. The 3 septembre 1838 I had the idea of the Char. I begined after a tour of Brittany, I suppose, or to the Havre. I begined the 4 nov. till 26 Xbre. The 26 dec. I send the 6 énormes cahiers to Kol [his friend, Colomb] for les faire voir to the bookseller...[2]

He sold the book to the publisher Ambroise Dupont for 2.500 francs, after being forced to cut it down at the latter's insistence. It appeared on the bookstalls April 6, 1839. On June 24, 1839 he set off again for Civita Vecchia.

His love affair with the Italy of his own day had been long over. Gone were the transports of the Milan days, suffused with Napoleonic splendor; gone the glamor that had persisted thereafter for a long while. To compensate for the lost dream, Stendhal immersed himself in the Italian past, the Italy of the *condottieri,* the Italy of passion, violence, heroism, even criminal daring: the era of the Cenci, of Vittoria Accoramboni — the land of crime, vice, even incest, of great chances and risks — the Italy that had attracted the Elizabethan and Jacobean playwrights — the Italy that was to become in the nineteenth century a subject of a new mythology, recreated by Jakob Burckhardt, Nietzsche, John Addington Symonds, and Walter Pater. For Stendhal the Italy of the fifteenth and sixteenth century served as a vivid contrast to the Italian present, sunk into an apathy in which feeling, daring, action had evaporated.

He discovered a scandalous Renaissance chronicle of the house of Farnese, *Origine della grandezza della famiglia Farnese,* and transplanted it into the post-Napoleonic era. Rome and Naples were transported into the small duchy of Parma and the environs of Lake Como. Autobiographical elements were to be woven into the narrative he now projected — *La Chartreuse de Parme.*

Was it some fierce irony that led Stendhal to choose the tiny duchy of Parma, then ruled by an epigonal figment of heroism — the widow of Napoleon Bonaparte, whose son was kept as a perpetual hostage in Vienna — and place at its head a reigning prince who modeled himself on Louis XIV?

Surely this was not to be merely a commentary on Parma, no more or less corrupt than the other duchies and kingdoms of Italy! This was an epic of "unheroism," a commentary on the world at large, with its complex politics and policies; a commentary on morality, on heroism, on intrigue, on hypocrisy — indeed, a study of a disintegrating society!

There was conscious design in Stendhal's mind and art as he opens his novel with the incomparable depiction of Waterloo, and our "unheroic" hero's presence and participation in that battle. Fabrizio del Dongo's pathetic, sometimes comic, often touching meandering on the great battlefield is in fact an obituary on what Stendhal conceived the ultimate defeat of European heroism. The overthrow of Napoleon, the rout of the French armies, the sense of betrayal — ring down the curtain on a great drama. When it rises again, and Fabrizio returns to Italy, it is all as if he had dreamt a bad dream. Had he really fought at Waterloo? Had he really caught a glimpse of Napoleon? Was this the war he had been dreaming of? The Napoleonic vision still haunts him, and his eyes are still glazed as he comes back to himself and to his country — and a world so utterly removed from his heroic dream — a world, as Stendhal sees it, filled with "âmes de boue," — "souls of mud."

As a suspected Bonapartist, Fabrizio is naturally in constant danger of arrest and worse at the hands of the Austrian puppets who are now in control of the Italian states, among whom are to be found his own father, the Marchese del Dongo, and Fabrizio's brother, Ascanio. On his side, Fabrizio has the support of his unhappy mother, and of his aunt, the widowed contessa Gina Pietranera, whose late husband had also been a "liberal." Gina, who has fallen in love with her nephew, works to establish his career in Parma, and with the aid of her lover, Count Mosca, eventually succeeds in having him made Archbishop.

The war that is now being carried on in and with the Court of Parma is one of intrigue, counter-intrigue, hypocrisy and double-dealing, in which true passion labors to counter the sordidness and perfidy that rule this little world. But even passion would have been helpless, did it not employ (alas!) more worldly weapons...

"Be a Lion or a Fox" — such is the battle-cry. Force and Guile! This is a story of "deromantization" of heroism, a handbook of Machiavellianism. Fabrizio is to be "educated" in the ways of life. Already on the battlefield he had encountered some preliminaries of this "education," when he finds himself robbed of his horse by French soldiers, having dreamt of military comradeship and loyalty in the spirit of the romances of Tasso and Ariosto! Sadly he admitted to himself, "So war was no longer that noble and common transport of souls dedicated to glory that he had imagined to himself from Napoleon's proclamations!" ... "I shall never be a hero," he confesses.

The "education" is now forcefully and rapidly advanced by his experiences in Parma. That duchy is ruled by an absolutist and unscrupulous prince, Ernesto IV, who fancies himself another Louis XIV. Actually, as well as symbolically, all lives within that small country revolve around the Court. Parma is the bastion of absolutism. It has its Bastille — the prison-fortress, the graveyard of liberals. It is the counterpart of the terrifying Spielberg in Austrian Bohemia, of the Peter and Paul Fortress of Saint-Petersburg, and of Spandau in Prussia.

Though he has in fact executed and imprisoned a number of "liberals," the reigning Prince Ernesto lives in constant dread of them, and it is this phobia that is utilized as a most useful instrument of the contending parties racing for place and influence at court. And around him the various forces and counter-forces weave their network of intrigue and conspiracy in which a-morality (if you wish) or immorality is used to counter an even baser a-morality, the difference being that the protagonists bring a higher degree of passion in their attempts to defeat the utter baseness of their opponents.

Stendhal's Parma is modelled on the state of affairs of the neighboring duchy of Modena, then ruled over by Francisco IV, grandson of Maria Theresa of Austria, a true archetype of the fictive Ernesto IV of Parma, a tyrant paramount, enemy of any "liberal" ideas and persons, principally of the Carbonari.

The duchy of Parma then can stand for any number of similar states, even some close to home, and its court can epitomize numerous other courts. Here, the court is a jungle, where the various animals strive for ascendancy and power. Some of these animals war with their sharp fangs; others with their cunning. In such a warfare there can be no question of absolute "innocence" — or let us put it more bluntly — absolute "integrity." It is warfare where there is no quarter given or expected, and woe to hm who is not armed to the teeth! Shrewdness, wit, guile, even deception — must war against brutal violence and unscrupulous chicanery. The miasmatic atmosphere leaves no one untouched. Noble natures must battle with ignoble means. Who shall escape the snares of duplicity when every life is threatened?

We have spoken of the "education" of Fabrizio del Dongo, our young "hero." He is one of the "innocent" who is here to learn the savage contrast between a romantic "Schwärmerei" — wild fantasy — and a world of horridly cold fact. He is fortunate in having two invaluable teachers, his beautiful, high-minded, impulsive, and unpredictable aunt, the widowed Gina Pietranera; and the equally high-minded, almost child-like, but wise Count Mosca, minister of State. These are among the "naturals" — children of Nature, of instinct, of passion, of action. Mosca is in love with Gina, but being married and separated from his wife, he cannot marry her. Gina, on her part, is in love with her nephew, Fabrizio, but she is fond and respectful of Count Mosca, and not averse to making plans for their union. He offers a practical solution: Gina is to marry the elderly, very wealthy Duca Sanseverina-Taxis, who is very desirous of obtaining the valuable courtier's ribbon of honor and a high official position. Once married, he will be appointed to some removed place, and will remain the nominal husband of Gina. She will be a Duchess, and near the Court alongside of Mosca. Her husband will be an ambassador somewhere.

But do you know that what you are proposing is highly immoral, the Countess said.

No more immoral than everything that is done in our court and a score of others. Absolute power has this advantage that it sanctifies everything in the eyes of the people. And what can be deemed absurd which nobody notices? Our policy in the next twenty years will consist in feeling fear of the Jacobins — and what a fear! Every year we shall fancy ourselves on the eve of 1793. You will hear, I hope, the speeches I make on this subject at my receptions! It'll be a fine show! Anything that will in the slightest diminish that fear will be supremely moral in the eyes of the nobles and the bigots. Now in Parma everyone who is not a noble or a bigot is in prison, or is preparing to go there...[3]

This is actual *Realpolitik!* No wonder Balzac saw the image of Metternich in the noble Count Mosca.

The Countess Gina is eager to advance the interest and the career of her beloved nephew, and there is no better road to success than the Church. So he is sent off to Naples to study theology, but not before he is presented with some valuable counsel as to his behavior at the Seminary:

Believe or not the things they teach you, but never raise any objection. Imagine that you are being taught the rules of the game of whist. Would you raise any objections to the rules of whist? I have told the count that you are a believer, and he was happy to hear it. It is useful both in this world and in the next . . . Believe blindly everything that they tell you at the Academy. Bear in mind that there are people who will make a careful note of your slightest objections . . .[4]

Gina does as Mosca proposed, and becomes the Duchess Sansaverina. Fabrizio is no less apt a pupil. He is on his way to becoming — what? Possibly and in time an archbishop? Unfortunately, he is also subject to passions, and having involved himself in a petty amour with an insignificant roving actress, he kills her jealous lover in self-defense and is forced to flee. He escapes to Bologna, where he enters a church in order to offer thanks to the Lord for his good fortune, and to confess his sins. But he too is practicing the morality of expedience:

Fabrizio asked pardon of God for many things, but, strangely enough it did not enter his mind to number among the sins the plan of becoming Archbishop, solely because Count Mosca was Prime Minister, and considered that office and the social status it conferred most fitting for the nephew of the Duchess.[5]

Apparently, in his catalogue of sins Simony was not included.

He cannot of course be aware that Prince Ernesto IV has his eyes on Duchess Gina, and knowing of Gina's affection for Fabrizio, sees in the case a wonderful opportunity of attaining his objective. Fabrizio will be brought to justice and the Duchess to her knees. Fabrizio is lured into a trap, arrested, and confined in the horrible Parma fortress. Here, from his window, he sees Clélia, daughter of the prison's governor, falls in love with her, exchanges messages, and declares himself. At the same time, there are other plots afoot — one of them on the part of the Duchess's enemies — to poison Fabrizio. The plot is foiled, and Fabrizio is enabled to escape. In the final examplars of spiritual casuistry we have no one else than the innocent Clélia herself. Conscience-stricken that she had violated her filial duties in having aided in Fabrizio's escape, she vows never to see him again, and agrees to marry the wealthy Marchese Crescenzi at her father's behest. But her love for Fabrizio persists. In time he becomes a celebrated preacher. Clélia's vow stands in the way of love's fulfilment, but passions have their own logic, as Stendhal insisted, and love finds a way out of the dilemma. She manages not to "see" him — for she meets him in the dark. Touchingly she admits him to a nocturnal rendez-vous. "Entre ici âme de coeur," she says . . .

"We are surrounded by tragic events," Count Mosca once said to Duchess Sanseverina in commenting on what might have been the outcome of one of Fabrizio's escapades. With greater relevance he might have been referring to the "tragedy" that permeates Parma, is of a much subtler kind. It is one that involves characters of dignity, even nobility, sometimes approaching grandeur, in actions which cannot but taint them. What saves them — Gina Sanseverina and Count Mosca — from utter improbity is that their actions, however ambiguous, are directed toward the higher realization of themselves — in love — and are the consequences of the capacity for experiencing true "passion." For it is this capacity for "passion" — even when it turns criminal — that still saves Italy for Stendhal. Poor as is the age of which he is writing, poor in true feelings and impulses, Italians are still — for Stendhal — a people that act on instinct, on rage. Not so the French, for whom everything is turned into a game. In Italy he still finds remnants of a true "heroism" — which everywhere else had disappeared after 1815. That is why he went back to the Renaissance of Italy, where "energy" and "passion" were still invested with their native grandeur, even in criminality.

But for all the irony, all the ambiguity and venial duplicities, Stendhal still succeeds in finding true heroic core in at least one peripheral character, the republican and agitator, Ferrante Palla, a remnant of Renaissance "virtù" — an outlaw in Parma, in hiding, with a sentence of death hanging over him. But even here, Stendhal's ambivalence cannot forbear giving him the semblance of an erratic enthusiast, not always in full control of his reason, the character of an idealistic dreamer. He is doomed to ultimate disenchantment, like Stendhal himself, doomed to discover that there are no republicans with whom to make a republic. He is "Italy's greatest poet," and also a "Tribune of the people" — who elicits from the Duchess Gina the appelation of "sublime."

That such uncompromising heroism is attributed to a failed republican is of itself a mark of Stendhal's own despair — a despair of Italy, a despair of the world, a despair that neither his superb irony, mockery, even comedy can fully conceal. Stendhal had seen the Carbonari movement brought to nought. Silvio Pellico's *Le mie prigioni* was ever in his mind as he was describing the prison-fortress of Parma. He had witnessed the failure of the uprisings in Bologna and Modena in the 1830's, failures, he believed, due to "mauvaise direction." A fragment of a novel, *Une Position sociale,* expresses the depth of his disillusionment with Italy and the Italians. He is describing the former Carbonaro, Prince Savelli:

Today, he is a ruined prince, and the times and his disappointed bones had made him a violent enemy of France, whom he could not forgive for not presenting Italy with the gift of liberty.

To which, Stendhal's *alter ego,* Roizand, replies:

But my dear friend, have you ever seen any of your wealthy friends giving a million to one of his poor friends? Undoubtedly, it would be nice if one did make such presents, but unfortunately it is not as yet customary. When one doesn't possess a sou, and one wants a million francs, one must take the trouble to earn it. There is not a word in our French Charter that did not cost us a thousand corpses. It's somewhat expensive, I must admit, but one can take it or leave it...[6]

Among other misconceptions, a legend widely disseminated claims that Stendhal was in reality non-political or a-political. This is only in part due to Stendhal's own ambiguities, or dualisms, for what he was saying publicly did not always tally with what he said privately or entered into his private diaries. He was a keen observer of events in England as well as in France. He abhorred Louis-Philippe and his government, and even hailed the attempt on the life of the king on the part of Fieschi. (He had a romantic respect for assassins!) He was a keen observer of the changing temper of the working-class population of England and France in the 1830's. In his *Mémoires d'un Touriste* he commented on the prevailing wretched working conditions in Lyon. In a note, not published until 1932, he remarked:

See what a succession of beautiful dramas has taken place within a few years! Fieschi, the rue Transnonain, the two great events of Lyon, so different from each other: the first revolt of 1831 had nothing political about it; the second, on the other hand, is almost solely the product of secret societies and republican plotting. When the workers wrote on their banners, Either live and work, or die fighting, they won four francs a day, and there was plenty of work for them.[7]

It is perhaps a mark of Stendhal's difficulties that in *La Chartreuse de Parme* one gets little sense of any population existing outside the court, the prison, or the intrigants. When the populace does make its appearance as a mass, in an uprising against the government, it is crushed by Count Mosca, who makes short shrift of the insurgents. It is also a significant fact that only a few years before Stendhal sat down to compose *La Chartreuse*, the two major leaders of the Italian Risorgimento had already made their appearance on the stage of history — Giuseppe Mazzini and Giuseppe Garibaldi, and Stendhal might have had their early disastrous exploits in mind — the failed liberation of Savoy and the escape of Garibaldi — under sentence of death — to South America.

Among the general reading public the publication of *La Chartreuse de Parme* caused no appreciable stir. Thus far he had had small acclaim for his writings. But there was one tribute he received that almost compensated for the many years of neglect. In the September 25, 1840 issue of the *Revue Parisienne* there appeared a long article entitled "Études sur M. Beyle" from the pen of Honoré de Balzac — chiefly devoted to the *Chartreuse.* Stendhal received it the following October. He had great cause for rejoicing. For here the "prince of French novelists," then at the height of his career, set out to do justice to one of his great fellow-writers.

Balzac hailed Stendhal as one of the "most distinguished masters of the literature of ideas," and the *Chartreuse de Parme* as an "extraordinary work." This is a book, he said, "where the sublime leaps from chapter to chapter. [Stendhal] has written a modern *Prince,* the novel that Machiavelli might have written, if he had been banished from Italy in the nineteenth century." "One is aware of perfection in everything."[8]

But there were also serious reservations. The conclusion of the book is hasty — which is only too true. But the most feeble element of the work, Balzac contended, was Stendhal's style. It was lacking in "images" — and in revising this work, the author would be well advised to pay closer attention to the writings of Chateaubriand and de Maistre. But Balzac recalled with approval that the author, once a liberal, now showed an attachment to monarchy, which, though treated with humor, displays a Frenchman's love.

Stendhal was deeply moved by the review. The letter in which he acknowledged Balzac's essay no longer exists, but there are three drafts extant of such a reply. The general sense of these suggests that Stendhal was even more appreciative of the criticism than of the praise. "You have felt an exaggerated pity for an orphan abandoned in the street," he wrote. "I imagined I would not be read before 1880."[9]

But while he agrees that some of the criticism of the contents is valid, Stendhal writes that he cannot accept Balzac's idea of a right style. For himself he can only say that he knew one rule alone — "A style can never be too clear or too simple." The alleged beautiful style of Chateaubriand seemed to him ridiculous as early as 1802, and utterly "false." Far from being careless, his own concern has been for precision, for he often reflected for a quarter of an hour before setting an adjective before its noun. He had an "amour exagéré pour la logique." "If I am not clear, my whole world goes to pieces."

Still, Stendhal set about revising the *Chartreuse* in accordance with some of Balzac's more acceptable suggestions, but he never completed the task. The reader of today is certainly conscious that the plot structure of the novel leaves something to be desired, that the conclusion — Clélia's death and Fabrizio's retirement to the Carthusian monastery (which explains the title of the book) — is unnecessarily hastened. So far as style is concerned, one must guard against taking Stendhal's own words too literally, when he states to Balzac that in composing the novel, and in order to achieve the right "tone," he would read two or three pages of the Code Civile, in order to achieve "naturalness." "I do not want to fascinate the soul of the reader by any factitious means..."[10]

He avoided deliberately the over-ripe rhetoric of such Romantics as Chateaubriand and Victor Hugo (sometimes visible in the pages of Balzac himself); he deliberately avoided long descriptive passages — whether of landscape or characters. Rhetoric is reduced to a minimum. There are no passionate love-scenes. The manipulation of the verb — for example — is highly conscious to hasten or delay action. With a minimum of distraction we are enabled to enter into the heart and thought-processes of the characters by means of what was later to be called the "interior monologue."

His public conscience — since he was living on the "Budget" — that is the government of Louis-Philippe — dictated that he be thought of as in favor of a constitutional monarchy rather than a republic. But for some years now, as early as 1834, he had been planning another novel of "education" — the making of a young conscience — set in France of his own day, the France of the July Monarchy. It was destined to remain unfinished. Originally titled *L'Orange de Malte,* it underwent various titular changes, finally emerging, posthumously, as a two-part incomplete *Lucien Leuwen*. It was a difficult (not to say, dangerous) thing he had undertaken, to write about contemporary France; time and again he attempted to return to it, only to leave off.

How closely the book touched on the times may be gathered from its very beginning, where Lucien Leuwen, son of a very wealthy and politically powerful banker, gets himself expelled from the École Polytechnique in June 1832 for his republican convictions, and thus commences his "education." It is an education both of consciousness and of the conscience (the French "conscience" stands for both). The dilemmas of conscience are persistent elements in the history of humanity. For conscience is consciousness in action, forced to make moral choices and act or not act upon them. *La Chartreuse de Parme* was the tragic comedy of conscience at war with an immoral world, but engaged in a battle that dissipated its potential heroism.

For a time Lucien proceeds in the manner of a Julien Sorel or a Fabrizio del Dongo. That is to say, having joined the Lancers Regiment at Nancy, he there comes under the influence of various political, social and religious forces at work in that provincial city. There are the republicans — few, and socially ostracized; and, at the other pole — the powerful, die-hard legitimists, divided in their loyalties between adherence to Charles X or Henri V, in either case implacable foes of the Juste-Milieu and Louis-Philippe. To advance himself socially and in love, Lucien undergoes a rigorous training in hypocrisy. As in the case of others of Stendhal's "heroes," the preliminaries of his great love affair with Mme de Chasteller are accompanied by the usual gaucheries and contretemps — this time a fall from his horse as he is showing off before her window. Such symbolic sexual timidity or backwardness is present throughout Stendhal's published and unpublished works up to this time. Mme de Chasteller is a fervent Carlist, and her relationship to Lucien arouses consternation in the camp of the Ultras, and they set about undoing it. They succeed.

As for the martial career of our young hero — shades of Marengo and Austerlitz! He participates in an army attack upon striking mill-workers and their miserable living quarters.

The laundry hanging in the windows to dry made one shudder, so wretched, so tattered and filthy. The window-panes were tiny and dirty, and in many of the windows old paper covered with writing and oiled had replaced the glass. Everywhere a shattering picture of poverty that cramped the heart, but not hearts that hoped to win a cross by meting out saber blows in this miserable little town... For the miliary, strategic, political, etc. details of this outstanding affair, see the newspapers of that time. The regiment covered itself with glory, and the workers gave evidence of the most signal cowardice.[11]

Lucien is only too well aware that for the sake of love and rank he is allowing his goal to be corroded; and he half-heartedly struggles against his natural impulses and spontaneous decencies — in Stendhal's words, "the danger of sincerity, music, and great forests" — that is — his best human instincts. He confesses to Mme de Chasteller: "All for the sake of getting nearer to your beautiful eyes I bought a missal, I fought a duel, and I cultivated the acquaintance of Dr. Du Poirier [the most contemptible of the local intriguers]." He is clear enough about the social stratum whose sole merits are a "fanatical belief in Henri V and the nobility, and a duplicity and stupidity toward the lower orders which amounted to a veritable crime against humanity." This is a society which numbers members like M. Sanréal, whose chief glory had been achieved in arresting a wretched peasant, "one of those to be shot without knowing why, by order of the Bourbons." He observes that the "Ultras" of the provinces are even more savage than those of Paris. "And here I was about to go forth," he reflects, "to sabre down the weavers, as M. de Vassignies put it so elegantly. If the affair gets hot, the colonel will receive the Cross of the Legion of Honor, and I — qualms of conscience."

And these are the first people of the universe! Leuwen thought, as he passed through the solitary and putrid streets of Nancy, on the way home. Great God! What must it be like in the small towns of Russia, Germany, and of England! What meanness! What atrocious and cold cruelties! There too rule is in the hands of that privileged class I find here, half-numbed and check-mated by their exile from the Budget. My father is right: One must live in Paris, and only with people who lead a pleasant life. They are happy, and therefore less inclined to evil. The soul of man is like a noisome swamp, if you don't rush past it, you go under.[12]

If Lucien Leuwen expected to find in Paris a haven for his conscience, he was soon to be disabused. Having left the army, he obtains, through his father's influence, a place in the office of the Ministry. But the elder M. Leuwen is nonplussed by his son's innocence. Is his son enough of a "rogue" to be a politician? Lucien decides in the affirmative. "His duplicity spoke well for the future." Since he believes that Mme de Chasteller had been deceiving him, he will bury his feelings in political activity. At once he discovers that his superior, Minister de Vaize, is playing the stock-market on the basis of diplomatic hunches, and that M. Leuwen is his banker. "So this is a thief," Lucien reflects. His father instructs him that thievery is a normal occurrence in the life of a politician, that everybody steals. (Such too was the opinion of the Duchess Sanseverina in the *Chartreuse*.) At the behest of M. Leuwen, Madame Grandet, who longs to see her husband a minister, becomes Lucien's mistress. This is a scene worthy of the highest dramatic skill of a Molière. To cap the sum of villainies, Lucien is now entrusted with the mission of frustrating the provincial election of a thoroughly honest candidate in favor of a scoundrel preferred by the Ministry. (Stendhal had in mind the candidacy of the remarkable democrat, the Abbé Grégoire, who, by the way, won the election to the Chamber of Deputies.)

We (and Lucien) are left in no doubt as to who the true rulers of France are. M. Leuwen senior makes no bones about it. "The Minister," he says, "is there to wait for me when necessary. He has ... greater need of me than I of him. He needs my bank and fears my salon." And Minister Vaize agrees:

He is the Talleyrand of the Bourse. His epigrams are law in that world, and since the July Revolution, that world comes closer and closer to the great world of fashion, the only one that should by rights have influence. The men of money have now taken the place of the great families of the Faubourg Saint-Germain.[13]

Such being the truth — and who would doubt the Banker and the Minister? — Stendhal has left it to Lucien's plebeian assistant to speak in the name of conscience — Stendhal's as well:

When one has the misfortune, he says, of living under a government of scoundrels, and a second misfortune, even greater in my opinion, of reasoning clearly and seeing the truth, one sees at once that under a government of ours, a government of knaves, even more so than that of the Bourbons and Napoleon, for it constantly betrays its first oath, agriculture and commerce are the only truly independent pursuits ... I prefer commerce. True, it has its own sordid and frightful aspects ..., but in the long run these frightful aspects ... are better than murdering honest bourgeois in the rue Transnonain, or, that which is even worse, justifying it in the pamphlets which we hawk.[14]

Stendhal knew he was treading on dangerous ground. Many of the characters of the book had their prototypes high in state affairs. "I shall not be able to print it as long as I serve under the Budget."[15]

Had Stendhal been able to complete and round out *Lucien Leuwen,* he would probably have created one of the very greatest of French novels of the nineteenth century. As it stands, it remains a brilliant portrait of the age, etched in acid, a novel full of sharp epigrams and aperçus, a superb satire, and a judgment passed on his times.

Stendhal's health, never of the best, underwent a sudden and ominous decline. In March 1841 he suffered a serious stroke, from which he partly recovered. He obtained leave to return to Paris, and though not too well, embarked once more on his usual rounds of visits. He was completing a new novel, *Lamiel,* and contracted in

1842 with Buloz of the *Revue des Deux Mondes* for another series of Italian tales. On March 22, 1842, returning from an official dinner, while walking on the rue Neuve-des-Capucines, he suddenly collapsed. He died the following day.

He had always considered himself more Italian than French, and in accordance with his wishes, his gravestone bore the inscription,

> Arrigo Beyle, Milanese,
> Visse, amò, scrisse.

He lies buried in the Montmartre cemetery.

For the inadequate recognition he was receiving in his own day, he sought to compensate by the dubious solace of posthumous fame. He set various dates for his literary resurrection, 1880, 1900, 1935. And he was not wrong. A new generation that rose in the wake of the great mid-century advances in science, in technology, and had experienced profound social changes, rediscovered Stendhal after 1880. The literary revolutions that followed the 1840's, the triumph of naturalism in art and letters served to reenforce his reestablishment, and deepen an appreciation of his pioneering work. The publication of hitherto suppressed or even unknown material enlarged not only the body of Stendhal's important writings, but the understanding of his profound psychological insights. His irony, wit, the remorseless analysis of his own self, as well as of his imaginary characters, startled with the prefiguration of modern psychological theories and practices. Few writers had pried so deeply into the hidden motives of human actions; few have so clearly analyzed their own shortcomings, inferiorities, their failed amours, their need for compensations, their ambivalences. He "deheroized" not only his fictional "heroes," but also himself. He saw through the sickness of the times, and suffered from the dilemma of someone who could live neither in the past nor the present. He was doomed to be the great "outsider." Like Lucien Leuwen, he was asking, "Must it be my fate to pass my life between the Royalists, and egoists in love with the past, and the Republicans, generous but tiresome fools, in love with the future?" He might have even more pregnantly said he was an eighteenth century man who, leaping over the nineteenth, found himself in the twentieth.

Some years before his death, in the throes of a deep depression, he wrote to Saint-Beuve:

I believe that there is a *God*. But he is evil and malevolent. I would be greatly astonished, if, after my death, I found him; and if he let me speak, I would certainly tell him off. If he existed, and were just, I would not behave differently. I would then benefit by his existence, for he would reward me for having behaved so as to procure for myself the great pleasures.[16]

He abhorred the France of his day — and King Louis-Philippe in particular.

O reader of 1880! he wrote in his private journal. Everything I am talking about will be forgotten by that time. The generous indignation that makes my heart throb and stops me from writing will seem ridiculous. If in 1880 there is a tolerable government, the shallows and rapids, the anxieties through which France will have passed in order to attain it will be forgotten. History will write only one word by the side of...[Louis Philippe's] name: The most knavish of K[ings].[17]

But where will *Le Rouge* be in 1880? It will have vanished in outer darkness.[18]

He was wrong.

IV.

PARIS: MAGNET AND HAVEN

Heinrich Heine:
A German Apollo in Paris

Adam Mickiewicz:
Poland's Poet-Prophet

José de Espronceda:
Spain's Childe Harold

1.

PARIS — MAGNET AND HAVEN

> Paris is not only the capital of France, but of the entire civilized world, and the gathering place of intellect. Here is gathered all that is great in love and hate, feeling and thought, knowledge and capacity, fortune and misfortune, past and present. Seeing the assemblage of famous and distinguished personalities, who are gathered here, one might deem Paris the Pantheon of the living. A new art, a new religion, a new life is here being created, and joyfully the creators of a new world bustle about here. Mighty deeds are in the offing and unknown deities are about to reveal themselves...
> — Heinrich Heine —

The July Revolution of 1830 had shaken all of Europe. Once more Paris and France seemed to have become the epicenters of a renewed earthquake. The fortresses of the Old Order were about to fall. A reborn France, it appeared, was about to lead all of Europe to freedom, the France that "lived the life of other nations rather than her own." "Faisons comme les Français!" the Belgians cried, and rose up against the domination of Holland. On October 4, they declared their independence, on October 10, they convoked a National Congress, and finally, on November 22, they declared a Constitutional Monarchy.

In November the Poles rose against the Russians in Warsaw. The struggle lasted until September 1831, and roused all of Europe to spirited support. In France the republicans clamored for direct intervention, and *Le National* appealed to Frenchmen: "The Poles

571

are calling for our help... Warriors! Frenchmen of the Revolution
and of the Empire! Youth! Come to our assistance! Women of
France come to the aid of the women of Poland!"[1]

Such dreams of intervention foundered on the realism of the
new French régime, which was in no mood to undertake a
revolutionary crusade. The Polish uprising was crushed. Like
disasters struck the insurgent movements of Italy, the Carbonari in
Rome, the revolutionaries of Modena, Bologna, and the Papal States.

The German lands too experienced convulsions, though in
general Prussia and Austria remained unmoved. In Brunswick,
Hesse-Cassel, and Saxony intimidated rulers granted constitutions;
in Brunswick the reigning Duke was deposed. But here too the tides
of reaction won the final victories.

Neither did England remain immune to the continental
earthquakes. And these were instrumental in hastening the passage
of the Reform Bill of 1832...

Paris became the haven of political refugees, failed revolutionaries
and patriots. Hither they came: Spaniards, Italians, Poles, Russians,
Germans. Paris became the goal of poets, musicians, painters and
sculptors — the ever cosmopolite center of international culture.
Paris was the unforgettable city of the French Revolution, of
Napoleon, and of the "glorious" July days. Paris was the city of
books, newspapers, theatres, the city of the outdoors, of the winding
streets and alleys replete with history, the city of cafés, of
conversations, of intellectual exchange. Here the foreigner could
find his own compatriots to quarrel with, to mourn with, to debate
with; and if so inclined, to join the international company of the
Saint-Simonians in the Salle Taitbout...

Indeed, there was no city like Paris in the world.

Among those who sought the freer air of Paris, were many
Jews, whose Ghetto-disabilities were once more resurrected after
1815 in German states, and whose feelings were graphically

described by the foremost journalist of the day, Ludwig Börne, as he recounted the difference between the status of his co-religionists during the Napoleonic era and under the Restoration:

...Before the battle began, [i.e. the "War of Liberation" against Napoleon] we in Frankfurt enjoyed, as did all others in Germany, wherever French legislation prevailed, rights equal to those of our Christian brothers...But when we returned from the War, we found our fathers and brothers, whom we had left as free citizens, slaves again. And so we have remained to this very day...We were deprived not only of our rights as citizens of the state, or those of our locality, but we do not enjoy those even of humanity, which are older than those of a civil society, and which no right can annul.[2]

2.

HEINRICH HEINE
A GERMAN APOLLO IN PARIS

A German Apollo — to see his high white forehead,
pure as a marble table, shadowed with great masses
of brown hair...His blue eyes sparkled with light
and inspiration; his round full cheeks, graceful in
contour, were not of the tottering romantic lividness
so fashionable at that date...A slight pagan
embonpoint, which was expiated later on by a truly
Christian emaciation, rounded the lines of his form.
He wore neither beard, nor moustache, nor whiskers;
he did not smoke nor drink beer, and, like Goethe,
even had a horror of these things.
> — Théophile Gautier —

In the summer of 1830 Heinrich Heine, then thirty-three years old, was taking the baths in Heligoland, on the North Sea, and here he heard the news of the July Revolution in France. He needed no second appeal. He had been ill at heart and in body, and the situation in Germany was becoming more and more oppressive. Yet, he should have had much cause for rejoicing. He was already a celebrated poet, for only three years before he had published a collection of his poems, the *Buch der Lieder*, and had at once leaped into the front ranks of German poets. In addition, he had completed the third volume of his *Travel Pictures*, which, in his own words, had become "the talk of Germany."

A Revolution in France! Now surely, he thought, things would happen in Germany. Europe was on fire. The Poles had risen! The Belgians had risen! Even in his own Germany, in Aix, Cologne, and in other cities there were rumblings. But as Heine waited, the revolutionary tide seemed to die out, and Europe was once more in retreat.

574

Were his own days in Germany numbered? For he was inscribed in the black books of the authorities. Like Börne, he too was a child of the Ghetto. Not the Ghetto of Frankfurt, with its walls and its terrifying gates, but of the spiritual ghetto of Düsseldorf, where he was born on December 13, 1797, which though not so constricting, still kept the Jews outside the pale of citizenship. Even his uncle, Salomon Heine of Hamburg, one of the wealthiest inhabitants of that city, and one of the most influential, possessed no civic rights. Young Heine came of a family that could not claim the prestige of wealth. He was soon to be made aware of what it meant to be a Jew. His parents had their eyes on the Hamburg Croesus, and destined him for the law, and for a brief time Heine dabbled in business, but with little success. His own talent and bent predestined him for the more arduous life of poet and writer — a profession that was not regarded highly by a hard-headed and practical business family. His university career brought him to Bonn, where he was fortunate to meet the critic and literary historian A. W. von Schlegel; then to Göttingen, and finally to Berlin. He became Herr Doktor Heinrich Heine. University life opened his eyes to the narrow chauvinism and the prevalent anti-Semitism of the student body and their societies, the Burschenschaften, their snobbery and intellectual poverty; though among their teachers in Berlin there was no lesser a figure than the philospher Hegel. There was, however, compensation here, particularly in the intellectual salons presided over by charming and intelligent women, mostly Jewish. There was Rahel Levine, the wife of Varnhagen von Ense; Mendelssohn's daughter, Dorothea Schlegel; Henriette Herz and her husband Dr. Marcus Herz (it was in their house that Ludwig Börne had lived when he was in Berlin). In these salons Heine met the intellectual élite of Germany.

He sought a deeper identification in Berlin, and for a time found it in the nascent Jewish cultural movement, of which the distinguished Jewish scholar, Leopold Zunz, was a presiding genius.

Here he learned from his co-religionists something of the history and achievements of the Jews. In the "Society for Jewish Culture and Science" he assimilated a great deal of what he was later to embody in unforgettable poetry and prose.

In 1822 he published his first volume of poems, the *Gedichte*, in the Romantic tradition of Byron, with the themes of love, death, the grave, and the supernatural. But already the future genius became evident in such masterpieces as "The Two Grenadiers" and "Belshazzar." The *Lyrical Intermezzo*, which followed two years later, contained some of his best-known and beautiful verses. Intrinsic gold in their own right, they glow even more brightly in the innumerable settings by composers. From the first of these, "Im wunderschönen Monat Mai," to the last, "Die alten, schönen Lieder," they have been repeated, passed from mouth to mouth, sometimes in ignorance of the author's name — "Lehn deine Wang an meine Wang," "Auf Flügeln des Gesanges," "Die Lotosblume," "Ich grolle nicht" — need one go on? No other German poet attracted so many composers.

These poems of Heine were his "confessio amantis," his confessional of a hopeless love that was to gnaw at his heart for the rest of his life. But for this love for Salomon Heine's beautiful daughter, Amalie, who, like her father, had little care for the poet or his poetry; and her calculated indifference, we should not have had these anguished, bitter, tear-laden gems, born of a profound experience.

In these and succeeding poems he was inaugurating a new era in German poetry. These were in reality tiny novels, compact, perfectly and deceptively simple, chiseled, so completely catching the manner and form of the folk-song and ballad, yet, adding one element forever to be associated with the poet — a subtle sophistication, irony, with a sting of self-mockery. He was a master of the synaesthetic — the mingling of the senses of sound, taste, touch and smell, as for example:

> Ich will meine Seele tauchen,
> In den Kelch der Lilie hinein;
> Die Lilie soll klingend hauchen
> Ein Lied von der Liebsten mein...

> I will steep my soul,
> Deep in the lily's chalice,
> The lily shall in sounds exhale,
> A song of my best beloved...

Add self-mockery, irony, bitterness, and disenchantment —
and you have Heine, the modern:

> Ich hab im Traum geweinet...

> In a dream my tears were falling;
> You were borne to your burial place.
> I woke, and still the teardrops
> Were streaming down my face.

> In a dream my tears were falling;
> I dreamed you were false to me.
> I woke, and for many hours
> Kept weeping bitterly.

> In a dream my tears were falling;
> I dreamed you were true to your vow.
> I woke, and my torrent of sorrow
> Is pouring even now.[3]

He was also revolutionizing German prose style in his *Travel Pictures*. In Heine's hands the narrative became something malleable, pliant, skilfully responding to the touches of seriousness, humor, satire, poignancy, and personal reaction, alternating prose and poetry. The discursive manner and informality allow him to break through the usually staid depictions of the traditional itinerary. He moves by association, reminiscence, and best of all, autobiographical recollection. As we go from one volume of these *Travel Pictures* to the next, the canvas broadens, so that when we reach the third and last, which includes his Italian experiences, we are already on the highway of history, politics, and aesthetics. He blends lightness, even flippancy, with seriousness. Thus the delicious description of his childhood in Düsseldorf includes the historic events of the Napoleonic invasion, and the change from an old order to the new:

In those days princes were not so care-ridden as they are now. Their crowns grew firmly on their heads, and at night they pulled night-caps over them, and slept peacefully. And the people slept peacefully at their feet, and on awaking each morning they said: "Good morning, father!" And the prince replied: "Good morning, my dear children!"

But suddenly all this changed. One morning, when we awoke at Düsseldorf and were about to say, "Good morning father!," our father was gone ... I went to the door and saw the French troops marching in — that glorious, gay nation, which has marched through the world with song and triumph ...[4]

So, too, the French drummer boy becomes the occasion of a subtle translation of a simple person's action into an enlarged canvas of politics. Monsieur Le Grand, the drummer, teaches young Heine French, as well as French history, by means of his drum:

Monsieur Le Grand knew only a little broken German, only the necessary phrases, such as bread, kiss, honor — but he could make himself perfectly understood on the drum. For instance, when I did not know the meaning of *liberté*, he would drum the *Marseillaise* — and I understood him. If I did not know the meaning of *égalité*, he beat the march, *Ça ira, ça ira — les aristocrats à la lanterne!* And I understood ... Once he wanted to explain to me the word *l'Allemagne*, and he drummed that very primitive and all too simple melody which is often played at fairs for dogs to dance to, *dumb, dumb, dumb* — I was angry, but I understood him.[5]

Such sentiments, tied to his adulation of Napoleon, were not calculated to endear him to his fellow-Germans, except those who like himself were groaning in the aftermath of the War of Liberation at the new oppressions, and the frequently broken promises of Prussian kings to give the people a new constitution.

It is in the third volume of the *Travel Pictures* that Heine entered upon the most serious reflections on the present and future course of history. Here he throws down the gauntlet to the autocratic régimes of Prussia and Austria, and though a fervent Bonapartist, does not hesitate to censure Napoleon's betrayal of freedom and the ideals of the French Revolution through his *coup-d'état* of the 18th of Brumaire. Before him he sees looming the "great battle of the times" — "Der grosse Kampf der Zeit." "And what is the great task of the day?" he asks. And he answers:

It is Emancipation. Not simply the emancipation of the Irish, the Greeks, the Frankfurt Jews, the West Indian blacks, and all such oppressed peoples, but the emancipation of the whole world, and especially of Europe, which has now come of age, and is tearing itself loose from the apron-strings of the privileged classes, the aristocracy...Every age has its own task, and when it is accomplished, mankind advances. The inequality which prevailed in an earlier day, imposed on Europe by feudalism, was perhaps necessary, or, in any case, a necessary condition for the progress of civilization. Today it is an obstacle, and revolts all civilized minds.[6]

He knew he was running risks. At any moment, he could easily be swept into one of the prison-fortresses like Spandau or Spielberg. It was time to leave Germany, time to leave his home in Lüneburg, time to leave Hamburg, the "cradle of his sorrows," and his beloved but unloving Amalie, now married to a substantial member of the Hamburg community.

On May 19, 1831 he crossed the Rhine.

Paris!

In Paris he found himself. He became a part of all he surveyed. He was a celebrated German poet, who could measure himself against any of his compatriot poets like Eichendorff, Moerike, or Uhland. He became a part of French society, and soon moved in circles that included the Rothschilds, Lafayette, Alexandre Dumas, and the outstanding poets and artists. By 1833, Sainte-Beuve, the critic, could write about him in the *National:* "M. Heine was not known to us before the July Revolution, but today he is practically naturalized here. He is one of us."[7]

In which other city of the world had there been such an aggregation of genius present at one and the same time? Fréderic Chopin arrived in December 1831; Franz Liszt had been in and out of Paris since 1823. Ludwig Börne was there — as was the phenomenal Paganini. As for the French, there was Berlioz, Delacroix, George Sand, Victor Hugo, Alfred de Musset — to name only a few. There were the enchanting salons, presided over by brilliant women, like the Princess Belgiojoso, where Heine would be at home soon, and where his wit — somewhat obstructed by his heavy German accent — could still sparkle. Théophile Gautier named him a "German Apollo."

From Paris he sent out his communications to Germany. From December 1831 to September 1832 he was the correspondent for Cotta's *Allgemeine Zeitung* in Augsburg, ever hopeful that the sharp-eyed censors would not interfere too heartlessly. Heine, in reporting on "The Conditions in France," had to tread cautiously, sometimes exposing himself to charges of ambiguity. Ludwig Börne, staunch and puritanical republican that he was, was provoked by what he believed to be Heine's aestheticism, hedonism, and political scepticism. And there was some truth in those animadversions, for it seemed that Heine was inclined toward some ideal monarchism politically, while his social sentiments and insights veered toward a social revolution, which he saw in the making. Yet, his reports on Louis-Philippe and his régime were sharply critical and perceptive. He saw in him the opportunist, and his vaunted course of the "juste-milieu" — a program of following a "middle course" — only a way of concealing the fact that he was — as Heine put it — the king of the "juste-millionaires." Keenly, Heine watched the manipulations of the Bourse — the stock-exchange — and its sensitive responses to the internal and external affairs of the country.

On June 5 and 6, 1832, there was an uprising of republicans in Paris on the occasion of the funeral of the Napoleonic general Lamarque. Here a handful of insurgents battled an assembled army of 60,000 men, and were ruthlessly cut down. On June 6 Heine visited the Paris Bourse.

When I arrived yesterday at the Bourse, in order to mail my letter, Heine reported, the entire speculator horde was assembled under its columns on the broad steps. The news had just come that the defeat of the patriots was assured, and the most saccharine satisfaction stole over all the faces — one might almost say that the entire Bourse was smiling. Amid the thunder of cannons, the Funds rose by ten sous.[8]

It was not only the salons of the upper crust that Heine was observing. As he wandered around Paris, he would attend various meetings such as that of the republican society, the *Amis du peuple* and listen to fervent speeches reminiscent of 1789, delivered by the firebrand Louis-Auguste Blanqui, who, in Heine's report, openly derided Louis-Philippe as "la boutique incarnée" — "the shop-keeper incarnate" — or he would attend the meetings of the Saint-Simonians, who had so deeply permeated his own thinking. In the streets of Paris he remarked on the numerous caricatures of the King, being displayed or hawked, the most celebrated of those depicting him as the "Pear." Louis-Philippe loved to parade as the "citizen-king," but Heine knew better. "Under his modest felt-hat he wears, as everyone knows, an unauthorized crown of the ordinary cast, and in his umbrella he is hiding the most absolute of scepters."[9] In pages worthy of Daniel Defoe, he described the ravages of cholera that swept through Europe in 1831 for the first time, sparing neither rich nor poor, great or small. Hegel succumbed to it, as did the French minister, Casimir Périer.

He had not forgotten his own country. Always his eyes and ears were fixed on Germany, sometimes with hope, more often with consternation and despair. He watched the land preeminent in philosophers, and wondered how soon those abstract transcendental theories of theirs were to be translated into action. He apprehended the potential thunderbolts that lay concealed in their seemingly celestial ruminations. Brilliantly he paralleled the political actions of the French alongside of the metaphysical speculations of the Germans, from "Kant . . . our Robespierre," to "Fichte, the Napoleon of philosophy, with his Ego . . ," "Schelling, and Hegel, "the Orléans of philosophy." And he concluded: "Thus, since we had successfully completed our cycle in philosophy, it was natural that we proceed to politics. Will we follow the same course?"[10]

No, he concluded there would be no German revolution in the immediate future, and the dreams of a German republic, harbored by so many of his fellow-Germans in exile or at home, were merely hollow, for

Belief in authority is not as yet extinct with them, and nothing fundamental drives them toward a republican government. They have not yet outgrown royalty . . . They have not yet experienced the misfortunes of the twenty-first of January [i.e., the execution of Louis XVI]; they still believe in persons; they believe in authority, in a supreme potentate, in the police, in the Holy Trinity, in the *Hallische Literaturzeitung,* in blotting paper, in wrapping paper, but most of all in parchment . . .[11]

He was brought to a more profound reflection on the nature of the historic process, and of Revolution itself. He apprehended the meaning of historical necessity.

Today is the product of yesterday. We must explore what yesterday has willed — if we would know what today wills . . . When the culture of a people and its attendant customs and needs are no longer in harmony with the established institutions, they of necessity come into fateful conflict, with the result that the latter are transformed. This phenomenon we call revolution. So long as the revolution is incomplete, so long as the transformation of institutions does not harmonize with the intellectual temper, the customs and needs of the people, the sickness of the body politic is not completely cured.[12]

Social thinkers of a succeeding generation will give a more precise definition of this particular aspect of revolution, but there can be no question that here Heine is laying bare the nature of social contradictions between antiquated institutions and the new necessities of a changing society that result in revolution.

The full extent of Heine's daring in these articles in the *Allgemeine Zeitung* may be gauged from the letter that Friedrich Gentz, secretary to Metternich, addressed to the publisher Cotta in the fall of 1832:

What an infamous adventurer like Heine, who I will grant is a poet whom, in fact, I admire as such, wishes and desires, while he treads the present régime of France in the mud, I am not inclined to investigate further, though it can all be easily surmised. But it seems to me that the boundless contempt with which these churls speak, among others and at this moment preeminently, of the most honorable section of the *Middle Classes,* should itself infuriate this class...For the priesthood and the nobility one no longer has any use; they are done for. Requiescant in pace! But when men like Périer and their adherents, that is employees, bankers, land-owners, and shop-keepers are even more shamefully held up to detestation than formerly the princes, dukes and barons, who then is left to govern the state?[13]

This was tantamount to an ultimatum and a prohibition of further publication, in which Cotta acquiesced. Heine's contributions came to an end in September 1832.

Heine rose to the occasion. He struck back by preparing an ungarbled edition of his *French Affairs*, in German and French, to which he appended a Preface, which was his *"J'accuse!"* His indignation was further aggravated by what had happened in Germany during May 27, 1832, when 25,000 men and women had gathered at Hambach to celebrate the anniversary of the winning of a Bavarian constitution. In the general fervor of the meeting demands were raised for moderate reforms, "one Germany," support for Poland, tributes to France. The meeting alarmed the German authorities, and the Federal Diet reacted by announcing that its authority superseded that of the individual states, and imposed a more rigid censorship, arrested the leaders of the demonstration, and suppressed their journals.

Heine's Preface was therefore not only a reply to the actions of Metternich, and Cotta's submission, but also an excoriation of Germany and its rulers, particularly Frederick William III, King of Prussia.

Poor German people! he wrote. While you were resting from the battles
you waged in the cause of your princes, and while you were burying your
dead who had fallen in the war, and were binding up each other's wounds,
smiling to see the blood run from your honest hearts, so full of joy and
faith ... in Vienna, in the old smithies of the aristocracy, the federal acts
were being forged! Strange! Even that prince who should have been most
grateful to the people, and who had therefore promised them, in this hour
of need, a representative constitution, a popular constitution, such as other
free people possess; — who promised it in black and white, with the most
positive words — that prince has succeeded in seducing the other German
princes, who like him, had obligated themselves to give their subjects a free
constitution. And they too broke their word and faith. Now he leans on the
Vienna federal act in order to be able to destroy the new-born German
constitution — he who dare not utter the word Constitution without
blushing. I speak of His Majesty, Frederick William, Third of the name,
King of Prussia.[14]

This was a declaration of war. It was not long thereafter, in
December 1835, that the Federal Diet promulgated its notorious
decree against the publications of the school of dissenting poets and
writers in German that was styled "Jung Deutschland" — "Young
Germany" — and that included a notable group of liberal authors,
Heine as well. Börne appeared in the list somewhat later. The
decree banned all their works, and proscribed their publication and
distribution in German lands.

There was no lack of occasions to provoke Heine. Although
seriously affected by the potential loss of a large sector of the
German reading public, he did not rest from his work. For the time
being, he had suspended the writing of poetry, and was devoting
himself to prose. As a matter of fact, his preoccupation with political
journalism and politics had served to mature his ideas. Three years
before the decree of 1835, he had begun two major works intended
to define cogently the character of German literature and philosophy
of the preceding era. These two books were to appear first in French
translations; then in garbled and censored German versions.

Die romantische Schule and *Zur Geschichte der Religion und Philosophie in Deutschland* are remarkable studies. They are summations as well as prognostic guideposts; they mark the end of an age and point the way to the future. They pronounce the end of the Romantic era, and announce the new forms under which both literature and philosophy are bound to appear. In certain other aspects, these books, especially the one on philosophy, are terrifying predictions of our own age. Like all of Heine's works, these, too, are highly personal, studded with brilliant bon-mots and aphorisms, but for all that, no less serious in evaluations and sharp aperçus. They are the products of a man who bridges two intellectual zones: that of the Romantics and that of the post-Romantics. Their author attempts to understand and help us understand the climate and the terrain out of which both the letters and philosophy of the Romantic period had their efflorescence. The philosophic standpoint from which Heine writes is in part that of the Saint-Simonians, particularly when he is concerned with the nature and goals of historic progress. He is no less candid about the metaphysical or cosmological preconceptions, the importance of the rehabilitation of flesh and matter, and the need, once and for all, to dispose of the traditional Judaeo-Christian separation of spirit and flesh, body and soul, bread and mind. Hence also the programmatic character of these works.

We promote, Heine wrote, the well-being of the material, the material well-being of the people, not because, like the materialists, we despise the spirit, but because we know that the divinity of man manifests itself also in his body. Human misery destroys or abases the body, which is the image of God — so that the spirit within perishes.

We interpret the great words of the Revolution which St. Just pronounced, "le pain est le droit du peuple" as meaning "le pain est le droit divin de l'homme." We do not contend for the human rights of the people, but for the divine rights of man...

I believe in progress. I believe that mankind is destined for happiness, and I have a better opinion of the deity than those pious souls who imagine that he created man only for suffering. Yes, here on earth I would establish by means of the blessings of free political and industrial institutions that beatific state which according to the opinion of the devout will be realized on the Day of Judgment and in Heaven.[15]

Unlike the German Romantics, Heine looked to the present and the future for a resolution of the great problems of the day. They saw the regeneration of mankind made possible only through a restoration of medieval Christianity. This was the so-called "Christian-Old-German movement." Heine traced the origins and the *raison-d'être* of this neo-medievalism to the condition of the German state — the "Misere" — the wretched straits in which the country found itself during the Napoleonic wars and the French domination, when the "vanquished princes grovelled at the feet of Napoleon," and the people sought salvation in religion and in a surrender to the will of God. For, as Heine added, "what other help could avail against Napoleon?" The Princes turned patriots, and preached patriotism to every other German. "And patriots we became, for we do as our princes ordain." Such too was the fate of the Romantic school of literature under the priesthood of the brothers Schlegel and their acolytes; they followed suit, resurrected an idealized national past of the Middle Ages, and became blood-brothers of German political medievalism and nationalism.

In justly celebrated passages, Heine proceeds to trace the course of German transcendental philosophy, the brilliant epoch which he saw as coming to an end with Hegel. Heine's lightness of tone cannot conceal the savage perceptiveness he brings to his analysis. First, there was the great religious revolution embodied in the Reformation.

It seems to me that a methodical people like the Germans had to commence with the Reformation. Thereafter they could occupy themselves with philosophy, and only when they had completed that task, were they in a position to pass on to political revolution. I find the sequence very reasonable. The heads which philosophy used for reflection could later be chopped off by the revolution, for its own purposes. But philosophy could never have used these heads if the revolution had first chopped them off.

Then comes the ominous prevision:

Don't worry, German republicans, — your German revolution will be no gentler or milder because it has been preceded by the *Critique* of Kant, the transcendental idealism of Fichte, and even the philosophy of nature [of Schelling]... The old stone gods will then arise from long forgotten ruins and rub the dust of a thousand years from their eyes, and Thor will leap to life with his giant hammer and smash the Gothic cathedrals!... Do not smile at the visionary who anticipates the same revolution in the realm of the visible as has taken place in the realm of the spiritual... A play will be performed in Germany which will make the French Revolution look like an innocent idyl.

And he addresses a warning to France, which he so greatly loved:

You have more to fear from a Germany set free than from the entire Holy Alliance with its Croats and Cossacks... Despite your present Romanticism you are really Classicists at heart, and you know Olympus well. Among the naked gods and goddesses who there rejoice over nectar and ambrosia, you may see one immortal who even amidst all this festivity and gaiety always wears a coat of mail and bears a helmet on her head and a spear in her hand.
    It is the Goddess of Wisdom.[16]

Journalism and his other prose writing kept him busy — as did his social engagements, no less than his amatory excursions. In 1834 he fell in love with a lovely nineteen-year old shop-girl, Crescentia Eugénie Mirat, whom he called Mathilde. To all intents and purposes she became his wife, though the union was not to be legalized until 1841. She was simple, naive, never fully aware that she was the companion of a great celebrity, but she fully compensated for her intellectual shortcoming by the loyalty and devotion she brought to the poet — then already beginning to show some serious symptoms of the physical disabilities that were to prove so tragic after 1848. She was a charming, voluptuous young woman, admired by Heine's German friends. With her Heine could indeed celebrate the Third Testament, the glorification of sensual love, that he had hymned in his Saint-Simonian poem:

Auf diesem Felsen bauen wir
Die Kirche von dem dritten
Dem dritten neuen Testament;
Das Leid is ausgelitten...

Upon this rock we'll build a church
To celebrate the splendid,
The Third and Final Testament;
Our sufferings are ended.

Destroyed is the duality
That long has bound us fast;
The stupid torment of the flesh
Is flung aside at last.

Do you hear God's word in the darkened sea?
Thousand-voiced He exclaims.
And can't you see above our heads.
The thousand God-lit flames?

The holy Lord is in the light,
And in the night's abysses;
And God is everything that is —
He throbs in our kisses.[17]

If one were to try to define Heine's religion at this time one might with justice call him a hedonistic Pantheist. But actually he was the embodiment of multiple ambiguities and contradictions. He was a Romantic and a post-Romantic; he was an aesthete, yet a severe critic of the age of "art" represented by Goethe. His "paganism" and his aestheticism warred with the ever-increasing awareness of the social and political pressures that seemed to him to be moving toward an eruption and presented urgent demands upon the poet for adequate responses. He often allowed his personal animosities to affect his sense of justice, and personal issues to overshadow larger principles he was so brilliant in perceiving and enunciating. To a number of his critics he appeared a weather-vane; yet when called upon, he could be as forthright, courageous, and uncompromising as any of his contemporaries. He was one of those who grew with the demands of the times; whose horizon was an ever-widening one. Though deeply involved in journalism — and he was one of those who revolutionized German prose style — he never forgot that he was also a preeminent poet, a poet who could appropriate contemporary historical issues and mould them into poetry.

He was by this time recognized as an international man of letters — as much French as German. He was always in need of money — both he and Mathilde were extravagant, and a meager stipend he received from his uncle supplemented his earnings as journalist and poet. From 1840 to 1848, he was the recipient of a subvention from the French government as a valuable "publiciste" and "correspondant de la Gazette d'Augsburg" — which was to cause him great humiliation and distress when finally revealed publicly on the outbreak of the Revolution.

He had longed to revisit Germany, to see his mother once more; his uncle Salomon, and old friends, and he realized that wish in the fall of 1843 and the summer of 1844. The city of Hamburg was no longer as he had left it; almost half had been burned out some time before. Memories of a former love — ineradicable — saddened him once more — a burden he was to bear till his dying day. But his poetic spirit was unquenchable, even, one might say — more enriched than ever. In Germany, and particularly Hamburg, he found the inspiration for some of his most scintillating sallies, particularly in the series of poems entitled *Germany: A Winter's Tale — Deutschland: ein Wintermärchen.*

Heine returned from his first visit to Germany with portions of *Germany — A Winter's Tale* in December 1843. During the preceding month, a young German publicist of twenty-six arrived in Paris, coming from the Rhenish provinces. This was Karl Marx, co-editor with Arnold Ruge of the *Franco-German Yearbooks,* which they were transferring to Paris. Marx was preparing to collaborate on another publication in that city, the radical semi-weekly German newspaper, *Vorwärts*. For years Marx had been an admirer of Heine's poetry, and it was not long before the two became friends. Heine was persuaded to contribute to the *Vorwärts*. It was here, that, during its short-lived existence (it fell foul of the French censorship) Heine published some of his best-known social and political poetry, and his finest satires. The whiplash of his wit was unsparing, and his targets ranged from King Frederick William IV of Prussia, King Ludwig of Bavaria, to German lethargy, Germany's corrupt bureaucracy, and the petty literary servitors of German absolutism. Here too was printed what is considered the most renowned social lyric of the century, "The Silesian Weavers," provoked by the uprising and the bloody suppression of the textile workers of that region. (Gerhart Hauptmann was to use the same subject for his drama, *The Weavers*.) The magnificent poem was both protest, battle-cry, and prophecy, and some of its lines were to be imprinted on the German consciousness for years to come, especially those relating to the "Doom" pronounced against God, King, and Fatherland; and the refrain, "We weave, we weave."

> Old Germany, your shroud's on our loom,
> And in it we weave the threefold doom:
> We weave; we weave!

> Altdeutschland, wir weben dein Leichentuch,
> Wir weben hinein den dreifachen Fluch,
> Wir weben, wir weben.[18]

His health might be bad — a progressive paralysis was making itself evident — but Heine's wit never shone more radiantly than now. In *Germany — A Winter's Tale* he could vie with the great satirists of all times — Aristophanes, Swift, Byron, Rabelais. Here he was the virtuoso playing all the stops of the instrument, the serious, the tender, the acid, even the scurrilous. This was an extraordinary travelogue in verse. The voyager is returning home.

He reaches the German border, so long yearned for — and he hears
German spoken, and a German song sung. A German "harp-girl" is
crooning about a world beyond and about human renunciation. Our
aroused poet counters with the song he is bringing:

> A new song, and a better song,
> Oh friends, I'll sing for you.
> Here on earth we mean to make
> Our Paradise come true...
>
> We mean to be happy here on earth —
> Our days of want are done.
> No more shall the lazy belly waste
> What toiling hands have won...
>
> Your Europe's betrothed to Liberty,
> That genius of beauty and grace. They
> Live in each other's passionate arms,
> They feast on their first embrace...[19]

The poet feels like Antaeus. Having touched his maternal soil
once more, he finds that his powers begin to grow. The customs
guards at the border start rummaging through his trunk.

> You fools, that search inside my trunk!
> Here's nothing you can find.
> The contraband that journeys with me
> I've stuck away in my mind.

Yes, in his head he carries countless treasures that no censor or
customs-inspector is likely to detect. And among these treasures is
this new poem he is planning, a manifesto, a fulfilment of the
promise of "a new song, and a better song" — a poem that answers
the needs of the times. A poem that aims high and low, and woe to
those whom the burnished and whetted arrows reach! Among them
will be King Frederick William IV of Prussia, who had ascended the
throne in 1840. That event had been accompanied by hosannahs
from many quarters, and pious hopes on the part of liberals that

now the long-promised constitution would be a reality. These hopes were soon dimmed, and doomed. Persecutions, censorship, imprisonments, instead of diminishing, increased. Courageous souls were forced into silence, or self-exile.

The poet, who had been accused by his enemies of prudential silences, was aroused as never before. He would hold back no longer. Let us follow him in his carriage, as it jolts along, the jog of the horses' hoofs almost echoed in the four-line colloquial stanza of Heine's poem. Along with the poet, we will sometimes doze off — and dream — mostly bad dreams, and with him awaken to once familiar places. We cross the Rhine, and converse with the Rhine-god. We come to ancient, hoary cities, with ancient, hoary monuments, cathedrals, palaces, tombs, testimonies to former grandeurs, and alas! present miseries. Here is Aachen, the imperial city of Charlemagne; here is Cologne with its towering but unfinished cathedral, filled with hoary trumpery and what Heine calls "the skeletons of superstition," a mouldy antiquity still worshipped by a posterity.

Here in Cologne it is that the poet discovers he is being followed by a mysterious figure — a kind of *Doppelgänger* — who hides an axe underneath his cloak. He is an executioner! Not an ordinary one, we discover, when the poet challenges him:

> "I am no scarecrow, no ghost of the Past
> Out of the grave arising;
> And I am no friend of rhetoric,
> Do little philosophizing.
>
> I'm of a practical character:
> The calm and silent kind.
> But know: I carry out, I do
> All that you've had in mind.
>
> And even though the years go by,
> I find no satisfaction
> Till thought becomes reality;
> You think, and I take action."

"Ich bin die Tat von deinen Gedanken." — "I am the deed —
offspring of your thoughts."

In his dream, Heine sees his thoughts come to life in action
— the executioner mercilessly hews down the monuments of the
"Three Holy Kings" in the Cologne Cathedral — a response to the
poet's bold address:

> Out! out of here! You should have crawled
> Down to your grave before.
> Life is now coming to confiscate
> The chapel's treasure-store.
>
> The future's joyous cavalry
> Shall here at last be housed.
> And if you're not willing, I'll turn to force:
> I'll club you till you're deloused...

In his imagination, at least, the word had become deed. The
transcendental philosophy of yore — the pride of the German
intellect — has at last descended to the earth. The word of
destruction has been uttered. There will be no restoration of the old.

Nor will Barbarossa, Emperor of the Holy Roman Empire,
return. Lying asleep with his hundreds of mighty warriors for
centuries now, he will not return to redeem Germany and restore
the Old Order, no matter how feverishly the Romantics call upon
him. With astonishment, then horror and outrage, Barbarossa
listens to our poet, as he recounts the fate of recent monarchs, who
lost their heads at the guillotine. The poet, in turn, berates the
Emperor:

> Sir Barbarossa! — I cried out loud —
> You're a mythical creation.
> Go, get some sleep! without your help
> We'll work out our salvation...
>
> It would be best if you stayed at home
> Here in the mountain-hall —
> Considering how matters stand,
> We need no king at all...

The poet finally arrives in Hamburg, and once again, after a thirteen-year separation, sees his mother, who overwhelms him with delicious cooking and searching questions. He consumes the food with gusto, and avoids the questions. In Hamburg he meets old acquaintances once more, his none-too-sympathetic uncle, his publisher, and — finally — in the street none other than the protecting goddess of Hamburg — Hammonia. She consents to reveal to him the otherwise hidden future of Germany, on the promise not to disclose it to others. The poem now makes a descent to a broad — almost scatological — humor, for the sacred vessel of revelation is a night-chair, out of which rise such mephitic odors as almost to overcome the poet.

What he saw of the future of Germany as he peered into the vessel — that must wait to be revealed another day, and to another generation.

> There is a new race growing up;
> Unrouged, unsinning youth!
> Freedom of thought, and freedom of joy —
> I'll let them know the truth...

The poem ends with an apostrophe to Kings to beware the wrath of poets, for they have the power — remember Dante! — of consigning them and their like to an inescapable and eternal stay in Hell...

The volume of poems in which *Germany — A Winter's Tale* was included — *Neue Gedichte* (also containing the political "Zeitgedichte" — "Poems for the Times") proved unexpectedly successful, and a second printing followed within a short time. There were, of course, also opprobrium, and charges that the poet had once more shown himself a disloyal and unpatriotic German, ready to sell out to the French, and a desecrater of the sacred black-red-and-gold German national standard. To which accusations Heine replied in the French edition of the poems:

Calm yourselves, he wrote. I will regard and respect your colors when they deserve it — when they no longer are an idle or servile pastime. Plant the black-red-and-gold banner on the heights of German thought, make it the standard of a free humanity, and I will offer my best heart's blood for it.

Complete, he continues, the work the French have begun, outstrip them in action as you already have done in thought, destroy servitude everywhere, become "God's redeemers," give back to the people, those disinherited of happiness, their dignity, and comsummate "the great work of the Revolution — universal Democracy." Then, indeed, will the great mission of German "universal sovereignty" have been realized.[20]

Four years after the publication of the *Neue Gedichte* new revolutions swept over all of Europe. In February 1848 Paris gave the starting signals for the uprisings. In May Heinrich Heine walked through the streets of his beloved city for the last time. The venereal disease he had contracted many years before now took its full toll. He became almost totally paralyzed, and blind. For eight years thereafter he was confined to his "mattress grave" — as he called it. For eight years his physical world was bounded by his sick-bed and the window or balcony to which he would be carried to peer once more with blinded eyes upon Paris. But his mind roved far and wide, and his creative genius never flagged. In spirit he was with the revolutionaries and with the failed revolution. He exulted in the heroic resistance of the Hungarians against Russians and Austrians; he heaped scorn and derision on his fellow-Germans on their subsequent relapse into their traditional "Gemütlichkeit" — their complacent and smug acceptance of a time-honored servility and tyranny.

> The wind's asleep, that howled so wild;
> At home it's quiet as could be;
> Germania, the great big child,
> Plays happily around his Christmas tree...

The wood and stream rest cozily,
By gentle moonlight comforted;
But — on a sudden — can it be
A shot? — perhaps it is a friend shot dead...

Poet, be still; your anguish grows —
You are so so sick... 'twere wiser not to speak.[21]

ADAM MICKIEWICZ
POLAND'S POET-PROPHET

He lived among us [Russians] as an alien, but he
nursed no hatred toward us in his soul. And we
loved him. Peaceful and kindly, he would join us at
our gatherings. With him we shared our pure
dreams and songs. He was inspired from above, and
from on high he looked on life. Often he spoke of
coming times, when nations, forgetting their strife,
would unite in one great family. Eagerly we listened
to the poet. He went to the west, and with blessings
we saw him off.
— Pushkin on Mickiewicz —

Among the European uprisings sparked by the Paris Revolution of
1830 none roused such sympathy and passion as that of the Poles
against Russia. The Warsaw rebellion broke out in November 1830,
and was not suppressed until September of the following year. The
valiant stand of a small nation against the Russian giant forcefully
affected the conscience of European and American democrats. The
country had suffered partitions at the hands of Prussia, Russia, and
Austria, and became symbolic of the fate of all small nations victims
of imperial competition and greed. On behalf of the Poles there
occurred demonstrations and agitations in many lands, but none so
powerful as those in France. The Polish insurgents staked their
hopes of victory on the military intervention of friendly powers,
especially of France. But none of them stirred. The defeat of the
rebellion was unfortunately abetted by the divisions within the
ranks of the Polish patriots, the more conservative elements

597

seeking a rapprochement with the Tsarist régime; the more radical democrats demanding the abdication of the Tsar, along with drastic social and political reforms. The Poles fought in the name and spirit of the French Revolution of July. As one of the insurgents put it, "The French Revolution is the final act, a closing of the great scene of the Middle Ages, and the first moment, the first light of dawn of a new Europe."[1] Such divisions were further compounded by the incompetence of the military and political leadership. Involved in their special interests, they failed to rally the peasant population with a program of social reform that would emancipate them from serfdom. Independence was the battle-cry of the day, not radical social change, though a sizable number of workers and artisans in Warsaw rallied to the cause, and joined the discontented army units who had precipitated the revolt. With the fall of Warsaw, the fate of Poland was sealed for many years to come.

As thousands of Polish refugees streamed across Europe, five thousand of them found their way to France, where they were lodged in various camps. Many of them came to Paris, which became the center of Polish agitation. Here too they brought the many divisions of opinion which had prevailed in their home country, probably in an aggravated and exacerbated form, as so often happens to a population in exile.

Polish leadership in France was divided between the conservative Prince Adam Czartoryski, who stood for compromise and accommodation with Russia, and Joachim Lelewel, Poland's outstanding historian, who agitated for national independence, and for radical social, political, and economic reforms.

Poland's tragedy also brought to France two of her most eminent artistic geniuses: Frédéric Chopin, her greatest musical figure, and Adam Mickiewicz (pr. Mitskévitch), her greatest poet.

Adam Mickiewicz arrived in Paris in August 1832. He was thirty-three years old, and already recognized as Poland's outstanding poet, though he was all but unknown outside of his own country and

Russia. His residence in France, his poetical productions there, and his activities were to spread his name far and wide. In fact, he became the voice of Poland, and his name was conjoined with that of Poland's national hero, Thaddeus Kościuśko, who had fought in the American Revolution, and had led the great Polish uprising of 1794.

In France Mickiewicz published his three major works; the politico-visionary "drama" of Poland's martyrdom, *Forefathers' Eve, Part III*; the messianic rhapsody of Poland's redemptory mission, *The Books of the Polish Nation and of the Polish Pilgrims*; and — most important of all — *Pan Tadeusz*, Poland's heroic epic. With the publication of the last of these in 1834, Mickiewicz practically ended his poetic career. Thereafter he embarked on his prophetic and messianic mission, on a kind of political apostolate, which was to end with his death of cholera in Turkey in 1855.

Unlike Chopin, Mickiewicz had in his youth experienced political persecution. While a young student at the University of Wilno, in Lithuania, which he had entered in 1815, he learned for the first time the meaning of national oppression, and what it meant to be a Pole. The University of Wilno was one of Europe's most eminent seats of learning, boasting scholars of great distinction, such as Joachim Lelewel. Naturally, the young students and many of their teachers were animated by a strong patriotic zeal. Student associations, ostensibly dedicated to literature and philosophy, also engaged in discussions of national and international issues. Mickiewicz became active in one such organization, the Philomaths, and by virtue of his conspicuous and recognized talent obtained a commanding position there. By 1823, he had already achieved fame with the publication of two volumes of poetry, which, while they may not have originated the Romantic movement in Polish letters, announced its fruition.

Though very much a part of the age, he did not nourish the customary *mal du siècle* — so much the fashion among his literary contemporaries. He was very much in the stream of international culture, the "offspring" of Goethe, Schiller, Sir Walter Scott, and greatly taken with those Scottish pseudo-Gaelic forgeries, Macpherson's "Ossian." But he was also a devout worshipper of Byron. These currents were enlarged in him by Poland's movement for national independence. What Greece was to Byron, Poland was to young Mickiewicz. The parallel went even beyond national aspirations, and involved a similarity of life-experiences. Like Byron, Mickiewicz was to die of disease, near a field of battle, in the process of rallying a military force to fight against Russia.

In Wilno, the watchful eye of the Russian master soon took note of what appeared to be illicit activities of the student body. Prince Constantine, brother of the Russian Tsar, was now Viceroy of Poland, and Nicolai Novosiltsov, his faithful watchdog, was Imperial Commissioner. In 1823 a rash act on the part of a young student, Michael Plater, provoked a major raid on the part of the police. He had dared express praise of the Polish Constitution of 1791. The young culprit was apprehended and drafted into the Russian army. Other youngsters were arrested and sentenced to various degrees of punishment. Members of the Philomaths were also apprehended, among them Mickiewicz. The arrests took place on October 23 and 24, 1823. Some of the sentences meted out were harsh; others comparatively mild. Prison and exile were the usual punishments. Mickiewicz was imprisoned for a while, and then, in October, exiled to Russia.

His punishment was not of the severer kind. He was scheduled for a teaching post under proper supervision. But otherwise he would be comparatively free. This was to be his first journey into the wide world — into the vastness which was Russia.

Actually he was not allowed to teach. But life in Russia proved pleasing, at times even exciting. Here he was brought in contact with a novel, live cultural environment, far wider than that of Wilno; and being known as a gifted poet, he was befriended by prominent Russians and Poles. Among the poems he had already produced was a romantic narrative, *Grażyna*, which celebrated the exploits of a Lithuanian heroine whose traitor husband had gone over to the enemy, the Teutonic Knights, and whom she replaces at the head of the Lithuanians, leads them to victory, and pays with her own life.

Adam Mickiewicz was very handsome, an engaging young man, fiery, eloquent, — and he readily made friends. Aside from the Poles, in St. Petersburg, he met and was particularly drawn to the artillery officer and poet, Kondratyi Ryleev, and his fellow soldier-poet, Alexander Bestuzhov, both members of the Northern Section of the Russian revolutionary movement. It is not unlikely that Mickiewicz also came to know their associates, as well as their political and social outlook.

He was sent down to Odessa, but not to teach. He was placed under the vigilant eye of Count Witte, curator of the college of Odessa, also an agent of the police. In Odessa Mickiewicz found a thriving Polish cultural colony, with many charming, affable, and intelligent women. Among them was the Countess Karolina Sobanska, at that moment the mistress of Count Witte, and about to be divorced from her husband. She was none other than the sister of Countess Evelina Hanska. Pushkin had been one of her many lovers, and she soon became Mickiewicz's mistress. Hard as exile might be, it seems to have offered Mickiewicz many compensating amenities! He was invited to accompany Count Witte on one of his tours to the Crimea, and here, Mickiewicz, like Pushkin before him, was brought face to face with new wonders: the sea, the Orient, and the peoples of southern Russia. Here he was inspired to compose the exquisite series of *Crimean Sonnets*, which were immediately translated into Russian, and established him as a poet of the first rank. The *Sonnets*, eighteen in number, were like eighteen pearls strung out, musical and rich in colors at the same time, masterpieces of the sonnet-form. In them one heard the surge of the ocean, and the poet's feverish response, reminiscent of the excitement of Byron and Heine. But here was Mickiewicz's own voice.

I fall upon the bosom of the ship, and hold it fast,
It seems my own bosom drives it faster than the gale,
So light! so fresh! so happy!
This is to know what a bird feels when it flies...

When he visited Moscow, he was welcomed in many of the salons, particularly that of the Princess Zanaida Volkonska. He associated with the most brilliant of literary men and women. Count Viazemsky, himself one of the translators of Mickiewicz's *Crimean Sonnets*, describes one such social evening to his wife:

The day before yesterday we spent the evening and the night at Pushkin's, with Zhukovski, Krylov, Khomiakov, Mickiewicz, Pletniev, and Nikolai Mukhanov. Mickiewicz gave an improvisation in French prose and amazed us, not of course by his phrasing, but by the force, richness and poetry of his thoughts... Wonderful was the effect of his improvisation. He was himself upset, and we listened with trembling and tears.[2]

Pushkin, of the same age as Mickiewicz, became one of the Polish poet's most fervent admirers. Mickiewicz arrived in Moscow just two days before the Decembrist uprising of the 25th. One can imagine what must have gone on in the souls of the two poets! Both of them were acquainted with a number of the participants. Was it on their minds when during one of the salon evenings Pushkin read scenes from his tragedy, *Boris Godunov*, and Mickiewicz exclaimed ecstatically, "Et tu, Shakespeare eris, si fata sinant," — "You, too, will be a Shakespeare, if the Fates allow"?

Moving between Moscow and St. Petersburg — everywhere, in fact, Mickiewicz was received with warmth and acclaim. He must have felt himself the equal of Pushkin and Zhukovsky. But amidst the sound of these plaudits, there must have mingled some dark inner voices of his own, especially after he had received letters from his former fellow-students, and from his friends likewise in exile. They were far away, somewhere in Orenburg or Ufa, leading a harsh existence, while he —? Was Mickiewicz succumbing to the flesh-pots of Egypt, and forgetting his former loyalties and allegiances?

No! he must have replied to his own heart. He was shamming gaiety; his heart was with them. He was composing epic romances, dealing with treason and expiation! He was still Poland's poet, and his new poem, *Konrad Wallenrod*, was to be the proof of it, and his own testament of faith. Here was the story of a hero, Konrad, a Lithuanian, who had been kidnapped as a child by the Teutonic Knights, and became Master of the Order. In a war on the Lithuanians he betrays his own high office, and brings about the victory of his putative foes at the sacrifice of his own life. Once more treason and redemption have become the central themes of his poetry. *Konrad Wallenrod* was published in 1828, strangely enough with the Russian censor's approval. But that old watch-dog Novosiltsov suspected perfidy. "The most artful treason," he said of the poem. Perhaps he was right, for in the uprising of 1830, the Warsaw cadets who stormed the Belvedere palace of Prince Constantine and forced him to flee in a cook's disguise, recited the words of that poem. "The word became flesh," one of the younger Poles exclaimed.[3]

He was restless, and wanted to leave Russia. The old Tsar Alexander was dead, the Decembrists had tried revolution and failed; had been executed or sent into long exile. Ryleev had been hanged; Bestuzhov exiled — he could not easily forget them. In May 1829 he received permission to leave Russia.

First he went to Berlin, where he tried to attend Hegel's lectures, but could make neither head or tail of them. Then he visited Weimar, met the octogenarian Goethe, whose birthday was being celebrated with a performance of *Faust*. Then on to Rome. He fell under the spell of the city, met many friends, and fell in love with Henriette, daughter of Count Anckwitz, and sued for her hand, and was rejected. After all, he was only a poet, and, in addition, an exile! But if he did not win her hand, she inspired him with her sweetness and her Christian fervor, and he felt within himself a renewal of his Catholic faith. Under the added influence of a Catholic priest, Choloniewski, he returned with redoubled zeal to Catholicism.

Then came 1830, the July Revolution in Paris, and in
November, the Polish uprising. Many of his friends, comrades,
fellow-students, he knew, were already under arms and in battle. But
he was tarrying... Now in Rome, now in Switzerland, briefly also in
Paris, and then in the Prussian territories close to the borders of
Poland — just on the other side of the war. His brother had been in
the war. Many of those he had known were dead... He did not
believe that his countrymen could win...

But — he was living a harrowing internal drama, whose
grievous content was the sense of his own "sin" — the sin of the
defector. Henceforth, the rest of his life would be an expiation
— through poetry and action. In Dresden, before heading again for
Paris, he commenced a dramatic poem, *Forefathers' Eve, Part III*, an
unrelated successor to two other previous portions. This was his
first act of expiation. Under pressure of the Prussian government,
he was forced to leave the German city.

He arrived in Paris on August 1, 1832, and was met by his
former professor, Joachim Lelewel. Now he was a refugee — like
many thousands, in a city that generously housed them, at this
moment the most hospitable city in the world. He had been away
from Poland since 1824. Like Chopin, he was never to see his
country again.

Mickiewicz had met the abbé Lamennais on his first visit to
Paris. Now, however, they were able to extend and reenforce the
common bond, spiritual and personal. Lamennais was deeply
affected by the Polish débacle. Mickiewicz was impressed by
Lamennais's personality, his sincerity, his religious fervor, and his
devotion to reform. They were both working in contiguous fields
— each of them searching for a revitalized Christianity, for a
religion of humanity. Here they were — once geographically almost
poles apart — marching by such diverse routes, and meeting now on
common ground, and on the common soil of France! Between them
was the interrelation not of master and pupil, but of intellectual and

moral equals, for Mickiewicz's *Books of the Polish Nation* was to serve as the inspiration of Lamennais's *Paroles d'un Croyant*. They could scarcely have foreseen the parallel course they were destined to follow; that at different times each of them would be journeying to Rome to bring this plea for political action and religious reform before the Pope, and even to try to win him over to the cause of Revolution.

Forefathers' Eve, Part III was published in Paris in 1832. Its theme is the martyrology of the poet's young companions of the Wilno school. The central figures of the poetic drama are Konrad, a poet, and Father Peter, a Catholic priest. The name Konrad was one that haunted Mickiewicz, and was always associated in his mind with a warring knight. It is possible that now it had acquired added sanctity by having also been the first name of Kondratyi Ryleev, another martyr. In Mickiewicz's poem, the protagonist, whose original name was Gustave, assumes the name of Konrad to mark his conversion from poet to warring knight — for Poland as well as for mankind, against the tyranny of Russian Tsarism.

The poem combines fantasy and realism. Angelic and diabolic forces contend over Konrad's soul. He is the embodiment of rebellion and overweening pride. He is both Prometheus and Lucifer. He despairs of God and defies him. The action of the poem takes place against a background of prison, prisoners, and tortures. While the imprisoned Konrad is asleep, the priest succeeds in exorcising the evil spirit of pride. Konrad comes to understand his true mission, the mission of liberating Poland, and beyond that the mission of redemption of all of Europe, and of the whole world. Shelley had immortalized the idea of Freedom and Liberation in *Prometheus Unbound*. Heine was dreaming his Utopian dream of a world transformed by a revolutionized and democratic Germany. In Mickiewicz's apocalyptic drama, the role of regenerator is reserved for a freed Poland. The future destiny of Poland is prefigured in Father Peter, with whose person and mission it is likely Mickiewicz identified himself. Might he not be the great liberating power himself?

Father Peter in a mystical vision foresees the coming of the savior:

> But see, a child escapes, grows up — he is our savior,
> The restorer of our land, born of a foreign mother.
> In his veins runs the blood of ancient warriors — and his name
> Shall be forty and four . . .

Was Mickiewicz using the arcane numerology to announce his own
New Coming? Commentators have interpreted the name of Adam,
which is Hebrew, as containing two consonants which translated
into numbers would make "forty and four" — the D being the
equivalent of 4, and the M of 40. Such a thought might not have been
far from the mind of Mickiewicz himself, judging from his later
writings and actions. The dramatic poem was never completed, but
its messianic import is clear enough. Poland will guide the world
through its own redemption to the redemption of mankind. Russia
is the Beast of the Apocalypse, and her destruction is foredoomed.
The "world's great age" — which Shelley had hymned — would
begin again.

Exile and oppression often breed mystical visions of liberation
at the hands of some "Messiah" — "the anointed one." The Jewish
Diaspora created a number of such "Redeemers," and East European
and Near-Eastern countries in past centuries have witnessed
millennary movement led by zealots and pretenders. False Messiahs,
such as Sabbetai-Zevi in the seventeenth, and Jakob Frank in the
eighteenth centuries, were among the more remarkable of such
visionaries. Their advent produced mass hysterias that affected
entire communities. Non-Jewish chiliastic phenomena were also
present in European history, sometimes particularly strong with
their appeals to the disinherited, and their promises of imminent
redemption. In such cities as Wilno, for example, the existence of an
outstanding community of Jewish scholars, many of whom were
deeply involved in the study of the Cabbala, undoubtedly also played
a part in and affected non-Jewish culture and thought. It is
impossible to conceive that Mickiewicz would not have come under
the influence of Jewish apocalyptic mysticism.

For the generality of the Polish people, Mickiewicz composed the *Books of the Polish Nation and of the Polish Pilgrims*, a strange rhapsody, utilizing a kind of biblical prose-poetry, and suggestive of the Prophets and Revelations. It was intended as a popular *vade-mecum* of Polish exiles, offering them the hope of inevitable liberation, and inspiring them with a sense of the true and grand mission of Poland. Poland is exalted as the only nation in modern history that had not bowed down to the empty idols worshipped by other nations — the idols of self-interest, but instead was the proclaimer to all other nations that "Whoever will come to me shall be free and equal, for I am Freedom ... They thought to slay Freedom in slaying Poland, but there will be a resurrection of Poland," and "after the Resurrection of the Polish Nation wars shall cease in all Christendom." Polish pilgrims are men and women who believe, love, and have hope. Ye live, Mickiewicz wrote, among strangers, many of them your enemies who do not understand the meaning of your mission. "Inquire not as to what shall be the government of Poland, but work for harmony, and end all discords ... Wear ye the long coats of the insurrections ... Ye have not to learn civilization from strangers, but ye are to teach them the true Christian civilization. The Jews will finally come to understand you and see the light of the new Christianity." And so the rhapsody ends with a Pilgrims' Litany:

> For a universal war for the Freedom of the peoples,
> > We beseech thee, O Lord,
> For the arms and the eagles of our nation,
> > We beseech thee, O Lord ...
> For the independence, unity, and freedom of our Fatherland,
> > We beseech thee, O Lord,
> In the name of the Father, Son and Holy Ghost. Amen.[4]

Strange, inspired, fantastic, and almost terrifying eschatology! Filled with contradictions, impractical adjurations, preaching at one and the same time Poland's exclusive role as savior of the world, and also the coming of a world free of war, inequality, and differences.

Here a theocratic future is built upon a national chauvinism, and yet promising a fulfilment of the best of human aspirations. Read in diverse ways, the book could be interpreted as a bible of Pan-Slavism, assigning to a Slavic nation the role of mankind's saviors; at the same time as it could also be interpreted as a call to revolutionary action.

There was, however, another side to Mickiewicz, a contrast to the mystic and oracular prophet. There was the Mickiewicz who scrutinized the present, and appraised it. Appended to *Forefathers' Eve, Part III*, was a series of poems called a "Digression." In remarkable lines, Mickiewicz was settling his accounts with Russia. Gone were the roseate memories of his days in Moscow and St. Petersburg in the warm companionship of social and intellectual celebrities. Gone, too, genial feelings he had experienced in the presence of Pushkin and Zhukovsky. These poems describe the journey of the poet and his companion, Konrad, to Russia, and their arrival in St. Petersburg.

The poet stands before a monument — the equestrian statue of Peter the Great, and alongside of him there is another figure:

> Hand in hand, two youths stood beneath one cloak,
> One rainy night. One was a pilgrim from the West,
> An unknown victim of the Tsarist might.
> The other was a Russian bard,
> Renowned for songs throughout the North —
> They knew each other well — but not long.
> They had been friends for several days...

Both gaze at the eminent Emperor, on his rearing charger, epitome of Russia's might and greatness. Who are these two youths? One, without doubt, is Mickiewicz himself. And the other, most probably Pushkin — though it might have been Ryleev. Into the Russian poet's lips Mickiewicz places a prophecy. They see how Tsar Peter has released the steed's reins, and how they both fly. Where is the steed headed?

And here a precipice checks his advance...
You guess that he will fall and be destroyed.
Thus he has galloped long, with tossing mane,
Like a cascade, leaping into the void,
That fettered by the frost, hangs dizzily.
But soon will shine the sun of liberty,
And from the west a wind will warm this land —
Will the cascade of tyranny then stand?[5]

In another poem, Mickiewicz is watching a military review, and observes how Tsarism had turned human beings into machines. Finally, rounding out the series of prophecies, he foresees the near future as unchaining the Neva river, and inundating the Tsarist realm ...

There is also a brief poem, "To my Russian Friends," — tender and bitter reminiscence — tender in recalling the executed Decembrist Ryleev, and the exiled Bestuzhov; bitter with castigation of time-serving poets who had been attacking the Polish patriots. The shafts were without doubt aimed at both Pushkin and Zhukovsky, who, in 1831, had published poems filled with hatred of Poland. But Pushkin, on his part, did not greatly resent Mickiewicz's attack, and to the end preserved affectionate memories and his high respect for the Pole. Pushkin's poem to Mickiewicz, which we have quoted at the head of this chapter, and which begins with the words, "He lived among us," concludes with "But now our gentle guest has become our enemy — and in order to please the turbulent rabble, imbues his verses with venom. The voice of the spiteful poet reaches us from afar, familiar voice! ... Oh God, illumine his heart with Thy truth and restore peace to his soul."[6] Despite official prohibition of Mickiewicz's works in Russia following the 1830's, his reputation and reception in Russia were never dimmed, and numerous translations continued appearing.

For world literature, however, Mickiewicz's attack on Russia had a very fruitful consequence and far-reaching import, for it occasioned Pushkin's magnificent poem, *The Bronze Horseman*.

If Mickiewicz harbored any illusions about Pope Gregory XVI's attitude toward his patriotic agitation, he was soon to be disenchanted. The papal encylical and brief which the Pope directed against Lamennais's *Paroles d'un Croyant* also adverted to Mickiewicz's *Books of a Polish Nation* as a "pamphlet full of temerity and malice." Such criticism was not calculated to endear the poet to the more conservative and devout of his countrymen.

Yet, not the least remarkable aspect of Mickiewicz's genius is the fact that despite all the spiritual and personal turmoils, the squabbles and bickering of his Paris compatriots, his own alternations of exultation and disaffection, he found the energy and persistence to bring to fruition his masterpiece, Poland's national epic, *Pan Tadeusz* (pr. Pon Tadéush). The poem was composed between 1832 and 1834. Yet even more remarkable is that feat for its being so utterly different in style and mood from the often frenzied prophetic and apocalyptic productions of the messianic poet. It started out as an idyl, but soon turned into an idyl-epic — idyl in its evocation of the poet's native countryside, and the past; epic in its intertwining of the life within the Lithuanian village with the historic fate and hopes of Poland. *Pan Tadeusz* appeared in 1834, and is the last of Mickiewicz's major poetic creations.

The opening of the epic poem, with its apostrophe, recreates the poet's land of birth, joining to it the passionate cry of the emigré:

> Litwo! Ojczyzno moja! ty jesteś jak zdrowie...
> (Litva! oychizno moya! ti yestesh yak zdrovie...)

> Litva! My country! You are like good health.
> Only he who has lost you, knows your worth.
> Today I see your splendor and all your beauty,
> For I long for you...

We are taken back to the small town of Soplicowo (Suplitsovo), actually Nowogródek (Novogrudek), Mickiewicz's birthplace. It is summer 1811, and the mood is one of recollected tranquillity. The poem ends in the spring of 1812, and the mood is one of excitement and hope. Napoleon is about to invade Russia. The great historic event has now obtruded itself on the pastoral landscape. The poem, begun under the influence of Goethe's narrative pastoral, *Hermann und Dorothea*, also set against a background of war, soon abandons its idyllic tone, and the figurative "shepherd's pipe" gives way to "trumpets stern." But at the conclusion, the idyllic element fuses with the war-like, for it celebrates both the union of two lovers, the protagonists of the story, and the arrival of the Polish soldiery eager to join Napoleon, from whose hands it is hoped Poland will receive her independence. The poem combines romance, melodrama, mystery, sports — and war. Though written out of the mood of deep depression following the catastrophe of 1832, despite its nostalgia and recollective sadness, the poem breathes a spirit of electrified hope.

Twenty-year old Master Thaddeus has returned to his estate at Soplicowo, which is in his uncle's charge. His father, Jacek Soplica, had disappeared, and it is at the latter's behest, somehow conveyed to his brother, the Judge, that Thaddeus is recalled from his studies in Wilno to reclaim his estate and marry a ward of the family, the young and beautiful Zosia. An element of mystery surrounds his father's whereabouts, but we soon learn that as a young squire of limited means he had wooed the daughter of a proud local magnate, Horeszko, and had been rejected in favor of a person of more befitting rank. Jacek's rage drives him to murder Horeszko, during a time of Polish insurrection, when the Russians are attacking Horeszko's castle. His subsequent life is one long expiation. He engages in patriotic work in support of Polish liberation and of Napoleon, returns to the village as a member of the Bernardine order, under the name of Father Robak. Eva, the woman he had loved and lost, had died in Siberian exile, and left behind a daughter — Zosia, now a ward of the Soplica household.

While all around them in Europe war is raging, the Polish and Lithuanian gentry, though under the Russian heel, engage in their own altercations, brawls, and feuds, like some medieval barons, and frequently take the law into their own hands, using their private armies of retainers, assisted by the lesser and impoverished gentry who are still full of arrogance and pride of ancestral rank. Sometimes there is a lull, and the interim is lightened by gargantuan feasts, drinking bouts, innumerable hunting expeditions, even a bear hunt, and other highly noisy amusements which often touch off serious conflicts.

But the life is not all turmoil and tumult. Nature around them is entrancing, and Mickiewicz with affectionate vividness evokes the sights, sounds, and scents of the fields, woods, grasses and flowers, with the passionate detailed observation reminiscent of Wordsworth. At times a freshness and peace pervade the scenes, as, for example, when the gentlefolk engage in gathering mushrooms, having for the occasion donned rustic habits. Mickiewicz even regales us with a lusty catalogue of mushrooms and flowers. The picture is lighteneed by the poet's humor, for he knows how to expose and laugh at the foibles of people, their pretentiousness, their boastfulness, and their fulsome oratory.

With zest Mickiewicz discourses of food and drink. There is a joyful and patriotic apostrophe to coffee — Polish coffee unmatched elsewhere, "black as coal, transparent as amber, fragrant as mocha, and thick as honey."

But alas! even Polish coffee cannot seal the divisons of that gentry society. A Horeszko heir, the "Count," launches a foray against the Soplicas to reassert his right to the possession of the Castle, and a bloody brawl erupts, Russian troops intervene, and in the course of the disturbance Father Robak, née Jacek Soplica, is wounded. He finally reveals his true identity and dies. All this time he had worked zealously to achieve a unity among his compatriots, wandering far and wide to recruit Polish forces in support of the imminent Napoleonic invasion. Here too, in Soplicowo, he had many secret and brave allies, among them the Jewish tavern-keeper, Yankiel.

Now Yankiel is an extraordinary person, perhaps the most remarkable Jewish figure in the literature of that period. Amid the numerous characters of *Pan Tadeusz* he stands out with particular prominence, in the world of the Catholic population, the gentry, the notaries, assessors, judges, counts and generals, Russians and Poles. He is a subsidiary figure that achieves grandeur. He is respected for his honesty and wisdom, and extraordinary disinterestedness; he is looked up to by both the Horeszkos and the Soplicas; he acts as arbiter in disputes, and among his co-religionists he officiates as a rabbi. He is a dedicated Polish patriot, and in the total confidence of Father Robak. He is a democrat and a lover of liberty.

But he is also an outstanding musician, master of the cembalon — the dulcimer. He speaks through this instrument, and speaks to all. Somewhere Mickiewicz must have come across his prototype; perhaps in Wilno, where there were many Jews like him filled with messianic hopes and longings...

And now it is spring of 1812 — the fateful moment has arrived. The cry resounds: "War! War!" Napoleon's armies are ready for their march into Russia, and Polish contingents arrive in Soplicowo to join them. Hopes fly sky-high, for Napoleon — "that man" — is the "god of war," who had been flinging his "thunder"

> From Libyan wastes to lofty Alpine peaks,
> Against Pyramids and Tabor,
> Marengo, Ulm, and Austerlitz,
> While Victory and Conquest sped before and after ...

Surely he was destined to bring salvation to Poland and the Poles, and crush the Russians.

Mickiewicz, too, exults:

> Oh Spring! Happy he who beheld you in our land! ...
> Born in servitude, bound in swaddling bands,
> But one such spring has been mine in my life ...

O year of years!
Long have you been heralded by marvels in the sky,
And long foretold by rumors among the folk...
I see you still, fair phatom of my dreams!

All looks well. The heroic General Dombrowski is here with his Polish army. The castle is teeming with soldiers and guests. Tadeusz is to be married to Zosia. At Zosia's entreaties, Yankiel consents to play the dulcimer. He strikes the chords of his instrument, and from it issues a history of Poland: the Poland of former bright hopes — like the achievement of the Constitution of May 1791, and the subsequent uprising; and the tragic Poland, the massacres perpetrated by the Russians against the Praga suburb of Warsaw.

Now Yankiel strikes up a heroic Polonaise, and a savage elegy.

The Master changed the pitch, and changed the strain.
Once more he looked and measured the strings with his eyes,
And joining hands, smote them with hammers two,
He struck the blows so hard, and yet so deftly,
The strings rang out with trumpets' blare aloft,
And from the trumpets to the heavens rose up — well-known —
Triumphant march, "Poland has not perished yet!"
And "March, march, Dombrowski to Poland's land!"
And all clapped hands, and "March, Dombrowski!" roared.[7]

There is music, too, in the verses themselves, and a transliteration can but vaguely suggest the forcefulness and vigor of Mickiewicz's heroic lines:

He struck the blows so hard and yet so deftly...

Uderzhenie tak shtuchne, tak potenzhne,
Zhe struny zadzvonily yak trombi moshenzhne,
I z tromb znana piosenka ku niebu vionenla,
Marsh triumfalny, "Yeshche Polska nie zginenla!"
"Marsh Dombrowski do Polski!"

Yankiel himself is overcome:

> The master, as if startled by his own lay,
> Dropped the hammers and raised his arms on high,
> His fox-skin cap slipped to his shoulders,
> His beard uplifted waved with majesty,
> His cheeks blazed with the fires of youth,
> And when his eyes alighted on Dombrowski,
> He covered them amidst a rush of tears.
> "General, long has our Litva waited your coming,
> Even as we Jews look toward our Messiah.
> Of you in olden times the minstrels sang to the folk,
> Of you the marvels in the sky forewarned,
> Live and wage war! Oh you our —"

He breaks down.

The festivities are capped by the announcement that Tadeusz and Zosia after their marriage would free their peasants and assign them land.

Such is the idealized world Mickiewicz's poetry portrayed. Peopled mostly by gentlefolk, one is forced to ask oneself — what of the peasants? They scarcely appear on the stage. In the poet's depiction of a totally unified population, there is no suggestion that many of the rich landowners feared a Napoleonic victory more than their oppressive Tsar.

Among the exiles in Paris, there were a number who took umbrage at Mickiewicz's seeming partiality toward the Polish gentry. Many of them missed, in Mickiewicz and his associates, references to the much needed social changes and they sensed an absence of truly revolutionary conviction. The most articulate of these critics, Mickiewicz's eminent fellow-poet, Julius Slowacki, composed an extravagant dramatic poem, *Kordian*, which was published in 1834. Here Slowacki presented a bitter, satirical, at times poignant replica of the romantic Pole, adrift on his dreams, an intellectual nihilist, and an unbridled egoist. It is these traits that Slowacki thought he discerned among the Polish emigrés. A sage attempts to convert Kordian from his wild phantasies, by calling upon him to come closer to the people, to try to understand them, and even come to love them. Kordian turns into an ardent Polish patriot, and even tries to persuade the Pope in favor of Poland's cause. Disenchanted, he turns terrorist, and prepares to assassinate Tsar Nicholas I. But on the verge of success, he breaks down completely. Such — Slowacki predicts — is the likely fate of romantic "messianic" revolutionaries who have no true, deep relation to the people of their nation.

There were, however, among the Polish refugees some who found the projects of their fellow-countrymen altogether too revolutionary, as well as utterly futile. Zigmunt Krasiński, a highly gifted poet and playwright, had as little use for the Polish gentry as he had for the radicals. His *Undivine Comedy* (1833), a kind of mystery play, mingled realism and phantasy in powerful poetic prose. The world is represented as on the verge of a cosmic débacle, as revolutionaries clash with aristocracy and gentry. The latter are depicted as utterly selfish and tyrannical and corrupt. So are the revolutionaries. Corrupt and godless. Allied with the revolutionaries are "Convert Jews," who, ostensibly dedicated to the revolutionary cause of Poland, are really aiming to achieve Judaic mastery of the world. Here are the prefigurations of all those monsters that the notorious *Protocols of the Elders of Zion* and Nazism were to turn into cosmic agents of the world's evil and disintegration. In the play, the revolutionaries triumph, but their victory is an empty one. The play ends as the dying revolutionary leader recognizes the futility of his efforts, and foresees the ultimate triumph of Jesus Christ.

Against such phantasies of cosmic despair, Mickiewicz's *Pan Tadeusz* stands out as a kind of "Pastoral Symphony" of almost radiant hope. Although this was the last of his important poetical compositions, he was not one to remain idle, or to wallow in the luxuries of a *Weltschmerz*, or in the sloughs of despond. Despite his mystical and messianic propensities, he remained a man of action to the last moment of his life. His years were not to be free of great sorrows, even tragedies. His marriage to the young Celina Szymanowska, daughter of the woman he had loved in Russia, proved catastrophic, for Celina was unbalanced mentally and subject to fits of insanity.

Mickiewicz himself in 1841, and for a few years thereafter, came under the magnetic sway of a Polish messianic illuminist, Andrzej Towiański (by some of his contemporaries suspected of being an agent of the Tsar). Possessed of a charismatic personality, Towiański is alleged to have effected a cure of Mickiewicz's insane wife. More and more Mickiewicz became dominated by the visionary and messianic, and he now amalgamated the figures of Napoleon Bonaparte, the Israelites, and Poland into unified bearers of the world's redemption. They would initiate a new and revolutionized Christianity that would change the world. He found a number of devotés, who gathered around himself and Towiański, in "conventicles."

Mickiewicz remained a most impressive personality, who deeply affected those who came in contact with him, through his integrity, his convictions, his patriotism, and his eloquence. He became something of a legend throughout Europe. In 1840 he was appointed to the chair of Slavic studies at the Collège de France — a signal honor, since the Collège did not then possess even a chair of German philology. Few lecturers enjoyed such distinguished audiences as now came to listen to the Polish poet discourse on Slavic civilization. George Sand was there (she composed one of the most perceptive studies of Mickiewicz's poetry), the historian Michelet, and the poet-philosopher Quinet (both the poet's colleagues at the Collège), Chopin, and the philosopher Victor Cousin. He electrified his hearers with his improvisations, for he always spoke extemporaneously, at times halting to find the right French expression, but "always succeeding."

The flowers of marvelous folk-lore mingled on his lips, fired by his Messianism. The Slav strength to suffer, to hope, to transform suffering into hope, lived within him. To listen to him was to see the coming of eternal Christianity on the morrow, if only we had faith and courage.[8]

So, one of his auditors.

What Mickiewicz's lectures lacked in scientific knowledge, they supplied with their wide philosophical scope and their eloquence. But soon, his radical pan-Slavism and his prophecies became obnoxious to the Russian government, which prevailed on that of France to terminate the poet's academic career. This was part of the currently aggravated governmental opposition to liberal thinkers, for both Michelet and Quinet soon lost their professorial chairs.

For the national aspirations of many European lands, aside from Poland, Mickiewicz became a symbolic figure; an inspiration, for example to Mazzini. The American Transcendentalist Margaret Fuller left testimony to an unforgettable experience when she met and spoke with him.

History does not wait on Messianic prophecies, and the sharp tensions — social and political — in France were soon to erupt in the February Revolution of 1848. Many writers and artists, Lamennais and George Sand among them, were soon propelled into new channels of thought and action. Mickiewicz was not one to stand aside. Perhaps this was the moment he had been waiting for. With all of Europe soon aflame, how could the emigrés fail to envision a total liberation of oppressed nationalities? Mickiewicz organized a Polish legion to fight against the Austrians in Italy. He obtained an interview with the Pope — Pius IX — then considered the rising dawn of Catholic liberalism — in behalf of Poland and a new order. He was soon to learn that there was nothing to be expected of the Vatican. He helped found and became the editor of a radical newspaper, *La Tribune des Peuples*, to which outstanding liberals and radicals contributed, and which was dedicated to the "idea of a holy war for the freeing of the peoples of Europe," but which was soon suppressed for its fiery radicalism.

He was discovering Socialism.

Socialism, he wrote, is a totally new word. Who brought it into being? We do not know. The most terrifying words are those whose origin people do not know, yet which the whole world repeats . . . Socialism appeared for the first time in the February days, in the peoples' programs. An unknown hand traced the word Socialism and a great fear took hold of all the self-satisfied Belshazzars of France . . . The old society and all those who represent it, without understanding the meaning of the word, read in it their death-sentence.[9]

Even the collapse of the revolutions did not abate his missionary zeal. Napoleon, Israel, and Poland remained the triadic elements of the world's salvation that no defeat could undo. On the outbreak of the Crimean War in 1854, he saw another crusade in the making, and he set about organizing a Polish and Jewish legion to join in the war against Russia. It was while engaged in this activity in Turkey, that he died of cholera on November 26, 1855. The town of Burgas was his Missolonghi.

Like Byron's, Mickiewicz's name and fame became international by-words. In the 1830's, upon the defeat of the Warsaw uprising, Ludwig Uhland, Germany's national bard, wrote a poem, "Mickiewicz."

> Mitten in der stillen Feier,
> Wird ein Saitengriff getan,
> Ha, wie schwillet die Leier
> Voller stets und mächtiger an . . .

> Hark, amidst the solemn hour,
> There was one who touched the lyre,
> Hear! a fuller, mightier music
> Surges from these magic chords.
> Here's a spirit sings life's renewal.
> What is dead is born again.
> Yes, the Master's song is warrant:
> "Poland has not perished yet!"

4.

JOSÉ DE ESPRONCEDA
SPAIN'S CHILDE HAROLD

> Romanticism! How many conflicting notions are
> aroused in our imagination when we hear that
> word! A magic talisman — it lures us sweetly like a
> beloved voice, like a celestial harmony. For others,
> Romantic means heresy, and worse... Romantic is
> Anti-Christ, Romantic is Beelzebub!
> — Eugenio de Ochoa, 1835 —

Victor Hugo, who had asserted that Romanticism was liberalism in
literature, would undoubtedly have rejoiced in its manifestation in
Spain. For in this country, Romanticism — a brief and belated
lightning stroke in a dreary and tumultuous historical panorama
— scorched for a moment both the political and cultural terrain. In
her literary productions, Spain, like the rest of absolutist Europe,
was bound to the pseudo-classical art of France in servile imitations,
— minor, but not inconsiderable formal bulwarks of conservatism.
It was not to this facet of Spain that Europe of the early nineteenth
century turned in the course of its cultural discovery and expansion.
The Romantics of Europe found new, rich treasures in Calderón,
Lope de Vega, and the medieval Spanish Romances. Cervantes had
long been known, admired, and imitated. Friedrich and August
Wilhelm von Schlegel in Germany, and John Gibson Lockhart and
Robert Southey in Great Britain, among others, brought new
excitement and joy with their translations and reinterpretations of
the great Baroque and medieval Spanish literary treasures.

620

It was now Spain's turn to seize upon the treasures that England and France had to offer, and it is out of these elements that Spanish Romanticism is born, fusing these with stores derived from Spain's own historic past, and the necessities and urgencies of the day.

And in the 1830's the latter were of great moment. The July Revolution of 1830 played a significant role in the life of many of the Spaniards. To turn toward France, and to be fired by the international reverberation of those great days was no longer to be tainted with the odium of being an *afrancesado* — a Francophile — so long associated with the aspersive meaning of "collaborator" during the War of Independence against Napoleon. To be *afrancesado* now, in the era of the Bourbon Restoration of Ferdinand VII, after 1823, meant recognition of an identity of interests and passions, as well as goals, cultural, political, and social, with the rest of the world — to enter once more into the orbit of modern history. The *afrancesados* were the "liberales" of this era; just as the "serviles" and the "apostolicos" were the absolutists and extreme royalists of 1814 and 1823.

But Spain's Romanticism is also the child of exile — exile of her liberal thinkers during the bitter and agonizing days of the Bourbon Restoration, which had been brought about with the aid of French bayonets under the Duc d'Angoulême. Her literature is a literature of despair as well as exaltation — on the one hand filled with the horror of betrayal by the returned monarchy, and on the other, with exaltation in memories of the War of Independence of 1810-1813; the heroism of May 2, 1808, the temporary achievement of the Constitution of 1812, the courageous resistance of the 1820's and the martyrdom of Riego and his associates.

One of the outstanding Spanish Romantics, Mariano José de Larra, a disciple of Lamennais and translator of his *Paroles d'un Croyant*, spoke the sentiments of other Romantics when he asked for a "new literature" that would be a just expression of the new society, "which we are building, altogether truthful, as our society is truthful, ... young, ... as the Spain which we are building." Literature, he insisted, was the effect and not the cause of historic circumstances. It should be a literature that is "the daughter of experience and history, scholarly, analytical, philosophical, profound, thinking all, saying all, in prose, in verse, the expression, in short, of the science of the age, of the progress of the century."[1]

This was, of course, the dream. To attempt to realize it in an atmosphere of disorder, disruption and chaos — first during exile, and in the midst of an ensuing civil war, and an unrest that was to beset Spain for many generations to come — was an almost impossible task.

The restoration of Ferdinand VII to the throne of Spain, though it brought back a ruthless and vindictive absolutism, did not in fact succeed in utterly stifling the opposition, especially among the younger generation. The hanging of Riego and the ignominious display of his corpse in Madrid; the executions by hanging and shooting of one hundred and twelve other liberals were to serve as unforgettable battle-cries for many years to come.

On the day of November 7, 1823, when Riego was being done to death, a group of young students stood in the Plaza de la Cebada, gazing at the frightful spectacle. Among them was the fifteen year old José de Espronceda, destined to become one of Spain's foremost Romantic poets, accompanied by his friend, Patricio Escosura, his future biographer. It was an experience neither of them would ever forget.

José de Espronceda was born in the fateful year of 1801, the son of a professional soldier. He might be said to have been cradled in the arms of Bellona, goddess of war, for he was brought into the world in the midst of an army campaign. His stalwart mother had accompanied her husband on an expedition sent to crush an insurrection in Aranjuez. The boy was born in a small village with the poetic name of Pajares de la Vega — Birds of the Plain — not far from Almendralejo. José was to remain a soldier all his life long, though in causes far removed from those his father espoused. The elder Espronceda was lieutenant-colonel in the service of the government.

José de Espronceda was fortunate in his education. At the Colegio San Mateo in Madrid, he came in contact with extraordinary teachers, the most remarkable of these being Don Alberto Lista, possessor of a luminous mind and a capacious heart, a scholar of great endowments and wide learning, and a human being who understood young students. When the Colegio was closed by order of the government because suspected of liberalism, Lista opened his own school, and here young Espronceda continued his education. He received a thorough training in classical and modern languages, and in other humanistic subjects. Not least crucial was the atmosphere of political liberalism that prevailed in the school. Outside, in Madrid and throughout the country there was an air of ominous oppression. There were the extremists of the right, who found King Ferdinand's severities too tame, and in their special organizations, such as "los Apostolicos," "El Angel Exterminador" and others — supported by the King's brother, Don Carlos and the latter's wife, Maria Francisca de Braganza — urged severer measures of repression, the restoration of the Inquisiton, and also fomented uprisings and disturbances throughout the countryside. After King Ferdinand's death in 1833, the Carlist pretender to the throne of Spain and his followers provoked a Civil War, to nullify the assumption of the throne by the legitimate heir Isabel II, then still a child under the regency of her mother, Maria Cristina. The country was to be torn apart for many years to come.

Within the younger spirits, however, the hearth of revolt remained unextinguished after 1823. Don Lista's students organized secret conspiratorial groups, met in obscure places, issued documents of protest, and soon became the objects of serious attention on the part of the police. Their associations were broken up; and though the punishments were mild, the warnings were sufficiently clear. Young Espronceda was condemned "to reclusion" in a convent in Guadalajara (a town in which his father was then stationed), but soon allowed to return to Madrid. In his confinement he began composing an epic poem, *Pelayo (Pelagius).* He was then sixteen.

He was undismayed, and unreformed, and more rebellious than ever. Between 1825 and 1827 we lose sight of him; but the fact that in 1827 he fled from Spain suggests a continuing political activity, possibly other conspiracies. He made his way to Portugal, which proved none too hospitable to Spanish refugees; and then to England. Tradition has it that it was in Portugal that Espronceda met Teresa Mancha, daughter of Colonel Epifanio Mancha, and fell in love with her. Some time in September 1827 he arrived in London, with a friend, Antonio Hernáiz. Here he found thousands of other Spaniards, in exile like himself, for England, then rivalling with France for the control of Spain, was welcoming potential allies.

Compared with Spain, England appeared a haven of freedom. The country was in a state of ferment over the pending Reform Bill, and our young Spaniards must have observed these agitations with special interest. Their own political activities were bound up with the fate of Spain, and the burning hopes of an overturn of the present Spanish régime. The presence in England of General Mina and Colonel Joaquín de Pablo transformed these hopes into an imminent reality.

For the young poet, England was also the land of Walter Scott, Lord Byron, Shakespeare, the misty poet of "Ossian." Of the older Romantics, Wordsworth and Coleridge were still alive; but the younger Romantics, Shelley, Keats, and Byron were gone. So far as English readers were concerned, never since the days of Spain's grandeur had there been such an interest in Spain, present and past. A number of British journals welcomed contributions from the newly arrived Spaniard. In the comparative quietness of England, Espronceda must have recalled his master, Lista's verses, in which the latter yearningly dreamt of a land "where quiet innocence passes her days in happy peace, where the law protects, without binding in chains, and authority is felt only in the good it dispenses and the evil it eschews."

> Ajenos climas busquemos, do tranquila inocencia
> en venturosa pas logra sus dias;
> do protege la ley sin echar lazos,
> y de la autoridád sólo se siente
> en el ben que dispensa o mal que evita.[2]

Espronceda's closest identification was with Byron, of course. He was later, whether in praise or blame, to be referred to as the Spanish Byron. But what literary figure, what painter or musician, had escaped that spell? To absorb the Byronic temper meant, for Espronceda, to become both poet and soldier. The opportunity for both engagements soon presented itself.

France was to complete what England had begun. He came to Paris in the tumultuous year of 1829. In the highly charged political and literary climate that prevailed here, Espronceda, who had mastered both English and French, had little difficulty in responding to the exhilaration and excitement of those hours. Here he was in the proximity of Victor Hugo, Vigny, Lamartine, and the Saint-Simonians; in the midst of the mounting rebellion that faced the régime of Charles X. The July Revolution appeared as the destined moment for Spain's resurrection as well. The doors that had sealed the Spanish refugees were now open, and France became the springboard for their entry into Spain.

Did Espronceda fight on the barricades of Paris during the July days? We do not know. His biographers believe that he did. Knowing what he was like, we may guess that his boiling blood would not long keep him from taking part in the revolution. His good friend, Balbino Corte, did take part, was wounded, and honored for his courage. It is not likely that Espronceda would have stood apart. Politics and insurrection were his life's blood.

The time seemed ripe now for some action that would rouse the Spaniards and bring about the overthrow of Ferdinand VII. Under the leadership of Colonel Joaquín de Pablo, an expedition of two hundred men was organized. Espronceda was a part of it. That he was a fiery opponent of the Spanish régime was long known to the Spanish authorities; the police had marked him down as a "revolucionario famoso," in 1829, and had made a search of his father's house.[3]

In October 1830 de Pablo and his troops crossed the Pyrenees, with the hope of arousing the Navarrese to rebellion. Vain hope! His own former troops, from whom he had anticipated support, turned against him. De Pablo was killed in action, and his followers were routed. Similar ventures in other parts of Spain also failed dismally. The populace of Spain failed to respond to their would-be liberators. Despondent, but not defeated, Espronceda returned to Paris, and in the following year, in the wake of the Polish uprising, he volunteered for a projected expedition designed to help the Poles. That project came to naught, despite the urgent clamors on the part of many Frenchmen, and the support of such important figures as General Lamarque and Lafayette. The venture foundered on the policies of expediency fostered by the "juste-milieu" of King Louis-Philippe.

There was nothing to do now but wait. Distance and time had not quenched the love between Teresa Mancha and Espronceda. He had met her again in London, where to escape destitution she had married a wealthy Spanish merchant. It was when the married couple visited Paris, that Teresa, the mother of two children, decided to leave home and family, to join the man she loved. We have no letters of the lovers, no journal of the poet to help us trace the course of that consuming passion, and its later decline. All that Espronceda left us some years later was love's tragic epitaph, three years after Teresa's death.

But while Espronceda waited, he was not inactive. Nor was the French police. Foreign political activists were under constant surveillance, and recently published materials testify to the fact that Espronceda was considered one of the twenty-five most dangerous Spaniards in Paris. There is reason to believe that he participated in the failed demonstration of September 19, 1831.[4]

Expelled from Paris, he was transferred to Bordeaux, and a short time thereafter found his way to London, then back to Paris.

In the meantime, the history of Spain was undergoing great changes. Ferdinand VII died in 1833. His brother, Don Carlos, was contesting the ascendency to the throne of the child Isabela and the regency of Maria Cristina. To gain popular support, Maria Cristina declared an amnesty, and made limited liberal concessions, ever ready to revoke them when time favored her. Espronceda took advantage of the amnesty to return to Spain, soon to be followed by Teresa. It would be useless to detail the distressing history of Spain during the next few years — when ministry followed ministry, and Maria Cristina was involved in a bitter struggle against the Carlist pretender and his ever-growing army of followers, at the same time as she was engaged in playing off her own statesmen against each other — the moderates against the "exaltados" — that is, the radicals. In 1840, the crisis reached a culmination when Maria Cristina was forced to abdicate as regent, and leave the country. Isabela II was declared queen, and minister Espartero took over the regency.

In the midst of these innumerable crises, Espronceda often found himself at odds with the government. He was himself an "exaltado," and his boldness often landed him in prison, or forced him into temporary exile from Madrid. But he was irrepressible as poet, editor, and politician. In 1840 appeared his volume of collected poems, the *Poesías Varias*, the gem of Spanish Romantic poetry. In 1841 he was appointed secretary to the Spanish legation in the Hague. At the same time he had been elected deputy to the Cortes from the province of Almería. A daughter, Blanca, was born to Teresa and Espronceda in 1834, but the love affair did not last, and they separated in 1836. Three years later Teresa died. Her end was a miserable one.

As a member of the Spanish Cortes, Espronceda dedicated himself to its humdrum duties with earnestness and fidelity, though he never neglected his literary or journalistic activities. He was cut off suddenly as a result of a mysterious throat ailment — other sources suggest an older chronic disease — on May 23, 1842, at the age of thirty-eight. Teresa was twenty-eight at the time of her death.

José de Espronceda stands out as the "representative man" of Spanish Romanticism.[5] In him is consummated that fusion that gives the movement its special character. With him, along with the other Romantics, it may be said that Spain once more rejoins the rest of the world in a shared aspiration and understanding. The Spanish struggle for independence of the 1820's had special significance for the rest of Europe, and its inspiration extended to Italy and Russia. Culturally Spain had given the European world Calderón, Lope de Vega, Cervantes, and the great art of Spain's baroque to absorb anew. Now Spain took sustenance from Romantic Europe, particulary from England and France, through an immediate personal contact with that world, now in the throes of a major change. The interlacing of cultures paralleled the interweaving of political ideas and actions. The Romantic ethic of individual personal defiance had been enlarged to encompass the wider needs of humanity. The Polish uprising, the barricades of the July days, the insurrections of Naples and Madrid, the Decembrist "revolution," — all these become parts of a common consciousness transcending the claims of a purely anarchic egoism. And these in turn are also intertwined with the intellectual and sentimental elements of the literature of the past and of the present. It is these elements that made up a good portion of Espronceda's private and public life, of his thoughts and actions, and of his poetry.

He apprehended, assimilated, and transformed; his range of interests was wide, and he took generously from the literary treasures of his own times and of Spain's past. The libertarian elements which Romanticism embodied in Lucifer, Don Juan, Faust, and the biblical Cain he knew how to employ and fuse into his Spanish background. One will find traces and echoes in his works of Byron — particularly of *Cain, Manfred*, and *Don Juan*; possibly of Goethe's *Faust*; of Victor Hugo, Lamartine, Vigny, as well as —

significantly — of the "people's poets" — Béranger and Auguste
Barbier. But they are all melted in his own crucibles, and transformed
by his own genius into original creations.

Espronceda's most ambitious work, *El Diablo Mundo* — *The
Satan World* — never completed, is a brilliant version of the Faust
legend, localized in Spain. The impress of Byron, Goethe, and
Voltaire is upon it, but the investing spirit is Espronceda's.
Originally planned as a kind of cosmic epic — satiric and serious at
the same time, partly also dramatic, it raises ultimate queries about
the nature of Man, the Universe, God, and Satan. Its world, though
peopled by timeless demons and supernatural agents, also encloses
the heyday timeliness of the real and actual Spain. The poet dreams,
and is beset by demoniac presences, restless queries, and finally by
the appearance of Lucifer, the eternal rebel and Nay-sayer — the
Lucifer closest to Byron rather than to the Mephistopheles of *Faust*.
In Espronceda he takes on the new form of Lucifer-Man. For, as
Lucifer explains to the poet, Man is Lucifer, Lucifer is Mankind:

> Yo siempre marcho contigo
> Y ese gusano que roe
> Tu corazón,...
> Soy yo...y mi infierno
> Es el corazón del hombre.

> I always walk by your side,
> And that worm that gnaws
> At your heart, that shadow
> Clouding your illusions,
> It is I, the fallen star,
> Angel of sorrows,
> King of evil, and my Hell
> Is the heart of Man.[6]

Lucifer, in Espronceda's poem, is not God's creation but
Man's. "You brought me into being," he asserts. "You placed me
within your storms, your griefs, your anxieties, blasphemies, impotence.

You made me your executioner, and it is you, mortal man, that divided the empire of the world between God and me. And yet you wander through the world asking futile questions..." For the eternal divisions that make up the nature of Man are Satanic elements — all bound up with his illusions and aspirations.

The superb lyrics of the opening sections are a filigree of music in words, suggestive of Shelley's *Prometheus Unbound*, and the opening of Goethe's *Faust*, broken into finally by the terrifying voice of Lucifer: "Quien es Dios?" "Who is this God?"

The Faustian story now takes over, as an old scholar, bitter with unanswered questions which time will no longer allow him to try to answer, is transformed into a beautiful youth, Adam, robust, fresh, and utterly innocent. But innocence gives way to experience.

The satirical portion of *El Diablo Mundo* now relates how our naked Adam is thrust into our world, and meets with the contumely and indignities that are meted out to moral purity and innocence. Espronceda without doubt was recalling the brilliant story of Voltaire, *L'Ingénu*, in which an American Huron, coming to France learns what a civilized world is like. The shocked populace of the Spanish city of Alcalá does not know what to make of this Adamic prodigy, and finally puts him in prison. For Adam may be some anarchist intent on undermining the state! He is instructed in the true nature of law, and were it not for the ministrations and intercession of a woman of the lower classes, who sells her body to an appropriate authority, Adam might have languished in jail till Doomsday. For such is Spanish justice! From her prisoner-father he learns the bitter lesson: "Homo homini lupus" — "Man is wolf to man," and that "our God is Lord omnipotent, and Money is his Lord-Lieutenant." He learns the nature of crime, discovers the great gulf that separates the rich from the poor; and has his first sight of death, and does not understand why human beings cannot be immortal, or why, being dead, they cannot be restored to life. Here the poem breaks off.

But in another fragment we learn how deeply Espronceda companions himself with Cain and Lucifer. These are the great Accusers. It is to the poet that the Angel speaks:

> Oh, hijo de Cain!...
> ...en ti la descendencia...
> Rebelde y generosa de Cain!
>
> Oh, Son of Cain!...
> You are the rebel and generous offspring of Cain

You, Poet, loftier than kings, whose thoughts dare ascend and even dare God himself, challenge and wrangle with Him, leave this world of sorrow and ascend with me, he urges — this world, which Espronceda describes, as one where "every grain of sand, every plant, every vile insect,... I hear hurling their bitter plaints of grief and sorrow..."[7]

"Quien es Dios?" Is he the Lord of the Empyrean, listening to the praise of the angelic hosts? Or the God of Vengeance? Or the God who created Man and the World, and then abandoned them to their own devices? Or is he Human Intelligence — daring, insatiable, always aspiring, restless to break the bars of the cage — which is the world? What is Man? A mystery. What is Life? Also a mystery...

One can imagine how deeply interlaced this dramatic poem was with his life's events, for Canto Two is entirely devoted to the beautiful and heart-rending apostrophe to the dead Teresa — certainly one of the most touching and desolating lyrics of Spanish Romanticism. Here orisons of past love turn in blasphemies, and love is tainted as the world itself. As in Tennyson's "Locksley Hall," where for the young rhapsodic lover, "Love took up the harp of life..., and smote the chords of Self," so for Espronceda, too, Love widened his heart and being to include all the world, and filled him with high and mighty purposes:

Yo amaba todo: Un doble sentimiento
Exaltaba mi ánimo, y sentía
En mi pecho un secreto movimiento
De grandes hechos generosos guía...

I loved all: a two-fold impulse
Raised my spirit, and I felt
Within my breast a secret motion
To great and generous deeds.
Liberty, with her immortal breath,
Sacred goddess, enkindled my soul,
And in my pure faith I saw within me
Promises of earthly glory and bliss.[8]

But then, came the revulsion, the disenchantment (we do not know the cause — perhaps misunderstanding, jealousy, estrangement — who dare guess?).

Tú fuiste un tiempo un cristalino río,
Manantial de purissima limpieza...

You were once a crystalline stream,
A source at once limpid and pure,
Then a torrent of somber taint,
Rushing betwen rock and bramble,
Ending at last, pool of fouled water,
Ending a fetid swamp...

The legend of Don Juan had originated in Spain, and had spread like wildfire throughout the European world. Espronceda's *El Estudiante de Salamanca* — *The Student of Salamanca* — completed some years before he embarked on *El Diablo Mundo*, turns Don Juan into a romantic anarch, living a terminal life, for whom there is neither yesterday nor tomorrow. Death does not affright him; he lives for the hour, and for himself. His heart is an "inn."

A majestic, satanic figure,
Lofty of countenance, Montemar strides,
A sublime spirit in his madness,
Provoking divine anger.

A weak vessel of impure matter,
With a soul that inspires and illumines it,
Matches it with God, and in daring flight
Soars toward His throne, and provokes Him to combat.

A lesser Cain, a tainted Lucifer, Montemar is immune to illusions, as he is to disenchantment. He defies society, and destroys the woman he loves. Out of love for him, she would bring him to repentance, but he denies both himself and God. Elvira is the damned and doomed Montemar's Beatrice. He has killed her brother, and one night wandering through the streets of the city, he encounters a white specter — a woman — and follows her. In an eerie scene he finds himself in the presence of his own corpse, and that of Elvira's brother, both being carried to their graves. Follows a witches' sabbath of madness, terrors, maelstroms of sounds and sights, ending in a spectral dance in which he takes part. He uncovers the visage of the woman he had been pursuing; she embraces and kisses him, and he discovers her to be a skeleton — Death! — his bride, his wife! He has denied love and humanity, and is consigned to damnation, while Elvira is enthroned among the angels.

This dramatic poem is Espronceda's *Symphonie Fantastique* — it is his *Damnation of Faust* — and the eerie spectacles are worthy of E.T.A. Hoffmann.

The dance of death is a *tour de force*, a *Walpurgisnacht*, rendered in varying cadences and rhymes with a master's technique, worthy of Hugo's *Orientales*. As the scenes move from the funereal wailing and the tears of love

Funebre
Llanto
De amor
Oyese
En tanto
En son...

and now accelerate and rise in volume in a constant crescendo, then mount towards a fortissimo of full horror, we find ourselves in the midst of "infernal noises," and in the presence of a "hundred spectres" —

> De pronto en horrendo estampido
> Desquirciarse la estancia sintiò
> Y al tremendo tartáreo ruido
> Cien espectros alzarse miró...

Don Félix de Montemar is now in his final death-throes — we are in the decrescendo of the "symphony" — the flame is dying out — the sounds are those of an expiring lyre — "light, brief sounds" —

> Y vió luego
> Una llama
> Que se inflama
> Y murió
> Y perdido
> Oyó el eco...
> Tal dulce
> Suspira
> La lira...
> Leve,
> Breva,
> Son.[9]

Espronceda was at one with life's "outsiders" — rebels, outcasts, and defiers of God and of society, and hymns them with bravado in poems dedicated to pirates, beggars, and executioners. He transforms Joseph de Maistre's executioner, society's instrument of terror, into a figure of giant proportions, as the very embodiment of history itself, a King of Kings, a warning even to those sitting on thrones.[10] But he was always deeply aware of the larger issues and the wider social strata of which these individuals were only a small part. Spain was ever before him, and he saw Spain in the larger context of contemporary history. He had witnessed the July days and had seen the heroism of the ordinary common people. He had watched them demonstrate in behalf of Poland in 1831 and 1832. He had seen them gunned down by Louis-Phillipe's gendarmerie. He had been present at the defeat and death of Colonel de Pablo and his followers; he had observed a band of two hundred soldiers standing up against a thousand. And he composed magnificent tributes to the people's courage and faith.

One of the noblest of these, "Al Dos da Mayo" — "The Second of May" — commemorates the Spanish people's resistance to the French in 1808, and he arraigns the self-seekers of the time (and of every time), who sought safety behind French bayonets, and then scornfully reviled and maligned what they called the "rabble." While writing this poem, he remembered Auguste Barbier's bitter verses recalling the July days of Paris, the dandies of the Boulevard de Gan, who afterwards paraded as "heroes" of that encounter.

> Que faisaient-ils, tandis qu'à travers la mitraille,
> Et sous le sabre détesté
> La grande populace et la sainte canaille
> Se ruaient á la immortalité?

> What did they do, when in the face of the cannon,
> And under the detested sabre,
> The great populace, the sainted *canaille*
> Was rushing toward immortality?

Espronceda, too, recalls the vilification of the "rabble" who had fought to defend the liberties of Spain.

"The rabble"!? he asks. "Canalla!" "You who denied glory to their burning fervor, and never saw the lightnings lighting up their inspired brows. Rabble! Yes, you, who in the midst of battle made boast of your infamy, cloaking your cowardly villainy in the security of cold reason, while in the meantime the 'rabble' . . . swept by a holy zeal shattered the chains of the earth . . . But why, thinking of those heroes does my heart break? Arise, "he calls out to the dead of 1808, "arise and behold the infamy and shame of your sons. The throne you erected is now that of an ungrateful king...Weep, your tongues cannot utter the cry of vengeance, your arms are limp...and my heart breaks, as I break the strings of my lyre."

> Y estallando las cuerdas de mi lira,
> Roto también mi corazón estalle.[11]

The dismay and disenchantment that swept the liberals and republicans following the accession of Louis-Philippe unmoored him, too, as he looked upon what seemed to him a disintegrating Europe:

> Miseria y avidez, dinero y prosa,
> En vil mercado convertido el mundo...
>
> Meanness and avarice, lucre and prose,
> The world turned into a huckster vile,
> The heart's generous passion sold on the mart,
> The trader King of Fate and Glory...
> And ancient Glory turned into carrion
> Dressed up in a gold-bordered winding sheet...
> Who will awaken you? What new accents,
> What trumpet call of Doom's day,
> Can move this rigid corpse:...
> I sit, another Jeremiah, a solitary,
> Amidst the cold ashes and silent ruins.
> Shall I break out in useless lamentations?
> No!
> I will sing.
> Mankind shall hear me.
> I will cry out, "Oh, shameful ones,
> Clear your brow of ancient vileness,
> And see!
> Your Glory is carrion no longer!"[12]

Many years later, toward the latter part of the nineteenth century, when both the political life and the literature of Spain experienced a renewal of spirit after the dismal years of internecine strife, and the paralysis of culture, the name and work of José de

Espronceda, his character and his life, were resuscitated in the works of the great novelists, such as Pérez Galdós and Pio Baroja, for they recognized in him the golden link that bound them to him, and with him in the common partnership of letters and liberalism. Today, in a revived Spain, he speaks more than ever as a contemporary.

V.

END OF AN EPOCH:
GOETHE, WEIMAR AND THE
TRANSFIGURATION OF FAUST

END OF AN EPOCH:
GOETHE, WEIMAR AND THE
TRANSFIGURATION OF FAUST

1.

> At bottom, we are all collective beings, say what you
> will...It is true that in my long life I have tried
> many things, and accomplished a number of which I
> can be proud. But to be honest, what do I have that
> is truly mine, other than the capacity and the
> inclination to see and hear, to discriminate and
> choose?...I do not attribute my works to my
> wisdom alone, but to hosts of things and persons
> who have nourished my work: the ignorant and the
> wise, the bright and the stupid, children and youths,
> as well as the mature, who told me what they
> thought, how they lived their lives; how they
> worked, and what they had experienced. And what I
> did was to harvest what others had sowed.
> — Goethe to Frédéric Soret, February 17, 1832 —

Johann Wolfgang von Goethe died on March 22, 1832. On July 22,
1831, he wrote in his diary: "Das Hauptgeschäft zu Stand gebracht,
letztes Mundum." "The main business attended to. Last fair copy
made."[1] He was speaking of the second part of *Faust*, which he had
just completed. The first part had begun to take shape around 1773!
It had taken sixty years to consummate the vast project. Such, too,
was the case with the *Wilhelm Meister* novels, the *Lehrjahre* and
Die Wanderjahre (The Apprenticeship and *The Years of Wandering)*,
which together had taken more than fifty years. It was as if Goethe,
as a young man, considered himself entitled to a special longevity.

641

He was born in 1749 in Frankfurt. The stars that "ruled at his nativity" looked favorably on him, provided him along with genius, a golden spoon. He came of a solid, well-to-do burgher family that boasted a line of important officials of his native city. Frankfurt was a "free city," a center of commerce and banking, one that was proud of its self-government.

Few of Goethe's literary contemporaries could have enjoyed such a set of favorable circumstances. The plight of writers of that day was indeed a wretched one. To take only one example, and that one of the greatest, Friedrich Schiller, in the neighboring Duchy of Württemberg, was to experience in his early lifetime the misery not only of poverty, but also of living in an autocratic state where career and fate were determined by the ruler's whim. He was saved only by flight.

Young Goethe grew up to be an extraordinarily handsome, engaging, and eloquent young man, who won the hearts of those he met. Under his father's pressure, Goethe entered upon the study of law — law then being a necessary stepping-stone to official employment — first at Leipzig, later at Strassburg. In the latter city he made the acquaintance of Johann Gottfried Herder, already celebrated as theologian and philosopher, who was to prove one of the most significant influences in Goethe's intellectual life. Herder's cultural interests ranged far and wide, and included cultural history, poetry as well as philosophy. Whatever his father's hopes and intentions, Goethe had others, and his practice of law did not continue very long. He was determined to be a poet, and fame came early. When he was twenty-four he became a celebrity with a tragedy, *Götz von Berlichingen*; and the following year, even more sensationally, with his novel, *Die Leiden des jungen Werther (The Sorrows of Young Werther)*.

Friedrich Schiller's *Die Räuber (The Robbers)*, which appeared eight years after *Götz* and Goethe's two works became the three "Bibles" of the literary movement of the eighteenth century known as the "Sturm und Drang," "Storm and Stress." Marked by volcanic and feverish expression, the movement was the articulate voice of young writers rebelling against the intellectual and political narrowness and repression of the country. Individualist in tone, it was more anarchist than revolutionary, often marked by notes of despair. As such, it was the precursor of the subsequent German Romantic School.

Götz von Berlichingen was, in fact, a robber-baron of the early sixteenth century. In Goethe's idealized transformation he became a rebel against absolute and oppressive authority, and a defender of the poor. Within the play, the cry of "Freiheit" is frequently uttered, and it remains Götz's battle-cry to the end. He dies crying out "Heavenly air — Freedom! Freedom!" And those around him exclaim mournfully, "The world is a prison... Woe to our times that have rejected you... Woe to posterity that fails to recognize your true worth."[2]

In an even greater measure, and to a much wider extent, did *Werther* work upon Goethe's generation and thereafter. Its impact became almost worldwide, gaining a universality far removed from the particularities of the German time and place. Its forceful depiction of a young man's hopeless love for another man's betrothed, its analysis of an intraversion, as well as description of the young man's humiliations at the hands of superior officials, and finally, Werther's suicide, aroused corresponding echoes in thousands of his readers, often resulting, as is well known, in parallel acts of self-destruction. It was indeed a book for the times. So, too, did Schiller's *Robbers* captivate the hearts in many countries with its own version of rebellion, typified in the creation of the figure of the "noble brigand" — expression of social rebellion. The young English poet, Coleridge, was brought to a state of excitement upon reading it, so that he could "weep aloud in a wild ecstasy!"[3]

It was at Leipzig that young Goethe began to develop that interest in science that was to become second nature with him for the rest of his life. At Strassburg Herder opened for him the profound meaning of the nature of "folk" and folk-poetry, and its manifestations in all peoples; he taught him the poetic greatness of the Old and New Testaments; and brought him a sense of the vastness and depth of various cultures.

Young Goethe soon showed himself the poet: song, ballad, as well as reflective and philosophical lyrics became his media, in addition to drama and the novel. He grew rapidly in self-awareness as a personality, strong, self-assured as person and poet. This sense of growing strength and independence he soon voiced in the poem of *Prometheus* (actually a portion of a drama he never completed), in which that Titan speaks in accents that are unmistakably those of the young poet, a Titan who dared defy Zeus and bring down fire to light and warm mankind, a Titan who was also creator of human beings who would be like himself; a Titan who dared assert:

> I know nothing more pitiful
> Under the sun
> Than ye gods...

and addressing Zeus himself, could exclaim:

> I, reverence thee?
> Hast thou assuaged the pains
> Of the heavily laden?
> Hast thou stilled the tears
> Of those anxious in spirit?...
>
> Who helped me
> From the Titans' insolence?
> Who rescued me from Death
> And slavery?
> Was it not thou thyself
> My sacred and glowing Heart?...

It was this poem that continued stirring generations of young hearts for many years...

Those years of the early 1770s were rich years. He was frequently in love, and frequently deeply loved. He loved and fled love. And he sang his loveliest songs. So it was in 1770 when he was in Strassburg, and met and loved Friederike Brion, and fled and sang. So again in 1772, when he met Charlotte Buff in Wetzlar, and immortalized her as Charlotte in *Werther*, and sang his moving "Willkommen und Abschied" ("Welcome and Farewell"); and so too when he became engaged to Lili Schönemann and parted, and composed "Neue Liebe, neues Leben" ("New Love, New Life"). In those years he was setting down the first sketches of *Faust* (the so-called *Urfaust*), with its unforgettable figure of Gretchen.

At about this time, the novelist Wilhelm Heinse described him as follows:

Goethe was with us, a beautiful youth of five-and-twenty, who is all genius and strength from head to foot, his heart full of feeling, his soul full of fire and eagle-winged...[4]

And the physiognomist Johann Kaspar Lavater:

What a glorious person Goethe would be beside a Prince! That's where he belongs. He could even be a King![5]

How could Lavater have foreseen that if Goethe was not destined to be King or stand beside a Prince, he would soon be standing beside a reigning Duke?

In the mouth of his *Faust*, Goethe had put eloquent words, almost as if to describe his own feelings at the time:

> Schon glüh ich wie vom neuen Wein
> Ich fühle Mut mich in die Welt zu wagen
> All Erden Weh und all ihr Glück zu tragen...

> I glow as if drunk with new-made wine,
> I feel the strength to meet the world head-on,
> To bear the woe, the whole world's bliss to bear,
> To battle storms, even in shipwreck's crash undaunted...

Why should he not have felt that way? The philosopher-theologian, Herder, had already advanced his ideas about the high dignity of the human being, and his "high destinies," and spoken of Man as a "son of gods, a sovereign of the earth."[5]

Goethe had weighty plans, and among them there were already sketches and lines of such plays as *Egmont* and *Torquato Tasso*. There were also preliminary pages of a novel. And as if Fate had been eavesdropping on him, there occurred an event which was to prove a turning point in his life. Duke Karl August of Weimar invited him to come to his court as his companion, and tutor, perhaps counsellor. In November 1775 Johann Wolfgang Goethe arrived in Weimar. He was then twenty-six, the Duke eighteen. Goethe could not have anticipated at that moment that the rest of his life, fifty-six years, with the exception of the two notable years in Italy, would be spent in or near Weimar.

Of the innumerable German states — great and small — the Duchy of Saxe-Weimar was one of the smallest and most insignificant for size and power. It is one of the paradoxes of history that during those years of Goethe's residence, it was destined to become an "Athens of the North," and achieve a historic significance never again equalled in its entire history.

It was not a Prussian or an Austrian court which Goethe was entering. The Duchy of Saxe-Weimar, as it was called, was but a pin-point in the large conglomeration of individual states, the whole of which was named the German Confederation. The Duchy included the university town of Jena, and the city of Eisenach. In the fashion of the times, despite its minute proportions, it was bureaucratic and feudal, as were the larger states, and its court protocol was not less bound to a rigid court-etiquette. It was — as we would say today — as "status-conscious" as any of its greater neighbors. Distinctions of class were rigidly and religiously observed; and the bureaucratic hierarchy ran from the top Geheimrat (true or real councillor) down to the ordinary crowd of Assessors, Revisors, reaching all the way to the bottom line of Kanzlist (really the ordinary clerk or copyist). To participate at court meals and ceremonies one had to be "hoffähig," that is, eligible for the court; at least, have a title.

Even Goethe had to wait a while before being admitted to the "Fürstliche Tafel" — the ducal table. First, he would have to be ennobled, which soon occurred, and he became "Johann Wolfgang von Goethe." In time he was made member of the Supreme Council, and eventually placed in charge successively of the mining commission, military commission, roads, and the treasury. Being Goethe, he fulfilled his duties with precision and devotion. However, for the first ten years he also acted as a kind of *maître des plaisirs* — the ceremonial arranger of royal receptions, court entertainments, masquerades, and other such presentations. During those years the creator-poet was dormant. But not his mind.

It was this little area of Weimar, the home of some five or six thousand inhabitants, really a village with small trade or industry, with unpaved somewhat odorous streets, and some seven hundred houses, and an extravagant court that he was to turn into a center of culture, cynosure and envy of the world! ...

Small as this world might be, there was the greater world that inhabited the Goethean personality. Though to his friends he might seem too much the "Courtier" — frequently in court-uniform, a decorated official, busy with marginal frivolities, the underground currents of his "self-development" kept on flowing in unceasing increase, as interests, startling to bystanders, appeared to be arising and flourishing. The process of his self-education, his "Selbstbildung," took on new forms, a search for a unified Weltanschauung — a world-view — a totality that would unify Nature for him, a totality that would include Art, Poetry, all creation. Now, in Weimar, that early interest in science became a passion which he could cultivate as he had long wished. His interests were to range far and wide, to include Botany, Geology, Mineralogy, Anatomy, Optics, and other aspects of Physics. He wished, in Bacon's words, to make "all knowledge his province." He strove in the recesses of his soul to emulate the example of the great Renaissance geniuses, men like Leonardo da Vinci and Michelangelo, to become a "sovr'uomo" —

— a "superman" — omniscient... And in time he was to make important discoveries that he felt confirmed him in his belief in the unity of all Nature and all Beings. Ever the observer of animate and inanimate nature, he discovered the intermaxillary bone in the human cranium; he anticipated a great many of our modern ideas of biology, particularly those connected with the theory of Evolution.

Always he was in search of the archetypal, the first principles and evidences of evolution and creation, the so-called "Ur". Here his poetic eye served him well. And his environs helped him greatly. The proximity of mines stimulated him in the study of mineral formations. He studied granite formations carefully. He studied botany, examined flower and leaf in search of similarities and differences — always in quest of some primal formation.

He also strove to create a "civilization" around him, to make of Weimar and Jena centers of culture. He was fortunate in having a sympathetic master, the Duke. So that soon around him he had attracted a group of notables unequalled at that time. There was Herder, and at nearby Jena Friedrich Schiller; the philosophers Fichte, Schelling, Hegel, the brothers Wilhelm and Alexander von Humboldt. Jena possessed scientists and laboratories.

Weimar gave Goethe a great deal, although it also took its toll. Karl August was generous materially, advanced him in councils, and later presented him with a theatre in which fully to realize his genius, and the genius and talents of others. Goethe acknowledged his debt in moving tributes. From being a companion, he had become the mentor of the Duke, feeling himself responsible for the Duke's inner development as a human being, and his outer development as ruler of his people. He had felt the need to curb the Duke's high spirits, his recklessness which verged on rashness. These and his better qualities the poet recalls in a memorable and touching birthday poem written in 1783, on the occasion of a revisit to the mines of Ilmenau, the restoration of which had been one of

Goethe's most cherished projects. This was the place in which they both hoped to create an "Eden." Adjuring the Duke to remember his responsibility, the poet adds

> Allein wer andre wohl zu leiten strebt,
> Muss fähig sein viel zu entbehren.

> But he who strives to guide others,
> Must be able to deny himself a great deal.[6]

And in a later poem, he acknowledges the Duke's generosity toward himself:

> Denn mir hat er gegeben, was Grosse selten gewähren . . .

> For he gave me what great ones seldom vouchsafe:
> Affection, leisure, trust, fields and garden and house . . .
> Never did Emperor, never King inquire after me,
> Only he, Karl August, was Augustus and Maecenas to me.[7]

Weimar also gave him the friendship and love of a remarkable woman, Frau von Stein, who for almost twelve years served as a kind of beloved and guardian-mother. This was to be the longest lasting relationship Goethe ever achieved with a woman before his meeting with Christiane Vulpius in 1788. It is significant to note that while after his arrival in Weimar, his other literary efforts faltered, or lingered unfulfilled for some years, his lyric gift continued as free, as magnificent as ever, and for Frau von Stein he wrote some of his most moving poems; as that beginning, "Warum gabst du uns die tiefen Blicke."

> Why, Fate, did you give us those deep glances,
> With which to view our future with apprehension,
> Never to trust our love, our earthly bliss,
> Which we deemed so blessed . . .[8]

For, he goes on, in her he saw a foretime sister or a wife; she who could read every lineament of his being, and could pour assuagement into his tumultuous blood.

Frau von Stein was thirty-three, and he twenty-six when they first met. She was raised at court, for her husband was Master of the Horse. She taught her young lover the graces consonant with behavior at the court; impressed upon him the seriousness of his duties as administrator; encouraged him in his other activities. He addressed her passionately as his "Lida," and coupled her name with that of Shakespeare: "To both of you I owe what I am." And in one of his plays written for the court theatre he inserted some lines from one of her love-letters, describing her state of mind. "Once more," she is quoted as saying, "I am restored to the world...Half a year ago I was ready to die. And now — no more!"[9]

We do not know the extent of their intimacy. We do know that he loved her deeply, more deeply than he had loved in a long time. Never before had his letters been so fervent, so passionate. Previously he had made it a habit to run away from his unmarried beloved women. What was he hoping for now? A *ménage à trois*? He had toyed with such ideas in his earliest plays. Once more he fled. No woman had so impressed herself on his life and work. His last farewell words to her were: "Lebe wohl du süsses Herz! Ich bin Dein." "Farewell sweet heart! I am yours."[10]

The plays he had in the making, still in their first versions, *Torquato Tasso* and *Iphigenie auf Tauris* are impregnated with her person. She is the Princess in the first of these; she is Iphigenie. When he completes them in Italy, and transposes them into verse, they will bear all the imprint of Frau von Stein. Such indeed was their union, which he called sealed "without vows, without sacrament." He had found all that he had sought for in his life. "There is nothing for me to seek. In you I have found all."[11] As for her, we have no written evidences of her own deep feelings. She destroyed all her letters he had returned to her in 1788...

Yet, for all that, he found it possible to go away, in expectation of a lengthy absence. But he had in fact grown weary of Weimar, grown weary of his official tasks; for, as he wrote her, "I was born to be a private person, and cannot understand how Fate has managed to involve me in public affairs and a ducal family.''[12] He was weary of provincial Weimar. But that there were other, even more profound, matters at stake — that we cannot doubt. He was not one to reveal the storms that raged within him. He was asking himself questions about his own destiny, his own creative career, and the future course of his own "Bildung". Was he being true to himself and to his vocation as poet?

No one could answer these questions but himself, and that only when he was far away. Not least, there was that body of unfinished work that demanded completion. In addition to the plays, there was the novel, centered on a young man of bourgeois extraction (was he not one himself?), seeking to find his way in life, its meaning, and goals. This was to be a novel closer to home, to realities he himself had experienced. It was to be a "Bildungsroman" — a novel of "education" for living, "Lebensbildung." He had been carrying the idea for such a novel around with him for a long while, and had even set down long portions of it. He had worked on it from 1777 till 1785. This fragment of the so-called "Ur-Meister," was to have its own special history. It remained in manuscript, and was lost sight of for many years, until finally recoverd in Zürich in 1910. When it was published, it appeared under the title of *Wilhelm Meisters theatralische Sendung. (Wilhelm Meister's Theatrical Mission)*. This was the antecedent of its two published successors, *Wilhelm Meisters Lehrjahre (Apprenticeship)* and *Wilhelm Meisters Wanderjahre (Years of Wandering)*, the first of which appeared in 1795, and the second in 1821. Another instance of a life-long endeavor...

2.

"September 3, 1786: At three o'clock in the morning I stole out
of Karlsbad; otherwise they would have kept me there and never let
me leave . . ." Thus Goethe. He was heading for Italy, the land of his
heart's desire. Had he not already, some time before, put into his
Mignon's lips the song that was henceforth to sound forth as the
eternal embodiment of that longing? "Kennst du das Land? . . ."where
the citrons bloom, and amid green verdure the golden oranges
glow? . . ." The days of the Privy Councillor, Legation Councillor,
Councillor Herr von Goethe, Herr Doktor von Goethe, and what not!
— were behind him. Ten long years of official tasks, reports,
meetings, journeys! Ten years during which his insides were
seething with repressed poetic projects! And here the great chance!
It was almost as if now his desire for further "Bildung" was to be
fulfilled. Herder had urged him to take along his papers, above all
his sketches for *Iphigenie*. And now, in his own words: "I separate
Iphigenie from the rest, and take it along to the lovely, warm land as
my companion."[13]

Over the Brenner Pass into Italy, in a carriage, with frightening
possibilities once you looked down into the gorges. But he is his own
man. Once more he feels his senses sharpened, his power of
observation and his eyes "clear, clean and bright," his spirit "elastic"
once more. Now he must attend to and on himself, he who was used
to meditating and commanding. "The sun is glowing, and one is
inclined once more to believe in a God."[14]

And, *sotto voce*, we add, "in Goethe Himself, too. . ."

He was entering the "classic" land, but inside him the heart of a
Romantic was beating. He had seen pictures of Italy in his father's
house (his father had been to Italy and had never forgotten the
experience), and now the reality of Italy was there. In September he
was in Venice. With enchantment he listened as his gondoliers sang

the verses of Tasso and Ariosto, set to the gondoliers' own melodies. He visited the art galleries. But for the first time he was also close to the sea. His interest in natural science had not abated, and he observed the water snails, limpets, and crabs. How wonderful were living things! he exclaimed. How fitted by Nature to their conditions — how *true*, how *being*. How his sceptical friends in Weimar would have been astounded at these interests!

He is sure that he had done right in coming here. Had he not done so, he felt he would have perished.

He hurried on, impatient, and spent only three days in Florence! Finally, Rome! Winckelmann had been there twenty years before; and for Goethe he was as alive as ever; Winckelmann who had made Europe aware of the true meaning of Greek art, though he was himself confined to an examination of Roman copies. For Winckelmann Rome was "the university for the whole world." Goethe trod the same streets, the same hills, and looked at the antiquities that had enthralled the older antiquarian. Goethe found a copy of Winckelmann's *History of Ancient Art,* and read it as he walked the ancient city. In Goethe's eyes Winckelmann stood for more than his grand achievement in the field of art-history. Here was an intense spirit that had risen from a low estate (he was the son of a shoemaker) and had achieved his goal through unparalleled effort, in the end to become a martyr (for he was murdered in Trieste on the eve of a triumphant return to Germany). But Winckelmann was also the embodiment of classic Hellenism, a true "pagan," an "ingenerate pagan," who, though a convert to Catholicism (a matter of expedience, according to Goethe, rather than conviction) shared Goethe's own antipathy toward Christianity and clericalism. For Goethe was revolted by the Italian paintings that depicted the martyrdom of Christian saints; and he paid scant attention to the churches and cathedrals.

Here, in Rome, he felt himself truly a "pagan." What he did not openly declare, except in his poetry, was the utter sense of release — release of himself sensually. In identifying himself with Winckelmann

(though not with the latter's homoeroticism), he was affirming a
new aspect of his life, the release of his own sexuality. For the first
time in his life he "let go." Whatever his relation to Frau von Stein
(and his letters to her from Italy are no less passionate), in his loves
at home he felt bound by ties that he could now free himself of. In his
Italian loves he felt free, knowing he could escape whenever he
wished. And he gave his eroticism full play. It must be remarked that
this liberation was the converse of the coin, the other side of which
also reflected the creative freedom he was now experiencing. That
new vitality and virility are evidenced in his tragedy of *Egmont*, on
which he had been working, which also celebrated the deep, free
love of Egmont and the bourgeois young woman, Klärchen, one of
Goethe's loveliest creations. The vitality he attributed to his hero,
Egmont, the *joie de vivre,* the recklessness, the freedom from care,
though in the play ending disastrously, was, in fact, a celebration of
his own free life in Italy, and the release from all constraints except
those of art.

Such were the elements of his "rebirth," as he calls it. He
wanders from one monument to another, from painting to painting.
Like Winckelmann, he was forced to make the best of Roman
replicas of Greek sculpture, unlike Keats, who could satisfy his soul
with the friezes of the Parthenon brought to England by Lord Elgin.
For the age of "scientific" archaelogy was just dawning, and still at
some distance loomed the major discoveries associated with the
excavations of Troy in Asia Minor, or Mycenae and Crete. In Italy
one could still come upon remains of Greek architecture at Paestum
and in Sicily. But Goethe was more than satisfied with what he could
find. He ordered a copy of a "colossal head of Jupiter." In the
Giustiniani Palace he stood riveted before the statue of Minerva.

Having the companionship of German artists in Rome and
elsewhere in Italy, he is drawn into sketching and painting, and by
the time he returns home he carries with him a rich store of his
own works.

Toward the end of February he arrived in Naples. He was overwhelmed by the beautiful landscape, and he recalled his father's own justified enthusiasm for the surroundings of the city. "I forgive all those who lose their senses," he wrote. "Naples is a paradise. Everyone lives a sort of inebriated self-forgetfulness."[15]

He witnessed the eruption of Vesuvius; visited the Greek temple at Paestum. Toward the end of March he was in Sicily, and in Palermo he was enchanted with the public gardens, "the most wonderful place in the world."[16] In Girgenti he visited the Temple of the Concordia and the ruins of the Temple of Juno. There was probably no busier man in the whole place; for he was taking notes, observing nature, sketching and, not least, occupied with his literary projects...

At no time of his life had he been happier. His ecstasy mounted as the days advanced. He felt restored in body and mind. "There is only one Rome in this world," he exclaimed. The idea that he would soon have to leave Italy desolated him. "How can I leave this place which has become my Paradise... For I am like one experiencing a transformed rebirth; I am renewed, and completed... The whole world is opening up for me... My life now is like a dream of youth... All that I have known for a long time is now, for the first time, becoming fully my own possession." In the presence of ancient works of art he senses an inward expansion of his personality. The bust of Medusa causes him to exclaim that "the mere idea that such a thing as this work is possible in this world is enough to 'double' the personality... When you think of me, think of me as a fortunate man." To Duke Karl August he wrote of himself as "again restored to poetic productivity."[17]

He was back in Rome. Soon it was time to go. Not the least painful element in his parting — from so many associations, friends, objects — was that from his "Milanese" beloved. None had endeared herself so intensely to him. He quotes lines from the Roman poet Ovid written when forced by Emperor Augustus to leave Rome,

Cum subit illius tristissima noctis imago...

When that saddest image comes to mind
Of the last night in the Roman city...
I cannot forbear the tears that come to my eye...[18]

And again to the Duke:

I can say in all truth that during this year and a half of isolation I have found myself. As what, will you ask? As the artist!...Through your continuous activity you have arrived at the knowledge as a prince of how people are to be properly made useful...Now accept me as your guest. Let me fill out at your side the full measure of my existence, my enjoyment of life; and my powers, like a freshly opened, fully gathered and purified mountain spring, will all the more easily be directed in accordance with your will.[19]

He was prepared to return, even if reluctantly. But he was returning as a poet. He asked to be relieved of his official duties. He believed he had attained to an integrated view of life, of the world, and of himself. He had attained to a totality. In his own words, his Roman experience had precipitated out all the dross of doubt, uncertainty. As he wrote in those early days of Rome, so now too he must have felt that "just as happened with me in my dealing with natural history, so now, here in Rome, the whole of world-history has become linked; and I account this my second birth-day, a true rebirth..."[20]

3.

On the 22nd of June, 1788, he was back in Weimar.

So, once more returned to the "murky" North, he felt depressed and disconcerted. Was he once more back among what his Mephistopheles was to call the "Northern phantoms"? Here, in Weimar nothing seemed to have changed. But, *he* was changed. How could he convey to his friends all that had happened to him? How open his deepest heart? To Herder he voiced his disillusionment:

From Italy, rich in forms, I was thrust back into formless Germany, and obliged to exchange a bright sky for a somber one. Instead of consoling me and drawing me to them, my friends brought me to the brink of despair. My rapture over objects that were far away, my torture, my complainings over what I had left and lost, seemed lost, seemed to offend them; I was wholly bereft of sympathy; no one understood my language.[21]

No one could appreciate how much he had lost in leaving Italy. Was it the spoiled favorite who was speaking? Partly, but mostly one who had come home to be hailed on the "change" which had come over him. But what had he really to complain of? He had been away for almost two years. He had left without prior warning. Could his friends be blamed if they looked askance at him? Frau von Stein, in particular, was out of sorts; even enraged. He had left her suddenly, and now like some feather-headed youth he expected to be hailed and taken to her bosom! After all, he was now thirty-nine. And she had to admit to being forty-five. She could scarcely feel consoled that she had been "immortalized" in those early passionate poems, and in the plays he was bringing back with him.

And now, not long after his return, came the *coup-de-grâce*, a dagger-thrust so powerful, and so mortal — for which there would never be forgiveness. Goethe met a young woman, Christiane Vulpius, twenty-five, and shortly thereafter he took her into his house as his companion. Christiane was of moderately humble origin, but not without education. She had been working in

Bertuch's artificial flower factory. She was intelligent, but no blue-stocking, and what proved even worse in the eyes of the court and its entourage, no "aristocrat." She was simple, unpretentious, fairly attractive, warm-hearted, and she loved Goethe. How was Frau von Stein to guess what had happened to her favorite in Italy, now in his thirty-seventh year, he who had probably for the first time in his life experienced the full freedom of sexual passion and its delights? In November, Christiane was a part of his household: consort, housekeeper, hostess, and lover. In December 1789 she bore him a son, Johann August Walter.

In December of that year Goethe had completed *Torquato Tasso,* in which, in its earlier form, Frau von Stein had played so great a part, and in which she had seen herself in the character of Princess Leonore. And was she not also the Iphigenie of his "Greek" drama, and might she not have stood as a foster-sister to Klärchen of *Egmont?* And now he was bosom-companion to one she rated as a "chamber-maid"! His friends also disapproved; even Schiller raised a moral eyebrow. The Duke, himself entwined in a "liason," half-shut his eyes.

Poor Christiane was ostrascized. But Goethe's mother, that remarkable woman, entertained friendly relations with her; she called her Goethe's "bed-fellow," and wrote kindly things about their young son.

While Goethe was away in Italy, rounding out his "self-education" — his "Lebensbildung" — events in the rest of Europe were moving toward a cyclonic climax. While he was polishing *Torquato Tasso* and giving it its final touches (a kind of farewell to Fau von Stein), the people of Paris stormed the Bastille in July 1789. Poor little Weimar, vassal of two mighty powers, Prussia and Austria, was not as yet aware how she, too, would be swept into the vortex of world-history.

4.

If he could not tell his Weimar friends, the court entourage, and others about the meaning of Italy, he, at least, knew what a rich store of wealth he was bringing back with him. Of course, he could show them the hundred and fifty or so drawings and paintings he had made. But he could hardly tell about his scientific findings, which, at times, he considered more significant. But he had also completed or was completing three plays, which he was sure would not have come into being without the Italian experience. They were his testaments; objectifications of himself, of his past, and his present. The three harked back to a historic past, *Egmont* and *Tasso* to the seventeenth century, and *Iphigenie auf Tauris* to ancient Greece.

In *Egmont* we hear the last echoing of the *Prometheus* poet, the poet speaking as rebel, as soldier, and as apostle of political freedom. But *Egmont* is also a tragedy of a personality with high-minded purposes and ideals, driven to defeat and death by his character that combines extreme courage and defiance, with a blindness with respect to reality, a recklessness and extravagance of feelings and actions, an unrealistic daring and bravado. He is a noble-minded defender of the civic rights of his Netherland fellow-citizens against the despotic encroachments of their Spanish rulers. Klärchen, the bourgeois young woman who is in love with him, and whom Egmont loves, is equally courageous and daring as she attempts to arouse the populace to rescue her lover, and wishes herself a man to be able to join him in battle. She is a kind of warrior-Gretchen, and takes her own life when Egmont is executed. He is free-handed and generous; he lives in self-deceptive security in the face of Spanish *Machtpolitik*. Like Götz von Berlichingen, he also dies with "Es lebe die Freiheit" on his lips. He loves life, and lives for the day in a state of chronic euphoria. But he is ignorant of other human hearts. He will not listen to the voice of sanity, that of

William of Orange, who warns him of his peril. With intrepidity and an astounding naiveté he voices his sentiments of freedom to the Duke of Alba, Spain's regent. He believes himself in the hands of an inscrutable and inescapable Fate, and speaks with reckless hyperbole:

As if lashed by invisible spirits, Time's sun-steeds draw us on in Fate's light chariot; and for us there is nothing but to take heart, and with reins firmly in hand, guide the chariot left or right, avoid a rock here, and a fall there. Where are we bound for? Who knows? We hardly know where we came from!...[22]

This is young Goethe recollected in what he believed to be a wiser tranquillity. It would be the last time Goethe would speak of Freedom in such heightened tones.

Just as Egmont is what we might today call extrovert, in such a degree is Tasso, the Renaissance poet of Ferrara, introvert. Torquato Tasso, the gifted author of *Jerusalem Delivered*, is at the other pole of Egmont. Here is a portrait of a sensitive, high-strung almost neurotic artist, who is unable to adjust to life around him, given as he is to almost morbid introspection, that finally degenerates into paranoia. Never at home in this world, or at the court of Alfonso, the Duke of Ferrara, he yearns for another world that lies in the past. He is estranged from other human beings. "Whither is fled the golden age?" he asks. And the Princess replies: "Dear friend, the golden age is gone. But the good ones of this earth will bring it back." The courtier Antonio, a tried man of the world, the voice of restraint, sanity, shrewdness; a wordly-wise master of policy, tries to bring moderation into the actions of the poet. But in vain. And Alfonso, the Duke, warns Tasso:

> Around us are abysses which Fate has dug,
> But the deepest of them lies within our hearts;
> And one is tempted to throw oneself below,
> I beg of you: Save your self from your other self:
> And the Man in you will win what Poet loses...[23]

Not even the Princess, the epitome of nobility, grace and wisdom, can save Tasso from himself. He is in love with her. She is Frau von Stein idealized, as is the Court; for Alfonso II is in reality another Karl August. Tasso ends a broken man...

> Only this is left me:
> Nature has vouchsafed us tears,
> The cry of pain, when a man no more can bear.
> But I am granted melody and word
> To wail the deepest fulness of my need,
> And if to others voices are denied.
> A God has granted me to speak my woe.[24]

The "classical" drama on Iphigenia was composed to celebrate the birth of a daughter to the Ducal pair in March 1779. It was written in a language that alternated between poetry and prose. The central character, naturally, was to be a woman, and the image of Frau von Stein was conveniently present. It was this version that Goethe took with him to Italy. Here toward the end of 1786 he labored on a revision, turned the prose into iambic pentameter, and completed the entire work toward the end of December.

Goethe's *Iphigenie auf Tauris* is only distantly related to the Euripides tragedy of the same name. In Euripides, Agamemnon's daughter is brought to Aulis to be sacrificed to appease Artemis, so that the fleet might sail for Troy. She is carried off by the goddess to the island of Tauris, where she becomes her priestess. The barbarous practice of King Thoas demands that every stranger appearing in Tauris be sacrificed to the goddess. Iphigenia's brother, Orestes, accompanied by his friend Pylades arrives. Orestes, who has murdered his mother, Clytemnestra, has been pursued by the Furies. Apollo counsels him to carry off the statue of Artemis lodged in Tauris and bring it back to Greece. Thus he would be finally cleansed and freed of the dreadful incubus which deprived him of his senses. They arrive in Tauris, are captured, and are destined for execution by the priestess of Artemis. But in the course of their interchange there is the celebrated "recognition."

The three lay plans to hoodwink the king, carry off the image of the goddess Artemis and flee. The pretext would be the need to cleanse at the shore of the sea the image desecrated by Orestes's presence. The plot succeeds, the King is outraged, but is deterred from pursuit and vengeance by the fortunate intervention of Athena.

Goethe uses only the slightest thread of this plot. For him the drama becomes a vehicle for proclaiming the gospel close to his heart, the gospel he believed was intrinsic to the Hellenic world, of humanity and humaneness — "Menschheit" and "Menschlichkeit." The bearer of this high message was to be a woman, Iphigenia, who was to combine with it the other article, that of Truth. The "barbarian" King Thoas of Tauris, the Scythian, is noble and dignified. He has extended asylum to Iphigenia, and has made her priestess of Diana. In addition he has suspended the cruel tradition of sacrificing strangers to the goddess while she is on the island, because he is in love with her. She, too, becomes an accomplice in the plot, but is overcome in the last moment, and reveals it to the King. He and Orestes are about to come to sword combat, when Iphigenia intervenes, and addresses Thoas:

> Let the sword fall from your hand, oh King,
> A moment's combat immortalizes the man,
> He falls, and poets chant his worth.
> But all the tears, the endless flow of tears,
> Of those left behind, the desolate wife,
> Those, no posterity numbers; no poet chants
> The thousand tear-sodden days and nights,
> When the still soul in vain calls for the lost,
> Too soon departed friend, and longs and pines . . .[25]

She has brought the weapon of Truth to war against cruelty and murder. And this too is a mighty deed, greater than those marked by sword and violence. She has dared the impossible; she too faces reproaches; for she will encounter greater evils if through her revelations none of the three is helped. "Through me," she pleads, "glorify the Truth!" And the King, bitterly recalling for her the history of her own house, the bloody house of Atreus,

> Dost believe that the brute Scythian,
> The barbarian, would heed the voice
> Of Truth and Humanity that Atreus
> The Greek contemned? ...[26]

In the end, Thoas acquiesces, and reluctantly exclaims, "Go!" But to Iphigenia this is not enough. She will not leave without his blessing. She calls upon the traditional laws of hospitality. And finally Thoas yields. "Farewell," he says.

Thus, the Scythian "barbarian" proves himself superior to the "civilized" Greeks who would sacrifice their own offspring in order to be able to set sail for war, or who do not recoil from gross deception.

This was Goethe's drama that was to be presented before the Court with full ceremony. While he was still at work on it in the little town of Apolda, he was writing: "I just can't get on with the play; it is damnable that the King of Tauris should be made to talk as if there were no starving stocking-weavers in Apolda."[27] Were the stocking-weavers on his mind as he was watching the opulent staging, costumes, and hearing his own stately language? ...

5.

Toward the end of his life Goethe confessed:

I have never known a more presumptuous man than myself, and the fact
that I say it shows it to be true. I never believed a thing had to be attained, I
always thought I had already attained it. If someone had set a crown on my
head, I should have taken it for granted. And yet just because of this I was
only a man like other people. It was only the fact that having undertaken
things beyond my powers, I tried to carry them out; that having received
beyond my deserts, I tried to be deserving, which differentiates me from a
truly insane person.[28]

Though uttered, no doubt, with tongue in cheek, there was
more than a grain of truth in that statement. It was particularly true
now, on his return from Italy. He felt more assured than ever before
that he was the architect of his own life, that now his life-formation,
his "Lebensbildung," lay before him as a challenge to himself to
prove that his decisions were the right ones.

He had anticipated that idea many years before, when he began
composing the novel that was to be a kind of autobiographical
testament, to be preoccupied with the problem of a person's life-
formation, education of character, and the search for one's true
vocation which would constitute his self-fulfilment.

That was the so-called "Urmeister," *Wilhelm Meister's Theatrical
Mission.* As appears from the title it was to deal with "education," in
this particular case education through the Theatre, the Drama.

Art as a formative influence in the building of a human being's
character had been a central preoccupation with thinkers in England
and Germany for many years. Friedrich Schiller had given that
conception probably its profoundest formulation in Goethe's own
lifetime.

We have already seen how deeply the intellectual and emotional
life of the Germans was involved with the problem of the "Ego"
— the salvation and preservation of the integrity of the personality
in the absence of a central unified political state. Such was the case in the

hectic days of the "Sturm und Drang" with its glorification of the individual "genius"; such too the case of the subsequent Romanticism, which combined elements of political and social revolt with the emphasis on the importance of the individual as a creative personality. Johann Gottfried Herder, Goethe's intellectual master, was perhaps the most powerful advocate of the idea of "self-cultivation," the idea that the individual was a potential "self-creator," and the "architect of one's life and fortune."[29] This was to be a kind of secular theology, spirituality without superstition, an attempt to approach the divine and at the same time preserve the human and humane, combining "Gottähnlichkeit" and the "Humanitätsideal" — achieving a semblance of Divinity and Ideal Humanity. In Herder, the religious element is notable, in others less so.

The shaping of one's self is therefore to be an art, like other arts, like sculpturing a statue, or making a poem, by an assimilation of the best that culture could offer, fusing the Greek "good" and the "beautiful."

"Bildung," "Kultur," and "Lebenskunst" — these became the established tenets for those who were in a position seriously to engage in such a development. This ideal became more and more secularized with the times. "Bildung" was the enhancement of the individual; "Kultur" that of a nation.

How important these elements became for German thinking will become evident later, for they were eventually assimilated into national "ideologies."[30] Goethe, through his portentous genius and influence, represented the crystallization of these elements for the future of German thought; with him the ideal became totally secularized, and a kind of "secular salvation."

All of Goethe's writings are, as he himself said, "fragments of an autobiography," and the original *Wilhelm Meister* — the "Urmeister" — is definitely that. His, too, was the passion for the theatre that young Meister reveals, when, as a child he was taken with his puppet-theatre; when, at the time of the French occupation during his boyhood, he attended the French theatre and hobnobbed with French actors; and now he almost prefigured his own future when, as in 1791, he was to become director, actor, impresario, court-dramatist of his own Weimar theatre.

Wilhelm Meisters theatralische Sendung is indeed a precious document. It has a spontaneity, a vigor, a freshness and directness that were only too often to be absent from its grander successors. Here Wilhelm is the young Goethe, the bourgeois son of a bourgeois father, sent out on a business mission. He becomes involved with a theatrical troupe, and fascinated by the theatre and a theatrical career, dreams of establishing a national theatre, and developing into a dramatic poet himself. He becomes a convert from the French classical drama to that of Shakespeare, a crucial conversion in Goethe's own life. Here we have a depiction of the rowdy, somewhat loose company of actors and actresses, a typical case of a wandering troupe. Here we meet with the enchanting person of Mignon, and the mysterious Harper. And here we have the inimitable songs of both. Here we have Wilhelm's transformation as he comes in contact with aristocratic life and abandons his former associates for a closer contact with the nobility. The pursuit of "Bildung" then becomes closely tied to an upper class, which becomes a precondition for it. Hence the celebrated apostrophe to upper-class existence and to "culture."

Thrice happy those whose birth lifts them above the lower stations of mankind, who need not, like so many good people, have to spend their lives in fret and worry...What comfort, what ease befalls those born to wealth!...Hail, then, the great ones of this earth! Hail those who draw near them and can draw from those springs, and partake of those advantages![31]

So he enters this "grand monde" as a member of the Count's troupe. Here he is made aware of the existence of Shakespeare, and his own creative talent as playwright and poet are awakened. His life is revolutionized. He makes *Hamlet* his own. His "Bildung" has been extended; he has entered two new worlds: that of the nobility, and that of Shakespeare. (That is, indeed, what Goethe himself felt when he coupled Frau von Stein and Shakespeare as the critical moments of his life.) Wilhelm hopes to remain in those two worlds for the rest of his life. Yet, he is still torn between his obligations to his father, and the family's business, and his ever-deepened interest in the theatre. His father's death, and the certainty that his brother-in-law would adequately administer the family's worldly affairs, decide him. Under pressure of his actor-associates he remains with his troupe. Here the manuscript ends. He will leave the bourgeois existence, and become actor, playwright, and poet... The sizable fragment of the *Theatralische Sendung* accompanied Goethe to Italy to await completion.

The fragment is a striking work. Seldom has Goethe again equalled the description of the actors' profession and life; nor did he ever surpass his depictions of such characters as Mignon, Philine, and others. They have the sharpness, sprightliness, even delicacy equalled only by the delineation of Gretchen in the *Urfaust*, or Klärchen of *Egmont*. There is a sense of true life around Wilhelm, a sense of individual characters and surroundings that is to be found only in some of the early scenes of *Faust* and the citizenry scenes of *Egmont*.

Goethe's own life was soon to be totally involved in the theatre. In 1791 he took over direction of the Court Theatre.

When Goethe returned to Weimar in November 1788 he found that Friedrich Schiller lived in the vicinity. Schiller came to Weimar in 1787. Their contacts at first scarcely presaged the intimacy and reciprocal impact that were to develop after 1794. Goethe used his influence to bring Schiller to the University of Jena, as professor of History, scarcely a highly remunerative office. All his life long Schiller had struggled, and hardship took its toll of his health. The occasional stipend that would fall to him from generous hands had to be eked out by hack work journalism. Unlike Goethe, who also had written his "Tyrannenhass" (Tyrant-hate) drama, *Götz von Belichingen* from the vantage ground of comfort,

Schiller had known and experienced both tyrant-hatred and tyranny, as well as poverty. He had managed after his flight from Württemberg to establish a dramatic career in Mannheim. He was already the author of significant plays, in addition to *The Robbers: Kabale und Liebe*, and the masterpiece, *Don Carlos*. He was also making a name for himself as a historian, and it was in that capacity that he officiated at Jena.

When he first met Goethe after the latter's return to Weimar, he was not impressed.

To be around Goethe for a stretch would make me very unhappy. Even toward his friends he exhibits few evidences of demonstrativeness. It is hard to get hold of him — to fasten on him. I believe that he is in fact an egoist to an extraordinary degree. He has the gift of captivating people, and can show himself highly obliging through smaller or greater attentions. He manifests his being beneficently, like a god, without giving himself — that seems to me a deliberate attitude, calculated to afford the deepest enjoyment of his own egoism.[32]

In time, Schiller's feelings, like those of Goethe, would change radically. But who will say that Schiller was utterly wrong? He had pierced to one element in Goethe's personality, the way in which Goethe's outward appearance and behavior frequently belied the turmoils and unrest that stormed within him, that found their outlet only in his creative work.

Soon, however, there was to be a close association, and the "Bildung" of each of the participants would be widened immeasurably. There was exchange and reciprocal appropriation. Schiller, the dramatist, the poet, the historian, the philosopher would, in Goethe's later words, supply the "half" that completed him, the kind of "doubling," one might say of the personality of which Goethe had spoken when in the presence of a masterpiece of art. They became Castor and Pollux, Dioscuri, a phenomenon not frequent in history. Schiller would be the gadfly spurring Goethe into activity when he seemed to lag. Goethe in turn offered the wisdom of long experience, the wider vision, and even more significantly, a theatre for Schiller's new works: *Wilhelm Tell, Die Jungfrau von Orleans, Wallenstein,* and *Die Braut von Messina.*

Goethe had come back from Italy not only inspired to greater literary activity, but also in almost the same degree, with a view of the world and Nature that was acquiring a greater and ever clearer shape. His scientific interests had, if anything, been extended, and now in the vicinity of Jena and its scientists and laboratories, he found new instruments for expanding and testing his new knowledge and theories. Like his own Faust, he sought for ultimate answers as to the nature of Being — whether in the physical or the animal world, answers as to origins and development; to find, one might almost say, the *Ding-an-Sich*, the ultimate Thing-in-Itself, the motive force or forces of the universe.

He was in search of the "Ur-Phenomenon." The "Ur" is the archetypal, the primordial, the prototypical. So that in Botany, he sought to discover the "Ur Pflanze," the plant that is at the root of all plant-life; in geology, to discover the "Ur-Gestein," the prototypical "stone" that would explain all subsequent formations — hence be a clue to the earth's creation and development; in like way the "Ur gestalt" the archtypal element of the animal and human world.

Had he been born later he would have said he was in quest of the key to the Evolution of all Creation. Had he devoted himself to science exclusively, he might have been a great scientist. As it is, he was wilfully divided, believing all too much in ready insights and guesses. So he had to content himself with being half-scientist, but a whole poet. It is remarkable that with so little true scientific "method" at his command, as well as instruments, he could make those discoveries in anatomy that would be of significance: he discovered the intermaxillary bone in the human skull, which convinced him of the interrelation between the human being and the rest of the animal world; he discovered the vertebral basis of the cranium. He was terribly shaken by the refusal of the world to accept his theories of Optics, of Light and Color, and his firm conclusion that he had overturned Newton's theories. Had he lived another ten or twenty years, how excited he would have been could he have witnessed the discovery of the "cell" by means of the microscope. Wasn't that really one of his own "Ur-organisms"? He felt he had a world of prophecies within him. His happiness in Italy was indescribable as he wrote home about his conception of the nature of the "Ur-plant."

The "Ur-Pflanze" will be the strangest creation in the world, which nature itself will begrudge me. With this model and the key to it you will be able to invent plants ad infinitum which will be consistent, i.e., even if they never existed they *could* exist.[33]

And on discovering the intermaxillary bone common to human beings and animals, he exclaimed:

Indeed, man is most intimately allied to animals. This co-ordination of the Whole makes every creature to be that which it is, and man is as much man through the form of his upper jaw, as through the form of the last joint of his little toe. And thus every creature is but a note of the greatest harmony, which must be studied in the Whole, or else it is nothing but a dead letter.[34]

Goethe was one of the first to speak of an "ice age." He sided with the so-called "Neptunists" as against the "Vulcanists," the latter of whom believed that the earth rose up as a result of volcanic explosions rather than massive inundations.

As for Nature, he writes,

It teaches and proves that the greatest, the most mysterious, and most magical moves along in a perfectly regular, simple, open fashion. It must in time heal the poor, unthinking, unknowing men of the thirst for the vaguely supernatural.[35]

The Archetype persists throughout Nature. The rarest form, he insists, preserves in secret the "Ur-bild" — the protypal image. The process of Nature is organic: Antithesis and Reconciliation, but not caprice or inconstancy. Order and Measure; Evolution without violence. In the second part of *Faust*, the Greek philosopher Thales speaks for Goethe when he asserts,

Nie war Natur in ihr lebendiges Fliessen
Auf Tag und Nacht und Stunden angewiesen;
Sie bildet regelnd jegliche Gestalt,
Und selbst im Grossen ist es nicht Gewalt.

Nature, in her living, fluid powers,
Was never bound by day, or night, or hours.
She makes each form by rules,
And even on a mighty scale, there is no violence.[36]

"As a Poet and Artist," Goethe wrote, "I am a polytheist; as a natural scientist, I am a pantheist."[37] If there is a God at work, He is within Nature. In this view he is at one with Spinoza and Giordano Bruno, the Renaissance "heretic" and philosopher. As Viëtor puts it, "Nature and spirit, phenomenon and essence, are one; the Infinite is distributed in purely finite, independent individual phenomena, which together constitute a great all-embracing unity. Unity in multiplicity is the essence of the world."[38]

When he came to seek the "archetypal" in Art and Poetry, Goethe believed he had found it in the ancient Greeks. Just as his Italian experience had heightened his understanding of processes acting in the world of Nature, the "Ur-type" — so his experience with Greek art, he thought, produced an understanding of the "Ur-form" — the "typical" — toward which all art should aspire. Here a number of diverse elements played a serious part in his determination: for one, the glorification of an ideal Hellenism, which was far removed from the actuality which was ancient Greece. Goethe brought to his own idealization his antagonism to his Romantic contemporaries. Keeping in mind Winckelmann's denomination of Greek art as the embodiment of "noble simplicity and serene greatness," Goethe could not fail to raise the banner against what he believed to be the essence of German Romanticism: wild unconstraint, even lawless freedom; and he found exemplars in such figures as the Schlegels and Heinrich von Kleist. Add to this element Goethe's time-long anti-Medievalism, his repugnance to

"Gothicism," and Gothic art, his abhorrence of all depictions of martyrdom and suffering, and it becomes clear why he found in the Greeks the high perfection of the "ideal." He ignored what might be called the "subterranean" elements of Greek life, the element of barbarism, the Bacchic orgies, and other aspects of its "Nachtseite" — its nocturnal preoccupations. So that it was an imperfect, though considering the times, a pardonably inadequate knowledge of Hellenism that dictated his almost categorical criteria of Art. On his analogies, Greek art conformed to his conception of the laws of Nature.

The Greeks, according to Goethe, were preoccupied with the concrete, the "real world," whereas moderns are not; the Greeks represented "existences," but moderns were concerned preeminently with "effects." "All eras in a state of decline are subjective; on the other hand, all progressive eras have an objective tendency."[39] On this occasion, when one considers the character of German Romanticism and its stormy subjectivism, Goethe was right. For Goethe even the Greek gods conformed to his ideal. The eyes of the Greeks were fixed on "this world" and the gods thereof. Their gods were their own progenitors, and their admiration for them seemed almost tantamount to an admiration of them as only "works of art." Only pagans, says the pagan Goethe, would be capable of such an attitude. Beauty was the ideal of that society, and they conceived beautiful man as nature's ultimate achievement. Greek art idealized the human form as it idealized the divine.

It was the contemplation of this "ideal" beauty in art that elevated the human spectator, raising him to something above and beyond himself. It "deified" him, just as the Greek artist "humanized" the god. For the Greeks brought the gods down from heaven. Consider the Olympian Jupiter whose statue, under that name was, according to tradition, worshipped reverently. "Der Gott war zum Menschen geworden, um den Menschen zum Gott zu erheben." "God had become human, in order to raise the human being to God."[40]

Here was the perfection to be striven for: abstraction and reality; the "type" and Nature; the abstract and the concrete — all raised to a level that lifts the onlooker above, while he still remains on the firm ground of reality. Human and yet divine, but always humane, this achievement offered a staggering contrast to the inebriated spirituality of Medieval art, and its modern prophets, such as Wackenroder and the Nazarene painters, and other Romantics.

6.

It is not hard to understand how Goethe conceived of Greek art as approximating the character of "Nature." "Quietness, serenity," were they not the very qualities that had made Keats feel faint when he contemplated the Elgin marbles, or the Greek vase? Nature, too, Goethe claimed, proceeded, as we have seen, not in volcanic eruption, but in a process of quiet evolution. Premature evolutionist that he was, how he would have recoiled from the theories of that Victorian who revolutionized all theories of the origins of Man — Charles Darwin! But Goethe imagined that history, too, must follow the peaceful course of peaceful Nature...

So it might seem from the terrains of the Weimar Court or from the lookouts of the Weimar hills. But alas! History refuses to conform to the dictates of poets, even if they do study natural phenomena.

Just at the moment when Goethe was completing *Torquato Tasso*, a storm broke over the whole European world. The Bastille of Paris fell on the fourteenth of July, 1789. The event shook thrones and hovels, shook kings and subjects, and, even Weimar...

It marked the beginning of a reign of war and upheavals that was to last almost uninterruptedly for a quarter of a century, from 1789 to 1815. We have seen how the event terrified, as well as inspired. In German lands we have seen how philosophers at first exulted, men like Fichte, Hegel; and in Goethe's close vicinity, Herder, and the poet Wieland. Herder hailed the march of the Spirit of the Times, hailed the fall of feudalism and class privilege, and the emergence of what he called "real folk," the emergence of the power of new classes. The event, in his eyes, equalled the introduction of Christianity, the Renaissance, and the Reformation.

And Goethe? He was silent. At least at first. Immersed in his contemplation of Nature's pacific ways, he could not understand what was happening, or perhaps he would not?... All his life long he loved and admired France and the French. Was he not himself an intellectual descendant of Voltaire, Rousseau, and Diderot?

But his journals and diaries of the day reveal nothing of what he might have felt or thought. It is as if deliberately, consciously, he wished to exclude the troublous ocean of history from his door, and close his ears to its roar and thunder...

No, Revolution could not be a part of the World-Process. But the revolutionary fever was catching on, even in Germany. The Rhineland was in a state of revolutionary uprising. As the European crisis deepened, Europe became the battle-ground of two camps: On one side revolutionary France; on the other, a coalition of Prussia, Austria, and other states, and eventually England, joined, of course, by the aristocratic French emigrés.

Nor could Weimar — that minute pendant of the great powers — escape the war. Adhering to his royal masters, Duke Karl August joined the Allied armies against France, Goethe followed. An insatiable observer of all things, he would find here, too, subjects for his mind's laboratory. So far as his full commitment to either cause, royalist or French, he appeared indifferent. To his friend, Friedrich Jacobi, he wrote on August 18, 1792, in the midst of the campaign: "Neither the death of the aristocratic or of the democratic sinners mattered one bit to me."[41] And during the momentous battle of Valmy, in which the royalist forces were thoroughly defeated by the French Republicans, Goethe appeared more interested in the rare species of stone in the neighborhood than in the military actions. Just as in the following year, during the more successful royalist assault on Mainz, he explored the charnel houses for bones that might be of use to him in his anatomical investigations. He was, it must be admitted, not indifferent to the toll of human beings that the war was taking.

He returned to Weimar and to his theatrical interests. But his political attitude had become more articulate, defined and rigid. He now expressed his political views in both verse and the drama. He had already in 1791 taken note of the unsavory scandal which had rocked the royal court of Versailles by the affair of the so-called

"Queen's Necklace," and in which the notorious Italian impostor
and charlatan, Cagliostro, was implicated, along with a number of
courtiers of both sexes. But Goethe was more deeply interested in
the intrigue, and only mildly in the corrupt state of the court, the
conduct of which he deprecated. But in 1793 he went forcefully into
the fray against the French Revolution with a series of topical plays
none of which could claim serious consideration today. In general,
his view of the French Revolution descends to a level of unworthy
triviality, travesty, or objurgation. The Revolutionaries are derogated
as "demagogues," "thieves," as members of a "mob," as the
"monstrous tyrant" — who prey either upon innocents or idiots to
mislead them. Such is the theme of *Der Bürgergeneral — The
Citizen-General* — which is a local farce taking place in a village
where a country-barber is overcome by revolutionary slogans and
parades as the Citizen-General, only in the end to be exposed,
laughed out of court, and admonished to behave, as are the rest of
the inhabitants of the village. Warned not to be "well-meaning
idiots," easy bait of demagogues, they are also advised to be good and
stay out of trouble. The local nobleman is spokesman for the sweet
status quo:

Children, love one another, tend your fields and run your houses diligently.
Let foreign countries look after themselves, and don't watch the political
skies except perhaps on Sunday and feast-days…In a country like ours
where the Prince holds aloof from no one, where all the classes think with
fairness of each other, where no one is prevented from using his abilities in
his own way, where useful knowledge and information are spread
everywhere, there will be no factions. What goes on in the world will attract
attention, but the seditious thoughts of whole nations will have no
influence. We shall be serenely grateful that we can see a clear sky overhead,
while disastrous storms are ravaging vast areas with their hail.[42]

Having thrown this adulatory side-remark at his own Duke
Karl August, Goethe who had produced the play at Weimar,
continued showing it at least once a year until 1803.

An unfinished play, *Das Mädchen von Oberkirch*, takes place in Strassburg, during the Revolution. The city is in the hands of the French revolutionaries, and the principal characters, aristocrats, are in danger of being dispossessed of their properties, or threatened with exile. The revolutionaries are described as "destroyers" and "terrible Jacobins." (This fanciful play, it seems, was to depict the honorable character of a young woman, Marie, who, to save her friends, accepts an offer to personate the revolutionary Goddess of Reason, then changes her mind in deference to honor.[43])

Some years later, in November 1799, Goethe attempted another drama, *Die natürliche Tochter (The Natural Daughter)* which brings on the stage a young woman of great moral dignity and "reine Menschlichkeit" — "the Pure Humane" — who is dedicated to the idea of a righteous kingship, which is at that time threatened by division and envy. The King is in need of faithful followers in an hour when "the low is swelling up, and the lofty is sinking."[44]

Goethe saw in the incendiary events only the working of the "mob" — "die rauhe Menge" — that endangered the sacred temples of Culture and Civilization. Such was to be his stand even to the end of his life, when he still inveighed against "Parisian equality" as an infectious disease, "a turbulence by the lowest elements," spreading "murderous, incendiary morals which destroyed and razed an idyllic existence, in so far as that was possible in the eighteenth century."[45]

While he was busy with sustaining righteous kings in *Die natürliche Tochter*, history was taking truly dramatic turns. A comet streaked across the sky full of ominous forebodings. On November 9, 1799, Napoleon Bonaparte effected his *coup d' état* of Brumaire. The mighty hand of the conqueror and his armies would sweep across the chessboard of Europe, brush aside king and knight, and reset the chessboard with fresh pieces...

Such an irresistible force had not been seen in the world for many centuries. It engulfed all of Europe; then extended to Africa. And it even threatened that enclave of seeming stability, little Weimar.

On October 14, 1806 took place the Battle of Jena. Prussia collapsed. In 1808 took place a Congress at Erfurt, "where four kings and thirty-four princes, including two emperors, including the Tsar of Russia," met with Napoleon.

In 1806 Napoleon's troops passed through Weimar, and even invested Goethe's home, where the faithful, courageous Christiane Vulpius managed to shy them away. It was in consideration of such heroism, and of dangers to come which might threaten his own life too, that Goethe decided to make Christiane his lawful wife, legally to secure her existence.

In October, Karl August of Saxe-Weimar joined other and mightier potentates to wait attendance on the Conqueror. For Goethe, who was also present, the master of Europe stood forth a giant. In Goethe's words he was the "one man" who had dissolved "the confusion made by thousands" — that is, broken the back of Revolution.

October 2: Goethe writes. "I am summoned to appear before the Emperor at eleven in the morning." And he continues:

The Emperor is seated at a round table, taking his breakfast. At his right stands, somewhat at a distance, Talleyrand; at his left, quite close Daru, with whom the Emperor is discussing matters of tribute. The Emperor motions to me. I approach, and stand at a seemly distance. After regarding me closely, he speaks. "Vous êtes un homme." I bow. He asks, "How old are you?" "Sixty years old." "You've preserved yourself well ... You've composed tragedies ..."

And so on. They converse of various things, among them Goethe's *Werther*, in which the Emperor cites a passage which he criticizes as "contrary to nature." Goethe agrees. The Emperor also discusses the so-called "Tragedies of Fate," then current in the theatre. "Why," says the Emperor, "do they bother with fate-tragedies? Politics is Fate."

October 17: "I receive the Order of the Legion of Honor."[46]

Such was the memorable interview. On another occasion Napoleon is reported to have invited Goethe to visit Paris. Goethe never did. One wonders whether that would have been benefit or detriment. One also wonders what might have happened to Goethe had he visited one or the other of those incomparable cities, London or Paris, and ventured outside the narrow precincts of Weimar...

For Goethe the figure of Napoleon loomed as no other person of the times. He had humbled the great ones of the world: Prussia and Austria; and he would also try to humble Russia. There seemed to be none to halt him.

How to account for him? Undoubtedly the man was no mere man. He must be driven by inscrutable and irresistible inner forces. Goethe sought to define such an indefinable phenomenon. He called that force a "daemon" — the Greek "daimon," meaning "genius" or "spirit," later degraded by medievalism to mean "evil spirit." The idea of the "daemon" became an important element in Goethe's psychological thinking.

The "daemon" is an inscrutable force; its unpredictable designs may tend toward evil; they may tend toward good. It is, in essence, amoral. Napoleon was a demoniac personality. Goethe tried to define it, as it manifested itself in Napoleon, ten years after Waterloo.

The darknesses and illuminations of man make his destiny. The demon ought to lead us every day with strings, and show us what to do on every occasion... Napoleon was the man! Always illuminated, always clear and decided, always with sufficient energy to carry through whatever he considered advantageous and necessary. His life was the stride of a demigod, from battle to battle, from victory to victory. It might be said of him that he lived in a state of continual illumination. His destiny was more brilliant than any the world had ever seen, or was likely to see...[47]

In another connection, he describes the amoral impulses that drive the "demonic" character:

...A titanic force emanates from them and they exercise an incredible power over every creature and even over the elements, and who can say how far their influence will extend? All the moral forces put together are powerless against them; it is in vain for the more enlightened section of humanity to brand them as deceived or deceivers; the masses will be attracted by them. Rarely if ever do their equals exist at the same time, and nothing can overcome them but the very universe against which they declare battle...[48]

But even demigods may be spurred by a daemon that is evil! Even demigods may miscalculate or overestimate their power. Came the Russian winter of 1812, and disaster. Nemesis, in the cloak of wintry weather and the Russian people, had achieved what others had been unable to do. Now the cries rang out: On to Paris! Freedom! National Liberation! Goethe remained cold to such cries. Napoleon's fortunes kept on falling: the defeat at Leipzig in October, 1813; abdication April 1814; exile to Elba... There were celebrations in 1814, when the Allied troops entered Paris, and the emigré nobles began returning. Goethe, the court-poet, strangely enough joined in the celebration. The Berlin theatrical manager, Iffland, invited him to compose a festival play, to celebrate the great victories, and the triumphant return of King Frederick William III from Paris to Berlin, along with Tsar Alexander. It was a strange undertaking for the poet; he had never had too much trust in the German people, whom he might like individually, but in the mass — not at all! He did not particularly like Prussia. He was suspicious of the so-called national movement of liberation; and, not least, he did not hate Napoleon or the French. But he set to work, anyway, and produced a "Greek" pageant-play, an allegory, *Epimenides Erwachen — The Awakening of Epimenides*. Epimenides, a half-mythical figure of the sixth century B.C., was reputed a priest, poet, and prophet of Crete, and to have slept for fifty-six years. In Goethe's play he has slept forty years and awakes to witness the devastation of the world around him and the end of war. This was to be a celebration of triumphant Peace, and a denunciation of War, the emissary of Hell, presumably Napoleon! The allegorical figures of Faith, Hope, and Charity were probably meant to stand for Tsar Alexander, Prussia, and Austria. The Chorus chants, "Brothers, rise to free the world!" "Comets beckon, the hour is ripe!" And to celebrate Victory, and the new Harmony, we hear voices rejoicing: "Now we are Germans once again. We are all renewed, reborn."

> Now let resound: The Lord is here;
> The night is filled with starry radiance;
> He, to bring us our salvation,
> Has striven, fought, and watched for us ...

It is not clear whether the Lord who has done all that is the Lord God, or the returning King of Prussia, whose promises of a constitution to the poor German people who had bled for his liberation were soon to be retracted ...

But again History played a mean, though rather brief trick on the victors. Napoleon came back! On March 19, 1815 he was back in Paris, and on March 30, 1815 the play was produced in Berlin! ... The following year it was produced in Weimar. Well, by that time Waterloo had once and for all decided Napoleon's fate ...

Then followed the Congress of Vienna. With some cynicism Goethe observed the machinations in that city, as the various predacious conquerors proceeded to slice up their prey. He retired to his own shell, and once more lost himself in botany, geology, anatomy and — poetry. He was satisfied that the status quo had been restored. He liked the "Holy Alliance," of which he said to his secretary-friend Eckermann that "nothing great and for humanity more beautiful had ever been invented."[49] Soon he was to support the restored French monarchy's intervention in Spain to bring back the Bourbons.

7.

But during those war years his literary output had not lagged. True, Schiller had died in 1805, and Goethe had lost an irreplaceable friend, critic, and counsellor. During that time he had concluded the first part of *Faust*, the first volumes of *Wilhelm Meisters Lehrjahre*; completed a novel, *Die Wahlverwandschaften (Elective Affinities)*; the first two volumes of his autobiography, *Dichtung und Wahrheit (Poetry and Truth)*, and numerous poems. Between Waterloo and the date of his death he was to be no less productive. There followed the *Italienische Reise (Journey to Italy)*, *Wilhelm Meisters Wanderjahre, (Wilhelm Meister's Years of Travel)*, the other volumes of his autobiography, numerous scientific works on Morphology and Optics; in poetry, some of his most enchanting verse and poetic sequences; and, finally, the second part of *Faust*. Long before his death he had become the end-goal of innumerable pilgrimages. Weimar became a shrine. Visitors streamed thither from Paris (Mickiewicz, among them), from England, from America, from Russia. He had in fact become something of a monument. He survived his wife Christiane, his son August von Goethe, Duke Karl August, Herder, and Hegel. He survived Napoleon. He outlived Beethoven.

He sought and found rejuvenation in love. He had once spoken of men who had been granted "a second puberty." He was one of these. He fell in love again and again. And once again he was inspired to poetry, much of it equal to anything he had ever written. Younger women attracted him, and were drawn to him. To young Minna Herzlieb we owe the "Sonnets" of 1810; to Marianne von Willemer, the astounding series called *West-östlicher Divan (West-Eastern Divan)* of 1814; and finally to Ulrike von Levetzow the intensely moving "Marienbad Elegy" of 1823.

England's foremost Orientalist, Sir William Jones, had in the seventies of the eighteenth century through his significant studies and translations of Arabic and Persian literature made the world aware of its richness. The German Romantics, especially the brothers Schlegel, had aided in the spread of a knowledge of Arabic, Persian and Hindu letters. Joseph von Hammer translated the poetry of the Persian poet Hafiz in 1812, and it was this version that Goethe utilized in writing his own *West-Eastern Divan*. Shams-uddin-Mohommed, the fourteenth century Persian poet, called himself Hafiz, "the one who knows" (i.e., the Koran), and his collection of poems was the "Divan." Here was poetry after Goethe's own heart, to con, to mull over, and then to make his own. For the *Divan* was a celebration of wine, love, and the goodness of a beneficent God. Some commentators had sought to find allegories and mystifications in the verses, making of wine and roses and love religious symbols. But for Goethe, Hafiz was the lusty hedonist, the extoller of life and its joys.

And in those troubled times Goethe was hankering after escape. The Orient opened its doors to him, just as Italy and Hellas had drawn him and assuaged him before. And so he began:

> Nord und West und Süd zersplittern,
> Throne bersten, Reiche zittern...

> North and West and South are sundered,
> Thrones are crashing, kingdoms tremble,
> Flee, oh flee, to eastern regions,
> To their pure, patriarchal air...

Drinking from the well of Life, he will have Love, Wine and Song, and become young again.

Yes, this was his poet, "You, Hafiz, though not pious, are blessed." and, he added, "In your way of poetizing, I shall find myself, and the way to inspire German hearts with new zest."[50]

In the vicinity of Frankfurt lived the family of von Willemer, Marianne and her husband. She was a woman of thirty; Johann Jakob Willemer was some twenty-five years older. She had been an actress and dancer, and had been taken in by him as a foster-daughter. Goethe met them in August 1814, shortly before they were married. And so, they fell in love, and Goethe named her with the Persian name of Suleika, and he became the Persian Hatem. To her he devoted an entire section of the work, the "Book Suleika," its most exquisite portion. The most remarkable aspect of their poetic interchange is that it includes a number of poems from her hand, for she proved herself an inspired poet too. He knew himself much older, and could only hope that the houris, the nymphs of the Mohammedan paradise, would generously receive him, for he was now transmuted into a youth by love. And so Hatem addresses Suleika:

> Locken, halten mich gefangen
> In dem Kreise des Gesichts!
> Euch geliebten braunen Schlangen
> Zu erwidern hab' ich nichts...

> Locks of hair, hold me captive
> In the circle of that face!
> My beloved, dear brown serpents
> To repay you I have nought.

> Nought but this my faithful heart
> That throbs with ever-youthful glow,
> For beneath the mists and snow-storms
> An Aetna rages on toward you...

> Bring on wine! and one more bumper!
> This brimming cup is meant for her!
> And if she find therein my ashes,
> She will say, He burned for me.[51]

It is fortunate that among the remarkable musical settings of these poems of the *West-Eastern Divan*, by Hugo Wolf, this one, in particular, is outstanding for its passionate, exquisite identification of composer and poet.

Marianne writes after one of their partings:

> Was bedeutet die Bewegung?
> Bringt der Ost mir frohe Kunde?...

What betokens this mild stirring:
Is is Eastwind's joyous tidings?
For the soft and cooling wings
Soothe my heart's deepest mourning.

Ah! the heart's deep truth alone
Love's sweet breath, a reborn Life...
Only his own lips can bring me.
Only his own breath convey.

And after their final parting:

West wind, — for your humid wings,
Oh, how deeply I envy you,
You can tidings bring to him,
How great pain a parting brings...[52]

Eight years later, in 1821, the poet fell in love again. He was approaching seventy-five, and the young woman, Ulrike von Levetzow, was seventeen. He even considered marriage, but the saner wisdom of mother and daughter prevailed; and there was another parting in 1823. Sobriety might smile condescendingly upon such an episode; and crusty, hard-shelled wisdom might shake its hoary locks, but who would not envy the young beloved one of the most moving love songs a poet ever indited, and who would not be grateful that aged love could produce such beauty. The farewell is contained in the "Marienbad Elegy."

The poet is addressing himself:

...So warst du denn im Paradies empfangen,
Als wärst du wert des ewing schönen Lebens:
Dir blieb kein Wunsch, kein Hoffen, kein Verlangen,
Hier war der Ziel des inningsten Bestrebens...

And you were thus received in Paradise
As worthy of a pure and endless life;
Nothing remained: no wish, no hope, no longing;
Here was the goal of all your inmost striving;

And he recalls:

> And on my lips the last kiss of all pressing,
> So clear in motion the loved one's image stays,
> With flaming script on my true heart inscribed...
>
> Mir ist das All, ich bin mir selbst verloren...
>
> To me the All, I to myself am lost,
> I who deemed myself favorite of gods.
> They tried me; sent me Pandora for a while,
> So rich in treasures; but richer more in warnings;
> They urged me on to those gift-bestowing lips,
> And wrested me from her, and sent me to my doom.[53]

The poignant words, the music, the feelings of the German poem are not the outpourings of an aging heart...

8.

Yet he had never resolved, nor could he resolve the problem of love. The pattern he had pursued from youth on had been one of passionate upheavals without resolution, or to put it bluntly, resolution through flight. Thus, too, with marriage. He united himself with Christiane, it is true, but that was a matter of expediency as well as gratitude, and in order to assure her legal rights after his death.

Flight meant creation. For him creation, whether in prose or verse or drama, meant crystallization and resolution.

Nearing old age, he was still beset by the problem of physical, sexual attraction. Once more he sought clarification in a work of art. He turned to the novel, and in 1820 published *Die Wahlverwandschaften (Elective Affinities)*. This was a puzzling, provocative, and intriguing work, for it is a kind of treatise on abnegation, renunciation, the sanctity of marriage, and the mystery of sexual attraction.

For the first time, too, Goethe allowed himself entry into romantic mysticism. He who had warred against romantic extravagances and enthusiasms, found himself entering into the domain of the "Night" — the Romantic "Nachtseite der Natur" — the nocturnal aspects of the human soul in its relation to Love. This time he draws on science for his analogy, and chemistry, in particular. Just as in a chemical solution, one element is attracted to, or repelled by another, so, too, Love exhibits similar phenomena.

Elective Affinities is remarkable also for being the only of his longer narrative works that has unity and coherence and a resolution; and a final integration of its elements. It is a narrative drama, in which two men and two women, a married couple and two unmarried characters, interact as if in a chemical retort. Nature and natural forces and the human will are the real actors. The moral issue is the responsibility of the human being toward oneself and society. Here magnetism, intuition, and what we today call extra-sensory perception play a great part — strange instruments for Goethe to handle, a man who had all his life insisted on "this-sidedness," clarity and order. The married couple, upper-class and highly intelligent, Charlotte and Eduard, are confronted by young Ottilie, Charlotte's niece, and an outsider, called the Captain. Mysterious, impenetrable forces, forces of attraction, begin to manifest themselves in the four. Charlotte is drawn to the Captain, and Eduard to Ottilie, who is being educated in a lycée, and is endowed with extraordinary qualities of sensitiveness, bordering on the mysterious. Eduard is a somewhat self-indulgent personality, a musical dilettante, but also quite attractive. The chemistry of the body and mind begins its work; the unconscious forces come to the fore as each of the characters falls in love with his or her counterpart: Charlotte with the Captain, and Eduard with Ottilie, and reciprocally. The mystical and the symbolic now take over as the child born to Charlotte and Eduard, conceived just at the time of their emotional alienation, resembles both the Captain and Ottilie. The baby is the product of a symbolic adultery. Left in the care of Ottilie, the child drowns, and Ottilie, now the center of the drama, who is passionately in love, renounces it and brings about her own death by starvation. Less dramatically Charlotte and the Captain both decide on a separation. The sanctity of marriage has been upheld; social laws have triumphed and been validated through these several renunciations.

9.

"Entsagung," "Renunciation" — that was to be a leading motive of his later works, those two other major narrative works concerned with the adventures of Wilhelm Meister, which had been trailing him from the 1770s almost to the end of his life. They — along with the enormous Faust dramas — may be said to form the two vast chapters of his final creative genius, each having an earlier portion that finds its interlocking sequel in later years, like two complementary epic works, one in prose, the other in dramatic verse. They are like two major attempts at Goethe's final interpretation of two worlds, of two parallel but distinct worlds, one that of a middle-class bourgeois character; the other of a "demonic" gigantic figure — both engaged in forms of "Lebensbildung."

These are the final testaments to his own generation as well as to posterity.

We may be permitted to call these two major works "epics" of self-creation and self-recreation. "Selbstbildung" in the course of years undergoes a transmutation in which characters pass from the philosophy of self-containment, and through "activity" find their way to the crucial conviction that the "self" is a fruitless element unless it interrelates with other "selves," with other members of society.

In the *West-Eastern Divan* the poet had chanted "Höchstes Glück der Erdenkinder sei nur die Persönlichkeit," "Let the highest bliss on earth be the Personality," and in another compelling poem he had described love in the symbol of the butterfly and the flame, the butterfly's immolation in the flame, as the spirit of renewal, of love-mating, symbolically the "Stirb und werde" — "Dying and becoming" — constant change and rebirth. Living means change, constant renewal; inertia is Death.[54]

Wilhelm Meister's Apprenticeship is a novel of revolt — the bourgeois young man striving toward the highest self-cultivation breaks with the life demands of middle-class existence, the life of the merchant, the trader; breaks down the barriers of what he conceived to be a sordid existence that does not offer the freedom of cultivation that is the property of the aristocracy. He believes he can find it in Art — the art of the theatre. In a letter Wilhelm writes to his brother-in-law, which is a kind of "declaration of independence," he declares for the theatrical career as the only path to the achievement of "culture." The bourgeois, he scornfully asserts, may not ask of a person, "What are you?" but only "What do you possess?" The only function the bourgeois possesses is that of being "useful." He can develop a very limited number of his capacities. Only the theatre and authorship offer opportunities for rounded self-cultivation of the personality.[55]

But Wilhelm's self-education is not altogether in his own hands. We discover that, unbeknownst, he is being observed and guided by others. These are the members of a kind of Masonic Order, the Society of the Tower. It is under their surveillance and direction that Wilhelm reaches the resolution of all his life's purposes. He discovers that actually he is not fitted for a theatrical career, neither as actor or as dramatist. He has committed errors. But what of that? He is instructed by a member of the Tower:

It is not the duty of the educator of the human heart to safeguard a person from error, but to guide the erring one; yes, even allow him to drain the cup of errors to the bottom.

And Wilhelm reflects: "Of which errors can he be speaking, except the one that pursued me all my life long, namely that I was seeking 'self-cultivation' where there was none to be found; that I imagined I could attain to a talent for which I had no disposition whatever."[56]

All those past experiences he has had he is now able to assimilate into his being and understanding: the chameleon character of the enchanting epicene person of Mignon, symbol of Italy itself; the protean, evanescent, lively, sprightly, mercurial Philine; the mysterious Harper, and all the others of his fellow-actors. He also comes to terms with Marianne, his first love, who, he had believed, had betrayed him. He finds out that he has been in the wrong. Marianne is dead, but she has left behind his "natural" son, whom Wilhelm now rediscovers.

Wilhelm "looked at the world no longer like a bird of passage." He makes plans for his son's future. "His years of apprenticeship were over, and along with the feelings of a father, he had also acquired all the virtues of a burgher." He recognizes the existence of a reciprocal influence betwen father and son. And he sets off for Italy.[57]

There are indications that the Society of the Tower was going to extend its moral and physical influence by establishing branches in other lands — perhaps even in America. The member who had had such a great part in Wilhelm's life, Jarno, is in fact setting forth on just such an enterprise...

Wilhelm Meisters Years of Wandering has an altogether wider scope. Here the individual characters take second place; in fact, they become shadowy. The pedagogue, the social thinker, the moralist — all these take over, and all of these are Goethe. We become aware, for the first time, of the social conditions subsisting; in this case those of the weaving industry in Switzerland, which is now being subjected to the same dire vicissitudes as other countries, but not in such an advanced stage. Machinery is replacing the cottage loom; capitalism is replacing individual enterprise. The cottager has no choice now: either he accepts the machine and goes into the factory, or he emigrates. Whereto? His eyes turn toward America.

There was a time when Goethe looked askance at emigration as a solution to economic crises. Now, however, he accepts the alternative of emigration, bitter as that may be. In fact, he almost conceives of America as a potential Utopia:

> America, you are more fortunate
> Than our old Continent.
> You have no ruined castles,
> No basalt monuments.
> You stand on no uncertain ground.

You do not suffer heart-pangs
Mid life's merriment,
From idle memories
And unprofitable strife.
Then use the present happily![58]

As the "Wanderbund" — "The Association of Emigrés" — are framing their Utopian charter, they specify that in the new country they would be forming a "Christian state," for it is part of their credo that Christianity stands for belief, love, hope, and complete acceptance of the holiness of Christ. "In this sense," the charter continues, "we cannot tolerate the presence of Jews in our midst; for how can we vouchsafe them a share of the highest culture, whose origin and tradition they deny?"[59] Among the ambiguities that characterize so much of Goethe's being, none is so startling as this unenlightened attitude toward Jews, expressed toward the end of his life. Where in Goethe's mind was the memory of Napoleon, who had extended civil rights to the Jews; where the traditions of the Enlightenment? Of Spinoza? Of Lessing? Where the young Goethe who had studied Yiddish and Hebrew?

One of the most interesting projects set forth in the book is the so-called Pedagogic Province, the educational institution into which Wilhelm entrusts his son, Felix. The institution tolerates "no religion based on fear." Religion, as it is practised here, is founded on "Reverence" — "Ehrfurcht." "Ehrfurcht" is manifested in a triple form: Reverence for that which is above; reverence for that which is our equal; reverence for that which is "below us." The last is reverence for poverty, contempt, shame and misery, suffering and death — even sin and crime. This is the so-called Sanctuary of Pain, "the Worship of Sorrow," "das Heiligtum des Schmerzes."[60]

Here too are taught the inescapable duties of practical activity and usefulness. "Where I am useful, there is my fatherland." Work and thought are conjoined; the reverence for labor is preached.

Wilhelm Meisters Wanderjahre is subtitled "Die Entsagenden," "The Renouncers." Renunciation consists in recognizing the boundaries, the limits of one's being, the extent of one's endowment and capabilities, and the values of "Time" — "God's greatest gift to mankind." Wilhelm finds his vocation, for he becomes a physician. He has attained to the autonomy of being; and he will now set his son Felix on the road to self-determination, "Selbstbestimmung." He has vindicated the appellation of being God's "Ebenbild" — God's "image." A doctor, he is enabled to save his son's life, and as he watches his son's reawakening, he exclaims: "Are you once again being born, you glorious image of the Lord; and once again you will experience damage and wounds, both without and within!" Wilhelm is now set upon the high road to life; he will be prepared to achieve a sense of the reality of the outer world, and find his own place in it as useful, creative participant. He will combine reverence for himself with those other three he had been taught at the Pedagogic Institute.

10.

To follow the course of the composition of *Faust* is to follow
Goethe's progress, from the early days of his maturing interest in
science, when Nature was still an "undeciphered, yet not
undecipherable" book, to the completion of the second part, the year
before his death, when Nature's book, if not yet totally deciphered,
was no longer a mystery that had resisted his understanding or
decipherment. It was an open book whose full penetration only
waited its time. He was on his way, if only Nature granted him
another lease on life.

Faust I and *Faust II* are like a journey on highways, byways and
detours; and as we move along we become aware that we are living
vicariously not only the transformations of the man Faust, but also
the transformations of Goethe himself. We go back to the young
Promethean of the early 1770s and we end with the aged Merlin, as
one admirer was to call him — a sixty years' span. The youth
reappears to us in the first *Faust*, the so-called *Urfaust* — sketches
that had been deemed lost forever, until rediscovered toward the
end of the nineteenth century. In *Faust I*, when it appeared in 1808,
we have the man in his maturity. In *Faust II* the Olympian, who in
the course of twenty years or so tried to refit the various threads of a
vast canvas, constituted of his vast experience, into a whole weft
that reveals variously the brilliance of the earlier days, but also large
spaces that show subdued and often somewhat dimmed evidences of
a declining power; a tapestry, nevertheless, so rich in diversity,
multiplicity of design and thought, startling contrasts, as to remain
an inspiring challenge, even if occasional riddle, but always a source
of amazement to this day.

The fragment, the so-called *Urfaust* (the *Proto-Faust*), already
reveals the master-hand of our pre-Weimar Prometheus. Young
Goethe projects on to the old scholar, Faust, his own dissatisfaction
with mere book-learning, his revulsion from pedantry; here he

reflects the ambition, the need to know, to penetrate into the secrets of Nature; here he is the defiant questioner, seeking answers to the world's riddles.

But here, too, is young Goethe, the lover, who merges his experiences in the character of Gretchen, and transfers to Faust his own sense of guilt, here heightened to heart-breaking tragedy.

> ... Am I not the runaway, the unhoused,
> The monster, void of purpose and peace,
> Who, like some cataract, rushing from rock to rock,
> In greedy rage roars onward toward the abyss ...
> Was it not enough for me to seize on crags
> And crumble them to atoms?
> What need had you to shatter her repose?
> And you Hell, was this the sacrifice you craved.
> Devil! help shorten these my hours of anguish,
> Let come soon what needs must come,
> And may her fate engulf me too,
> And both together perish in the ruin.[61]

The completion of the first part of *Faust* lingered. It seemed as if the work needed intense spurs before it could see the light of day. And such preconditions appeared. One was the Italian journey. The other the challenge of Schiller's presence. *Faust: Ein Fragment* appeared in 1790; *Faust: Der Tragödie erster Teil*, in 1808. The Italian experience, as we have seen, was critical for Goethe's emotional development, especially in freeing him erotically. It made possible to uncover Faust's dualism that speaks in his self-description: "Zwei Seelen wohnen ach! in meiner Brust" — "Alas! two souls reside in my breast!" — the one urging him upwards, the other downwards; the Faust of the Witches' Sabbath as well as of the ideal aspirations. Schiller's urgent presence and critical acumen hastened the process to completion.

The publication of Goethe's *Faust* in 1808 was a momentous event, and was soon recognized as such. It is not necessary here to enter upon a history of its diffusion, practically all over the world. It became, as we know, the most powerful "myth" of the nineteenth century.

The attraction of *Faust I* is not hard to explain. The play contained so great a variety of themes and styles as to satisfy the most fastidious intellectual as well as the more popular palate. It was at once "philosophical" and immediately personal. It called forth immediate identification and empathy. It touched all chords of the heart. It has humor. It has high solemnity, high seriousness. It has Faust, and it has Gretchen, and not least it has Mephistopheles! Its verse-form is doggerel, lyric, sublime unrhymed lines. It has vulgarity, obscenity and pathos. It has God and Satan. It is a microcosm. It has a Promethean character and a Witches' Sabbath.

The Prologue in Heaven, with its choral hymning by the Archangels, is probably the most sublime poetry Goethe ever created:

> Die Sonne tönt nach alter Weise,
> In Brudersphären Wettgesang...

In Bayard Taylor's translation:

> The sun-orb sings in emulation,
> Amid brother-spheres, his ancient round:
> His path predestined through creation
> He ends with step of thunder-sound...

As each archangel in turn rehearses his praises in celestial ecstasy, Mephistopheles intrudes himself and enters into a quite genial colloquy with the Lord, like Satan in the *Book of Job*. It will end in a friendly wager. Mephistopheles challenges the Lord's possession of Faust: Whose will Doctor Faust be? The Lord's or the Devil's? The Lord agrees to the wager:

> Es irrt der Mensch so lang er strebt...

> So long as Man strives he still will err...
> But a good man in his darkest yearnings
> Is still aware of the one good way...

From sublimity, and genial celestial good-humor, we now descend to doggerel, as we meet Faust in his musty study. The discontented, all-knowing old scholar declaims against his ignorance and useless knowledge, and berates pedantry.

Habe nun ach! Philosophie...

Alas! I've studied Philosophy,
Jurisprudence, Medicine,
And sad to say, Theology...
And here poor fool with all my lore
I stand no wiser than before...

He turns to magic so that he might learn "what binds the world in its inmost being," to search out its energies and seeds. He will seek out the source, the very God-Nature — the animating principle of the Universe.

Faust's is a dual nature.

Two souls, alas! reside within my breast,
And each would fain dissever from the other,
One with harsh love-lust holds fast
Tenacious to the world; the other with might
Rises from the dust to lofty ancestral regions.

Torn between the earthy and the heavenly, Faust proves an easy prey for Mephistopheles. For Mephistopheles is Faust's earth-bound half.

And who is this Mephistopheles? Is he that hater of light (as the Greek origin of the name suggests)? Or, the destroyer (as a Hebrew derivation indicates)? He is, of course, in Goethe, far removed from the early "Devil" of medieval comedy, or even Marlowe's Renaissance tragedy, *Dr. Faustus*. He is no obscene, motley fool, clown, buffoon, or tumbler. Nor is he Lucifer, the bearer of light. He is a philosopher of the "evil" side of Nature, doomsday preacher of negation and destruction, the cynical, sometimes gay onlooker on human follies. He is the negative that mocks the fantasy flights of Faust, his lofty pretensions, his cosmic ambitions and his sentimentality. He knows himself to be what he is:

Ein Teil von jener Kraft
Der stets das Gute will und stets das Böse schafft...

> Part of the power
> That always wills the Bad, and always works the Good.

> I am the Spirit that denies,
> And justly so, for all that has arisen
> Deserves to be destroyed...
> It were better far were naught created...
> Destruction, in short, — what you call evil,
> That is my true element.

He is the self-described "favorite son of Chaos." And he is also a cosmic dialectician, a logician.

> I am a portion of that portion, once the All,
> A part of that darkness that brought forth the Light.

Yet, he sadly recognizes he is fighting a futile battle, for despite all those thousands that he has "buried," creation and recreation still proceed... There are elements in Faust he will never comprehend, though he can mock them: his cosmic urges and his highly-charged exultations, such as:

> I glow as if inspired by new-made wine,
> I feel the strength to meet the world head-on,
> To bear earth's woes, earth's bliss to share,
> And even strive with the might of storms,
> Undaunted even in the shipwreck's crash...

> And all that to mankind is allotted,
> I will enjoy within my inner self,
> And in my spirit grasp the highest and the lowest,
> Heap on my bosom all their weal and woe
> And my own self to all their selves expand,
> And like themselves perish in the end.

Mephistopheles will give Faust everything his heart desires (even if he doesn't fully understand) and Faust, in return will grant him his soul after death, but only

> When to the fleeting moment I can say,
> Stay with me! — you are so fair;
> Then you may bind me with your bonds,
> Then will I gladly hasten to my end...

He will be shown the "little" world and the "great" world; the high and the low, even the lowest, such as a Witches' Sabbath on the Brocken mountain, where obscenity reigns free; but first they must go to the Witches' Kitchen, where he will be turned from an old man into a blooming youth. Here in the magic mirror he sees a beautiful woman, and for the rest of his life, for good and evil, he will be ravished by woman's beauty...

And thus equipped with youth and with the indispensable company of Mephistopheles, Faust ventures out into the world to explore all and exploit all, but most fully to exploit his own now imperious Ego. He is ready to plunge into the lower depths of sensuality which as a poor old scholar he had never tasted; he will "allay those glowing passions" that boil within him. "For only restlessness proves the man." Mephistopheles will give him plenty of opportunities to be restless...

> Fair Lady, may I dare,
> Offer arm and escort on your way?

> I'm neither lady, nor am I fair:
> And unescorted I'll find my way.

Here the "tragedy" of Faust begins. An engaging young man, no doubt of a higher class, accosts a pretty young woman of the burgher class — her name is Gretchen — who is modesty herself. With an auxiliar like Mephistopheles, how can the assault fail? As Heine would have said: "Es ist eine alte Geschichte." "It's an old, old story." And in this case, too, it leads to a heart-break, infanticide, and death by execution. There are few, if any characters in all of Goethe's writings that possess the simplicity, innocence, and intuitive delicacy of Gretchen, this child of Nature. Like so many children of nature, Gretchen falls a prey to high sophistication, abetted by Hell.

When she naïvely asks him about his "religion," Faust, the natural philosopher, becomes, in Rousseau's manner, expansive: "Gefühl ist alles!" "Feeling is all!" She, untainted by philosophy, knows what feeling is, for she is its truest embodiment, and she gets herself entangled in its web. Even Faust is moved at times as he gazes around her small room. He senses its "holiness." "Within this very poverty, what plenty; within this prison, what heavenly bliss!" And in a momentary self-realization he asks himself, "Why is your heart so heavy? What has brought you here?" Having Mephistopheles as an aid, it is not difficult for Faust to seduce Gretchen. How can she escape, when she is trapped between a philosopher and the Devil? She sings her loveliest songs, like "Der König in Thule" and "Meine Ruh' ist hin," which the whole world knows. And so, in the process of scouring the universe for experiences, Faust brings death to Gretchen; to her mother, through a sleeping potion; and to her brother, in a duel. A somewhat high price, one might think, to pay for the expansion of Faust's ego. But we may be partially consoled: for this time celestial voices from Above reply to Mephistopheles' words about Gretchen's ultimate fate, "She is judged!" with "She is saved!" The last words we hear are Gretchen's cry of "Heinrich! Heinrich!" Such is the tragic ending of *Faust I*. Now, we ask (as did the rest of the world), how will Faust himself end?

11.

"Den lieb ich, der Unmöglichkeit begehrt," — "Him I love who craves impossibility." Thus one of the characters speaks in the second part of *Faust*. So, undoubtedly, Goethe himself reflected, as he set about completing his Faust tragedy. After all, he had been pursuing impossibilities all his life long.

"In this tragedy," Goethe is speaking to the historian Heinrich Luden, "when it is finally completed, I hope to represent the spirit of world-history. I hope to offer a true picture of the life of humanity, embracing Past, Present, and Future. In the person of Faust, Humanity will be idealized. He will be depicted as the representative of Humanity."[62]

Let us now imagine we are looking at Goethe, the supreme alchemist, like some modern Paracelsus, standing before an enormous alembic in his laboratory, mixing various ingredients from a whole life's abundance. He is in process of distilling the elixir that is to be *Faust, Part II*. Into the vessel he pours elements that have come from his own laboratory, his personal self, his poetry, philosophy, science, history. He is intent on producing a work that will challenge and perhaps match the great epics of Europe, Homer's, Lucretius's, Dante's and Milton's. He is almost violating his own sacred edict about "Beschränkung" — "self-limitation" — that an artist must practice, for he pours into the retort all the various forms of the arts he has mastered: the epic, dramatic, the lyric, the burlesque, the sublime, in an intoxicating variety of metrical designs. Out of his scientific trove he drops grains of geology, botany, osteology; seasoning the whole with Spinoza and other philosophers. The laboratory is filled with the fumes of creation, and the spirits evoked take on various shapes, and soon occupy all the spaces, terrifying at times, amazing, beautiful as well. It is time to send them out into life. Two of these we recognize as familiar: Faust and Mephistopheles. The others we await with impatience.

Gone is the sleepy medieval German town we have known hitherto. We are being thrust into the "larger" world, taken on a cosmic tour. Time and Space are annihilated. We move back and forth in history; we move into the very depths of the earth.

First, we must reawaken Faust from his deep sleep. Spirits hover over him, Ariel, among them, chanting.

Faust awakens to new life, reinvigorated and rededicated, now determined "ever to strive toward the highest existence." He has an arduous journey before him, as he leaves the little world of yesterday, for the macrocosm, the larger world now set before him. His "sacred discontent" — as it has been called — will now drive him into experiences he could never before have imagined.

First of all, he is thrust into past history: into the decaying Feudalism of a medieval Imperial Court. The entire country is in a process of disintegration; the treasury is on the verge of bankruptcy; the people in a state of utter disarray and distress. All is chaos. The Emperor of this Holy Roman Empire is incompetent, a spendthrift, and at a total loss. Fortunately two strangers appear who are possessed of what seem to be miraculous powers. They rescue the country from financial disaster: they discover for the Emperor hidden stores of wealth in the ground; they teach him modern financial speculation; the printing of paper money. The populace goes wild, craving enrichment. The Emperor is restored in his confidence, and now demands entertainment. And for such, there are no superiors to the two miracle workers. Faust becomes a *maître des plaisirs*, a master of ceremonies, and with the assistance of his companion, prepares stunning pageants, which are nothing short of marvels, as they are also puzzling. They far exceed in splendor those Goethe used to prepare for the court of Karl August.

The Emperor is insatiable, He desires nothing less than to see Paris and Helen of Sparta. One major dramatist of the Renaissance, Christopher Marlowe, had ventured to reinvoke ancient Greece in the person of Helen for his own Faustus. He has immortalized her forever in Faustus's entranced invocation:

"Was this the face that launched a thousand ships?"
— an apostrophe that required no further descriptive epithets.

Goethe's Faust, who has similar longings, undertakes this
arduous task. It will be no easy journey into the nethermost world of
the Greeks. Thither Mephistopheles dare not accompany him, for
he is a "Northern" spirit, at home only with the foul witches of the
Germans. Faust must go alone. For the first time he is appalled. To
obtain access to Helen, he must go down deep into the earth, and
encounter the primal elements of creation, the Earth Mothers, "die
Mütter." They are the "Urgestalten" — the archetypal forces of
creation; they are the Roman "Terrae Matres." Paracelsus's "Matrix
Rerum" — the roots and sources and ultimate mysteries of all
creation. Whither the way? Faust inquires of Mephistopheles. And
the latter:

> The way? No way.
> Into the Untrodden, not to be trodden,
> To the Unbeseechable, not to be beseeched,
> Driven about by endless solitudes.
> Dost know the meaning of Solitude and Wastes?

But Faust is not to be dissuaded:

> Let us go!
> We'll plumb the deepest depths.
> Whatever befall,
> In your Naught I hope to find the All.

In the realm of the Mothers he will find the sacred and miraculous
tripod which will enable him to call up immortal Helen, along with
Paris. So now, it is Faust who is the great magician, entertaining the
Emperor and his court, and lo! here they are. The masque of Paris
and Helen amazes all. And as Paris, according to history, makes a
move to carry off Helen, Faust breaks out of his role as theatrical
manager, and intervenes. Immediately there is an explosion,
everything disappears, and Faust is left unconscious. Once having
seen Helen, he will never recover...

Thereafter, there is no end to the wonders that will befall Faust. Now he is back in his old study, more moth-eaten than ever. He is lying, still unconscious, as Mephistopheles presides in Faust's shabby fur cloak, the academe, once more beset by an eager and arrogant scholar. Nearby is a laboratory, where Wagner, Faust's old disciple, is at his retorts. He is about to complete a rare experiment, which is coming to fruition. He is making a "homunculus" — an artificial human being! Still not fully born, but fully intelligent, he moves about in his glass container, in full possession of a mind! All he needs is to be reborn as a human being. He floats in the air, and it is he who will show Faust and Mephistopheles the way to ancient Hellas. Homunculus gives the sleeping Faust a preview-dream of Hellenic beauty. He shows him Leda being courted by the swan, Zeus. Asleep, Faust is air-borne on the long journey to Greece. First they must attend a classical Witches' Sabbath — the Classical Walpurgisnacht. No reader not armed with a nether-world Baedeker — a guide to Greek mythological spirits — dare enter here, for he will meet with such a repletion of the supernatural as to make him giddy. Even Mephistopheles almost goes out of his mind as he meets griffins, lamiae, giant ants, sphinxes, sirens, wraiths, vampyres and no end! There are also two philosophers of Greece, violently debating, à la Goethe, the question of the origin of the earth: Anaxagoras being Vulcanist, and Thales Neptunist. Here Goethe's imagination runs riot, and were it not for the presence of Mephistopheles and his inimitable humor, the reader's patience would be sadly taxed. Poor Mephisto! He is baffled, perplexed, provoked, badgered by these foreign denizens of Hades...

It is a relief to find Faust again, still hungering for Helen. "Without her," he wails, "I cannot live." When we see him, he is a medieval grand baron, lord of a castle-fortress, with a mighty retinue. At this moment, he is in Sparta, and his quarters adjoin those of the palace of Menelaus, the husband of Helen. Helen has returned from Troy not long before, accompanied by Trojan slave-girls. In lofty hexameters she recounts her history, as she awaits her husband who has just brought her back, and, as we learn, destines her for the block. Fortunately, there is rescue at the gate. Faust is there. And Helen advances into the castle-courtyard to await the grace of the Germanic war-lord. Medieval Germany joins hands and hearts with Hellenic beauty, and both are now enthroned in a Grecian Arcadia. Splendors of wealth are laid at her feet, no doubt the deserved spoils of medieval marauding. The Arcadian union soon produces an offspring, the glorious, lovely Euphorion, a wonderful creature, who inherits Helen's beauty and Faust's restlessness. Euphorion, who is the representative of modern genius, must be forever skipping, and flying almost as if he had wings. Euphorion, we are told, is Lord Byron, the Romantic, the rebel, the aristocrat, the poet after Goethe's heart, the battler for Greek liberation, and its martyr. But Byron died at Missolonghi, before he could even enter battle. In Goethe's drama he is wingless and yet attempts to fly, he falls to earth and is killed. He leaves behind his cloak and his lyre and Helen disappears along with him, leaving behind her veil. A chorus intones a moving threnody to Byron. But he is gone. And Helen too is gone forever.

And now what? asks Mephistopheles. You've hovered close to the moon with your dream. Is it *that* you are aiming for?

Faust has grown older, and perhaps wiser. No! he replies,

> No! this earthly sphere
> Allows room enough for earthly deeds;
> Astounding works we will achieve;
> I feel new strength for boldest daring . . .
> Power, domains I'll win . . .
> The Doing is all, and Glory naught.

He has mighty plans. He will henceforth work within this world. A vast project challenges him now. He has watched the ocean eroding the shore. What if he, Faust, would pit his strength against the

waters, against the "aimless power of the intractable elements"? He
will shut the ocean from the land. But where to get the power and
the land? Mephistopheles has the answer. There is a war going on.
The Holy Roman Emperor is in trouble. Incompetent as he is,
ineffectual and wasteful, he has brought the Empire to the brink of
collapse, and now is threatened by a rival, who is gathering strength
because of the discontent of the subjects. Help the Emperor,
Mephistopheles advises, and he will give you all you desire, land and
power. As a result of their aid, the Emperor is saved, his enemies
defeated. And Faust is a mighty potentate, and begins to assert his
power. He has a vast domain on the ocean front, far as the eye can
see. But the inebriation of power has taken possession of him; the
need to acquire more. He commands vessels that sweep the oceans
and bring back rich booty. He has added piracy to his achievements.
His evil demon assures him, Might has become Right. If you have
Power, Right is on your side. People ask *what* is being done, not
how! And he adds the very modern maxim:

> War, Trade, and Piracy are one,
> A solid Trinity, hard to tear apart.

Faust is on the verge of being an empire-builder . . . Whatever stands
in his way must be swept aside. The marvelous view he has over his
terrain is obstructed by a modest cottage and a mean chapel. The
cottage is occupied by an old couple, Philemon and Baucis. The
clanging of the chapel bell is disturbing to his ears. He can hear it in
his palace. It will be necessary to move the cottage and the old couple
elsewhere. Mephistopheles harkens to his master's voice, and his
violent minions do their work, but unfortunately in the process of
removal, a fire breaks out and cottage, chapel, and the two old
people and their guest perish. Faust is momentarily made sad . . .

Is Mephistopheles responsible, or is he indeed Faust's imperial
and imperious unconscious? Was he in fact working out unspoken
intentions?

As, from his balcony, Faust contemplates the fires burning, shadows begin to gather around him. Four hags approach him: Want, Necessity, Guilt, and Care. The first three cannot enter the rich man's castle. Care finds her way through the keyhole. And there beyond is another figure, skulking — Death. Faust senses the presence of Care, and gives way to fresh reflections, looking anew for the key to his existence. He has begun to realize that the Freedom he believed he posessed was an illusion. He has been chained to Magic and Mephistopheles. Care asks, "Have you never known Care?" No, Faust replies. He has roamed throughout the world, indulging every desire, yet he was never truly satisfied. Now he is wiser; his range is more circumscribed. The beyond is illusion; here, here on earth there is room for achievement. If he could only free himself, he says,

> Could I but unlearn those magic spells,
> Could I but face thee Nature as Man alone,
> It were well worth to be Human again . . .

He realizes at last that enslaved to Mephistopheles he has surrendered the essential quality of being human and being a part of humanity — the freedom to be a human being, "ein Mensch."

Though endowed with physical sight, he has, like all other human beings — so Care affirms — been blind. She breathes upon him, and he is truly blinded. At the same time he regains his sight — he gains *insight*. Within him, he now knows, all is light. He will assert his true humanity — set to work on his mighty enterprise.

> For this is Wisdom's final word:
> Only he deserves his Freedom and his Life
> Who daily conquers them afresh.

His sightless imagination now foresees the future: There, where the swamplands are, there where the seas have eaten away the shores, he will create a fertile land.

> Such a throng would I gladly see,
> Standing on a free soil with people free,
> Then might I justly to the Moment say:
> Remain awhile, you are so fair!
> Then traces of my earthly days
> In aeons cannot perish!
> In such fore-feeling of Fortune's lofty gift,
> I now enjoy the highest moment's bliss.

He had wagered with Mephistopheles that the instant he would wish a Moment to stand still, he would forfeit his soul. Though that moment is now as of the future, his anticipation of it is there. The effort, the will, and the striving are there. Faust will not be doomed, nor can his soul be forfeit. Faust dies.

But Mephistopheles, not knowing the decisions of Higher Powers (how could he?), stands watch, as Faust's grave is being dug by minions of the nether world. He will catch Faust's soul as it leaves the body. He has the certificate of possession in his hand. But Highest Wisdom has sent angels to distract the enemy, and Faust's soul is carried aloft. Poor Mephistopheles!

Faust is transfigured. Choirs of holy anchorites, Fathers of the Church, angels and other celestial beings, as well as penitent sinners now deceased, hymn their prayers, while Faust ascends. There are petitions to the Virgin Mary. Among the petitioner-penitents is Gretchen, now become the most forceful of Faust's intercessors:

> Encircled by seraphic spirit-choirs,
> The new-born scarcely is aware,
> Scarcely sensing the new fresh life,
> As like the heavenly hosts he grows.
> See how the earth-bound tie is loosening,
> He now casts off the earthly husk.
> With primal force of youthful beauty,
> He strides in bright ethereal garb,
> Dazzled by the new day's effulgence,
> Grant me, Virgin, the boon of guiding him.

And the Mater gloriosa:

> Come rise up to ever higher spheres,
> Once made aware of thee, he'll follow...

The mystic choir concludes:

> Alles vergängliche
> Ist nur ein Gleichnis...

> All that is transient
> Is but a symbol,
> Earth's unfulfilled
> Here finds completion;
> The indescribable
> Here it is done;
> Eternal Womanhood
> Draws us upward and on.

Faust is saved.

> For he who ever onward strives
> Is worthy of salvation.

"Man errs as long as he strives," the Lord had told Mephistopheles in the Prologue in Heaven. And for Goethe the principle of activity, of doing had always been his vital concern. Supineness, inaction, passiveness had been repugnant to him. We shall recall how in the first part of *Faust*, the hero translated the Gospel words, "In the Beginning was the Word," into "In the Beginning was the Deed," and set out to act upon this affirmation. In *Wilhelm Meister* Action is again set forth as an important element in a character's education. "To be active is a human being's first principle."

Later, another very significant element was added. Action became conjoined with "innocence." Thus in the *West-Eastern Divan* we read that the "true life lies in the innocence of action," that Action is "conscienceless" — for conscience belongs not to the actor but to the observer. Activity is eternally innocent, guiltless, and amoral.

It is this, too, that becomes one of the guiding principles of Faust's actions and behavior, and a clue to his psychology. His actions are absolute in the treatment of Philemon and Baucis, even if he himself is not the direct agent. When he further aggrandizes his domains through his unlimited power, he is "acting," but acting as some grand potentate. His final philanthropic project for the benefit of mankind is not marked by a special interest for human improvement as such, but rather seems the benevolent act of an enlightened despot, who is for doing *for* people, but not doing *with* them.

It is, however, a grand achievement of Faust's to come to the conclusion that the greater part of his life has not had the qualities of absolute individuality, or freedom, always bound, as he was, to Mephistopheles, or his own "lower" being, utterly dominated by his higher principle of "selfness." His long journey has taken him toward "Menschheit" and "Menschlichkeit," though when he envisions a "free people" on a "free soil" we have the impression that a Monarch is about to grant Freedom as a gift to his underlings or subjects. And when Faust toward the end is giving orders to his workers, he appears to be ordering "vassals" — "Knechte" — happy at the crowd "that is drudging and moiling for me."

This is to say, that Goethe's *Faust* is a perplexing work. One wonders at Faust's apotheosis with its quasi-Christian, almost Catholic conclusion. Has the "pagan" Goethe turned Christian mystic? Is he saying now, Action is not enough to justify salvation; salvation requires Divine Grace for its fulfilment? Are we then on the verge of a conclusion that parallels Dante's vision in the *Paradiso*? And is Gretchen the analogue of Dante's Beatrice? What, indeed, is the "eternal feminine" that leads us all aloft, where there is Perfection, where the imperfect of the earth achieves an almost Platonic wholeness, completion? Is it Dante's Divine Love, "L'amor, che move il sole e l'altre stelle" — "the Love that moves the sun and the other stars"?

We may assume that "das ewig Weibliche" is in Goethe's mind the coalescence of many qualities, many of them earthly, many of them more abstract. Of course, it is the idealization and the ideal that Goethe always sought in woman and woman's love: Helen of Sparta, Gretchen the German; Frau von Stein the aristocrat; and those other innumerable lovely women who kept on enchanting him and were enchanted by him, and kept on forgiving him and from whom he was escaping. But, we believe, it is also an "Urgestalt," that vital, final principle he sought in Nature: the all-enclosing Harmony of Nature, and its motive power. "Das Weibliche," then, may be thought of as the eternally forgiving and understanding Mother, that takes the errant son to her bosom. Finally, may it not stand for the principle of Love itself? The Love that transcends understanding, but which is solely the possession of woman?

Enigma or no, *Faust* in both parts is a work of sufficient grandeur and substance to feed the imagination and intellect of a whole world. If the first portion has more to offer to the emotions and empathies of its readers and spectators, the second offers innumerable stimuli to the intellect, and much too, for the emotions. We are thinking in particular of the last scene of *Faust II*, which may be called the journey toward Faust's "humanization."

If Goethe's *Faust* was, as one of his distinguished editors claims, "a testament to the German people," it was to prove an ambiguous one; fertile, for posterity, of varied contradictory interpretations and practical uses. Was Faust to be identified with Germany, as many others were to claim, being the very image of "heilige Unzufriedenheit" — "sacred discontent" — and all his unscrupulousness and near-criminal actions "only a veil for his noblest strivings, which Mephistopheles cannot understand"?[63]

Or is Faust, as the philosopher George Santayana believed, guided in his philanthropic interests solely by "arbitrary passion," by a "selfish illusion," "passionate wilfulness," and "aggressive and criminal" in his statesmanship and public spirit.[64]

Later German ideologists, and nationalists, preferred to see in Faust another Siegfried, the embodiment of Germany as a "Machtstaat," — "a Power-State," and the political expresion of "Might is Right."[65] For, in fact, Faust does reveal before his death the attributes of a "Machtmensch," the "heroism of Power," close enough to the image of a benevolent monarch that Goethe himself cherished in the person of Karl August.

And might others be blamed if they saw in the conclusion of the drama and the transfiguration a veiled pessimism on the part of Goethe himself, and a picture of a world in decay, sliding toward chaos and dissolution, but waiting for another Napoleon to appear and restore Order?

Thus the "myth" of Faust took many forms. In music, Hector Berlioz consigned Faust to punishment in Hell in his symphonic poem, *The Damnation of Faust*. Others, like Arrigo Boito, made Mephistopheles the central character, in *Mefistofele*. Franz Liszt remained faithful to the original, and voted for salvation in his *Faust Symphony*.

In literature, the progeny of Faust and the Faustian "myth" is practically countless. It stretches from Goethe's immediate successors, like the Austrian poet Nikolaus Lenau, through the nineteenth and into the twentieth century, in hundreds of variants. We must rest content with naming only two of recent birth, and let them stand as representative: to wit, Thomas Mann's *Doctor Faustus* and Mikhail Bulgakov's *Master and Margarita*, both deeply stamped by contemporary historical events.

12.

As he looked around him in old age, Goethe found little consolation in the world as it had turned out to be. Chaos seemed to be king. He saw restlessness all around him, despite the apparent quiet and peace his much vaunted "Holy Alliance" had guaranteed. He was afraid of revolution and revolutionaries. He even deprecated a republication of his early *Prometheus* drama, because it might be misunderstood as a "gospel" by "our revolutionary youth." This was uttered in 1820. "It might," he wrote to the composer Zelter, "fall into the hands of the Berlin and Mainz Commissions, who might look upon my youthful high-jinks with wry faces."[66]

The age seemed "absurd" and barbarous. He himself and his generation, he thought, belonged to an epoch that would never return.[67]

It is scarcely surprising therefore that the July Revolution of 1830 only confirmed him in his bleak outlook. There is an incident, recited by Frédéric Soret, tutor to Weimar princes, and a frequent visitor of Goethe's, that is well known and characteristic of the later Goethe. Soret reports:

News of the July Revolution reached Weimar, and set up consternation all over. In the course of the afternoon I visited Goethe. "What do you think of the great event," Goethe called out to me. "The volcano has erupted; everything is in flames. It is no longer a matter of closed doors."

Soret admitted it was a terrible thing, and went on to deplore the conditions in France that had brought it on.

"We seem not to be speaking of the same matter," Goethe interrupted. "I'm not speaking of *that*. I'm concerned with something altogether different. I'm speaking of the terrible upheaval that has taken place in the French Academy of Sciences! The very momentous dispute between Cuvier and Geoffroy de Saint-Hilaire!"

This was a scientific controversy about the consequences to be drawn from the "organic structure of molluscs and fishes."[68]

Grand and universal as Goethe might be, he reveals his attachment to another age, as well as his own limitations, not only politically, but also aesthetically. In no other respect is this so well brought out as in his particular estimation of the person and work of Beethoven. Beethoven was after all one of the few personalities in the arts of that age worthy to stand beside Goethe as another Titan. Goethe had met Beethoven in Teplitz, a watering place, in 1812. The composer had sent him the incidental music to *Egmont*, which Goethe admired. Beethoven had been somewhat outraged on seeing Goethe's almost servile behavior in the presence of royalty and aristocracy. Goethe, on his side, found Beethoven's personality too abrasive and unconstrained. He was repelled by Beethoven's piano performance, finding in it "the yearning and restlessness which bursts all bonds and loses itself in the infinite." Young Felix Mendelssohn had played an arrangement of the C-Minor Symphony for him, and Goethe had judged it "beautiful and mad enough to drive one crazy." Other compositions of Beethoven Goethe "admired with horror."[69] It was a strange, new world that Beethoven was disclosing...Goethe felt more at ease with his own composer, Zelter.

Indefatigable almost to the very end, putting the last touches to his *Faust*, returning to Ulrike a bundle of her letters with a short poem, handling with fondness the new edition of his works in forty volumes, and as ever fascinated by his favorite sciences; always sociable, welcoming visitors and friends to the table (alas! Christiane was no longer alive, she had died in 1816), let us see him at the end, as one of his friends, Chancellor Friedrich Müller, saw him. He is leaving the company after a short expedition near the Dornburg Castle, going down to examine minerals:

After such a conversation it is fitting for old Merlin to renew his friendship with the Ur-elements. Moved and very happy we watched for a long time as, wrapped in his light grey overcoat, he made his way solemnly down to the valley below, stopping here and there at some rock or some individual plant, and testing the former with his mineralogical hammer. The mountains were already long shadows in which gradually he disappeared from view like a ghostly apparition.[70]

He had once said that he had so many plans afoot, that Nature owed him another existence. No one could charge him with ever having wasted this one.

NOTES

Notes

Part One: Waterloo and After.

I. The Anguish of Transition and Waterloo.

1. François-René Chateaubriand, *The Memoirs of Chateaubriand* tr. Robert Baldick (N.Y., 1961), 277.

2. *Ibid.,* 232.

3. Hedva Ben-Israel, *English Historians and the French Revolution,* (Cambridge, England, 1968), 47.

4. E.J. Hobsbawm, *The Age of Revolution: Europe 1789-1848* (NY, 1969), 106.

5. J.L. Talmon, *Political Messianism: The Romantic Phase* (London, 1960), 200.

6. Hobsbawm, 1.

7. Mack Walker, *Metternich's Europe* (N.Y., 1968), 113, 116-117.

II. "The Sceptered Isle" and "The Dark Satanic Mills."

8. Asa Briggs, *The Age of Improvement* (N.Y., 1961), 12.

9. Frederick Engels, *The Condition of the Working-Class in England* (Karl Marx, *On England,* Moscow, 1953), 49.

10. J.B. Priestley, *The Prince of Pleasure and his Regency 1811-1820* (N.Y., 1969), 77.

11. Alvin Redman, *The House of Hanover* (N.Y., 1968), 152.

12. *Ibid.,* 143.

13. Robert Owen, *The Life of Robert Owen Written by Himself...* (N.Y.,1967), I, 116.

14. Robert Fulford, *George IV* (London, 1949), 97.

15. J.L. and Barbara Hammond, *The Age of the Chartists 1831-1854* (London, 1930), 18.

16. F.M.L. Thompson, *English Landed Society in the Nineteenth* Century (London, 1963), passim.

17. William Wordsworth, *The Prelude* (Version of 1805), ed. Ernest de Selincourt (Oxford, 1933), Books IX and X.

18. *Ibid.,* Bk. VII.

19. *The Poetry and Prose of William Blake,* ed. Geoffrey Keynes (London, 1948), 870-876.

20. Jacob Bronowski, *William Blake and the Age of Revolution* (New York, 1965), 52-53.

21. Blake, "Marginalia to Watson's Apology," *Poetry and Prose,* 760.

22. To Thomas Butts, Jan. 10, 1802, *ibid.,* 853.

23. Blake, "The Marriage of Heaven and Hell."

24. "Vala, or the Four Zoas, Night the Second."

25. "Songs of Experience, London."
26. Bronowski, 97.
27. *Ibid.,* 121.
28. "Vala, Night the Seventh."
29. Mark Schorer, *William Blake: The Politics of Vision* (N.Y., 1959), 341.
30. "America."
31. "Auguries of Innocence."
32. "The Everlasting Gospel."
33. Schorer, 176-177.
34. "Jerusalem."
35. "Vala, Night the Ninth."
36. "Jerusalem," ch. 1.
37. Preface to "Jerusalem."
38. "Vala, Night the Ninth."
39. Byron, "The Bride of Abydos."
40. Keats, "Sleep and Poetry."
41. Robert Gittings, *John Keats* (Boston, 1968), 85.
42. *Ibid.,* 84.
43. *The Letters of John Keats,* ed. Hyder E. Rollins (Cambridge, Mass., 1958), I, 383.
44. B.R. Haydon, *The Autobiography and Journals,* ed. Malcolm Elwin (N.Y., 1950), 75-79.
45. Keats, "On seeing the Elgin Marbles for the first time."
46. To George and Tom Keats, December 1817, *Letters* (ed. Rollins) I, 191.
47. To Tom Keats, *ibid.,* I, 320.
48. To the George Keatses, Sept. 18, 1819, *ibid.,* 193-194.
49. To George Keats, Oct. 14, 1818; *ibid.,* I, 394.
50. To J.H. Reynolds, April 18, 1817; *ibid.,* I, 133.
51. "Epistle to John Hamilton Reynolds."
52. Gittings, 216, 233.
53. To J.A. Hessey, Oct. 8, 1818; *The Letters of John Keats,* ed. Maurice Buxton Forman (Oxford, 1952), 221.
54. *Ibid.,* May 11, 1817; *ibid.,* 30.
55. To Benjamin Bailey, July 18, 1818; *ibid.,* 191-192.
56. To George Keats, Oct. 24, 1818; *ibid.,* 239-240.
57. Gittings, 143.
58. To Woodhouse, Oct. 27, 1818; *Letters* (ed. Forman), 227.
59. To Fanny Brawne, July 25, 1819; *Letters* (ed. Rollins), II, 133.
60. B.R. Haydon, *Autobiography,* 317.
61. "Lamia."
62. "Ode to a Nightingale."
63. To George and Tom Keats, Dec. 1817; *Letters* (ed. Forman), 71.
64. To the George Keatses, Sept. 24, 1819; *ibid.,* 425.
65. To Benjamin Bailey, Nov. 22, 1817; *Letters* (ed. Rollins), I, 184-185.
66. To George Keats, April 21, 1819; *Letters* (ed. Forman), 335-336.

67. May 3, 1818; *Letters* (ed. Rollins), 282.

68. To Woodhouse, Oct. 21, 1818; *ibid.,* I, 380.

69. Gittings, 380.

70. February 1820; *Letters* (ed. Forman), 468.

71. Théophile Gautier, "L'Art."

72. Kenneth Neill Cameron, *The Young Shelley: Genesis of a Radical* (N.Y., 1962), 288.

73. Shelley, Preface to "The Revolt of Islam."

III. France: The Furnace of World History.

1. Victor Hugo, *Les Misérables,* II, 94.

2. Friedrich Sieburg, *Chateaubriand,* tr. Violet M. Macdonald (N.Y., 1961), 186.

3. See, in particular, George Rudé, *The Crowd in the French Revolution,* passim.

4. Hobsbawm, 68n.

5. Frederick B. Artz, "The Electoral System in France during the Bourbon Restoration," in James Frigugletti and Emmet Kennedy, *The Shaping of Modern France* (N.Y., 1969), 205.

6. Artz, 21n.

7. Edgar Quinet, *Histoire de mes idées,* in Bernard Guyon, *La Pensée politique...de Balzac* (Paris, 1967), 51.

8. Chateaubriand, *Le Génie du Christianisme, Oeuvres complètes* (Paris, 1849-1860), II, 100.

9. George Brandes, *Main Currents of Nineteenth Century Literature: III. The Reaction in France* (N.Y., 1923), 85.

10. *Memoirs,* 20.

11. Joseph de Maistre, *Principe génerateur...,* A. and F. Bayet, *Les Écrivains politiques du XIXe siècle* (Paris, 1935), 119, 121.

12. "Considerations on Political Institutions," *Works,* tr. Jack Lively (N.Y., 1965), 77.

13. Bayet, 124.

14. *Works,* 89.

15. "A Study of Sovereignty," *Works,* 108, 113, 103.

16. "Considerations...," *Works,* 59.

17. *Ibid.,* 191-192.

18. "Reflexions sur le Protestantisme," de Maistre, *Du Pape, les Soirées de Saint-Petersbourg* (Paris, 1957), 119.

19. "Du Pape," 166, 172-174.

20. *Oeuvres de Saint-Simon...,* (Paris, 1865-1878) XV, 247-248.

21. Frederick Engels, *Socialism; Utopian and Scientific,* in Karl Marx, *Selected Works* (Moscow, 1935) I, 148-149.

22. *Lettres d'un Habitant de Genève,* Frank E. Manuel, *The New World of Henri Saint-Simon* (Cambridge, Mass., 1956), 133.

23. *Ibid.*, 223.

24. *L'Industrie, Oeuvres de...Saint Simon* (Paris, Editions Anthropos, 1966), II, 21.

25. Mathurin Dondo, *The French Faust: Henri Saint-Simon* (New York, 1955), 146.

26. Manuel, 192.

27. *L'Organisateur, Oeuvres* XX, 17-26.

28. J.L. Talmon, *Political Messianism*, 64.

29. *Le Nouveau Christianisme*, Albert Fried and Ronald Sanders, *Socialist Thought: A Documentary History* (Edinburgh, 1964), 78; 102.

30. From the Memoirs of Hippolyte Auger, Manuel, 191.

31. *Oeuvres* (Paris, 1966), I, 121.

32. Pierre Jean de Béranger, "Les Fous," (1833).

33. Charles Gide, Introduction to *Selections from the Works of Fourier* (London, 1901), 12-13.

34. *Ibid.*, 15.

35. Engels, 150.

36. *Théorie de l'Unité Universelle*, Gide, 86-87.

37. *Ibid.*, 88-89.

38. *Théorie de Quatre Mouvements, ibid.*, 100.

39. Engels, 150.

40. *Quatre Mouvements...*, Gide, 55.

41. *Unité Universelle, ibid.*, 139; 142.

42. Talmon, 154-155.

43. Gide, 200.

44. *Ibid.*, 77.

45. *Ibid.*, 78-80.

46. Talmon, 143.

47. Théophile Gautier, *Souvenirs Romantiques,* "Victor Hugo" (Paris, 1920), 17; A.F. Davidson, *Victor Hugo: His Life and Character* (London, 1912), 75.

48. André Maurois, *Olympio, ou la Vie de Victor Hugo* (Paris, 1954), 94.

49. As recollected by his future father-in-law, Pierre Foucher, cited in Raymond Escholier, *Victor Hugo raconté par ceux qui l'on vu* (Paris, 1931), 99.

50. Gautier, 23.

51. *Cromwell,* Act III, sc. 4.

52. François Pierre Guillaume Guizot, *Vie de Shakespeare* in *Oeuvres complètes de Shakespeare* (Paris, 1872), Vol. I.

53. Alexandre Dumas, *The Road to Monte Cristo,* ed. Jules Eckert Goodman (N.Y., 1956), 109-110.

54. Jacques Barzun, *Berlioz and the Romantic Century* (Boston, 1950), I, 86.

55. Victor Pavie, in a letter to his father, February 26, 1830 in Victor Hugo, *Oeuvres Complètes* (Paris, 1957-1969), III, 1276.

56. *Hernani,* Act V, sc. 2.
57. *Ibid.,* Act V, sc. 2.
58. *Les Orientales,* IV: "Enthousiasme."

IV. Germany — The Dissevered Self.

1. Ludwig Börne, *Sämtliche Schriften* (Düsseldorf, 1964-1968), I, 165.
2. Johann Gottlieb Fichte, *Erste Einleitung in die Wissenschaftslehre, Deutsche Literatur: Reihe Romantik,* (Weimar etc., 1925 ff.), II, 87; 96.
3. Brandes, *Main Currents,* II, 189.
4. Novalis, *Schriften,* ed. Paul Kluckhohn (Leipzig, 1929), II, 382, 384, 350.
5. "Hymnen an die Nacht."
6. *"Blütenstaub," ibid.,* II, 17; Brandes, 189.
7. Walter Silz, *Early German Romanticism,* (Cambridge, Mass., 1929), 161.
8. Novalis, *Heinrich von Ofterdingen,* Part I, ch. 5.
9. *Die Christenheit oder Europa,* Schriften II, 83.
10. *Ibid.,* 77, 67.
11. "Blütenstaub," *ibid.,* II, 17.
12. *Deutsche Literatur: Reihe Romantik,* I, 83.
13. *Ibid.,* 61.
14. Brandes, 69.
15. *Lucinde, Deutsche Literatur: Reihe Romantik,* IV. "Lebenskunst," 208-209; 215.
16. Friedrich Schlegel, "Fragmente über Liebe and Ehe," *ibid.,* 153.
17. Raymond Immerwahr, in S.S. Prawer, *The Romantic Period in Germany* (London, 1970), 53-54.
18. Ludwig Tieck, *Franz Sternbald,* cited in Hans Kals, *Die soziale Frage in der Romantik* (Köln, 1974), 97.
19. *Ibid.,* 98.
20. Fichte to his wife, September 1799, *Deutsche Literatur: Reihe Romantik,* I, 102.
21. Eudo C. Mason, *Deutsche und Englische Romantik* (Göttingen, 1966), 46.
22. Kleist to Christian Ernst Martini, Potsdam, July 18, 19, 1799: *Werke,* ed. Erich Schmidt (Leipzig, n.d.), V, 31.
23. November 25, 1800, *ibid.,* 168.
23a. March 22, 1801, *ibid.,* 104-105.
24. July 21, 1801, *ibid.,* 242.
25. May 1, 1802, to Ulrike von Kleist, *ibid.,* 287.
26. Helmut Sembdner (ed.), *Heinrich von Kleists Lebensspuren* (Frankfurt, 1977), 59.
27. *Ibid.,* 79.
28. *Ibid.,* 302-304.
29. *Werke* V, 249.
30. *Der Prinz von Homburg,* Act I, sc. 1.

31. *Ibid.*, Act III, sc. 5.

32. Heinrich Heine, *Buch Le Grand*, ch. 3; *Sämtliche Werke*, ed. Walzel (Leipzig, 1912), IV, 144.

33. *Briefe, Werke* V, 359.

34. *Penthesilea*, sc. 22.

35. *Käthchen von Heilbronn*, Act IV, sc. 2.

36. *Lebensspuren*, 376-377.

37. See below, "The First Revolution and Alexander Pushkin," pp. 355-414.

38. Hegel, *Aesthetik* I, 150-152, cited in Fredric James, *Marxism and Form* (Princeton, 1971), 352-353.

39. Heinrich Heine, *Die romantische Schule, Werke* VII, 106.

40. *Ibid.*, 105.

41. Hoffmann, *Antonie; Dichtungen und Schriften*, ed. Walter Harich (Weimar, 1924), I, 247.

42. *Kater Murr, ibid.*, V, 79-80.

43. On Hoffmann and France, see below section on "Berlioz," 146 f.

44. *Kater Murr*, ch. 3.

45. *Berganza.*

46. Heine, *Die romantische Schule*, Bk. II, *Werke* VII, 106-107.

47. Ulrich Haussermann, *Friedrich Hölderlin* (Reinbeck bei Hamburg, 1961), 70.

48. "Die Völker schwiegen und schlummerten," *Sämtliche Werke* (Stuttgart, 1946-1977, I, 138.

49. "Hymne an die Freiheit," *Sämtliche Werke*, ed. N.V. Heilingrath (Berlin, 1922), I, 143-147.

50. "Hymne an die Menschheit," *ibid.*, I, 134-137.

51. "Hymne an die Freiheit," *ibid.*, I, 143-147.

52. *Ibid.*, I, 191-193.

53. To Neuffer, June 1796, *ibid.*, II, 372-374.

54. *Ibid.*, II, 376.

55. *Ibid.*, III, 490.

56. *Hyperion, ibid.*, II, 282-287.

57. *Ibid.*, II, 183-187.

58. *Ibid.*, II, 122-123.

59. To Johann Gottfried Ebel, Frankfurt, Jan. 10, 1797, *ibid.*, VI, 146-148.

60. "Skizze zur Fortsetzung," *ibid.*, III, 227.

61. *Der Tod des Empedokles, ibid.*, III, 83.

62. *Empedokles*, "Zweite Fassung," ("Second Version"), *ibid.*, III, 873.

63. "Erste Fassung," (First Version"), *ibid.*, III, 143-147.

64. Pierre Bertaux, "Hölderlin und die französische Revolution," *Hölderlin Jahrbuch* XV, (1967-1968), 15.

65. *Empedokles auf dem Aetna, Werke*, ed. Heilingrath II, 222-223.

66. "Der Archipelagus," *ibid.*, IV, 99.

67. "Gesang der Deutschen," *ibid.*, IV, 129-131.

68. "Der Rhein," *ibid.*, IV, 39-40.

69. "Brot und Wein, *ibid.*, IV, 124-125.

70. *Ibid.*, 125.

71. "Dichtermut," *ibid.*, IV, 39-40.

72. "Ganymed," *ibid.*, IV, 69.

73. E.T.A. Hoffman, *Dichtungen und Schriften* (ed. Walther Harich, Weimar, 1924), XII, 14; 19.

74. Silz, 16.

75. George Simmel, *Schopenhauer und Nietzsche* (München, 1920), 148-149.

76. Maynard Solomon, *Beethoven* (N.Y., 1977), 133.

77. *Ibid.*, 325.

78. Ernst Ludwig Schellenberg, *Das Buch der deutschen Romantik* (Berlin, 1924), 83.

79. Eichendorff, "Mondnacht," "Klage," "An die Dichter, "Der Wegelagerer"; and Brandes, 223.

79a. Eichendorff, *Neue Gesamtausgabe der Werke* (Cotta, 1957), II, 1043.

80. Wilhelm Heinrich Wackenroder and Ludwig Tieck, *Herzensergiessungen* ... (Leipzig, 1921), 51, 127-128; 131-132; 143.

81. Schellenberg, 230; 244; 259.

82. *Ibid.*, 230.

83. Camillo von Klenze, *From Goethe to Hauptmann* (N.Y., 1926), 98.

84. Josef Görres, *Die teutschen Volksbucher,* in *Deutsche Literatur, Reihe Romantik,* X, 133-134; 148; 151.

85. Karl Ludwig Haller, *Restauration der Staatswissenschaften,* cited in Jacques Droz, *Le Romantisme politique en Allemagne* (Paris, 1963), 191.

86. Goetz A. Briefs, "The Economic Philosophy of Romanticism," *Journal of the History of Ideas,* II (1941), 283.

87. Adam Müller, *Elemente der Staatskunst, Romantik X, Deutsche Vergangenheit und deutscher Staat,* 229.

88. Adam Müller, in the *Deutsche Staatsanzeigen,* cited in Droz, *Le Romantisme politique,* 154-155.

89. Adam Müller, in Droz, 164.

90. Briefs, 287.

91. "Bonaventura," *Nachtwachen,* "Ninth Night," *Deutsche Literatur: Reihe Romantik,* XVI, 69-70.

92. *Ibid.*, "Sixth Night," 46.

93. *Ibid.*, "Sixteenth Night," 114-115. (Latest research assigns the *Nachtwachen* to a certain Friedrich G. Wetzel, a prolific writer, who is remembered today solely by this work. See also Jeffrey L. Sammons, *Die Nachtwachen von Bonaventure* (The Hague, 1965).

94. Grillparzer and Lenau will be considered in a succeeding volume of *Heroic Imagination.*

95. Ferdinand Raimund, *Das Mädchen aus der Feenwelt, Gesammelte Werke* (Gütersloh, 1962), Act II; Act III.

96. *Der Alpenkönig, oder der Menschenfeind,* Act II.

V. "Skeleton of a Titanic Form": The Italy of Giacomo Leopardi and Alessandro Manzoni.

1. Giacomo Leopardi, *Opere*, ed. S. and G. Solmi (Milano, 1966), II, 957, n. 3; I. Origo and Heath-Stubbs, Leopardi, *Selected Poetry and Prose* (N.Y., 1967), 72.
2. J.H. Whitfield, *Giacomo Leopardi* (Oxford, 1954), 190.
3. *Ibid.*, 31-32.
4. *Ibid.*, 26.
5. Origo, 24, n. 1.
6. Leopardi, "Le Ricordanze" ("Memories"), *Poesie e Prose* (Firenze, n.d.), 175-176.
7. Origo, 19.
8. "Il Pensiero Dominante."
9. Whitfield, 160-161; Origo, 59.
10. Byron, *Manfred*, Act II, sc. IV.
11. Origo, 91.
12. Whitfield 173-174.
13. *Ibid.*, 107.
14. Leopardi, "A Se Stesso" ("To Himself").
15. John Ruskin, *Praeterita* (London, 1949), II, ch. 3.
16. Luigi Settembrini, *Lezioni di letteratura italiana* III, 354, cited in Origo, 73.
17. Manzoni, *I Promessi Sposi* (Milano, 1877), ch. 8.
18. *Ibid.*, chs., 24; 8.
19. *Ibid.*, chs., 7; 11; 18.
20. *Ibid.*, ch. 14.
21. Archibald Colquhoun, *Manzoni and His Times* (London, 1954), 184.
22. *Ibid.*, 183.
23. George Martin, *Verdi* (N.Y., 1953), 431.
24. *Ibid.*, 437.
25. Silvio Pellico, *Le mie Prigioni* (Paris, 1837), ch. 92.
26. *Ibid.*, ch. 99.

VI. The Agony of Spain.

1. Hermann Baumgarten, *Geschichte Spaniens* (Leipzig, 1969), II, 584.
2. *Ibid.*, 585.
3. Antonia Vallentin, *This I Saw: The Life and Times of Goya* (N.Y., 1949), 330.
4. See, in particular, the articles by Edith F. Helman, "The Elder Moratín and Goya," and "The Younger Moratín and Goya," in the *Hispanic Review*, XXIII (1955), 218-230, and XXVII (1959), 103-122.
5. Enrico Crispaldi, article "Goya," in *Enc. of World Art*, VI, 653.
6. Vallentin, 160-161.
7. Crispaldi, 659.
8. Edith Helman, *Transmundo de Goya* (Madrid, 1963), 52.
9. Vallentin, 273.

VII. Russia — The First Revolution and Alexander Pushkin.

1. Anatole G. Mazour, *The First Russian Revolution* (Stanford, 1969), 55.
2. James H. Billington, *The Icon and the Axe* (N.Y., 1966), 293.
3. *Ibid.*, 167, 169.
4. Mazour, 105.
5. *Ibid.*, 115.
6. *Ibid.*, 154; 164.
7. *Ibid.*, 207.
8. Michel-R. Hofman, *Les Grands romanciers russes* (Paris, 1967), 58.
9. Pushkin, "Besy," ("The Demons").
10. David Magarshack, *Pushkin* (N.Y., 1967), 44-45.
11. *Ibid.*, 50.
12. Henri Troyat, *Pushkin* (N.Y., 1970), 124.
13. Franklin A. Walker, "K.F. Ryleev: A Self-Sacrifice for Revolution," *Slavonic and East European Review*, XLVII (1969), 436-446.
14. *Letters of Alexander Pushkin*, tr. J. Thomas Shaw (Madison, 1967), 79; 81. (Rough draft to unknown correspondent, March, 1821).
15. Ernest J. Simmons, *Pushkin* (Cambridge, Mass., 1937), 100-101.
16. *Pushkin on Literature*, ed. Tatiana Wolff (London, 1971), 44; 47. The names of the revolutionaries were abbreviated for security reasons, and their identity is conjectural.
17. Magarshack, 129.
18. Simmons, 179.
19. *Ibid.*, 185-186.
20. Troyat, 230-231.
21. *Ibid.*, 251.
22. Troyat, 295-296.
23. *Eugene Onegin*, ch. VII, 36.
24. "Prorok," ("The Prophet").
25. Simmons, 320-321.
26. Troyat, 280.
27. V. Nabokov, *Eugene Onegin*, (N.Y., 1964), III, 312.
28. A.S. Pushkin, *Eezbranniye Socheeneneeya (Selected Works)*, (Moscow, 1979), II, 165; and Nabokov, V, 212.
29. Vissarion Belinsky, *Selected Philosophical Works* (Moscow, 1948), 274.
30. *Pushkin on Literature*, 221-222.
31. *Ibid.*, "Notes on Popular Drama," (1830), 263-264.
32. *Ibid.*, 263-264.
33. John Bayley, *Pushkin*, 152.
34. Simmons, 290.
35. Mikhail Lermontov, "Smert Poeta," ("Death of a Poet").
36. Pushkin "Osen," ("Autumn").

Part Two: The Rising Tide: 1830-1848.
I-II. Barricades. 1830 and the Artist.

1. Vincent W. Beach, "Charles X and the Application of Article X of the Charter," in Friguglietti, *The Shaping of Modern France,* 213.
2. Jean Louis de Courson, *1830: La Revolution Tricolore* (Paris, 1965), 23.
3. David H. Pinkney, "A New Look at the French Revolution of 1830," in Friguglietti, 217-222.
4. T.E.B. Howarth, *Citizen King: The Life of Louis Philippe* (London, 1961), 113; 117.
5. Courson, 11-12.
6. *Ibid.,* 146.
7. Alexandre Dumas, *The Road to Monte Cristo: A Condensation from the Memoirs of Alexandre Dumas,* ed. John Eckert Goodman (N.Y., 1956), 151.
8. Courson, 234.
9. *Ibid.,* 250.
10. *Ibid.,* 260.
11. *Ibid.,* 339.
12. Jacques Barzun, *Berlioz and the Romantic Century,* I, 135.
13. Alfred Chabaud, *Jules Michelet* (Paris, 1929), 17-18.
14. *The Poetry and Prose of Heinrich Heine,* ed. Frederic Ewen (N.Y., 1948), 394-396.
15. Karl Gutzkow, cited in Jost Hermand, *Das junge Deutschland* (Stuttgart, 1966), 14-15.
16. Jacques Laffitte, *Mémoirs,* cited in Courson, 166.
17. John Stuart Mill, Letters to the *Examiner,* August 1830, cited in Iris Wessel Mueller, *John Stuart Mill and French Thought* (Urbana, Ill., 1956), 19-20.
18. Stendhal, *Correspondance,* ed. V. del Litto (Paris, 1967), II, 187 (August 15, 1830).
19. Robert M. Adams, *Stendhal: Notes on a Novelist* (N.Y., 1959), 4.
20. Fernand Rude, *Stendhal, et la pensée sociale de son temps* (Paris, 1967), 196.
21. *Correspondance* I, 998.
22. Matthew Josephson, *Stendhal* (Garden City, 1946), 319.
23. Alfred de Musset, *Confession d'un enfant du siècle, Oeuvres complètes en Prose* (Paris, 1957), 65-68.
24. Stendhal, *Le Rouge et le Noir,* Part II, ch. 1.
25. *Ibid.,* Part I, ch. 10.
26. *Ibid.,* Part II, ch. 41.
27. *Ibid.,* Part II, ch. 22.
28. *Ibid.,* Part II, ch. 44.
29. See below, pp. 550ff.
30. Hector Berlioz, *A Selection from his Letters,* tr. Humphrey Searle (N.Y., 1966), 10; *Mémoires* (Paris, 1969), I. ch. XXVI, 166.

31. *A Selection from his Letters,* 26.

32. *Fragments from the Literary Remains of a Young Physicist,* cited in Gwendolyn Bays, *The Orphic Vision* (Lincoln, Nebraska, 1964), 55.

33. *Ibid.,* 79.

34. Thomas De Quincey, *Confessions of an English Opium-Eater, Works* (Edinburgh, 1878), I, 193; 195; 212-213; 266-269.

35. *A Selection from his Letters,* 33.

36. *Ibid.,* 33.

37. Jacques Barzun, *Berlioz and His Century* (N.Y., 1956), 51-52.

38. *Mémoires* I, 177-178.

39. *A Selection from his Letters,* 42-43.

40. Barzun, 257.

41. *Ibid.,* 387.

42. *Les plus belles lettres de Eugène Delacroix,* ed. Edouard Roditi (Paris, 1963), 100-101.

43. Jean Alazard, article "Delacroix" in the *Encycl. of Word Art,* IV, 284; 252.

44. *Ibid.,* 283.

45. Jean-Louis Bory, in René Huyghe, *Delacroix* (Paris, 1963), 90.

46. Claude Roger-Marx, in Huyghe, 216.

47. Alazard, 284.

48. *Ibid.,* 284.

49. Delacroix, *Journal,* ed. André Jouhin (Paris, 1932), I, 96-97.

50. Jean Cau, in Huyghe, 20.

51. *Ibid.,* 22.

52. *Journal* I, 280-290; René Hardy in Huyghe, 145ff.

53. Hardy, 156; *Journal* I, 340 (February 14, 1850).

54. *Journal* I, 289-290.

55. Hardy, 156.

56. Charles Baudelaire, "L'oeuvre et la vie d'Eugène Delacroix," *Oeuvres complètes,* ed. Y.G. Le Dantec (Paris, 1961), 868.

57. *Ibid.,* 871.

58. *Ibid.,* 871.

III. France: 1831-1848.
I. Honoré de Balzac and the Quest of the Absolute.

1. Auguste Comte, *Cours de Philosophie Positive* (Paris, 1852), I, 16.

2. Francis Darwin, *Life and Letters of Charles Darwin* (N.Y., 1959), I, 56.

3. Thomas S. Kuhn, "Energy Conservation as an Example of Simultaneous Discovery," in *Critical Problems in the History of Science,* ed. Marshall Clagett (Madison, 1962), 321.

4. Cited in Dora B. Weiner, *Raspail, Scientist and Reformer* (N.Y., 1968), 112.

5. Balzac, *Phsiologie du mariage, L'Oeuvre de 'Balzac,* ed. Albert Béguin (Paris, 1955), XII, 912; 915; 866-867.

6. *Ibid.*, 885-886.
7. Bernard Guyon, *La Pensée politique et sociale de Balzac* (Paris, 1967), 108.
8. *Ibid.*, 8; 499-500.
9. *Ibid.*, 121; Balzac, *Correspondance* (Paris, 1960-1969), I, 142-143.
10. Balzac, *Code des gens honnêtes, Oeuvres diverses* (ed. Conard), I, 65; Guyon, 208.
11. *Correspondance* I, 266-268.
12. Guyon, 438.
13. *Ibid.*, 438.
14. Balzac, *Ferragus, L'Oeuvre de Balzac* (ed. Béguin) II.
15. Balzac, *La Peau de chagrin, L'Oeuvre* VII.
16. *Ibid.*, VII, 1227-1228.
17. *Ibid.*, 1154-1155.
18. Michel Carrouges, *L'Oeuvre* VII, 961
19. Linda Rudich, "Une Interprétation de *La Peau de chagrin, L'Année Balzacienne,* 1971, 105-133.
20. Balzac, *Louis Lambert, L'Oeuvre* I, 76.
21. *Ibid.*, 135.
22. Théophile Gautier, *Portraits Contemporains,* "Balzac" (Paris, 1874), 72.
23. Balzac, *Gambara, L'Oeuvre* VII.
24. *Correspondance,* I, 567-568.
25. *Lettres à Madame Hanska,* ed. Roger Pierrot (Paris, 1967), I, 6.
26. *Ibid.*, 14-17, November 7, 1832.
27. *Correspondance* II, 390; Paris, October 11, 1833.
28. *Ibid.*, I, 471-472.
29. *Lettres à Madame Hanska,* I, 269-270.
30. *La Peau de chagrin, L'Oeuvre* VII.
31. Balzac, "Les Artistes," cited in Pierre Barbéris, *Balzac et le mal du siècle* (Paris, 1970), II, 1174-1176.
32. Balzac, *Gobseck, L'Oeuvre* VI.
33. *Eugénie Grandet, L'Oeuvre* V.
34. *Les Paysans, L'Oeuvre* III.
35. *Le Curé de Tours, L'Oeuvre* VI.
36. *Père Goriot, L'Oeuvre* IV.
37. *Le Curé de Village, L'Oeuvre* VII.
38. *La Fille aux yeux d'or (The Girl with the Golden Eyes), L'Oeuvre,* I.
39. *Le Père Goriot, L'Oeuvre* IV.
40. *Ibid.*
41. *César Birotteau, L'Oeuvre* II.
42. *La Maison Nucingen, L'Oeuvre* VI.
43. *La Duchesse de Langeais, L'Oeuvre* VI.
44. *Les Paysans, L'Oeuvre* III.

45. *Ibid.*
46. *Le Médecin de campagne, L'Oeuvre* VI.
47. *Ibid.*
48. *Illusions perdues, L'Oeuvre* IV.
49. "Avant-Propos," *La Comédie Humaine* (ed. Pleiade, Paris, 1951), I, 7.
50. *Ibid.,* 8-9.
51. *Ibid.,* 16.
52. *Le Médecin de campagne,* ch. 1.
53. *Le Curé de village, L'Oeuvre* VII.

2. George Sand and the Quest of the Self.

1. Franco Venturi, *Roots of Revolution* (N.Y., 1964), 74.
2. Balzac, *Correspondance* I, 264.
3. The "pre-original" version of the *Physiologie du mariage,* cited by Madeleine Fargeaud, *Balzac et la Recherche de l'Absolu* (Paris, 1968), 434.
4. Balzac, *Une Fille d'Eve,* ch. 1.
5. George Sand, *Correspondance* (Paris, 1964), I, 690-691 (August 15, 1830); 705-706 (September 17, 1830).
6. *Correspondance* (1966) II, 103-105 (June 13, 1832).
7. George Sand, *Indiana,* chs. 21; 23.
8. *Correspondance* II, 741.
9. *Lélia* (edition of 1833), ch. 23.
10. *Ibid.,* Part III, ch. 1.
11. *Ibid.,* Part II, ch. 32.
12. William Makepeace Thackeray, *The Paris Sketchbook* (N.Y. and London, 1898), 191.
13. Curtis Caute, *George Sand* (Boston, 1975), 340.
13a. "De la littérature en politique et la politique en littérature," (February 1, 1831), *Oeuvres complètes* (Paris, 1957), 777.
14. "Dédicace" of *La Coupe et les lèvres.*
15. Musset, "Tristesse."
16. *Le National,* letter by editor Vignerie, August 4, 1833, cited in S. Charléty, *La Monarchie de Juillet* (Paris, 1921), 98-99.
17. Auguste Laveille, *Un Lamennais Inconnu* (Paris, 1898), 308.
18. W. G. Roe, *Lamennais and England* (Oxford, 1966), 10.
19. Lamennais, *Paroles d'un Croyant,* ed. Yves Le Hir (Paris, 1949), XXXVIII, XXIV, XXXIV.
20. *Ibid.,* XX.
21. Letter to Count Lützow (Austrian Ambassador in Rome), cited in Alec R. Vidler, *Prophecy and Papacy* (N.Y., 1954), 149-150.
22. Lamennais, *Modern Slavery,* tr. W. J. Linton (London, 1840), 14-22.
23. *Correspondance de Liszt et de Madame d'Agoult* (Paris, 1933), I, 78.
24. Humphrey Searle, *The Music of Liszt* (N.Y., 1966) 12-13; 24.
25. Charléty, 123.
26. André Maurois, *Lélia* (N.Y., 1953), 206.

27. Wladimir Karénine, *George Sand* (Paris, 1912), II, 200.

28. Balzac, *Correspondance* II, 678-679, n. 2 (cited from Mélanie de Metternich's Journal of May 20, 1835).

29. *La Lélia de 1839*, ed. P. Reboul (Paris, 1960), ch. 60.

30. *Mauprat* (1836), ch. 10.

31. Georg Weerth, *Fragment eines Romans*.

32. *Le Compagnon du Tour de France*, chs. 24; 33.

33. *Mauprat*, ch. 7.

34. *Ibid.*, ch. 25.

35. *Correspondance* III, 596.

36. Frédéric Chopin, *Selected Correspondence*, ed. Arthur Hedley (N.Y. 1963), 141.

37. H. Remsen Whitehouse, *A Revolutionary Princess: Christine Belgiojoso Trivulzio* (N.Y. 1906).

38. See Ethel Saniel Brook, *The Social and Political Ideas of Countess d'Agoult* (Doctoral Dissertation, Columbia University, 1969).

39. *Journal Intime*, 45-46; Maurois, *Lélia*, 240-241.

40. April Fitzlyon, *The Price of Genius: The Life of Pauline Viardot* (London, 1964), 105.

3. Stendhal — Journey's End: "La Chartreuse de Parme."

1. Stendhal, *Vie de Henri Brulard*, ch. 1.

2. *La Chartreuse de Parme*, ed. Pierre Jourda (Paris, 1933), I, xii.

3. *Ibid.*, ch. 6.

4. *Ibid.*, ch. 6.

5. *Ibid.*, ch. 12.

6. *Une Position sociale, Romans*, ed. S. S. de Sacy (Paris, 1969), II, 472.

7. Fernand Rude, *Stendhal et la pensée sociale de son temps*, 236.

8. Balzac, "Études sur M. Beyle," *Oeuvres diverses*, ed. Bouteron and Lognon (Paris, 1940), III, 372-374.

9. Stendhal, *Correspondance* (Paris, 1968), III, 393.

10. *Ibid.*, 10.

11. *Lucien Leuwen*, Part I, ch. 27.

12. *Ibid.*, ch. 22.

13. *Ibid.*, ch. 42.

14. *Ibid.*, ch. 49.

15. From a note written February 17, 1835, cited in Matthew Josephson, *Stendhal* (Garden City, 1946) 399.

16. *Correspondance* II, 765; to Sainte-Beuve, from Civita Vecchia, December 21, 1834.

17. *Vie de Henri Brulard*, ch. 13.

18. *Ibid.*, ch. 15.

III. Paris: Magnet and Haven.
1-2. Heinrich Heine: A German Apollo in Paris.

1. Charléty, 34.
2. Ludwig Börne, *Briefe aus Paris*, No. 78; *Sämtliche Schriften*, ed. Inge and Peter Rippmann (Düsseldorf, 1964-1968) III, 580.
3. Translated by Aaron Kramer, in Frederic Ewen, *The Poetry and Prose of Heinrich Heine* (N.Y., 1948) 78.
4. Heine, *Reisebilder* II, *Sämtliche Werke*, ed. Oskar Walzel (Leipzig, 1912) IV, 135; Ewen, *Heine,* 303-304.
5. *Werke* IV, 166; Ewen, *Heine,* 309.
6. *Reisebilder* III, 298; Ewen, 812-813.
7. G. Ras, *Börne und Heine als politische Schriftsteller* (Groningen, 1927), 63.
8. Heine, *Französische Zustände, Sämtliche Werke* VI, 271.
9. *Ibid.,* 159.
10. "Einleitung zu Kahldorf über den Adel," (1831), *ibid.,* V, 391.
11. *Französishe Zustände,* 236; Ewen, 758.
12. *Werke,* 175; Ewen, 822-823.
13. Cited in Hans Kaufmann, *Heinrich Heine,* in *Werke und Briefe* (Berlin, 1964), 59.
14. *Französische Zustände,* "Vorrede," 91-92; Ewen, 749.
15. Heine, *Religion und Philosophie in Deutschland, Sämtliche Werke* VII, 265-266; Ewen, 808; 32.
16. *Werke,* 348-354; Ewen 759-762.
17. *Sämtliche Werke* II, 36; English translation by Aaron Kramer, in Ewen, 112-113.
18. "Die schlesischen Weber" ("The Silesian Weavers") tr. Aaron Kramer, in Ewen, 244.
19. "Deutschland: Ein Wintermärchen" ("Germany — A Winter's Tale"), tr. Aaron Kramer, in Ewen, 177-240.
20. "Vorwort," *Sämtliche Werke* II, 275-278; 447-448.
21. "Oktober 1849," tr. Aaron Kramer; Ewen, 242; 254.

3. Adam Mickiewicz — Poland's Poet-Laureate.

1. J.B. Ostrowski, Jan. 14, 1831, cited in R. F. Leslie, *Polish Politics and the Revolution of November, 1830* (London, 1956) 149.
2. Gleb Struve, "Mickiewicz in Russia, *Slavonic and East-European Review* XXVI (1947), 133.
3. Wiktor Weintraub, *The Poetry of Adam Mickiewicz* (The Hague, 1954), 132.
4. Mickiewicz, *Books of the Polish Nation,* in R.P. Noyes, *Poems by Adam Mickiewicz* (N.Y., 1944), 377-491.
5. "The Monument of Peter the Great."
6. John N. Washburn, "The Russians on Mickiewicz," in Manfred Kridl (ed.), *Adam Mickiewicz: Poet of Poland* (N.Y., 1969), 155.

7. *Pan Tadeusz*, Bk. XII.
8. Cited in Daniel Halévy, *Jules Michelet* (Paris, 1928), 36.
9. *La Tribune des Peuples*, April 15, 1849, cited in Léon Kolodziej, *Adam Mickiewicz* (Paris, 1970), 180.

4. José de Espronceda — Spain's Childe Harold.

1. Cited in Hans Jeschke, *Die romanischen Literaturen*, in *Handbuch der Literatur-wissenschaften* (Potsdam, 1935f.) 352; Enrique Pineyro, *El Romanticismo en España* (Paris, n.d.), 34-35.
2. "El emigrado de 1823," cited in *Obras Completas de Espronceda*, ed. D. Jorge Campos (Madrid, 1954), XVII.
3. Cascales y Muñoz, "Apuntes y materiales para la Biografia de Don José de Espronceda," *Revue Hispanique* XXIII (1910), 93.
4. Pedro Ortiz Armengol, *Espronceda y los Gendarmes*, 116-117.
5. Pineyro, 139.
6. *El Diablo Mundo*, "Introducción."
7. *Ibid.*, "El Angel y el Poeta."
8. *Ibid.*, Canto II: " A Teresa."
9. *El Estudiante de Salamanca*, Part IV.
10. "El Verdugo" ("The Executioner"). For de Maistre, see above 146f.
11. "Al Dos de Mayo."
12. "A la Degradación de Europa."

V. End of an Epoch: Goethe, Weimar, and the Transfiguration of Faust.

1. *Goethes Werke*, ed. Robert Petsch (Leipzig, 1926) V, 42.
2. *Götz von Berlichingen*, Act V.
3. See Frederic Ewen, *The Prestige of Schiller in England* (N.Y., 1932).
4. Cited in G.H. Lewes, *The Life of Goethe* (edition of 1864, reprinted N.Y., 1965), 177.
5. Cited in *J.G. Herder on Social and Political Culture*, tr. and ed. by F.M. Barnard (Cambridge, England, 1969), 265.
6. "Ilmenau," *Werke* (ed. Petsch) I, 282-287.
7. "Venezianische Epigramme" 34b., *Werke* I, 178-178.
8. *Werke* II, 309-310.
9. Goethe, *Die Geschwister, Werke* VI, 397-398.
10. Johann Wolfgang von Goethe, *Briefe*, ed. Rudolf Bach (München, 1958), 226-227; Carlsbad, Sept. 26, 1786.
11. *Ibid.*, 216, August 18, 1785.
12. *Ibid.*, 191, September 17, 1782.
13. Goethe, *Italienische Reise, Werke* XVII, 37; 50.
14. *Ibid.*, 53.
15. *Ibid.*, 226.
16. *Ibid.*, 257.

17. *Werke* XVII, 12; 31; 98; 228; 367; 377; 384.

18. *Ibid.,* 563.

19. *Goethes Werke, Briefe* (Zürich, 1949), XIX, 104-109.

20. *Italienische Reise, Werke* (ed. Petsch), XVII, 169.

21. George Brandes, *Wolfgang Goethe,* tr. Allen W. Porterfield (N.Y., 1925), I, 243.

22. Goethe, *Egmont, Werke* VI, Act II, sc. 2.

23. *Torquato Tasso, Werke* VII, Act V. sc. 2.

24. *Ibid.,* Act V. sc. 5.

25. Goethe, *Iphigenie auf Tauris, Werke* VII, Act V, sc. 6.

26. *Ibid.,* Act V, sc. 3.

27. *Werke* VII, 10.

28. Richard Friedenthal, *Goethe: His Life and Times* (N.Y., 1965), 485.

29. For important discussions of this aspect of "self-cultivation," see W.H. Bruford, *Culture and Society in Classical Weimar* and *The German Tradition of Self-Cultivation* (Cambridge, England, 1962 and 1975 respectively).

30. See our later section on Faust (post) and Hans Schwerte, *Faust und das Faustische* (Stuttgart, 1962).

31. *Wilhelm Meisters theatralische Sendung, Werke* X, 231.

32. *Werke* I, 29.

33. *Italienische Reise, Werke* XVII, 337.

34. Letter to Carl Ludwig von Knebel, November 17, 1784; *Briefe,* ed. Rudolf Bach, 208-209; November 17, 1784.

35. To Knebel, Dec. 15, 1784; cited Brandes I, 428-429.

36. *Faust II,* Act II, sc. 4.

37. *Werke* I, 378.

38. Karl Viëtor, *Goethe the Poet* (Cambridge, Mass., 1949), 47.

39. *Goethes Gespräche mit Eckermann (Goethe's Conversations with Eckermann)* ed. Erich Zenker (Berlin, 1955), 224 (Jan. 29, 1826).

40. Goethe, *Winckelmann, Werke* (Hamburg ed., 1953), XII, 103.

41. *Briefe, Gedenkausgabe der Werke,* ed. Ernst Beutler (Zürich, 1949), XIX, 192-193.

42. Goethe, *Der Bürgergeneral, Werke* VII, sc. 14.

43. *Das Mädchen von Oberkirch, Werke* VIII, 475-486.

44. *Die natürliche Tochter, Werke,* VII, Act I, sc. 5.

45. Wilhelm Mommsen, *Die politischen Anschauungen Goethes* (Stuttgart, 1948), 114, n. 1.

46. Goethe, "Selbstbiographische Einzelheiten," *Werke* XVI, 378-381.

47. *Goethes Gespräche mit Eckermann (Conversations)* (Berlin, 1955), March 11, 1828.

48. Goethe, *Dichtung und Wahrheit,* Part IV, *Werke* XVI, 310-311.

49. Mommsen, 166; 167; *Gespräche mit Eckermann,* 248 (Jan. 3, 1827).

50. Goethe, *West-östlicher Divan, Werke* III, 21; 38.

51. *Ibid.,* "Buch Suleika," 89.
52. *Ibid.,* 94-97.
53. "Trilogie der Leidenschaft: Elegie," *Werke* II, 90-95.
54. *West-östlicher Divan, Werke* III, 86; 33.
55. *Wilhelm Meisters Lehrjahre, Werke* XI, Bk. V, ch. 3, 288-291.
56. *Ibid.,* Bk. VII, ch. 9, 478-479.
57. *Ibid.,* Bk. VIII, ch. 1, 484-485.
58. "Den Vereinigten Staaten" ("To the United States"), *Werke* II, 416.
59. *Wilhelm Meisters Wanderjahre,* Bk. III, ch. 11; *Werke* XII, 379. See also Max Waldman, *Goethe and the Jews* (N.Y., 1934).
60. *Ibid.,* Bk. II, ch. 2, 175-184.
61. *Goethes Urfaust, Werke* V, 543, lines 1411ff.
62. Cited in Georg Lukács, *Goethe und seine Zeit* (Berlin, 1955), 180.
63. Robert Petsch, *Goethes Werke,* V, 36.
64. George Santayana, *Three Philosophical Poets* (Cambridge, Mass., 1910), 185.
65. For the course of the Faust "myth" see Hans Schwerte, *Faust und das Faustische* (Stuttgart, 1962).
66. To Zelter, May 11, 1820; Goethe, *Gedenkausgabe* (Zürich, 1951), *Briefe* XXI, 393.
67. Mommsen, 277.
68. Frédéric Soret, in *Gespräche mit Eckermann* (Berlin, 1955), 700-701.
69. Cited in Viëtor, 153.
70. Cited in Friedenthal, 474-475.

Index

(An asterisk (*) denotes a major entry)